International Management

FOURTH EDITION

INTERNATIONAL MANAGEMENT

Managing Across Borders and Cultures

Helen Deresky

State University of New York–Plattsburgh

Upper Saddle River, New Jersey 07458

Library of Congress Cataloging-in-Publication Data

Deresky, Helen
    International management: managing across borders and cultures / Helen
Deresky.
      p. cm.
    Includes bibliographical references and index.
    ISBN 0-13-009053-0
     1. International business enterprises—Management.   2. International business
enterprises—Management—Case studies.   3. Industrial management.   I. Title

HD62.4.D47 2003
658′.049—dc21

2002021820

Editor-in-Chief: Jeff Shelstad
Project Manager: Jessica Sabloff
Editorial Assistant: Kevin Glynn
Media Project Manager: Michele Faranda
Marketing Manager: Shannon Moore
Marketing Assistant: Christine Genneken
Managing Editor (Production): John Roberts
Production Editor: Maureen Wilson
Permissions Coordinator: Suzanne Grappi
Associate Director, Manufacturing: Vincent Scelta
Production Manager: Arnold Vila
Manufacturing Buyer: Michelle Klein
Cover Design: Maureen Eide
Cover Illustration/Photo: Cartesia/Getty Images, Inc./PhotoDisc, Inc.
Cover Printer: Phoenix
Full-Service Project Management and Composition: UG/GGS Information Services, Inc.
Printer/Binder: Courier–Westford

Credits and acknowledgments borrowed from other sources and reproduced, with permission, in this textbook appear in Booknotes and Credits.

Pearson Education LTD.
Pearson Education Australia PTY, Limited
Pearson Education Singapore, Pte. Ltd
Pearson Education North Asia Ltd
Pearson Education, Canada, Ltd
Pearson Educación de Mexico, S.A. de C.V.
Pearson Education-Japan
Pearson Education Malaysia, Pte. Ltd

10 9 8 7 6 5 4 3 2 1
ISBN 0-13-009053-0

Brief Contents

Contents

PART THREE: FORMULATING AND IMPLEMENTING
STRATEGY FOR INTERNATIONAL AND
GLOBAL OPERATIONS   219

Preface

The hyper-competitive global arena of the twenty-first century mandates that managers develop the skills necessary to design and implement global strategies, to conduct effective cross-national interactions, and to manage daily operations in foreign subsidiaries. Companies operating abroad often report that their global strategy is undermined by expatriate failure—the ineffective management of intercultural relations. This means that the fate of overseas operations depends at least in part on the international manager's cultural skills and sensitivity, and the ability to carry out the company's strategy within the host country's business practices.

Clearly, the skills needed for effective management of people and processes in a global context are crucial for the twenty-first century. There is thus a pronounced need for a comprehensive textbook that addresses the actual management functions and behaviors necessary to develop global vision and management skills at both an organizational—**strategic**—(macro) level, and the **interpersonal** (micro) level. *International Management: Managing Across Borders and Cultures,* Fourth Edition, fills this need.

This text places the student in the role of a manager of any nationality, encouraging the student to take a truly global perspective in dealing with dynamic management issues in both foreign and diverse host environments. Cross-cultural management and competitive strategy is evaluated in the context of global changes—the European Union, the North American Free Trade Agreement (NAFTA), the liberalization of eastern Europe, and the evolving marketplace of the Commonwealth of Independent States—that require new management applications. Throughout, the text emphasizes how the variable of culture interacts with other national and international factors to affect managerial processes and behaviors. In addition, the growing competitive influence of technology is emphasized throughout the text, and with boxes featuring the use of e-business for global competitive strategic positioning.

This textbook is designed for undergraduate and graduate students majoring in international business or general management. Graduate students might be asked to focus more heavily on the comprehensive cases that end each part of the book, and to complete the term project in greater detail. It is assumed, though not essential, that most students using *International Management: Managing Across Borders and Cultures,* Fourth Edition, will have taken a basic principles of management course. Although this text is primarily intended for business students, it is also useful for practicing managers and for students majoring in other areas, such as political science or international relations, who would benefit from a background in international management.

NEW TO THIS EDITION

Although the entire text has been reworked to reflect current research, current events, and company examples from the field of international management, specific revisions to the text material include:

> **Streamlined text**—from 13 to 11 chapters, with particular focus on global strategic positioning, effective cross-cultural understanding and management, and developing and retaining an effective global management cadre.

Comprehensive cases—twelve of the fifteen comprehensive cases are new and current; ten are exclusive to this book and three are favorites rolled over from the third edition. There is an emphasis on technology in several of the cases. The selection of cases has drawn from a broad array of geographical locations for the settings: France, Malaysia, Germany, Japan, China, Canada, West Indies, South Africa, Singapore, Burma, Indonesia, and "the world." The integrative case presents the student-manager with a variety of strategic, cultural, and social responsibility issues involved in making a decision about the setting up a factory in Mexico.

E-Business—the increasing emphasis on technology in global business transactions is highlighted in every chapter with text coverage, such as that in Chapter 6, "Using E-Business for Global Expansion," and with E-biz boxes in every chapter.

New chapter opening profiles, management focus boxes, chapter-ending cases, and comparative section.

DISTINCTIVE TEXT FEATURES

➤ **Comprehensive Cases,** which place the student in the decision-making role of the manager regarding issues of strategy, culture, HRM, social responsibility, technology, and politics in the global arena. Examples are TelSys International, which deals with a cross-cultural negotiation situation set in Malaysia and which can be used as a negotiation simulation; SoftBank Corp., a Japanese company, on the subject of Internet and web-related acquisitions; West Indies Yacht Club Resort, which deals with challenges of expatriate assignments and cross-cultural leadership and motivation; and the DaimlerChrysler AG case.

➤ **Chapter Opening Profiles** giving practical and current illustrations of the chapters topics—such as "Nokia's China Strategy," and "The Rise of the NAFTA Manager."

➤ **Comparative Management in Focus Sections** providing in-depth comparative applications of chapter topics in specific countries—such as "Interdependence: Borderland Amexica," "Labor Relations in Germany," and "Communicating with Arabs."

➤ **Management Focus Boxes** that give management and company examples around the world and highlight the chapter topics—such as "In Japan and India, E-Business Must Be Localized," "Technology Shift Adds to Culture Clash in France," "Nextlink Enables Global Strategy Implementation," "Unions without Borders? The Case of the Duro Bag Factory in Rio Bravo," and "Leadership in a Digital World."

➤ **E-Biz Boxes** explaining the application of IT—specifically B2B—around the world, such as "Airbus Joins Global Aerospace B2B Exchange," "B2B Markets: Fast Negotiations and Transactions," and "Bikeworld Goes Global Using FedEx Technologies and Shipping."

➤ **Chapter-Ending Cases:** short cases, such as "The EU Grounds the GE-Honeywell Merger," "Toyota's Tough Boss," and "The Venezuelan Coup."

➤ **Experiential Exercises** that challenge students on topics such as ethics in decision making, cross-cultural negotiations, and strategic planning are at the end of each chapter.

➤ **Internet Exercises** pertaining to selected topics throughout the book are on the book's Web site to help students explore chapter content in more detail and relate what they've learned to real-world situations. Go to http://www.prenhall.com/Deresky.

➤ **Integrative Term Project,** outlined at the end of the text, provides a vehicle for research and application of the course content.

➤ **Integrative Case:** AT&T Consumer Products: The Mexico Decision

SUPPLEMENTS PACKAGE

Instructor's Manual with Test Item File: For each chapter, the Instructor's Manual provides a comprehensive lecture outline, chapter discussion questions, and "Student Stimulation" questions and exercise, as well as additional Teaching Resources and Lecture Notes annotated in the lecture outline. There are also additional Experiential Exercises for selected chapters. The Test Item File consists of multiple choice questions (with page references for instructors), discussion questions, and longer essay questions.

Instructor's Resource CD-ROM, Including PowerPoint Slides: The Instructor's Resource CD-ROM contains the computerized Test Item File, PowerPoint Electronic Transparencies, and Instructor's Manual. A revised, comprehensive package of text outlines and figures corresponding to the text, the PowerPoint Electronic Transparencies, are designed to aid the educator and supplement in-class lectures. Containing all of the questions in the printed Test Item File, Test Manager is a comprehensive suite of tools for testing and assessment. Test Manager allows educators to easily create and distribute tests for their courses, either by printing and distributing through traditional methods or by on-line delivery via a Local Area Network (LAN) server.

PH International Custom Video: This video, drawn from Prentice Hall's custom On Location! video series, features experts discussing a wide range of issues in the global marketplace. By focusing on the ways in which well-known companies (including Yahoo!, MTV Europe, Sebago Shoes, and Nivea) become successful beyond their home markets, these videos bring to life chapter concepts and terms, tying them together in a real-world context.

Companion Web Site: The companion web site for this text, located at http://www.prenhall.com/Deresky, contains valuable resources for both students and professors, including an interactive student study guide.

ACKNOWLEDGMENTS

The author would like to acknowledge, with thanks, the individuals who made this text possible. For the fourth edition, these people include the following:

Dr. Dharma deSilva
Wichita State University

Prof. David Ricks
University of Missouri–St. Louis

Dr. Tim Wilkinson
University of Akron

Dr. Yong Zhang
Hofstra University

Helen Deresky

Assessing the Environment— Political, Economic, Legal, Technological

Opening Profile: Nokia's China Strategy: Exchanging Technology for Market Access

The Finnish company's China chairman talks about the challenges of doing business under Beijing's watchful eye

When Folke Ahlback, chairman of Nokia (China) Investment Company, arrived in Beijing six years ago, the local office consisted of about 250 staffers working in a former Beijing movie theater. Since then, he's built Nokia's China operation into a sales powerhouse with 5,000 employees. In 1999, it contributed 14 percent of Nokia Corporation's global sales.

Small wonder Nokia has invested more than $1 billion in the Chinese market. Already, there are more than 70 million wireless subscribers in the Middle Kingdom, with 2 million new users signing up each month. Ahlback, also a Nokia senior vice president, recently spoke about his company's operations in China with Irene M. Kunii, a *Business Week* correspondent covering telecommunications. Here are excerpts from their conversation.

Q: Has there been any downturn in your China business?
A: There have been no cancellations of orders. Growth has continued to climb steadily. . . . We're satisfied since China's gross domestic product is on the 8 percent level.

Q: Nokia seems to have good relations with its Chinese partners. Why is that? And how many partners are there?
A: Chinese and Finns have some common characteristics. They don't brag and are modest. They are aware that life isn't easy. It makes you a little more humble. We have seven joint ventures, and all but one are state-owned.

Q: You're transferring sophisticated technology to these partners. Aren't you concerned that they might take your market share in the future?
A: Because the telecom industry is so important [in China], there are rules and regulations. You transfer technology and you get market access. It's a mix between a central and a planned economy. We've learned that every country has its own characteristics. In 1998, China became the second most important market for Nokia [after the United States].

Q: How much market share do Chinese handset makers have?
A: The MII's [Ministry of Information Industry] task is to make sure that 30 percent will be Chinese. It's likely to be in the range of 5 percent to 10 percent now.

Q: Are you concerned that China is backing the development of yet another third-generation, or 3G, cellular standard, TD-SCDMA?
A: We are firm believers that . . . regardless of what choice will be made, the point is to make an evolutionary path to wideband CDMA (or W-CDMA, the 3G standard backed by Japan and Europe). If we don't do this, we haven't achieved our path.

Q: But what of this new standard under development with Siemens?

A: As with any standard, there are two steps. First is to make it a standard. We welcome the fact that China is involved in standardization. Consumers are interested only in features, and not the technology. So the test for TD-SCDMA will be the market. Nokia is supporting this standard and is involved in R&D.

Q: Will the mobile Internet take off in China the way it has in Japan? As you know, there the emphasis is on entertainment sites.

A: China is a big country, and it's [in the process of] building one of the world's biggest and most modern mobile-phone systems. But it is a developing country, so it will be very careful about how it's going to use it. So, for 3G, we shouldn't talk about content but rather how to enhance the business. The target for the Chinese government is to make investment decisions that will help industry to be more efficient.

Q: Does that mean Chinese won't be downloading games to their handsets?

A: The Chinese government's first concern is to give the Chinese [mobile] infrastructure to business. They'll get the state-of-the-art technology first. Then the government will give consumers what they want. Big consumer segments will want the same as everyone else. The whole of Chinese society would like to be connected [to the mobile Internet.]

Q: Will Chinese companies contribute to the development of content and applications for the mobile Net?

A: We think there will be hundreds of companies [doing this] in China and thousands worldwide. I'm sure the Chinese government wants Chinese businesses to play a big role in wireless cellular operations.

Q: Would it be possible for Nokia to operate independently in China and thus protect its intellectual property?

A: In China, it's very advisable to work with partners. I would not advise anyone to go to China without a partner for such a complicated business like telecoms. After building a business together, your joint-venture partner becomes your trusted partner.

Q: That's fine, but look what happened to the foreign partners of mobile operator China Unicom [which had its foreign joint-venture agreements with Unicom terminated last year].

A: It was political. They developed an investment structure that went against the government's policies, so Chinese officials decided they should dissolve it.

Q: Is this a good place to set up a business in terms of being able to hire promising engineers?

A: In China, we have a big supply of educated people. It didn't take us long to ramp up operations—less than 12 months per factory. Between 1996 [and] 1999, we have built manufacturing capability in China, not only for China but also the world. We made China a manufacturing center, along with the U.S. and Europe.

SOURCE: Edited by Thane Peterson, www.businessweek.com, January 22, 2001.

The Jack Welch of the future cannot be me. I spent my entire career in the United States. The next head of General Electric will be somebody who spent time in Bombay, in Hong Kong, in Buenos Aires. We have to send our best and brightest overseas and make sure they have the training that will allow them to be the global leaders who will make GE flourish in the future.

—JACK WELCH, IN A SPEECH TO GE EMPLOYEES, 2001

Managers in the twenty-first century are being challenged to operate in an increasingly complex, interdependent, and dynamic global environment. Those involved in global business have to adjust their strategies and management styles to those regions of the world in which they want to operate, whether directly or through some form of alliance. This global arena is illustrated in the opening profile—an interview with Folke Ahlback, chairman of the Finnish company, Nokia (China) Investment Company.[1] Typical challenges that he has faced are those involving politics, culture, and the use, transfer, and protection of technology. In addition, the opportunities and risks of the global marketplace increasingly bring with them the societal obligations of operating in a global community. An example is the dilemma faced by Western drug manufacturers, which came to the forefront in spring 2001, of how to fulfill their responsibilities to stockholders, acquire capital for research, protect their patents, and also be good global citizens by responding to the cry for free or low-cost drugs for AIDS in poor countries.[2] Managers in those companies are struggling to find ways to balance their social responsibilities, their image, and their competitive strategies.

To compete aggressively, firms must make considerable investments overseas—not only capital investment but also investment in well-trained managers with the skills essential to working effectively in a multicultural environment. In any foreign environment, managers need to handle a set of dynamic and fast-changing variables, including the all-pervasive variable of culture that affects every facet of daily management. Added to that "behavioral software" is the challenge of the burgeoning use of technological software and the borderless Internet, which are rapidly changing the dynamics of competition and operations.

Global management, then, is the process of developing strategies, designing and operating systems, and working with people around the world to ensure sustained competitive advantage. Those management functions are shaped by the prevailing conditions and ongoing developments in the world, as outlined in the following sections.

THE GLOBAL BUSINESS ENVIRONMENT

Globalism

Business competitiveness has now evolved to a level of sophistication that many term **globalism**—global competition characterized by networks that bind countries, institutions, and people in an interdependent global economy. The invisible hand of global competition is being propelled by the phenomenon of an increasingly borderless world. As described by Kenichi Ohmae, "The nation-state itself—that artifact of the eighteenth and nineteenth centuries—has begun to crumble, battered by a pent-up storm of political resentment, ethnic prejudice, tribal hatred, and religious animosity."[3]

As a result of global economic integration, extrapolation of current trends will lead to world exports of goods and services of $11 trillion by the year 2005, or 28 percent of world gross domestic product (GDP).[4] As reported by the World Trade Organization, differences in regional output growth rates have narrowed as economic activity picked up in Western Europe and the transition economies.[5] It is clear that world trade is phenomenal and growing and, importantly, is increasingly including the developing nations.

Almost all firms around the world are affected to some extent by globalism. Firms from any country now compete with your firm both at home and abroad, and your domestic competitors are competing on price by outsourcing resources anywhere in the world. It is essential, therefore, for managers to go beyond operating only in their domestic market because by doing so they are already behind the majority of managers who recognize that they must have a global vision for their firms and that vision starts with preparing themselves with the skills and tools of managing in a global environment. Companies that desire to remain globally competitive and to expand their operations to other countries will have to develop a top management cadre who have experience operating abroad and who understand what it takes to do business in other countries and to work with people in and from other cultures.

As another indicator of globalism, foreign direct investment has grown more than three times faster than the world output of goods. The European Union (EU) has now caught up with the United States to share the position of the world's largest investor. The United Kingdom has been the most active source of merger and acquisition investment. The United States is the largest home for foreign investment, with China the second largest recipient. Many global companies produce and sell their global brands more "overseas" than in the domestic market. As of 2002, Nestlé, for example, has 50 percent of its sales outside of the home market, Coca-Cola has 80 percent, and Procter and Gamble 65 percent. Investment by global companies around the world means that this aspect of globalism benefits developing economies—through the transfer of financial, technological, and managerial resources, and through the development of local allies, which later become self-sufficient and have other operations. Global companies are becoming less tied to specific locations, and their operations and allies are spread around the world, as they source and coordinate resources and activities in the most suitable areas, and as technology allows faster and more flexible interactions and greater efficiencies.

Small companies are also affected by and, in turn, affect globalism. They play a vital role in contributing to their national economies—through employment, new job creation, development of new products and services, and international operations, typically exporting. The vast majority (about 98 percent) of businesses in developed economies are small and medium-sized enterprises (SMEs), which are typically referred to as those companies having fewer than 500 employees. Although many small businesses are affected by globalism only to the extent that they face competing products from abroad, an increasing number of entrepreneurs are being approached by potential offshore customers, thanks to the burgeoning number of trade shows, federal and state export initiatives, and the growing use of Websites, with the ease of making contact and placing orders on-line. In the United States, for example, more than half of the companies with annual revenue under $100 million export their products.[6]

Regional Trading Blocs—The TRIAD

Much of today's world trade takes place within three regional free-trade blocs (Western Europe, Asia, and North America), called the TRIAD market, grouped around the three dominant currencies (the euro, the yen, and the dollar).[7] One researcher summarizes the impact this new order has had on our perception of national boundaries in the following way:

> Today, if you look closely at the world TRIAD companies inhabit, national borders have effectively disappeared and, along with them, the economic logic that made them useful lines of demarcation in the first place.[8]

The European Union (EU)

> We are very conscious about the euro because our main market is Europe; we told clients that as soon as they are ready, we will be ready [by pricing his products in euros].
>
> —WILLY LIN, MILOS MANUFACTURING, HONG KONG (FAMILY-OWNED KNITWEAR COMPANY) *FAR EASTERN ECONOMIC REVIEW*, SEPTEMBER 3, 1998

With 12 of the 15 member states of the European Community adopting a common currency and monetary policy, the EU—a single, borderless Western European market—is now a reality. And, as negotiations continued in 2001, voting rights were being negotiated for up to 13 new members to join the EU.[9] With the euro now a legally tradable currency, Europe's business environment is being transformed. The vast majority of legislative measures have been adopted to create an internal market with free movement of goods and people among the European Union (EU) countries, creating the largest and most integrated common market in the world, with 376 million consumers. But the elimination of internal tariffs and customs, as well as financial and commercial barriers, has not eliminated national pride. Although most people in Western Europe are being thought of simply as Europeans, they still think of themselves first as British, French, Danish, or Italian and are wary of giving up too much power to centralized institutions or of giving up their national culture.

Global managers face two major tasks. One is strategic (dealt with more fully in Chapter 6)—how firms outside of Europe can deal with the implications of the EU and of what some have called a "Fortress Europe"—that is, a market giving preference to insiders. The other task is cultural—how to deal effectively with multiple sets of national cultures, traditions, and customs within Europe, such as differing attitudes about how much time should be spent on work versus leisure activities.

Asia

Japan and the Four Tigers—Singapore, Hong Kong, Taiwan, and South Korea, each of which has abundant natural resources and labor—provide most of the capital and expertise for Asia's developing countries.[10] Economists are observing a growing integration of the region, with Japan as a catalyst and a dominant—but welcome—partner.

In the 1980s and early 1990s, much of Asia's economic power and competitive edge was attributed to Japan's *keiretsu* and South Korea's *chaebol*. Both are large conglomerates of financially linked groups of companies that play a significant role in their countries' economies. Japanese keiretsus—Mitsubishi and Toyota, to name two of the most powerful—are regarded in Washington as forms of trade barriers.[11] Recently, however, Japan's economic slide has been partially attributed to the closed system of the keiretsu, including political protection and influence for the keiretsu, and dubious financial backing. As a result, such conglomerates have been forced to break up and restructure. As an example, in March 2000 Toshiba Corporation announced a three-year reorganization plan.[12]

In all, the economic woes of Southeast Asia have severely slowed the growth in the region and have had a ripple effect on the sales and earnings of companies around the world. However, in 2001, Washington and Tokyo renewed efforts towards a more open marketplace.[13]

North America

The goal of the North American Free Trade Agreement (**NAFTA**) between the United States, Canada, and Mexico, was to bring faster growth, more jobs, better working conditions, and a cleaner environment for all as a result of increased exports and trade. This trading bloc—"one America"—has 360 million consumers and has the potential for expansion in South America as trade liberalization among the Latin American countries progresses.[14]

Reflecting optimism about investment opportunities resulting from the NAFTA, foreign companies have invested billions in Mexico. To take advantage of increased trade, American companies have set up new manufacturing facilities in Mexico or extended their manufacturing and assembly operations in the **maquiladoras**—U.S. manufacturing facilities that have operated just south of the Mexican-American border since the 1960s under special tax concessions. Many Mexican and American companies have set up joint ventures, such as the one between Wal-Mart and Cifra, the largest retailers in the United States and Mexico, respectively; in fact, as of 2001, WalMex was Mexico's biggest chain.[15] Already known as "Detroit South," the car industry south of the border is taking over more and more factory production for the Big Three carmakers in the United States, taking advantage of lower Mexican wages. However, recurring problems with the infrastructure continue to put downward pressure on trade.

Other Regions in the World

Sweeping political, economic, and social changes around the world present new challenges to global managers. The worldwide move away from communism, together with the trend toward privatization, has had an enormous influence on the world economy; economic freedom is a critical factor in the relative wealth of nations.

One of the most striking changes today is that almost all nations have suddenly begun to develop decentralized, free-market systems in order to manage a global economy of intense competition, the complexity of high-tech industrialization, and an awakening hunger for freedom.[16]

Central and Eastern Europe

An area greatly affected by these recent developments is the Central and Eastern European bloc, where communism proved unworkable and finally crumbled. World attention is now focused on a new market of 430 million people whose invitingly low wage rates offer investors an unexplored, low-cost manufacturing opportunity. Many impediments remain that will hamper business growth, however, because East European countries lack the capitalist structure and systems to reproduce Western management practices easily. As one researcher notes, "Market research is unfamiliar. The closest thing to a market survey that many East Europeans have experienced is a government interrogation."[17] However, growing stability and economic gains in Central Europe—Poland, Hungary, and the Czech Republic—are attracting a flood of foreign investment. These include an Opel car plant in southern Poland, expansion by IBM of its disk-drive plant in Hungary, and a new TV plant by Matsushita in the Czech Republic.[18]

China

China has enjoyed recent success as an export powerhouse, a status built on its strengths of low costs and a constant flow of capital. Its GDP growth rate, though slowing, was the fastest growth rate in the world for several consecutive years.

President Jiang Zemin has made state-enterprise reform his priority, though it can hardly be called mass privatization. His plan is to save China's 1,000 largest state enterprises and privatize or dissolve smaller, money-losing ones. His goal is to invigorate Chinese industry so it can compete in the global economy. As a result, millions of surplus industrial workers will lose their jobs, and the others will no longer receive free lifelong social benefits.[19] In September 2001, China completed its 15-year quest to become a member of the World Trade Organization (WTO). The deal, which will open China's state-dominated economy to imports and also increase their exports, became effective in 2002; lower tariffs will make foreign products more affordable for the Chinese, opening up huge, untapped markets.[20]

Unfortunately, privatization is not as easy as it sounds. Whether in Pakistan, China, Russia, or Argentina, the problems involved with selling state-owned companies—monsters of inefficiency that have incurred colossal losses over the years—are not easily solved.

Less Developed Countries

Change in less developed countries (**LDCs**) has come about more slowly as they struggle with low gross national product (GNP) and low per capita income, as well as the burdens of large, relatively unskilled populations and high international debt. Their economic situation and the often unacceptable level of government intervention discourage the foreign investment they need. Many countries in Central and South America, the Middle East, India, and Africa desperately hope to attract foreign investment to stimulate economic growth. For firms willing to take the economic and political risks, there is considerable potential for international business in the LDCs. Assessing the risk-return tradeoffs and keeping up with political developments in these developing countries are two of the many demands on international managers.

Information Technology

From his London office, Richard J. Callahan, the U.S. West International chief, . . . begins a turbocharged conference call with seven division presidents in five countries. They hash over cellular-phone sales in the Czech Republic, forecast long-distance hookups in Russia, and give a thumbs-up to opening an office in Japan.[21]

Of all the developments propelling global business today, the one that is transforming the international manager's agenda more than any other is the rapid advance in **information technology** (**IT**). The speed and accuracy of information transmission are changing the nature of the global manager's job by making geographic barriers less relevant. Indeed, the necessity of being able to access IT is being recognized by managers and families around the world, who are giving priority to being "plugged in" over other lifestyle accoutrements, as shown in the accompanying photograph. This family in Shanghai lives in a one-room apartment with no bathroom or cooking facilities. Instead, the Hei family has invested in a PC, cell phone, pager, TV, and VCR. The "father" runs his printing business with the cell phone; Dan, the son, studies computer science at the university.

Information can no longer be centrally or secretly controlled by governments; political, economic, market, and competitive information is available almost instantaneously to anyone around the world, permitting informed and accurate decision making. Even cultural barriers are being gradually lowered by the role of information in

The Hei family in Shanghai chooses high-tech conveniences over bathroom and cooking conveniences.
SOURCE: Rick Smolan and Jennifer Erwitt, "One Digital Day" (Sausalito, Calif.: Against All Odds Productions, 1998), reprinted in Fortune, *June 8, 1998.*

educating societies about one another. Indeed, as consumers around the world become more aware, through various media, of how people in other countries live, their tastes and preferences begin to converge:

> Global brands of colas, blue jeans, athletic shoes and designer ties and handbags are as much on the mind of the taxi driver in Shanghai as they are in the home of the schoolteacher in Stockholm.[22]

The explosive growth of information technology is both a cause and an effect of globalism. The information revolution is boosting productivity around the world. In addition, use of the Internet is propelling electronic commerce around the world, as discussed later in this chapter. Companies around the world are linked electronically to their employees, customers, distributors, suppliers, and alliance partners in many countries. Technology, in all its forms, gets dispersed around the world by multinational corporations (MNCs) and their alliance partners in many countries. However, some of the information intended for electronic transmission is currently subject to export controls by a EU directive intended to protect private information about its citizens. So, perhaps IT is not yet "borderless" after all, but rather is subject to the same norms, preferences, and regulations as "human" cross-border interactions.

Workforce Diversity

In many countries around the world, the workforce is becoming increasingly diverse because of the erosion of rigid political boundaries, the rapidity of travel, and the quick spread of information. Propelled by globalism, the world labor force is undergoing considerable change as a result of (1) the increasing movement across borders of workers at all skill levels; (2) the rising average age of employees; and (3) the addition of great numbers of women to the workforce (particularly in developing countries), many with higher levels of education.[23] In the United States, for example, demographic information from the Bureau of Labor Statistics indicates that, by the year 2050, Hispanic Americans will represent 25 percent, and Asian/Pacific Americans 9 percent, of the U.S. population.[24] Thus, workforce diversity is becoming a crucial managerial issue. In essence, cross-cultural management worldwide is as much the task of managing multiculturalism at home as it is of managing a workforce in a foreign country. It often means both: one manages in a foreign environment and, while there, manages a culturally diverse local workforce.

Effective management increasingly depends on the ability to design and implement programs, throughout an organization, that value diversity and pluralism. Such programs enable the organization to enjoy the benefits of multiculturalism, including the possibility of more creativity, innovation, and flexibility; they heighten sensitivity to foreign customers and provide a greater and more varied pool of talent.[25]

Exhibit 1-1   An Open Systems Model: The Contingency Role of the Global Manager

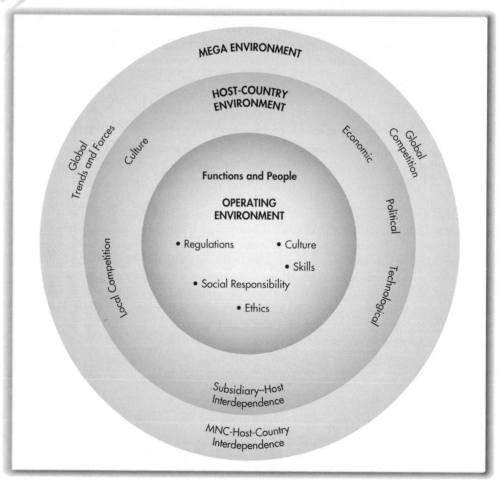

The Global Manager's Role

Whatever your level of involvement, you need to understand the global business environment and its influence on the manager's role. This complex role demands a contingency approach to dynamic environments, each of which has its own unique requirements. Within the larger context of global trends and competition, the rules of the game for the global manager are set by each country (as depicted in Exhibit 1-1): its political and economic agenda, its technological status and level of development, its regulatory environment, its comparative and competitive advantages, and its cultural norms. The astute manager will analyze the new environment, anticipate how it may affect the future of the home company, and then develop appropriate strategies and operating styles.

THE POLITICAL AND ECONOMIC ENVIRONMENT

Proactive globally oriented firms maintain an up-to-date profile of the political and economic environment of the countries in which they maintain operations (or have plans for future investment). In the early 1990s, the formerly rigid ideological systems of capitalism, communism, and socialism underwent profound changes, and the lines of demarcation between those systems increasingly blurred. It is now best to measure such systems along a continuum of economic systems—from those that operate primarily according to market forces (such as the United States) to those that use central planning for resource allocation (such as the People's Republic of China). Near the center of the continuum lie the industrialized Western European countries and Japan. Some countries in Africa, Asia, and Latin America are continuing to develop their market mechanisms and economic systems to improve their economic health.

An important aspect of the political environment is the phenomenon of ethnicity—a driving force behind political instability around the world. In fact, many uprisings and conflicts that are thought to be political in nature are actually expressions of differences among ethnic groupings. Often, it is religious disputes that lie at the heart of those differences. Uprisings based on religion operate both in conjunction with ethnic differences (as probably was the case in the former Yugoslavia), or separate from them (as in Northern Ireland). Many terrorist activities are also based on religious differences, as in the Middle East. Managers must understand the ethnic and religious composition of the host country in order to anticipate problems of general instability, as well as those of an operational nature—such as effects on your workforce, on production and access to raw materials, and on your market.[26] For example:

> In Pakistan one must understand the differences between Punjabi and Sindi. In Malaysia it is essential to recognize the special economic relationship between Chinese and Malay. In the Philippines it is important to understand the significant and lead financial role played by the Filipino-Chinese.[27]

Political Risk

> Increasingly, investors are understanding that projects can be derailed by little "p" political risk . . . the death from 1,000 cuts.[28]

The managers of a global firm need to investigate the political risks to which they expose their company in certain countries—and the implications of those risks for the economic success of the firm. **Political risks** are any governmental action or politically motivated event that could adversely affect the long-run profitability or value of a firm.[29] The Middle East, as we have seen, has traditionally been an unstable area where political risk heavily influences business decisions.

In unstable areas, multinational corporations weigh the risks of nationalization or expropriation. **Nationalization** refers to the forced sale of the MNC's assets to local buyers, with some compensation to the firm, perhaps leaving a minority ownership with the MNC. **Expropriation**, very rare in the last decade, occurs when the local government seizes the foreign-owned assets of the MNC, providing inadequate compensation; or, in the case of no compensation, it is confiscation. In countries that have a proven history of stability and consistency, the political risk to a multinational corporation is relatively low. The risk of expropriation is highest in countries that experience continuous political upheaval, violence, and change. Events that affect all foreign firms doing business in a country or region are called macropolitical risk events. In the Middle East, Iraq's invasion of Kuwait in 1990 abruptly halted all international business with and within both of those countries and caught businesses wholly unprepared. In China, the Tiananmen Square crackdown on student protestors in 1989 interrupted much foreign business in the Far East. After years of increasing international investment in China (the United States had reached the $3 billion mark in direct foreign investment at the time of the crackdown), many companies closed and withdrew their personnel. Concerned about the government's response to student unrest, these businesses were wary about the future.[30]

The political uncertainty and unrest in the newly independent countries of Eastern Europe are a prime example of the risk-return tradeoff that companies must assess. The attraction in Russia, for example, though it struggles in its transition to a market economy, is the considerable potential profits available to investors in the consumer goods sector which can accrue from the pent-up demand for goods for 150 million people who are beginning to realize some economic growth.[31] The continuing uncertainty has also not deterred Japan from setting up bases in Eastern Europe to penetrate the European Community market.[32]

In many regions, terrorism poses a severe and random political risk to company personnel and assets and can, obviously, interrupt the conduct of business. According to Micklous, **terrorism** is "the use, or threat of use, of anxiety-inducing . . . violence for ideological or political purposes."[33] The increasing incidence of terrorism, especially in Latin America, concerns MNCs. In particular, the kidnapping of business executives has become quite common. Those events that affect one industry or company or only a few companies are called **micropolitical risk events**.[34] These types of events have become more common than macrorisk events. Such micro action is often called creeping expropriation, indicating a government's gradual and subtle action against foreign firms.[35] This is when the "death from a 1,000 cuts" comes in—"when you haven't been expropriated, but it takes ten times longer to do anything."[36] Typically, such continuing problems with an investment present more difficulty for foreign firms than major events that are insurable by political-risk insurance agencies. The following list describes seven typical political risk events common today (and possible in the future).

1. Expropriation of corporate assets without prompt and adequate compensation
2. Forced sale of equity to host-country nationals, usually at or below depreciated book value

3. Discriminatory treatment against foreign firms in the application of regulations or laws.

4. Barriers to repatriation of funds (profits or equity)

5. Loss of technology or other intellectual property (such as patents, trademarks, or trade names)

6. Interference in managerial decision making

7. Dishonesty by government officials, including canceling or altering contractual agreements, extortion demands, and so forth.[37]

Political Risk Assessment

International companies must conduct some form of **political risk assessment** to manage their exposure to risk and to minimize financial losses. Typically, local managers in each country assess the potentially destabilizing issues and evaluate their future impact on the company, making suggestions for dealing with possible problems. Corporate advisors then establish guidelines for each local manager to follow in handling these problems. Dow Chemical has a program in which it uses line managers trained in political and economic analysis as well as executives in foreign subsidiaries to provide risk analyses of each country.[38]

Risk assessment by multinational corporations usually takes two forms. One is through the use of experts or consultants familiar with the country or region under consideration. Such consultants, advisers, and committees usually monitor important trends that may portend political change, such as the development of opposition or destabilizing political parties. They then assess the likelihood of political change and develop several plausible scenarios to describe alternative political conditions in the future.

A second and increasingly common means of political risk assessment used by MNCs is through the development of their own internal staff and in-house capabilities. This type of assessment may be accomplished by having staff assigned to foreign subsidiaries or affiliates monitor local political activities or by hiring people with expertise in the political and economic conditions in regions critical to the firm's operations. Frequently, both means are used. The focus must be on monitoring political issues before they become headlines; the ability to minimize the negative effects on the firm—or to be the first to take advantage of opportunities—is greatly reduced once CNN has put out the news.

No matter how sophisticated the methods of political risk assessment become, however, nothing can replace timely information from people on the front line. In other words, sophisticated techniques and consultations are useful as an addition to, but not as a substitute for, the line managers in the foreign subsidiaries, many of whom are host-country nationals. These managers represent the most important resource for current information on the political environment and how it might affect their firm because they are uniquely situated at the meeting point of the firm and the host country. Prudent MNCs, however, weigh the subjectivity of these managers' assessments and also realize that similar events will have different effects from one country to another.

An additional technique, the assessment of political risk through the use of computer modeling, is now becoming fairly common. One firm, American Can, uses a program called PRISM (primary risk investment screening matrix). This program digests information from overseas managers and consultants on 200 variables and reduces them to an index of economic desirability and an index of political and economic stability. Those countries with the most favorable PRISM indices are then considered by American Can for investment.[39] Such a program, of course, is only as good as its input data—which is often of doubtful quality because of inadequate information systems in many countries and because the information is processed subjectively.

To analyze their data on potential risks, some companies attempt to quantify variables into a ranking system for countries. They use their staff or outside consultants to allocate a minimum and a maximum score for criteria they deem important to them (1) on the political and economic environment, (2) on domestic economic conditions, and (3) on external economic relations. The sum of the individual scores for each variable represents a total risk evaluation range for each country.[40]

An actual risk ranking of selected countries is shown in Exhibit 1-2. The country risk assessment is a comparative ranking of those countries based on factors such as GDP growth, trade policy, and foreign investment climate—that is, economic, not just political, factors. The comparison is on a scale of 1 to 5, with 5 being the highest ranking, or lowest relative risk. Thus, Russia and Turkey have the most risk in the overall rating of these countries, with Singapore and the Netherlands having relatively low risk.[41]

One drawback of these quantitative systems is that they rely on information based primarily on past events. They are therefore limited in their ability to predict political events in a volatile environment.

Still another method, more rapidly responsive to and predictive of political changes, is called the early-warning system. This system uses lead indicators to predict possible political dangers, such as signs of violence or riots, developing pressure on the MNC to hire more local workers, or pending import-export restrictions.[42] The early-warning analysis is typically separated into macrorisk and microrisk elements.

In addition to assessing the political risk facing a firm, alert managers also examine the specific types of impact that such risks may have on the company. For an autonomous international subsidiary, most of the impact from political risks (nationalization, terrorism) will be at the level of the ownership and control of the firm because its acquisition by the host country would provide the state with a fully operational business.[43] For global firms, the primary risks are likely to be from restrictions (on imports, exports, currency, and so forth), with the impact at the level of the firm's transfers (or exchanges) of money, products, or component parts.[44]

Managing Political Risk

After assessing the potential political risk of investing or maintaining current operations in a country, managers face perplexing decisions on how to manage that risk. On one level, they can decide to suspend their firm's dealings with a certain country at a given point—either by the **avoidance** of investment or by the withdrawal of current investment (by selling or abandoning plants and assets). On another level, if they decide that the risk is relatively low in a particular country or that a high-risk environment is worth the potential returns, they may choose to start (or maintain) operations there and to accommodate that risk through **adaptation** to the political regulatory environment. That adaptation can take many forms, each designed to respond to the concerns of a given local area. Some means of adaptation suggested by Taoka and Beeman are given here:

1. **Equity sharing** includes the initiation of joint ventures with nationals (individuals or those in firms, labor unions, or government) to reduce political risks.
2. **Participative management** requires that the firm actively involve nationals, including those in labor organizations or government, in the management of the subsidiary.
3. **Localization of the operation** includes the modification of the subsidiary's name, management style, and so forth, to suit local tastes. Localization seeks to transform the subsidiary from a foreign firm to a national firm.
4. **Development assistance** includes the firm's active involvement in infrastructure development (foreign-exchange generation, local sourcing of materials or parts, management training, technology transfer, securing external debt, and so forth).[45]

In addition to avoidance and adaptation, two other means of risk reduction available to managers are **dependency** and **hedging**. Some means that managers might use to maintain dependency—keeping the subsidiary and the host nation dependent on the parent corporation—are as follows:

1. **Input control** means that the firm maintains control over key inputs, such as raw materials, components, technology, and know-how.
2. **Market control** requires that the firm keep control of the means of distribution (for instance, by only manufacturing components for the parent firm or legally blocking sales outside the host country).
3. **Position control** involves keeping certain key subsidiary management positions in the hands of expatriate or home-office managers.
4. **Staged contribution strategies** mean that the firm plans to increase, in each successive year, the subsidiary's contributions to the host nation (in the form of tax revenues, jobs, infrastructure development, hard-currency generation, and so forth). For this strategy to be most effective, the firm must inform the host nation of these projected contributions as an incentive.[46]

Finally, even if the company cannot diminish or change political risks, it can minimize the losses associated with these events by hedging. Some means of hedging are as follows:

1. **Political risk insurance** is offered by most industrialized countries. In the United States, the Overseas Private Investment Corporation (OPIC) provides coverage for new investments in projects in friendly, less developed countries. Insurance minimizes losses arising from specific risks—such as the inability to repatriate profits, expropriation, nationalization, or confiscation—and from damage as a result of war, terrorism, and so forth.[47] The Foreign Credit Insurance Association (FCIA) also covers political risks caused by war, revolution, currency inconvertibility, and the cancellation of import or export licenses. However, political risk insurance only covers the loss of a firm's assets, not the loss of revenue resulting from expropriation.[48]

2. **Local debt financing** (money borrowed in the host country), where available, helps a firm hedge against being forced out of operation without adequate compensation. In such instances, the firm withholds debt repayment in lieu of sufficient compensation for its business losses.

Multinational corporations also manage political risk through their global strategic choices. Many large companies diversify their operations both by investing in

Exhibit 1-2   Comparative Country Risk Rankings

Country	Overall Rating	Political Risk	GDP Growth	Per Capita Income	Trade Flow with U.S.
Italy	4.13	5	3	5	4
Denmark	4.25	5	3	5	2
Netherlands	4.63	5	3	5	4
Japan	4.19	5	3	5	5
Australia	4.5	5	4	5	4
Ireland	4.38	5	3	5	3
Germany	4.5	5	3	5	5
Sweden	4	5	3	5	3
France	4.38	5	3	5	5
Switzerland	4.5	5	3	5	4
Singapore	4.88	5	5	5	5
Belgium	4.38	5	3	5	4
United Kingdom	4.63	5	3	5	5
Canada	4.38	5	3	4	5
Israel	4	4	4	4	4
Malaysia	3.75	4	4	—	4
Chile	2.88	4	3	—	2
Thailand	3.5	4	4	—	4
South Korea	3.63	4	4	3	5
Spain	3.5	4	3	4	3
Hong Kong	4.5	4	4	5	4
Saudi Arabia	3.38	4	3	2	4
Taiwan	4.13	4	4	4	5
Turkey	2.13	3	—	—	2
South Africa	2.75	3	3	—	2
Argentina	3.25	3	4	3	3
Poland	2.75	3	4	—	2
Indonesia	2.63	3	4	—	3
Philippines	3	3	4	—	4
Costa Rica	2.38	3	3	—	2
Czech Republic	2.75	3	3	—	—
Colombia	3.25	3	4	3	3
India	2.75	3	3	—	3
China	2.88	3	4	—	5
Mexico	3.38	3	3	2	5
Brazil	3	3	4	—	4
Egypt	2.38	2	3	—	2
Venezuela	2.38	2	2	—	4
Peru	2.56	2	4.5	—	2
Russia	2	—	—	2	2

SOURCE: Data from T. Morrison, W. Conaway, and J. Douress, Dun & Bradstreet's *Guide to Doing Business Around the World* (Englewood Cliffs, N.J: Prentice-Hall, 1997).

Exhibit 1-2   (cont.)

Country	Monetary Policy	Trade Policy	Protection of Property Rights	Foreign Investment Climate
Italy	4	4	4	4
Denmark	5	4	5	5
Netherlands	5	5	5	5
Japan	5	4	4	2.5
Australia	5	4	5	4
Ireland	5	4	5	5
Germany	5	4	5	4
Sweden	4	4	4	4
France	5	4	5	3
Switzerland	5	4	5	5
Singapore	5	5	4	5
Belgium	5	4	5	4
United Kingdom	5	4	5	5
Canada	5	4	5	4
Israel	3	4	4	5
Malaysia	5	4	4	4
Chile	3	3	3	4
Thailand	5	3	3	4
South Korea	5	3	3	2
Spain	3	4	3	4
Hong Kong	4	5	5	5
Saudi Arabia	5	3	3	3
Taiwan	5	4	4	3
Turkey	—	3	2	4
South Africa	4	3	3	3
Argentina	4	3	3	3
Poland	2	3	3	4
Indonesia	3	2	3	2
Philippines	4	2	4	4
Costa Rica	2	2	3	3
Czech Republic	3	4	3	4
Colombia	4	3	3	3
India	4	2	3	3
China	3	2	2	3
Mexico	4	3	3	4
Brazil	3	3	3	3
Egypt	4	2	2	3
Venezuela	2	2	3	3
Peru	2.5	2.5	3	3
Russia	—	3	3	3

Ranking Scale: 1–5, with 5 = best, or lowest risk.

many countries and by operating through joint ventures with a local firm or government or through local licensees. By involving local people, companies, and agencies, firms minimize the risk of negative outcomes due to political events. (We discuss these and other global strategies in Chapters 6 and 7.)

Managing Terrorism Risk

> Terrorists attack New York City World Trade Center and The Pentagon.
> —NEWS SOURCES AROUND THE WORLD, SEPTEMBER 11, 2001

> Eighty countries lost citizens in the World Trade Center.
> —SECRETARY COLIN POWELL, SEPTEMBER 23, 2001

No longer is the risk of terrorism for global businesses focused only on certain areas such as South America or the Middle East. That risk now has to be considered in countries such as the United States, which had previously been regarded as safe. Many companies from Asia and Europe had office branches in the towers of the World Trade Center in New York; most of those offices, along with the employees from those countries, were destroyed in the attack. Thousands of lives and billions of dollars were lost, not only by those immediately affected by the attack, but also by countless small and large businesses impacted by the ripple effect; global airlines and financial markets were devastated.

As incidents of terrorism accelerate around the world, such as the year 2000 bombing of the U.S.S. *Cole* in Yemen, many companies are also increasingly aware of the need to manage the risk of terrorism. Both IBM and Exxon try to develop a benevolent image in high-risk countries through charitable contributions to the local community. They also try to maintain low profiles and minimize publicity in the host countries by using discreet corporate signs at the company sites, for instance.[49] Some companies have put together teams to monitor the patterns of terrorism around the world. Kidnappings are common in Latin America (as a means of raising money for political activities). Abductions in Colombia hit a record 3,029 in 2000.[50] In the Middle East, airplane hijackings, kidnapping of foreigners, and blackmail (for the release of political prisoners) are common. In Western Europe, terrorists typically aim bombs at U.S. banks and computer companies. Almost all MNCs have stepped up their security measures abroad, hiring consultants in counterterrorism (to train employees to cope with the threat of terrorism) and advising their employees to avoid U.S. airlines when flying overseas.[51]

Economic Risk

> The Chilean power companies, forestry firms, soda bottlers and supermarkets that plowed billions of dollars into Argentina are now retrenching or revising their strategies. The moves follow Argentina's currency devaluation, which brought the economy to a virtual standstill and sapped the population of much of its remaining buying power.
> —WALL STREET JOURNAL, FEBRUARY 20, 2002, P.A.17.[52]

Closely connected to a country's political stability is its economic environment—and the relative risk that it may pose to foreign companies. A country's level of economic development generally determines its economic stability and therefore its relative risk to a foreign firm. Most industrialized nations pose little risk of economic instability; less developed nations pose more risk. This risk was illustrated when Argentina's economic woes, expected to result in the country's economy shrinking up to 15 percent in 2002, negatively affected foreign firms doing business there.

A country's ability or intention to meet its financial obligations determines its economic risk. The economic risk incurred by a foreign corporation usually falls into one of two main categories; its subsidiary (or other investment) in a specific country may become unprofitable (1) if the government abruptly changes its domestic monetary or fiscal policies or (2) if the government decides to modify its foreign-investment policies. The latter situation would threaten the company's ability to repatriate its earnings and would create a financial or interest-rate risk.[53] Furthermore, the risk of exchange-rate volatility results in currency translation exposure to the firm when the balance sheet of the entire corporation is consolidated and may cause a negative cash flow from the foreign subsidiary. Currency translation exposure occurs when the value of one country's currency changes relative to that of another. For a U.S. company operating in Mexico, the peso devaluation meant that the company's assets in that country were worth less when translated into dollars on the financial statements; but the firm's liabilities in Mexico were also less. When exchange-rate changes are radical, as with the devaluation of the Russian ruble in 1998, there are repercussions around the world. Not only is it unfortunate for the Russian people whose money can buy so much less, but it also means that Russian firms do not have enough buying power to purchase products from overseas, which means that the sales of foreign companies will decline. On the other hand, foreign companies have more purchasing power in Russia to outsource raw materials, labor, and so on.

Because every MNC operating overseas exposes itself to some level of economic risk, often affecting its everyday operational profitability, managers constantly reassess the level of risk the company may face in any specific country or region of the world. Four methods of analyzing economic risk, or a country's creditworthiness, are recommended by John Mathis, a professor of international economics who has also served as senior financial policy analyst for the World Bank. These methods are (1) the quantitative approach, (2) the qualitative approach, (3) a combination of both of these approaches, and (4) the checklist approach.

The *quantitative method*, says Mathis, "attempts to measure statistically a country's ability to honor its debt obligation."[54] This measure is arrived at by assigning different weights to economic variables in order to produce a composite index used to monitor the country's creditworthiness over time and to make comparisons with other countries. A drawback of this approach is that it does not take into account different stages of development among the countries it compares.

The *qualitative approach* evaluates a country's economic risk by assessing the competence of its leaders and analyzing the types of policies they are likely to implement. This approach entails a subjective assessment by the researcher in the process of interviewing those leaders and projecting the future direction of the economy.

The *checklist approach*, explains Mathis, "relies on a few easily measurable and timely criteria believed to reflect or indicate changes in the creditworthiness of the country."[55] Researchers develop various vulnerability indicators that categorize countries in terms of their ability to withstand economic volatility. Most corporations recognize that neither this, nor any single approach, can provide a comprehensive economic risk profile of a country. Therefore they try to use a combination of approaches.

In 2001, companies around the world were still feeling the effects of their exposure to economic risk in Asian countries as their economic decline that began with Thailand in 1997 deepened and as it appeared that Japan was not taking sufficiently radical steps to turn its economy around. At that time, the reverberations, felt around the world in its effects on the earnings of MNCs and on the world's stock markets, reconfirmed for everyone the interdependence of world economies, and clarified the points of interface between world economic issues and business, and indeed that of the individual's welfare. The Comparative Management in Focus section further details this situation.

Comparative Management in Focus

Global Managers Respond to Economic Slide in Indonesia[56]

"In one month, you see your net income wiped out before your eyes."
—JOHN VONDRAS, U.S. WEST MANAGER IN INDONESIA.

As one Asian economy after another appeared to be melting down in 1998, one of the first to fall, and the hardest hit, was Indonesia, the world's fourth largest country. The result was devastating for the people in Indonesia as the rupiah lost 75 percent of its value over a period of just a few months. Inflation seemed to be out of hand, and the country faced considerable unrest and rioting. It wasn't long before President Suharto was forced to resign.

Foreign companies operating in Indonesia were also hit hard; their managers struggled with how to respond to the events and how much economic risk to take in anticipation of the potential long-term rewards of a vast market opening up to foreigners. Japanese and British companies have an even greater investment to date in Indonesia than do U.S. companies, which alone have invested some $9 billion there. Lured by abundant natural resources, companies such as Goodyear Tire & Rubber have long had a presence in Indonesia. Unocal has been there for 30 years and plans to stay. Barry Lane of Unocal notes that "Major infrastructure projects are so integrated into a country, it's not like we could pack up our bags and leave at any moment." Interdependence of country and foreign investment is further evidenced by Freeport McMoRan, Inc., which mines copper, gold, and silver in the Irian Jaya province. That region is the company's entire mining resource, and the company is the largest corporate taxpayer for Indonesia.

One of the managers caught in the downdraft was John Vondras, U.S. West's top manager in Indonesia, in charge of running a 500,000-line telephone system in Indonesia. His problems were many; as a result of the devaluation of the rupiah, the company was losing a great deal in dollar terms, even though local revenues in rupiahs were up 26 percent. In addition, his joint venture has to repay a $615 million loan in U.S. dollars, even though it earns revenues in rupiahs. "In one month," says Vondras, "you see your net income wiped out before your eyes."[57]

A number of companies, such as a KFC franchise, were in partnership with a member of the Suharto family, which in the past was often the only entry mode for foreign firms trying to gain a foothold in Indonesia. Other companies, such as General Motors, have been able to get out of this relationship. GM, which has been making cars in Indonesia since 1994, was able to buy out its Indonesian partner, a Suharto half-brother, in 1997. Although the local partner—unable to withstand the Asian economic crisis—has since gone bankrupt, GM has been able to keep afloat. However, GM cars lost two-thirds of their dollar value within a few days. GM now makes monthly price revisions in anticipation of currency exchange fluctuations. Other strategies adopted to combat the problem have been to increase the local content of GM cars in order to take advantage of lower local costs. Bill Botwick, president of GM's Indonesian operation, says he is hanging in there for the long run because they expect to have a good market share.

As the IMF pressures the Indonesian government to privatize state-owned companies in the banking, telecommunications, mining, steel, ship-building, and aerospace sectors, investment opportunities will become available and help to reverse the economic decline. Meanwhile, foreign managers there are assessing their exposure to continued economic risk compared to the potential long-term market opportunities.

THE LEGAL ENVIRONMENT

The prudent global manager consults with legal services, both locally and at her or his headquarters, to comply with host-country regulations and to maintain cooperative long-term relationships in the local area. If the manager waits until a problem arises, little legal recourse may be available outside of local interpretation and enforcement. Indeed, this has been the experience of many foreign managers in China, where financial and legal systems remain rudimentary in spite of attempts to show the world a capitalist face. Managers there often simply ignore their debts to foreign companies as they did under the old socialist system.[58] The painful lesson to many foreign companies in China is that they are losing millions because Beijing often does not stand behind the commitments of its state-owned enterprises. Although still no guarantee, the risk of massive losses may be minimized, among other ways, by making sure you get approval from related government offices (national, provincial, and local), seeing that you are not going to run amok of long-term government goals, and getting loan guarantees from the headquarters of one of Beijing's main banks.[59] In addition, one cannot assume that there will be legal recourse in China. Mr. Cheng, an American businessman who grew up in Hunan, was thrown in jail in China because a Chinese businessman changed his mind about investing in Mr. Cheng's safety-helmet factory in Zhuhai. Only after two months and his son's visit to the U.S. Embassy in Beijing was Mr. Cheng freed. Mr. Cheng asks, "[without even a trial], how could the court render a decision just one hour after Mr. Liu and my general manager had signed a new contract?"[60] Some of the contributing factors, he has realized since then, were the personal connections—*guanxi*—involved and the fact that some courts offer their services to the business community for profit. In addition, many judges get their jobs through nepotism rather than by virtue of a law degree.

Although the regulatory environment for the international manager consists of the many local laws and the court systems in those countries in which he or she operates, certain other legal issues are covered by international law—the law that governs relationships between sovereign countries, the basic units in the world political system.[61] One such agreement, which regulates international business by spelling out the rights and obligations of the seller and the buyer, is the United Nations Convention on Contracts for the International Sale of Goods (CISG). This convention became law on January 1, 1988, and applies to contracts for the sale of goods between countries that have adopted the convention.

Generally speaking, the manager of the foreign subsidiary or foreign operating division will comply with the host country's legal system. Such systems, derived from common law, civil law, or Muslim law, are a reflection of the country's culture, religion, and traditions. Under **common law**, used in the United States and 26 other countries of English origin or influence, past court decisions act as precedents to the interpretation of the law and to common custom. **Civil law** is based on a comprehensive set of laws organized into a code. Interpretation of these laws is based on reference to codes and statutes. About 70 countries, predominantly in Europe (e.g., France and Germany), are ruled by civil law, as is Japan. In Islamic countries, such as Saudi Arabia, the dominant legal system is Islamic law; based on religious beliefs, it dominates all aspects of life. **Islamic law** is followed in approximately 27 countries and combines, in varying degrees, civil, common, and indigenous law.[62]

Contract Law

In China, the old joke goes, a contract is a pause in the negotiation.
—VANESSA CHANG, KPMG PEAT MARWICK[63]

A **contract** is an agreement by the parties concerned to establish a set of rules to govern a business transaction. Contract law plays a major role in international business transactions because of the complexities arising from the differences in the legal systems of participating countries and because the host government in many developing and communist countries is often a third party in the contract. Both common-law and civil-law countries enforce contracts, although their means of resolving disputes differ. Under civil law, it is assumed that a contract reflects promises that will be enforced without specifying the details in the contract; under common law, the details of promises must be written into the contract to be enforced.[64] Astute international managers recognize that they will have to draft contracts in legal contexts different from their own, and so they prepare themselves accordingly by consulting with experts in international law before going overseas. In China, for example, "The risk is, you could have a contract torn up or changed. We're just going to have to adjust to that in the West," says Robert Broadfoot, who heads the Political & Economic Risk Consultancy in Hong Kong. He says that Western companies think they can avoid political risk by spelling out every detail in a contract, but "in Asia, there is no shortcut for managing the relationship."[65] In other words, the contract is in the relationship, not on the paper, and the way to ensure the reliability of the agreement is to nurture the relationship.

Even a deal that has been implemented for some time may start to get watered down at a time when you cannot do anything about it. A Japanese-led consortium experienced this problem after it built an expressway in Bangkok. The Thai government later lowered the toll that it had agreed could be charged for use of the road. This is a subtle form of expropriation, since a company cannot simply pack up a road and leave.[66] Neglect regarding contract law may leave a firm burdened with an agent who does not perform the expected functions, or a firm may be faced with laws that prevent management from laying off employees (often the case in Belgium, Holland, Germany, Sweden, and elsewhere).[67]

Other Regulatory Issues

Differences in laws and regulations from country to country are numerous and complex. These and other issues in the regulatory environment that concern multinational firms are discussed briefly here.

Countries often impose protectionist policies, such as tariffs, quotas, and other trade restrictions, to give preference to their own products and industries. The Japanese have come under much criticism for protectionism, which they use to limit imports of foreign goods while they continue exporting consumer goods (e.g., cars, electronics) on a large scale. The American auto industry continues to ask the U.S. government for protection from Japanese car imports. Calls to "buy American," however, are thwarted by the difficulty of identifying cars that are truly American-made; the intricate web of car-manufacturing alliances between Japanese and American companies often makes it difficult to distinguish the maker.

A country's tax system influences the attractiveness of investing in that country and affects the relative level of profitability for an MNC. Foreign tax credits, holidays, exemptions, depreciation allowances, and taxation of corporate profits are additional considerations the foreign investor must examine before acting. Many countries have signed tax treaties (or conventions) that define terms such as income, source, and residency and spell out what constitutes taxable activities.

The level of government involvement in the economic and regulatory environment varies a great deal among countries and has a varying impact on management practices. In Canada, the government has a significant involvement in the economy. It has a powerful role in many industries, including transportation, petrochemicals, fishing, steel, textiles, and building materials—forming partly owned or wholly owned enterprises. Wholly owned businesses are called Crown Corporations (Petro Canada, Ontario Hydro Corporation, Marystown Shipyard, Saskatchewan Telephones, and so forth), many of which are as large as the major private companies. The government's role in the Canadian economy, then, is one of both control and competition.[68] Government policies, subsidies, and regulations directly affect the manager's planning process, as do other major factors in the Canadian legal environment, such as the high proportion of unionized workers (30 percent). In Quebec, the law requiring official bilingualism imposes considerable operating constraints and expenses. For a foreign subsidiary, this regulation forces managers to speak both French and English and to incur the costs of language training for employees, translators, the administration of bilingual paperwork, and so on.[69]

THE TECHNOLOGICAL ENVIRONMENT

The effects of technology around the world are pervasive—both in business and in private lives. In many parts of the world, whole generations of technological development are being skipped over—for example, many people will go straight to a digital phone without ever having had their houses wired under the analog system. Even in a remote village such as Bario, Malaysia—still lacking traditional roads in 2001—an information highway is under way.[70] Advances in information technology are bringing about increased productivity—for employees, for companies, and for countries.

Now that we are in a global information society, it is clear that corporations must incorporate into their strategic planning and their everyday operations the accelerating macro-environmental phenomenon of **technoglobalism**—in which the rapid developments in information and communication technologies (**ICTs**) are propelling globalization and vice versa.[71] Investment-led globalization is leading to global production networks, which results in global diffusion of technology to link parts of the value-added chain in different countries. That chain may comprise parts of the same firm, or it may comprise suppliers and customers, or technology-partnering alliances among two or more firms. Either way, technological developments are facilitating, indeed necessitating, the network firm structure that allows flexibility and rapid response to local needs. Clearly, the effects of technology on global trade and business transactions cannot be ignored; in addition, the **Internet** is propelling electronic commerce around the world. The ease of use and pervasiveness of the Internet raises difficult questions about ownership of intellectual property, consumer protection, residence location, taxation, and other issues.[72]

New technology specific to a firm's products represents a key competitive advantage to firms and challenges international businesses to manage the transfer and diffusion of proprietary technology, with its attendant risks. Whether it is a product, a process, or a management technology, an MNC's major concern is the **appropriability of technology**—that is, the ability of the innovating firm to profit from its own technology by protecting it from competitors.

An MNC can enjoy many technological benefits from its global operations. Advances resulting from cooperative research and development (R&D) can be transferred among affiliates around the world, and specialized management knowledge can be integrated and shared. However, the risk of technology transfer and pirating is considerable and costly. Although firms face few restrictions on the creation and dissemination of technology in developed countries, less developed countries often impose restrictions on licensing agreements, royalties, and so forth, and have other legal constraints on patent protection.

In Germany, for example, royalties on patents are limited to 10 percent of sales, but the patent and trademark durations are 20 years and 10 years, respectively, with 45 percent being the highest tax bracket allowed on royalties. Less developed countries tend to be comparatively more restrictive on the patent and trademark durations and on the range of unpatentable items. Egypt has no limits on royalties but will only patent production processes, and then only for 15 years.

In most countries, governments use their laws to some extent to control the flow of technology. These controls may be in place for reasons of national security. Other countries, LDCs in particular, use their investment laws to acquire needed technology (usually labor-intensive technology to create jobs), to increase exports, to use local technology, and to train local people.

The most common methods of protecting proprietary technology are the use of patents, trademarks, trade names, copyrights, and trade secrets. Various international conventions do afford some protection in participating countries; over 80 countries adhere to the International Convention for the Protection of Industrial Property, often referred to as the Paris Union, for the protection of patents. However, restrictions and differences in the rules in some countries not signatory to the Paris Union, as well as industrial espionage, pose continuing problems for firms trying to protect their technology. In 2002, Western pharmeceutical companies were embroiled in the difficult battle to protect their patents for drugs, while some less developed economies felt they had a right to override patents in order to provide low-cost drugs to fight the AIDS epidemic.

One risk to a firm's intellectual property is the inappropriate use of the technology by joint-venture partners, franchisees, licensees, and employees (especially those who move to other companies). Some countries rigorously enforce employee secrecy agreements.

As another major consideration, global managers will want to evaluate the appropriateness of technology for the local environment—especially in less developed countries. Studying the possible cultural consequences of the transfer of technology, managers must assess whether the local people are ready and willing to change their values, expectations, and behaviors on the job to use new technological methods, whether applied to production, research, marketing, finance, or some other aspect of business. Often, the decision regarding the level of technology transfer is dominated by the host government's regulations or requirements. In some instances, the host country may require that foreign investors import only their most modern machinery and methods so that the local area may benefit from new technology. In other cases, the host country may insist that foreign companies only use labor-intensive processes—this can help to reduce high unemployment in the area. When the choice is left to international managers, experts in economic development recommend that managers make an informed choice of appropriate technology. The choice of technology may be capital-intensive, labor-intensive, or intermediate, but the key is that it should suit the level of development in the area and the needs and expectations of the people who will use it.[73]

As an example of the successful use of appropriate technology, we can mention a small manufacturer of detergent in India called Patel. Patel has taken over three-quarters of the detergent market from Lever, a multinational company whose Surf brand detergent had formerly dominated the market in India. Managers at Patel realized that, although Surf was a high-quality, high-priced product, it was not suitable for a poor country. They set up a chain of stores in which people mixed their own detergent ingredients by hand. This primitive method has enabled Patel to tailor its technology to the conditions and expectations in India and to outsell Lever on the basis of price; its annual sales are now over $250 million.[74]

Global E-Business

> What happened to the Net's borderless economy? . . . The Internet promises frictionless trade, clarity of pricing, and a medium where language problems are minimized. We're still very far away from that point, though.
>
> —www.businessweek.com, AUGUST 27, 2001

In spite of global trade's lower pace of advancement over the Internet than initially expected, without doubt the Internet has had a considerable impact on how companies buy and sell goods around the world—mostly raw materials and services going to manufacturers. Internet-based electronic trading and data exchange is changing the way companies do business, breaking down global barriers of time, space, logistics, and culture. It has introduced a new level of global competition by providing efficiencies through reducing numbers of suppliers and slashing administration costs throughout the value chain. **E-business** is "the integration of systems, processes, organizations, value chains and entire markets using Internet-based and related technologies and concepts."[75] **E-commerce** refers directly to the marketing and sales process. Firms use e-business to help build new relationships between businesses and customers.[76] The Internet and e-business provide a number of uses and advantages in global business, including the following:[77]

1. Convenience in conducting business worldwide; facilitating communication across borders contributes to the shift toward globalization and a global market.
2. An electronic meeting and trading place, which adds efficiency in conducting business sales.

3. A corporate Intranet service, merging internal and external information for enterprises worldwide.
4. Power to consumers as they gain access to limitless options and price differentials.
5. A link and efficiency in distribution.[78]

Although most of the early attention was on e-commerce, experts now believe the real opportunities are in business-to-business (**B2B**) transactions. And while the scope, complexity, and sheer speed of the B2B phenomenon, including e-market-places, have global executives scrambling to assess the impact and their own competitive roles, estimates for growth in the e-business marketplace may have been overzealous. The global economic slowdown and its resultant dampening of corporate IT spending have caused various research groups such as AMR Research and the Gartner Group to revise downwards their projections for B2B Internet transactions, as shown in Exhibit 1-3. Still the growth projections are considerable, with an estimated $6 trillion in B2B transactions expected in 2004.

While we hear mostly about large companies embracing B2B, it is noteworthy that a large proportion of the current and projected B2B use is by small and medium-sized firms. This is shown in Exhibit 1-4, broken down by three common purposes—supply chain, procurement, and distribution channel.

Exhibit 1-3

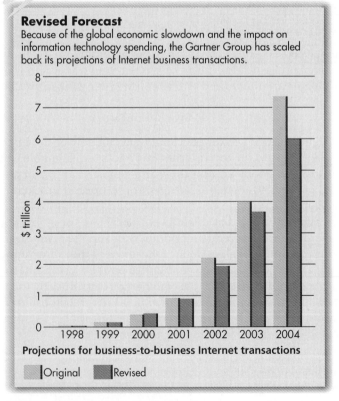

SOURCE: *The New York Times,* March 26, 2001.

Exhibit 1-4

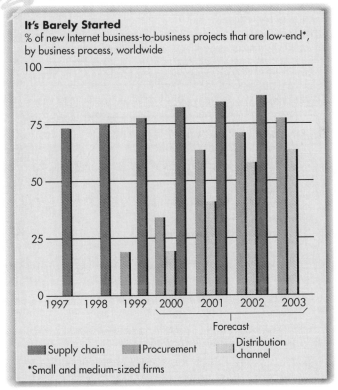

It's Barely Started
% of new Internet business-to-business projects that are low-end*,
by business process, worldwide

Supply chain   Procurement   Distribution channel

Forecast

*Small and medium-sized firms

SOURCE: *The Economist*, November 11, 2000.

Of course, a successful Internet strategy—especially on a global scale—is not easy. Potential problems abound, as experienced by the European and U.S. companies surveyed by Forrester Research and shown in Exhibit 1-5. These problems include internal obstacles and politics, difficulties in regional coordination and in balancing global versus local e-commerce, and cultural differences. Such a large-scale change in organizing business clearly calls for absolute commitment from the top, empowered employees with a willingness to experiment, and good internal communications.[79]

Barriers to the adoption and progression of e-business around the world include lack of readiness of partners in the value chain, such as suppliers. Typically, companies must invest in increasing their trading partners' readiness and their customers' capabilities if they want to have an effective marketplace. Other barriers are cultural. In Europe, for example:

> Europe's e-commerce excursion has been hindered by a laundry list of cultural and regulatory obstacles, like widely varying tax systems, language hurdles and currency issues.
> —E-COMMERCE REPORT, *THE NEW YORK TIMES*, MARCH 26, 2001

Exhibit 1-5

Why It Isn't Easy
"What is the major pain in doing global e-commerce?"
% of 40 US and European companies interviewed

- Internal obstacles and politics
- Balance of global v local e-commerce
- Regional co-ordination
- Cultural differences
- Inadequate service provider
- Transition of global to web strategy
- Global logistics
- Complicated product to deliver

SOURCE: *The Economist*, November 11, 2000.

In other areas of the world, barriers to creating global e-businesses include differences in infrastructure systems such as physical infrastructures, information, and payment infrastructures. In those countries, innovation is required to use local systems for implementing a web strategy; examples are given in the Management Focus section.

For these reasons, B2B e-business is likely to expand globally faster than B2C. In addition, consumer e-commerce depends on each country's level of access to computers and the Internet, as well as the relative efficiency of home delivery.

Other problems relate to the difficulty within industries of agreeing on common formats for transmitting data—a problem experienced by Milan Turk, Jr., director of global customer business development for Procter and Gamble.[80]

In spite of various problems, use of the Internet to facilitate and improve global competitiveness continues to be explored and discovered. In the public sector in Europe, for example, the European Commission has started advertising tender invitations on-line in order to transform the way public sector contracts are awarded, using the Internet to build a truly single market:

> With public procurement accounting for 11.5 percent of the European Union's GDP, the initiative could result in increased cross-border trade, improved transparency and openness, and better value-for-money for taxpayers.
>
> —*THE FINANCIAL TIMES*, www.ft.com/eprocurement, WINTER 2000

Management Focus

IN JAPAN AND INDIA, E-BUSINESS MUST BE LOCALIZED

Credit cards are not widely used for e-commerce in Japan—less than 10 percent of transactions are conducted using credit cards. Bank transfers and COD are the most popular payment mechanisms. But many consumers in Japan regularly use convenience stores to pay utility and other bills. Thus, 7-Eleven Japan has a payment acceptance service for products and services purchased from Web merchants. Consumers can select "Payment at a 7-Eleven Store" as one of the payment options and print out a payment slip that they present at their nearest 7-Eleven store.

Now, 7-Eleven Japan is going one step further by allowing consumers to pick up and pay for merchandise bought on the Web at any of its 8,000 7-Eleven stores in Japan. This venture, called 7dream.com, may become the dominant fulfillment and payment infrastructure for e-commerce in Japan.

7-Eleven stores may become e-commerce kiosks, payment centers, and fulfillment centers. Similar opportunities await operators of public call office (PCO) booths in India, which can be converted into combination Internet cafes and collection centers for e-commerce shipments.

Consider an even more basic problem with B2B e-commerce in countries like India. Many small businesses in India do not have Internet access or even personal computers. So, how can a U.S.-based B2B firm connect with Indian suppliers? Limited Internet penetration seems to be a fatal constraint, until you realize that what India *does* have is abundant cheap labor. So a B2B e-commerce venture can afford to have real people visiting each small supplier in India, manually collecting orders, invoices, and payments. This information can be entered into a Net-based transaction system that can communicate with the U.S.-based buyers. At the Indian end of the network, "humanware" can substitute for hardware and software. The insight is to substitute capital for labor.

SOURCE: Mohanbir, Sawhney and Mandal Sumant, "Go Global," *Business* 2.0, May 2000, pp. 178–213.

Other global professional service organizations are successfully using all aspects of e-business and are helping their clients to do so. One example is PricewaterhouseCoopers. The company's employees, operating in over 150 countries, provide clients with expertise in solving complex business problems, including the sectors of Global Human Resources, Business Process Outsourcing, Financial Advisory, Audit and Advisory, Management Consulting, and Global Tax Services.[81]

As the PricewaterhouseCoopers executives claim, e-business is not only a new Website on the Internet, but "a source of significant strategic advantage; one that will distinguish one company from another and transform business relationships as they are known today."[82] Hoping to capture this strategic advantage, the European Airbus venture—a public and private sector combination—has joined a global aerospace B2B exchange for aircraft parts, as detailed in the accompanying *E-Biz Box*. The exchange illustrates two major trends in global competition—those of cooperative global alliances, even among competitors, to achieve synergies, and the use of technology to enable those connections and synergies.

Conclusion

A skillful global manager cannot develop a suitable strategic plan or consider an investment abroad without first assessing the environment—political, legal,

E-Biz Box

EUROPE'S AIRBUS JOINS GLOBAL AEROSPACE B2B EXCHANGE

France's Airbus Industrie is joining the Global Aerospace and Defense Exchange for aircraft parts under development by Boeing, Lockheed Martin, Raytheon, and BAE Systems. The open aerospace and defense exchange is based on the Commerce One MarketSite Portal Solution, which provides an electronic marketplace where buyers and sellers around the world can conduct business. The founding industry partners have an agreement to share equal ownership stakes in the new entity, with adjustments over time to be based on each partner's flow of its e-commerce through the exchange. Commerce One has a 5 percent equity; and 20 percent equity has been set aside for other industry participants and employees of the new venture.

The partner companies, their manufacturers, and their suppliers expect to realize enormous cost savings in the $400 billion industry by buying and selling parts over the Internet in the on-line exchange. The companies involved currently do business with over 37,000 suppliers, hundreds of airlines, and national governments globally, all of which will be invited to join the Web-based marketplace. Most commercial airplanes contain up to six million parts and are supported by millions of pages of technical data. The partners expect to be able to deliver greater value and to realize significantly lower transaction costs. The exchange will also be an e-marketplace for the indirect products and services that the partner companies, the airlines, and their suppliers need for daily operations.

Plans for the Website now include the world's five largest aerospace companies and the biggest manufacturers of commercial airliners, Boeing and Airbus. Airbus Industrie is a European consortium comprising France's Aerospatiale Matra, Germany's DaimlerChrysler Aerospace, Spain's Construcciones Aeronauticas, and UK's BAE Systems.

While the combined exchange is being developed, the partners involved continue their own e-commerce sites, such as Raytheon's www.Everythingaircraft.com and Airbus Online Services. Meanwhile, other alliances among various partners continue, such as that between Aerospatiale, DaimlerChrysler Aerospace, and Construcciones, which formed the European Aeronautic Defence and Space Company. The company also plans to pull Italy's Finmeccanica into the fold. The Brits, retaining their usual independence, have decided to keep their aerospace company BAE Systems, 20 percent owner of Airbus, independent.

But no-one said it would be easy. Commerce One, developer of the five-member Global aerospace site, faces considerable technical hurdles because of the tremendous red tape and regulatory clearances involved with aerospace transactions.

SOURCES: Adapted from: www.commerceone.com, www.Airbus.com, www.herring.com, www.FT.com, www.Boeing.com, www.baesystems.com, www.raytheon.com, and www.lockheedmartin.com (all 2000).

regulatory, and technological—in which the company will operate. This assessment should result not so much in a comparison of countries as in a comparison of (1) the relative risk and (2) the projected return on investments among these countries. Similarly, for ongoing operations, both the subsidiary manager and headquarters management must continually monitor the environment for potentially unsettling events or undesirable changes that may require the redirection of certain subsidiaries or the entire company. Some of the critical factors affecting the global manager's environment (and therefore requiring monitoring) are listed in Exhibit 1-6.

Environmental risk has become the new frontier in global business. The skills of companies and the measures taken to manage their exposure to environmental risk on a world scale will soon largely replace their ability to develop, produce, and market global brands as the key element in global competitive advantage.[83]

Exhibit 1-6   The Environment of the Global Manager

Political Environment	Economic Environment
Form of government	Economic system
Political stability	State of development
Foreign policy	Economic stability
State companies	GNP
Role of military	International financial standing
Level of terrorism	Monetary/fiscal policies
Restrictions on imports/exports	Foreign investment
Regulatory Environment	**Technological Environment**
Legal system	Level of technology
Prevailing international laws	Availability of local technical skills
Protectionist laws	Technical requirements of country
Tax laws	Appropriability
Role of contracts	Transfer of technology
Protection for proprietary property	Infrastructure
	Environmental protection

Cultural Environment (see Part 2)

As we shall see, the managerial functions and the daily operations of a firm are also affected by a subtle, but powerful, environmental factor in the host country—that of culture. The pervasive role of culture in international management will be discussed fully in Part 2.

In the next chapter we will assess some more subtle, but critical, factors in the global environment—those of social responsibility and ethical behavior. We will consider such questions as: What is the role of the firm in the future of other societies and their people? What stakeholders do managers need to consider in their strategic and operational decisions in other countries? How do the expectations of firm behavior vary around the world, and should those expectations influence the international manager's decisions? What role does long-term global economic interdependence play in the firm's actions in other countries?

SUMMARY OF KEY POINTS

1. Competing in the twenty-first century requires firms to invest in the increasingly refined managerial skills needed to perform effectively in a multicultural environment. Managers need a global orientation to meet the challenges of world markets and rapid, fundamental changes in a world of increasing economic interdependence.

2. Global management is the process of developing strategies, designing and operating systems, and working with people around the world to ensure sustained competitive advantage.

3. One major direction in world trade is the development of regional free-trade blocs. The TRIAD market refers to the three trade blocs of Western Europe, Asia, and North America.

4. New markets and trading opportunities are emerging in Eastern Europe (in countries like Hungary and those of the Commonwealth of Independent States), in China, and in less developed countries.

5. Drastic worldwide changes present dynamic challenges to global managers, including the political and economic trend toward the privatization of businesses, rapid advances in information technology, and a growing culturally diverse workforce.

6. Global managers must be aware of political risks around the world. Political risks are any governmental actions or politically motivated events that adversely affect the long-run profitability or value of a firm.

7. Political risk assessment by MNCs usually takes two forms—consultation with experts familiar with the area and the development of internal staff capabilities. Political risk can be managed through (1) avoiding or withdrawing investment; (2) adapting to the political regulatory environment; (3) maintaining the host country's dependency on the parent corporation; and (4) hedging potential losses through political risk insurance and local debt financing.

8. Economic risk refers to a country's ability to meet its financial obligations. The risk is that the government may change its economic policies, thereby making a foreign company unprofitable or unable to repatriate its foreign earnings.

9. The regulatory environment comprises the many different laws and courts of those nations in which a company operates. Most legal systems derive from the common law, civil law, or Muslim law.

10. Use of the Internet in e-commerce—in particular in business-to-business transactions—and for intracompany efficiencies, is rapidly becoming an important factor in global competitiveness.

11. The appropriability of technology is the ability of the innovating firm to protect its technology from competitors and to obtain economic benefits from that technology. Risks to the appropriability of technology include technology transfer and pirating and legal restrictions on the protection of proprietary technology. Intellectual property can be protected through patents, trademarks, trade names, copyrights, and trade secrets.

DISCUSSION QUESTIONS

1. Discuss examples of recent macropolitical risk events and the effect they have or might have on a foreign subsidiary. What are micropolitical risk events? Give some examples and explain how they affect international business.

2. What means can managers use to assess political risk? What do you think is the relative effectiveness of these different methods? At the time you are reading this, what countries or areas do you feel have political risk sufficient to discourage you from doing business there?

3. Can political risk be "managed"? If so, what methods can be used to manage such risk, and how effective are they? Discuss the lengths you would go to manage political risk relative to the kinds of returns you would expect to gain.

4. Explain what is meant by the economic risk of a nation. Use a specific country as an example. Can economic risk in this country be anticipated? How?

5. Discuss the importance of contracts in international management. What steps must a manager take to ensure a valid and enforceable contract?

6. Discuss the effects of various forms of technology on international business. What role does the Internet play? Where is all this leading us? Explain the meaning of the appropriability of technology. What role does this play in international competitiveness? How can managers protect the proprietary technology of their firms?

7. Discuss the risk of terrorism. What means can managers use to reduce the risk or the effects of terrorism? Where in the world, and from what likely sources, would you anticipate terrorism?

APPLICATION EXERCISES

1. Do some further research on the technological environment. What are the recent developments affecting businesses and propelling globalization? What problems have arisen regarding use of the Internet for global business transactions, and how are they being resolved?
2. Consider recent events and the prevailing political and economic conditions in the Commonwealth of Independent States (the former Soviet Union). As a manager who has been considering investment there, how do you assess the political and economic risks at this time? What should be your company's response to this environment?

EXPERIENTIAL EXERCISE

In groups of three, represent a consulting firm.

You have been hired by a diversified multinational corporation to advise on the political and economic environment in different countries. The company wants to open one or two manufacturing facilities in Europe to take advantage of the EU agreement. Consider a specific type of company and two specific countries in Europe and present to the class the types of risks that would be involved and what steps the firm could take to manage those risks. Which country do you recommend?

INTERNET RESOURCES

Visit the Deresky companion Website at http://prenhall.com/Deresky for this Chapter's Internet resources.

CASE STUDY: THE EU GROUNDS THE GE-HONEYWELL MERGER

Political and legal differences around the world can hit home and restrict strategic alliances even between two domestic companies. Enter the era of the global reach of regulatory bodies. General Electric and Honeywell—two American corporations—had planned the $41 billion deal and gained approval from the Department of Justice in the United States. But the European Commission, the executive arm of the EU, has jurisdiction over mergers between firms with combined revenues of $4.2 billion, of which $212 million must be within Europe.[1] The GE-Honeywell deal fell within these criteria. GE, for example, employs 85,000 people in Europe and had $25 billion in revenue in 2000.

Whereas the U.S. antitrust regulation tends to focus on whether such alliances will hurt consumers, the European antitrust regulators focus on the potential harm to business competition. Commissioner Mario Monti's decision to block the deal in June 2001 was based largely on a concern about potential "bundling." The concern was that GE would "use its clout to tie two core products into a single package—jet engines and Honeywell avionics—and sell it at a price lower than European competitors could match."[2] While the European Commission admitted that customers might benefit from lower prices in the short term, they were more worried about the long-run competitiveness of GE's rivals and the future of the aerospace industry. The EC wanted GE to remedy this potential scenario by selling off several businesses such as GE Capital Aviation Services ("Gecas"), an anti-aircraft and leasing business. Whereas GE had suggested various structural remedies to the concerns about Gecas, the Commission remained wary about the potential effects of vertical integration.[3] Noel Forgeard, CEO of Airbus Industrie, the European planemaker that would have an interest in the competitive issues, said that he did not oppose the GE-Honeywell deal after discussing with Jack Welch how the deal would be structured.[4]

Monti indicated that he would accept fewer divestments in other areas as long as he got the structural commitments he wanted regarding Gecas. At that point, however, "G.E. is now offering to sell businesses with $1 billion in revenues—half its original offer—and has taken off the table most of Honeywell's avionics and aerospace products."[5]

On June 14, 2001, Jack Welch, the highly successful chairman and CEO of GE, who postponed his retirement to see the deal with Honeywell to fruition, said:

"We have always said there is a point at which we wouldn't do the deal. The Commission's extraordinary demands are far beyond that point. This shows you are never to old to get surprised."[6]

Paul O'Neill, U.S. Treasury secretary, stated that the Commission's proposal to block the deal was "off the wall. . . . They are the closest thing you can find to an autocratic organisation that can successfully impose their will on things that one would think are outside their scope of attention."[7] However, Monti, obviously disturbed by what he called attempts to bring about political intervention in the European antitrust case, later stated that the GE-Honeywell situation was a rare case of disagreement between the transatlantic competition authorities.[8]

References

1. M. Elliott, "How Jack Fell Down," *Time*, July 16, 2001.
2. *Wall Street Journal*, July 3, 2001.
3. "Lex: GE/Honeywell," *Financial Times*, www.FT.com, June 29, 2001.
4. *Wall Street Journal*, June 18, 2001.
5. "GE-Honeywell: Flight-Paths Diverge," www.FT.com, July 5, 2001.
6. Ibid.
7. *Wall Street Journal*, June 18, 2001.
8. "GE-Honeywell," www.FT.com.

Case Questions

1. How did it happen that regulators on different sides of the Atlantic, but from similar free-market democracies, arrived at such divergent views regarding this kind of antitrust situation in the first place? What is there in the different historic, political, legal, and business practices background that gave rise to this situation? Are there differences in the approach to globalization?

2. What are the implications and potential fallout of the European Commission's decision for strategic planning of other companies around the world?

3. Does this mean that companies can now be governed in every way by any of the countries or regions in which they do business, or is there hope of future "globalization" of regulations such as these?

4. What do you suggest that potential merger companies should do to avoid this kind of problem in the future?

C h a p t e r 2

Managing Interdependence: Social Responsibility and Ethics

Outline

Opening Profile: AIDS: Nestlé's New Moral Dilemma in Africa

For the Nestlé Corporation of Switzerland, its 2001 moral dilemma regarding distribution of its baby formula in Africa was an ironic turnaround from its 1981 dilemma. Then, a seven-year boycott of Nestlé's baby products and a United Nations code on selling baby formula in LDCs pressured Nestlé to change its marketing strategy for Similac baby formula. Nestlé had promoted Similac in LDCs as a replacement for breast milk, giving out free samples of the baby formula without proper instructions for preparing it. Public outcry arose over the massive number of infant deaths that resulted primarily from the lack of information about sterilizing the bottles and the water to mix with the formula and from the lack of facilities to do so. In addition, poverty-stricken mothers resorted to overdiluting the formula or not buying any more when the samples ran out; meanwhile, they found that their own breast milk had stopped flowing from lack of use.[1] Nestlé agreed to a voluntary marketing code and pledged not to distribute free or low-cost formula.

In 2001, however, many believed that Unicef should reconsider that code because of the modern scourge of AIDS in Africa. The problem is that mothers infected with the AIDS virus are transmitting it to their babies through breastfeeding, with estimates of infected babies well over a million.[2] And, while Nestlé has volunteered to donate free formula to HIV-infected women, UNICEF still refuses to endorse the $3 billion infant-formula industry. So, even though the situation has changed, unless Unicef also changes the requirements, Nestlé does not want to go against the code and risk a repeat of the situation 20 years ago.[3]

Global interdependence is a compelling dimension of the global business environment, creating demands on international managers to take a positive stance on issues of social responsibility and ethical behavior, economic development in host countries, and ecological protection around the world.

Managers today are usually quite sensitive to issues of social responsibility and ethical behavior because of pressures from the public, from interest groups, from legal and governmental concerns, and from media coverage. It is less clear where to draw the line between socially responsible behavior and the corporation's other concerns, or between the conflicting expectations of ethical behavior among different countries. In the domestic arena, managers are faced with numerous ethical complexities. In the international arena, such concerns are compounded by the larger numbers of stakeholders involved, including customers, communities, and owners in various countries.

Our discussion will focus separately on issues of social responsibility and ethical behavior, but there is considerable overlap between them. The difference is a matter of scope and degree. Whereas ethics deals with decisions and interactions on an individual level, decisions about social responsibility are broader in scope, tend to be made at a higher level, affect more people, and reflect a general stance taken by a company or a number of decision makers.

THE SOCIAL RESPONSIBILITY OF MNCs

As illustrated in the opening profile, multinational corporations have been and—to a lesser extent—continue to be at the center of debate regarding social responsibility, particularly the benefits versus harm wrought by their operations around the world, especially in less developed countries. The criticisms of MNCs have been lessened in recent years by the decreasing economic differences among countries, by the emergence of LDC multinationals, and by the greater emphasis on social responsibility by MNCs. However, concerns still remain about the exploitation of LDCs, fueled by such incidents as the Union Carbide gas leak in Bhopal, India, in December 1984, which killed 2,500 people and injured over 200,000 others. Such incidents raise questions about the use of hazardous technology in developing economies.

Issues of social responsibility continue to center on the poverty and lack of equal opportunity around the world, the environment, consumer concerns, and employee safety and welfare. Many argue that, since MNCs operate in a global context, they should use their capital, skills, and power to play a proactive role in handling worldwide social and economic problems and that, at the least, they should be concerned with host-country welfare. Others argue that MNCs already have a positive impact on LDCs by providing managerial training, investment capital, and new technology as well as by creating jobs and improving the infrastructure. Certainly, multinational corporations (now often called transnational corporations [TNCs]) constitute a powerful presence in the world economy and often have a greater capacity than local governments to induce change. The sales, debts, and resources of the largest multinationals exceed the gross national product, the public and private debt, and the resources, respectively, of some nations.[4]

The concept of international social responsibility includes the expectation that MNCs concern themselves with the social and economic effects of their decisions. The issue is how far that concern should go and what level of planning and control that concern should take. Such dilemmas are common for MNC managers. Del Monte managers, for example, realize that growing pineapples in the rich coastal lands of Kenya brings mixed results there. Although badly needed foreign-exchange earnings are generated for Kenya, there are adverse effects for poor Kenyans living in the region because less land is available for subsistence agriculture to support them.[5]

Opinions on the level of social responsibility that a domestic firm should demonstrate range from one extreme—the only responsibility of a business is to make a profit, within the confines of the law, in order to produce goods and services and serve its shareholders' interests[6]—to another extreme—companies should anticipate and try to solve problems in society. In between these extremes are varying positions described as socially reactive, in which companies respond, to some degree of currently prevailing social expectations, to the environmental and social costs of their actions.[7] Carroll's classic model illustrates the relationships among the social issues involved, the categories of social responsibilities, and the four levels of the philosophy of reaction, or responsiveness—reaction, defense, accommodation, and proaction.[8] Carroll's model is shown in Exhibit 2-1. The levels of philosophy (proaction, accommodation, etc.), at the top, correspond to the levels of social responsibility on the side in the same order as shown (from top to bottom). Thus, usually a company with a proactive philosophy will put in the extra effort to fulfill discretionary responsibilities, whereas a company with a defensive philosophy will not be concerned beyond its legal responsibilities. In applying those dimensions to the typical social issues facing a corporation, the model suggests that typically a company with a defensive philosophy toward the social issue of discrimination only meets its legal responsibilities as they are brought to bear by outside forces, as compared with a company with a proactive philosophy, which would meet its ethical and discretionary responsibilities by setting up positive programs to value diversity in the company. For example, lawsuits in 1997–1998 forced the Denny's chain of restaurants in the United States to diversify its

Exhibit 2-1   A Three-Dimensional Model of Corporate Social Responsibility

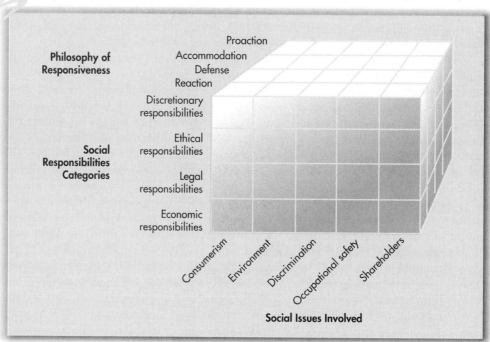

SOURCE: Adapted from A. B. Carroll, "A Three-Dimensional Conceptual Model of Corporate Performance," *Academy of Management Review* 4 (1979): 497–505.

management structure, whereas a more proactive stance would have called for that change to be made much earlier, perhaps as the growing diversity of its clientele was noted.

The stance toward social responsibility that a firm should take in its international operations, however, is much more complex—ranging perhaps from assuming some responsibility for economic development in a subsidiary's host country to taking an active role in identifying and solving world problems. The increased complexity regarding the social responsibility and ethical behavior of firms across borders is brought about by the additional stakeholders in the firm's activities through operating overseas. As illustrated in Exhibit 2-2, managers are faced with not only considering stakeholders in the host country, but also with weighing their rights against the rights of their domestic stakeholders. Most managerial decisions will have a tradeoff of the rights of these stakeholders—at least in the short term. For example, a decision to discontinue using children in Pakistan to sew soccer balls means the company will pay more for adult employees, and therefore reduce the profitability to its owners. That same decision—while taking a stand for human rights according to the social and ethical expectations in the home country and bowing to consumers' demands—may mean that those children and their families go hungry or are forced into worse working situations. Another decision to keep jobs at home to satisfy local employees and

Exhibit 2-2   MNC Stakeholders

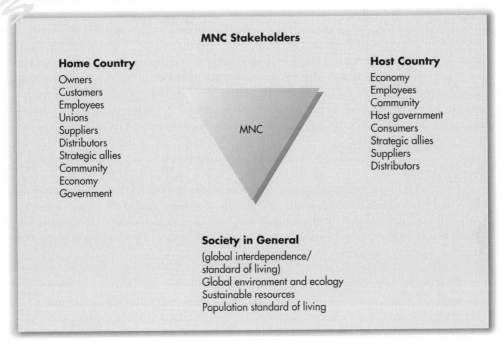

MNC Stakeholders

Home Country
Owners
Customers
Employees
Unions
Suppliers
Distributors
Strategic allies
Community
Economy
Government

MNC

Host Country
Economy
Employees
Community
Host government
Consumers
Strategic allies
Suppliers
Distributors

Society in General
(global interdependence/
standard of living)
Global environment and ecology
Sustainable resources
Population standard of living

unions will mean higher prices for consumers and less profit for stakeholders. In addition, if competitors take their jobs to cheaper overseas factories, then a company may go out of business, which will mean no jobs at all for the domestic employees and a loss for the owners.

With the growing awareness of the world's socioeconomic interdependence, global organizations are beginning to recognize the need to reach a consensus on what should constitute moral and ethical behavior. Some think that such a consensus is emerging because of the development of a global corporate culture—an integration of the business environments in which firms currently operate.[9] This integration results from the gradual dissolution of traditional boundaries and from the many intricate interconnections among MNCs, internationally linked securities markets, and communication networks.[10]

Although it is very difficult to implement a generalized code of morality and ethics in individual countries, such guidelines do provide a basis of judgment regarding specific situations. Bowie uses the term *moral universalism* to address the need for a moral standard that is accepted by all cultures.[11] He says that this approach to doing business across cultures is far preferable to other approaches, such as ethnocentrism or ethical relativism. With an ethnocentric approach, a company applies the morality used in its home country—regardless of the host country's system of ethics.

A company subscribing to ethical relativism, on the other hand, simply adopts the local moral code in whatever country it is operating. With this approach, companies run into value conflicts, such as continuing to do business in China despite home-country objections to China's continued violation of human rights. In addition, public pressure in the home country often forces the MNC to act in accordance with ethnocentric value systems anyway. In one instance, public outcry in the United States and most of the world resulted in major companies (IBM, General Motors, Coca-Cola, and Eastman Kodak) either selling or discontinuing their operations in South Africa during the 1980s to protest that country's apartheid policies. More recently, the Food and Drug Administration (FDA) has been pressuring U.S. manufacturers of silicone-filled breast implants (prohibited in the United States for cosmetic surgery because of health hazards) to adopt a voluntary moratorium on exports. While Dow Corning has ceased its foreign sales—citing its responsibility to apply the same standards internationally as it does domestically—the other three major manufacturers continue to export the implants, often from their factories in other countries.

The difficulty, even in adopting a stance of moral universalism, is in deciding where to draw the line—which kinds of conflicts of values, asks Wicks, are "conversation stoppers" or "cooperation enders"? Individual managers must at some point decide, based on their own morality, when they feel a situation is simply not right and withdraw their involvement.

> There are practical limitations on our ability to act in the modern world, . . . but a systematic infringement of basic personal rights is generally grounds for ending cooperation. Less blatant violations, or practices which are not abhorrent to our basic values, are treated as items which are negotiable.[12]

MNC Responsibility Toward Human Rights

Whereas many situations regarding the morality of the MNC's presence or activities in a country are quite clear, other situations are not, especially when dealing with human rights. The role of MNCs in pulling out of South Africa in the 1980s as part of the movement against apartheid has now played out, and many are cautiously returning to the now multiracial democracy. In many other areas of the world, the question of what role MNCs should play regarding human rights is at the forefront. So loud has been the cry about products coming from so-called sweatshops around the world that President Clinton established an Anti-Sweatshop Code of Conduct, which includes a ban on forced labor, abuse, and discrimination, and requires companies to provide a healthy and safe work environment and to pay at least the prevailing local minimum wage, among other requirements. A group has been named to monitor compliance; enforcement is difficult, of course, but publicity helps! The Department of Labor publishes the names of companies that comply with the code, including Nike, Reebok, Liz Claiborne, Wal-Mart, and Phillips-Van Heusen.[13] Those companies can be identified on the department's home page Website (http://www.gov./nosweat.htm). Even so, in a study commissioned by Nike in 2000 to review personnel activities at its contractors in Indonesia, it was found that:

> 56 percent of the 4,004 workers told researchers that they had witnessed supervisors verbally, sexually, or physically abusing other employees.
> —*WALL STREET JOURNAL*, FEBRUARY 22, 2001

The study, by nonprofit Global Alliance, concludes that workers at the Indonesian factories contracted by Nike had limited access to medical care, were exposed to sexual molestation by managers, and were often forced to work overtime.[14] What constitutes "human rights" is clouded by the perceptions and priorities of people in different countries. While the United States often takes the lead in the charge against what they consider human rights violations around the world, other countries point to the homelessness and high crime statistics in the United States. Often the discussion of human rights centers around Asia because many of the products in the West are imported from Asia by Western companies using manufacturing facilities located there.[15] It is commonly held in the West that the best chance to gain some ground on human rights issues is for large MNCs and governments around the world to take a unified stance; many global players now question the morality of trading for goods that have been produced by forced labor or child labor. Although laws in the United States ban prison imports, shady deals between the manufacturers and companies acting as intermediaries make it difficult to determine the origin of many products— and make it easy for companies wanting access to cheap products or materials to ignore the law. However, under pressure from their labor unions (and perhaps their conscience), a number of large image-conscious companies have established corporate codes of conduct for their buyers, suppliers, and contractors and have instituted strict procedures for auditing their imports.[16] Reebok has audited all its suppliers in Asia. Levi Strauss has gone a step further. After sending teams of investigators around the world, Levi announced a new company policy: "We should not initiate or renew contractual relationships in countries where there are pervasive violations of basic human rights."[17] The Management Focus section "Levi Takes a Stand for Human Rights" offers more insight into Levi's practices.[18]

Codes of Conduct

A considerable number of organizations have developed their own codes of conduct; some have gone further to group together with others around the world to establish standards to improve the quality of life for workers around the world. Companies such as Avon, Sainsbury Plc., Toys 'R' Us and Otto Versand have joined with the Council on Economic Priorities (CEP) to establish SA8000 (Social Accountability 8000, on the lines of the manufacturing quality standard ISO9000). Their proposed global labor standards would be monitored by outside organizations to certify whether plants are meeting those standards, among which are the following:

- ➤ Do not use child or forced labor.
- ➤ Provide a safe working environment.
- ➤ Respect workers' rights to unionize.
- ➤ Do not regularly require more than 48-hour work weeks.
- ➤ Pay wages sufficient to meet workers' basic needs.[19]

In addition, there are four international codes of conduct that provide some consistent guidelines for multinational enterprises (MNEs). These codes were developed by the International Chamber of Commerce, the Organization for Economic Cooperation and Development, the International Labor Organization, and the United Nations Commission on Transnational Corporations. Getz has integrated these four codes and organized their common underlying principles, thereby estab-

Management Focus

LEVI TAKES A STAND FOR HUMAN RIGHTS

Levi Strauss & Co., the world's largest supplier of brand-name apparel, has been exporting jeans and jobs around the world for years, but recently it also decided to export human rights.

During the 1980s, Levi paid little attention to working conditions at its contract factories—until 1991, in fact, when it was informed that a contractor on the island of Saipan was keeping imported Chinese women in conditions of near slavery. The contractor was working them 11 hours a day for 7 days a week, paying them below the local minimum wage. Levi terminated that contract. Following that, the company—which exports about 50 percent of its jeans and shirts overseas—decided to investigate its 400 foreign contractors in 1992: Levi found that about 25 percent of them were treating their workers badly, and child labor was being used in places such as Bangladesh. After that, Levi adopted strict guidelines for its foreign contractors, such as:

- Suppliers must provide safe and healthy conditions that meet Levi's standards.
- Suppliers must pay workers no less than prevailing local wages.
- Company inspectors will make surprise visits to contractors to ensure compliance.

Levi was the first MNC to impose such guidelines, covering the treatment of workers and the environmental impact of production, on its contractors abroad. The company backed up its new stance with threats to cancel contracts with violators. The company inspectors, such as Im Choong Hoe, travel around Southeast Asia to Levi's contracted factories, from Indonesia to Bangladesh—not examining the quality of the products, but looking for health and safety hazards and any abuses of worker rights. But Im Choong Hoe and other inspectors try to work with contractors to improve the situation rather than to impose hardship among the workers. For example, when Im Choong found that one of Levi's contractors in Bangladesh employed children, Levi decided to pay the children while they attended school on the factory site until age 14, rather than insist that the contractor fire them and bring hardship to their families.

In 1993, Levi withdrew its contracts in China and Burma, citing pervasive violation of human rights and continuing labor inequities. Of course, Levi was also concerned with its image in the eyes of its customers. Levi Strauss knew that its brand and reputation would suffer and that customers would not want to buy a shirt made by children in Bangladesh or by forced labor in China. Robert Haas, chairman and CEO of Levi, notes that he has found that decisions focusing only on cost factors don't best serve the long-term interests of the company or its shareholders. Benefits that he feels have accrued from Levi's values-driven approach include improved loyalty, trust, and retention among its employees, business partners, suppliers, and customers, as well as more credibility among leaders in new markets.

SOURCE: F. Gibney, "The Trouble with China," *Newsweek*, May 17, 1993; B. Dumaine, "Exporting Jobs and Ethics," *Fortune*, October 5, 1992; G. P. Zachary, "Levi Tries to Make Sure Contract Plants in Asia Treat Workers Well," *Wall Street Journal*, July 28, 1994; R. D. Haas, "Ethics in the Trenches," *Across the Board* (May 1994): 12–13.

lishing MNE behavior toward governments, publics, and people, as shown in Exhibit 2-3 (the originating institutions are in parentheses). She concludes, "As international organizations and institutions (including MNEs themselves) continue to refine the codes, the underlying moral issues will be better identified, and appropriate MNE behavior will be more readily apparent."[20]

Exhibit 2-3   International Codes of Conduct for MNEs

MNE and Host Governments

Economic and developmental policies

- MNEs should consult with governmental authorities and national employers' and workers' organizations to assure that their investments conform to the economic and social development policies of the host country. (ICC; OECD; ILO; UN/CTC)
- MNEs should not adversely disturb the balance-of-payments or currency exchange rates of the countries in which they operate. They should try, in consultation with the government, to resolve balance-of-payments and exchange rate difficulties when possible. (ICC; OECD; UN/CTC)
- MNEs should cooperate with governmental policies regarding local equity participation. (ICC; UN/CTC)
- MNEs should not dominate the capital markets of the countries in which they operate. (ICC; UN/CTC)
- MNEs should provide to host government authorities the information necessary for correctly assessing taxes to be paid. (ICC; OECD)
- MNEs should not engage in transfer pricing policies that modify the tax base on which their entities are assessed. (OECD; UN/CTC)
- MNEs should give preference to local sources for components and raw materials if prices and quality are competitive. (ICC, ILO)
- MNEs should reinvest some profits in the countries in which they operate. (ICC)

Laws and regulations

- MNEs are subject to the laws, regulations, and jurisdiction of the countries in which they operate. (ICC; OECD; UN/CTC)
- MNEs should respect the right of every country to exercise control over its natural resources, and to regulate the activities of entities operating within its territory. (ICC; OECD; UN/CTC)
- MNEs should use appropriate international dispute settlement mechanisms, including arbitration, to resolve conflicts with the governments of the countries in which they operate. (ICC; OECD)
- MNEs should not request the intervention of their home governments in disputes with host governments. (UN/CTC)

- MNEs should resolve disputes arising from expropriation by host governments under the domestic law of the host country. (UN/CTC)

Political involvement

- MNEs should refrain from improper or illegal involvement in local political activities. (OECD; UN/CTC)
- MNEs should not pay bribes or render improper benefits to any public servant. (OECD; UN/CTC)
- MNEs should not interfere in intergovernmental relations. (UN/CTC)

MNEs and the Public

Technology transfer

- MNEs should cooperate with governmental authorities in assessing the impact of transfers of technology to developing countries and should enhance the technological capacities of developing countries. (OECD; UN/CTC)
- MNEs should develop and adapt technologies to the needs and characteristics of the countries in which they operate. (ICC; OECD; ILO)
- MNEs should conduct research and development activities in developing countries, using local resources and personnel to the greatest extent possible. (ICC; UN/CTC)
- When granting licenses for the use of industrial property rights, MNEs should do so on reasonable terms and conditions. (ICC; OECD)
- MNEs should not require payment for the use of technologies of no real value to the enterprise. (ICC)

Environmental protection

- MNEs should respect the laws and regulations concerning environmental protection of the countries in which they operate. (OECD; UN/CTC)
- MNEs should cooperate with host governments and with international organizations in the development of national and international environmental protection standards. (ICC, UN/CTC)
- MNEs should supply to appropriate host governmental authorities, information concerning the environmental impact of the products and processes of their entities. (ICC; UN/CTC)

Exhibit 2-3   (cont.)

MNEs and Persons

Consumer protection

- MNEs should respect the laws and regulations of the countries in which they operate with regard to consumer protection. (OECD; UN/CTC)
- MNEs should preserve the safety and health of consumers by disclosure of appropriate information, proper labeling, and accurate advertising. (UN/CTC)

Employment practices

- MNEs should cooperate with host governments' efforts to create employment opportunities in particular localities. (ICC)
- MNEs should support representative employers' organizations. (ICC; ILO)
- MNEs should try to increase employment opportunities and standards in the countries in which they operate. (ILO)
- MNEs should provide stable employment for their employees. (ILO)

- MNEs should establish nondiscriminatory employment policies and promote equal employment opportunities. (OECD; ILO)
- MNEs should give priority to the employment and promotion of nationals of the countries in which they operate. (ILO)
- MNEs should assure that adequate training is provided to all employees. (ILO)
- MNEs should contribute to the managerial and technical training of nationals of the countries in which they operate, and should employ qualified nationals in managerial and professional capacities. (ICC; OECD; UN/CTC)
- MNEs should respect the right of employees to organize for the purpose of collective bargaining. (OECD; ILO)

- MNEs should provide workers' representatives with information necessary to assist in the development of collective agreements. (OECD; ILO)
- MNEs should consult with workers' representatives in all matters directly affecting the interests of labor. (ICC)
- MNEs, in the context of negotiations with workers' representatives, should not threaten to transfer the operating unit to another country. (OECD; ILO)
- MNEs should give advance notice of plant closures and mitigate the resultant adverse effects. (ICC; OECD; ILO)
- MNEs should cooperate with governments in providing income protection for workers whose employment has been terminated. (ILO)
- MNEs should provide standards of employment equal to or better than those of comparable employers in the countries in which they operate. (ICC; OECD; ILO)
- MNEs should pay, at minimum, basic living wages. (ILO)
- MNEs should maintain the highest standards of safety and health, and should provide adequate information about work-related health hazards. (ILO)

Human rights

- MNEs should respect human rights and fundamental freedoms in the countries in which they operate. (UN/CTC)
- MNEs should not discriminate on the basis of race, color, sex, religion, language, social, national and ethnic origin, or political or other opinion. (UN/CTC)

- MNEs should respect the social and cultural objectives, values, and traditions of the countries in which they operate. (UN/CTC)

International agency sources:
OECD: The Organization for Economic Cooperation and Development Guidelines for Multinational Enterprises.
ILO: The International Labor Office Tripartite Declarations of Principles Concerning Multinational Enterprises and Social Policy.
ICC: The International Chamber of Commerce Guidelines for International Investment.
UN/CTC: The United Nations Universal Declaration of Human Rights.
The UN Code of Conduct on Transnational Corps.

ETHICS IN GLOBAL MANAGEMENT

> The computer is on the dock, it's raining, and you have to pay $100 [bribe]
> to get it picked up.
>
> —WM. C. NORRIS, CONTROL DATA CORPORATION

Globalization has multiplied the ethical problems facing organizations. Yet business ethics have not yet globalized. Attitudes towards ethics are rooted in culture and business practices. American businesses have a high degree of institutionalized ethics, such as codes of ethics and tax breaks for socially responsible behavior. Swee Hoon Ang found, for example, that, while East Asians tended to be less ethical than their expatriate counterparts from the United States and Britain, it was because they consider deception as amoral and acceptable if it has a positive effect on larger issues such as the company, the extended family, or the state.[21] For an MNC, it is very difficult to reconcile consistent and acceptable behavior around the world with home-country standards. One question, in fact, is whether they even should be reconciled; it seems that the United States is the driving force to legislate moral business conduct overseas.[22]

The term **international business ethics** refers to the business conduct or morals of MNCs in their relationships with individuals and entities.[23] Such behavior is based largely on the cultural value system and the generally accepted ways of doing business in each country or society, as we have discussed throughout this book. Those norms, in turn, are based on broadly accepted guidelines from religion, philosophy, the professions, and the legal system. Should managers of MNC subsidiaries, then, base their ethical standards on those of the host country or those of the home country—or can the two be reconciled? What is the moral responsibility of expatriates regarding ethical behavior, and how do these issues affect business objectives? How do expatriates simultaneously balance their responsibility to various stakeholders—to owners, creditors, consumers, employees, suppliers, governments, and societies? The often conflicting objectives of host and home governments and societies also must be balanced.[24]

The approach to these dilemmas varies among MNCs from different countries. While the American approach is to treat everyone the same by making moral judgments based on general rules, managers in Japan and Europe tend to make such decisions based on shared values, social ties, and their perception of their obligations.[25] According to many U.S. executives, there is little difference in ethical practices among the United States, Canada, and Northern Europe. According to Bruce Smart, former U.S. undersecretary of Commerce for International Trade, the highest ethical standards seem to be practiced by the Canadians, British, Australians, and Germans. As he says "a kind of noblesse oblige still exists among the business classes in those countries"—compared with the prevailing attitude among many American managers which condones making it whatever way you can.[26] Another who experienced few problems with ethical practices in Europe is Donald Petersen, former CEO of Ford Motor Company; but he warns us about underdeveloped countries, in particular those under a dictatorship, where bribery is generally accepted practice.[27] Petersen's experience has been borne out by research, which draws on 14 surveys from 7 independent institutions, by Transparency International, a German non-governmental organization (NGO) that fights corruption. The organization's year 2001 Corruption Perceptions Index (shown in Exhibit 2-4) shows results of research on the level of corruption among public officials and politicians in various countries,

Exhibit 2-4 The 2001 Corruption Perceptions Index

Country Rank	Country	2001 CPI Score	Country Rank	Country	2001 CPI Score	Country Rank	Country	2001 CPI Score
1	Finland	9.9	31	Hungary	5.3	61	Malawi	3.2
2	Denmark	9.5		Trinidad & Tobago	5.3		Thailand	3.2
3	New Zealand	9.4		Tunisia	5.3	63	Dominican Rep	3.1
4	Iceland	9.2	34	Slovenia	5.2		Moldova	3.1
	Singapore	9.2	35	Uruguay	5.1	65	Guatemala	2.9
6	Sweden	9.0	36	Malaysia	5.0		Philippines	2.9
7	Canada	8.9	37	Jordan	4.9		Senegal	2.9
8	Netherlands	8.8	38	Lithuania	4.8		Zimbabwe	2.9
9	Luxembourg	8.7		South Africa	4.8	69	Romania	2.8
10	Norway	8.6	40	Costa Rica	4.5		Venezuela	2.8
11	Australia	8.5		Mauritius	4.5	71	Honduras	2.7
12	Switzerland	8.4	42	Greece	4.2		India	2.7
13	United Kingdom	8.3		South Korea	4.2		Kazakhstan	2.7
14	Hong Kong	7.9	44	Peru	4.1		Uzbekistan	2.7
15	Austria	7.8		Poland	4.1	75	Vietnam	2.6
16	Israel	7.6	46	Brazil	4.0		Zambia	2.6
	USA	7.6	47	Bulgaria	3.9	77	Cote d'Ivoire	2.4
18	Chile	7.5		Croatia	3.9		Nicaragua	2.4
	Ireland	7.5		Czech Republic	3.9	79	Ecuador	2.3
20	Germany	7.4	50	Colombia	3.8		Pakistan	2.3
21	Japan	7.1	51	Mexico	3.7		Russia	2.3
22	Spain	7.0		Panama	3.7	82	Tanzania	2.2
23	France	6.7		Slovak Republic	3.7	83	Ukraine	2.1
24	Belgium	6.6	54	Egypt	3.6	84	Azerbaijan	2.0
25	Portugal	6.3		El Salvador	3.6		Bolivia	2.0
26	Botswana	6.0		Turkey	3.6		Cameroon	2.0
27	Taiwan	5.9	57	Argentina	3.5		Kenya	2.0
28	Estonia	5.6		China	3.5	88	Indonesia	1.9
29	Italy	5.5	59	Ghana	3.4		Uganda	1.9
30	Namibia	5.4		Latvia	3.4	90	Nigeria	1.0

2001 CPI Score relates to perceptions of the degree of corruption as seen by businesspeople, academics, and risk analysts, and ranges between 10 (highly clean) and 0 (highly corrupt). A more detailed description of the CPI methodology is available at www.gwdg.de/~uwvw/2001.htm

SOURCE: Transparency International, 2001.

as perceived by businesspeople, academics, and risk analysts. The conclusion from that study was that:

> There is a worldwide corruption crisis. . . . Some of the richest countries in the world scored 9 or higher out of a clean score of 10. But 55 countries— among the world's poorest—scored less than 5, suggesting high levels of perceived corruption in government and public administration.
> —TRANSPARENCY INTERNATIONAL PRESS RELEASE, PARIS, JUNE 27, 2001.

E-Biz Box

EU IMPOSES CROSS-BORDER ELECTRONIC DATA PRIVACY

Most people in the United Sates have wished for more privacy of personal data; they receive mailings, solicitations, and other information about themselves that make them wonder where that source acquired the personal information. Not so in Europe. In fact, the Europeans are determined that they won't get on any unwanted mailing list from the United States or elsewhere. As of October 25, 1998, when the European Union Directive on Data Protection went into effect, commissioners in Brussels have resolved to prosecute companies and block websites that fail to live up to Europe's standards on data privacy. The directive guarantees European citizens absolute control over data concerning them. A U.S. company wanting personal information must get permission from that person and explain what the information will be used for; the company must also guarantee that the information won't be used for anything else without the person's consent. EU citizens have the right, under this directive, to file suits against a company if they feel it is abusing their private data and force them to change it.

Such protections seem admirable, but free marketers across the ocean are worried about the prospect of Europe being able to regulate the computer databases and the Internet, which are vital to the information economy. They feel that regulations should be agreed upon for a global system. It is a stalemate situation of protection of privacy versus freedom of information, which is protected by the First Amendment in the United States. At the heart of the standoff is a basic cultural difference: Europeans trust their governments over companies, whereas in the Untied States, it is the opposite. Already, European inspectors travel to Sioux City, South Dakota, to Citigroup's giant data processing center, where computers store financial information about millions of German credit card holders, to make sure that Citigroup is complying with the privacy data protection law. Citigroup accepted the supervision as a condition to market a credit card in Germany.

U.S. companies are concerned that the EU directive will force them to establish separate data networks for Europe, making it impossible to conduct business as usual with EU member countries. The privacy rules are already having an effect—prohibiting U.S. airlines and hotels, for example, from storing information about their clients that they would normally use to provide better service for them. Third parties to business transactions, such as FedEx delivering a package across the ocean, could also be held responsible. There is considerable concern that the EU directive will imperil the future of electronic commerce.

The question of protection of export of private data is but one of the complexities brought about by the use of technology in international business. For now, on your next trip to Europe, bringing back the contact information that you entered on your laptop computer is illegal!

SOURCE: "Rules of Global Economy Are Set in Brussels," *Wall Street Journal*, April 23, 2002; "Europe's Privacy Cops," *Business Week*, November 2, 1998; "Eurocrats Try to Stop Data at the Border," *Wall Street Journal*, October 30, 1998.

The biggest single problem for MNCs in their attempt to define a corporatewide ethical posture is the great variation of ethical standards around the world. Many practices that are considered unethical or even illegal in some countries are accepted ways of doing business in others. More recently, this dilemma has taken on new forms because of the varied understandings of the ethical use of technology around the world, as illustrated in the accompanying E-Biz Box.

U.S. companies are often caught between being placed at a disadvantage by refusing to go along with a country's accepted practices, such as bribery, or being subject to criticism at home for using "unethical" tactics to get the job done. Large companies that have refused to participate have led the way in taking a moral stand because of their visibility, their potential impact on the local economy, and, after all, their ability to afford such a stance.[28]

Whereas the upper limits of ethical standards for international activities are set by the individual standards of certain leading companies—or, more realistically, by the moral values of their top managers—it is more difficult to set the lower limits of those standards. Laczniak and Naor explain:

> The laws of economically developed countries generally define the lowest common denominator of acceptable behavior for operations in those domestic markets. In an underdeveloped country or a developing country, it would be the actual **degree of enforcement** of the law that would, in practice, determine the lower limit of permissible behavior. (boldface added)[29]

The bribery of officials is prohibited by law in many countries, but it still goes on as an accepted practice; often, it is the only way to get anything done. In such cases, the MNC managers have to decide on what standard of behavior they will follow. What about the $100 bribe to get the computer off the rainy dock? According to William Norris, he told his managers to pay the $100 because to refuse would be taking things too far. Generally, Control Data did not yield to such pressure, though they say they lost sales as a result.[30]

Questionable Payments

A specific ethical issue for managers in the international arena is that of **questionable payments**. These are business payments that raise significant questions of appropriate moral behavior either in the host nation or in other nations. Such questions arise out of differences in laws, customs, and ethics in various countries, whether the payments in question are political payments, extortion, bribes, sales commissions, or "grease money"—payments to expedite routine transactions.[31] Other common types are payments to speed the clearance of goods at ports of entry and to obtain required certifications. They are called different names in different countries: tokens of appreciation, *la mordida* (the bite, in Mexico), *bastarella* ("little envelope" in Italy), *pot-de-vin* (jug of wine in France). For the sake of simplicity, we will categorize all these different types of questionable payments as some form of bribery. In Mexico, for example, companies make monthly payments to the mail carriers, or their mail gets "lost."

In South Korea, for example, the bribery scandal that put former president Roh Tae Woo behind bars in 1996 spread to the top 30 chaebol (which account for 14 percent of South Korea's gross domestic product). Any ensuing changes to the close relationship between politics and business in South Korea are likely to reshape, and perhaps slow down, the Korean economy. But executives in those chaebols say they still expect to pay the *Huk Kab*, or "rice-cake expenses," which run thousands of dollars, as "holiday gifts" to cabinet ministers as a hedge against disadvantageous treatment.

Exhibit 2-5 shows results from research by Transparency International, resulting in the Bribe Payers Index (BPI). This ranks the leading exporting countries in terms of the degree to which their companies are perceived to be paying bribes abroad. That organization's conclusion is:

> The scale of bribe-paying by international corporations in the developing countries of the world is massive
> —PETER EIGEN, CHAIRMAN, TRANSPARENCY INTERNATIONAL

Exhibit 2-5   Bribe Payers Index (BPI)

Rank	Country	Score	Rank	Country	Score
1	Sweden	8.3	11	Singapore	5.7
2	Australia	8.1	12	Spain	5.3
2	Canada	8.1	13	France	5.2
4	Austria	7.8	14	Japan	5.1
5	Switzerland	7.7	15	Malaysia	3.9
6	Netherlands	7.4	16	Italy	3.7
7	United Kingdom	7.2	17	Taiwan	3.5
8	Belgium	6.8	18	South Korea	3.4
9	Germany	6.2	19	China	3.1
9	United States	6.2			

Score: 1 (high levels of bribery) to 10 (perceived level of negligible bribery)
SOURCE: Transparency International, 2000.

The dilemma for Americans operating abroad is how much to adhere to their own ethical standards in the face of foreign customs or how much to follow local ways to be competitive. Certainly, in some societies, gift giving is common to bind social and familial ties, and such gifts incur obligation. However, Americans must be able to distinguish between harmless practices and actual bribery, between genuine relationships and those used as a coverup. To help them distinguish, the **Foreign Corrupt Practices Act (FCPA)** of 1977 was established, which prohibits U.S. companies from making illegal payments or other gifts or political contributions to foreign government officials for the purposes of influencing them in business transactions. The goal was to stop MNCs from contributing to corruption in foreign government and to upgrade the image of the United States and its companies operating overseas. The penalties include severe fines and sometimes imprisonment. Many managers feel the law has given them a more even playing field, and so they have been more willing to do business in certain countries where it seemed impossible to do business without bribery and kickbacks.

Unfortunately, bribery continues, mostly on a small scale, where it often goes undetected. But the U.S. government does vigorously pursue and prosecute bribery cases. Even the mighty IBM's Argentine subsidiary has been accused of paying a bribe of $249 million to get the contract to install computers at all the branches of Argentina's largest commercial bank, Banco de la Nacion.[32] Companies from the United States claim that they are placed at a competitive disadvantage in Latin America and elsewhere because their competitors overseas do not face the same home-country restrictions on bribery.

If we agree with Carson that "accepting a bribe involves the violation of an implicit or explicit promise or understanding associated with one's office or role, and that, therefore, accepting (or giving) a bribe is always prima facie wrong," then our decisions as a manager, salesperson, or whatever are always clear, no matter where we are.[33]

If, however, we acknowledge that in some cases—in "morally corrupt contexts," as Philips calls them—"there may be no prima facie duty to adhere to the agreements implicit in one's role or position," then the issue becomes situational and a matter of judgment, with few consistent guidelines.[34] If our perspective, continues Philips, is that "the action purchased from the relevant official does not count as a violation of his [or her] duty," then the American managers or other foreign managers involved are actually victims of extortion rather than guilty of bribery.[35] That is the position taken by Gene Laczniak of Marquette Company, who says that it is just part of the cost of doing business in many countries to pay small bribes to get people simply to do their jobs. But he is against paying bribes to persuade people to make a decision that they would not otherwise have made.[36]

Whatever their professed beliefs, many businesspeople are willing to engage in bribery as an everyday part of meeting their business objectives. Many corporate officials, in fact, avoid any moral issue by simply "turning a blind eye" to what goes on in subsidiaries. Some companies avoid these issues by hiring a local agent who takes care of the paperwork and pays all the so-called fees in return for a salary or consultant's fee.[37] However, while the FCPA does allow "grease" payments to facilitate business in a foreign country, if those payments are lawful there, other payments prohibited by the FCPA are still subject to prosecution even if the company says it did not know that its agents or subsidiaries were making such payments—the so-called reason to know provision.[38]

Critics of the FCPA contend that the law represents an ethnocentric attempt to impose U.S. standards on the rest of the world and puts American firms at a competitive disadvantage.[39] Indeed, the United States is the only country prohibiting firms from making payments to secure contracts overseas.[40] In any event, many feel that business activities that cannot stand scrutiny are clearly unethical, corrupt, and, in the long run, corrupting.[41] Bribery fails three important tests of ethical corporate actions: (1) Is it legal? (2) Does it work (in the long run)? (3) Can it be talked about?[42]

Many MNCs have decided to confront concerns about ethical behavior and social responsibility by developing worldwide practices that represent the company's posture. Among those policies are the following:

➤ Develop worldwide codes of ethics.
➤ Consider ethical issues in strategy development.
➤ Given major, unsolvable, ethical problems, consider withdrawal from the problem market.
➤ Develop periodic "ethical impact" statements.[43]

Most of the leadership in developing ethical postures in international activities comes from the United States. Although this move toward ethics and social responsibility is spreading, both in the United States and around the world, problems still abound in many countries.

Heightened global competition encourages companies to seek advantages through questionable tactics. A 1995 Commerce Department study revealed many incidents of improper inducements by companies and governments around the world (such as Germany's Siemens and the European airframe consortium Airbus Industrie) which undercut U.S. companies. Yet American companies are not all clean. In October 1995, Lockheed Martin Corporation's former vice president was sentenced to 18 months in prison and given a $125,000 fine for bribing a member of the Egyptian Parliament to win an order for three C-130 cargo planes.[44] So much for Lockheed's consent decree to refrain from corrupt practices, which they signed 20 years ago following their bribery scandal in Japan.

Japan also continues to have its share of internal problems regarding the ethical behavior of its officials and businesspeople. In the scandal involving Nippon Telephone and Telegraph Company (NTT), the chairman of the board of NTT was involved in obtaining cut-rate stock in a real estate subsidiary of the Recruit Company in exchange for helping the company obtain two U.S. supercomputers. When the stock went public, the chairman and other NTT executives made a lot of money, and they were later arrested and charged with accepting bribes.[45] As the scandal unfolded, it appeared that government members were involved, including the prime minister, Noboru Takeshita, who had received $1.4 million in questionable, albeit legal, donations from the Recruit Company. Takeshita subsequently resigned, as did other government officials, and the incident became known as Recruitgate, in reference to the Watergate scandal that forced President Nixon to resign.[46]

Making the Right Decision

How is a manager operating abroad to know what is the "right" decision when faced with questionable or unfamiliar circumstances of doing business? The first line of defense is to consult the laws of both the home and the host countries—such as the FCPA. If any of those laws would be violated, then you, the manager, must look to some other way to complete the business transaction, or withdraw altogether. Second, you could consult the International Codes of Conduct for MNEs, as shown in Exhibit 2-3. These are broad and cover various areas of social responsibility and ethical behavior; even so, many issues are subject to interpretation.

If legal consultation does not provide you with a clear answer about what to do, you should consult the company's code of ethics (if there is one). You, as the manager, should realize that you are not alone in making these kinds of decisions. It is also the responsibility of the company to provide guidelines for the actions and decisions made by its employees. In addition, you are not the first, and certainly not the last, to be faced with this kind of situation—which also sets up a collective experience in the company about what kinds of decisions your colleagues typically make in various circumstances. Those norms or expectations (assuming they are honorable) can supplement the code of ethics or substitute for the lack of a formal code. If your intended action runs contrary to the norms or the formal code, then discontinue that plan. If you are still unsure of what to do, you have the right and the obligation to consult your superiors. Unfortunately, often the situation is not that clear cut, or your boss will tell you to "use your own judgment." Sometimes your superiors back at the home office just want you to complete the transaction to the benefit of the company and don't want to be involved in what you have to do to consummate the deal. It is at this point that, if your dilemma continues, you must fall back to your own moral code of ethics. One way to consider the dilemma is to ask yourself what are the rights of the various stakeholders involved (see Exhibit 2-2), and how should you weigh those rights. First, does the proposed action (rigged contract bid, bribe, etc.) harm anyone? What are the likely consequences of your decision in both the short run and long run? Who would benefit from your contemplated action? What are the benefits to some versus potential harm to others? In the case of a rigged contract bid through bribery, for example, people are put at a disadvantage, especially over the long term with a pattern of this behavior. This is because if competition is unfair, not only are your competitors harmed by losing the bid, but also the consumers of the products or services are harmed because they will pay more to attain them than they would under an efficient market system.

In the end, you have to follow your own conscience and decide where to draw the line in the sand in order to operate with integrity—otherwise the line moves further and further away with each transgression. In addition, what can start with a small bribe or coverup here—a matter of personal ethics—can, over time, and in the aggregate of many people covering up, result in a situation of a truly negligent, and perhaps criminal, stance toward social responsibility to society, as that revealed by investigations of the tobacco industry in the United States. Indeed, executives are increasingly being held personally and criminally accountable for their decisions; this is true even for people operating on the board of directors of a company.

MANAGING INTERDEPENDENCE

Because multinational firms (or other organizations, such as the Red Cross) represent global interdependency, their managers at all levels must recognize that what they do, in the aggregate, has long-term implications for the socioeconomic interdependence of nations. Simply to describe ethical issues as part of the general environment does not address the fact that managers need to control their activities at all levels—from simple, daily business transactions involving local workers, intermediaries, or consumers to global concerns of ecological responsibility—for the future benefit of all concerned. Whatever the situation, the powerful long-term effects of MNC and MNE action (or inaction) should be planned for and controlled—not haphazardly considered part of the side effects of business. The profitability of individual companies depends on a cooperative and constructive attitude toward global interdependence.

Foreign Subsidiaries in the United States

Much of the preceding discussion has related to U.S. subsidiaries around the world. However, to highlight the growing interdependence and changing balance of business power globally, we should also consider foreign subsidiaries in America. Since much criticism about a lack of responsibility has been directed toward MNCs with headquarters in the United States, we need to think of these criticisms from an outsider's perspective. The number of foreign subsidiaries in the United States has grown and continues to grow dramatically; foreign direct investment (FDI) in the United States by other countries is in many cases far more than U.S. investment outward. Americans are thus becoming more sensitive to what they perceive as a lack of control over their own country's business.

Things look very different from the perspective of Americans employed at a subsidiary of some overseas MNC. Interdependence takes on a new meaning when people "over there" are calling the shots regarding strategy, expectations, products, and personnel. Often, Americans' resentment over different ways of doing business by "foreign" companies in the United States inhibits cooperation, which gave rise to the companies' presence in the first place.

Today, managers from all countries must learn new ways, and most MNCs are trying to adapt. Sadahei Kusumoto, president and CEO of the Minolta Corporation, says that Japanese managers in the United States need to recognize that they are "not in Honshu [Japan's largest island] anymore" and that one very different aspect of management in the United States is the idea of corporate social responsibility.[47]

In Japan, corporate social responsibility has traditionally meant that companies take care of their employees, whereas in the United States the public and private sectors are expected to share the responsibility for the community. Part of the explanation for this difference is that American corporations get tax deductions for corporate philanthropy, whereas Japanese firms do not; nor are Japanese managers familiar with community needs. For these and other reasons, Japanese subsidiaries in the United States have not been active in U.S. philanthropy. However, Kusumoto pinpoints why they should become more involved in the future:

> In the long run, failure to play an active role in the community will brand these companies as irresponsible outsiders and dim their prospects for the future.[48]

Whether Kusomoto's motives for change are humanitarian or just good business sense does not really matter. The point is that he recognizes interdependence in globalization and acts accordingly.

Managing Subsidiary—Host-Country Interdependence

When managing interdependence, international managers must go beyond general issues of social responsibility and deal with the specific concerns of the MNC subsidiary—host-country relationship. Outdated MNC attitudes that focus only on profitability and autonomy are shortsighted and usually result in only short-term realization of those goals. MNCs must learn to accommodate the needs of other organizations and countries:

> Interdependence rather than independence, and cooperation rather than confrontation are at the heart of that accommodation . . . the journey from independence to interdependence managed badly leads to dependence, and that is an unacceptable destination.[49]

Most of the past criticism levied at MNCs has focused on their activities in LDCs. Their real or perceived lack of responsibility centers on the transfer-in of inappropriate technology, causing unemployment, and the transfer-out of scarce financial and other resources, reducing the capital available for internal development. In their defense, MNCs help LDCs by contributing new technology and managerial skills, improving the infrastructure, creating jobs, and bringing in investment capital from other countries by exporting products. The infusion of outside capital provides foreign-exchange earnings that can be used for further development. The host government's attitude is often referred to as a love-hate relationship: it wants the economic growth that MNCs can provide, but it does not want the incursions on national sovereignty or the technological dependence that may result.[50] Most criticisms of MNC subsidiary activities, whether in less developed or more developed countries, are along these lines:

1. MNCs raise their needed capital locally, contributing to a rise in interest rates in host countries.
2. The majority (sometimes even 100 percent) of the stock of most subsidiaries is owned by the parent company. Consequently, host-country people do not have much control over the operations of corporations within their borders.

3. MNCs usually reserve the key managerial and technical positions for expatriates. As a result, they do not contribute to the development of host-country personnel.

4. MNCs do not adapt their technology to the conditions that exist in host countries.

5. MNCs concentrate their research and development activities at home, restricting the transfer of modern technology and know-how to host countries.

6. MNCs give rise to the demand for luxury goods in host countries at the expense of essential consumer goods.

7. MNCs start their foreign operations by purchasing existing firms rather than by developing new productive facilities in host countries.

8. MNCs dominate major industrial sectors, thus contributing to inflation by stimulating demand for scarce resources and earning excessively high profits and fees.

9. MNCs are not accountable to their host nations but only respond to home-country governments; they are not concerned with host-country plans for development.[51]

Specific MNCs have been charged with tax evasion, union busting, and interference in host-country politics. Of course, MNCs have both positive and negative effects on different economies. For every complaint about MNC activities (whether about capital markets, technology transfer, or employment practices), we can identify potential benefits, as shown in Exhibit 2-6.

Numerous conflicts arise between MNC companies or subsidiaries and host countries, including conflicting goals (both economic and noneconomic) and con-

Exhibit 2-6 MNC Benefits and Costs to Host Countries

Benefits	Costs
Capital Market Effects	
■ Broader access to outside capital	■ Increased competition for local scarce capital
■ Foreign-exchange earnings	■ Increased interest rates as supply of local capital decreases
■ Import substitution effects allow governments to save foreign exchange for priority projects	■ Capital service effects of balance of payments
■ Risk sharing	
Technology and Production Effects	
■ Access to new technology and R&D developments	■ Technology is not always appropriate
■ Infrastructure development and support	■ Plants are often for assembly only and can be dismantled
■ Export diversification	■ Government infrastructure investment is higher than expected benefits
Employment Effects	
■ Direct creation of new jobs	■ Limited skill development and creation
■ Opportunities for indigenous management development	■ Competition for scarce skills
■ Income multiplier effects on local community business	■ Low percentage of managerial jobs for local people
	■ Employment instability because of ability to move production operations freely to other countries

SOURCE: R. H. Mason and R. S. Spich, *Management: An International Perspective* (Homewood, Ill. Irwin, 1987), 202.

flicting concerns, such as the security of proprietary technology, patents, or information. Overall, the resulting tradeoffs create an interdependent relationship between the subsidiary and the host government, based on relative bargaining power. The power of MNCs is based on their large-scale, worldwide economies, their strategic flexibility, and their control over technology and production location. The bargaining chips of the host governments include their control of raw materials and market access and their ability to set the rules regarding the role of private enterprise, the operation of state-owned firms, and the specific regulations regarding taxes, permissions, and so forth.[52]

MNCs run the risk of their assets becoming hostage to host control, which may take the form of nationalism, protectionism, or governmentalism. Under nationalism, for example, public opinion is rallied in favor of national goals and against foreign influences. Under protectionism, the host institutes a partial or complete closing of borders to withstand competitive foreign products, using tariff and nontariff barriers, such as those used by Japan. Under governmentalism, the government uses its policy-setting role to favor national interests, rather than relying on market forces. An example is Britain's decision to privatize its telephone system.[53]

Ford Motor Company came up against many of these controls when it decided to produce automobiles in Spain. The Spanish government set specific restrictions on sales and export volume: the sales volume was limited to 10 percent of the previous year's total automobile market, and the export volume had to be at least two-thirds of the entire production in Spain. Ford also had to agree that it would not broaden its model lines without the authorization of the government.[54]

The intricacies of the relationship and the relative power of an MNC subsidiary and a host-country government are situation specific. Clearly, such a relationship should be managed for mutual benefit; a long-term, constructive relationship based on the MNC's socially responsive stance should result in progressive strategic success for the MNC and economic progress for the host country. The effective management of subsidiary–host-country interdependence must have a long-term perspective. Although temporary strategies to reduce interdependence via controls on the transnational flows by firms (for example, transfer-pricing tactics) or by governments (such as new residency requirements for skilled workers) are often successful in the short run, they result in inefficiencies that must be absorbed by one or both parties, with negative long-term results.[55] In setting up and maintaining subsidiaries, managers are wise to consider the long-term trade-offs between strategic plans and operational management. By finding out for themselves the pressing local concerns and understanding the sources of past conflicts, they can learn from mistakes and recognize the consequences of the failure to manage problems. Furthermore, managers should implement policies that reflect corporate social responsibility regarding local economic issues, employee welfare, or natural resources.[56] At the least, the failure to manage interdependence effectively results in constraints on strategy. In the worst case, it results in disastrous consequences for the local area, for the subsidiary, and for the global reputation of the company.

The interdependent nature of developing economies and the MNCs operating there is of particular concern when discussing social responsibility because of the tentative and fragile nature of the economic progression in those countries. MNCs need to set a high moral standard and lay the groundwork for future economic development. At the minimum they should ensure that their actions will do no harm. Some recommendations by De George for MNCs operating in and doing business with developing countries are as follows:

1. Do no intentional harm. This includes respect for the integrity of the ecosystem and consumer safety.
2. Produce more good than harm for the host country.
3. Contribute by their activity to the host country's development.
4. Respect the human rights of their employees.
5. To the extent that local culture does not violate ethical norms, respect the local culture and work with and not against it.
6. Pay their fair share of taxes.
7. Cooperate with the local government in developing and enforcing just background (infrastructure) institutions (i.e., laws, governmental regulations, unions, and consumer groups, which serve as a means of social control).[57]

One issue that illustrates conflicting concerns about social responsibility is the interdependence between Mexico and the United States which has resulted from the North American Free Trade Agreement (NAFTA), as discussed in the following section.

Comparative Management in Focus

Interdependence: "Borderland Amexica"

In Laredo, Texas, 8,000 trucks a day haul the global economy north and south . . . through a town that once didn't bother to pave the streets.

—*TIME*, JUNE 11, 2001

By 2001, about half of all new jobs created in Mexico since the NAFTA stemmed directly from that agreement, fostering a burgeoning middle class of consumers.

—*FORTUNE INVESTORS' GUIDE*, DECEMBER 18, 2000

The evidence abounds, as of 2002, that the North American Trade Agreement has created increasing interdependence and business and cultural convergence. This is particularly apparent along what has become known as borderland—a rapidly growing and intermeshed community along the Mexican-U.S. border where five or six "twin-cities" house tax-advantaged factories called *maquiladoras*. According to the National Association of Maquiladoras, there are 3,611 foreign-owned factories that employ over 1.3 million people in Mexico.[58]

Companies that used to outsource production in Asia have been enticed by the benefits of the NAFTA to do so in Mexico instead, many of them just across the border. About 800,000 people cross the border each day—to work, shop, or seek services. *Time* magazine observes that this borderland is essentially its own country—"Amexica"—where the United States blends into Mexico. In fact, those authors question why there is a border at all because of the growing integration and interdependence of those people and businesses and culture on both sides of the border.[59] Firetrucks, schools, hospitals, groceries, and so on, service both sides of the border. Economic and environmental interdependence are evident in cities such as Juarez-El Paso, where there are over 400 assembly plants from Ireland to Japan, and two million people drink the same water and breathe the same air.[60] However, while Mexico does not want to discourage continued investment, and there is a burgeoning middle class in some areas, in other areas extreme poverty and environmental pollution prevail. With the minimum wage set at the equivalent of $4.20 *a day*, a family of four has a difficult time surviving in many of those areas, where it is estimated that at least $20 a day is needed to support them.[61] Critics of the NAFTA say that whatever economic benefits there are have come at the expense of Mexican workers and the Mexican environment, and that "little has been done to improve the lives of the poorest Mexicans."[62] Mexico's president Vicente Fox, a former Coca-Cola executive, argues that the solution is "the narrowing of wage differentials among Mexico, the United States, and Canada."[63] In booming Juarez, for example, pay is still only about $1.25 an hour. However, some companies, such as Delphi automotive Systems, are helping to fund affordable homes close to the plants—a move that has reduced employee turnover at Delphi from 10 percent a month to 1.2 percent a year.[64]

It may be too soon to judge the long-run success of the NAFTA, but early results do reinforce the interdependent nature of the agreement, the three economies (Mexico, United States, and Canada), and the relative level of success attained for business firms, environmental issues, and people. Now, several years since the NAFTA took effect, the Mexican border factories have boomed, and many of those jobs are now high-tech, bringing training and a higher standard of living for many Mexicans. Indeed, President Fox set 2001 budget goals of 4 to 5 percent GDP growth.[65] An investigation produced for the Economic Strategy Institute concluded that

> the extremely optimistic and pessimistic predictions made by proponents and opponents of the NAFTA have not come true, but both the United States and Mexico are benefiting.
> —JOHN MUTTI, ECONOMICS PROFESSOR,
> *AUTOMOTIVE NEWS*, FEBRUARY 12, 2001

The study also concluded that NAFTA has promoted trade and greater efficiency in the member countries and the world as a whole.

It seems that because of lower labor costs for "foreign" companies, the devalued peso, and the NAFTA-reduced tariff levels, the NAFTA had a mitigating effect on the Mexican economic crisis.[66] In addition, in a touch of irony, Asia's problems caused some global companies to relocate factories from Asia to Mexico. In fact, Mexico has overtaken mainland China as the volume leader of exports of textiles and garments to the United States. But do the trade numbers tell it all? Perhaps we can compare perspectives from south and north of the border by looking at some examples and issues.

From the South Looking North

> It's not like ten years ago, when we wanted to talk to [U.S.] customers and no one would talk to us. Now, big [U.S.] customers are calling us.
> —VICTOR ALMEIDA, CEO, INTERCERAMIC[67]

The Almeida family of Interceramic (Internacional de Cerámica SA, Chihuahua, Mexico) always wanted to export to the United States, but it took the heightened interest in Mexico through the NAFTA agreement to give them their breakthrough.

The manufacturer of glazed floor and wall tile is just one of the many savvy Mexican firms making inroads into the U.S. market. But in many ways it is harder for Mexican managers to go north than it is for U.S. managers to go south. While they both face the same sorts of cross-cultural managerial problems, Mexican companies are typically at a competitive disadvantage in the United States because they are not as advanced in technology or efficiency as American firms.

Interceramic, a traditional Mexican family business, had to learn the hard way that business is done differently in the United States. Victor Almeida, the CEO, found that contractors buy most of the tile in the United States, compared to the homeowner in Mexico, and that customers in the United States demanded a much better level of service.[68] He had to convince U.S. distributors that Interceramic had high-quality products and that the company was reliable, and it took some time to find the right U.S. managers to represent the company and interact with people on both sides of the border. He encouraged the U.S. managers to be more like Mexicans by showing their emotions more openly. In addition, he opened offices in Texas so that the export managers could be closer to the customer and thus get more input to custom-design the tiles to suit American tastes. Although it has taken a few years, Almeida's efforts are now paying off, and he attributes much of that to the NAFTA, as well as to his hard work.

But it's a different story for smaller, less efficient firms: many simply cannot compete with the resources of technology and access to capital that U.S. firms are bringing to Mexico. Corner stores and small businesses are getting driven out by the Wal-Marts, Grossmans, and Dunkin' Donuts—the same competitive situation that has hit towns in the United States. Mexican factories are finding it difficult to compete for employees with companies like GM which are offering subsidized housing. However, other businesses, in towns such as Nuevo Laredo, are booming as a result of servicing large companies such as Wal-Mart (known locally as Walmex, Mexico's biggest chain as of 2001).[69]

From the North Looking South

If you don't have trustworthy Mexican partners, you can get into trouble here; only idiots try to figure it out themselves.

—R. HECKMANN, CEO, U.S. FILTER[70]

"For every factory opened in Mexico (whether by Asian, Canadian, European, or American firms), the U.S. wins service, transportation, or distribution jobs."[71] American firms that supply components to those factories are also profiting from the boom south of the border. This is because primary components in products such as VCRs must be made in North America to benefit from the NAFTA. U.S. and Mexican companies also benefit from orders for supplies from European and Asian firms.

Although many Canadian and U.S. companies are expanding into Mexico, taking advantage of the increased confidence and opportunities resulting from passage of the NAFTA, most firms face an uphill battle because they make incorrect assumptions about the similarity of the market and distribution system. Problems include corruption, American arrogance, red tape on both sides of the border, and misunderstandings about the Mexican culture and how to do business there.

Coupling these problems with those in the infrastructure, it is easy to see why many foreign firms have had difficulties expanding into Mexico, often giving up. While it is easier now to get a business phone line, transportation and mail systems are still behind American expectations, and bill collecting often must be done in person because of numerous problems with the mail and required documentation. Electricity is sometimes cut off without notice, and the legal system is so difficult to figure out that foreigners risk going to jail without being accused of a crime. Mexican partners and alliances seem to be the answer—as even the giant Wal-Mart Stores Inc. found out when it ran into so many distribution problems in Mexico that it decided it would cost no more in the long run to use local distributors.

So why do American companies bother? Typically because they want to take advantage of market expansion opportunities. One example is U.S. Filter, a water-purification company whose target in Mexico is "90 million people who can't trust their tap water, and a slew of companies under government pressure to clean up waste water."[72]

Interdependence—South-North Strategic Alliances

Richard Heckmann, U.S. Filter's CEO, realized early on that alliances with trustworthy Mexican partners provided the answer to many problems and to achievement of the interdependent goals of both countries and their firms. He knew, for example, that the political reality was that Mexican officials would favor their ties to Mexican firms and steer bids to those companies. So he contracted a Mexican construction company, Plar SA, with strong political connections. In order to reach his smaller potential customers, Heckmann has formed a joint venture with Enrique Anhalt, a local Mexico City water-purification supplier to 250 manufacturers and other customers with small systems, assuming that when they upgrade they will turn to a local supplier. Plar SA benefits from the deal by getting technical and financial help from U.S. Filter to upgrade its technology.

The environmental cleanup efforts in Mexico clearly exhibit the interdependence of the NAFTA and will benefit everyone in the long run. Funding from the United States is helping with projects such as the sewage-treatment plants at 11 cities south of the border. In turn, that business is going to many U.S. environmental-services companies, such as San Diego Gas & Electric Company, which is building natural gas pipelines to Mexicali and Tijuana to supply clean fuel to industrial plants.

The auto industry is another agent of massive change in Mexico, building an industrial base south of the border that will help strengthen the Mexican economy. "The auto industry has the unusual ability to . . . jump start a middle class," according to David Cole, director of the University of Michigan's automotive studies office.[73] Although the average Ford worker in Hermosillo still earns considerably less than his counterpart in Wayne,

Michigan, that wage does represent a considerable increase for Mexican workers. In addition, every new auto plant in Mexico trains thousands of Mexicans, most of them new to factory work. While those factors don't console auto workers in the United States who have lost their jobs, they do mean that American auto manufacturers can be more globally competitive.

There is likely to be increasing interdependence among the Americas in the future as agreements open up further trade with other South American countries such as Chile, Brazil, and Uruguay. These countries are also tearing down their internal trade barriers, in a wave that may eventually form a free-trade zone from Alaska to Tierra del Fuego—a proposed "super NAFTA."[74] South Americans are realizing that they may get left out in the cold as both the European Community and North America form their own huge markets. In addition, 34 nations in North, Central and South America, and the Caribbean are negotiating a Free Trade Area of the Americas (FTAA) as a proposed expansion of the NAFTA.[75]

Managing Environmental Interdependence

International managers—and all people for that matter—can no longer afford to ignore the impact of their activities on the environment. As Ward and Dubois put it:

> Now that mankind is in the process of completing the colonization of the planet, learning to manage it intelligently is an urgent imperative. [People] must accept responsibility for the stewardship of the earth. The word stewardship implies, of course, management for the sake of someone else. . . . As we enter the global phase of human evolution, it becomes obvious that each [person] has two countries, his [or her] own and the planet earth.[76]

Effectively managing environmental interdependence includes considering ecological interdependence as well as the economic and social implications of MNC activities. There is an ever-increasing awareness of, and a mounting concern, worldwide, about the effects of global industrialization on the natural environment. This concern was evidenced by the gathering of world leaders at the Earth Summit in Rio de Janeiro to discuss and decide on action for ecological preservation. Government regulations and powerful interest groups are demanding ecological responsibility regarding the use of scarce natural resources and production processes that threaten permanent damage to the planet. MNCs have to deal with each country's different policies and techniques for environmental and health protection. Such variations in approach reflect different levels of industrialization, living standards, government–business relations, philosophies of collective intervention, patterns of industrial competition, and degrees of sophistication in public policy.[77] For an MNC to take advantage of less stringent regulations (or expectations) is not only irresponsible but also invites disaster, as illustrated by the Union Carbide accident in Bhopal.

In recent years, the export of hazardous wastes from developed countries to less developed ones has increased considerably. One instance was the dumping of over 8,000 drums of waste, including drums filled with polychlorinated biphenyl (PCB), a highly toxic compound, in Koko, Nigeria.[78] While not all dumping is illegal, the large international trade in hazardous wastes (as a result of the increasing barriers to domestic disposal) raises disturbing questions regarding social responsibility. Although the importer of waste must take some blame, it is the exporter who shoulders the ultimate responsibility for both generation and disposal. Often, companies choose to dispose of hazardous waste in less developed countries to take advantage of weaker regulations and lower costs. Until we have strict international regulation of trade in hazardous wastes, companies should take it upon themselves to monitor their activities, as Singh and Lakhan demand:

> To export these wastes to countries which do not benefit from waste-generating industrial processes or whose citizens do not have lifestyles that generate such wastes is unethical. It is especially unjust to send hazardous wastes to lesser developed countries which lack the technology to minimize the deleterious effects of these substances.[79]

The exporting of pesticides poses a similar problem, with the United States and Germany being the main culprits. The United States exports about 200 million pounds of pesticides each year that are prohibited, restricted, or not registered for use in the United States.[80] One MNC, Monsanto Chemical Corporation, for example, sells DDT to many foreign importers, even though its use in the United States has been essentially banned. Apart from the lack of social responsibility toward the people and the environment in the countries that import DDT, this action is also irresponsible to American citizens because many of their fruits and meat products are imported from those countries.[81]

These are only two of the environmental problems facing countries and large corporations today. According to Graedel and Allenby, the path to truly sustainable development is for corporations to broaden their concept of industrial ecology:

> The concept [of industrial ecology] requires that an industrial system be viewed not in isolation from its surrounding systems, but in concert with them. It is a systems view in which one seeks to optimize the total materials cycle from virgin material, to finished material, to component, to product, to obsolete product, and to ultimate disposal.[82]

Essentially, this perspective supports the idea that environmental citizenship is necessary for a firm's survival as well as responsible social performance.[83]

It is clear, then, that MNCs must take the lead in dealing with ecological interdependence by integrating environmental factors into strategic planning. Along with an investment appraisal, a project feasibility study, and operational plans, such planning should include an environmental impact assessment.[84] At the least, MNC managers must deal with the increasing scarcity of natural resources in the next few decades by (1) looking for alternative raw materials, (2) developing new methods of recycling or disposing of used materials, and (3) expanding the use of byproducts.[85]

Multinational corporations already have had a tremendous impact on foreign countries, and this impact will continue to grow and bring about long-lasting changes. Even now, U.S. MNCs alone account for about 10 percent of the world's GNP. Because of interdependence at both the local and global level, it is not only moral but also in the best interest of MNCs to establish a single clear posture toward social and ethical responsibilities worldwide and to ensure that it is implemented. In a real sense, foreign firms enter as guests in host countries and must respect the local laws, policies, traditions, and culture as well as those countries' economic and developmental needs.

Conclusion

When research findings and anecdotal evidence indicate differential attitudes toward ethical behavior and social responsibility across cultures, MNCs must take certain steps. For example, they must be careful when placing a foreign manager in a country whose values are incongruent with his or her own because this could lead to conflicts with local managers, governmental bodies, customers, and suppliers. As discussed earlier, expatriates should be oriented to the legal and ethical ramifications of questionable foreign payments, the differences in environmental regulations, and the local expectations of personal integrity. They should also be supported as they attempt to integrate host-country behaviors with the expectations of the company's headquarters.[86]

Social responsibility, ethical behavior, and interdependence are important concerns to be built into management control—not as afterthoughts but as part of the ongoing process of planning and controlling international operations for the long-term benefit of all.

In Part 2, we will focus on the pervasive and powerful influence of culture in the host-country environment in which the international manager operates. In Chapter 3, we will examine the nature of culture—what are its various dimensions and roots? How does culture affect the behavior and expectations of employees and what are the implications for how managers operating in other countries should behave?

SUMMARY OF KEY POINTS

1. The concept of international social responsibility includes the expectation that MNCs should be concerned about the social and economic effects of their decisions on activities in other countries.

2. Moral universalism refers to the need for a moral standard that is accepted by all cultures.

3. Concerns about MNC social responsibility revolve around issues of human rights in other countries, such as South Africa and China. Many organizations develop codes of conduct for their approach to business around the world.

4. International business ethics refers to the conduct of MNCs in their relationships to all individuals and entities with whom they come into contact. Ethical behavior is judged and based largely on the cultural value system and the generally accepted ways of doing business in each country or society. MNC managers must decide whether to base their ethical standards on those of the host country or those of the home country and whether these different standards can be reconciled.

5. MNCs must balance their responsibility to various stakeholders, such as owners, creditors, consumers, employees, suppliers, governments, and societies.

6. Questionable payments are those payments that raise significant questions about appropriate moral behavior in either the host nation or other nations. The Foreign Corrupt Practices Act prohibits most questionable payments by U.S. companies doing business in other countries.

7. Managers must control their activities relative to interdependent relationships at all levels—from simple, daily business transactions involving local workers, intermediaries, or consumers to global concerns of ecological responsibility.

8. The MNC–host-country relationship is generally a love-hate relationship from the host country's viewpoint in that it wants the economic growth that the MNC can provide but does not want the dependency and other problems that result.

9. The failure to effectively manage interdependence will result in constraints on strategy, in the least, or in disastrous consequences for the local area, the subsidiary, and the global reputation of the company.

10. Managing environmental interdependence includes the need to consider ecological interdependence as well as the economic and social implications of MNC activities.

APPLICATION EXERCISE

Do some research to find out the codes of conduct of two MNCs. Compare the issues that they cover and share your findings with the class. After several students have presented their findings, prepare a chart showing the commonalities and differences of content in the codes presented. How do you account for the differences?

EXPERIENTIAL EXERCISE

Consider the ethical dilemmas in the following situation and decide what you would do. Then meet in small groups of students and come to a group consensus. Discuss your decisions with the class.

> I am CEO of an international trading company in Turkey. One state-owned manufacturing company (Company A) in one of the Middle East countries opened a tender for 15,000 tons PVC granule K value 70. Company A makes all its purchases through tenders. For seven years in that market my company has never been able to do any business with Company A (though we have sold many bulk materials to other state-owned companies in that market). One of our new managers had a connection with the purchasing manager of Company A, who promised to supply us with all of our competitors' bids if we pay him a 2 percent commission on all of our sales to his company. Our area manager accepted this arrangement. He got the competing bids, made our offer, and we got the tender. I learned of this situation when reviewing our income and expenses chart, which showed the 2 percent commission.
>
> What shall I do, given the following: (1) If I refuse to accept the business without any legitimate reasons (presently there are none) my company will be black-listed in that country—where we get about 20 percent of our gross yearly profit. (2) If I accept the business and do not pay the 2 percent commission, the purchasing manager will make much trouble for us when he receives our shipment. I am sure that he will not release our 5 percent bank guarantee letter about the quality and quantity of the material. (3) If I accept the business and pay the 2 percent commission, it will go against everything I have achieved in the 30 years of my career.

You have three ethical problems here: First, your company has won a rigged bid. Second, you must pay the person who rigged it or he will make life miserable for you. And third, you have to decide what to do with the area manager who accepted this arrangement.

SOURCE: J. Delaney and D. Sockell, "Ethics in the Trenches," *Across the Board* (October 1990): 17.

CASE STUDY: BALANCING HUMAN RIGHTS AROUND THE WORLD: NIKE AND REEBOK

Nike and Reebok—two major footwear companies familiar to most people—outsource their footwear production around the world. But they each structure the outsourcing process differently.

Nike

Nike managers refer to their company as a "network firm"—one that is connected to other companies that produce their products. Nike employs 8,000 people in management, design, sales, and promotion, and leaves production in the hands of some 75,000 workers around the world, hired by independent contractors. Most of Nike's outsourced goods come from Indonesia and Vietnam, where wages are low and enforcement of labor laws are lax.

Recently, Nike has come under fire for its continuous relationship with some Korean and Vietnamese subcontractors who were accused of mistreating their workers. In Korea there were reports of women being forced to kneel down and hold their hands up for 25 minutes, and another woman being subjected to having her mouth taped shut because of talking during working hours. In Vietnam, it was reported that a supervisor molested workers and that employees, mostly young females were getting paid about $0.20 an hour and working six days a week (below the minimum wage in Vietnam).

These are just a few of the reported incidents involving Nike's "network firms." But Nike has kept the company out of the spotlight because it does not actually own these factories—it just does business with them. Nike has no plans to change its operations, and the company has used high-profile figures to downplay the problem. John Thompson, Georgetown basketball coach, hired by Nike, viewed a Vietnam plant and stated that he did not see any of the kinds of things he had heard about.

After these reports, Nike joined the list of companies adhering to the Anti-sweatshop Code of Conduct. In May 1998, Nike announced a new Code of Conduct and plans to select partners to participate in monitoring practices in Indonesia, China, and Vietnam. The company also announced in the fall of 1998 that it would lift wages for its entry-level factory workers in Indonesia by 22 percent to offset Indonesia's devalued currency.

Reebok

Reebok, a global athletic sports and fitness company, prides itself on its commitment to human rights. The company is also committed to finding partners who will use ethical manufacturing policies. Reebok helped establish The Task Force on Global Manufacturing Practices to organize, research, and develop recommendations for action.

Reebok has set stringent standards for production of their goods: the Reebok Human Rights Production Standards. Reebok will seek compliance with set standards in the selection of subcontractors, contractors, suppliers, and other business partners. Some of these standards include the following (summarized) as set out on their home page (http://www.reebok.com):

Working Hours/Overtime: Reebok only seeks partners who do not require more than 60-hour work weeks . . . and prefer those who use a 48-hour work week.

Forced or Compulsory Labor: Reebok will not work with or purchase materials from companies that use labor required as a means of political coercion or as a punishment for holding or expressing political views.

Fair Wages: Reebok searches for partners who share its belief in fair wages and benefits. Reebok will not select partners who pay less than minimum wage required by local law or pay their workers less than prevailing local industry practices.

Child Labor: Reebok will not work with business partners that employ children in the production of goods (under 14 years of age).

Safe and Healthy Work Environment: Reebok seeks business partners who provide workers with a safe and healthy workplace, and who do not expose workers to hazardous conditions.

Partners: Reebok will seek business partners who allow them full knowledge of the production facilities used and will undertake affirmative measures, such as on-site inspection of production facilities, to implement and monitor these standards.

One example of Reebok's commitment has been in reassessing its soccer business. After learning that as much as 20 percent of the soccer ball stitching in Pakistan may have been done by children, Reebok has tried to do its part in ending the poor conditions that have promoted child labor. After soliciting several proposals from soccer ball manufacturers in Pakistan, Reebok signed an agreement with Reed and Associates and Moltex Rubber Works to establish a new manufacturing facility. The terms of the agreement are that all work on the balls will be done inside the plant and that all workers will be at least 15 years old and will be paid at least the minimum wage in Pakistan.

Case Questions

1. How do you assess the approach of Nike and of Reebok to outsourcing around the world? Can you apply the term *ethnocentrism* or the term *ethical relativism* to either of these cases? What are your thoughts on the concept of "moral universalism" as it may pertain to these situations?

2. Do a "stakeholder analysis" for each company separately (Nike and Reebok). Lay out the categories of stakeholders and detail for each the "stake" of each party—the rights, obligations, incentives, and motivations. What is, or should be, their role in the dilemma of outsourcing production from countries in which there may be a "sweatshop" situation?

3. Return to your answers to question 1. Now assess the impact—the changes in "stake"—that your recommendations would have on each of the stakeholders you identified in question 2.

   Who benefits and who loses through the use of so-called sweatshops for outsourcing production? What do you think the future holds for this situation?

4. What actions can consumers take to end "sweatshops"? Do you think they should take action? What would be the results for the various stakeholders? Do you think the negative publicity about Nike has caused positive change in the company's policies?

Case Sources

Robert Senser, "Human Rights for Workers Bulletin." http://ourworld.compuserve.com/homepages/HRW/bu10.htm;

Reebok: "Reebok Production Standards," http://www.reebok.com/humanrights/products.htm;

Reebok home page: http://www.reebok.com;

http://www.Nikebiz.com;

"A Floor under Foreign Factories?" *Business Week*, November 2, 1998.

Comprehensive Cases

Case 1 Aung Sein: An Entrepreneur in Myanmar

Aung Sein,[1] a citizen of Myanmar,[2] an ethnic Chinese and an entrepreneur, was having difficulty with his disposable glove business. Using a machine of his own design, Aung Sein believed he could produce enough disposable gloves to satisfy the demand in Myanmar. Many workers in Myanmar were being needlessly exposed to injury and infection because of the shortage of disposable gloves. But the Ministry of Trade (the agency that makes all major purchases for the Myanmar Government) would not buy his gloves. Aung Sein decided to evaluate the costs, benefits and risks of attempting to induce the Ministry of Trade to buy his gloves.

Until he found a way to market his disposable gloves, Aung Sein concentrated his efforts on the management of a travel agency he owned with 13 other Myanmar citizens of Chinese ancestry. In addition to organizing group tours for foreigners, his agency had contracted with a gold mining venture owned by Singaporeans. Aung Sein's agency arranged logistics support (transportation, lodging, food, laborers, etc.) for the construction and operation of a new mine in Northern Myanmar. The travel agency provided Aung Sein and his partners with opportunities to earn foreign exchange, while revenues from the disposable glove business would be in local currency only.

Aung Sein came from an entrepreneurial family. His father walked to Myanmar through the rugged mountain ranges from China when he was fifteen years old. He arrived in Myanmar, not speaking the language and owning only the clothes he wore. Aung Sein's father married a Burmese girl and raised a family. He and his wife eventually owned a grocery store in Scott Market, the main shopping place for foreigners and the well-to-do in Yangon.[3] In the 1960s, the Myanmar Government took over the Scott Market store. Aung Sein's parents moved to the smaller city of Nyaunglebin, some 100 miles south of Yangon. With their savings they were able to send all of their children to college.

Aung Sein, the third of eight children, always had a desire to succeed. "My father expected me to become a physician. I enrolled in the Rangoon Medical Institute after graduating from the university with honors. When I became a physician in 1987, I entered private practice instead of joining the government health service. I operated a clinic in partnership with a pediatrics professor from the Health Institute. I was an owner, manager, and practicing physician." The conflict between his role as a business manager and his responsibilities to his patients bothered Aung Sein. "Many people who needed medical attention had no money. We tried to treat as many as we could, but the clinic could not survive without making money." Finally Aung Sein decided that he would pursue his entrepreneurial instincts. He quit the clinic and stopped practicing medicine.

SOURCE: By Robert W. Hornaday, The University of North Carolina at Charlotte. This case is intended as a basis for classroom discussion rather than to illustrate effective or ineffective handling of an administrative situation.

[1]A pseudonym.
[2]Formerly named Burma.

[3]Formerly named Rangoon, the capital city.

Aung Sein's measure of success was to own a large house in downtown Yangon and to employ enough people so that he could devote his time to planning entrepreneurial ventures. Others would attend to the operational details. He was always on the alert for entrepreneurial opportunities.

Aung Sein developed two guiding principles: (1) "Search for what the people want." and (2) "Sell those things to them at minimum investment for maximum profit." Aung Sein did not consider these principles to be heartless capitalism. Instead he described a win–win situation where both he and his customers become better off through his efforts. In addition, he hoped to provide employment to many people and to train them so they could compete in the world market. He had ideas for solar energy sources for remote villages and the production of ball point pens and electrical fixtures.

THE DISPOSABLE GLOVE BUSINESS

One of Aung Sein's first ventures was the production of disposable gloves. These items were not produced in Myanmar and had to be imported—an expensive process requiring scarce foreign exchange. Because of the expense, many workers who should have used disposable gloves did not. These gloves are of the type often worn by cafeteria workers in the United States. They are not surgically sterile, greatly lowering the cost.

Medical personnel such as midwives, paramedics, and laboratory workers should regularly wear disposable gloves to prevent infection from patients, laboratory specimens, autopsy procedures, and blood used for transfusions. The spread of AIDS in Myanmar increased the need for cheap disposable gloves that fit either hand and have a sensitive touch and feel. Other workers who regularly handle caustic materials (lead-acid batteries, insecticides, herbicides, etc.) could also benefit from wearing disposable gloves.

The Myanmar Ministry of Trade was importing about 100,000 disposable gloves monthly from companies in the United Kingdom, the United States, Japan, and India at a price of five dollars per one hundred gloves. An unknown number of gloves were also being smuggled across the border from China at a price of $3.50 per one hundred gloves. Midwives and laboratory workers used about 30% and 25%, respectively, of the imported gloves. The supply of gloves was clearly not meeting demand. Workers in Myanmar needed about 50,000 disposable gloves per day, or about 1.5 million gloves per month.

Seeing this unmet demand as an opportunity, Aung Sein built his disposable glove machine. The first model was hand-operated using plastic pellets as raw material. "My wife and I made the gloves and packaged them at home. I hooked up an electric motor to the glove-making machine to speed things up."

Financing

Aung Sein's total investment in his machinery was Kyat[4] 37,000 (about US$350). "To you Americans this doesn't sound like much, but in Myanmar, this is a lot of money. I had to borrow from a money lender at rates of 5% to 10% per month," said Aung Sein.

Aung Sein priced his gloves for Kyat 50 per box of 50 gloves—about one fifth the price of imported gloves. The cost of electricity was negligible, since Aung Sein surreptitiously hooked up his machine to his inexpensive household electric line avoiding the major expense of installing a commercial electric line.

"The Ministry of Trade wouldn't buy my gloves, but I sold about 1,000 boxes to private physicians," recalled Aung Sein. This provided a small profit of Kyat 27,000 (about US$250 to Aung Sein and his wife). To make his glove operation self sufficient by hiring production and marketing personnel, Aung Sein estimated that he would need an operating profit of $1,000 per month.

Disposable Glove Operations—First Year 1994/1995

	Per Unit	Total (1,000 boxes)
Selling Price	Kyat 50	Kyat 50,000
Raw Materials	Kyat 14	Kyat 14,000
Packaging	Kyat 5	Kyat 5,000
Total Cost	Kyat 19	Kyat 19,000
Operating Profit	Kyat 31	Kyat 31,000
Debt Principal and Interest		Kyat 4,000
Total Profit (Loss)		Kyat 27,000

Marketing Difficulties

Aung Sein focused his marketing efforts on the Ministry of Trade, the governmental agency with contracting authority. "They will not buy. No sale.

---

[4]The Myanmar currency. Pronounced "chawt."

My gloves have been approved by the Ministry of Health and my friends in the medical profession have tested the gloves. They all think my gloves are good. When I visit the Ministry of Trade, everybody is polite. They agree my gloves meet their needs and they say they will contact me with an order, but nothing ever happens."

Aung Sein suspected that the reason that the Ministry of Trade bureaucrats were not interested is that they kept a percentage of the foreign exchange dollars that flowed through their hands on purchases of disposable gloves from foreign sources. If they bought his gloves using kyats, they would suffer personal financial losses. In addition, if purchasing agents secured disposable gloves within Myanmar, they might be pressured to procure other disposable medical supplies within Myanmar, further cutting the foreign exchange dollars that flowed through the Ministry of Trade.

To sell disposable gloves to the Ministry of Trade, Aung Sein has concluded that he would be forced to arrange payments to government officials. Payoffs could take the form of outright cash payments, gifts of expensive items such as automobiles or household appliances, or the deposit of foreign exchange in foreign banks in Bangkok or Singapore for the use of government officials when they or their families traveled outside Myanmar.

Aung Sein believed that his glove business would be good for Myanmar. "My countrymen need these gloves," he said. "Maybe I could provide some jobs." The only way to sell large quantities of gloves, however, was through the Ministry of Trade. To get officials to buy his gloves, Aung Sein felt that he would have to offer them the same inducements they were receiving from smugglers. He sat down to estimate how much Ministry of Trade officials received from smuggled gloves and whether he could still make a profit by offering similar payoffs.

EXHIBIT: A NOTE ON MYANMAR

Through the 1990s, Myanmar had a military government, a dominant religion (Therevada Buddhism) with political clout, a large, underpaid government bureaucracy, and a history of bloody ethnic conflict. In common with most of Southeast Asia, Myanmar's economic system suffered from serious problems of corruption and smuggling. For those doing business with governments in this region, conventional wisdom pegged the "normal" payoff to bureaucrats at between 10% and 20% of the contract price.

Background

Rich in natural and agricultural resources, Myanmar was once the wealthiest country in Southeast Asia and the world's largest rice exporter. During the last days of British colonial rule before World War II Myanmar had the highest literacy rate of any nation between Suez and Japan. The country is bisected by the Irawaddy River system, which provides a rich source of hydroelectric power, water for irrigation, and over 1000 miles of inland navigation from the Indian Ocean on the south to the Chinese border on the north.

But Myanmar did not produce economic development and growth to match its fast growing neighbors in Southeast Asia such as Thailand, Malaysia, and Singapore. In 1987, the United Nations General Assembly classified Myanmar as a "least developed nation" along with Chad, Ethiopia, Nepal, and Bangladesh. The U.S. State Department in 1996 estimated the gross domestic product per person in Myanmar to be somewhere between 200 and 300 U.S. dollars.

Maintenance of law and order has always been a major issue in Myanmar. The Burmese are the dominant ethic group, but comprise only about 68% of the population. Over the centuries, other ethnic groups have fiercely attempted to maintain their autonomy. A small but vigorous Chinese minority has controlled most of the private sector economy. Ethnic Chinese also have usually held many key positions in government and education.

Experts agreed that political problems caused Myanmar's economic malaise. The multiparty governmental system adopted after independence from the British in 1947 could neither maintain internal order nor sustain economic development. Finally, in 1962, the army took direct control under General Ne Win who remained a virtual dictator for 25 years. Ne Win declared that Myanmar would follow a strange mixture of European-style socialism and populist isolationism that appealed to the xenophobic strain among Burmese farmers.

The most striking aspect of this "Burmese Way to Socialism" was isolation from the rest of the world. Ne Win abruptly canceled foreign aid projects, including international exchange agreements such as the Fulbright program. Tourism was severely curtailed and citizens of Myanmar had great difficulty getting permission to travel abroad for any reason. Ne Win built a wall around Myanmar.

A detailed description of the political and economic turmoil these policies produced is beyond the scope of this note. The standard of living of most people dropped below that of the pre-war colonial period. Prices for gasoline and electricity skyrocketed. Black markets proliferated and influential individuals became wealthy amid widespread economic decline and poverty.

Ne Win's policies exacerbated the situation. Private companies were nationalized. English was banned from the schools (it was returned in the 1970s). The national currency (kyat) was pegged at an artificially high level. Strong currency controls cut the flow of foreign exchange. The result was economic disaster. The lack of foreign exchange, the inflated value of the kyat, and an overgrown, corrupt bureaucracy combined to create formidable obstacles to any entrepreneurial activity.

In 1988, serious civil disturbances broke out. Police were unable to restore order. Regular army units, fresh from border combat with insurgent groups, shot down hundreds (perhaps thousands) in several major urban areas. Ne Win stepped down and a group of generals staged a coup. Ruling through the State Law and Order Restoration Committee (SLORC) the army leaders promised elections in 1990. An opposition coalition defeated the SLORC party in the 1990 election. SLORC, however, refused to turn over power and continued to govern Myanmar by decree, bypassing regular legal and political institutions, placing opposition leader Ang San Suu Kyi under house arrest.

Foreign governments began to abandon aid projects in Myanmar in the wake of the 1988 riots. The suppression of dissident groups and the inability or unwillingness of the Myanmar government to control the opium trade on the border with Thailand led to the departure of most foreign donors, including the Asian Development Bank, the United States Agency for International Development (USAID), and Japanese aid agencies. The United States withdrew its ambassador. Private foreign companies, while not forbidden to do business with Myanmar, received no assistance from governmental sources such as the World Bank, the International Monetary Fund, or the U.S. Export Import Bank. The departure of foreign donors was a major blow. Myanmar was more isolated than ever.

Recognizing the economic reasons behind the 1988 disturbances, SLORC abandoned the command economy of the Burmese Way to Socialism and moved towards a market economy. The government eased visa restrictions on those entering and leaving Myanmar. Regulations were changed to encourage foreign investment, including provisions for foreign ownership of Myanmar corporations. Many of these reforms were aimed at encouraging foreign donors to return. Whether Myanmar's leaders could foster economic growth without further bloodshed was unclear.

The Foreign Exchange Problem

All businesses in Myanmar were vexed by the exchange rate problem in the 1990s. The Myanmar kyat was a restricted currency that could not be traded outside Myanmar. The Myanmar Government maintained the kyat at a greatly inflated exchange rate—about six kayt to one U.S. dollar in 1996. The government required Myanmar citizens to deposit their money in kyat accounts at the official exchange rate in one of seven banks authorized to handle foreign exchange. The purpose of these restrictions was to keep foreign exchange capital from fleeing country.

The tourist industry is usually a major source of foreign exchange for developing countries. Myanmar fits this profile. The country has world-class tourist destinations such as towering pagodas, ancient temple complexes, scenic lakes and mountains, and the Irawady River. In the 1990s, however, Myanmar's transportation infrastructure was practically nonexistent. Roads, airlines, hotels, and restaurants needed to be drastically improved before large numbers of tourists chose Myanmar as a vacation destination.

To encourage tourism, the Myanmar Government sold dollar-denominated foreign exchange certificates (FECs) at par for U.S. dollars. The FECs could be converted to kyat at a legal "parallel market" rate of 120 kyats to the dollar that closely followed the black market exchange rate. Most facilities (hotels, airlines, shops, restaurants, etc.) that catered to foreign tourists in Myanmar preferred payment in FECs, not kyat. Of course, there was also a brisk black market in U.S. currency. The U.S. State Department reported that one hundred dollar bills were in great demand and commanded a premium price when exchanged for kyat, in some instances 140 kyat to the U.S. dollar in mid-1996.

Myanmar citizens who maintained foreign exchange accounts could withdraw their money in FECs only for specific purchases such as the purchase of airline tickets or for commodities sold at special retail outlets. Any other withdrawals had to be in kyat at the rate of six to the dollar. This enabled the Myanmar Government, in effect, to confiscate foreign exchange earnings from its citizens and use that foreign exchange for governmental international transactions.

While the government forced citizens to sell their dollars for kyat at the official exchange rate, converting kyat back into dollars was a different proposition. The government severely limited the amount of foreign exchange it would sell at six kyats to the dollar. Myanmar citizens could not export foreign exchange. For instance, as of mid-1996, a citizen of Myanmar desiring to travel outside the country could convert only US$65.00 using kyat at the official exchange rate. Businesses that desired to convert kyat back into dollars faced similar restrictions. The Myanmar Government's currency policies provided ample opportunity for individuals and businesses to get around official restrictions

through smuggling, bribery, and the flourishing black market.

The most popular way to get around currency restrictions is to overbill or underbill on goods and services purchased or sold on foreign markets. To keep foreign exchange from coming into a country with currency restrictions a firm might underbill. For example, a tourist business might make a group tour deal with an agent in Bangkok for $100,000 asking the Bangkok agent to make out the invoice for $80,000 to show to Myanmar authorities and deposit the remaining $20,000 in a Bangkok bank account owned by the Myanmar tourist business.

Conversely, to get foreign exchange out a Myanmar business would overbill a purchase made from foreigners. Assume the same tourist business buys tour buses from a Japanese firm for $80,000. The Myanmar business might ask the Japanese to state the price on the invoice as $100,000. The Myanmar firm would send $100,000 in foreign exchange. The Japanese firm would take $80,000 as payment and deposit the extra $20,000 in a Bangkok bank account for the Myanmar business.

Overbilling and underbilling practices are not unique to developing countries. For example, "kickbacks" to suppliers are a frequent source of ethical and legal problems in the United States.

Case 2   Treating AIDS—The Global Ethical Dilemma

Ninety percent of the world's 33 million HIV/AIDS cases are in Africa, Latin America and Asia. The vast majority of infected people in those areas can't afford the cocktails of miracle drugs that can make AIDS a chronic disease rather than a death sentence.[1]

The dilemma for drug companies, governments, and world health organizations is how to make those cocktails—which cost about $750 a month in the United States—affordable in countries such as South Africa, where annual income is around $6,000 per capita, and where 8 percent of the 38 million people there are infected with the AIDS

virus.[2] Western drug companies are faced with issues of social responsibility in both the short- and the long-term. In the short term they are faced with concerns of compassion for people who can be treated with their drugs, pressure from health organizations around the world, global competition, and the need to maintain a benevolent image. For the long term, the pharmaceutical industry is faced with maintaining sufficient revenue to support the goal of developing a cure for AIDS and other diseases—a process that takes years of research and development.

In a related concern the pharmaceutical industry is fighting to protect intellectual-property rights—the patents on their drugs that protect the companies from generic copies. This goes to the heart of what drug companies are in business to do: to invest large sums of money over a long period to develop drugs, which are then patented so that those companies can recoup their investment cost. The executives of those companies feel that if they cannot maintain global patent protection, then their businesses would not survive. This in itself is a dilemma for world health, because who, then, would develop and produce the drugs the world needs? Those managers also have the responsibility to maximize shareholder wealth.

This complex, global situation continues to unfold with various parties trying to find a solution to the overall problem, which comes down to one of who should pay for AIDS drugs around the world?

For its part, the South African government passed a law in 1997 to empower the government to secure cheaper drugs for its people by allowing small local companies to copy patented drugs. The provision was also made to allow AIDS drugs to be imported from countries such as India which do not enforce patent rights.[3] Needless to say, this led to an ongoing legal battle with the multinational drug companies with branches in South Africa. In an attempt to combat such actions, in May 2000, five major multinational pharmaceutical companies offered to sell the AIDS combination therapies at reduced prices to developing nations.[4] However, the annual cost of $1,000 was still regarded as too high for most patients. In addition, those companies pointed out that the administration of therapies is far more complicated and expensive than simply handing out pills. Various groups, such as Oxfam and Doctors Without Borders (a humanitarian group of doctors who volunteer their time) continue to pressure drug companies to reduce their prices further for poor countries; they also have been working to enable generic versions to be imported to those countries without trade penalties.[5]

On another front in this war, an Indian company, Cipla Ltd., announced in February 2001 that it would provide its generic version of the triple-combination therapy to Doctors Without Borders at a cost of $350 per patient per year. Indian law allows that local firms there can manufacture drugs without regard to whether they are patented in other countries, "if they employ processes different from the original patented process."[6]

Through its action, Cipla has triggered a price war, causing GlaxoSmithKline and Merck to match prices for poor countries. Yusuf Hamied, Cipla's chairman, is glad to see that trend because he is concerned about the alarming rate of increase of cases of HIV in India—currently 4 million—and says that his company could not produce enough by itself.[7] He believes that patents should only be between countries that are technological equals. He states that:

> . . . patent laws are national laws; they are not international laws. There is no one patent that applies to the whole world; patent laws are designed with national interests in mind. . . . Every country must be allowed to decide its own destiny.[8]

This was the reasoning that led India to change its patent law in 1972 to prohibit product patents in food and health. However, if India is to be allowed to join the WTO it will have to change its patent laws by 2005, making many of its drugs illegal, although its process patents can run for seven years after that.

South African and India are claiming a state of "national emergency," which allows governments to ignore foreign patents under WTO's rules. In Brazil, also, local pharmaceutical firms, under pressure from the Brazilian government, have been making their own anti-retroviral drugs and distributing them free to patients. As a result, AIDS deaths have dropped by 50 percent since 1994.[9]

Western pharmaceutical companies regard the actions by the Brazilian and Indian governments as infringing on their intellectual property rights. The counterargument is that because most of those large companies sell anti-AIDS drugs mostly to wealthy countries, it is not necessary for them to keep up their prices.[10]

In April 2001, the world pharmaceutical industry dropped its lawsuit against the South African government, because the primary companies (Merck & Co., GlaxoSmithKline PLC, Bristol-Myers Squibb Co., Boehringer Ingelheim GmbH, and Abbott Laboratories) concluded that, by fighting it, their image was being severely tarnished by the general opinion in the world about their insensitivity to the plight of poor people.[11] The suit had been filed by the industry in 1998 challenging the

South African law allowing generic drugs to be imported without the permission of the patent holders.[12] The agreement to drop the suit was based on a promise by the South African government to comply with the WTO rules in implementing the disputed medicines law.[13] Confounding efforts by many parties, however, has been the attitude by President Thabo Mbeki toward the AIDS problem in his country. He has stated on several occasions that he believes that AIDS is "simply a disease of poverty, not of infection with the HIV virus."[14] Foot dragging over approval of the use of free drugs offered by Boehringer for 90,000 expectant mothers is creating the impression that the South African government, in the end, lacks the political will to use the AIDS drugs.[15]

The South African government came under further pressure in January 2002 when Doctors Without Borders (the Nobel-prize winning humanitarian group, Medicins sans Frontieres—MSF) took action that ignored the South African patent law. Supported by local AIDS activists in Johannesburg, the group demanded the government make the drugs more widely available and imported cheap generic drugs from Brazil to use in their clinic near Capetown.[16] Although western manufacturers "have steadily dropped their prices, to the point where executives say they are making no profit or are selling their drugs at a loss," those prices are still being undercut by generic manufacturers in India, Thailand, and Brazil.[17] The MSF group is no doubt counting on the belief that the two companies holding patents on the drugs they imported from Brazil to South Africa—GlaxoSmithKline PLC and Boehringer Ingelheim GmbH—will not sue such a well-respected charitable organization. Even so, Glaxo executives expressed surprise because their company has an agreement with a South African generics producer to manufacture some of Glaxo's drugs.[18] The problem, however, is that South African regulatory approval has not yet been granted for such drugs. Such obstructionist tactics are coming under fire from the MSF group. Although the South African Department of Health claims that about 25 percent of the country's adults are infected with HIV, president Mbeki continues to question whether HIV causes AIDS and even whether AIDS is actually the leading cause of death in South Africa, a

stance that is bringing criticism and pressure form various groups in the country.[19] The South African government refused to pay for the drugs imported by the Treatment Action Campaign (TAC) for use by the MSF doctors, at a cost of $3.20 to $1.55 per daily treatment.[20]

Meanwhile, as this situation of global interdependence brings challenges of social responsibility conflicting with capitalism, the UN has established a board to oversee the global fund for HIV, tuberculosis and malaria, now at $1.9bn. Although there is pressure to use that money to buy generic drugs, the World Health Organization is working toward more agreement with the major pharmaceutical companies for them to intensify their efforts to find cures for diseases of developing countries.[21]

CASE QUESTIONS

1. Do a stakeholder analysis of this global situation; that is, name the various parties involved and explain the goals of each, the rationale for their positions, and the short- and long-term implications of the situation each party faces.

2. What ethical philosophy should apply to this situation—moral ethnocentrism, ethical relativism, or moral universalism? Explain the rationale for your answer and relate it to the parties you identified in question #1.

3. Is a universal code of ethics possible for the global pharmaceutical industry? Explain how that could work.

4. Using Carroll's Three Dimensional Model of Corporate Social Responsibility on page 38, explain the initial position taken by the western pharmaceutical companies on each of the three dimensions (social responsibilities categories, social issues involved, philosophy of responsiveness). In what ways, if any, had that position changed by the end of the case write-up?

5. What should, or can, the managers of the western pharmaceutical companies do to resolve this problem? Is it entirely their responsibility? What other parties could, or should, help pay for the drugs? Draw up a plan of action from the perspective of a company executive.

6. Do a follow-up on this case situation. What has happened since February 2002? Has the position of the companies as you described in question #4 changed? If so, how? What changes have there been for the other major stakeholders?

ENDNOTES

1. D. Rosenberg and John Barry, "No Money, No Meds: South Africa Needs Access to Cheap AIDS Medicine, but Drug Companies Want a Say in What They Get and How They Get It," *Newsweek* (July 12, 1999), v134, i2, p32.
2. Ibid.
3. Ibid.
4. "AIDS and the Drug Companies," *America* (March 26, 2001), v184, i10, p3.
5. Ibid.
6. Ibid.
7. K. S. Jayaraman, "Opinion Interview: Yusuf Hamied, Chairman of Indian Drug Company, Cipla," *New Scientist* (March 31, 2001), v169, i2284, p42.
8. Ibid.
9. *America.*
10. Ibid.
11. R. Block and G. Harris, "Drug Makers Agree to Drop South Africa Suit," *Wall Street Journal* (April 19, 2001).
12. Ibid.
13. Ibid.
14. Ibid.
15. Ibid.
16. M. Schoofs, "Doctor Group Defies South Africa AIDS Policy," *Wall Street Journal* (January 30, 2002).
17. Ibid.
18. Ibid.
19. Ibid.
20. S. Boseley, "AIDS Drugs Bring Hope to S. Africa; AIDS Activists Bring Gift of Life to South Africa," *The Guardian—United Kingdom* (January 30, 2002).
21. Ibid.

Case 3   Footwear International

John Carlson frowned as he studied the translation of the front-page story from the afternoon's edition of the *Meillat*, a fundamental newspaper with close ties to an opposition political party. The story, titled "Footwear's Unpardonable Audacity," suggested that the company had knowingly insulted Islam by including the name of Allah in a design used on the insoles of sandals it was manufacturing. To compound the problem, the paper had run a photograph of one of the offending sandals on the front page. As a result, student groups were calling for public demonstrations against Footwear the next day. As managing director of Footwear Bangladesh, Carlson knew he would have to act quickly to defuse a potentially explosive situation.

SOURCE: Reproduced by permission of the author. (Copyright © R. William Blake, Faculty of Business Administration, Memorial University of Newfoundland, St. Johns, Canada.)

FOOTWEAR INTERNATIONAL

Footwear International is a multinational manufacturer and marketer of footwear. Operations span the globe and include more than 83 companies in 70 countries. These include shoe factories, tanneries, engineering plants producing shoe machinery and moulds, product development studios, hosiery factories, quality control laboratories, and approximately 6,300 retail stores and 50,000 independent retailers.

Footwear employs more than 67,000 people and produces and sells in excess of 270 million pairs of shoes every year. The head office acts as a service center and is staffed with specialists drawn from all over the world. These specialists, in areas such as marketing, retailing, product development, communications, store design, electronic data processing, and business administration, travel for much of the year to share their expertise with the various companies. Training and technical education, offered through company-run colleges and the training facility at headquarters, provide the latest skills to employees from around the world.

Although Footwear requires standardization in technology and the design of facilities, it also encourages a high degree of decentralization and autonomy in its operations. The companies are virtually self-governing, which means their allegiance belongs to the countries in which they operate. Each is answerable to a board of directors that includes representatives from the local business community. The concept of "partnership" at the local level has made the company welcome internationally and has allowed it to operate successfully in countries where other multinationals have been unable to survive.

BANGLADESH

With a population approaching 110 million in an area of 143,998 square kilometers (see Exhibit C3-1), Bangladesh is the most densely populated country in the world. It is also among the most impoverished, with a 1987 per capita gross national product of $160 and a high reliance on foreign aid.

Exhibit C3-1

More than 40 percent of the gross domestic product is generated by agriculture, and more than 60 percent of its economically active population works in the agriculture sector. Although the land in Bangladesh is fertile, the country has a tropical monsoon climate and suffers form the ravages of periodic cyclones. In 1988, the country experienced the worst floods in recorded history.

The population of Bangladesh is 85 percent Muslim, and Islam was made the official state religion in 1988. Approximately 95 percent of the population speaks Bengali, with most of the remainder speaking tribal dialects.

Bangladesh has had a turbulent history in the 20th century. Most of the country was part of the British-ruled East Bengal until 1947. In that year, it joined with Assam to become East Pakistan, a province of the newly created country of Pakistan. East Pakistan was separated from the four provinces of West Pakistan by 1,600 kilometers of Indian territory, and although the East was more populous, the national capital was established in West Pakistan. Over the following years, widespread discontent built in the East whose people felt that they received a disproportionately small amount of development funding and were under-represented in government.

Following a period of unrest starting in 1969, the Awami League, the leading political party in East Pakistan, won an overwhelming victory in local elections held in 1970. The victory promised to give the league, which was pro-independence, control in the National Assembly. To prevent that happening, the national government suspended the convening of the Assembly indefinitely. On March 26, 1971, the Awami League proclaimed the independence of the People's Republic of Bangladesh, and civil war quickly followed. In the ensuing conflict, hundreds of thousands of refugees fled to safety across the border in India. In December, India, which supported the independence of Bangladesh, declared war, and 12 days later Pakistan surrendered. Bangladesh had won its independence, and the capital of the new country was established at Dhaka. In the years immediately following independence, industrial output declined in major industries as the result of the departure of many of the largely non-Bengali financier and managerial class.

Throughout the subsequent years, political stability proved elusive for Bangladesh. Although elections were held, stability was threatened by the terrorist tactics resorted to by opposition groups from both political extremes. Coups and countercoups, assassinations, and suspension of civil liberties became regular occurrences.

Since 1983, Bangladesh had been ruled by the self-proclaimed President General H. M. Ershad. Despite demonstrations in 1987 that led to a state of emergency being declared, Ershad managed to retain power in elections held the following year. The country remains politically volatile, however. Dozens of political parties continually maneuver for position, and alliances and coalitions are the order of the day. The principal opposition party is the Awami League, an alliance of eight political parties. Many of the parties are closely linked with so-called opposition newspapers, which promote their political positions. Strikes and demonstrations are frequent and often result from cooperation among opposition political parties, student groups, and unions.

FOOTWEAR BANGLADESH

Footwear became active in what was then East Bengal in the 1930s. In 1962, the first major investment took place with the construction of a footwear manufacturing facility at Tongi, an industrial town located 30 kilometers north of Dhaka. During the following years, the company expanded its presence in both conventional and unconventional ways. In 1971, the then managing director became a freedom fighter, while continuing to oversee operations. He subsequently became the only foreigner to be decorated by the government with the "Bir Protik" in recognition of both his and the company's contribution to the independence of Bangladesh.

In 1985, Footwear Bangladesh went public and two years later spearheaded the largest private-sector foreign investment in the country, a tannery and footwear factory at Dhamrai. The new tannery produced leather for local Footwear needs and the export market, and the factory produced a variety of footwear for the local market.

By 1988, Footwear Bangladesh employed 1,800 employees and sold through 81 stores and 54 agencies. The company introduced approximately 300 new products a year to the market using their in-house design and development capability. Footwear managers were particularly proud of the capability of the personnel in these departments, all of whom were Bangladeshi.

Annual sales in excess of 10 million pairs of footwear gave the company 15 percent of the national market in 1988. Revenues exceeded $30 million and after-tax profit was approximately $1 million. Financially, the company was considered a medium contributor within the Footwear organization. With a population approaching 110 million, and per capita consumption of one pair of shoes every two years, Bangladesh was perceived as offering Footwear enormous potential for growth both through consumer education and competitive pressure.

Exhibit C3-2   Translation of the Meillat Story*

Unpardonable Audacity of Footwear

In Bangladesh a Sandal with Allah as Footwear trade mark in Arabic designed in calligraphy has been marketed although last year Islam was made the State Religion in Bangladesh. The Sandal in black and white contains Allah in black. Prima facie it appears it has been designed and the Alif "the first letter in Arabic" has been jointly written. Excluding Alif it reads LILLAH. In Bangladesh after the Satan Rushdie's[†] Satanic Verses which has brought unprecedented demonstration and innumerable strikes (Hartels). This International shoe manufacturing organization under Jewish ownership with the design of Allah has made religious offense. Where for sanctity of Islam one million people of Afghanistan have sacrificed their lives and wherein occupied Palestine many people have been gunned down by Jews for sanctity of Islam in this country the word Allah under this guise has been put under feet.

Last night a group of students from Dhaka university came to Meillat office with a couple of pairs of Sandal. The management staff of Footwear was not available over telephone. This sandal has got two straps made of foam.

*The translation is identical to that which Carlson was given at work.
†Salman Rushdie was the author of the controversial book The Satanic Verses. The author had been sentenced to death, in absentia, by Ayatollah Khomeini, the late leader of Iran, for crimes against Islam.

Exhibit C3-3 The Temple Bells and the Design Used on the Sandal

Company name and logo*

The company's name and logo appeared prominently on the insole of the sandal. Both of the images in the exhibit were redrawn from copies of facsimiles sent to headquarters by John Carlson.

Exhibit C3-4 The Arabic Spelling of Allah*

This exhibit was redrawn from a facsimile sent to headquarters by John Carlson.

The managing director of Footwear Bangladesh was John Carlson, one of only four foreigners working for the company. The others were the managers of production, marketing, and sales. All had extensive and varied experience within the Footwear organization.

THE INCIDENT

On Thursday, June 22, 1989, John Carlson was shown a copy of that day's *Meillat*, a well-known opposition newspaper with pro-Libyan leanings. Under the headline "Footwear's Unpardonable Audacity," the writer suggested that the design on the insole of one model of sandal produced by the company included the Arabic spelling of the word *Allah* (see Exhibit C3-2). The story went on to suggest that Footwear was under Jewish ownership and to link the alleged offense with the gunning down of many people in Palestine by Jews. The story highlighted the fact that the design was on the insole of the sandal and therefore, next to the bottom of the foot, a sign of great disrespect to Muslims.

Carlson immediately contacted the supervisor of the design department and asked for any information he could provide on the design on the sandals. He already knew that they were from a medium-priced line of women's footwear that had the design on the insole changed often as a marketing feature. Following his investigation, the supervisor reported that the design had been based on a set of Chinese temple bells that the designer had purchased in the local market. Pleased by the appearance of the bells, she had used them as the basis for a stylized design, which she submitted to her supervisor for consideration and approval (see Exhibit C3-3).

All the employees in the development and marketing department were Muslims. The supervisor reported that the woman who had produced the offending design was a devout Bengali Muslim who spoke and read no Arabic. The same was true of

Exhibit C3-5   Translation of the Student Group's Proclamation*

The audacity through the use of the name "Allah" in a sandal.

Let Rushdie's Jewish Footwear Company be prohibited in Bangladesh.

Dear people who believe in one God it is announced in the holy Quran Allahs name is above everything but shoe manufacturing Jewish Footwear Shoe Company has used the name Allah and shown disrespect of unprecedented nature and also unpardonable audacity. After the failure of Rushdie's efforts to destroy the beliefs of Muslims in the Quran, Islam and the prophet (SM) who is the writer of Satanic verses the Jewish People have started offending the Muslims. This time it is a fight against Allah. In fact Daud Haider, Salman Rushdie Viking Penguin and Footwear Shoe Company all are supported and

financed by Jewish community. Therefore no compromise with them. Even at the cost of our lives we have to protest against this conspiracy.

For this procession and demonstration will be held on 23rd, June Friday after Jumma prayer from Baitul Mukarram Mosque south gate. Please join this procession and announce we will not pardon Footwear Shoe Company's audacity. Footwear Shoe Company has to be prohibited, don't buy Jewish products and Footwear shoes. Be aware Rushdie's partner.

Issued by Bangladesh Islamic Jubashibir (Youth Student Forum) and Bangladesh Islamic Satrashbir (Student Forum)

SOURCE: *The translation is identical to that which Carlson was given at work.

almost all the employees in the department. The supervisor confirmed to Carlson that numerous people in the department had seen the new design prior to its approval, and no one had seen any problem or raised any objection to it. Following the conversation, Carlson compared the design to the word *Allah*, which he had arranged to have written in Arabic (see Exhibit C3-4).

Carlson was perplexed by the article and its timing. The sandals in question were not new to the market and had not been subject to prior complaints. As he reread the translation of the *Meillat* article, he wondered why the Jewish reference had been made when the family that owned Footwear International was Christian. He also wondered if the fact that students from the university had taken the sandals to the paper was significant.

As the day progressed, the situation got worse. Carlson was shown a translation of a proclamation that had been circulated by two youth groups calling for demonstrations against Footwear to be held the next day (see Exhibit C3-5). The proclamation linked Footwear, Salman Rushdie, and the Jewish community, and ominously stated that "even at the cost of our lives we have to protest against this conspiracy."

More bad news followed. Calls had been made for charges to be laid against Carlson and four others under a section of the criminal code that forbade "deliberate and malicious acts intended to outrage feelings of any class by insulting its religion or religious believers" (see Exhibit C3-6). A short time later, Carlson received a copy of a statement

Exhibit C3-6   Section 295 of the Criminal Code

295-A. *Deliberate and malicious acts intended to outrage religious feelings of any class by insulting its religion or religious believers.* Whoever, with deliberate and malicious intention of outraging the religious feelings of any class of [the citizens of Bangladesh], by words, either spoken or written, or by visible representations, insults, or attempts to insult the religion or religious beliefs of that class, shall be punished with imprisonment . . .

. . . In order to bring a matter under S. 295-A it is not the mere matter of discourse or the written expression but also the manner of it which has to be looked to. In other words the expressions should be such as are bound to be regarded by any reasonable man as grossly offensive and provocative and maliciously and deliberately intended to outrage the feelings of any class of citizens. . . . If the injurious act was done voluntarily without a lawful excuse, malice may be presumed.

Exhibit C3-7   The Statement of the Plaintiff

> The plaintiff most respectfully states that:
>
> 1) The plaintiff is a lawyer, and a Bangladeshi Citizen and his religion is Islam. He is basically a devout Muslim. According to Islamic tradition he regularly performs his daily work.
>
> 2) The first accused of this . . . is the Managing Director of Footwear Shoe Company, the second accused is the Production Manager of the said company, the third accused is the Marketing Manager, the fourth accused is the Calligrapher of the said company and last accused is the Sales Manager of the said company. The said company is an international organization having shoe business in different countries.
>
> 3) The accused persons deliberately wanted to outrage the religion of Muslims by engraving the calligraphy of "Allah'" in Arabic on a sandal thereby to offend the religion of majority this Muslim Country. By marketing this sandal with the calligraphy of "Allah" they have offended the religious feelings of millions of Muslims. It is the solemn religious duty and responsibility of every devout Muslim to protect the sanctity of "Allah." The plaintiff first saw the sandal with this calligraphy on 22nd June 1989 at Elephant road shop.
>
> The accused persons collectively and deliberately wanted this calligraphy under the feet thereby to offend the religion of mine and many other Muslims and have committed a crime under provisions of section 295A of the Penal Code. At the time of the hearing the evidence will be provided.
>
> Therefore under the provisions of section 295A of the Penal Code the accused persons to be issued with warrant of arrest and be brought to court for justice.
>
> The names of the Witnesses
>
> 1)
> 2)
> 3)

that had been filed by a local lawyer although no warrants were immediately forthcoming (see Exhibit C3-7).

While he was reviewing the situation, Carlson was interrupted by his secretary. In an excited voice, she informed him that the prime minister was being quoted as calling the sandal incident an "unforgivable crime." The seriousness of the incident seemed to be escalating rapidly, and Carlson wondered what he should do to try to minimize the damage.

CASE QUESTIONS

You are in John Carlson's position. Analyze the situation facing Footwear, and prepare a detailed plan of action to deal with your immediate responsibilities as well as the entire situation and a long-term plan. The following suggestions may help you develop your plan:

➤ Use a stakeholder analysis to assess the role and objectives of various interest groups and evaluate what is going on and why, and to look beyond the immediate situation.

➤ Consider what role or roles local politics play in the Footwear case, and who are the principal actors in this real-life business drama.

➤ What issues are of greatest concern to Footwear Bangladesh? To Footwear International?

Note: These events actually happened. Ask your professor for the information on the follow-up events. Do you think this situation could happen again?

C h a p t e r   3

Understanding the Role of Culture

Outline

Opening Profile: Telmex's Cultural Advantage Undermined by Global Competition

We speak to our customers in a language they can understand about benefits they can understand.

—FRANCISCO CAMACHO, TELMEX MANAGER, WALL STREET JOURNAL, 1998

This is a watershed in the history of telecommunications competition in Mexico.

—ROLAND ZUBIRAN, PRESIDENT OF ALESTRA, www.FT.com, JANUARY 2, 2001

The United States is pressing its case at the W.T.O. claiming the Mexican telecom market has kept U.S. companies from competing.

—WALL STREET JOURNAL, FEBRUARY 13, 2002

When U.S. phone giants AT&T and MCI Comunications started up long-distance business in Mexico in 1997, they got a surprising lesson about competition from Télefonos de México SA (Telmex), the former state-owned monopoly. At that time, AT&T and MCI (now MCI Worldcom, Inc. after the merger) had a combined market share of about 25 percent.

Apparently, Telmex has shown them how to do business in the developing world by understanding its markets and its people. The company used its understanding of the way of life of Mexican people, took advantage of its familiarity with Mexico's feeble regulatory and legal systems, and engaged in smart marketing.

Much of Telmex's success, according to AT&T and MCI executives, comes from intricate cultural understanding in a country where influence often counts more than the law.

In 2001, however, the tables turned on Telmex, ending years of legal clashes designed to open up Mexico's $12 billion telecom market. Avantel and Alestra (partly owned by U.S. carriers Worldcom and AT&T) had claimed that Telmex was operating a near-monopoly. The United States had a complaint before the World Trade Organization. Mexico's antitrust agency declared that Telmex was in fact dominant in its services, but Telmex still evaded court efforts to restrict its reach. However, Telmex eventually agreed to provide fair access. This set the stage for President Vicente Fox's efforts to open up a new era of investment and economic development. Mexico has a population of 97 million, but only 11.5 million telephone lines—one of the lowest penetration rates compared with other large Latin American countries. As part of the agreement, Alestra and Avantel agreed to pay Telmex for past interconnection fees, amounting to $180 million.

As of February 2001, however, Teléfonos de México S.A. still controlled 98 percent of local lines and 81 percent market share for long-distance service. Perhaps its cultural savvy has given it a foothold difficult to penetrate by outsiders.

SOURCES: www.FT.com, "Mexican Telcos Agree Pact," January 2, 2001; "Pacts May Give AT&T, Worldcom, Better Access in Mexico Market," *The Dallas Morning News*, January 8, 2001, in www.Chicagotribune.com, January 28, 2001; "U.S. Phone Giants Find Telmex Can Be a Bruising Competitor," *Wall Street Journal*, October 23, 1998.

This chapter's Opening Profile describes how an understanding of the local culture and business environment can give managers an advantage in competitive industries; foreign companies—no matter how big—can ignore those aspects to their peril. Such differences in culture and the way of life in other countries necessitate that managers develop international expertise to manage on a contingency basis according to the host-country environment. Powerful, interdependent factors in that environment—political, economic, legal, technological, and cultural—influence management strategy, functions, and processes.

A critical skill for managing people and processes in other countries is **cultural savvy**—that is, a working knowledge of the cultural variables affecting management decisions. Managers have often seriously underestimated the significance of cultural factors. According to numerous accounts, many blunders made in international operations can be attributed to a lack of cultural sensitivity.[1] Examples abound. Scott Russell, senior vice president for human resources at Cendant Mobility in Danbury, Connecticut, recounts the following.

> An American company in Japan charged its Japanese HR manager with reducing the workforce. The Japanese manager studied the issue but couldn't find a solution within cultural Japanese parameters; so when he came back to the Americans, he reduced the workforce by resigning— which was not what they wanted.[2]

Cultural sensitivity, or **cultural empathy**, is an awareness and an honest caring about another individual's culture. Such sensitivity requires the ability to understand the perspective of those living in other (and very different) societies and the willingness to put oneself in another's shoes.

International managers can benefit greatly from understanding the nature, dimensions, and variables of a specific culture and how these affect work and organizational processes. This cultural awareness enables them to develop appropriate policies and determine how to plan, organize, lead, and control in a specific international setting. Such a process of adaptation to the environment is necessary to implement strategy successfully. It also leads to effective interaction in a workforce of increasing cultural diversity, in both the United States and other countries.

Company reports and management studies make it clear that a lack of cultural sensitivity costs businesses money and opportunities. One study of U.S. multinational corporations found that poor intercultural communication skills still constitute a major management problem; American managers' knowledge of other cultures lags far behind their understanding of other organizational processes.[3] In a synthesis of the research on cross-cultural training, Black and Mendenhall found that up to 40 percent of expatriate managers leave their assignments early because of poor performance or poor adjustment to the local environment. About half of those who do remain are considered only marginally effective. Furthermore, they found that cross-cultural differences are the cause of failed negotiations and interactions, resulting in losses to U.S. firms of over $2 billion a year for failed expatriate assignments alone.[4]

We also have evidence, however, that cross-cultural training is effective in developing skills and enhancing adjustment and performance. In spite of such evidence, U.S. firms do little to take advantage of such important research and to incorporate it into their ongoing training programs, whose purpose is ostensibly to prepare managers before sending them overseas. Too often, the importance of such training in developing cultural sensitivity is realized much too late, as seen in the following account of the unhappy marriage between America's AT&T and Italy's Olivetti, the office-equipment maker:

> One top AT&T executive believes that most of the problems in the venture stemmed from cultural differences. "I don't think we or Olivetti spent enough time understanding behavior patterns," says Robert Kayner, AT&T group executive. "We knew the culture was different, but we never really penetrated. We would get angry, and they would get upset." Mr. Kayner says AT&T's attempts to fix the problems, such as delays in deliveries, were transmitted in curt memos that offended Olivetti officials. "They would get an attitude, 'Who are you to tell us what to do,'" he says. Or the Olivetti side would explain its own problems, and AT&T managers would simply

respond, "Don't tell me about your problems. Solve them." AT&T executives are the first to admit, now, that one of the greatest challenges of putting a venture together is that partners frequently see the world in very different—and potentially divisive—ways.[5]

In this chapter, we will provide a conceptual framework with which companies and managers can assess relevant cultural variables and develop cultural profiles of various countries. We will then use this framework to consider the probable effects of cultural differences on an organization and their implications for management. To do this, we need to examine the powerful environmental factor of cultural context. First, we explore the nature of culture, its variables and dimensions, and then we consider specific differences in cultural values and their implications for the on-the-job behavior of individuals and groups. We will discuss cultural variables in general in this chapter. The impact of culture on specific management functions and processes will be discussed in later chapters as appropriate.

CULTURE AND ITS EFFECTS ON ORGANIZATIONS

As generally understood, **the culture of a society** comprises the shared values, understandings, assumptions, and goals that are learned from earlier generations, imposed by present members of a society, and passed on to succeeding generations. This shared outlook results, in large part, in common attitudes, codes of conduct, and expectations that subconsciously guide and control certain norms of behavior.[6] One is born into, not with, a given culture, gradually internalizing its subtle effects through the socialization process. Culture results in a basis for living grounded in shared communication, standards, codes of conduct, and expectations.[7] Over time, cultures evolve as societies adapt to transitions in their external and internal environments and relationships. A manager assigned to a foreign subsidiary, for example, must expect to find large and small differences in the behavior of individuals and groups within that organization. As depicted in Exhibit 3-1, these differences result from the societal, or sociocultural, variables of the culture, such as religion and language, in addition to prevailing national variables, such as economic, legal, and political factors. National and sociocultural variables thus provide the context for the development and perpetuation of cultural variables. These cultural variables, in turn, determine basic attitudes toward work, time, materialism, individualism, and change. Such attitudes affect an individual's motivation and expectations regarding work and group relations, and they ultimately affect the outcomes that can be expected from that individual.

The way these sets of variables can interact is illustrated by a policy change made by KLM Royal Dutch Airlines, where the organizational culture responded to national cultural values and accepted practices. The culture of social responsiveness in the Netherlands was incorporated into business policy when the airline revised its travel-benefits policy for families of employees. For some time, many KLM stewards had protested the rule that only immediate family were eligible for low fares on KLM flights. They found it discriminatory that even just-married heterosexual spouses received the benefit, while long-term homosexual partners were not eligible. Upon reconsideration, KLM responded that any couple who formally registered as living together, which is a normal legal practice in the Netherlands, would be eligible for the low fares. However, a year had to elapse between partners before a new partner could be registered. By changing its policy, KLM put the emphasis on committed relationships rather than on marital status or sexual preference.[8]

Exhibit 3-1   Environmental Variables Affecting Management Functions

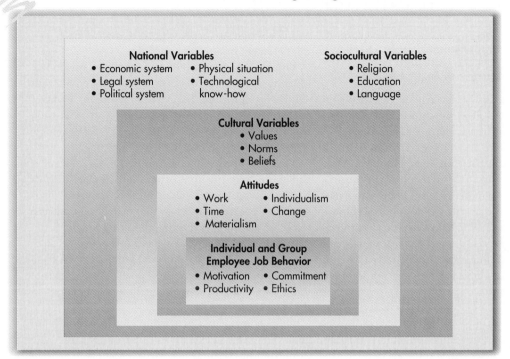

As of 2001, McDonald's had 58 restaurants in Russia. Their experience with setting up businesses there for the last 11 years since the first restaurant opened in Moscow demonstrates the combined effects of national and cultural variables on work. There, local employees require lengthy training to serve up "Bolshoi Maks" in the "McDonald's way." Unfortunately, Russians are still for the most part not familiar with working under the capitalist system; they have been victims of the inertia brought about by the old system of central planning for so long that productivity still remains low. As a result, Russians have few goods to buy, and the new free-market prices are so high that there is little motivation for them to work for rubles that won't buy anything.[9]

It is clear that cultural variables—shared beliefs, values, and attitudes—can greatly affect organizational processes. One example of how culture affects organizational processes is frequently evident as the use of technological applications in those processes spreads around the world. The result can be culture–technology clashes, as illustrated in the accompanying E-Biz Box. Which organizational processes are most affected, and how, is the subject of ongoing cross-cultural management research and debate.[10] Some argue that the effects of culture are more evident at the individual level of personal behavior than at the organizational level, as a result of convergence.[11] Convergence describes the phenomenon of the shifting of individual management styles to become more similar to one another. The convergence argument is based on the belief that the demands of industrialization and worldwide coordination and competition tend to factor out differences in organizational-level processes, such as choice of technology and structure. In a 2000 study of Japanese and Korean firms, Lee, Roehl and Choe found that globalization and firm size were sources of convergence of management styles.[12] These factors are discussed in more detail later in this chapter.

E-Biz Box

ASIA'S CULTURE-INTERNET CLASH

> Many managers in Asia cling to the standard corporate practice of doling out information on a need-to-know basis.
> —www.businessweek.com, OCTOBER 23, 2000

Asia is a world leader in wireless technology, broadband communications, and electronic government; it has tremendous potential as a center for B2B e-commerce. Yet advancements into e-business are hindered by a culture–Internet clash. There are several problem areas.

While Asia is home to 60 percent of the world's people—creating the potential for huge pan-Asian e-marketplaces—those people speak hundreds of languages, creating a web of Babble. Also, the Internet is about giving workers access to information so they can move at Net speed. Yet many managers in Asia cling to the standard corporate practice of doling out information on a need-to-know basis.

Another hindrance to e-commerce is the way Asian companies deal with suppliers. Supply chains in Asia typically involve three or four middlemen—twice as many as in Europe. In Japan, for instance, retailers pay for what they receive and wholesalers eat the cost of missing items. To protect themselves, wholesalers get dozens of workers to unpack boxes, count the contents, and repack the boxes before they are shipped. Wholesalers, therefore, see the Internet as a threat to their jobs.

Costs of connecting to the Internet are high, also hindering e-business. While logging on in Hong Kong and Seoul is still a third more expensive than that in the United States, Japan is even worse off. Leased lines are three times pricier in Tokyo than in New York and twice the cost of those in Germany. Meanwhile, the phone system is so underpowered in India that most businesses can't even get Internet connections.

Other problems include commercial transactions, which in Asia still involve cash or letters of credit, with written receipts often required. In addition, a lack of comprehensive credit services also means that each e-marketplace buyer and seller must be painstakingly screened, which can take weeks.

E-Zaiko, for example, a venture between Mitsui & Company, and Itochu Corporation, two of Japan's largest trading houses, has created an electronic marketplace for excess inventory that matches buyers and sellers of clothing, furniture, and other goods. It is a first in Japan, and e-Zaiko has a ready-made list of clients from its keiretsu industrial groups. Yet the company must reach thousands of small businesses that don't even have computers, let alone connections to the Internet.

One company that isn't waiting for its customers to get wired is Asia-Steel.com. For the past few years, CEO Justin Chu has been giving away computers to get customers hooked into their on-line service. The Hong Kong company, which lets buyers and sellers trade steel electronically, has handed out more than 1,000 PCs to steel mills in China and trained purchasing managers to use them, resulting in attracting 200,000 tons of steel to its site per month.

To close the Internet divide, Asian companies need deep pockets, strong connections between their on-line and off-line businesses, and, most importantly, tremendous skill at translating to the Web the networks of business relationships that make Asia a complicated place to operate.

SOURCE: Adapted from www.businessweek.com "The Net Is Transforming the West, But Companies in the East Lag Behind," October 23, 2000.

The effects of culture on specific management functions are particularly noticeable when we attempt to impose our own values and systems on another society. Exhibit 3-2 gives some examples of the values typical of U.S. culture, compares some common perspectives held by people in other countries, and shows which management functions might be affected, clearly implying the need for the differential management of organizational processes. For example, American managers plan activities,

Exhibit 3-2   U.S. Values and Possible Alternatives

Aspects of U.S. Culture*	Alternative Aspect	Examples of Management Function Affected
The individual can influence the future (where there is a will there is a way).	Life follows a preordained course, and human action is determined by the will of God.	Planning and scheduling
The individual can change and improve the environment.	People are intended to adjust to the physical environment rather than to alter it.	Organizational environment, morale, and productivity
An individual should be realistic in his or her aspirations.	Ideals are to be pursued regardless of what is "reasonable."	Goal setting and career development
We must work hard to accomplish our objectives (Puritan ethic).	Hard work is not the only prerequisite for success; wisdom, luck, and time are also required.	Motivation and reward system
Commitments should be honored (people will do what they say they will do).	A commitment may be superseded by a conflicting request, or an agreement may only signify intention and have little or no relationship to the capacity for performance.	Negotiating and bargaining
One should effectively use one's time (time is money that can be saved or wasted).	Schedules are important, but only in relation to other priorities.	Long- and short-range planning
A primary obligation of an employee is to the organization.	The individual employee has a primary obligation to his or her family and friends.	Loyalty, commitment, and motivation
The employer or employee can terminate the relationship.	Employment is for a lifetime.	Motivation and commitment to the company
The best-qualified people should be given the positions available.	Family, friendship, and other considerations should determine employment practices.	Employment, promotions, recruiting selection, and reward

*Aspect here refers to a belief, value, attitude, or assumption that is a part of a culture in that it is shared by a large number of people in that culture.
SOURCE: Excerpted from *Managing Cultural Differences* by Philip R. Harris and Robert T. Moran, 5th ed. Copyright © 2000 by Gulf Publishing Company, Houston, TX. Used with permission. All rights reserved.

schedule them, and judge their timely completion based on the belief that people influence and control the future, rather than assuming that events will occur only at the will of Allah, as managers in an Islamic nation might believe.

Many people in the world understand and relate to others only in terms of their own culture. This unconscious reference point of one's own cultural values is called a **self-reference criterion**.[13] The result of such an attitude is illustrated in the following story:

> Once upon a time there was a great flood, and involved in this flood were two creatures, a monkey and a fish. The monkey, being agile and experienced, was lucky enough to scramble up a tree and escape the raging

waters. As he looked down from his safe perch, he saw the poor fish struggling against the swift current. With the very best of intentions, he reached down and lifted the fish from the water. The result was inevitable.[14]

The monkey assumed that its frame of reference applied to the fish and acted accordingly. Thus, international managers from all countries must understand and adjust to unfamiliar social and commercial practices—especially the practices of that mysterious and unique nation, the United States. Japanese workers at a U.S. manufacturing plant learned to put courtesy aside and interrupt conversations with Americans when there were problems. Europeans, however, are often confused by the Americans' apparent informality, which then backfires when the Europeans do not get work done as the Americans expect.[15]

As a first step toward cultural sensitivity, an international manager should understand her or his own culture. This awareness helps to guard against adopting either a parochial or an ethnocentric attitude. **Parochialism** occurs when a Frenchman, for example, expects those from or in another country to automatically fall into patterns of behavior common in France. **Ethnocentrism** describes the attitude of those who operate from the assumption that their ways of doing things are best—no matter where or under what conditions they are applied. Companies both large and small have demonstrated this lack of cultural sensitivity in countless subtle (and not so subtle) ways, with varying disastrous effects.

Procter & Gamble was one such company. In an early Japanese television commercial for Camay soap, a Japanese woman is bathing when her husband walks into the bathroom. She starts telling him about her new beauty soap. Her husband, stroking her shoulder, hints that he has more on his mind than suds. The commercial, which had been popular in Europe, was a disaster in Japan. For the man to intrude on his wife "was considered bad manners," says Edwin L. Artzt, P&G's vice chairman and international chief. "And the Japanese didn't think it was very funny." P&G has learned from its mistakes and now generates about half of its revenue from foreign sales.[16]

After studying his or her own culture, the manager's next step toward establishing effective cross-cultural relations is to develop cultural sensitivity. Managers not only must be aware of cultural variables and their effects on behavior in the workplace but also must appreciate cultural diversity and understand how to build constructive working relationships anywhere in the world. In the next sections, we will explore cultural variables and dimensions. In later chapters, we will suggest specific ways in which managers can address these variables and dimensions to help build constructive relationships.

CULTURAL VARIABLES

Given the great variety of cultures and subcultures around the world, how can a student of cross-cultural management, or a manager wishing to be culturally savvy, develop an understanding of the specific nature of a certain people? With such an understanding, how can a manager anticipate the probable effects of an unfamiliar culture within an organizational setting and thereby manage human resources productively and control outcomes?

One approach is to develop a cultural profile for each country or region with which the company does or is considering doing business. Developing a cultural profile requires some familiarity with the cultural variables universal to most cul-

Management Focus

TECHNOLOGY SHIFT ADDS TO CULTURE CLASH IN FRANCE

It seemed for a while that technology would minimize business differences across borders. But when IT spending took a downward spiral, conflicts more pronounced in the "old economy" in Europe returned, along with quashed expectations. This was experienced by U.S. managers of high-technology companies in France, for example. One of these managers was Henri Poole. As reported in *BusinessWeek Online*, Poole was hired in May 2000 to be CEO of a French software company in Paris, called MandrakeSoft.[1] But, when technology lost its luster, his American management style ran afoul of French Old World feathers, causing him to leave the company less than a year after he started.

Americans and others often assume that European business culture is similar to that in the United States, but that is a mistake; there are considerable differences even among the EU countries themselves. The French, for example, place great importance on status—education, the arts, and one's social status, along with the titles and other outward signs of their status. They are less motivated by the typical American work ethic; more important to them are people, the quality of life, vacations, and so on. Personal qualities are more important to them than achievements.[2] They regard Americans' emphasis on competition as ruthless and power-seeking. At the same time, the French are more authoritative in business dealings, with centralized decision making, compared with the democratic style of American managers, although the French do enjoy a healthy debate.[3] Flexibility in business practices in France is also limited by excessive bureaucracy and regulations, and employees are so protected that it is very difficult to fire anyone.[4]

Unfortunately, many American managers, like Poole, assumed that the language of technology would supersede the importance of the French native tongue and the language of their culture, resulting in a disappointing relationship.

[1]"Yankee, We Want You, Yankee, Go Home," www.Businessweek.com, July, 2001.

[2]P. R. Harris and R. T. Moran, *Managing Cultural Differences*, 5th ed. (Houston, Tex: Gulf Publishing Co., 2000).
[3]Ibid; Farud Ekasgnawum *Competing Globally*, (Woburn, Mass: Butterworth-Heinemann, 2001).
[4]"Yankee, We Want You"; Harris and Moran.

tures. From these universal variables, managers can identify the specific differences found in each country or people—and hence anticipate their implications for the workplace.

Managers should never assume that they can successfully transplant American, or Japanese, or any other country's styles, practices, expectations, and processes. Instead, they should practice a basic tenet of good management—contingency management. Contingency management requires managers to adapt to the local environment and people and to manage accordingly. That adaptation can be complex because the manager may confront differences not only in culture, but also in business practices and shifts in the technological environment, as illustrated in the accompanying Management Focus.

Subcultures

Managers should recognize, of course, that generalizations in cultural profiles will produce only an approximation, or stereotype, of national character. Many countries comprise diverse subcultures whose constituents conform only in varying degrees to the national character. In Canada, distinct subcultures include anglophones and francophones (English-speaking and French-speaking people) and indigenous Canadians. The United States, too, has varying subcultures. Americans abroad are almost always dealt with in the context of the stereotypical American, but at home Americans recognize differences among themselves due to ethnic, geographic, or other subcultural backgrounds. Americans should apply the same insight toward people in other countries and be extremely careful not to overgeneralize or over-simplify. For example, although Americans tend to think of Chinese as homogeneous in their culture, there are considerable differences among Chinese people owing to regional diversity—including distinct ethnic groups with their own local customs and a multitude of dialects. A study by Ralston et al. concluded that, although adherence to traditional Confucian values was common to all regions, regions differed considerably on variables such as individualism and openness to change (with Guangzhou and Shanghai ranking the highest on those dimensions, followed by Beijing and Dalian and then Chengdu and Lanzhou).[17] This implies that Chinese in Guangzhou and Shanghai may be somewhat more "westernized" and more open to doing business with westerners.

Above all, good managers treat people as individuals, and they consciously avoid any form of stereotyping. However, a cultural profile is a good starting point to help managers develop some tentative expectations—some cultural context—as a backdrop to managing in a specific international setting. It is useful, then, to look at what cultural variables have been studied and what implications can be drawn from the results.

Universal Cultural Variables

To develop cultural profiles we first need to be familiar with the kinds of universal cultural variables found in most societies that make up unique clusters and provide a snapshot of the overall character of a specific group. Although there are countless individual variables, one approach to categorizing interdependent variables is given by Harris and Moran, who have identified eight categories that form the subsystems in any society.[18] This systems approach to understanding cultural and national variables—and their effects on work behavior—is consistent with the model shown in Exhibit 3-1. The following sections describe these eight categories and explain their implications.

Kinship   A kinship system is the system adopted by a given society to guide family relationships. Whereas in the United States this system consists primarily of the nuclear family (which is increasingly represented by single-parent families), in many other parts of the world the kinship system consists of an extended family with many members, spanning several generations. This extended, closely knit family, typical in many Eastern nations, may influence corporate activities in cases where family loyalty is given primary consideration—such as when contracts are awarded or when employees are hired (and a family member is always selected over a more suitable candidate from outside the family). In these family-oriented societies, such practices are pervasive and are taken for granted. Foreign managers often find themselves locked out of important decisions when dealing with family businesses. If, however, they take the time to learn the local cultural expectations regarding families, they will notice predictable patterns of behavior and be better prepared to deal with them. Such traditional practices are exemplified in the experience of an Asian MBA, educated in the

United States, when he presented a more up-to-date business plan to his uncle, the managing director of a medium-sized firm in India:

> The family astrologer attended the meeting and vetoed the plan. Later, the nephew persisted and asked the astrologer to reconsider the plan. The astrologer recommended various ceremonies after which the astral signs would probably bend toward the plan.[19]

Education   The formal or informal education of workers in a foreign firm, received from whatever source, greatly affects the expectations placed on those workers in the workplace. It also influences managers' choices about recruitment and staffing practices, training programs, and leadership styles. Training and development programs, for example, need to be consistent with the general level of educational preparation in that country.

Economy   Whatever the economic system, the means of production and distribution in a society (and the resulting effects on individuals and groups) has a powerful influence on such organizational processes as sourcing, distribution, incentives, and repatriation of capital. At this time of radically changing political systems, it appears that the drastic differences between capitalist and socialist systems will have less effect on MNCs than in the past.

Politics   The system of government in a society, whether democratic, communist, or dictatorial, imposes varying constraints on an organization and its freedom to do business. It is the manager's job to understand the political system and how it affects organizational processes, to negotiate positions within that system, and to manage effectively the mutual concerns of the host country and guest company. As demonstrated by the difficulties that McDonald's had in training Russian workers for its Moscow restaurant (discussed earlier in the chapter), the political and economic subsystems of a country often dominate other cultural systems.

Religion   The spiritual beliefs of a society are often so powerful that they transcend other cultural aspects. Religion commonly underlies both moral and economic norms. In the United States, the effects of religion in the workplace are limited (other than a generalized belief in hard work, which stems from the Protestant work ethic), whereas in other countries religious beliefs and practices often influence everyday business transactions and on-the-job behaviors. For example, in a long-standing tradition based on the Qur'an and the sayings of Muhammad, Arabs consult with senior members of the ruling families or the community regarding business decisions. Hindus, Buddhists, and some Muslims believe in the concept of destiny, or fate. In Islamic countries, the idea of *insha Allah*, that is, "God willing," prevails. In some Western countries, religious organizations, such as the Roman Catholic Church, play a major cultural role through moral and political influence.

One of the ways that the Islamic faith affects the operations of international firms involves the charging of interest:[20]

> The kingdom of Saudi Arabia observes Sharia, which is Islamic law based on both the Qur'an and the Hadith—the traditions of the Prophet Muhammad. Under these codes, interest is banned, and both the giver

and the taker of interest are equally damned. This means that the modern Western banking system is technically illegal. A debate has begun on the interpretation of the concept of interest. The kingdom's religious scholars, the ulema, view all interest, or rib'a, as banned. Some have challenged that interpretation as too restrictive, however, and have called for a more liberal interpretation. Their view is that Muhammad referred only to excessive interest when he condemned usury. Should something come of this debate, it would help establish a legal framework for dealing with Saudi Arabia's banking problems, such as steep drops in profits, and end the legal limbo of Western-style banking in the kingdom.[21]

Associations   Many and various types of associations arise out of the formal and informal groups that make up a society. Whether these associations are based on religious, social, professional, or trade affiliations, managers should be familiar with them and the role they may play in business interactions.

Health   The system of health care in a country affects employee productivity, expectations, and attitudes toward physical fitness and its role in the workplace. These expectations will influence managerial decisions regarding health care benefits, insurance, physical facilities, sick days, and so forth.

Recreation   Closely associated with other cultural factors, recreation includes the way in which people use their leisure time, as well as their attitudes toward leisure and their choice of whom to socialize with. Workers' attitudes toward recreation can affect their work behavior and their perception of the role of work in their lives.

CULTURAL VALUE DIMENSIONS

Cultural variables result from unique sets of shared values among different groups of people. Most of the variations between cultures stem from underlying value systems, which cause people to behave differently under similar circumstances. **Values** are a society's ideas about what is good or bad, right or wrong—such as the widespread belief that stealing is immoral and unfair. Values determine how individuals will probably respond in any given circumstance. As a powerful component of a society's culture, values are communicated through the eight subsystems just described and are passed from generation to generation. Interaction and pressure among these subsystems (or more recently from foreign cultures) may provide the impetus for slow change. The dissolution of the Soviet Union and the formation of the Commonwealth of Independent States is an example of extreme political change resulting from internal economic pressures and external encouragement to change.

Project GLOBE Cultural Dimensions

Recent research results on cultural dimensions have been made available by the GLOBE (Global Leadership and Organizational Behavior Effectiveness) Project team. The team comprises 170 researchers who have collected data over seven years on cultural values and practices and leadership attributes from 18,000 managers in 62 countries. Those managers were from a wide variety of industries and sizes of organizations from every corner of the globe. The team identified nine cultural dimensions that distinguish one society from another and have important managerial implications: assertiveness, future orientation, performance orientation, humane orientation, gender differentiation, uncertainty avoidance, power distance, institutional collectivism versus individualism, and in-group collectivism. Only the first four will be discussed here; since the others are similar dimensions to those researched by Hofstede, presented in the next section, we wish to avoid confusion for the reader. (Other research results from the GLOBE project are presented in subsequent chapters where applicable, such as in the Leadership section in Chapter 11.) The descriptions are as follows and selected results are shown in Exhibit 3-3.[22]

Exhibit 3-3   Selected Cultural Dimensions Rankings from the Globe Research Project

Country Rankings on Assertiveness

Least Assertive Countries in GLOBE		Medium Assertive Countries in GLOBE		Most Assertive Countries in GLOBE	
Sweden	3.38	Egypt	3.91	Spain	4.42
New Zealand	3.42	Ireland	3.92	U.S.	4.55
Switzerland	3.47	Philippines	4.01	Greece	4.58
Japan	3.59	Ecuador	4.09	Austria	4.62
Kuwait	3.63	France	4.13	Germany (Former East)	4.73

Country Rankings on Performance Orientation

Least Performance-Oriented Countries in GLOBE		Medium Performance-Oriented Countries in GLOBE		Most Performance-Oriented Countries in GLOBE	
Russia	2.88	Sweden	3.72	U.S.	4.49
Argentina	3.08	Israel	3.85	Taiwan	4.56
Greece	3.20	Spain	4.01	New Zealand	4.72
Venezuela	3.32	England	4.08	Hong Kong	4.80
Italy	3.58	Japan	4.22	Singapore	4.90

Country Rankings on Future Orientation

Least Future-Oriented Countries in GLOBE		Medium Future-Oriented Countries in GLOBE		Most Future-Oriented Countries in GLOBE	
Russia	2.88	Slovenia	3.59	Denmark	4.44
Argentina	3.08	Egypt	3.86	Canada (English-speaking)	4.44
Poland	3.11	Ireland	3.98	Netherlands	4.61
Italy	3.25	Australia	4.09	Switzerland	4.73
Kuwait	3.26	India	4.10	Singapore	5.07

Country Rankings on Humane Orientation

Least Humane-Oriented Countries in GLOBE		Medium Humane-Oriented Countries in GLOBE		Most Humane-Oriented Countries in GLOBE	
Germany (Former West)	3.18	Hong Kong	3.90	Indonesia	4.69
Spain	3.32	Sweden	4.10	Egypt	4.73
France	3.40	Taiwan	4.11	Malaysia	4.87
Singapore	3.49	U.S.	4.17	Ireland	4.96
Brazil	3.66	New Zealand	4.32	Philippines	5.12

SOURCE: Mansour Javidan and Robert J. House, "Cultural Acumen for the Global Manager: Lessons from Project GLOBE," *Organizational Dynamics* (Spring 2001): 289–305.

Assertiveness   This dimension refers to how much people in a society are expected to be tough, confrontational, and competitive versus modest and tender. Austria and Germany, for example, are highly assertive societies that value competition and have a "can-do" attitude. This compares with Sweden and Japan, less assertive societies, which tend to prefer warm and cooperative relations and harmony. The GLOBE team concluded that those countries have sympathy for the weak and emphasize loyalty and solidarity.

Future Orientation   This dimension refers to the level of importance a society attaches to future-oriented behaviors such as planning and investing in the future. Switzerland and Singapore, high on this dimension, are inclined to save for the future and have a longer time horizon for decisions. This perspective compares with societies such as Russia and Argentina, which tend to plan more in the shorter term and place more emphasis on instant gratification.

Performance Orientation   This dimension measures the importance of performance improvement and excellence in society and refers to whether people are encouraged to strive for continued improvement. Singapore, Hong Kong, and the United States score high on this dimension; typically, this means that people tend to take initiative and have a sense of urgency and the confidence to get things done. Countries like Russia and Italy have low scores on this dimension; they hold other priorities ahead of performance, such as tradition, loyalty, family and background, associating competition with defeat.

Humane Orientation   This dimension measures the extent to which a society encourages and rewards people for being fair, altruistic, generous, caring, and kind. Highest on this dimension are the Philippines, Ireland, Malaysia, and Egypt, indicating a focus on sympathy and support for the weak. In those societies paternalism and patronage are important, and people are usually friendly, tolerant, and value harmony. This compares with Spain, France, and the former West Germany, which scored low on this dimension; people in these countries give more importance to power and material possessions, as well as self-enhancement.

Clearly, research results such as these are helpful to managers seeking to be successful in cross-cultural interactions. Anticipating cultural similarities and differences allows managers to develop the behaviors and skills necessary to act and decide in a manner appropriate to the local societal norms and expectations.

Hofstede's Value Dimensions

Earlier research resulted in a pathbreaking framework for understanding how basic values underlie organizational behavior; this framework was developed by Hofstede, based on his research on over 116,000 people in 50 countries. He proposed four value dimensions: (1) power distance, (2) uncertainty avoidance, (3) individualism, and (4) masculinity.[23] We should be cautious when interpreting these results, however, because his research findings are based on a sample drawn from one multinational firm, IBM, and because he does not account for within-country differences in multicultural countries. Although we introduce these value dimensions here to aid in the understanding of different cultures, their relevance and application to management functions will be discussed in later chapters.

The first of these value dimensions, **power distance**, is the level of acceptance by a society of the unequal distribution of power in institutions. In the workplace, inequalities in power are normal, as evidenced in hierarchical boss–subordinate relationships. However, the extent to which subordinates accept unequal power is societally determined. In countries in which people display high power distance (such as Malaysia, the Philippines, and Mexico), employees acknowledge the boss's authority simply by respecting that individual's formal position in the hierarchy, and they seldom bypass the chain of command. This respectful response results, predictably, in a centralized structure and autocratic leadership. In countries where people display low power distance (such as Austria, Denmark, and Israel), superiors and subordinates are apt to regard one another as equal in power, resulting in more harmony and cooperation. Clearly, an autocratic management style is not likely to be well received in low power-distance countries.

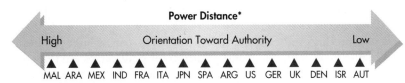

Power Distance*

High   Orientation Toward Authority   Low

MAL ARA MEX IND FRA ITA JPN SPA ARG US GER UK DEN ISR AUT

*Not to scale—indicates relative magnitude.
Note: ARA = Arab Countries
    AUT = Austria

SOURCE: Based on G. Hofstede, "National Cultures in Four Dimensions," *International Studies of Management and Organization*, Spring–Summer 1983.

The second value dimension, **uncertainty avoidance**, refers to the extent to which people in a society feel threatened by ambiguous situations. Countries with a high level of uncertainty avoidance (such as Japan, Portugal, and Greece) tend to have strict laws and procedures to which their people adhere closely, and there is a strong sense of nationalism. In a business context, this value results in formal rules and procedures designed to provide more security and greater career stability. Managers have a propensity for low-risk decisions, employees exhibit little aggressiveness, and lifetime employment is common. In countries with lower levels of uncertainty avoidance (such as Denmark, Great Britain, and, to a lesser extent, the United States), nationalism is less pronounced, and protests and other such activities are tolerated. As a consequence, company activities are less structured and less formal, some managers take more risks, and there is high job mobility.

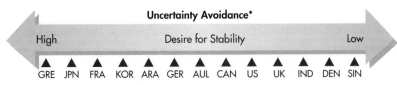

Uncertainty Avoidance*

High   Desire for Stability   Low

GRE JPN FRA KOR ARA GER AUL CAN US UK IND DEN SIN

*Not to scale—indicates relative magnitude.
Note: AUL = Australia

SOURCE: Based on G. Hofstede, 1983.

The third of Hofstede's value dimensions, **individualism**, refers to the tendency of people to look after themselves and their immediate family only and to neglect the needs of society. In countries that prize individualism (such as the United States, Great Britain, and Australia), democracy, individual initiative, and achievement are highly valued; the relationship of the individual to organizations is one of independence on an emotional level, if not on an economic level.

In countries such as Pakistan and Panama, where low individualism prevails—that is, where collectivism predominates—one finds tight social frameworks, emotional dependence on belonging to "the organization," and a strong belief in group decisions. People from a collectivist country, like Japan, believe in the will of the group rather than that of the individual, and their pervasive collectivism exerts control over individual members through social pressure and the fear of humiliation. The society valorizes harmony and saving face, whereas individualistic cultures generally emphasize self-respect, autonomy, and independence. Hiring and promotion practices in collectivist societies are based on paternalism rather than achievement or personal capabilities, which are valued in individualistic societies. Other management practices (such as the use of quality circles in Japanese factories) reflect the emphasis on group decision-making processes in collectivist societies.

Hofstede's findings indicate that most countries scoring high on individualism have both a higher gross national product and a freer political system than those countries scoring low on individualism—that is, there is a strong relationship among individualism, wealth, and a political system with balanced power. Other studies have found that the output of individuals working in a group setting differs between individualistic and collectivist societies. In the United States, a highly individualistic culture, social loafing is common—that is, people tend to perform less when working as part of a group than when working alone.[24] In a comparative study of the United States and the People's Republic of China (a highly collectivist society), Earley found that the Chinese did not exhibit as much social loafing as the Americans.[25] This result can be attributed to Chinese cultural values, which subordinate personal interests to the greater goal of helping the group succeed.

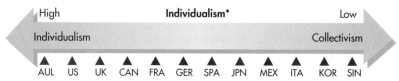

*Not to scale—indicates relative magnitude.
Based on Hofstede, 1983.

The fourth value dimension, **masculinity**, refers to the degree of traditionally "masculine" values—assertiveness, materialism, and a lack of concern for others—that prevail in a society. In comparison, femininity emphasizes "feminine" values—a concern for others, for relationships, and for the quality of life. In highly masculine societies (Japan and Austria, for example), women are generally expected to stay home and raise a family. In organizations, one finds considerable job stress, and organizational interests generally encroach on employees' private lives. In countries with low masculinity (such as Switzerland and New Zealand), one finds less conflict and job stress, more women in high-level jobs, and a reduced need for assertiveness. The United States lies somewhat in the middle, according to Hofstede's research. American women typically are encouraged to work and usually are able to get some support for child care (through day-care centers and maternity leaves).

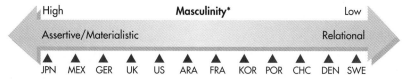

*Not to scale—indicates relative magnitude.
Based on Hofstede, 1983.

The four cultural value dimensions proposed by Hofstede do not operate in isolation; rather, they are interdependent and interactive—and thus complex—in their effects on work attitudes and behaviors. For example, in a 2000 study of small to medium-sized firms in Australia, Finland, Greece, Indonesia, Mexico, Norway and Sweden, based on Hofstede's dimensions, Steensma, Marino, and Weaver found that "entrepreneurs from societies that are masculine and individualistic have a lower appreciation for cooperative strategies as compared to entrepreneurs from societies that are feminine and collectivist. Masculine cultures view cooperation in general as a sign of weakness and individualistic societies place a high value on independence and control."[26] In addition, they found that high levels of uncertainty avoidance prompted more cooperation, such as developing alliances to share risk.

Geographic Clusters   Nath and Sadhu summarized and categorized by geographic region the four value dimensions by Hofstede as well as other cultural dimensions, as shown in Exhibit 3-4.

Based on a synthesis of Hofstede's research and other cluster studies, Ronen and Shenkar developed eight country clusters grouped according to the similarities found in those studies of employee attitudes toward (1) the importance of work goals, (2) need fulfillment and job satisfaction, (3) managerial and organizational variables, and (4) work role and interpersonal orientation.[27] These country clusters are shown in Exhibit 3-5. In addition, at that time (1985) per capita gross national product (GNP) was used to determine placement in the figure, with the most highly developed countries close to the center. This may indicate some relationship between a country's level of development and its generally accepted values and attitudes, although the variables are too complex to draw conclusions about any direction of causality among them.

Trompenaars' Value Dimensions

Fons Trompenaars also researched value dimensions; his work was spread over a ten-year period, with 15,000 managers from 28 countries, representing 47 national cultures. Some of those dimensions, which we are not discussing elsewhere and which affect daily business activities, are shown in Exhibit 3-6, along with the descriptions and the placement of nine of the countries in approximate relative order.[28] If we view the placement of these countries along a range from personal to societal, based on each dimension, some interesting patterns emerge.[29] One can see from the exhibit that the same countries tend to be at similar positions on all dimensions, with the exception of the emotional orientation.

Looking at Trompenaars' dimension of **universalism versus particularism,** we find that the universalistic approach applies rules and systems objectively, without consideration for individual circumstances, whereas the particularistic approach—more common in Asia and in Spain, for example—puts the first obligation on rela-

Exhibit 3-4   The Cultural Milieu

| Region/Country | Hofstede's Dimensions | | | | Other Dimensions |
	Individualism-Collectivism	Power Distance	Uncertainty Avoidance	Masculinity-Femininity	
North America (USA)	Individualism	Low	Medium	Masculine	
Japan	Collectivism	High and low	High	Masculine and feminine	*Amae* (mutual dependence): authority is respected, but superior must be a warm leader
Europe:					
Anglo	Individualism	Low/medium	Low/medium	Masculine	
Germanic West Slavic West Urgic	Medium individualism	Low	Medium/high	Medium/ high masculine	
Near Eastern Balkanic	Collectivism	High	High	Medium masculine	
Nordic	Medium/high individualism	Low	Low/medium	Feminine	
Latin Europe	Medium/high individualism	High	High	Medium masculine	
East Slavic	Collectivism	Low	Medium	Masculine	
China	Collectivism	Low	Low	Masculine and feminine	Emphasis on tradition, Marxism, Leninism, and Mao Zedong thought
Africa	Collectivism	High	High	Feminine	Colonial traditions; tribal customs
Latin America	Collectivism	High	High	Masculine	Extroverted; prefer orderly customs and procedures

SOURCE: Raghu Nath and Kunal K. Sadhu, "Comparative Analysis, Conclusions, and Future Directions," in *Comparative Management—A Regional View,* ed. Raghu Nath (Cambridge, Mass.: Ballinger Publishing Company, 1988), 273.

tionships and is more subjective. Trompenaars found, for example, that people in particularistic societies are more likely to pass on insider information to a friend than those in universalistic societies.

In the **neutral versus affective** dimension, the focus is on the emotional orientation of relationships. The Italians, Mexicans, and Chinese, for example, would openly express emotions even in a business situation, whereas the British and Japanese would consider such displays unprofessional; they, in turn would be regarded as hard to "read."

As far as involvement in relationships goes, people tend to be either **specific or diffuse** (or somewhere along that dimension). Managers in specific-oriented cultures—the United States, United Kingdom, France—separate work and personal

Exhibit 3-5   Clusters of Countries Based on Attitudinal Dimensions

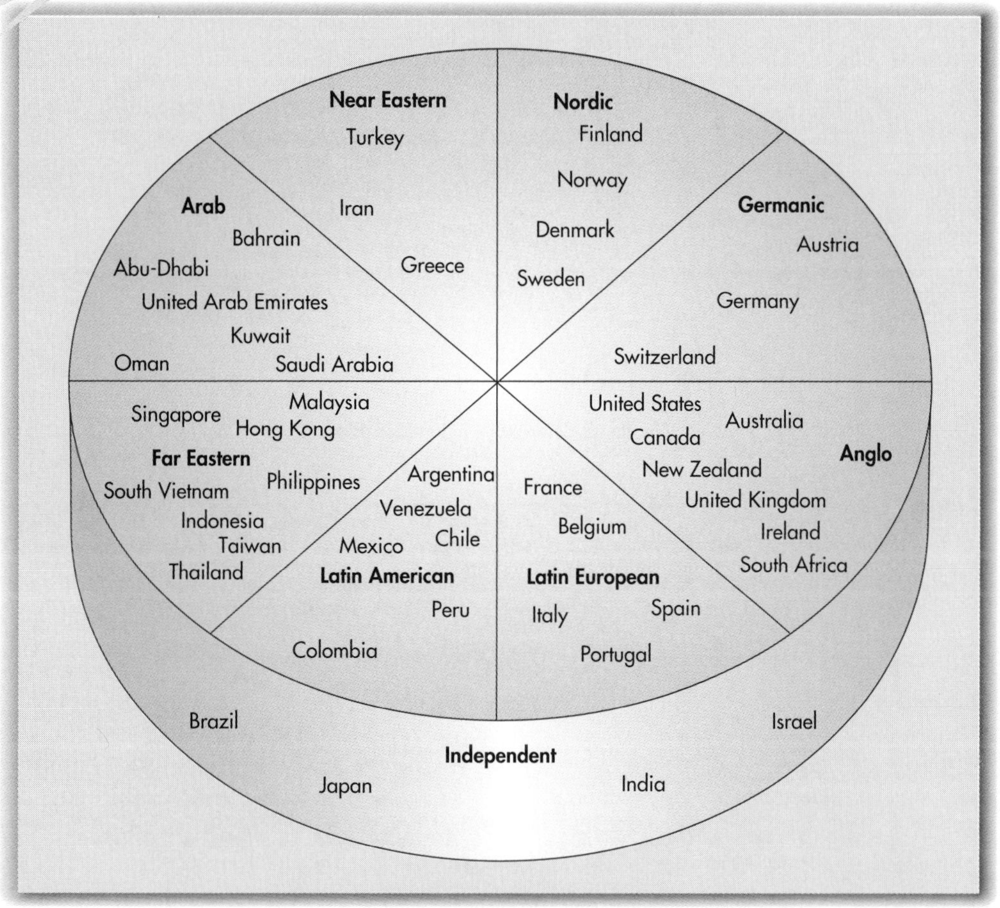

SOURCE: S. Ronen and O. Shenkar, "Clustering Countries on Attitudinal Dimensions: A Review and Synthesis," *Academy of Management Review* (September 1985): 449.

issues and relationships; they compartmentalize their work and private lives, and they are more open and direct. In diffuse-oriented cultures—Sweden, China—there is spillover from work into personal relationships and vice versa.

In the **achievement versus ascription** dimension, the question that arises is what is the source of power and status in society? In an achievement society, the source of status and influence is based on individual achievement—how well one performs the job and what level of education and experience one has to offer. Therefore, women, minorities, and young people usually have equal opportunity to attain position based on their achievements. In an ascription-oriented society, people ascribe status on the basis of class, age, gender, and so on; one is more likely to be born into a position of influence. Hiring in Indonesia, for example, is more likely to be based on who you are than is the case in Germany, or Australia.

Exhibit 3-6 Trompenaars' Value Dimensions

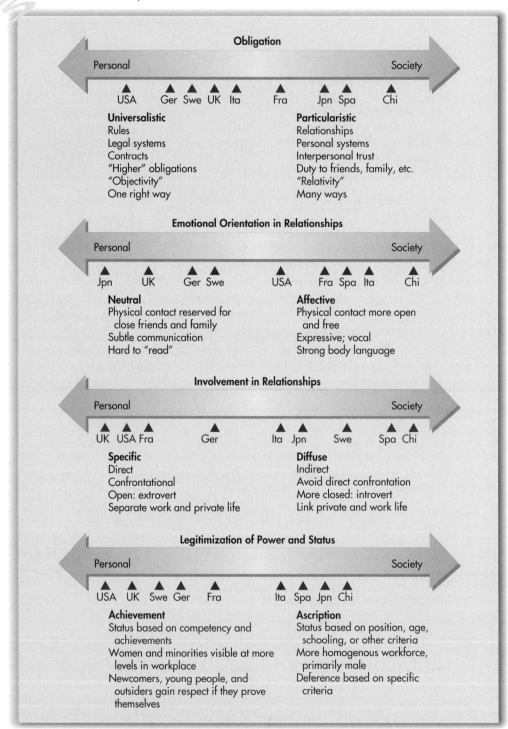

SOURCE: Adapted from Lisa Hoecklin, *Managing Cultural Differences* (Wokingham, England: Addison-Wesley), and The Economist Intelligence Unit, 1995. Based on Trompenaars, 1993.

It is clear, then, that a lot of what goes on at work can be explained by differences in people's innate value systems, as described by Hofstede and Trompenaars, based on their research. Awareness of such differences and how they influence work behavior can be very useful to you as a future international manager.

Critical Operational Value Differences

After studying various research results about cultural variables, it helps to identify some specific culturally based variables that cause frequent problems for Americans in international management. Important variables are those involving conflicting orientations toward time, change, material factors, and individualism. We try to understand these operational value differences because they strongly influence a person's attitudes and probable response to work situations.

Time   Americans often experience much conflict and frustration because of differences in the concept of time around the world—that is, differences in temporal values. To Americans, time is a valuable and limited resource; it is to be saved, scheduled, and spent with precision, lest we waste it. The clock is always running—time is money. Therefore, deadlines and schedules have to be met. When others are not on time for meetings, Americans may feel insulted; when meetings digress from their purpose, Americans tend to become impatient. Similar attitudes toward time are found in Western Europe and elsewhere.

In many parts of the world, however, people view time from different and longer perspectives, often based on religious beliefs (such as reincarnation, in which time does not end at death), on a belief in destiny, or on pervasive social attitudes. In Latin America, for example, a common attitude toward time is **mañana**, a word that literally means "tomorrow." A Latin American person using this word, however, usually means an indefinite time in the near future. Similarly, the word **bukra** in Arabic can mean "tomorrow" or "some time in the future." While Americans usually regard a deadline as a firm commitment, Arabs often regard a deadline imposed on them as an insult. They feel that important things take a long time and therefore cannot be rushed. To ask an Arab to rush something, then, would imply that you have not given him an important task or that he would not treat that task with respect. International managers have to be careful not to offend people—or lose contracts or employee cooperation—because they misunderstand the local language of time.

Change   Based largely on long-standing religious beliefs, values regarding the acceptance of change and the pace of change can vary immensely among cultures. Western people generally believe that an individual can exert some control over the future and can manipulate events, particularly in a business context—that is, individuals feel they have some internal control. In many non-Western societies, however, control is considered external; people generally believe in destiny, or the will of Allah, and therefore adopt a passive attitude or even feel hostility toward those introducing the "evil" of change. In societies that place great importance on tradition (such as China), one small area of change may threaten an entire way of life. Webber describes just how difficult it is for an Asian male, concerned about tradition, to change his work habits:

> To the Chinese, the introduction of power machinery meant that he had to throw over not only habits of work but a whole ideology; it implied dissatisfaction with the ways of his father's way of life in all its aspects. If the old loom must be discarded, then 100 other things must be discarded with it, for there are somehow no adequate substitutes.[30]

The New Idea
SOURCE: Courtesy McDonald's Corporation

International firms are agents of change throughout the world. Some changes are more popular than others; as the photo shows, McDonald's hamburgers are apparently one change the Chinese are willing to accept.

Material Factors   Americans consume resources at a far greater rate than most of the rest of the world. Their attitude toward nature—that it is there to be used for their benefit—differs from the attitudes of Indians or Koreans, for example, whose worship of nature is part of their religious belief. Whereas Americans often value physical goods and status symbols, many non-Westerners find these things unimportant; they value the aesthetic and the spiritual realm. Such differences in attitude have implications for management functions, such as motivation and reward systems, because the proverbial carrot must be appropriate to the employee's value system.

Individualism   In general, Americans tend to work and conduct their private lives independently, valuing individual achievement, accomplishments, promotions, and wealth above any group goals. In many other countries, individualism is not valued (as previously discussed in the context of Hofstede's work). In China, for example, much

Exhibit 3-7   Fundamental Differences between Japanese and Mexican Culture That Affect Business Organizations

Dimension	Japanese Culture	Mexican Culture
Hierarchical nature	Rigid in rank and most communication; blurred in authority and responsibility	Rigid in all aspects
Individualism vs. collectivism	Highly collective culture; loyalty to work group dominates; group harmony very important	Collective relative to family group; don't transfer loyalty to work group; individualistic outside family
Attitudes toward work	Work is sacred duty; acquiring skills, working hard, thriftiness, patience and perseverance are virtues	Work is means to support self and family; leisure more important than work
Time orientation	Balanced perspective; future oriented; monochronic in dealings with outside world	Present oriented; time is imprecise; time commitments become desirable objectives
Approach to problem solving	Holistic, reliance on intuition, pragmatic, consensus important	Reliance on intuition and emotion, individual approach
Fatalism	Fatalism leads to preparation	Fatalism makes planning, disciplined routine unnatural
View of human nature	Intrinsically good	Mixture of good and evil

SOURCE: J. J. Lawrence and Ryh-song Yeh, "The Influence of Mexican Culture on the Use of Japanese Manufacturing Techniques in Mexico," *Management International Review* 34, no. 1 (1994): 49–66.

more of a "we" consciousness prevails, and the group is the basic building block of social life and work. For the Chinese, conformity and cooperation take precedence over individual achievement, and the emphasis is on the strength of the family or community—the predominant attitude being "we all rise or fall together."

International managers often face conflicts in the workplace as a result of differences in these four basic values of time, change, materialism, and individualism. If these operational value differences and their likely consequences are anticipated, managers can adjust expectations, communications, work organization, schedules, incentive systems, and so forth, to provide for more constructive outcomes for the company and its employees. Some of these operational differences between Japanese and Mexican cultures are shown in Exhibit 3-7. Note, in particular, the factors of time, individualism change (fatalism), and materialism (attitudes toward work) expressed in the exhibit.

THE INTERNET AND CULTURE

This is how many Koreans become versed in the Internet [at PC parlors].
—WON JUN YOUNG, MANAGER, YECA STATION (A PARLOR THAT SELLS
THE USE OF PCS FOR GAMES, SHARE TRADING, TEMPORARY OFFICES)
www.businessweek.com SEPTEMBER 25, 2000

We would be remiss if we did not acknowledge the contemporary phenomenon of the increasingly pervasive use of the Internet in society, for it seems to be encroaching on many of the social variables discussed earlier—in particular associations, education, and the economy. In South Korea, for example, where information technology makes up about 10 percent of the $400 billion economy and is expected to reach 20 percent by 2010, there is an obsession for anything digital. This phenomenon seems to be changing the lives of many Koreans. Teenagers, used to hanging out at the mall, now do so at the country's 20,000 PC parlors to watch movies, check e-mail, and surf the Net for as little as $1. Korean housewives are on a waiting list for ADSL lines when the $35 billion high-speed government telecommunications project is completed in 2005. By then 95 percent of Korean households will have Internet access.[31]

At the same time that the Internet is affecting culture, culture is also affecting how the Internet is used. One of the pervasive ways that culture is determining how the Internet may be used in various countries is through the local attitude to **information privacy**—the right to control information about oneself—as observed in the following quote:

> You Americans just don't seem to care about privacy, do you?
> —SWEDISH EXECUTIVE, WINTER 2001.[32]

While Americans collect data about consumers' backgrounds and what they buy, often trading that information with other internal or external contacts, the Swedes, for example, are astounded that this is done, especially without governmental oversight.[33] The Swedes are required to register all databases of personal information with the Data Inspection Board (DIB), their federal regulatory agency for privacy, and to get permission from that board before that data can be used. Indeed, the Swedish system is typical of most countries in Europe in their societal approaches to privacy.[34] One example of a blocked data transfer occurred when Sweden would not allow American airlines to transmit passenger information, such as wheelchair need and meal preferences, to the United States.[35] Some of the differences between the European and American approaches to privacy are shown in Exhibit 3-8.

Exhibit 3-8 European and U.S. Approaches toward Consumer Information Privacy

	U.S.	Europe
Legislative Approach	sectoral	omnibus
Regulatory Structure	self-help with voluntary control	centralized agency (commissioner, registration, or licensing)
Data Subjects' Rights	none or opt-out (determined by sector)	inspection/correction, opt-out (sometimes opt-in)
Privacy's Role in Society	contractual	human rights issue

SOURCE: H. Jeff Smith, "Information Privacy and Marketing: What the U.S. Should (and Shouldn't) Learn from Europe" *California Management Review* 43, 2 (Winter 2001).

Generally, in Europe, each person must be informed, and given the chance to object, if the information about that person is going to be used for direct marketing purposes or released to another party. That data cannot be used for secondary purposes if the consumer objects.

> In Italy, data cannot be sent outside—even to other EU countries—without the explicit consent of the data subject.
> In Spain, all direct mail has to include the name and address of the data owner so that the data subject is able to exercise his rights of access, correction, and removal.[36]

The manner in which Europe views information privacy has its roots in culture and history, leading to a different value set regarding privacy. The preservation of privacy is considered a human right, perhaps partially as a result of an internalized fear about how personal records were used in war times in Europe. In addition, research by Smith on the relationship between level of concern about privacy and Hofstede's cultural dimensions revealed that high levels of uncertainty avoidance were associated with the European approach to privacy, whereas higher levels of individualism, masculinity, and power distance were associated with the U.S. approach.[37]

It seems, then, that societal culture and the resultant effects on business models can render the assumptions about the "global" nature of information technology incorrect. U.S. businesspeople, brought up on a strong diet of the market economy, need to realize that they will often need to "localize" their use of IT to different value sets about its use.

DEVELOPING CULTURAL PROFILES

Managers can gather considerable information on cultural variables from current research, personal observation, and discussions with people. From these sources, managers can develop cultural profiles of various countries—composite pictures of working environments, people's attitudes, and norms of behavior. As we have previously discussed, these profiles are often highly generalized; many subcultures, of course, may exist within a country. But managers can use these profiles to anticipate drastic differences in the level of motivation, communication, ethics, loyalty, and individual and group productivity that may be encountered in a given country. More such homework may have helped the GM-Daewoo joint venture in Korea, which is coming to an end after years of acrimonious relations. Executives from both sides acknowledge that they "seriously underestimated the obstacles posed to their three-continent car-making experiment by divergent cultures and business aspirations, not to mention the different languages."[38]

It is relatively simple to pull together a descriptive profile for American culture, even though regional and individual differences exist, because we know ourselves and because researchers have thoroughly studied American culture. The results of one such study by Harris and Moran are shown in Exhibit 3-9, which provides a basis of comparison with other cultures and thus suggests the likely differences in workplace behaviors.

Exhibit 3-9   Americans at a Glance

1. *Goal and achievement oriented*—Americans think they can accomplish just about anything, given enough time, money, and technology.
2. *Highly organized and institutionally minded*—Americnas prefer a society that is strong institutionally, secure, and tidy or well kept.
3. *Freedom-loving and self-reliant*—Americans fought a revolution and subsequent wars to preserve their concept of democracy, so they resent too much control or interference, especially by government or external forces. They believe in an ideal that all persons are created equal; though they sometimes fail to live that ideal fully, they strive through law to promote equal opportunity and to confront their own racism or prejudice.

    They also idealize the self-made person who rises form poverty and adversity, and think they can influence and create their own futures. Control of one's destiny is popularly expressed as "doing your own thing." Americans think, for the most part, that with determination and initiative, one can achieve whatever one sets out to do and thus fulfill one's individual human potential.
4. *Work oriented and efficient*—Americans possess a strong work ethic, though they are learning in the present generation to enjoy leisure time constructively. They are conscious of time and efficient in doing things. They tinker with gadgets and technological systems, always searching for easier, better, more efficient ways to accomplish tasks.
5. *Friendly and informal*—Americans reject the traditional privileges of royalty and class, but defer to those with affluence and power. Although informal in greeting and dress, they are a noncontact culture (e.g., avoid embracing in public usually) and maintain a certain physical/psychological distance with others (e.g., about 2 feet).
6. *Competitive and aggressive*—Americans in play or business generally are so oriented because of their drives to achieve and succeed. This is partially traced to their heritage of having to overcome a wilderness and hostile elements in their environment.
7. *Values in transition*—traditional American values of family loyalty, respect and care of the aged, marriage and the nuclear family, patriotism, material acquisition, forthrightness, and the like are undergoing profound reevaluation as people search for new meanings.
8. *Generosity*—Although Americans seemingly emphasize material values, they are a sharing people, as has been demonstrated in the Marshall Plan, foreign aid programs, refugee assistance, and their willingness at home and abroad to espouse a good cause and to help neighbors in need. They tend to be altruistic and some would say naive as a people.

SOURCE: From *Managing Cultural Differences* by Philip R. Harris and Robert T. Moran, 5th ed. Copyright © 2000 by Gulf Publishing Company, Houston, TX. Used with permission. All rights reserved.

It is not so easy, however, to pull together descriptive cultural profiles of peoples in other countries unless one has lived there and been intricately involved with those people. But managers can make a start by using what research and literature is available on a comparative basis. The following section provides brief, generalized country profiles based on a synthesis of research, primarily from Hofstede[39] and England,[40] as well as numerous other sources.[41] These profiles illustrate how to synthesize information and gain a sense of the character of a society—from which implications may be drawn about how to manage more effectively in that society. More extensive implications and applications related to managerial functions are drawn in later chapters.

___

Profiles in Culture

Comparative Management in Focus

JAPAN

> Now I have to stand firmly on my own and think for myself. I wish I had realized this earlier in life. . . . Building my life around the company was a big mistake.
> —AKIO KUZUOKA, 40-YEAR EMPLOYEE AT A JAPANESE COMPANY.
> *WALL STREET JOURNAL*, DECEMBER 29, 2000.

In 2002, we see evidence in cities of changes in Japan's business culture as a result of economic decline and global competition (discussed at the end of this section). However, the underlying cultural values still predominate—for now anyway.

Much of the Japanese culture—and the basis of working relationships—can be explained by the principle of *wa*, "peace and harmony." This principle, embedded in the value they attribute to *amae* ("indulgent love"), probably originated in the Shinto religion, which focuses on spiritual and physical harmony. *Amae* results in *shinyo*, which refers to the mutual confidence, faith, and honor necessary for successful business relationships. Japan ranks high on pragmatism, masculinity, and uncertainty avoidance, and fairly high on power distance. At the same time, much importance is attached to loyalty, empathy, and the guidance of subordinates. The result is a mix of authoritarianism and humanism in the workplace, similar to a family system. These cultural roots are evident in a very homogeneous managerial value system, with strong middle management, strong working relationships, strong seniority systems that stress rank, and an emphasis on looking after employees. The principle of *wa* carries forth into the work group—the building block of Japanese business. The Japanese strongly identify and thus seek to cooperate with their work groups. The emphasis is on participative management, consensus problem solving, and decision making with a patient, long-term perspective. Open expression or conflict is discouraged, and it is of paramount importance to avoid the shame of not fulfilling one's duty. These elements of work culture result in a devotion to work, collective responsibility, and a high degree of employee productivity.

If we extend this cultural profile to its implications for specific behaviors in the workplace, we can draw a comparison with common American behaviors. As shown in Exhibit 3-10, most of those behaviors seem to be opposite to those of their counterparts; it is no wonder that there are many misunderstandings and conflicts in the workplace between Americans and Japanese. For example, a majority of the attitudes and behaviors of many Japanese stems from a high level of collectivism, compared with a high level of individualism common to Americans. This contrast is highlighted in the center of Exhibit 3-10 by "maintain the group," compared with "protect the individual." In addition, the strict social order of the Japanese permeates the workplace in adherence to organizational hierarchy and seniority and in loyalty to the firm. This contrasts markedly with the typical American responses to organizational relationships and duties based on equality. In addition, the often blunt, outspoken American businessperson offends the indirectness and sensitivity of the Japanese for whom the virtue of patience is paramount, causing the silence and avoidance that so

Exhibit 3-10   The American–Japanese Cultural Divide

Japanese	American	
	Japanese	**American**	
Patience	Man within nature	Man controlling nature	**Action**
	Caution	Risk-taking	
	Incremental improvement	Bold initiative	
	Deliberation	Spontaneity	
	Adherence to form	Improvisation	
	Silence	Outspokenness	
	Memorization	Critical thinking	
	Emotional sensitivity	Logical reasoning	
	Indirectness	Clarity and frankness	
	Assuaging	Confronting	
	Avoiding	Threatening	
Harmony	Consensus building	Decisiveness	**Freedom**
	Conformity	Individuality	
	Group convention	Personal principle	
	Trusted relationships	Legal safeguards	
	Collective strength	Individual independence	
	Maintain the group	Protect the individual	
	Modest resignation	Righteous indignation	
	Saving face	Being heard	
	Oppressive unanimity	Chaotic anarchy	
	Humble cooperation	Proving oneself	
Hierarchy	Rewarding seniority	Rewarding performance	**Equality**
	Loyalty	Track record	
	Generalists	Specialists	
	Obligations	Opportunities	
	Untiring effort	Fair effort	
	Shame	Guilt	
	Dependency	Autonomy	
	Dutiful relationships	Level playing field	
	Industrial groups	Industrial competition	
	Strict ranking	Ambiguous/informal ranking	
	Racial differentiation	Racial equality	
	Gender differentiation	Gender equality	

SOURCE: R. G. Linowes, "The Japanese Manager's Traumatic Entry into the United States: Understanding the American-Japanese Cultural Divide," *The Academy of Management Executive VII*, no. 4 (November 1993): 24.

frustrates Americans.[42] As a result, Japanese businesspeople tend to think of American organizations as having no spiritual quality and little employee loyalty, and of Americans as assertive, frank, and egotistic. Their American counterparts, in turn, respond with the impression that Japanese businesspeople have little experience and are secretive, arrogant, and cautious.[43]

In 2001, however, anecdotal evidence indicates that some convergence with Western business culture is taking place—resulting from Japan's economic contraction and subsequent bankruptcies. Focus on the group, lifetime employment, and a pension has given way to a more competitive business environment with job security no longer guaranteed and an emphasis on performance-based pay. This has led Japan's "salarymen" to recognize the need for personal responsibility on the job and in their lives. Although only a few years ago emphasis was on the group, Japan's long economic slump seems to be causing some cultural restructuring of the individual. Corporate Japan is changing from a culture of consensus and groupthink to touting the need for an "era of personal responsibility" as a solution to revitalize its competitive position in the global marketplace.[44]

> To tell you the truth, it's hard to think for yourself, says Mr. Kuzuoka . . . [but, if you don't] . . . in this age of cutthroat competition, you'll just end up drowning.[45]

GERMANY

The reunited Germany is somewhat culturally diverse inasmuch as the country borders several nations. Generally, Germans rank quite high on Hofstede's dimension of individualism, although their behaviors seem less individualistic than those of Americans. They score fairly high on uncertainty avoidance and masculinity and have a relatively small need for power distance. These cultural norms show up in the Germans' preference for being around familiar people and situations; they are also reflected in their propensity to do a detailed evaluation of business deals before committing themselves.

Christianity underlies much of German culture—over 96 percent of Germans are Catholics or Protestants. This may be why Germans tend to like rule and order in their lives, and why there is a clear public expectation of the acceptable and the unacceptable way to do things. Public signs everywhere in Germany dictate what is allowed or *verboten* (forbidden). Germans are very strict with their use of time, whether for business or pleasure, frowning on inefficiency or on tardiness. In business, Germans tend to be assertive, but they downplay aggression. Decisions are not as centralized as one would expect, with hierarchical processes often giving way to consensus decision making. However, there is strict departmentalization in organizations, with centralized and final authority at the departmental manager level. Hall and Hall describe the German preference for closed doors and private space as evidence of the affinity for compartmentalization in organizations and in their own lives. They also prefer more physical space around them in conversation than do most other Europeans, and they seek privacy in aural distance. German law prohibits loud noises in public areas on weekend afternoons. Germans are conservative, valuing privacy, politeness, and formality; they usually use last names and titles for all except those close to them.

In negotiations, Germans want detailed information before and during discussions, which can become lengthy. Factors such as voice and speech control are given much weight. But since Germany is a low-context society, communication is explicit, and Americans find negotiations easy to understand.[46]

SOUTH KOREA

Koreans rank high on collectivism and pragmatism, fairly low on masculinity, moderate on power distance, and quite high on uncertainty avoidance. Although greatly influenced by American culture, Koreans are still very much bound to the traditional Confucian teachings of spiritualism and collectivism. Korea and its people have undergone great changes, but the respect for family, authority, formality, class, and rank remain strong. Koreans are quite aggressive and hard-working, demonstrative, friendly, and very hospitable. For the most part, they do not subscribe to participative management. Family and personal relationships are important, and connections are vital for business introductions and transactions. Business is based on honor and trust; most contracts are oral. Although achievement and competence are important to Koreans, a driving force in relationships is the priority of guarding both parties' social and professional reputations. Thus, praise predominates, and honest criticism is rare.

Further insight into the differences between American and Korean culture can be derived from the following excerpted letter from Professor Jin K. Kim in Plattsburgh, New York, to his high school friend, MK, in South Korea, who just returned from a visit to the United States. MK, whom Dr. Kim had not seen for 20 years, is planning to emigrate to the United States, and Dr. Kim wants to help ward off his friend's culture shock by telling him about American culture from a Korean perspective.

Dear MK,

I sincerely hope the last leg of your trip home from the five-week fact-finding visit to the United States was pleasant and informative. Although I may not have expressed my sense of exhilaration about your visit through the meager lodging accommodations and "barbaric" foods we provided, it was sheer joy to spend four weeks with you and Kyung-Ok. (Please refrain from hitting the ceiling. My use of your charming wife's name, rather than the usual Korean expression, "your wife" or "your house person," is not an indication of my amorous intentions toward her as any red-blooded Korean man would suspect. Since you are planning to immigrate to this country soon, I thought you might as well begin to get used to the idea of your wife exerting her individuality. Better yet, I thought you should be warned that the moment the plane touches American soil, you will lose your status as the center of your familial universe.) At any rate, please be assured that during your stay here my heart was filled with memories of our three years together in high school when we were young in Pusan.

During your visit, you called me, on several occasions, an American. What prompted you to invoke such a reference is beyond my comprehension. Was it my rusty Korean expressions? Was it my calculating mind? Was it my pitifully subservient (at least when viewed through your cultural lens) role that I was playing in the family life? Or, was it my familiarity with some facets of the American cultural landscape? This may sound bewildering to you, but it is absolutely true that through all the years I have lived in this country, I never truly felt like an American. Sure, on the surface, our family followed closely many ritualistic routines of the American culture: shopping malls, dining out, PTA, Little League, picnics, camping trips, credit card shopping sprees, hot dogs, etc.

But mentally I remained stubbornly in the periphery. Naturally, then, my subjective cultural attitudes stayed staunchly Korean. Never did the inner layers of my Korean psyche yield to the invading American cultural vagaries, I thought. So, when you labeled me an American for the first time, I felt a twinge of guilt.

Several years ago, an old Korean friend of mine, who settled in the United States about the same time I did, paid a visit to Korea for the first time in some 15 years. When he went to see his best high school friend, who was now married and had two sons, his friend's wife made a bed for him and her husband in the master bedroom, declaring that she would spend the night with the children. It was not necessarily the sexual connotation of the episode that made my friend blush; he was greatly embarrassed by the circumstance in which he imposed himself to the extent that the couple's privacy had to be violated. For his high school friend and his wife, it was clearly their age-old friendship to which the couple's privacy had to yield. MK, you might empathize rather easily with this Korean couple's state of mind. But it would be a gross mistake even to imagine there may be occasions in your adopted culture when a gesture of friendship breaks the barrier of privacy. Zealously guarding their privacy above all, Americans are marvelously adept at drawing the line where friendship—that elusive "we" feeling—stops and privacy begins. . . .

Indeed, one of the hardest tasks you will face as an "alien" is how to find that delicate balance between your individuality (for example, privacy) and your collective identity (for example, friendship or membership in social groups).

Privacy is not the only issue that stems from this individuality-collectivity continuum. Honesty in interpersonal relationships is another point that may keep you puzzled. Americans are almost brutally honest and frank about issues that belong to public domains; they are not afraid of discussing an embarrassing topic in most graphic details as long as the topic is a matter of public concern. Equally frank and honest gestures are adopted when they discuss their own personal lives once the presumed benefits from such gestures are determined to outweigh the risks involved. Accordingly, it is not uncommon to encounter friends who volunteer personally embarrassing and even shameful information lest you find it out from other sources. Are Americans equally straightforward and forthcoming in laying out heartfelt personal criticisms directed at their friends? Not likely. Their otherwise acute sense of honesty becomes significantly muted when they face the unpleasant task of being negative toward their personal friends. The fear of an emotion-draining confrontation and the virtue of being polite force them to put on a facade or mask.

The perfectly accepted social behavior of telling "white lies" is a good example. The social and personal virtues of accepting such lies are grounded in the belief that the potential damage that can be inflicted by directly telling a friend the hurtful truth far outweighs the potential benefit that the friend could gain from it. Instead of telling a hurtful truth directly, Americans use various indirect communication channels to which their friend is likely to be tuned. In other words, they publicize the information in the form of gossip or behind-the-back recriminations until it is transformed into a sort of collective criticism against the target individual. Thus objectified and collectivized, the "truth" ultimately reaches the target individual with a minimal cost of social discomfort on the part of the teller. There is nothing vile or insidious about this communication tactic, since it is deeply rooted in the concern for sustaining social pleasantry for both parties.

This innocuous practice, however, is bound to be perceived as an act of outrageous dishonesty by a person deeply immersed in the Korean culture. In the Korean cultural context, a trusted personal relationship precludes such publicizing prior to direct, "honest" criticism to the individual concerned, no matter what the cost in social and personal unpleasantry. Indeed, as you are well aware, MK, such direct reproach and even recrimination in Korea is in most cases appreciated as a sign of one's utmost love and concern for the target individual. Stressful and emotionally draining as it is, such a frank expression of criticism is done out of "we" feeling. Straight-talking friends did not want me to repeat undesirable acts in front of others, as it would either damage "our reputation" or go against the common interest of "our collective identity." In Korea, the focus is on the self-discipline that forms a basis for the integrity of "our group." In America, on the other hand, the focus is on the feelings of two individuals. From the potential teller's viewpoint, the primary concern is how to maintain social politeness, whereas from the target person's viewpoint, the primary concern is how to maintain self-esteem. Indeed, these two diametrically opposed frames of reference—self-discipline and self-esteem—make one culture collective and the other individualistic.

It is rather amazing that for all the mistakes I must have made in the past twenty years, only one non-Korean American friend gave me such an "honest" criticism. In a sense, this concern for interpersonal politeness conceals their disapproval of my undesirable behavior for a time and ultimately delays the adjustment or realignment of my behavior, since it is likely to take quite a while for the collective judgment to reach me through the "publicized" channels of communication. So many Korean immigrants express their indignation about their American colleagues who smile at them but who criticize them behind their backs. If you ever become a victim of such a perception, MK, please take heart that you are not the only one who feels that pain.

MK—The last facet of the individualism-collectivism continuum likely to cause a great amount of cognitive dissonance in the process of your assimilation to American life is the extent to which you have to assert your individuality to other people. You probably have no difficulty remembering our high school principal, K. W.

Park, for whom we had a respect-contempt complex. He used to lecture, almost daily at morning assemblies, on the virtue of being modest. As he preached it, it was a form of the Confucian virtue of self-denial. Our existence or presence among other people, he told us, should not be overly felt through communicated messages (regardless of whether they are done with a tongue or pen). . . . One's existence, we were told, should be noticed by others in the form of our acts and conduct. One is obligated to provide opportunities for others to experience one's existence through what he or she does. Self-initiated effort for public recognition or self-aggrandizement was the most shameful conduct for a person of virtue.

This idea is interesting and noble as a philosophical posture, but when it is practiced in America, it will not get you anywhere in most circumstances. The lack of self-assertion is translated directly into timidity and lack of self-confidence. This is a culture where you must exert your individuality to the extent that it would make our high school principal turn in his grave out of shame and disgust. Blame the size of the territory or the population of this country. You may even blame the fast-paced cadence of life or the social mobility that moves people around at a dizzying speed. Whatever the specific reason might be, Americans are not waiting to experience you or your behaviors as they exist. They want a "documented" version of you that is eloquently summarized, decorated, and certified. What they are looking for is not your raw, unprocessed being with rich texture; rather, it is a slickly processed self, neatly packaged and, most important, conveniently delivered to them. Self-advertising is encouraged almost to the point of pretentiousness. Years ago in Syracuse, I had an occasion to introduce a visiting Korean monk-scholar to a gathering of people who wanted to hear something about Oriental philosophies. After taking an elegantly practiced bow to the crowd, this humble monk declared, "My name is . . . Please teach me, as I do not know anything." It took quite a bit of probing and questioning for us to extract something to chew on from that monk with the mysterious smile. Contrast this with an American colleague of mine applying for a promotion several years ago, who literally hauled in two cabinets full of documented evidence of his scholarly achievements.

The curious journey toward the American end of the individualism-collectivism continuum will be inevitable, I assure you. The real question is whether it will be in your generation, your children's, or their children's. Whenever it happens, it will be a bittersweet revenge for me, since only then will you realize how it feels to be called an American by your best high school chum.

CULTURE AND MANAGEMENT STYLES AROUND THE WORLD

As an international manager, once you have researched the culture of a country in which you may be going to work or do business, and have developed a cultural profile, it is useful then to apply that information to develop an understanding of the expected management styles and ways of doing business that predominate in that region, or with that type of business setting. Two examples follow: Saudi Arabia and Chinese Small Family Businesses.

Saudi Arabia

Understanding how business is conducted in the modern Middle East requires an understanding of the Arab culture, since the Arab peoples are the majority there and most of them are Muslim. The Arab culture is intertwined with the pervasive influence of Islam. Even though not all Middle Easterners are Arab, the Arab culture and management style predominates in the Gulf region. Shared culture, religion, and language underlie behavioral similarities throughout the Arab world. Islam "permeates Saudi life—Allah is always present, controls everything, and is frequently referred to in conversation."[47] Employees may spend over two hours a day in prayer, part of the life patterns that intertwine work with religion, politics, and social life.

Arab history and culture is based on tribalism, with its norms of reciprocity of favors, support, obligation, and identity passed on to the family unit, which is the primary structural model. Family life is based on closer personal ties than in the West. Arabs value personal relationships, honor, and saving face for all concerned; these values take precedence over the work at hand or verbal accuracy. "Outsiders" must realize that establishing a trusting relationship and respect for the Arab social norms has to precede any attempts at business discussions. Honor, pride, and dignity are at the core of "shame" societies such as the Arabs. As such, shame and honor provide the basis for social control and motivation. Circumstances dictate what is right or wrong and what is acceptable behavior.[48]

Exhibit 3-11   Behavior That Will Likely Cause Offense in Saudi Arabia

- Bringing up business subjects until you get to know your host, or you will be considered rude.
- Commenting on a man's wife or female children over 12 years of age.
- Raising colloquial questions that may be common in your country but possibly misunderstood in Saudi Arabia as an invasion of privacy.
- Using disparaging or swear words and off-color or obscene attempts at humor.
- Engaging in conversations about religion, politics, or Israel.
- Bringing gifts of alcohol or using alcohol, which is prohibited in Saudi Arabia.
- Requesting favors from those in authority or esteem, for it is considered impolite for Arabs to say no.
- Shaking hands too firmly or pumping—gentle or limp handshakes are preferred.
- Pointing your finger at someone or showing the soles of your feet when seated.

SOURCE: P. R. Harris and R. T. Moran, *Managing Cultural Differences*, 5th ed. (Houston: Gulf Publishing, 2000).

Exhibit 3-12   The Relationship between Culture and
Managerial Behaviors in Saudi Arabia

Cultural Values	Managerial Behaviors
Tribal and family loyalty	Work group loyalty Paternal sociability Stable employment and a sense of belonging A pleasant workplace Careful selection of employees Nepotism
Arabic language	Business as an intellectual activity Access to employees and peers Management by walking around Conversation as recreation
Close and warm friendships	A person rather than task and money orientation Theory Y management Avoidance of judgment
Islam	Sensitivity to Islamic virtues Observance of the Qur'an and Sharia Work as personal or spiritual growth
Majlis	Consultative management A full and fair hearing Adherence to norms
Honor and shame	Clear guidelines and conflict avoidance Positive reinforcement Training and defined job duties Private correction of mistakes Avoidance of competition
An idealized self	Centralized decision making Assumption of responsibility appropriate to position Empathy and respect for the self-image of others
Polychronic use of time	Right- and left-brain facility A bias for action Patience and flexibility
Independence	Sensitivity to control Interest in the individual
Male domination	Separation of sexes Open work life; closed family life

SOURCE: R. R. Harris and R. T. Moran, *Managing Cultural Differences* 4th ed. (Houston: Gulf Publishing, 1996).

Arabs avoid open admission of error at all costs because weakness (***muruwwa***) is a failure to be manly. It is sometimes difficult for westerners to get at the truth because of the Arab need to avoid showing weakness; instead Arabs paint a desired or idealized situation. Shame is also brought on someone who declines to fulfill a request or a favor; therefore, a business arrangement is left open if something has yet to be completed.

The communication style of Middle Eastern societies is high context (that is, implicit and indirect), and their use of time is polychronic—many things can be going on at the same time, with constant interruptions commonplace. The imposition of deadlines is considered rude, and business schedules take a back seat to the perspective that events will occur "sometime" when Allah wills (*bukra insha Allah*). Arabs give primary importance to hospitality; they are cordial to business associates and lavish in their entertainment, constantly offering strong black coffee (which you should not refuse) and banquets before considering business transactions. Westerners must realize the importance of personal contacts and networking, socializing and building close relationships and trust, practicing patience regarding schedules, and doing business in person. Exhibit 3-11 gives some selected actions and nonverbal behaviors that may offend Arabs. The relationship between cultural values and norms in Saudi Arabia and managerial behaviors is illustrated in Exhibit 3-12.

Chinese Small Family Businesses

The predominance of small businesses in China and the region highlights the need for managers from around the world to gain an understanding of how such businesses operate. Many small businesses—most of which are family or extended-family businesses—become part of the value chain (suppliers, buyers, retailers, etc.) within industries in which "foreign" firms may compete.

Exhibit 3-13 presents a general framework for comparing Western and Chinese cultures; shown are the resulting differences in Chinese attitudes and behavior, along with the implications for managers. Further discussion of the Chinese culture continues in Chapter 5 in the context of negotiation. Here we will point out some specifics of Chinese management style and practices in particular as they apply to small businesses. It is important to point out that no matter what size company, but especially in small businesses, it is the all-pervasive presence and use of *guanxi* that provides the little red engine of business transactions in China. *Guanxi* means connections—the network of relationships the Chinese cultivate through friendship and affection; it entails the exchange of favors and gifts to provide an obligation to reciprocate favors. There is an unwritten code among those who share a *guanxi* network.[49] The philosophy and structure of Chinese businesses comprise paternalism, mutual obligation, responsibility, hierarchy, familialism, personalism, and connections.[50] Autocratic leadership is the norm, with the owner using his or her power, but also with a caring about other people which may predominate over efficiency.[51]

According to Lee, the major differences between Chinese management styles and those of their Western counterparts are human-centeredness, family-centeredness, centralization of power, and small size.[52] Their human-centered management style puts people ahead of a business relationship and focuses on friendship, loyalty, and trustworthiness.[53] The family is extremely important in Chinese culture, and small businesses tend to be run like a family.

The centralized power structure in Chinese organizations, unlike those in the West, splits into two distinct levels—at the top is the boss and a few family members, and at the bottom are the employees, with no ranking among the workers.[54]

As Chinese firms in many modern regions in the Pacific Rim seek to modernize and compete locally and globally, a tug of war has begun between the old and the new—the traditional Chinese management practices, and the increasingly "imported" Western management styles. As discussed by Lee, this struggle is encapsulated in the

Exhibit 3-13   A Summary of Western and Chinese Cultural Differences
and the Implications for Management

Comparing pertinent features of the West with that of China, we can make the following
distinctions:

The West	China
Individual rights	Individual duty and collective obligations
Rule by law	Rule by personality and imperial authority
The collective right to grant, question, and reject political authority	Unquestioning submission to hereditary authority backed by force
Political and ethnic pluralism	Monolithic power and homogeneity
Cultural interaction	Cultural isolation
Sufficient resources to support early urbanization, specialization of labor, and large-scale trade	An agrarian, subsistence economy and endless hardship, both natural and imposed
An external orientation	An internal orientation
Physical and social mobility	Permanence *in situ*
Reliance on reason and the scientific method	Reliance on precedent, intuition, and wisdom
An aggressive, active approach to nature, technology, and progress	Passive, fatalistic submission

Resulting differences in Chinese values, attitudes, and behavior with managerial implications:

1. Larger power distance—a greater willingness to accept the authority of others
2. Collectivism
    a. Deriving satisfaction less from task competence and achievement and more from a sense of contribution to a group effort
    b. More value placed on the comfort and availability of mutual support and affiliation with a group than on independence, self-reliance, privacy and personal space
    c. More cooperativeness and less competitiveness as individuals
    d. Harmony and humility rather than aggressiveness
    e. High-content communication rather than directness and forthrightness
    f. Recognition of group, rather than individual, performance
    g. More relativistic, particularistic ethical standards
3. An external locus of control
4. More reliance on accumulated wisdom than on reason and objectivity
5. Holistic thinking and synthesis rather than linear thinking and analysis

SOURCE: J. Scarborough, "Comparing Chinese and Western Cultural Roots: Why East is East and . . . ," *Business Horizons* (November–December 1998): 15–24.

different management perspectives of the old and young generations, as shown in Exhibit 3-14. A two-generational study of Chinese managers by Ralston et al. also found generational shifts in work values in China. They concluded that the new generation manager is more individualistic, independent, and risk-taking in the pursuit of profits. However, they also found the new generation holding on to their Confucian values, concluding that the new generation may be viewed as "crossverging their Eastern and Western influences, while on the road of modernization."[55]

Exhibit 3-14 Chinese Management Philosophies: The Old and the New

Old Generation	Young Generation
Claim that they have more experiences	Claim that they have more education
Perceive that their role is to intervene for the workers and help them	Perceive that their role is to hire competent workers and expect them to perform
Believe that is it the boss's responsibility to solve problems	Believe that it is the individual's responsibility to solve problems
Stress that a boss has the obligation to take care the workers	Stress that workers have responsibility to perform the job well
Emphasize that individuals should conform to majority	Emphasize that individuals should maximize their talents and potentials
Believe that work cannot be divided clearly and like to be involved in everything	Believe that a boss should mind his or her own work and leave the workers to do their job
Perceive that work is more important than designation and organizational structure	Perceive that designation and organizational structure are important in order to get the work done
Believe that managers should help the workers solve their problems	Believe that managers should set objectives and achieve them
Complain that the young generation likes to use complicated management methods	Complain that the old generation does things on ad hoc basis
Perceive that the young generation likes to change and expects immediate results	Perceive that the old generation is static and resistant change
Worry that the young generation is not experienced in running the business	Frustrated that the old generation still holds on strongly to their power
Emphasize that they have to take care of the old workers in the process of the company's growth	Emphasize that they have to gain acceptance from their peers
Emphasize that ethics are important in business	Emphasize that strategy is important in business
Anticipate that the young generation is going to have many difficulties if they adopt Western concepts of management	Frustrated that the old generation does not let them test out their concepts of management
Believe that one's ability is limited and one should be contented with what one has	Believe that there are a lot of opportunities for achievement and growth

SOURCE: Dr. Jean Lee, "Culture and Management—A Study of Small Chinese Family Business in Singapore," *Journal of Small Business Management* (July 1996).

Conclusion

We have examined various cultural values and have discussed how managers can understand them with the help of cultural profiles. Now we will turn our attention to the applications of this cultural knowledge to management in an international environment (or, alternatively in a domestic multicultural environment)—especially as relevant to cross-cultural communication (Chapter 4), negotiation and decision making (Chapter 5), and motivating and leading (Chapter 11). Culture and communication are essentially synonymous; what happens when people from different cultures communicate, and how can the international manager understand the underlying process and adapt her or his style and expectations accordingly? For the answers, read on to the next chapter.

SUMMARY OF KEY POINTS

1. The culture of a society comprises the shared values, understandings, assumptions, and goals that are passed down through generations and imposed by members of the society.

2. Cultural and national differences strongly influence the attitudes and expectations and therefore the on-the-job behavior of individuals and groups.

3. Managers must develop cultural sensitivity to anticipate and accommodate behavioral differences in different societies.

4. Managers must avoid parochialism—an attitude that assumes one's own management techniques are best in any situation or location and that other people should follow one's patterns of behavior.

5. Harris and Moran take a systems approach to understanding cultural and national variables and their effects on work behavior. They identify eight subsystems of variables: kinship, education, economy, politics, religion, associations, health, and recreation.

6. From his research in 50 countries, Hofstede proposes four underlying value dimensions that help to identify and describe the cultural profile of a country and affect organizational processes. These are power distance, uncertainty avoidance, individualism, and masculinity. Through the research of Hofstede and others, we can cluster countries based on intercultural similarities.

7. On-the-job conflicts in international management frequently arise out of conflicting values and orientations regarding time, change, material factors, and individualism.

8. Managers can use research results and personal observations to develop a character sketch, or cultural profile, of a country. This profile can help managers anticipate how to motivate people and coordinate work processes in a particular international context.

DISCUSSION QUESTIONS

1. What is meant by the culture of a society, and why is it important that international managers understand it? Do you notice cultural differences among your classmates? How do those differences affect the class environment? your group projects?

2. Describe the four dimensions of culture proposed by Hofstede. What are the managerial implications of these dimensions?

3. Discuss the types of operational conflicts that could occur in an international context because of different attitudes toward time, change, material factors, and individualism. Give examples relative to specific countries.

4. Give some examples of countries in which the family and its extensions play an important role in the workplace. How are managerial functions affected, and what can a manager do about this influence?

5. Discuss collectivism as it applies to the Japanese workplace. What managerial functions does it affect?

APPLICATION EXERCISES

1. Develop a cultural profile for one of the countries in the following list. Form small groups of students and compare your findings in class with those of another group preparing a profile for another country. Be sure to compare specific find-

ings regarding religion, kinship, recreation, and other subsystems. What are the prevailing attitudes toward time, change, material factors, and individualism?

Any African country
People's Republic of China
England
Mexico
France
India

2. In small groups of students, research Hofstede's findings regarding the four dimensions of power distance, uncertainty avoidance, masculinity, and individualism for one of the pairs of countries listed below. (Your instructor can assign the countries to avoid duplication.) Present your findings to the class. Assume you are a U.S. manager of a subsidiary in the foreign country and explain how differences on these dimensions are likely to affect your management tasks. What suggestions do you have for dealing with these differences in the workplace?

United States and Brazil
United States and Italy
United States and People's Republic of China
United States and Russia

EXPERIENTIAL EXERCISES

1. A large Baltimore manufacturer of cabinet hardware had been working for months to locate a suitable distributor for its products in Europe. Finally invited to present a demonstration to a reputable distributing company in Frankfurt, it sent one of its most promising young executives, Fred Wagner, to make the presentation. Fred not only spoke fluent German but also felt a special interest in this assignment because his paternal grandparents had immigrated to the United States from the Frankfurt area during the 1920s. When Fred arrived at the conference room where he would be making his presentation he shook hands firmly, greeted everyone with a friendly *guten tag*, and even remembered to bow the head slightly as is the German custom. Fred, a very effective speaker and past president of the Baltimore Toastmasters Club, prefaced his presentation with a few humorous anecdotes to set a relaxed and receptive atmosphere. However, he felt that his presentation was not very well received by the company executives. In fact, his instincts were correct, for the German company chose not to distribute Fred's hardware products.
   What went wrong?
2. Bill Nugent, an international real estate developer from Dallas, had made a 2:30 P.M. appointment with Mr. Abdullah, a high-ranking government official in Riyadh, Saudi Arabia. From the beginning things did not go well for Bill. First, he was kept waiting until nearly 3:45 before he was ushered into Mr. Abdullah's

SOURCE: Gary P. Ferraro, *The Cultural Dimensions of International Business* 2nd ed. (Englewood Cliffs, N.J.: Prentice Hall, 1994).

office. And when he finally did get in, several other men were also in the room. Even though Bill felt that he wanted to get down to business with Mr. Abdullah, he was reluctant to get too specific because he considered much of what they needed to discuss sensitive and private. To add to Bill's sense of frustration Mr. Abdullah seemed more interested in engaging in meaningless small talk rather than dealing with the substantive issues concerning their business.

How might you help Bill deal with his frustration?

3. Tom Forrest, an up-and-coming executive for a U.S. electronics company, was sent to Japan to work out the details of a joint venture with a Japanese electronics firm. During the first several weeks, Tom felt that the negotiations were proceeding better than he had expected. He found that he had very cordial working relationships with the team of Japanese executives, and in fact, they had agreed on the major policies and strategies governing the new joint venture. During the third week of negotiations Tom was present at a meeting held to review their progress. The meeting was chaired by the president of the Japanese firm, Mr. Hayakawa, a man in his mid-40s, who had recently taken over the presidency from his 82-year-old grandfather. The new president, who had been involved in most of the negotiations during the preceding weeks, seemed to Tom to be one of the strongest advocates of the plan that had been developed to date. Also attending the meeting was Hayakawa's grandfather, the recently retired president. After the plans had been discussed in some detail, the octogenarian past president proceeded to give a long soliloquy about how some of the features of this plan violated the traditional practices on which the company had been founded. Much to Tom's amazement, Mr. Hayakawa did nothing to explain or defend the policies and strategies that they had taken weeks to develop. Feeling extremely frustrated, Tom then gave a fairly strong argued defense of the plan. To Tom's further amazement, no one else in the meeting spoke up in defense of the plan. The tension in the air was quite heavy and the meeting adjourned shortly thereafter. Within days the Japanese firm completely terminated the negotiations on the joint venture.

How could you help Tom better understand this bewildering situation?

INTERNET RESOURCES

Visit the Deresky Website at http://prenhall.com/Deresky for this chapter's Internet resources.

CASE STUDY: TROUBLE AT COMPUTEX CORPORATION

Mr. Peter Jones
Vice President—Europe
Computex Corporation
San Francisco/USA
Göteborg.

The writers of this letter are the headcount of the Sales Department of Computex Sweden, A.S., except for the Sales Manager.

SOURCE: Martin Hilb, University of St. Gallen, Switzerland.

We have decided to bring to your attention a problem which unsolved probably will lead to a situation where the majority among us will leave the company within a rather short period of time. None of us want to be in this situation, and we are approaching you purely as an attempt to save the team to the benefit of ourselves as well as Computex Corporation.

We consider ourselves an experienced, professional, and sales-oriented group of people. Computex Corporation is a company which we are proud to work for. The majority among us have been employed for several years. Consequently, a great number of key customers in different areas of Sweden see us as representatives of Computex Corporation. It is correct to say that the many excellent contacts we have made have been established over years; many of them are friends of ours.

These traits give a very short background because we have never met you. What kind of problem forces us to such a serious step as to contact you?

Problems arise as a result of character traits and behavior of our General Manager, Mr. Miller.

Firstly, we are more and more convinced that we are tools that he is utilizing in order to "climb the ladder." In meetings with us individually, or as a group, he gives visions about the future, how he values us, how he wants to delegate and involve us in business, the importance of cooperation and communication, etc. When it comes to the point, these phrases turn out to be only words.

Mr. Miller loses his temper almost daily, and his outbursts and reactions are not equivalent to the possible error. His mood and views can change almost from hour to hour. This fact causes a situation where we feel uncertain when facing him and consequently are reluctant to do so. Regarding human relationships, his behavior is not acceptable, especially for a manager.

The extent of the experience of this varies within the group due to our location. Some of us are seldom in the office.

Secondly, we have experienced clearly that he has various means of suppressing and discouraging people within the organization.

The new "victim" now is our Sales Manager, Mr. Johansson. Because he is our boss, it is obvious that we regret such a situation, which to a considerable extent influences our working conditions.

There are also other victims among us. It is indeed very difficult to carry through what is stated in our job descriptions.

We feel terribly sorry and wonder how it can be possible for one person almost to ruin a whole organization.

If this group consisted of people less mature, many of us would have left Computex Corporation already. So far only one has left the company due to the above reasons.

From September 1, two new Sales Representatives are joining the company. We regret very much that new employees get their first contact with the company under the present circumstances. An immediate action is therefore required.

It is not our objective to get rid of Mr. Miller as General Manager. Without going into details, we are thankful for what he has done to the company from a business point of view. If he could control his mood, show some respect for his colleagues, keep words, and stick to plans, we believe that we can succeed under his leadership.

We are fully aware of the seriousness of contacting you, and we have been in doubt whether or not to contact you directly before talking to Mr. Miller.

After serious discussions and considerations, we have reached the conclusion that a problem of this nature unfortunately cannot be solved without some sort of action from the superior. If possible, direct confrontation must be avoided. It can only make things worse.

We are hoping for a positive solution.

Six of Your Sales Representatives in Sweden

Peter Jones let out a long sigh as he gazed over the letter from Sweden. "What do I do now?" he thought, and began to reflect on the problem. He wondered who was right and who was wrong in this squabble, and he questioned whether he would ever get all the information necessary to make a wise decision. He didn't know much about the Swedes, and was unsure whether this was strictly a work problem or a "cross-cultural" problem. "How can I tease those two issues apart?" he asked himself, as he locked his office and made his way down the hallway to the elevator.

As Peter pulled out of the parking garage and onto the street, he began to devise a plan to deal with the problem. "This will be a test of my conflict management skills," he thought. "No doubt about it!" As he merged into the freeway traffic from the on-ramp and began his commute home, he began to wish that he had never sent Miller to Sweden in the first place. "But would Gonzalez or Harris have done any better? Would I have done any better?" Few answers seemed to come to him as he plodded along in the bumper-to-bumper traffic in Interstate 440.

Case Question

You are Peter. How would you deal with this problem now? What should have been done differently in the first place?

Communicating across Cultures

Outline

**Opening Profile: Oriental Poker Face:
Eastern Deception or Western Inscrutability?**

Among many English expressions that are likely to offend those of us whose ancestry may be traced to the Far East, two stand out quite menacingly for me: "Oriental poker face" and "idiotic Asian smile." The former refers to the supposedly inscrutable nature of a facial expression that apparently reflects no particular state of mind, while the latter pokes fun at a face fixed with a perpetually friendly smile. Westerners' perplexity, when faced with either, arises from the impression that these two diametrically opposed masquerading strategies prevent them from extracting useful information—the type of information that at least they could process with a reasonable measure of confidence—about the feelings of the person before them. An Asian face that projects no signs of emotion, then, seems to most westerners nothing but a facade. It does not matter whether that face wears an unsightly scowl or a shining ray; a facial expression they cannot interpret poses a genuine threat.

Compassionate and sympathetic to their perplexity as I may be, I am also insulted by the Western insensitivity to the significant roles that subtle signs play in Asian cultures. Every culture has its unique modus operandi for communication. Western culture, for example, apparently emphasizes the importance of direct communication. Not only are the communicators taught to look directly at each other when they convey a message, but they are also encouraged to come right to the point of the message. Making bold statements or asking frank questions in a less than diplomatic manner (i.e., "That was really a very stupid thing to do!" or "Are you interested in me?") is rarely construed as rude or indiscreet. Even embarrassingly blunt questions such as "Senator Hart, have you ever had sexual intercourse with anyone other than your wife?" are tolerated most of the time. Asians, on the other hand, find this direct communicative style quite unnerving. In many social interaction situations, they avoid direct eye contact. They "see" each other without necessarily looking directly at each other, and they gather information about inner states of mind without asking even the most discreet or understated questions. Many times they talk around the main topic, and, yet, they succeed remarkably well in understanding one another's position. (At least they believe they have developed a reasonably clear understanding.)

To a great extent, Asian communication is listening-centered; the ability to listen (and a special talent for detecting various communicative cues) is treated as equally important as, if not more important than, the ability to speak. This contrasts clearly with the American style of communication that puts the utmost emphasis on verbal expression; the speaker carries most of the burden for ensuring that everyone understands his or her message. An Asian listener, however, is prone to blame himself or herself for failing to reach a comprehensive understanding from the few words and gestures performed by the speaker. With this heavier burden placed on the listener, an Asian speaker does not feel obliged to send clearly discernible message cues (at least not nearly so much as he or she is obliged to do in American cultural contexts). Not obligated to express themselves without interruption, Asians use silence as a tool in communication. Silence, by most Western conventions, represents discontinuity of communication and creates a feeling of discomfort and anxiety. In the Orient, however, silence is not only comfortably tolerated but is considered a desirable form of expression. Far from being a sign of displeasure or animosity, it serves as an integral part of the communication process, used for reflecting on messages previously exchanged and for carefully crafting thoughts before uttering them.

It is not outlandish at all, then, for Asians to view Americans as unnecessarily talkative and lacking in the ability to listen. For the Asian, it is the American who projects a mask of confidence by being overly expressive both verbally and nonverbally. Since the American style of communication places less emphasis on the act of listening than on speaking, Asians suspect that their American counterparts fail to pick up subtle and astute communicative signs in conversation. To a cultural outlook untrained in reading those signs, an inscrutable face represents no more than a menacing or amusing mask.

SOURCE: Dr. Jin Kim, State University of New York–Plattsburgh. Copyright © 1995 by Dr. Jin Kim. Used with permission of Dr. Kim.

Cultural communications are deeper and more complex than spoken or written messages. The essence of effective cross-cultural communication has more to do with releasing the right responses than with sending the "right" messages.

—HALL AND HALL[1]

> Multi-local online strategy . . . is about meeting global business objectives by tuning into the cultural dynamics of their local markets.
>
> —"THINK GLOBALLY, INTERACT LOCALLY,"
> NEW MEDIA AGE, SEPTEMBER 9, 1999[2]

As the Opening Profile suggests, communication is a critical factor in the cross-cultural management issues discussed in this book, particularly those of an interpersonal nature, involving motivation, leadership, group interactions, and negotiation. Culture is conveyed and perpetuated through communication in one form or another. Culture and communication are so intricately intertwined that they are, essentially, synonymous.[3] By understanding this relationship, managers can move toward constructive intercultural management.

Communication, whether in the form of writing, talking, listening, or through the Internet, is an inherent part of a manager's role and takes up the majority of the manager's time on the job. Studies by Mintzberg demonstrate the importance of oral communication; he found that most managers spend between 50 and 90 percent of their time talking to people.[4] The ability of a manager to communicate effectively across cultural boundaries will largely determine the success of international business transactions or the output of a culturally diverse workforce. It is useful, then, to break down the elements involved in the communication process, both to understand the cross-cultural issues at stake and to maximize the process.

THE COMMUNICATION PROCESS

The term **communication** describes the process of sharing meaning by transmitting messages through media such as words, behavior, or material artifacts. Managers communicate to coordinate activities, to disseminate information, to motivate people, and to negotiate future plans. It is of vital importance, then, that the receiver interprets the meaning of a particular communication in the way the sender intended. Unfortunately, the communication process, as shown in Exhibit 4-1, involves stages during which the meaning can be distorted. Anything that serves to undermine the communication of the intended meaning is typically referred to as **noise**.

The primary cause of noise stems from the fact that the sender and the receiver each exist in a unique, private world called her or his life space. The context of that private world, based largely on culture, experience, relations, values, and so forth, determines the interpretation of meaning in communication. People filter, or selectively understand, messages consistent with their own expectations and perceptions of reality and their values and norms of behavior. The more dissimilar the cultures of those involved, the more likelihood of misinterpretation. In this way, as Samovar, Porter, and Jain state, cultural factors pervade the communication process:

> Culture not only dictates who talks with whom, about what, and how the communication proceeds, it also helps to determine how people encode messages, the meanings they have for messages, and the conditions and circumstances under which various messages may or may not be sent, noticed, or interpreted. In fact, our entire repertory of communicative behaviors is dependent largely on the culture in which we have been raised. Culture, consequently, is the foundation of communication. And, when cultures vary, communication practices also vary.[5]

Exhibit 4-1   The Communication Process

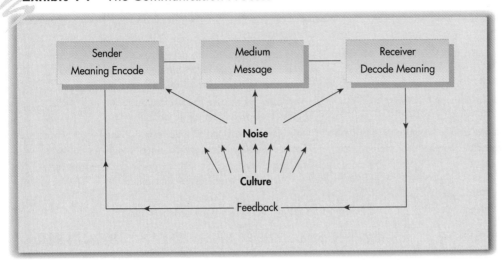

Communication, therefore, is a complex process of linking up or sharing the perceptual fields of sender and receiver; the perceptive sender builds a bridge to the life space of the receiver.[6] After the receiver interprets the message and draws a conclusion about what the sender meant, he or she will, in most cases, encode and send back a response, making communication a circular process.

The communication process is rapidly changing, however, as a result of technological developments, therefore propelling global business forward at a phenomenal growth rate. These changes are discussed later in this chapter.

Cultural Noise in the Communication Process

In Japanese there are several words for "I" and several words for "you" but their use depends on the relationship between the speaker and the other person. In short, there is no "I" by itself; the "I" depends on the relationship.

—H. C. TRIANDIS, IN *THE BLACKWELL HANDBOOK OF CROSS-CULTURAL MANAGEMENT*, M. GANNON AND K. NEWMAN EDS. (OXFORD, ENGLAND: BLACKWELL PUBLISHERS, 2002).

Because our focus here is on effective cross-cultural communication, we need to understand what cultural variables cause noise in the communication process. This knowledge of **cultural noise** will enable us to take steps to minimize that noise and so improve communication.

When a member of one culture sends a message to a member of another culture, **intercultural communication** takes place. The message contains the meaning intended by the encoder. When it reaches the receiver, however, it undergoes a transformation in which the influence of the decoder's culture becomes part of the meaning.[7] Let's take a look at an example (Exhibit 4-2) of intercultural communication in which the meaning got all mixed up. Note how the attribution of behavior differs for each participant.

Exhibit 4-2   Cultural Noise in International Communication

Behavior	Attribution
American: "How long will it take you to finish this report?"	*American*: I asked him to participate. *Greek*: His behavior makes no sense. He is the boss. Why doesn't he tell me?
Greek: "I don't know. How long should it take?"	*American*: He refuses to take responsibility. *Greek*: I asked him for an order.
American: "You are in the best position to analyze time requirements."	*American*: I press him to take responsibility for his actions. *Greek*: What nonsense: I'd better give him an answer.
Greek: "10 days."	*American*: He lacks the ability to estimate time; this time estimate is totally inadequate.
American: "Take 15. Is it agreed? You will do it in 15 days?"	*American*: I offer a contract. *Greek*: These are my orders: 15 days.

In fact, the report needed 30 days of regular work. So the Greek worked day and night, but at the end of the 15th day, he still needed to do one more day's work.

American: "Where is the report?"	*American*: I am making sure he fulfills his contract. *Greek*: He is asking for the report.
Greek: "It will be ready tomorrow."	(Both attribute that it is not ready.)
American:"But we agreed it would be ready today."	*American*: I must teach him to fulfill a contract. *Greek*: The stupid, incompetent boss! Not only did he give me the wrong orders, but he doesn't even appreciate that I did a 30-day job in 16 days.
The Greek hands in his resignation.	The American is surprised. *Greek*: I can't work for such a man.

SOURCE: Adapted from H. C. Triandis, *Interpersonal Behavior* (Monterey, Calif., Brooks/Cole, 1997), 248; reported in Simcha Ronen, *Comparative and Multinational Management* (New York: John Wiley and Sons, 1986), 101–102.

Attribution is the process in which people look for the explanation of another person's behavior. When they realize that they do not understand another, they tend, say Hall and Hall, to blame their confusion on the other's "stupidity, deceit, or craziness."[8]

In the situation depicted in Exhibit 4-2, the Greek employee gets frustrated and resigns after experiencing communication problems with his American boss. How could this outcome have been avoided? We do not have much information about the people or the context of the situation, but we can look at some of the variables that might have been involved and use them as a basis for analysis.

THE CULTURE–COMMUNICATION LINK

Trust in Communication

The key ingredient in a successful alliance is trust.

—JAMES R. HOUGHTON, FORMER CHAIRMAN OF CORNING, INC.,
ORGANIZATIONAL DYNAMICS, SPRING 2001

Effective communication, and therefore collaboration in alliances across national boundaries, depends on the informal understandings among the parties which are based on the trust that has developed between them. However, the meaning of trust and how it is developed and communicated vary across societies. In China and Japan, for example, business transactions are based on networks of long-standing relationships based on trust, rather than the formal contracts and arms-length relationships typical of the United States. When there is trust between parties there is implicit understanding behind communications. This understanding has numerous benefits in business, including encouraging them to overlook cultural differences and minimize problems. It allows them to adjust to unforeseen circumstances with less conflict than would be the case with formal contracts, and it facilitates open communication in exchanging ideas and information.[9] From his research on trust in global collaboration, John Child suggests the following guidelines for cultivating trust:

> ➤ Create a clear and calculated basis for mutual benefit. There must be realistic commitments and good intentions to honor them.
> ➤ Improve predictability: strive to resolve conflicts and keep communication open.
> ➤ Develop mutual bonding through regular socializing and friendly contact.[10]

What can managers anticipate with regard to the level of trust in communications with people in other countries? If trust is based on how trustworthy we consider a person to be, then it must vary according to that society's expectations about whether that culture supports the norms and values that predispose people to behave credibly and benevolently. Are there differences across societies in those expectations of trust? Research by the Wold Values Study Group of 90,000 people in 45 societies provides some insight on cultural values regarding predisposition to trust.[11] Exhibit 4-3 shows the percentage of respondents in each society who responded that "most people can be trusted." As you can see, the Nordic countries and China had the highest predisposition to trust, while Brazil, Turkey, Romania, Slovenia, and Latvia had the lowest.

The GLOBE Project

Results from the GLOBE research on culture, discussed in Chapter 3, provide some insight into culturally appropriate communication styles and expectations for the manager to use abroad. GLOBE researchers Javidan and House make the following observations.[12] For people in societies that ranked high on performance orientation, for example, the United States, presenting objective information in a direct and explicit way is an important and expected manner of communication; this compares with people in Russia or Greece—which ranked low on performance-orientation—for whom hard facts and figures are not readily available or taken seriously. In those cases, a more indirect approach is preferred. People from countries ranking low on assertiveness, such as Sweden, also recoil from explicitness; their preference is for much two-way discourse and friendly relationships.

People ranking high on the "humane" dimension, such as those from Ireland and the Philippines, make avoiding conflict a priority and tend to communicate with the goal of being supportive of people rather than of achieving objective end results. This compares to people from France and Spain whose agenda is achievement of goals.

The foregoing has provided examples of how to draw implications for appropriate communication styles from the research findings on cultural differences across

Exhibit 4-3   Levels of General Trust in People

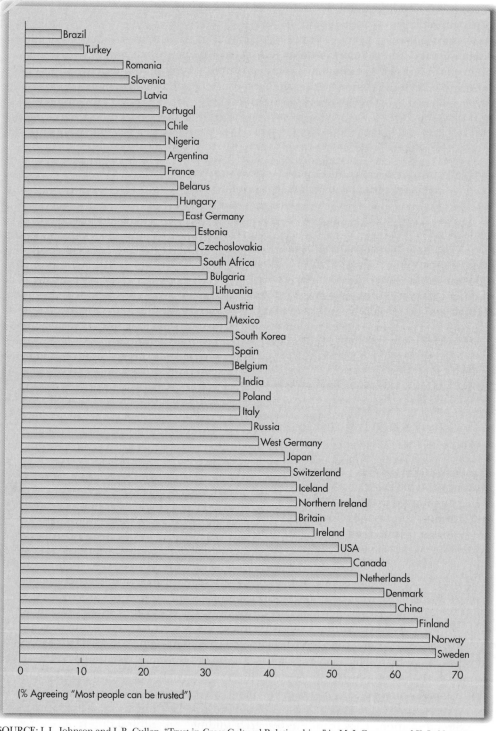

(% Agreeing "Most people can be trusted")

SOURCE: J. L. Johnson and J. B. Cullen, "Trust in Cross-Cultural Relationships," in M. J. Gannon and K. L. Newman, *The Blackwell Handbook of Cross-Cultural Management* (Oxford, England: Blackwell Publishers, 2002), p. 349.

societies. Astute global managers have learned that culture and communication are inextricably linked and that they should prepare themselves accordingly. Most will also suggest that you watch and listen carefully to how your hosts are communicating and to follow their lead.

Cultural Variables in the Communication Process

On a different level, it is also useful to be aware of cultural variables that can affect the communication process by influencing a person's perceptions; some of these variables have been identified by Samovar and Porter and discussed by Harris and Moran, Ronen, and others.[13] These variables are as follows: attitudes, social organization, thought patterns, roles, language (spoken or written), nonverbal communication (including kinesic behavior, proxemics, paralanguage, and object language), and time. Although we discuss these variables separately, their effects are interdependent and inseparable, or, as Hecht, Andersen, and Ribeau put it: "Encoders and decoders process nonverbal cues as a conceptual, multichanneled gestalt."[14]

Attitudes   We all know that our attitudes underlie the way we behave and communicate and the way we interpret messages from other people. Ethnocentric attitudes are a particular source of noise in cross-cultural communication. In the incident described in Exhibit 4-2, both the American and the Greek are clearly attempting to interpret and convey meaning based on their own experiences of that kind of transaction. The American is probably guilty of stereotyping the Greek employee by quickly jumping to the conclusion that he is unwilling to take responsibility for the task and the scheduling.

This problem, stereotyping, occurs when a person assumes that every member of a society or subculture has the same characteristics or traits. Stereotyping is a common cause of misunderstanding in intercultural communication. It is an arbitrary, lazy, and often destructive way to find out about people. Astute managers are aware of the dangers of cultural stereotyping and deal with each person as an individual with whom they may form a unique relationship.

Social Organization   Our perceptions can be influenced by differences in values, approach, or priorities relative to the kind of social organizations to which we belong. These organizations may be based on one's nation, tribe, or religious sect, or they may consist of the members of a certain profession. Examples of such organizations include the Academy of Management or the UAW (United Auto Workers).[15]

Thought Patterns   The logical progression of reasoning varies widely around the world and greatly affects the communication process. Managers cannot assume that others use the same reasoning processes, as illustrated by the experience of a Canadian expatriate in Thailand:

> While in Thailand a Canadian expatriate's car was hit by a Thai motorist who had crossed over the double line while passing another vehicle. After failing to establish that the fault lay with the Thai driver, the Canadian flagged down a policeman. After several minutes of seemingly futile discussion, the Canadian pointed out the double line in the middle of the road and asked the policeman directly, "What do these lines signify?" The policeman replied, "They indicate the center of the road and are there so

I can establish just how far the accident is from that point." The Canadian was silent. It had never occurred to him that the double line might not mean "no passing allowed.[16]

In the Exhibit 4-2 scenario, perhaps the American did not realize that the Greek employee had a different rationale for his time estimate for the job. Because the Greek was not used to having to estimate schedules, he just took a guess, which he felt he had been forced to do.

Roles   Societies differ considerably in their perception of a manager's role. Much of the difference is attributable to their perception of who should make the decisions and who has responsibility for what. In our example, the American assumes that his role as manager is to delegate responsibility, to foster autonomy, and to practice participative management. He is prescribing the role of the employee without any consideration of whether the employee will understand that role. The Greek's frame of reference leads him to think that the manager is the boss and should give the order about when to have the job completed. He interprets the American's behavior as breaking that frame of reference, and therefore he feels that the boss is "stupid and incompetent" for giving him the wrong order and for not recognizing and appreciating his accomplishment. The manager should have considered what behaviors Greek workers would expect of him and then either played that role or discussed the situation carefully, in a training mode.

Language   Spoken or written language, of course, is a frequent cause of miscommunication, stemming from a person's inability to speak the local language, a poor or too-literal translation, a speaker's failure to explain idioms, or a person missing the meaning conveyed through body language or certain symbols. Even among countries that share the same language, there can be problems in the subtleties and nuances inherent in the use of the language, as noted by George Bernard Shaw: "Britain and America are two nations separated by a common language." This problem can exist even within the same country among subcultures or subgroups.[17]

Many international executives tell stories about lost business deals or lost sales because of communication blunders:

> When Pepsi Cola's slogan "Come Alive with Pepsi" was introduced in Germany, the company learned that the literal German translation of "come alive" is "come out of the grave."
> A U.S. airline found a lack of demand for its "rendezvous lounges" on its Boeing 747s. They later learned that "rendezvous" in Portuguese refers to a room that is rented for prostitution.[18]

More than just conveying objective information, language also conveys cultural and social understandings from one generation to the next.[19] Examples of how language reflects what is important in a society include the 6,000 different Arabic words used to describe camels and their parts and the 50 or more classifications of snow used by the Inuit Eskimos.

Inasmuch as language conveys culture, technology, and priorities, it also serves to separate and perpetuate subcultures. In India, 14 official and many unofficial languages are used, and over 800 languages are spoken on the African continent.

Because of increasing workforce diversity around the world, the international business manager will have to deal with a medley of languages. For example, assembly-line workers at the Ford plant in Cologne speak Turkish and Spanish as well as German. In Malaysia, Indonesia, and Thailand, many of the buyers and traders are Chinese. Not all Arabs speak Arabic; in Tunisia and Lebanon, for example, French is the commercial language.[20]

International managers need either a good command of the local language or competent interpreters. The task of accurate translation to bridge cultural gaps is fraught with difficulties, as Schermerhorn discovered in his study of 153 Hong Kong Chinese bilinguals. He found a considerable difference in interpretation and response according to whether the medium used was Chinese or English, even after many experts were involved in the translation process.[21]

Even the direct translation of specific words does not guarantee the congruence of their meaning, as with the word "yes" used by Asians, which usually means only that they have heard you, and, often, that they are too polite to disagree. The Chinese, for example, through years of political control, have built into their communication culture a cautionary stance to avoid persecution by professing agreement with whatever opinion was held by the person questioning them.[22]

Politeness and a desire to say only what the listener wants to hear create noise in the communication process in much of the world. Often, even a clear translation does not help a person to understand what is meant because the encoding process has obscured the true message. With the poetic Arab language—replete with exaggeration, elaboration, and repetition—meaning is attributed more to how something is said rather than what is said.

In our situation with the American supervisor and Greek employee, it is highly likely that the American could have picked up some cues from the employee's body language, which probably implied problems with the interpretation of meaning. Let's now look at how body language may have created noise in this case.

Nonverbal Communication   Behavior that communicates without words (although it often is accompanied by words) is called **nonverbal communication**. People will usually believe what they see over what they hear—hence the expression, "a picture is worth a thousand words." Studies show that these subtle messages account for between 65 and 93 percent of interpreted communication.[23] Even minor variations in body language, speech rhythms, and punctuality, for example, often cause mistrust and misperception of the situation among cross-national parties.[24] The media for such nonverbal communication can be categorized into four types: (1) kinesic behavior, (2) proxemics, (3) paralanguage, and (4) object language.

The term **kinesic behavior** refers to body movements—posture, gestures, facial expressions, and eye contact. Although such actions may be universal, their meaning often is not. Because kinesic systems of meaning are culturally specific and learned, they cannot be generalized across cultures. Most people in the West would not correctly interpret many Chinese facial expressions; sticking out the tongue expresses surprise, a widening of the eyes shows anger, and scratching the ears and cheeks indicates happiness.[25] Research has shown for some time, however, that most people worldwide can recognize displays of the basic emotions of anger, disgust, fear, happiness, sadness, surprise, and contempt.[26]

Many businesspeople and visitors react negatively to what they feel are inappropriate facial expressions, without understanding the cultural meaning behind them.

In his studies of cross-cultural negotiations, Graham observed that the Japanese feel uncomfortable when faced with the Americans' eye-to-eye posture. They are taught since childhood to bow their heads out of humility, whereas the automatic response of Americans is "look at me when I'm talking to you!"[27]

Subtle differences in eye behavior (called oculesics) can throw off a communication badly if they are not understood. Eye behavior includes differences not only in eye contact but also in the use of eyes to convey other messages, whether or not that involves mutual gaze. Edward T. Hall, author of the classic *The Silent Language*, explains the differences in eye contact between the British and the Americans. During speech, Americans will look straight at you, while the British keep your attention by looking away. They will then look at you when they have finished speaking, which signals that it is your turn to talk. The implicit rationale for this is that you can't interrupt people when they are not looking at you.[28]

It is helpful for American managers to be aware of the many cultural expectations regarding posture and how they may be interpreted. In Europe or Asia, a relaxed posture in business meetings may be taken as bad manners or the result of poor upbringing. In Korea you are expected to sit upright, with feet squarely on the floor, and to speak slowly, showing a blending of body and spirit.

Managers can also familiarize themselves with the many different interpretations of hand and finger signals around the world, some of which may even represent obscene gestures. Of course, we cannot expect to change all of our ingrained, natural kinesic behavior, but we can be aware of what it means to others. And we can learn to understand the kinesic behavior of others and the role it plays in their society, as well as how it can affect business transactions. Misunderstanding the meanings of body movements—or an ethnocentric attitude toward the "proper" behavior—can have negative repercussions, as illustrated in the Opening Profile of this chapter.

Proxemics deals with the influence of proximity and space on communication—both personal space and office space or layout. Americans expect office layout to provide private space for each person, and usually a larger and more private space as one goes up the hierarchy. In much of Asia, the custom is open office space, with people at all levels working and talking in close proximity to one another. Space communicates power in both Germany and the United States, evidenced by the desire for a corner office or one on the top floor. The importance of French officials, however, is made clear by a position in the middle of subordinates, communicating that they have a central position in an information network, where they can stay informed and in control.[29]

Do you ever feel vaguely uncomfortable and start slowly moving backward when someone is speaking to you? This is because that person is invading your "bubble"—your personal space. Personal space is culturally patterned, and foreign spatial cues are a common source of misinterpretation. When someone seems aloof or pushy, it often means that she or he is operating under subtly different spacial rules.

Hall and Hall suggest that cultural differences affect the programming of the senses and that space, perceived by all the senses, is regarded as a form of territory to be protected.[30] South Americans, Southern and Eastern Europeans, Indonesians, and Arabs are **high-contact cultures**, preferring to stand close, touch a great deal, and experience a "close" sensory involvement. On the other hand, North Americans, Asians, and Northern Europeans are **low-contact cultures** and prefer much less sensory involvement, standing further apart and touching far less. They have a "distant" style of body language.[31]

Interestingly, high-contact cultures are mostly located in warmer climates, and low-contact cultures in cooler climates. Americans are relatively nontouching, automatically standing at a distance so that an outstretched arm will touch the other person's ear.[32] Standing any closer than that is regarded as invading intimate space. However, Americans and Canadians certainly expect a warm handshake and maybe a pat on the back for closer friends, though not the very warm double handshake of the Spaniards (clasping the forearm with the left hand). The Japanese, considerably less haptic (touching), do not shake hands; an initial greeting between a Japanese and a Spanish businessperson would be uncomfortable for both parties if they were untrained in cultural haptics.

When considering high- and low-contact cultures, we can trace a correlation between Hofstede's cultural variables of individualism and collectivism and the types of kinesic and proxemic behaviors people display. Generally, people from individualistic cultures are more remote and distant, whereas those from collectivist cultures are interdependent—they tend to work, play, live, and sleep in close proximity.[33]

The term **paralanguage** refers to how something is said rather than the content—the rate of speech, the tone and inflection of voice, other noises, laughing, or yawning. The culturally aware manager learns how to interpret subtle differences in paralanguage, including silence. Silence is a powerful communicator. It may be a way of saying no, of being offended, or of waiting for more information to make a decision. There is considerable variation in the use of silence in meetings. While Americans get uncomfortable after 10 or 15 seconds of silence, Chinese prefer to think the situation over for 30 seconds before speaking. The typical scenario between Americans and Chinese, then, is that the American gets impatient, says something to break the silence, and offends the Chinese by interrupting his chain of thought and comfort level with the subject.[34] Graham, a researcher on international negotiations, taped a bargaining session held at Toyota's U.S. headquarters in California. The American executive had made a proposal to open a new production facility in Brazil and was waiting for a response from the three Japanese executives, who sat with lowered eyes and hands folded on the table. After about 30 seconds—an eternity to Americans, accustomed to a conversational response time of a few tenths of a second—the American blurted out that they were getting nowhere, and the meeting ended in a stalemate. More sensitivity to cultural differences in communication might have led him to wait longer or perhaps to prompt some further response through another polite question.[35]

The term **object language**, or **material culture**, refers to how we communicate through material artifacts, whether architecture, office design and furniture, clothing, cars, or cosmetics. Material culture communicates what people hold as important. In Mexico, a visiting international executive or salesperson is advised to take time out, before negotiating business, to show appreciation for the surrounding architecture, which is prized by Mexicans.

Time   Another variable that communicates culture is the way people regard and use time (discussed in Chapter 3). To Brazilians, relative punctuality communicates the level of importance of those involved. To Middle Easterners, time is something controlled by the will of Allah.

To initiate effective cross-cultural business interactions, managers should know the difference between **monochronic time systems** and **polychronic time systems** and how they affect communications. Hall and Hall explain that in monochronic cultures

(Switzerland, Germany, and the United States), time is experienced in a linear way, with a past, a present, and a future, and time is treated as something to be spent, saved, made up, or wasted. Classified and compartmentalized, time serves to order life. This attitude is a learned part of Western culture, probably starting with the Industrial Revolution. Monochronic people, found in individualistic cultures, generally concentrate on one thing at a time, adhere to time commitments, and are accustomed to short-term relationships.

In contrast, polychronic systems tolerate many things occurring simultaneously and emphasize involvement with people. Two Latin friends, for example, will put an important conversation ahead of being on time for a business meeting, thus communicating the priority of relationships over material systems. Polychronic people—Latin Americans, Arabs, and those from other collectivist cultures—may focus on several things at once, be highly distractible, and change plans often.[36]

The relationship between time and space also affects communication. Polychronic people, for example, are likely to hold open meetings, moving around and conducting transactions from one party to another, rather than compartmentalizing meeting topics, as do monochronic people.

We can discuss endless nuances and distinctions regarding cultural differences in nonverbal communication. The various forms are listed in Exhibit 4-4; wise intercultural managers will take careful account of the role that such differences might play.

What aspects of nonverbal communication might have created noise in the interactions between the American supervisor and the Greek employee in Exhibit 4-2? Undoubtedly, there were some cues in the kinesic behavior of each person that could have been picked up. It was the responsibility of the manager, in particular, to notice any indications from the Greek that could have prompted him to change his communication pattern or assumptions. Face-to-face communication permits the sender of the message to get immediate feedback, verbal and nonverbal, and thus to have some idea as to how that message is being received and whether additional information is needed. What aspects of the Greek employee's kinesic behavior or paralanguage do you think might have been evident to a more culturally sensitive manager? Did both parties' sense of time affect the communication process?

Exhibit 4-4   Forms of Nonverbal Communication

- Facial expressions
- Body posture
- Gestures with hands, arms, head, etc.
- Interpersonal distance (proxemics)
- Touching, body contact
- Eye contact
- Clothing, cosmetics, hairstyles, jewelry
- Paralanguage (voice pitch and inflections, rate of speech, and silence)
- Color symbolism
- Attitude toward time and the use of time in business and social interactions
- Food symbolism and social use of meals

Context

A major differentiating factor that is a primary cause of noise in the communication process is that of **context**—which, as you will see, actually incorporates many of the variables just discussed The context in which the communication takes place affects the meaning and interpretation of the interaction. Cultures are known to be high- or low-context cultures, with a relative range in between.[37] In **high-context cultures** (Asia, the Middle East, Africa, and the Mediterranean), feelings and thoughts are not explicitly expressed; instead, one has to read between the lines and interpret meaning from one's general understanding. Two such high-context cultures are those of South Korea and Arab cultures. In such cultures, key information is embedded in the context rather than made explicit. People make assumptions about what the message means through their knowledge of the person or the surroundings. In these cultures, most communication takes place within a context of extensive information networks resulting from close personal relationships. In **low-context cultures** (Germany, Switzerland, Scandinavia, and North America), where personal and business relationships are more compartmentalized, communication media have to be more explicit. Feelings and thoughts are expressed in words, and information is more readily available.

In cross-cultural communication between high- and low-context people, a lack of understanding may preclude reaching a solution, and conflict may arise. Germans, for example, will expect considerable detailed information before making a business decision, whereas Arabs will base their decision more on knowledge of the people involved—the information is still there, but it is implicit.

People in high-context cultures expect others to understand unarticulated moods, subtle gestures, and environmental clues that people from low-context cultures simply do not process. Misinterpretation and misunderstanding often result.[38] People from high-context cultures perceive those from low-context cultures as too

Exhibit 4-5   Cultural Context and Its Effects on Communication

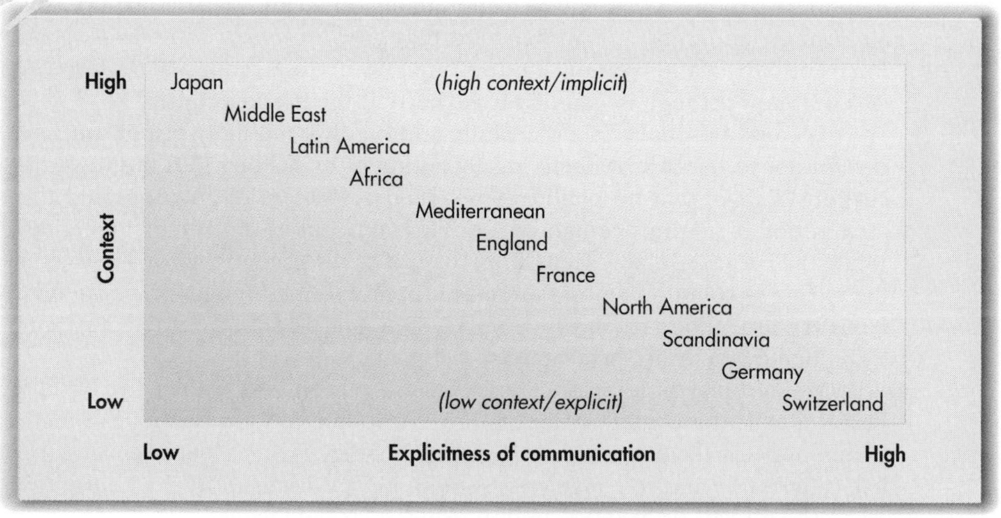

SOURCE: Based on information drawn from Edward T. Hall and M. R. Hall, *Understanding Cultural Differences* (Yarmouth, ME: Intercultural Press, 1990); and Martin Rosch, "Communications: Focal Point of Culture," *Management International Review* 27, no. 4 (1987): 60.

talkative, too obvious, and redundant. Those from low-context cultures perceive high-context people as nondisclosing, sneaky, and mysterious.[39] Research indicates, for example, that Americans find talkative people more attractive, whereas Koreans, high-context people, perceive less verbal people as more attractive. Finding the right balance between low- and high-context communication can be tricky, as Hall and Hall point out: "Too much information leads people to feel they are being talked down to; too little information can mystify them or make them feel left out."[40] Exhibit 4-5 shows the relative level of context in various countries.

The importance of understanding the role of context and nonverbal language to avoid misinterpretation is illustrated in the following section.

Comparative Management in Focus

Communicating with Arabs

In the Middle East, the meaning of a communication is implicit and inter-woven, and consequently much harder for Americans, accustomed to explicit and specific meanings, to understand.

Arabs are warm, emotional, and quick to explode: "sounding off" is regarded as a safety valve.[41] In fact, the Arabic language aptly communicates the Arabic culture, one of emotional extremes. The language contains the means for overexpression, many adjectives, words that allow for exaggeration, and metaphors to emphasize a position. What is said is often not as important as how it is said.[42] Eloquence and flowery speech are admired for their own sake, regardless of the content. Loud speech is used for dramatic effect.

At the core of Middle Eastern culture are friendship, honor, religion, and traditional hospitality. Family, friends, and connections are very important on all levels in the Middle East and will take precedence over business transactions. Arabs do business with people, not companies, and they make commitments to people, not contracts. A phone call to the right person can help to get around seemingly insurmountable obstacles. An Arab expects loyalty from friends, and it is understood that giving and receiving favors is an inherent part of the relationship; no one says no to a request for a favor. A lack of follow-through is assumed to be beyond the friend's control.[43]

Because hospitality is a way of life and highly symbolic, a visitor must be careful not to reject it by declining refreshment or rushing into business discussions. Part of that hospitality is the elaborate system of greetings and the long period of getting acquainted, perhaps taking up the entire first meeting. While the handshake may seem limp, the rest of the greeting is not. Kissing on the cheeks is common among men, as is handholding between male friends. However, any public display of intimacy between men and women is strictly forbidden by the Arab social code.

Women play little or no role in business or entertainment; the Middle East is a male-dominated society, and it is impolite to inquire about women. Other, nonverbal taboos include showing the soles of one's feet and using the left (unclean) hand to eat or pass something. In discussions, slouching in a seat or leaning against a wall communicates a lack of respect.

The Arab society also values honor. Harris and Moran explain: "Honor, social prestige, and a secure place in society are brought about when conformity is achieved. When one fails to conform, this is considered to be damning and leads to a degree of shame."[44] Shame results not from just doing something wrong, but from having others find out about that wrongdoing. Establishing a climate of honesty and trust is part of the sense of honor. Therefore, considerable tact is needed to avoid conveying any concern or doubt. Arabs tend to be quite introverted until a mutual trust is built, which takes a long time.[45]

In their nonverbal communication, most Arab countries are high-contact cultures. Arabs stand and sit closer and touch people of the same sex more than westerners. They do not have the same concept of "public" and "private" space, or as Hall puts it: "Not only is the sheer noise level much higher, but the piercing look of the eyes, the touch of the hands, and the mutual bathing in the warm moist breath during conversation represent stepped-up sensory inputs to a level which many Europeans find unbearably intense.[46] On the other hand, the distance preferred by North Americans may leave an Arab suspicious of intentions because of the lack of olfactory contact.[47]

The Muslim expression *bukra insha Allah*—"tomorrow if Allah wills"—explains much about the Arab culture and its approach to business transactions. A cultural clash typically occurs when an American tries to give an Arab a deadline. "'I am going to Damascus tomorrow morning and will have to have my car tonight,' is a sure way to get the mechanic to stop work," explains Hall, "because to give another person a deadline in this part of the world is to be rude, pushy, and demanding."[48] In such instances, the attitude toward time communicates as loudly as words.

In verbal interactions, managers need to be aware of different patterns of Arab thought and communication. Compared to the direct, linear fashion of American communication, Arabs tend to meander: they start with social talk, discuss business for a while, loop round to social and general issues, then back to business, and so on.[49] American impatience and insistence on sticking to the subject will "cut off their loops," triggering confusion and dysfunction.

Exhibit 4-6 illustrates some of the sources of noise that are likely to interfere in the communication process between Americans and Arabs.

For people doing business in the Middle East, the following are some useful guidelines for effective communication:

➤ Be patient. Recognize the Arab attitude toward time and hospitality—take time to develop friendship and trust, for these are prerequisites for any social or business transactions.

➤ Recognize that people and relationships matter more to Arabs than the job, company, or contract—conduct business personally, not by correspondence or telephone.

➤ Avoid expressing doubts or criticism when others are present—recognize the importance of honor and dignity to Arabs.

➤ Adapt to the norms of body language, flowery speech, and circuitous verbal patterns in the Middle East, and don't be impatient to "get to the point."

➤ Expect many interruptions in meetings, delays in schedules, and changes in plans.[50]

Exhibit 4-6   Miscommunication between Americans and Arabs Caused by Cross-Cultural Noise

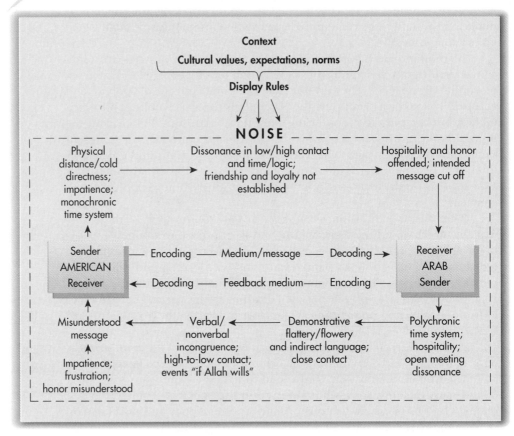

Communication Channels

In addition to the variables related to the sender and receiver of a message, the variables linked to the channel itself and the context of the message must be taken into consideration. These variables include fast or slow messages and information flows, as well as different types of media.

Information Systems   Communication in organizations varies according to where and how it originates, the channels and the speed at which it flows, whether it is formal or informal, and so forth. The type of organizational structure, the staffing policies, and the leadership style will affect the nature of an organization's information system.

As an international manager, it is useful to know where and how information originates and the speed at which it flows, both internally and externally. In centralized organizational structures, as in South America, most information originates from top managers. Workers take less responsibility to keep managers informed than in a typical company in the United States, where delegation results in information flowing from the staff to the managers. In a decision-making system where many people are involved, such as the *ringi* system of consensus decision making in Japan, there is a systematic pattern for information flow that the expatriate needs to understand.[51]

Context also affects information flow. In high-context cultures (such as in the Middle East), information spreads rapidly and freely because of the constant close contact and the implicit ties among people and organizations. Information flow is often informal. In low-context cultures (such as Germany or the United States), information is controlled and focused, and thus it does not flow so freely.[52] Compartmentalized roles and office layouts stifle information channels; information sources tend to be more formal.

It is crucial for an expatriate manager to find out how to tap into a firm's informal sources of information. In Japan, employees usually have a drink together on the way home from work, and this becomes an essential source of information. However, such communication networks are based on long-term relationships in Japan (and in other high-context cultures). The same information may not be readily available to "outsiders." A considerable barrier in Japan separates strangers from familiar friends, a situation that discourages communication.

Americans are more open and talk freely about almost anything, whereas Japanese will disclose little about their inner thoughts or private issues. Americans are willing to have a wide "public self," disclosing their inner reactions verbally and physically. In contrast, the Japanese prefer to keep their responses largely to their "private self." The Japanese expose only a small portion of their thoughts; they reduce, according to Barnlund, "the unpredictability and emotional intensity of personal encounters."[53] Barnlund depicts this difference diagrammatically, as shown in Exhibit 4-7, which illustrates the cultural clash between the public and private selves in intercultural communication between Americans and Japanese. The plus and minus signs indicate the areas of agreement or disagreement (respectively) resulting when each party forces its cultural norms of communication on the other. In the American style, the American's cultural norms of explicit communication impose on the Japanese by invading the person's private self. The Japanese style of implicit communication causes a negative reaction from the American because of what is perceived as too much formality and ambiguity, which wastes time.[54]

Cultural variables in information systems and context underlie the many differences in communication style between Japanese and Americans. Exhibit 4-8 shows some specific differences. The Japanese *ningensei* ("human beingness") style of communication refers to their preference for humanity, reciprocity, a receiver-orientation, and an underlying distrust of words and analytic logic.[55] The Japanese believe that true intentions are not readily revealed in words or contracts, but are in fact masked by them. In contrast to the typical American's verbal agility and explicitness, Japanese behaviors and communications are directed to defend and give face for everyone concerned; to do so, they avoid public disagreements at all costs. In cross-cultural negotiations this last point is essential.

The speed with which we try to use information systems is another key variable that needs attention to avoid misinterpretation and conflict. Americans expect to give and receive information very quickly and clearly, moving through details and stages in a linear fashion to the conclusion. They usually use various media for fast messages—letters giving all the facts and plans up front, faxes, and familiar relationships. In contrast, the French use the slower message channels of deep relationships, culture, and sometimes mediators to exchange information. A French written communication will

Exhibit 4-7   Intercultural Communication Conflicts
between Americans and Japanese

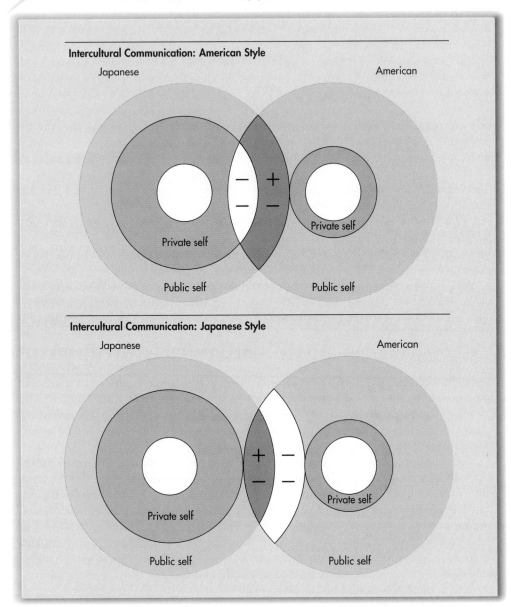

SOURCE: Dean C. Barnlund, "Public and Private Self in Communicating with Japan," *Business Horizons* (March–April 1989): 37.

Exhibit 4-8   Difference between Japanese and American Communication Styles

Japanese *Ningensei* Style of Communication	U.S. Adversarial Style of Communication
1. Indirect verbal and nonverbal communication	1. More direct verbal and nonverbal communication
2. Relationship communication	2. More task communication
3. Discourages confrontational strategies	3. Confrontational strategies more acceptable
4. Strategically ambiguous communication	4. Prefers more to-the-point communication
5. Delayed feedback	5. More immediate feedback
6. Patient, longer term negotiators	6. Shorter term negotiators
7. Uses fewer words	7. Favors verbosity
8. Distrustful of skillful verbal communicators	8. Exalts verbal eloquence
9. Group orientation	9. More individualistic orientation
10. Cautious, tentative	10. More assertive, self-assured
11. Complementary communicators	11. More publicly critical communication
12. Softer, heartlike logic	12. Harder, analytic logic preferred
13. Sympathetic, empathetic, complex use of pathos	13. Favors logos, reason
14. Expresses and decodes complex relational strategies and nuances	14. Expresses and decodes complex logos, cognitive nuances
15. Avoids decision making in public	15. Frequent decision making in public
16. Makes decisions in private venues, away from public eye	16. Frequent decision in public at negotiating tables
17. Decisions via *ringi* and *nemawashi* (complete consensus process)	17. Decisions by majority rule and public compromise is more commonplace
18. Uses go-betweens for decision making	18. More extensive use of direct person-to-person, player-to-player interaction for decisions
19. Understatement and hesitation in verbal and nonverbal communication	19. May publicly speak in superlatives, exaggerations, nonverbal projection
20. Uses qualifiers, tentative, humility as communicator	20. Favors fewer qualifiers, more ego-centered
21. Receiver/listening-centered	21. More speaker- and message-centered
22. Inferred meanings, looks beyond words to nuances, nonverbal communication	22. More face-value meaning, more denotative
23. Shy, reserved communicators	23. More publicly self-assertive
24. Distaste for purely business transactions	24. Prefers to "get down to business" or "nitty gritty"
25 Mixes business and social communication	25. Tends to keep business negotiating more separated from social communication
26. Utilizes *matomari* or "hints" for achieving group adjustment and saving face in negotiating	26. More directly verbalizes management's preference at negotiating tables
27. Practices *haragei* or belly logic and communication	27. Practices more linear, discursive, analytical logic; greater reverence for cognitive than for affective

SOURCE: A Goldman, "The Centrality of 'Ningensei' to Japanese Negotiating and Interpersonal Relationships: Implications for U.S. Japanese Communication," *International Journal of Intercultural Relations* 18, no. 1 (Winter 1994).

be tentative, with subsequent letters slowly building up to a new proposal. The French preference for written communication, even for informal interactions, echoes the formality of their relationships—and results in a slowing down of message transmission that often seems unnecessary to Americans. Jean-Louis Reynal, a plant manager at Citroen, explains that "it wouldn't be too much of an exaggeration to say that, until they are written, until they are entrusted to the blackboard, the notepad, or the flip chart, ideas have no reality for the French manager. You could even say that writing is an indispensable aid to 'being' for us."[56]

In short, it behooves Americans to realize that, because most of the world exchanges information through slower message media, it is wise to schedule more time for transactions, develop patience, and learn to get at needed information in more subtle ways—after building rapport and taking time to observe the local system for exchanging information.

We have seen that cross-cultural misinterpretation can result from noise in the actual transmission of the message—the choice or speed of media. Interpreting the meaning of a message can thus be as much a function of the transmission channel (or medium) as it is of examining the message itself.

INFORMATION TECHNOLOGY— GOING GLOBAL AND ACTING LOCAL

All information is local; IT systems can connect every corner of the globe, but IT managers are learning they have to pay attention to regional differences.[57]
—*COMPUTERWORLD*, APRIL 10, 2000

Deploying B2B e-commerce technology [globally] . . . becomes exponentially more difficult because systems must address concerns not germane to domestic networks, such as language translation, currency conversion and even cultural differences.[58]
—*INTERNET WEEK*, OCTOBER 9, 2000

Using the Internet as a global medium for communication has enabled companies of all sizes to quickly develop a presence in many markets around the world—and in fact has enabled them to "go global." However, their global reach cannot alone translate into global business. Those companies are learning that they have to adapt their e-commerce and their enterprise resource planning (ERP) applications to regional idiosyncrasies beyond translation or content management issues; even asking for a name or e-mail address can incur resistance in many countries where people do not like to give out personal information.[59] While communication over the Internet is clearly not as personal as face-to-face cross-cultural communication, those transactions must still be regionalized and personalized to adjust to differences in language, culture, local laws, and business models, as well as differences in the level of development in the local telecommunications infrastructure. And yet, if the Internet is a global medium for communication, why do so many U.S. companies treat the Web as a U.S.-centric phenomenon? Giving preference to some geographic regions, languages, and cultures is "a short-sighted business decision that will result in diminished brand equity, market share, profits and global leadership."[60] With an annual predicted growth rate of 70 percent in non-English language sites and usage, this would put English-language sites in the minority somewhere around 2002–2003.[61]

It seems essential, then, that a global on-line strategy must also be multilocal. The impersonal nature of the Web must somehow be adapted to local cultures in order to establish relationships and create customer loyalty. Effective technological communication requires even more cultural sensitivity than face-to-face communication because of the inability to assess reactions and get feedback, or even to retain contact in many cases. It is still people, after all, who respond to and interact with other people through the medium of the Internet, and those people interpret and respond according to their own languages and cultures as well as local business practices and expectations. In Europe, for example, there are significant differences in business cultures and e-business technology, which have slowed e-business progress there. However, some companies are making progress in pan-European integration services, such as *leEurope*, which aims to cross language, currency and cultural barriers. *leEurope* is building a set of services "to help companies tie their back-end e-business systems together across European boundaries through a series of mergers involving regional e-business integrators in more than a dozen countries."[62]

One global company that has successfully added a multilocal on-line strategy to its long-established bricks and mortar facilities is Manheim Auctions, Inc., featured in the accompanying E-Biz Box.

MANAGING CROSS-CULTURAL COMMUNICATION

Steps toward effective intercultural communication include the development of cultural sensitivity, careful encoding, selective transmission, careful decoding, and appropriate followup actions.

Developing Cultural Sensitivity

When acting as a sender, a manager must make it a point to know the receiver and to encode the message in a form that will most likely be understood as intended. On the manager's part, this requires an awareness of his or her own cultural baggage and how it affects the communication process. In other words, what kinds of behaviors does the message imply, and how will they be perceived by the receiver? The way to anticipate the most likely meaning that the receiver will attach to the message is to internalize honest cultural empathy with that person. What is the cultural background—the societal, economic, and organizational context—in which this communication is taking place? What are this person's expectations regarding the situation, what are the two parties' relative positions, and what might develop from this communication? What kinds of transactions and behaviors is this person used to? Cultural sensitivity (discussed in Chapter 3) is really just a matter of understanding the other person, the context. and how the person will respond to the context.

Careful Encoding

In translating his or her intended meaning into symbols for cross-cultural communication, the sender must use words, pictures, or gestures that are appropriate to the receiver's frame of reference. Of course, language training is invaluable, but senders should also avoid idioms and regional sayings (such as "go fly a kite" or "foot the bill") in a translation, or even in English when speaking to a non-American who knows little English.

E-Biz Box

MANHEIM AUCTIONS, INC., ADDS LOCALIZED B2B SYSTEM TO ITS GLOBAL OPERATIONS

With headquarters in Atlanta, Georgia, Manheim Auctions is the largest and highest volume wholesale automobile auction company in the world. The company operates more than 115 auction facilities worldwide, and employs over 30,000 people. Manheim remarkets vehicles for wholesale consignors. These sellers include car dealers, manufacturers, rental car operators, fleet/lease companies and financial institutions. The buyers of the vehicles are licensed franchise and independent auto dealers. Thousands of dealers conduct business using Manheim's global network, which shares a massive database of vehicle information, including prices, histories and digital photos—through www.Manheimauctions.com and www.Autotrader.com , as well as localized addresses.[63]

Mainheim has had its share of challenges as it attempts to localize its "cyberlots" while expanding globally. New partners in the United Kingdom and Australia, for example, unknown to Manheim, had lines of business that Manheim's on-line site did not support. The company also had to make adjustments for different measurement standards, such as kilometers, and different terminology for car parts, such as a "boot" in the United Kingdom instead of "trunk."[64] In addition, with feedback from its Australian acquisition partner, Manheim made changes to its corporate logo, shown here. Those partners down under naturally felt left out when they saw that the globe logo showed only North and South America.[65]

Exhibit 4-9

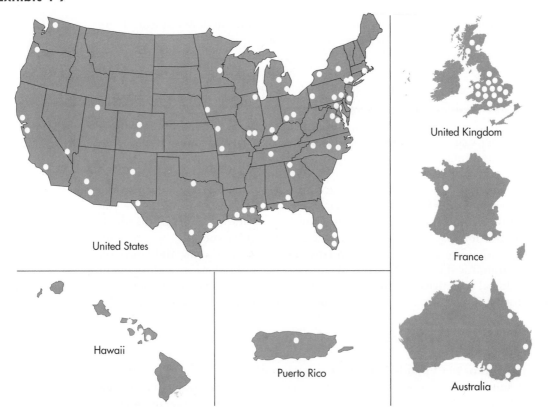

*With more than **115** locations worldwide, Manheim's global network shares a massive database of vehicle information including prices, histories, and digital photos.*

SOURCE: www.manheimauctions.com/HTML/history.html.

Literal translation, then, is a limited answer to language differences. Even among English-speaking countries, words may have different meanings—as experienced by a U.S. banker in Australia after a business dinner. To show appreciation, he said he was full (interpreted by his hosts as drunk); as the silence spread at the table, he tried to correct himself by saying he was stuffed (a word used locally only in a sexual context).[66] Ways to avoid such problems are to speak slowly and clearly, avoid long sentences and colloquial expressions, and explain things in several different ways and through several media, if possible.[67] However, even though English is in common use around the world for business transactions, the manager's efforts to speak the local language will greatly improve the climate. Sometimes people from other cultures resent the assumption by English-speaking executives that everyone else will speak English.

Language translation is only part of the encoding process; the message also is expressed in nonverbal language. In the encoding process, the sender must ensure congruence between the nonverbal and the verbal message. In encoding a message, therefore, it is useful to be as objective as possible and not to rely on personal interpretations. To further clarify their message, managers can hand out written summaries of verbal presentations and use visual aids—graphs or pictures. A good general guide is to move slowly, wait, and take cues from the receivers.

Selective Transmission

The type of medium chosen for the message depends on the nature of the message, its level of importance, the context and expectations of the receiver, the timing involved, and the need for personal interaction, among other factors. Typical media include e-mail, letters or memos, reports, meetings, telephone calls, teleconferences, videoconferences, or face-to-face conversations. The secret is to find out how communication is transmitted in the local organization—how much is downward versus upward or vertical versus horizontal, how the grapevine works, and so on. In addition, the cultural variables discussed earlier need to be considered: whether the receiver is from a high- or low-context culture, whether he or she is used to explicit or implicit communication, and what speed and routing of messages will be most effective.

For the most part, it is best to use face-to-face interaction for relationship building or for other important transactions, particularly in intercultural communications, because of the lack of familiarity between parties. Personal interactions give the manager the opportunity to get immediate verbal and visual feedback and to make rapid adjustments in the communication process.

International dealings are often long-distance, of course, limiting the opportunity for face-to-face communication. However, personal rapport can be established or enhanced through telephone calls or videoconferencing and through trusted contacts. Modern electronic media can be used to break down communication barriers by reducing waiting periods for information, clarifying issues, and allowing instant consultation. Global telecommunications and computer networks are changing the face of cross-cultural communication through the faster dissemination of information within the receiving organization. Ford of Europe uses videoconferencing for engineers in Britain and Germany to consult about quality problems. Through the television screen, they examine one another's engineering diagrams and usually find a solution that gets the factory moving again in a short time.[68]

Careful Decoding of Feedback

Timely and effective feedback channels can also be set up to assess a firm's general communication about the progression of its business and its general management principles. The best means to get accurate feedback is through face-to-face interaction because this allows the manager to hear, see, and sense immediately how a message is being interpreted. When visual feedback on important issues is not possible or appropriate, it is a good idea to use several means of attaining feedback, in particular, employing third parties.

Decoding is the process of translating the received symbols into the interpreted message. The main causes of incongruence are (1) the receiver misinterprets the message, (2) the receiver encodes his or her return message incorrectly, or (3) the sender misinterprets the feedback. Two-way communication is thus essential for important issues so that successive efforts can be made until an understanding has been achieved. Asking other colleagues to help interpret what is going on is often a good way to break a cycle of miscommunication.

Perhaps the most important means to avoiding miscommunication is to practice careful decoding by improving one's listening and observation skills. A good listener practices projective listening, or empathetic listening—listening without interruption or evaluation to the full message of the speaker, attempting to recognize the feelings behind the words and nonverbal cues, and understanding the speaker's perspective.

At the MNC level, avenues of communication and feedback among parent companies and subsidiaries can be kept open through telephone calls, regular meetings and visits, reports, and plans—all of which facilitate cooperation, performance control, and the smooth running of the company. Communication among far-flung operations can be best managed by setting up feedback systems and liaison people. The headquarters people should maintain considerable flexibility in cooperating with local managers and allowing them to deal with the local context as they see fit.

Followup Actions

Managers communicate both through action and inaction. Therefore, to keep open the lines of communication, feedback, and trust, managers must follow through with action on what has been discussed and then agreed upon—typically a contract, which is probably the most important formal business communication. Unfortunately, the issue of contract follow-through is a particularly sensitive one across cultures because of the different interpretations regarding what constitutes a contract (perhaps a handshake, perhaps a full legal document) and what actions should result. Trust, future communications, and future business are based on such interpretations, and it is up to the manager to understand them and to follow through on them.

The management of cross-cultural communication depends largely on a manager's personal abilities and behavior. Those behaviors that researchers indicate to be most important to **intercultural communication effectiveness** (ICE) are listed here, as reviewed by Ruben:

1. respect (conveyed through eye contact, body posture, voice tone and pitch)
2. interaction posture (the ability to respond to others in a descriptive, nonevaluative, and nonjudgmental way)
3. orientation to knowledge (recognizing that one's knowledge, perception, and beliefs are valid only for oneself and not for everyone else)

4. empathy
5. interaction management
6. tolerance for ambiguity
7. other-oriented role behavior (one's capacity to be flexible and to adopt different roles for the sake of greater group cohesion and group communication)[69]

Whether at home or abroad, certain personal capabilities facilitate effective intercultural communication; these abilities can help the expatriate to adapt to the host country and enable productive working relations to develop in the long term. Researchers have established a relationship between personality traits and behaviors and the ability to adapt to the host-country's cultural environment.[70] What is seldom pointed out, however, is that communication is the mediating factor between those behaviors and the relative level of adaptation the expatriate achieves. The communication process facilitates cross-cultural adaptation—through this process, expatriates learn the dominant communication patterns of the host society. Therefore, we can link those personality factors shown by research to ease adaptation with those necessary for effective intercultural communication.

Kim has consolidated the research findings of these characteristics into two categories: (1) **openness**—traits such as open-mindedness, tolerance for ambiguity, and extrovertedness; and (2) **resilience**—traits such as having an internal locus of control, persistence, a tolerance of ambiguity, and resourcefulness.[71] These personality factors, along with the expatriate's cultural and racial identity and the level of preparedness for change, comprise that person's potential for adaptation. The level of preparedness can be improved by the manager before his or her assignment by gathering information about the host country's verbal and nonverbal communication patterns and norms of behavior. Kim incorporates these factors in a communication model of cross-cultural adaptation. Exhibit 4-10 shows the major variables that affect the level of communication competence achieved between the host and the expatriate. These are the adaptive predisposition of the expatriate and the conditions of receptivity and conformity to pressure in the host environment. These factors affect the process of personal and social communication, and, ultimately, the adaptation outcome. Explains Kim: "Three aspects of strangers' adaptive change—increased functional fitness, psychological health, and intercultural identity—have been identified as direct consequences of prolonged communication-adaptation experiences in the host society."[72] In Chapter 10, we will point out areas where the firm has responsibility to improve the employee/managerial ability to adapt.

In identifying personal and behavioral specifics that facilitate ICE, however, we cannot lose sight of the whole picture. We must remember the basic principle of contingency management, that is, that managers operate in a system of many interacting variables in a dynamic context. Studies show that situational factors—such as the physical environment, time constraints, degree of structure, feelings of boredom or overwork, and anonymity—are strong influences on intercultural communication competence.[73]

It is this interdependence of many variables that makes it difficult for intercultural researchers to isolate and identify factors for success. Although managers try to understand and control up front as many factors as possible that will lead to management effectiveness, often they only find out what works from the results of their decisions.

Exhibit 4-10   A Communication Model of Cross-Cultural Adaptation

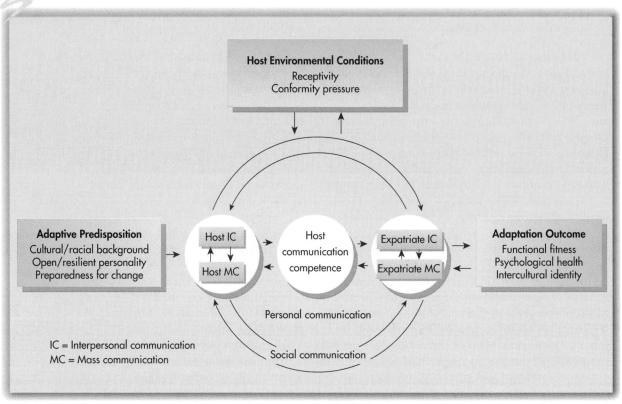

SOURCE: Adapted from Young Yun Kim, *Communication and Cross-Cultural Adaptation* (Clevedon, England: Multilingual Matters, 1988): 79.

Conclusion

Effective intercultural communication is a vital skill for international managers and domestic managers of multicultural workforces. Because we have learned that mis-communication is much more likely to occur among people from different countries or racial backgrounds than among those from similar backgrounds, we try to be alert to how culture is reflected in communication—in particular by developing cultural sensitivity and an awareness of potential sources of cultural noise in the communication process. A successful international manager is thus attuned to these variables and is flexible enough to adjust his or her communication style to best address the intended receivers—that is, to do it "their way."

Cultural variables and the manner in which culture is communicated underlie the processes of negotiation and decision making. How do people around the world negotiate—what are their expectations and their approach to negotiations? What is the importance of understanding negotiation and decision-making processes in other countries? Chapter 5 will address these questions and make suggestions for the international manager to handle these important tasks.

SUMMARY OF KEY POINTS

1. Communication is an inherent part of a manager's role, taking up the majority of the manager's time on the job. Effective intercultural communication largely determines the success of international transactions or the output of a culturally diverse workforce.

2. Culture is the foundation of communication, and communication transmits culture. Cultural variables that can affect the communication process by influencing a person's perceptions include attitudes, social organizations, thought patterns, roles, language, nonverbal language, and time.

3. Language conveys cultural understandings and social norms from one generation to the next. Body language, or nonverbal communication, is behavior that communicates without words. It accounts for 65 to 93 percent of interpreted communication.

4. Types of nonverbal communication around the world are kinesic behavior, proxemics, paralanguage, and object language.

5. Effective cross-cultural communication must take account of whether the receiver is from a country with a monochronic or a polychronic time system.

6. Variables related to channels of communication include high- and low-context cultures, fast or slow messages and information flows, and various types of media.

7. In high-context cultures, feelings and messages are implicit and must be accessed through an understanding of the person and the system. In low-context cultures, feelings and thoughts are expressed, and information is more readily available.

8. The effective management of intercultural communication necessitates the development of cultural sensitivity, careful encoding, selective transmission, careful decoding, and followup actions.

9. Certain personal abilities and behaviors facilitate adaptation to the host country through skilled intercultural communication.

10. Communication over the Internet must still be localized to adjust to differences in language, culture, local laws, and business models.

DISCUSSION QUESTIONS

1. How does culture affect the process of attribution in communication?
2. What is stereotyping? Give some examples. How might people stereotype you? How does a sociotype differ from a stereotype?
3. What is the relationship between language and culture? How is it that people form different countries who speak the same language may still miscommunicate?
4. Give some examples of cultural differences in the interpretation of body language. What is the role of such nonverbal communication in business relationships?
5. Explain the differences between monochronoic and polychronic time systems. Use some examples to illustrate their differences and the role of time in intercultural communication.
6. Explain the differences between high- and low-context cultures, giving some examples. What are the differential effects on the communication process?
7. Discuss the role of information systems in a company, how and why they vary from country to country and the effects of these variations.

APPLICATION EXERCISES

1. Form groups in your class, multicultural if possible. Have each person make notes about his or her perceptions of (1) Mexican Americans, (2) Native Americans,

(3) African Americans, (4) Americans of European descent. Discuss your notes and draw conclusions about common stereotypes. Discuss any differences and why stereotyping occurs.

2. Invite some foreign students to your class. Ask them to bring photographs, slides, and so forth of people and events in their native countries. Have them explain the meanings of various nonverbal cues, such as gestures, dress, voice inflections, architecture, and events. Discuss with them any differences between their explanations and the attributions you assigned to those cues.

3. Interview a faculty member or a businessperson who has worked abroad. Ask him or her to identify factors that facilitated or inhibited adaptation to the host environment. Ask whether more preparation could have eased the transition and what, if anything, that person would do differently before another trip.

EXPERIENTIAL EXERCISE: Script for Juan Perillo and Jean Moore

Scene I: February 15, San Juan, Puerto Rico

Juan: Welcome back to Puerto Rico, Jean. It is good to have you here in San Juan again. I hope that your trip from Dayton was a smooth one.

Jean: Thank you, Juan. It's nice to be back here where the sun shines. Fred sends his regards and also asked me to tell you how important it is that we work out a firm production schedule for the next three months. But first, how is your family? All doing well, I hope.

Juan: My wife is doing very well, but my daughter, Marianna, broke her arm and has to have surgery to repair the bone. We are very worried about that because the surgeon says she may have to have several operations. It is very difficult to think about my poor little daughter in the operating room. She was out playing with some other children when it happened. You know how roughly children sometimes play with each other. It's really amazing that they don't have more injuries. Why, just last week, my son . . .

Jean: Of course I'm very sorry to hear about little Marianna, but I'm sure everything will go well with the surgery. Now, shall we start work on the production schedule?

Juan: Oh, yes, of course, we must get started on the production schedule.

Jean: Fred and I thought that June 1 would be a good cutoff date for the first phase of the schedule. And we also thought that 100 A-type computers would be a reasonable goal for that phase. We know that you have some new assemblers whom you are training, and that you've had some problems getting parts from your suppliers in the past few months. But we're sure you have all those problems worked out by now and that you are back to full production capability. So, what do you think? Is 100 A-type computers produced by June 1 a reasonable goal for your people?

Juan: (hesitates a few seconds before replying) You want us to produce 100 of the newly designed A-type computers by June 1? Will we also be producing our usual number of Z-type computers, too?

Jean: Oh, yes. Your regular production schedule would remain the same as it's always been. The only difference is that you would be producing the new A-type computers, too. I mean, after all, you have a lot of new employees, and you have all the new

SOURCE: L. Catlin and T. White, *International Business: Cultural Sourcebook and Case Studies* (Cincinnati, Ohio: South-Western Co., 1994).

manufacturing and assembling equipment, that we have in Dayton. So, you're as ready to make the new product as we are.

Juan: Yes, that's true. We have the new equipment and we've just hired a lot of new assemblers who will be working on the A-type computer. I guess there's no reason we can't meet the production schedule you and Fred have come up with.

Jean: Great, great. I'll tell Fred you agree with our decision and will meet the goal of 100 A-type computers by June 1. He'll be delighted to know that you can deliver what he was hoping for. And, of course, Juan, that means that you'll be doing just as well as the Dayton plant.

Scene II: May 1, San Juan, Puerto Rico

Jean: Hello, Juan. How are things here in Puerto Rico? I'm glad to have the chance to come back and see how things are going.

Juan: Welcome, Jean. It's good to have you here. How is your family?

Jean: Oh, they're fine, just fine. You know, Juan, Fred is really excited about that big order we just got from the Defense Department for 50 A-type computers. They want them by June 10, so we will ship them directly to Washington from San Juan as the computers come off your assembly line. Looks like it's a good thing we set your production goal at 100 A-type computers by June 1, isn't it?

Juan: Um, yes, that was certainly a good idea.

Jean: So, tell me, have you had any problems with the new model? How are your new assemblers working out? Do you have any suggestions for changes in the manufacturing specs? How is the new quality control program working with this model? We're always looking for ways to improve, you know, and we appreciate any ideas you can give us.

Juan: Well, Jean, there is one thing . . .

Jean: Yes? What is that?

Juan: Well, Jean, we have had a few problems with the new assemblers. Three of them have had serious illnesses in their families and have had to take off several days at a time to nurse a sick child or elderly parent. And another one was involved in a car accident and was in the hospital for several days. And you remember my daughter's surgery? Well, her arm didn't mend properly, and we had to take her to Houston for additional consultations and therapy. But, of course, you and Fred knew about that.

Jean: Yes, we were aware that you had had some personnel problems and that you and your wife had had to go to Houston with Marianna. But what does that have to do with the 50 A-type computers for the Defense Department?

Juan: Well, Jean, because of all these problems, we have had a few delays in the production schedule. Nothing serious, but we are a little bit behind our schedule.

Jean: How far behind is "a little bit"? What are you trying to tell me, Juan? Will you have 50 more A-type computers by June 1 to ship to Washington to fill the Defense Department order?

Juan: Well, I certainly hope we will have that number ready to ship. You know how difficult it can be to predict a precise number for manufacturing, Jean. You probably have many of these same problems in the Dayton plant, don't you?

EXERCISE QUESTIONS

1. What went wrong for Jean in Puerto Rico? Could this have been avoided? What should she have done differently.

2. Replay the role of Jean and Juan during their conversation, establishing a more constructive communication and management style than Jean did previously.

INTERNET RESOURCES

Visit the Deresky companion Web site at http://prenhall.com/Deresky for this chapter's Internet resources.

CASE STUDY: ELIZABETH VISITS GPC'S FRENCH SUBSIDIARY

Elizabeth Moreno is looking out the window from her business class seat somewhere over the Indian Ocean on Thai Air en route to Paris—Orly International Airport from the Philippines, where she has just spent a week of meetings and problem solving in a pharmaceutical subsidiary of the Global Pharmaceutical Company (GPC). (The Philippines trip is covered in the Chapter 12 case study.)

GPC has the lion's share of the worldwide market in the ethical pharmaceutical products. Ethical drugs are those that can be purchased only through a physician's prescription. In the United States, GPC has research and manufacturing sites in New York, New Jersey, Pennsylvania, and Michigan. The company also has subsidiaries in Canada, Puerto Rico, Australia, Philippines, Brazil, England, and France. GPC has its administrative headquarters in Pennsylvania.

Because of the dispersed geographic locations of its subsidiaries, GPC's top scientists and key managers log thousands of jet miles a year visiting various offices and plants. Its top specialists and executives regularly engage in multisite real-time video and telephone conferences as well as using electronic mail along with faxes, modems, and traditional mail to keep in touch with key personnel.

Despite these technological advances, face-to-face meetings and on-site consultations are used widely. In the case of the French subsidiary, nothing can take the place of face-to-face consultations. the French manager is suspicious of figures in the balance sheet, of the telephone, of his subordinates, of what he reads in the newspaper, and of what Americans tell him in confidence. In contrast, the American trusts all these (Hill 1994, 60). This is the reason GPC regularly sends its scientists and executives to France.

Elizabeth Moreno is one of the key specialists within GPC. Her expertise in chemical processing is widely known not only within her company but also in the pharmaceutical industry worldwide. She has been working at GPC for more than 12 years since finishing her advanced degree in chemistry from a university in the Midwest. While working for GPC, she has been given more and more responsibilities leading to her current position as vice president of chemical development and processing.

From a hectic visit in the Philippines, her next assignment is to visit the French subsidiary plant for one week to study a problem with shelf-life testing of one of its newest antiallergy capsules. It seems that product's active ingredient is degrading sooner than the expiration date. During her stay, she will conduct training for chemists in state-of-the-art techniques for testing as well as training local managers in product statistical quality control. These techniques are now currently used in other GPC locations.

To prepare for her foreign assignments, Elizabeth attended a standard three-hour course given by her company's human resource management department on

---

SOURCE: This case was prepared by Edwin J. Portugal, MBA, Ph.D., who teaches multinational management at State University of New York–Potsdam. It is intended to be used as a basis for discussion on the complexity of multicultural management and not to illustrate effective versus ineffective management styles. Copyright © 1995 by Edwin J. Portugal.

dealing with cross-cultural issues. Moreover, she recalls reading from a book on French management about the impersonal nature of French business relations. This was so much in contrast with what she just has experienced from her visit in the Philippine subsidiary. The French tend to regard authority as residing in the role and not in the person. It is by the power of the position that a French manager gets things done (Hill 1994, 58). With this knowledge, she knows that her expertise and her position as vice president will see her through the technical aspects of the meeting that are lined up for the few days she will be in Paris.

French manager view their work as an intellectual challenge that requires application of individual brainpower. What matters to them is the opportunity to show one's ability to grasp complex issues, analyze problems, manipulate ideas, and evaluate solutions (Hill 1994, 214).

There are a few challenges for Elizabeth on this assignment. She is not fluent in French. Her only exposure to France and the language was a two-week vacation in Paris she spent with her husband a couple of years ago. But in her highly technical field, the universal language is English. So, she believes that she will not have much difficulty in communicating with the French management to get her assignment successfully completed.

Americans place high value on training and education. In the United States, the field of management has principles that are generally applicable and can be taught and learned. In contrast, the French place more emphasis on the person who can adapt to any situation by virtue of his intellectual quality (Hill 1994, 63). Expertise and intellectual ability are inherent in the individual and simply cannot be acquired through training or education.

It appears that Elizabeth will be encountering very different ways of doing business in France. While she thought about the challenges ahead, her plane landed at the Paris—Orly International Airport. She whisked through customs and immigration without any delays. There was no limousine waiting for her at the arrival curbside. Instead she took the train to downtown Paris and checked into an apartment hotel that was reserved for her in advance of her arrival.

After a week in Paris, she is expected back in her home office to prepare reports to GPC management about her foreign assignments.

Case Questions

1. What can Elizabeth Moreno do to establish a position of power in front of French managers to help her accomplish her assignment in five days? Explain.
2. What should Elizabeth know about high-context versus low-context cultures in Europe? Explain.
3. What should Elizabeth include in her report, and what should be the manner in which it is communicated, so that future executives and scientists avoid communications pitfalls? Explain.
4. How can technical language differ from everyday language in corporate communications? Explain.
5. How does this business trip compare to her previous trip to the Philippines?

Case Bibliography

Hill, Richard, *Euro-Managers & Martians: The Business Cultures of Europe's Trading Nations* (Brussels: Europublications, Division of Europublic, SA/NV, 1994).

C h a p t e r 5

Cross-Cultural Negotiation and Decision Making

Opening Profile: Sparks Fly at Enron's Power Plant in India

> We faced a lot of naysayers throughout the entire process, and people who thought
> we could never pull it off.
>
> —REBECCA MARK, CHAIRPERSON ENRON'S INTERNATIONAL UNIT,
> WALL STREET JOURNAL, FEBRUARY 1999

> Raghu Dhar, editor of India's largest television network, says Enron offered him a $1
> million a year job to silence his reports of how Enron—with the help of two U.S.
> administrations—pushed for and built the plant, even though it would quadruple
> Indian electricity bills while guaranteeing big profits at no risk to Enron.
>
> —CBS NEWS 60 MINUTES REPORT, APRIL 14, 2002

It took three years, to February 1999, for Rebecca Mark and her team at Enron's International
Unit to bring its Dabhol power plant in India back into operation. In 1996, the Indian government
had canceled the partially built plant because of pressure from environmentalists and a derailed
economic reform plan that had placed the Dabhol plant as the first foreign-owned power
project. But Ms. Mark's persistence eventually brought about consensus to reignite economic
reform and to get the Dabhol plant going again. Enron submitted a proposal in 1997 to build five
to seven additional power plants in India. The first phase, the Dabhol plant, was completed in
December 1998.

Ms. Mark had worked on the relationship between Enron International and India, with an
on-again, off-again relationship, since the early 1990s, when the Indian government began to be
more open toward foreign investment. Prior to that, Gandhi's philosophy of *swadeshi*, meaning
self-reliance, had perpetuated protectionism for its domestic industries. Ms. Mark had an ambitious
plan to construct a $3 billion, 2,015-megawatt power plant in Dabhol, in Maharashtra State. She
negotiated extensively with the Maharashtra State government and members of India's civil service. She needed 170 different state and federal permits, along with layers of legal and tax paperwork. She commented on this process:

> I've had tea with every bureaucrat in India . . . people don't understand how to get
> things done in India. Politicians lay out a plan, but that's different from working
> through the system.
>
> —C. HILL, INSTITUTIONAL INVESTOR, JANUARY 1998

As of April 2001, Enron's 2,364-megawatt plant at Dabhol was the biggest foreign investment in India.
However, officials at Enron—the Houston-based company—announced on April 9, 2001, that it had
lost confidence in the state company that is contractually obliged to buy the output of its Maharashtra
plant. The problem was that the energy Enron sold to local utilities cost four times the going rate.
Although there had been an agreement for the Maharashtra officials to pay partly in U.S. dollars, no
one foresaw the decline of the rupee or the surge in oil prices. The bill ran up to Rs.2.25 billion (33
million pounds), and a Maharashtra government plea to the federal government to bail out the state
fell on deaf ears. As a result, the plant shut down, and Enron chairman Kenneth Lay demanded a
billion-dollar bailout from the central government in India. While India's federal power minister, Suresh
Prabhu, states that the bill will be paid, there are broader ramifications of this situation for foreign
investors and for India's ability to attract them.

It seems that Ms. Mark's tireless negotiations with government officials may have been accompanied by pressure tactics and bribery, which in the end led to a no-win situation for both India and
Enron. From the beginning, the deal overwhelmingly favored Enron. The contract called for Enron to
be paid for all the power produced, whether or not it was needed or used. In addition, although India
has abundant coal resources for cheap power generation, Enron ran the plant on liquefied natural gas
shipped by tanker from one of its own subsidiaries in the Middle East. Further (according to a consultant to the Indian government, and reported on CBS "60 Minutes") Enron told the government officials in Delhi that if they did not sign Enron's deal, the U.S. government would not continue to support

India on the foreign exchange financial front. Through it all, Enron has always maintained that the power plant would be beneficial to India.

SOURCES: CBS News, "60 Minutes" report. April 14, 2002. "India: 'Force Majeure' Clause Invoked in Enron Power Case," report by Indian new agency PTI, BBC Monitoring Service, U.K., April 9, 2001; "Enron Threat to Withdraw from India," www.FT.com April 10, 2001; "Who Benefited from 'Sweetheart' Deal with Enron?" *Hindustan Times*, India, January 22, 2001; "A Power Play India Can't Afford to Lose," www.businessweek.com, January 31, 2001; *Business Week*, January 8, 2001; "Enron's Plant in India Was Dead; This Month, It Will Go on Stream," *Wall Street Journal*, February 5, 1999; C. Hill, "How Rebecca Mark Solved India," *Institutional Investor*, January 1998.

Global managers negotiate with parties in other countries to make specific plans for strategies (exporting, joint ventures, and so forth), and for continuing operations. While the complexities of cross-cultural negotiations among firms around the world present challenge enough, managers also sometimes are faced with negotiating with various governmental agencies. This kind of situation is illustrated in the opening profile of Enron's Dabhol plant, where negotiators were faced with shifting political agenda over time, internal political conflicts between state and national governments, and multiple layers of bureaucratic hurdles. The high-level political negotiations between the United States and China to gain the return of the U.S. military crew from the plane that was forced to land there in April 2001 is another example of complex situations fraught with both political agenda and cultural nuances, such as the need for the Chinese to "save face" by demanding an apology.

Managers must prepare for strategic negotiations. Next the operational details must be negotiated—the staffing of key positions, the sourcing of raw materials or component parts, the repatriating of profits, to name a few. As globalism burgeons, the ability to conduct successful cross-cultural negotiations cannot be overemphasized. Failure to negotiate productively will result in lost potential alliances and lost business at worst, confusion and delays at best.

During the process of negotiation—whether before, during, or after negotiating sessions—all kinds of decisions are made, both explicitly or implicitly. A consideration of cross-cultural negotiations must therefore include the various decision-making processes that occur around the world. Negotiations cannot be conducted without decisions being made.

This chapter will examine the processes of negotiation and decision making as they apply to international and domestic cross-cultural contexts. Our objective is a better understanding of successful management.

NEGOTIATION

Effecting strategy depends on management's ability to negotiate productively—a skill widely considered one of the most important in international business. In the global arena, cultural differences produce great difficulties in the negotiation process. Ignorance of native bargaining rituals, more than any other single factor, accounts for our unimpressive sales efforts with the Japanese and others.[1] Important differences in the negotiation process from country to country include (1) the amount and type of preparation for a negotiation, (2) the relative emphasis on tasks versus interpersonal relationships, (3) the reliance on general principles rather than specific issues, and

Exhibit 5-1   Stakeholders in Cross-Cultural Negotiations

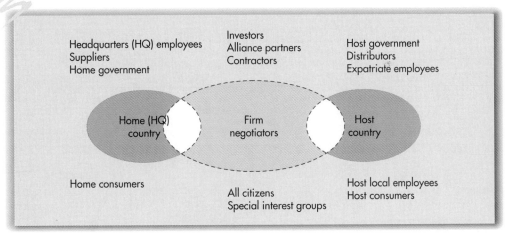

(4) the number of people present and the extent of their influence.[2] In every instance, managers need to familiarize themselves with the cultural background and underlying motivations of the negotiators—and the tactics and procedures they use—to control the process, make progress, and therefore maximize company goals.

The word **negotiation** describes the process of discussion between two or more parties aimed at reaching a mutually acceptable agreement. For long-term positive relations, the goal should be to set up a **win-win situation**—that is, to bring about a settlement beneficial to all parties concerned. This process, difficult enough when it takes place among people of similar backgrounds, is even more complex in international negotiations because of differences in cultural values, lifestyles, expectations, verbal and nonverbal language, approaches to formal procedures, and problem-solving techniques. The complexity is heightened when negotiating across borders because of the greater number of stakeholders involved. These stakeholders are illustrated in Exhibit 5-1. In preparing for negotiations, it is critical to avoid **projective cognitive similarity**—that is, the assumption that others perceive, judge, think, and reason in the same way when, in fact, they do not because of differential cultural and practical influences. Instead, astute negotiators empathetically enter into the private world or cultural space of their counterparts, while willingly sharing their own view of the situation.[3]

THE NEGOTIATION PROCESS

The negotiation process comprises five stages, the ordering of which may vary according to the cultural norms; for most people relationship-building is part of a continuous process of preparation in any event: (1) preparation, (2) relationship building, (3) the exchange of task-related information, (4) persuasion, and (5) concessions and agreement.[4] Of course, in reality these are seldom distinct stages, but rather tend to overlap; negotiators may also revert to an earlier stage temporarily. With that in mind, it is useful to break down the negotiation process into stages to discuss the issues relevant to each stage and what international managers might expect, so that they might more successfully manage this process. These stages are shown in Exhibit 5-2 and discussed in the following sections.

Exhibit 5-2   The Negotiation Process

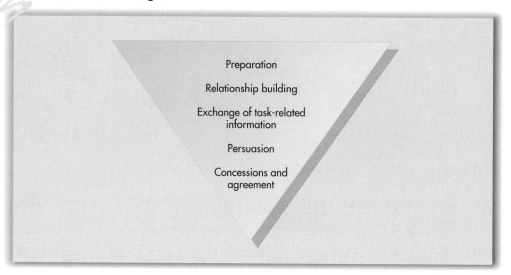

Stage One: Preparation

The importance of careful preparation for cross-cultural negotiations cannot be overstated. To the extent that time permits, a distinct advantage can be gained if negotiators familiarize themselves with the entire context and background of their counterparts (no matter where the meetings will take place) in addition to the specific subjects to be negotiated. Because most negotiation problems are caused by differences in culture, language, and environment, hours or days of tactical preparation for negotiation can be wasted if these factors are not carefully considered.[5]

To understand cultural differences in negotiating styles, managers first need to understand their own styles and then determine how their style differs from the norm in other countries. They can do this by comparing profiles of those perceived to be successful negotiators in different countries. Such profiles reflect the value system, attitudes, and expected behaviors inherent in a given society. Later sections in this chapter will describe and compare negotiating styles around the world.

Variables in the Negotiating Process

Adept negotiators do some research to develop a profile of their counterparts so that they know, in most situations, what to expect, how to prepare, and how to react. Exhibit 5-3 shows 12 variables to consider when preparing to negotiate. These variables can, to a great degree, help managers understand the deep-rooted cultural and national motivations and traditional processes underlying negotiations with people from other countries.

After developing thoughtful profiles of the other party or parties, managers can plan for the actual negotiation meetings. Prior to the meetings, they should find out as much as possible about (1) the kinds of demands that might be made, (2) the composition of the "opposing" team, and (3) the relative authority that the members possess. After this, the managers can gear their negotiation strategy specifically to the other side's firm, allocate roles to different team members, decide on concessions, and prepare an alternative action plan in case a negotiated solution cannot be found.[6]

Exhibit 5-3   Variables in the Negotiation Process

1. *Basic conception of negotiation process*: Is it a competitive process or a problem-solving approach?

2. *Negotiator selection criteria*: Is selection based on experience, status, expertise, personal attributes, or some other characteristic?

3. *Significance of type of issues*: Is it specific, such as price, or is the focus on relationships or the format of talks?

4. *Concern with protocol*: What is the importance of procedures, social behaviors, and so forth in the negotiation process?

5. *Complexity of communicative context*: What degrees of reliance is placed on nonverbal cues to interpret information?

6. *Nature of persuasive arguments*: How do the parties attempt to influence each other? Do they rely on rational arguments, on accepted tradition, or on emotion?

7. *Role of individuals' aspirations*: Are motivations based on individual, company, or community goals?

8. *Bases of trust*: Is trust based on past experience, intuition, or rules?

9. *Risk-taking propensity*: How much do the parties try to avoid uncertainty in trading information or making a contract?

10. *Value of time*: What is each party's attitude toward time? How fast should negotiations proceed, and what degree of flexibility is there?

11. *Decision-making system*: How does each team reach decisions—by individual determination, by majority opinion, or by group consensus?

12. *Form of satisfactory agreement*: Is agreement based on trust (perhaps just a handshake), the credibility of the parties, commitment, or a legally binding contract?

SOURCE: Adapted from S. E. Weiss and W. Stripp, *Negotiation with Foreign Business Persons: An Introduction for Americans with Propositions on Six Cultures* (New York University Faculty of Business Administration, February 1985).

In some situations, however, the entire negotiation process is something people have to learn from scratch. After the splintering of the Soviet Union into 15 independent republics, managers from the Newmont Mining Corporation of Denver, wishing to form a joint venture to refine gold deposits in Uzbekistan, found themselves at a standstill. Officials in Uzbekistan had never negotiated a business contract and had no one to tell them how to proceed.[7]

Following the preparation and planning stage, which is usually done at the home office, the core of the actual negotiation takes place on-site in the foreign location (or at the manager's home office if the other team has decided to travel there). In some cases, a compromise on the location for negotiations can signal a cooperative strategy, which Weiss calls "Improvise an approach: Effect Symphony"—a strategy available to negotiators familiar with each others' culture and willing to put negotiation on an equal footing. Weiss gives the following example of this negotiation strategy:

> For their negotiations over construction of the tunnel under the English Channel, British and French representatives agreed to partition talks and alternate the site between Paris and London. At each site, the negotiators were to use established, local ways, including the language, . . . thus punctuating approaches by time and space.[8]

In this way, each side was put into the context and the script of the other culture about half the time.

The next stage of negotiation—often given short shrift by Westerners—is that of relationship building. In most parts of the world, this stage usually has either taken place already or is concurrent with other preparations.

Stage Two: Relationship Building

The process of relationship building is regarded with much more significance in most parts of the world than it is in the United States. American negotiators are, generally speaking, objective about the specific matter at hand and usually want to waste no time in getting down to business and making progress. This approach, well understood in the United States, can be disastrous if the foreign negotiators want to take enough time to build trust and respect as a basis for negotiating contracts. In such cases, American efficiency interferes with the patient development of a mutually trusting relationship—the very cornerstone of an Asian business agreement.[9]

In many countries, such as Mexico and China, personal commitments to individuals, rather than the legal system, form the basis for the enforcement of contracts. Effective negotiators allow plenty of time in their schedule for such relationship building with bargaining partners. This process usually takes the form of social events, tours, and ceremonies, along with much light conversation, or nontask sounding, while both sides get to know one another. In such cultures, one patiently waits for the other party to start actual business negotiations, aware that relationship building is, in fact, the first phase of negotiations.[10] It is usually recommended that managers new to such scenarios use an intermediary—someone who already has the trust and respect of the foreign managers and who therefore acts as a "relationship bridge." Middle Easterners, in particular, prefer to negotiate through a trusted intermediary, and for them as well, initial meetings are only for the purpose of getting acquainted. Arabs do business with the person, not the company, and therefore mutual trust must be established.

In their bestseller on negotiation, *Getting to Yes*, Fisher and Ury point out the dangers of not preparing well for negotiations:

> In Persian, the word "compromise" does not have the English meaning of a midway solution which both sides can accept, but only the negative meaning of surrendering one's principles. Also, a "mediator" is a meddler, someone who is barging in uninvited. In 1980, United Nations Secretary-General Kurt Waldheim flew to Iran to deal with the hostage situation. National Iranian radio and television broadcast in Persian a comment he was to have made upon his arrival in Tehran: "I have come as a mediator to work out a compromise." Less than an hour later, his car was being stoned by angry Iranians.[11]

As a bridge to the more formal stages of negotiations, such relationship building is followed by posturing—that is, general discussion that sets the tone for the meetings. This phase should result in a spirit of cooperation. To help ensure this result, negotiators must use words like respect and mutual benefit rather than language that would suggest arrogance, superiority, or urgency.[12]

Stage Three: Exchanging Task-Related Information

In the next stage, exchanging task-related information, each side typically makes a presentation and states its position; a question-and-answer session usually ensues, and alternatives are discussed. From an American perspective, this represents a straightforward, objective, efficient, and understandable stage. However, Copeland and Griggs point out that negotiators from other countries continue to take a more indirect approach at this stage. Mexican negotiators are usually suspicious and indirect, presenting little substantive material and more lengthy, evasive conversation. French negotiators enjoy debate and conflict and will often interrupt presentations to argue about an issue even if it has little relevance to the topic being presented. The Chinese also ask many questions of their counterparts, and they delve specifically and repeatedly into the details at hand; conversely, the Chinese presentations contain only vague and ambiguous material. For instance, after about 20 Boeing officials spent 6 weeks presenting masses of literature and technical demonstrations to the Chinese, the Chinese said, "Thank you for your introduction."[13]

The Russians also enter negotiations well prepared and well versed in the specific details of the matter being presented. To answer their (or any other side's) questions, it is generally a good idea to bring along someone with expertise to answer any grueling technical inquiries. Russians also put a lot of emphasis on protocol and expect to deal only with top executives.

Adler suggests that negotiators should focus not only on presenting their situation and needs but also on showing an understanding of their opponents' viewpoint. Focusing on the entire situation confronting each party encourages the negotiators to assess a wider range of alternatives for resolution, rather than limiting themselves to their preconceived, static positions. She suggests that to be most effective, negotiators should prepare for meetings by practicing role reversal.[14]

Stage Four: Persuasion

In the next phase of negotiations, persuasion, the hard bargaining starts. Typically, both parties try to persuade the other to accept more of their position and to give up some of their own. Often, some persuasion has already taken place beforehand in social settings and through mutual contacts. In the Far East, details are likely to be worked out ahead of time through the backdoor approach (*houmani*). For the most part, however, the majority of the persuasion takes place over one or more negotiating sessions. International managers usually find that this process of bargaining and making concessions is fraught with difficulties because of the different uses and interpretations of verbal and nonverbal behaviors. Although variations in such behaviors influence every stage of the negotiation process, they can play a particularly powerful role in persuasion, especially if they are not anticipated.

Studies of negotiating behavior have revealed the use of certain recognizable *tactics*, which skilled negotiators recognize and use. Exhibit 5-4 shows the results of a study comparing the use of various tactics (promises, threats, and so forth) among the Japanese, Americans, and Brazilians. The results indicate that the Japanese and the Americans tend to be more alike in the use of these behaviors, whereas the Japanese and the Brazilians are less alike. For example, the Brazilians use fewer promises and commitments than the Japanese or the Americans (only half as many), but they use commands far more often. The Japanese and the Americans use threats twice as often as the Brazilians, and they use commands only about half as often as the Brazilians. The Brazilians and the Japanese seldom behave similarly.

Other, less savory tactics are sometimes used in international negotiations. Often called *dirty tricks*, these tactics, according to Fisher and Ury, include efforts to mislead "opponents" deliberately.[15] Some negotiators may give wrong or distorted factual information or use the excuse of ambiguous authority—giving conflicting impressions about who in their party has the power to make a commitment. In the midst of

Exhibit 5-4 Differences among Japanese, American, and Brazilian Verbal Negotiating Behavior

Bargaining Behaviors and Definition	Frequency per Half-Hour Bargaining Session		
	Japanese	American	Brazilian
Promise. A statement in which the source indicated his or her intention to provide the target with a reinforcing consequence that source anticipates target will evaluate as pleasant, positive, or rewarding.	7	8	3
Threat. Same as promise, except that the reinforcing consequences are thought to be noxious, unpleasant, or punishing.	4	4	2
Recommendation. A statement in which the source predicts that a pleasant environmental consequence will occur to the target. Its occurrence is not under the source's control.	7	4	5
Warning. Same as recommendation, except that the consequences are thought to be unpleasant.	2	1	1
Reward. A statement by the source that is thought to create pleasant consequences for the target.	1	2	2
Punishment. Same as reward, except that the consequences are thought to be unpleasant.	1	3	3
Positive normative appeal. A statement in which the source indicates that the target's past, present, or future behavior was or will be in conformity with social norms.	1	1	0
Negative normative appeal. Same as positive normative appeal, except that the target's behavior is in violation of social norms.	3	1	1
Commitment. A statement by the source to the effect that its future bids will not go below or above a certain level.	15	13	8
Self-disclosure. A statement in which the source reveals information about itself.	34	36	39
Question. A statement in which the source asks the target to reveal information about itself.	20	20	22
Command. A statement in which the source suggests that the target perform a certain behavior.	8	6	14

SOURCE: From John L. Graham, "The Influence of Culture on the Process of Business Negotiations in an Exploratory Study," *Journal of International Business Studies* (Spring 1985): 88.

hard bargaining, the prudent international manager will follow up on possibly misleading information before taking action based on trust.

Other rough tactics are designed to put opposing negotiators in a stressful situation physically or psychologically so that they are more likely to give in. These include uncomfortable room temperatures, too-bright lighting, rudeness, interruptions, and other irritations. Specific bargaining pressures include extreme or escalating demands, threats to stop negotiating, calculated delays, and a take-it-or-leave-it attitude. In a survey of 18 U.S.-Korean joint ventures, for example, U.S. executives reported that the behavior of the Koreans during the course of negotiations was often "abusive," resulting in "shouting matches, desk pounding, and chest beating."[16]

International negotiators must keep in mind, however, that what might seem like dirty tricks to Americans is simply the way other cultures conduct negotiations. In some South American countries, for example, it is common to start negotiations with misleading or false information.

The most subtle behaviors in the negotiation process, and often the most difficult to deal with, are usually the nonverbal messages—the use of voice intonation, facial and body expressions, eye contact, dress, and the timing of the discussions. **Nonverbal behaviors** are ingrained aspects of culture used by people in their daily lives; they are not specifically changed for the purposes of negotiation. In a comparative study of the nonverbal negotiating behaviors of Japanese, Americans, and Brazilians, Graham assessed the relative frequency of the use of silent periods, conversational overlaps, facial gazing (staring at people's faces), and touching. He found that the Brazilians interrupted conversation about twice as often as the Japanese and the Americans and used much more touching and facial gazing. Needless to say, they scored low on silent periods. The Japanese tended to use more silent periods and interruptions than the Americans but less facial gazing. The Japanese and the Americans evidenced no touching whatsoever, other than handshaking, during a 30-minute period.[17]

Although we have discussed persuasion as if it were always a distinct stage, it is really the primary purpose underlying all stages of the negotiation process. In particular, persuasion is an integral part of the process of making concessions and arriving at an agreement.

Stage Five: Concessions and Agreement

In the last stage of negotiation, concessions and agreement, tactics vary greatly across cultures. Well-prepared negotiators are aware of various concession strategies and have decided ahead of time what their own concession strategy will be. Familiar with the typical initial positions that various parties are likely to take, they know that the Russians and the Chinese generally open their bargaining with extreme positions, asking for more than they hope to gain, whereas the Swedes usually start with what they are prepared to accept.

Research in the United States indicates that better end results are attained by starting with extreme positions. With this approach, the process of reaching an agreement involves careful timing of the disclosure information and of concessions. Most people who have studied negotiations believe that negotiators should disclose only the information that is necessary at a given point and that they should try to obtain information piece by piece to get the whole picture gradually without giving away their goals or concession strategy. These guidelines will not always work in intercultural negotiations because the American process of addressing issues one at a time, in a linear fashion, is not common in other countries or cultures. Negotiators in the Far East, for example, approach issues in a holistic manner, deciding on the whole deal at the end, rather than making incremental concessions.

Again, at the final stage of agreement and contract, cultural values determine how these agreements will be honored. Whereas Americans take contracts very seriously, Russians often renege on their contracts. The Japanese, on the other hand, consider a formal contract to be somewhat of an insult and a waste of time and money in legal costs, since they prefer to operate on the basis of understanding and social trust.[18]

UNDERSTANDING NEGOTIATION STYLES

Global managers can benefit from studying differences in negotiating behaviors (and the underlying reasons for them), which can help them recognize what is happening in the negotiating process. Exhibit 5-5 shows some examples of differences among North American, Japanese, and Latin American styles. Brazilians, for example, generally have a spontaneous, passionate, and dynamic style. They are very talkative and particularly use the word *no* extensively—more than 40 times per half hour compared with 4.7 times for Americans and only 1.9 times for the Japanese. They also differ markedly from the Americans and Japanese by their use of extensive physical contact.[19]

The Japanese are typically skillful negotiators. They have spent a great deal more time and effort studying American culture and business practices than Americans have spent studying Japanese practices. A typical example of this contrast was apparent at recent trade negotiations between Japan and the United States in 1994. Charlene Barshefsky—a tough American international lawyer—had never visited Japan before being sent there as a trade negotiator and had little knowledge of its counterparts. But

Exhibit 5-5   Comparison of Negotiation Styles—Japanese, North American, and Latin American

Japanese	North American	Latin American
Emotional sensitivity highly valued	Emotional sensitivity not highly valued	Emotional sensitivity valued
Hiding of emotions	Dealing straightforwardly or impersonally	Emotionally passionate
Subtle power plays; conciliation	Litigation not so much as conciliation	Great power plays; use of weakness
Loyalty to employer; employer takes care of employees	Lack of commitment to employer; breaking of ties by either if necessary	Loyalty to employer (who is often family)
Face-saving crucial; decisions often on basis of saving someone from embarrassment	Decisions made on a cost-benefit basis; face-saving does not always matter	Face-saving crucial in decision making to preserve honor, dignity
Decision makers openly influenced by special interests	Decision makers influenced by special interests but often not considered ethical	Execution of special interests of decision expected, condoned
Not argumentative; quiet when right	Argumentative when right or wrong, but impersonal	Argumentative when right or wrong; passionate
What is down in writing must be accurate, valid	Great importance given to documentation as evidential proof	Impatient with documentation as obstacle to understanding general principles
Step-by-step approach to decision making	Methodically organized decision making	Impulsive, spontaneous decision making
Good of group is the ultimate aim	Profit motive or good of individual ultimate aim	What is good for group is good for the individual
Cultivate a good emotional social setting for decision making; get to know decision makers	Decision making impersonal; avoid involvements, conflict of interest	Personalism necessary for good decision making

SOURCE: From Pierre Casse, *Training for the Multicultural Manager: A Practical and Cross-Cultural Approach to the Management of People* (Washington, D.C.: Society for Intercultural Education, Training, and Research, 1982).

Mr. Okamatsu, as most Japanese negotiators, was very familiar with America. He had lived in New York for three years with his family and had spent many years handling bilateral trade disputes between the two countries. The different styles of the two negotiators were apparent in the negotiations. Ms. Barshefsky wanted specific import goals. Mr. Okamatsu wanted to talk more about the causes of trade problems rather than set specific targets, which he called the "cooperative approach." Ms. Barshefsky snapped that the approach was nonsense and "would analyze the past to death, with no link to future change."[20]

Such differences in philosophy and style between the two countries reflect ten years of anger and feelings of betrayal in trade negotiations. John Graham, a California professor who has studied international negotiating styles, says that the differences between American and Japanese styles are well illustrated by their respective proverbs: the American believes that "the squeaking wheel gets the grease," and the Japanese say that "the pheasant would not be shot but for its cry."[21] The Japanese are calm, quiet, patient negotiators; they are accustomed to long, detailed negotiating sessions. Whereas Americans often plunge straight to the matter at hand, the Japanese instead prefer to develop long-term, personal relationships. The Japanese want to get to know those on the other side and will spend some time in **nontask sounding**—general polite conversation and informal communication before meetings (*nemawashi*).

In negotiations, the Japanese culture of politeness and hiding of emotions can be disconcerting to Americans when they are unable to make straightforward eye contact or when the Japanese maintain smiling faces in serious situations. It is important that Americans understand what is polite and what is offensive to the Japanese (and vice versa). Americans must avoid anything that resembles boasting because the Japanese value humility, and they must avoid physical contact or touching of any sort.[22] Consistent with the culture-based value of maintaining harmony, the Japanese are likely to be evasive or even leave the room rather than give a direct negative answer.[23] Fundamental to the Japanese culture is a concern for the welfare of the group; anything that affects one member or part of society affects the others. Thus, the Japanese view decisions carefully in light of long-term consequences; they use objective, analytic thought patterns; and they take time for reflection.[24]

Further insight into negotiating styles around the world can be gained by comparing the North American, Arab, and Russian styles. As shown in Exhibit 5-6, basic cultural values often shed light on the way information is presented, whether and how concessions will be made, and the general nature and duration of the relationship.

For North Americans, negotiations are businesslike; their **factual appeals** are based on what they believe is objective information, presented with the assumption that it is understood by the other side on a logical basis. Arabs use **affective appeals** based on emotions and subjective feelings; Russians employ **axiomatic appeals**—that is, their appeals are based on the ideals generally accepted in their society. The Russians are tough negotiators; they stall for time until they unnerve Western negotiators by continuously delaying and haggling. Much of this approach is based on the Russians' different attitude toward time. Because Russians do not subscribe to the Western belief that "time is money," they are more patient, more determined, more dogged negotiators. They try to keep smiles and other expressions of emotion to a minimum to present a calm exterior.[25]

In contrast to the Russians, Arabs are more interested in long-term relationships and therefore are more likely to make concessions. Compared with westerners, Arabs have a casual approach to deadlines and frequently lack the authority to finalize a deal.[26]

Exhibit 5-6   Comparison of Negotiation Styles—North Americans, Arabs, Russians

	North Americans	Arabs	Russians
Primary negotiating style and process	Factual: appeals made to logic	Affective: appeals made to emotions	Axiomatic appeals made to ideals
Conflict: opponents' arguments countered with . . .	Objective facts	Subjective feelings	Asserted ideals
Making concessions	Small concessions made early to establish a relationship	Concessions made throughout as a part of the bargaining process	Few, if any, small concessions made
Response to opponent's concessions	Usually reciprocate opponent's concessions	Almost always reciprocate opponent's concessions	Opponent's concessions viewed as weakness and almost never reciprocated
Relationship	Short-term	Long-term	No continuing relationship
Authority	Broad	Broad	Limited
Initial position	Moderate	Extreme	Extreme
Deadline	Very important	Casual	Ignored

SOURCE: Adapted from E. S. Glenn, D. Witmeyer, and K. A. Stevenson, "Cultural Styles of Persuasion," *International Journal of Intercultural Relations* 1 (1984).

Successful Negotiators Around the World

Following are selected profiles of what it takes to be a successful negotiator, as perceived by people in their home country. These are profiles of American, Indian, Arab, Swedish, and Italian negotiators, according to Pierre Casse, and give some insight into what to expect from the different negotiators and what they expect from others.[27]

American Negotiators

According to Casse, a successful American negotiator acts as follows:

1. Knows when to compromise
2. Takes a firm stand at the beginning of the negotiation
3. Refuses to make concessions beforehand
4. Keeps his or her cards close to his or her chest
5. Accepts compromises only when the negotiation is deadlocked
6. Sets up the general principles and delegates the detail work to associates
7. Keeps a maximum of options open before negotiation
8. Operates in good faith
9. Respects the "opponents"
10. States his or her position as clearly as possible
11. Knows when he or she wishes a negotiation to move on

12. Is fully briefed about the negotiated issues
13. Has a good sense of timing and is consistent
14. Makes the other party reveal his or her position while keeping his or her own position hidden as long as possible
15. Lets the other negotiator come forward first and looks for the best deal.

Indian Negotiators

Indians, says Casse, often follow Gandhi's approach to negotiation, which Gandhi called *satyagraha*, "firmness in a good cause." This approach combines strength with the love of truth. The successful Indian negotiator thus acts as follows:

1. Looks for and says the truth
2. Is not afraid of speaking up and has no fears
3. Exercises self-control ("The weapons of the satyagraha are within him.")
4. Seeks solutions that will please all the parties involved ("Satyagraha aims to exalt both sides.")
5. Respects the other party ("The opponent must be weaned from error by patience and sympathy. Weaned, not crushed; converted, not annihilated.")
6. Neither uses violence nor insults
7. Is ready to change his or her mind and differ with himself or herself at the risk of being seen as inconsistent and unpredictable
8. Puts things into perspective and switches easily from the small picture to the big one
9. Is humble and trusts the opponent
10. Is able to withdraw, use silence, and learn from within
11. Relies on himself or herself, his or her own resources and strengths
12. Appeals to the other party's spiritual identity ("To communicate, the West moves or talks. The East sits, contemplates, suffers.")
13. Is tenacious, patient, and persistent
14. Learns from the opponent and avoids the use of secrets
15. Goes beyond logical reasoning and trusts his or her instinct as well as faith

Arab Negotiators

Many Arab negotiators, following Islamic tradition, use mediators to settle disputes. A successful Arab mediator acts in the following way:

1. Protects all the parties' honor, self-respect, and dignity
2. Avoids direct confrontations between opponents
3. Is respected and trusted by all
4. Does not put the parties involved in a situation where they have to show weakness or admit defeat
5. Has the necessary prestige to be listened to
6. Is creative enough to come up with honorable solutions for all parties
7. Is impartial and can understand the positions of the various parties without leaning toward one or the other
8. Is able to resist any kind of pressure that the opponents could try to exercise on him
9. Uses references to people who are highly respected by the opponents to persuade them to change their minds on some issues ("Do it for the sake of your father.")
10. Can keep secrets and in so doing gains the confidence of the negotiating parties

11. Controls his temper and emotions (or loses it when and where necessary)
12. Can use conferences as mediating devices
13. Knows that the opponents will have problems in carrying out the decisions made during the negotiation
14. Is able to cope with the Arab disregard for time
15. Understands the impact of Islam on the opponents who believe that they possess the truth, follow the Right Path, and are going to "win" because their cause is just

Swedish Negotiators
Swedish negotiators, according to Casse, are:

1. Very quiet and thoughtful
2. Punctual (concerned with time)
3. Extremely polite
4. Straightforward (they get straight down to business)
5. Eager to be productive and efficient
6. Heavy-going
7. Down to earth and overcautious
8. Rather flexible
9. Able to and quite good at holding emotions and feelings
10. Slow at reacting to new (unexpected) proposals
11. Informal and familiar
12. Conceited
13. Perfectionist
14. Afraid of confrontations
15. Very private

Italian Negotiators
Italians, says Casse, value a negotiator who acts as follows:

1. Has a sense of drama (acting is a main part of the culture)
2. Does not hide his or her emotions (which are partly sincere and partly feigned)
3. Reads facial expressions and gestures very well
4. Has a feeling for history
5. Does not trust anybody
6. Is concerned about the *bella figura*, or the "good impression," he or she can create among those who watch his or her behavior
7. Believes in the individual's initiatives, not so much in teamwork
8. Is good at being obliging and *simpatico* at all times
9. Is always on the qui vive, the "lookout"
10. Never embraces definite opinions
11. Is able to come up with new ways to immobilize and eventually destroy his or her opponents
12. Handles confrontations of power with subtlety and tact
13. Has a flair for intrigue
14. Knows how to use flattery
15. Can involve other negotiators in complex combinations

Comparing such profiles is useful. Indian negotiators, for example, are humble, patient, respectful of the other parties, and very willing to compromise, compared with Americans, who are firmer about taking stands. An important difference between Arab negotiators and those from most other countries is that the negotiators are mediators, not the parties themselves; hence, direct confrontation is made impossible. Successful Swedish negotiators are conservative and careful, dealing with factual and detailed information. This profile contrasts with Italian negotiators, who are expressive and exuberant but less straightforward than their Swedish counterparts.

MANAGING NEGOTIATION

Skillful global managers need to assess many factors when **managing negotiation**. They must understand the position of the other parties in regard to their goals—whether national or corporate—and whether these goals are represented by principles or specific details. They should have the ability to recognize the relative importance attached to completing the task versus developing interpersonal relationships. Managers also need to know the composition of the teams involved, the power allotted to the members, and the extent of the teams' preparation. In addition, they must grasp the significance of personal trust in the relationship. As stated earlier, the culture of the parties involved affects their negotiating styles and behavior and thus the overall process of negotiation. However, whatever the culture, research by Tse, Francis, and Walls has found person-related conflicts to "invite negative, more relation-oriented (versus information-oriented) responses," leading them to conclude that:

> The **software of negotiation**—that is, the nature and the appearance of the relationship between the people pursuing common goals—needs to be carefully addressed in the negotiation process.[28]

This is particularly true when representatives of individual-focused cultures (such as the Americans) and group-focused cultures (such as the Chinese) are on opposite sides of the table. Many of these cultural-based differences in negotiations came to light in Husted's recent study on Mexican negotiators' perceptions of the reasons for the failure of their negotiations with U.S. teams. The summary findings are shown in Exhibit 5-7. However, Husted believes that "many of the perceived differences relate to the typical differences found between high-context and low-context cultures."[29] In other words, the Mexican managers' interpretations were affected by their high-context culture, with the characteristics of an indirect approach, patience in discussing ideas, and maintenance of dignity. Instead, the low-context Americans conveyed an impatient, cold, blunt communicative style. To maintain the outward dignity of their Mexican counterparts, Americans need to approach negotiations with Mexicans with patience and tolerance and to refrain from attacking ideas because these attacks may be taken personally.

The relationships among the factors of cross-cultural negotiation discussed in this chapter are illustrated in Exhibit 5-8.

The successful management of intercultural negotiations requires that a manager go beyond a generalized understanding of the issues and variables involved. She or he must (1) gain specific knowledge of the parties in the upcoming meeting, (2) prepare accordingly to adjust to and control the situation, and (3) be innovative.[30]

Exhibit 5-7 Bargaining with the Gringos
Mexican Managers' Perceptions of Causes of Failure of Negotiations with
Americans

	Very Important (%)	Important (%)	Moderately Important (%)	Total (%)
Problems with U.S. team				
Lack of authority of U.S. team to make decisions	37.0	20.0	15.0	72.0
U.S. team's failure to resolve doubts of Mexican team	34.0	26.0	14.0	74.0
U.S. team's lack of sincerity	41.0	20.0	9.0	70.0
Eigenvalue: 2.9009/Percent of var.: 26.4/Cum. var.: 26.4				
Negotiation process				
Differences in negotiation styles	26.5	28.4	22.5	77.4
U.S. team quoting unreasonable prices	52.5	17.8	8.9	79.2
Mexican lack of knowledge of delivery systems	42.0	19.0	11.0	72.0
Mexican lack of preparation	40.6	21.8	9.9	72.3
Eigenvalue: 2.3577/Percent of var.: 21.4/Cum. var.: 47.8				
Cultural barriers				
Differences in business practices	24.5	29.4	22.5	76.4
Communication barriers	37.3	17.6	12.7	67.6
Eigenvalue: 1.7976/Percent of var.: 16.3/Cum. var.: 64.1				
Language problems	41.2	21.6	5.9	68.7
Eigenvalue: 1.0763/Percent of var.: 9.8/Cum. var.: 73.9				
Price constraints				
Mexican team's inability to lower the price	32.0	22.0	18.0	72.0
Eigenvalue: 1.0433/Percent of var.: 9.5/Cum. var.: 83.4				

SOURCE: Bryan W. Husted, "Bargaining with the Gringos: An Exploratory Study of Negotiations between Mexican and U.S. Firms," *International Executive* 36(5) (September–October 1994): 625–644.

Research has shown that a problem-solving approach is essential to successful cross-cultural negotiations, whether abroad or in the home office, although the approach works differently in various countries.[31] This problem-solving approach requires that a negotiator treat everyone with respect, avoid making anyone feel uncomfortable, and not criticize or blame the other parties in a personal way that may make someone feel shame—that is, lose face.

Research by the Huthwaite Research Group reveals how successful negotiators, compared to average negotiators, manage the planning process and their face-to-face behavior. The group found that during the planning process, successful negotiators consider a wider range of options and pay greater attention to areas of common ground. Skillful negotiators also tend to make twice as many comments regarding long-term issues and are more likely to set upper and lower limits regarding specific points. In their face-to-face behavior, skillful negotiators make fewer irritating comments—such as "we're making you a generous offer,"—make counterproposals

Exhibit 5-8   Cross-Cultural Negotiation Variables

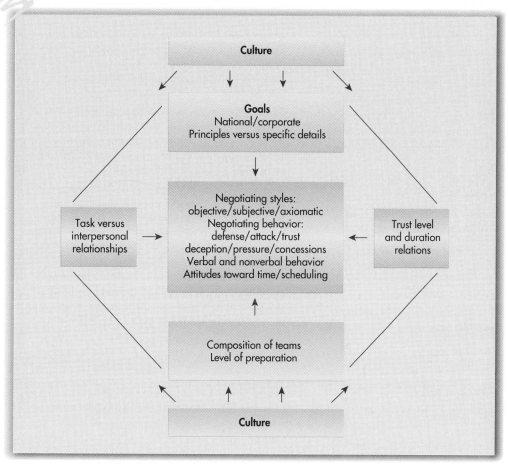

less frequently, and use fewer reasons to back up arguments. In addition, skilled negotiators practice active listening—asking questions, clarifying their understanding of the issues, and summarizing the issues.[32]

Using the Web to Support Negotiations

Modern technology can provide support for the negotiating process, though it can't take the place of the essential face-to-face ingredient in many instances. A growing component for electronic commerce is the development of applications to support the negotiation of contracts and resolution of disputes. As Web applications develop, they may provide support for various phases and dimensions, such as:

> Multiple issue, multiple party business transactions of a buy-sell nature, international dispute resolution (business disputes, political disputes), internal company negotiations and communications, among others.[33]

Management Focus

SAMSUNG'S E-CHAEBOL

Korea's **Samsung**, the trading arm of South Korea's family-run conglomerate, or **chaebol**, is using the Internet to transform its role as a middleman into a global e-marketplace player. Samsung anticipates $7 billion in trades in 2002 from its five on-line marketplaces, listed below, up from $2.8 billion in 2001.[1] Transactions through these trading auctions reduce the need for personal negotiating, which often is problematic from one country to another.

SAMSUNG'S E-MARKETPLACES[2]

FishRound: On-line marketplace for frozen fish. Samsung owns 70 percent. Trading fee is 1 percent.

FishRound.com provides a full range of services, including Consulting, Auction, Procurement, Logistics, Financing, and MRO Services (ship repair bunkering).

GSX Trades steel on the spot market. Samsung one of majority owners. Trading fee 0.375 percent.

ChemCross: Trades industrial chemicals in Asia. They are in the refining, petrochemical and polymer industry. Owned by Samsung and 60 Asian chemical manufacturers. Fee is 0.3 to 0.55 percent.

CareCamp: Korea's top e-marketplace for medical equipment for hospitals and other medical institutions. 50 percent owned by Samsung, and 50 percent by hospitals, suppliers, and doctors. Trading fee is from 1 percent to 3 percent.

Textopia: A textile e-marketplace for buying and selling fiber, yarn, and other raw materials. Composed of five categories: Open market (for meeting new business partners and exchange and auction services; Private Network (customized for collaborating partners); Functions (for after-contract services: inspection, logistics, insurance, and financing); Information (a guide for business deals); and My Topia (tips for transaction management). Trading fee is less than 1 percent.

---

[1]www.Samsung.com; *BusinessWeek ebiz*/August 6, 2001.

[2]www.Fishround.com; www.GSX.com; www.Chemcross.com; www.Textopia.com; www.CareCamp.com; *BusinessWeek ebiz*/August 6, 2001.

Negotiation Support Systems (NSS) can provide support for the negotiation process by:

➤ Increasing the likelihood that an agreement is reached when a zone of agreement exists (solutions that both parties would accept).

➤ Decreasing the direct and indirect costs of negotiations, such as costs caused by time delays (strikes, violence), and attorneys' fees, among others.

➤ Maximizing the chances for optimal outcomes.[34]

One Web-based support system, developed at Carleton University in Ottawa, Canada—called INSPIRE—provides applications for preparing and conducting negotiations, and for renegotiating options after a settlement. Users can specify preferences and assess offers; the site also has graphical displays of the negotiation process.[35]

E-Negotiation

Increasingly, the negotiation process is being carried out through e-commerce, as more and more e-marketplaces replace middlemen in trading around the world. One example is the Samsung e-Chaebol, discussed in the accompanying Management Focus.

Negotiating with the Chinese

The Chinese way of making decisions begins with socialization and initiation of personal guanxi rather than business discussion. The focus is not market research, statistical analysis, facts, Power point presentations, or to-the-point business discussion. My focus must be on fostering guanxi.

—SUNNY ZHOU, GENERAL MANAGER OF
KUNMING LIDA WOOD AND BAMBOO PRODUCTS.[36]

When westerners initiate business negotiations with representatives from the People's Republic of China, cultural barriers confront both sides. The negotiation process used by the Chinese—although there are variations among the Cantonese, Shanghainese, and northern Chinese—is dramatically different from that of the Americans. For instance, the Chinese put much greater emphasis than Americans on respect and friendship, on saving face, and on group goals. Long-term goals are more important to the Chinese than the specific current objectives typical of Western negotiators.[37] Even though market forces are starting to have more influence in China, political and economic agendas are still expected to be considered in negotiations. Research by Xinping Shi of 198 managers in Beijing, 185 in Shanghai, and 189 in Guangzhou shows that prevailing economic conditions, political pervasiveness, and "constituent shadow" are key practical factors which, added to a cultural factors, make up the context affecting Chinese negotiations. ("Constituent shadow" refers to the influence that constituents such as political and state agencies have on the negotiating parties in China.) These antecedent factors, when filtered through the specific negotiator's profile, result in various behaviors, processes, and outcomes from those negotiations. Moreover, little difference in those factors was found among the different regions in China. Exhibit 5-9 shows these environmental factors and the relationships among the factors involved in Western-Chinese business negotiation.

Exhibit 5-9   Influences on Western-Chinese Business Negotiations

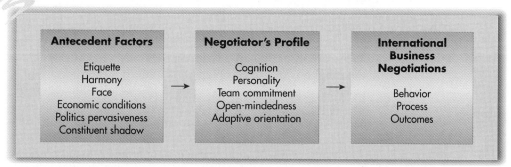

SOURCE: Xinping Shi, "Antecedent factors of International Business Negotiations in the China Context," *Management International Review* H/r no. 2 (April 2001): 182.

Businesspeople report two major areas of conflict in negotiating with the Chinese—the amount of detail the Chinese want about product characteristics, and their apparent insincerity about reaching an agreement. In addition, Chinese negotiators frequently have little authority, frustrating Americans who do have the authority and are ready to conclude a deal.[38] This situation arises because Chinese companies report to the government trade corporations, which are involved in the negotiations and often have a representative on the team. The goals of Chinese negotiators remain primarily within the framework of state planning and political ideals. Although China is tending to become more profit-oriented, most deals are still negotiated within the confines of the state budget allocation for that project rather than on the basis of a project's profitability or value. It is crucial, then, to find out which officials—national, provincial, local—have the power to make, and keep, a deal. According to James Broering of Arthur Andersen, who does much business in China, "companies have negotiated with government people for months, only to discover that they were dealing with the wrong people."[39]

Research shows that for the Chinese, the negotiation process is greatly affected by three cultural norms: their ingrained politeness and emotional restraint; their emphasis on social obligations; and their belief in the interconnection of work, family, and friendship. Because of the Chinese preference for emotional restraint and saving face, aggressive or emotional attempts at persuasion in negotiation are likely to fail. Instead, the Chinese tendency to avoid open conflict will more likely result in negative strategies such as discontinuing or withdrawing from negotiation.[40] At the heart of this kind of response is the concept of **face**—it is essential for foreigners to recognize the role that face behavior plays in negotiations. There are two components of face—*lien* and *mien-tzu*. *Lien* refers to a person's moral character; it is the most important thing defining that person, and without it one cannot function in society. It can only be earned by fulfilling obligations to others. *Mien-tzu* refers to one's reputation or prestige, earned through accomplishments or through bureaucratic or political power.[41] Giving others one's time, gifts, or praise enhances one's own face. In negotiations, it is vital that you do not make it obvious that you have "won" because that means that the other party has "lost" and will lose face. One must therefore make token concessions and other attempts to show that respect must be demonstrated, and modesty and control must be maintained; otherwise anyone who feels he or she has "lost face" will not want to deal with you again. The Chinese will later ignore any dealings or incidents that caused them to lose face, maintaining the expected polite behavior out of social consciousness and concern for others. When encountering an embarrassing situation, they will typically smile or laugh in an attempt to save face, responses that are confusing to Western negotiators.[42]

The Chinese emphasis on social obligations underlies their strong orientation toward collective goals. Therefore, appeals to individual members of the Chinese negotiating team, rather than appeals to benefit the group as a whole, will probably backfire.[43] The Confucian emphasis on the kinship system and the hierarchy of work, family, and friends explains the Chinese preference for doing business with familiar, trusted people and trusted companies. "Foreign" negotiators, then, should focus on establishing long-term, trusting relationships, even at the expense of some immediate returns.

Deeply ingrained in the Chinese culture is the importance of harmony for the smooth functioning of society. Harmony is based primarily on personal relationships, trust, and ritual. After the Chinese establish a cordial relationship with foreign negotiators, they use this relationship as a basis for the give-and-take of business discussions. This implicit cultural norm is commonly known as *guanxi*, which refers to the intricate, pervasive network of personal relations that every Chinese carefully cultivates. It is the primary means of accomplishing things and getting ahead.[44] In other words, *guanxi* establishes obligations to exchange favors in future business activities.[45] Even within the Chinese bureaucracy, *guanxi* prevails over legal interpretations. Although networking is important anywhere to do business, the difference in China is that "*guanxi* networks are not just commercial, but also social, involving the exchange both of favor and affection."[46] Firms that have special *guanxi* connections and give preferential treatment to one another are known as members of a *guanxihu* network.[47] Sunny Zhou, general manager of Kumming Lida Wood and Bamboo Products, states that when he shops for lumber, "the lumber price varies drastically, depending on whether one has strong guanxi with the local administrators."[48]

Western managers should thus anticipate extended preliminary visiting (relationship building), in which the Chinese expect to learn more about them and their trustworthiness. The Chinese also use this opportunity to convey their own deeply held principles. They attach considerable importance to mutual benefit.[49] The Chinese expect Western firms to sacrifice corporate goals and above-average profits to Chinese national goals and principles, such as meaningful friendship, Chinese national development, and the growth and enhancement of the Chinese people. Misunderstandings occur when Americans show polite acceptance of these general principles without understanding their significance—because they do not have any obvious relationship to American corporate goals, such as profit. Nor do such principles seem relevant to practical decisions on plant locations, employee practices, or sourcing.[50]

Americans often experience two negotiation stages with the Chinese—the technical and the commercial. During the long technical stage, the Chinese want to hammer out every detail of the proposed product specifications and technology. If there are two teams of negotiators, it may be several days before the commercial team is actually called in to deal with aspects of production, marketing, pricing, and so forth. However, the commercial team should sit in on the first stage to become familiar with the Chinese negotiating style.[51] The Chinese negotiating team is usually about twice as large as the Western team; about a third of the time is spent discussing technical specifications, and another third on price negotiations, with the rest devoted to general negotiations and posturing.[52]

The Chinese are among the toughest negotiators in the world. American managers must anticipate various tactics, such as their delaying techniques and their avoidance of direct, specific answers: both ploys are used to exploit the known impatience of Americans. The Chinese frequently try to put pressure on Americans by "shaming" them, thereby implying that the Americans are trying to renege on the friendship—the basis of the implicit contract. Whereas westerners come to negotiations with specific and segmented goals and find it easy to compromise, the Chinese are reluctant to negotiate details. They find it difficult to compromise and trade because they have entered negotiations with a broader vision of achieving development goals for China, and they are offended when westerners don't internalize those goals.[53] Under these circumstances, the Chinese will adopt a rigid posture, and no agreement or contract is final until the negotiated activities have actually been completed.

Patience, respect, and experience are necessary prerequisites for anyone negotiating in China. For the best outcomes, older, more experienced people are more acceptable to the Chinese in cross-cultural negotiations. The Chinese want to deal with the top executive of an American company, under the assumption that the highest officer has attained that position by establishing close personal relationships and trust with colleagues and others outside the organization. Western delegation practices are unfamiliar to them, and they are reluctant to come to an agreement without the presence of the Chinese foreign negotiator.[54] From the Western perspective, confusing jurisdictions of government ministries hamper decisions in negotiations.[55] Americans tend to send specific technical personnel with experience in the task at hand; therefore, they have to take care in selecting the most suitable negotiators. In addition, visiting negotiating teams should realize that the Chinese are probably negotiating with other foreign teams, often at the same time, and will use that setup to play one company's offer against the others. On an interpersonal level, Western negotiators must also realize that, while a handshake is polite, physical contact is not acceptable in Chinese social behavior; nor are personal discussion topics such as one's family. However, it is customary to take small gifts as tokens of friendship. Pye offers the following additional tips to foreigners conducting business with the Chinese:[56]

➤ Practice patience.

➤ Accept prolonged periods of stalemate.

➤ Refrain from exaggerated expectations and discount Chinese rhetoric about future prospects.

➤ Expect the Chinese to try to manipulate by shaming.

➤ Resist the temptation to believe that difficulties may have been caused by one's own mistakes.

➤ Try to understand Chinese cultural traits, but realize that a foreigner cannot practice them better than the Chinese.

Managing Conflict Resolution

Much of the negotiation process is fraught with conflict—explicit or implicit—and such conflict can often lead to a standoff, or a lose-lose situation. This is regrettable, not only because of the situation at hand, but also because it probably will shut off future opportunities for deals between the parties. Much of the cause of such conflict can be found in cultural differences between the parties—in their expectations, in their behaviors, and particularly in their communication styles.

As discussed in Chapter 4, much of the difference in communication styles is attributable to whether you belong to a high-context or low-context culture (or somewhere in between, as shown in Exhibit 4-4). In low-context cultures such as that in the United States, conflict is handled directly and explicitly, and is also regarded as separate from the person negotiating. That is, the negotiators draw a distinction between the people involved and the information or opinions they are representing. They also tend to deal on the basis of factual information and logical analysis. That approach to conflict is called **instrumental oriented**.[57] In high-context cultures, such as in the Middle East, the approach to conflict is **expressive oriented**—that is, the situation is handled indirectly and implicitly, and there is no clear delineation of the situation from the person handling it. Those negotiators do not want to get in a confrontational situation because it is regarded as insulting and would cause a loss of "face," so they tend to use evasion and avoidance if they cannot reach agreement through emotional appeals. Their avoidance and inaction conflict with the expectations of the low-context negotiators who are looking to move ahead with the business at hand and arrive at a solution.

The differences between high- and low-context cultures which often lead to conflict situations are summarized in Exhibit 5-10. Most of these variables were discussed earlier in this chapter or in Chapter 4 on communication. They overlap because the subjects and culture and communication are really inseparable, and negotiation differences and conflict situations arise from variables in culture and communication.

The point here is, how can a manager from France, from Japan, or from Brazil, for example, manage conflict situations? The solution, as discussed before, lies mainly in your ability to know and understand the people and the situation you will face. Be

Exhibit 5-10   Sources of Conflict between Low-Context and
High-Context Cultures

Key Questions	Low-Context Conflict	High-Context Conflict
Why	Analytic, linear logic; instrumental oriented; dichotomy between conflict and conflict parties	Synthetic, spiral logic; expressive oriented; integration of conflict and conflict parties
When	Individualistic oriented; low collective normative expectations; violations of individual expectations create conflict potentials	Group oriented; high collective normative expectations; violations of collective expectations create conflict potentials
What	Revealment; direct, confrontational attitude; action and solution oriented	Concealment; indirect nonconfrontational attitude; "face" and relationship oriented
How	Explicit communication codes; line-logic style: rational-factual rhetoric; open, direct strategies	Implicit communication codes; point-logic style: intuitive-effective rhetoric; ambiguous, indirect strategies

SOURCE: W. Gudykunst, L. Stewart, and S. Ting-Toomey, *Communication, Culture, and Organizational Processes.* Copyright © 1985 by Sage Publications, Inc. Reprinted by permission of Sage Publications, Inc.

E-Biz Box

B2B MARKETS: FAST NEGOTIATIONS AND TRANSACTIONS

Over 80 percent of on-line downloads are business-to-business (B2B) transactions. B2B e-commerce—in which transactions between businesses are conducted on-line—offers a number of inherent advantages over traditional commerce. First, it's cheaper to process the nuts and bolts of transactions—purchase orders, proposals, billing statements, fund transfers—when customers are serving themselves on-line. In addition, large buyers such as manufacturers can find better prices if they set up reverse-bidding systems on the Internet that pit suppliers against each other.

For sellers who participate in these markets, there's a lower comfort level with the customer, but there are opportunities for more flexible pricing—at least in theory. And the Internet helps everyone reach more potential trading partners.

The Internet adds new dynamics to the traditional one-to-one model for business transactions. Many vendors sell directly from their sites—virtually all computer-related companies now provide an on-line storefront—but more sophisticated virtual market-places seek to bring buyers and sellers together in one place. By doing this, they hope to increase pricing efficiencies. Some B2B marketplaces are vertically oriented, seeking to capture a large share of a single industry's transactions. Others are horizontal—offering, for instance, places where small businesses can purchase telephone service, office supplies and insurance.

These on-line markets where buyers and sellers negotiate prices are called exchanges. They generally use some sort of bidding or reverse-bid system, and prices fluctuate based on demand. These types of exchanges work well with commodity-type goods that are easily definable. Other B2B sites make comparison shopping possible by aggregating catalogs from more than one vendor.

Typically, B2B sites are supported by membership, subscription, or transaction fees, along with revenue from advertisers. Like stock markets, on-line B2B markets seek to drive volume to their sites to create liquidity and thus efficient pricing.

SOURCE: Adapted from A. Palazzo, *B2B Markets Basics*, www.business.com and www.FT.com, January 28, 2001.

prepared by developing an understanding of the cultural context in which you will be operating. What are the expectations of the persons with whom you will be negotiating? What kinds of communication styles and negotiating tactics should you expect, and how will they differ from your own? It is important to bear in mind your own expectations and negotiating style and to be aware of the other parties' expectations about your behavior. Try to consider in advance what it will take to arrive at a win-win solution. Often it helps to use the services of a host-country adviser or mediator, who may be able to help with early diffusion of a conflict situation.

One contemporary tool in negotiation and decision making that helps to avoid circumstances of conflict is the on-line B2B marketplace; exchanges, where buyers and sellers negotiate prices, speed up the decision-making and transaction process, as described in the accompanying E-Biz Box.

DECISION MAKING

Negotiation actually represents the outcome of a series of small and large decisions. The decisions include those made by each party before actual negotiations start—in determining, for example, the position of the company and what fallback proposals it may suggest or accept. The decisions also include incremental decisions, made during the negotiation process, on how to react and proceed, when to concede, and on what to agree or disagree. Negotiation can thus be seen as a series of explicit and implicit decisions, and the subjects of negotiation and decision making become interdependent.

For instance, sometimes just the way a decision is made during the negotiation process can have a profound influence on the outcome, as this example shows:

> In his first loan negotiation, a banker new to Japan met with seven top Japanese bankers who were seeking a substantial amount of money. After hearing their presentation, the American agreed on the spot. The seven Japanese then conferred among themselves and told the American they would get back to him in a couple of days as to whether they would accept his offer or not. The American banker learned a lesson he never forgot.[58]

The Japanese bankers expected the American to negotiate, to take time to think it over, and to consult with colleagues before giving the final decision. His immediate decision made them suspicious, so they decided to reconsider the deal.

There is no doubt that the speed and manner of decision making affect the negotiation process. In addition, how well negotiated agreements are implemented is affected by the speed and manner of decision making. In that regard, it is clear that the effective use of technology is playing an important role, especially when dealing with complex cross-border agreements in which the hundreds of decision makers involved are separated by time and space.

The role of decision making in management, however, goes far beyond the finite occasions of negotiations. It is part of the manager's daily routine—from operational-level, programmed decisions requiring minimal time and effort to those nonprogrammed decisions of far broader scope and importance, such as the decision to enter into a joint venture in a foreign country.

The Influence of Culture on Decision Making

It is crucial for international managers to understand the influence of culture on decision-making styles and processes. Culture affects decision making both through the broader context of the nation's institutional culture, which produces collective patterns of decision making, and through culturally based value systems that affect each individual decision maker's perception or interpretation of a situation.[59]

The extent to which decision making is influenced by culture varies among countries. For example, Hitt, Tyler, and Park have found a "more culturally homogenizing influence on the Korean executives' cognitive models" than on those of U.S. executives, whose individualistic tendencies lead to different decision patterns.[60] The ways that culture influences an executive's decisions can be studied by looking at the variables involved in each stage of the rational **decision-making process**. These stages are (1) defining the problem, (2) gathering and analyzing relevant data, (3) considering alternative solutions, (4) deciding on the best solution, and (5) implementing the decision.

One of the major cultural variables affecting decision making is whether a country assumes an **objective approach** or a **subjective approach**. Whereas the Western approach is based on rationality (managers interpret a situation and consider alternative solutions based on objective information), this approach is not common throughout the world. Latin Americans, among others, are more subjective, basing decisions on emotions.

Another cultural variable that greatly influences the decision-making process is the **risk tolerance** of those making the decision. Research shows that people from Belgium, Germany, and Austria have a considerably lower tolerance for risk than people from Japan or the Netherlands—whereas American managers have the highest tolerance for risk.[61]

One important variable in the decision-making process is the manager's perception of the **locus of control** over outcomes—whether that locus is internal or external. Some managers feel they can plan on certain outcomes because they are in control of events that will direct the future in the desired way. In contrast, other managers believe that such decisions are of no value because they have little control over the future—which lies in the hands of outside forces, such as fate, God, or nature. American managers believe strongly in self-determination and perceive problem situations as something they can control and should change. However, managers in many other countries, Indonesia and Malaysia among them, are resigned to problem situations and do not feel that they can change them. Obviously, these different value systems will result in a great difference in the stages of consideration of alternative actions and choice of solution, often because certain situations may or may not be viewed as problems in the first place.

Another variable that affects the consideration of alternative solutions is how managers feel about staying with familiar solutions or trying new ones. Many managers, particularly those in Europe, value decisions based on past experiences and tend to emphasize quality. Americans, on the other hand, are more future oriented and look toward new ideas to get them there.

Approaches to Decision Making

In addition to affecting different stages of the decision-making process, value systems influence the overall approach of decision makers from various cultures. The relative level of **utilitarianism** versus **moral idealism** in any society affects its overall approach to problems. Generally speaking, utilitarianism strongly guides behavior in the Western world. Research has shown that Canadian executives are more influenced by a short-term, cost-benefit approach to decision making than their Hong Kong counterparts. Canadian managers are considerably more utilitarian than leaders from the People's Republic of China, who approach problems from a standpoint of moral idealism; they consider the problems, alternatives, and solutions from a long-term, societal perspective rather than an individual perspective.[62]

Another important variable in companies' overall approach to decision making is that of autocratic versus participative leadership. In other words, who has the authority to make what kinds of decisions? A country's orientation—whether it is **individualistic** or **collectivist** (as discussed in Chapter 3)—influences the level at which decisions are made. In many countries with hierarchical cultures—Germany, Turkey, and India, among others—authorization for action has to be passed upward through echelons of management before final decisions can be made. Most employees in these countries simply expect the autocrat—the boss—to do most of the decision making and would not be comfortable otherwise. Even in China, which is a highly collectivist society, employees expect **autocratic leadership** because their value system presupposes the superior to be automatically the most wise. In comparison, in Sweden, decision-making authority is very decentralized. Americans talk a lot about the advisability of such **participative leadership**, but in practice they are probably around the middle between autocratic and participative management styles.

Arab managers have long traditions of consultative decision making, supported by the Qur'an and the sayings of Muhammed. However, such consultation occurs more on a person-to-person basis than in group meetings, and thus diffuses potential opposition.[63] Although business in the Middle East tends to be transacted in a highly personalized manner, the final decisions are made by the top leaders, who feel that they must impose their will for the company to be successful. In comparison, in cultures like Japan's that emphasize collective harmony, participatory or group decision making predominates, and consensus is important. The best-known example is the bottom-up (rather than top-down) decision-making process used in most Japanese companies, described in more detail in the next section.

One final area of frequent incongruence concerns the relative speed of decision making. A country's culture affects how fast or slow decisions tend to be made. The relative speed may be closely associated with the level of delegation, as just discussed—but not always. The pace at which decisions are made can be very disconcerting for outsiders. North Americans and Europeans pride themselves on being decisive; managers in the Middle East, with a different sense of temporal urgency, associate the importance of the matter at hand with the length of time needed to make a decision. Without knowing this cultural attitude, a hasty American would insult an Egyptian; a quick decision, to the Egyptian, would reflect a low regard for the relationship and the deal.

Exhibit 5-11 illustrates, in summary form, how all the variables just discussed can affect the steps in the decision-making process.

Exhibit 5-11   Cultural Variables in the Decision-Making Process

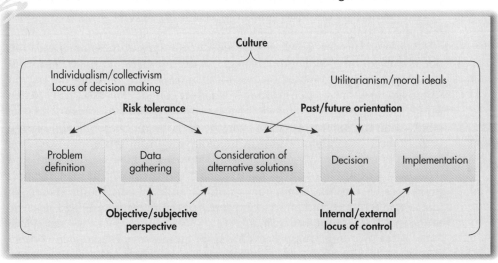

**Comparative
Management
in Focus**

Decision Making in Japanese Companies

Japanese companies are involved in joint ventures throughout the world, especially with American companies. The GM-Toyota joint venture agreement process, for example, was the result of over two years of negotiation and decision making. In this new company and in similar companies, Americans and Japanese are involved in decision making at all levels on a daily basis. The Japanese decision-making process greatly differs not only from the American process but from that of many other countries—especially at the higher levels of their organizations.

An understanding of the Japanese decision-making process—and indeed of many of their management practices—requires an understanding of their national culture. As previously discussed, much of the Japanese culture, and therefore the basis of Japanese working relationships, can be explained by the principle of *wa*, meaning "peace and harmony." This principle is one aspect of the value they attribute to **amae**, meaning "indulgent love," a concept probably originating in the Shinto religion, which focuses on spiritual and physical harmony. *Amae* results in **shinyo**, which refers to the mutual confidence, faith, and honor required for successful business relationships. The principle of *wa* influences the work group, the basic building block of Japanese work and management. The Japanese identify strongly with their work groups, where the emphasis is on cooperation, participative management, consensus problem solving, and decision making based on a patient, long-term perspective. Open expression of conflict is discouraged, and it is of utmost importance to avoid embarrassment or shame—to lose face—as a result of not fulfilling one's obligations. These elements of work culture generally result in a devotion to work, a collective responsibility for decisions and actions, and a high degree of employee productivity. It is this culture of collectivism and shared responsibility that underlies the Japanese *ringi* system of decision making.

In the **ringi** system, the process works from the bottom up. Americans are used to a centralized system, where major decisions are made by upper-level managers in a "top-down" approach typical of individualistic societies. The Japanese process, however, is dispersed throughout the organization, relying on group consensus.

The *ringi* process is one of gaining approval on a proposal by circulating documents to those concerned throughout the company. It usually comprises four steps: proposal, circulation, approval, and record.[64] Usually, the person who originates the written proposal, which is called a **ringi-sho**, has already worked for some time to gain informal consensus and support for the proposal within the section and then from the department head.[65] The next step is to attain a general consensus in the company from those who would be involved in implementation. To this end, department meetings are held, and if necessary, expert opinion is sought. If more information is needed, the proposal goes back to the originator, who finds and adds the required data. In this way, much time and effort—and the input of many people—go into the proposal before it becomes formal.[66]

Up to this point, the process has been an informal one to gain consensus, called the **nemawashi** process. Then the more formal authorization procedure begins, called the *ringi* process. The *ringi-sho* is passed up through successive layers of management for approval—the approval made official by seals. In the end, many such seals of approval are gathered, thereby ensuring collective agreement and responsibility and giving the proposal a greater chance of final approval by the president. The whole process is depicted in Exhibit 5-12.

The *ringi* system is cumbersome and very time-consuming prior to the implementation stage, although implementation is facilitated because of the widespread awareness of and support for the proposal already gained throughout the organization. But its slow progress is problematic when decisions are time-sensitive. This process is the opposite of the Americans' top-down decisions, which are made quite rapidly and without consultation, but which then take some time to implement because unforeseen practical or support problems often arise.

Exhibit 5-12   Decision-Making Procedure in Japanese Companies

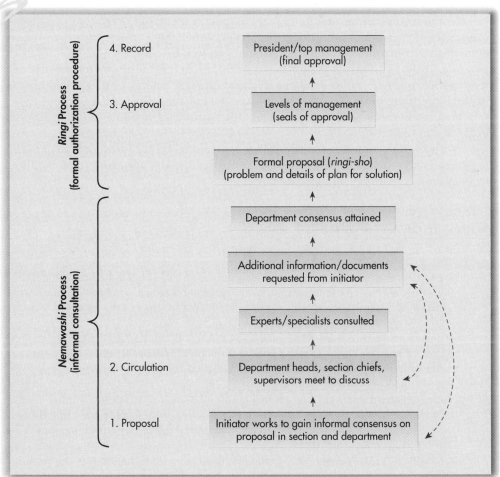

Another interesting comparison is often made regarding the planning horizon (aimed at short- or long-term goals) in decision making between the American and Japanese systems. The Japanese spend considerable time in the early stages of the process defining the issue, considering what the issue is all about, and determining whether there is an actual need for a decision. They are more likely than Americans to consider an issue in relation to the overall goals and strategy of the company. In this manner, they prudently look at the "big picture" and consider alternative solutions, instead of rushing into quick decisions for immediate solutions, as Americans tend to do.[67]

Of course, in a rapidly changing environment, quick decisions are often necessary—to respond to competitors' actions, a political uprising, and so forth—and it is in such contexts that the *ringi* system sometimes falls short because of its slow response rate. The system is, in fact, designed to manage continuity and to avoid uncertainty, which is considered a threat to group cohesiveness.[68]

Conclusion

It is clear that competitive positioning and long-term successful operations in a global market require a working knowledge of the decision-making and negotiating process of managers from different countries. These processes are complex and often interdependent. Although managers may make decisions that do not involve negotiating, they cannot negotiate without making decisions, however small, or they would not be negotiating. In addition, managers must understand the behavioral aspects of these processes to work effectively with people in other countries or with a culturally diverse workforce in their own country.

With an understanding of the environment and cultural context of international management as background, we move next in Part 3 to planning and implementing strategy for international and global operations.

SUMMARY OF KEY POINTS

1. The ability to negotiate successfully is one of the most important in international business. Managers must prepare for certain cultural variables that influence negotiations, including the relative emphasis on task versus interpersonal relationships, the use of general principles versus specific details, the number of people present, and the extent of their influence.

2. The negotiation process typically progresses through the stages of preparation, relationship building, exchange of task-related information, persuasion, and concessions and agreement. The process of building trusting relationships is a prerequisite to doing business in many parts of the world.

3. Culturally based differences in verbal and nonverbal negotiation behavior influence the negotiation process at every stage. Such tactics and actions include promises, threats, initial concessions, silent periods, interruptions, facial gazing, and touching; some parties resort to various dirty tricks.

4. The effective management of negotiation requires an understanding of the perspectives, values, and agenda of the other parties and the use of a problem-solving approach.

5. Decision making is an important part of the negotiation process as well as an integral part of a manager's daily routine. Culture affects the decision-making process both through a society's institutions and through individuals' risk tolerance, their objective versus subjective perspective, their perception of the locus of control, and their past versus future orientation.

6. The Internet is increasingly being used to support the negotiation of contracts and resolution of disputes. Web sites that provide open auctions take away the personal aspects of negotiations, though those aspects are still essential in many instances.

DISCUSSION QUESTIONS

1. Discuss the stages in the negotiation process and how culturally based value systems influence these stages. Specifically,

   - explain the role and relative importance of relationship building in different countries
   - discuss the various styles and tactics that can be involved in exchanging task-related information
   - describe differences in culturally based styles of persuasion
   - discuss the kinds of concession strategies a negotiator might anticipate in various countries

2. Discuss the relative use of nonverbal behaviors, such as silent periods, interruptions, facial gazing, and touching, by people from various cultural backgrounds. How does this behavior affect the negotiation process in a cross-cultural context?

3. Describe what you would expect in negotiations with the Chinese and how you would handle various situations.

4. What are some of the differences in risk tolerance around the world? What is the role of risk propensity in the decision-making process?

5. Explain how objective versus subjective perspectives influences the decision-making process. What role do you think this variable has played in all of the negotiations and decisions between Iraq and the United Nations?

6. Explain differences in culturally based value systems relative to the amount of control a person feels he or she has over future outcomes. How does this belief influence the decision-making process?

EXPERIENTIAL EXERCISES

Exercise

1. Multicultural Negotiations

Goal

To experience, identify, and appreciate the problems associated with negotiating with people of other cultures.

SOURCE: Egidio A. Diodati, assistant professor of Management at Assumption College in Worcester, Massachusetts, in C. Harvey and M. J. Allard, *Understanding Diversity* (New York: HarperCollins Publishers, 1995). Used with permission.

Instructions

1. Eight student volunteers will participate in the role play: four representing a Japanese automobile manufacturer and four representing an American team that has come to sell microchips and other components to the Japanese company. The remainder of the class will observe the negotiations.

2. The eight volunteers will divide up into the two groups and then separate into different rooms, if possible. At that point, they will be given instruction sheets. Neither team can have access to the other's instructions. After dividing up the roles, the teams should meet for 10 to 15 minutes to develop their negotiation strategies based on their instructions (from the instructor's manual).

3. While the teams are preparing, the room will be set up using a rectangular table with four seats on each side. The Japanese side will have three chairs at the table with one chair set up behind the three. The American side of the table will have four chairs side-by-side.

4. After the preparation time is over, the Japanese team will be brought in, so they may greet the Americans when they arrive. At this point, the Americans will be brought in and the role play begins. Time for the negotiations should be 20 to 30 minutes. The rest of the class will act as observers and will be expected to provide feedback during the discussion phase.

5. After the negotiations are completed, the student participants from both sides and the observers will complete their feedback questionnaires. Class discussion of the feedback questions will follow.

Feedback Questions for the Japanese Team

1. What was your biggest frustration during the negotiations?
2. What would you say the goal of the American team was?
3. How would you rate the success of each of the American team members in identifying your team's needs and appealing to them?

> Mr. Jones, Vice President and Team Leader
>
> Mr./Mrs. Smith, Manufacturing Engineer
>
> Mr./Mrs. Nelson, Marketing Analyst
>
> Mr./Mrs. Frost, Account Executive

4. What would you say the goal of the Japanese team was?
5. What role (e.g., decider, influencer, etc.) did each member of the American team play?

> Mr. Jones
>
> Mr./Ms. Smith
>
> Mr./Mrs. Nelson
>
> Mr./Mrs. Frost

6. What strategy should the American team have taken?

Feedback Questions for the American Team

1. What was your biggest frustration during the negotiations?
2. What would you say the goal of the Japanese team was?

3. How would you rate the success of each of the American team members?

   Mr. Jones, Vice President and Team Leader
   Mr./Mrs. Smith, Manufacturing Engineer
   Mr./Mrs. Nelson, Marketing Analyst
   Mr./Mrs. Frost, Account Executive

4. What would you say the goal of the American team was?
5. What role (e.g., decider, influencer, etc.) did each member of the Japanese team play?

   Mr. Ozaka
   Mr. Nishimuro
   Mr. Sheno
   Mr. Kawazaka

6. What strategy should the American team have taken?

Feedback Questions for the Observers

1. What was your biggest frustration during the negotiations?
2. What would you say the goal of the Japanese team was?
3. How would you rate the success of each of the American team members?

   Mr. Jones, Vice President and Team Leader
   Mr./Mrs. Smith, Manufacturing Engineer
   Mr./Mrs. Nelson, Marketing Analyst
   Mr./Mrs. Frost, Account Executive

4. What would you say the goal of the American team was?
5. What role (e.g., decider, influencer, etc.) did each member of the Japanese team play?

   Mr. Ozaka
   Mr. Nishimuro
   Mr. Sheno
   Mr. Kawazaka

6. What strategy should the American team have taken?

Exercise 2: Japanese Decision Making

Time: Two class meetings

Goal

To allow students to experience the process and results of solving a problem or initiating a project using the Japanese decision processes of *nemawashi* and *ringi*.

Preparation

Review Chapters 4 and 5; study section "Decision Making in Japanese Companies," in Chapter 5.

Introduction

The Professor explains the exercise and designates or elicits two specific subjects or projects to be resolved by the class. These could be current problems on campus, for example. (One project may be used, but that would mean that half the class would be sitting around waiting during the first stage. Also, by using two projects, each group can experience being a primary group and a secondary group.)

First Class—*Nemawashi*

Example for a Class of 30

Stage 1: Three groups of five students meet to draw up a plan to resolve issue No. 1. The other three groups of five meet to draw up a plan to resolve issue No. 2.

Stage 2: Results for the two projects are switched to the other groups—secondary groups (*Kacho*). The *Kacho* discuss the plan suggested by the primary groups. They may request additional information from the primary groups.

Stage 3: Groups or individuals may meet outside of class as they wish in order to discuss their assigned project or problem before the second class meeting. Outside experts or sources may be consulted.

Second Class

Formal proposal: *Ringi-sho*—submitted for project one and project two. Each plan must be signed by all class members, representing a consensus decision. Professor discusses plans with class to assess feasibility and likelihood of approval by university president. Any minor changes are resolved and approval is indicated.

Feedback: Ask the class how effective they felt this process to be in their environment and culture. What problems did they encounter? What do they feel about the outcomes compared to other ways in which they would have approached those problems? Would they choose the same decision-making process for another project?

INTERNET RESOURCES

Visit the Deresky companion Website at http://prenhall.com/Deresky for this chapter's Internet resources.

CASE STUDY: MARTINEZ CONSTRUCTION COMPANY IN GERMANY

(Martinez Construction & Konstruktion Dreizehn)

Juan Sanchez glanced out the window of the Boeing jetliner and admired the countryside passing below. The overcast skies failed to dampen his enthusiasm for the challenges and opportunities he and his company now faced. Two generations of local services had done little to prepare Martinez Construction for the coming days. Nevertheless, Juan remained confident that once the spirit of cooperation and trust was established, the new German operation would be a success.

SOURCE: Term project by Ann Eubanks, and Derek Bonen Clark, graduate students at the State University of New York—Plattsburgh, Spring 1995. Copyright © 1995 by Helen Deresky. This case and the characters represented in it are fictional. The case is presented as a basis for educational discussion rather than to illustrate either effective or ineffective handling of an administrative situation.

Martinez Construction

Martinez Construction is a well-established construction company in eastern Spain. Founded in Barcelona in the mid-1940s, its reputation and quality of service ensured growing profits for decades. However, a recent decline in contracts has resulted in a growing awareness of the dependence the business has on local economic conditions.

Diego Martinez, president and son of the founder of Martinez Construction, now faces a growing certainty that the survival and continued growth of the family business depend on expansion into the international marketplace. In Barcelona, Diego had met many German tourists. They seemed to enjoy the warm sunshine of Spain. He also knew that many German companies now conducted business in Spain. So, it was natural that when his company started thinking globally they were drawn to the new German states. The recent collapse of communism and subsequent opening of new markets in Eastern Europe provided what seemed like an excellent opportunity for expansion. After all, why shouldn't Martinez Construction take advantage of the cheap labor and raw materials?

More information was needed, however. Martinez Construction representatives contacted banks, commercial departments of foreign consulates, chambers of commerce, and the Treuhandanstalt's Investor Services department. They also depended on accountants, lawyers, consultants, and others to provide advice. After the initial research and discussion of the alternatives with other members of management, Diego has come to the conclusion that the best approach to this venture will be through the acquisition of an existing company from the Treuhandanstalt (THA). This decision was made after concluding that Martinez Construction lacked the resources necessary to risk a greenfield operation. Added to this was the certainty that an alliance with other German companies would not allow Martinez Construction to established itself as a serious competitor in the international construction market.

Diego chose his brother-in-law and manager of the Barcelona branch of Martinez Construction. Juan Sanchez, to act as the negotiator for the company with the THA. Although Juan is unfamiliar with German business practices, Diego feels that Juan's friendly demeanor and expertise in the needs of the company will ensure the establishment of the necessary trust to build a strong cooperative venture with the THA.

Juan will be accompanied by Diego's nephew and projected manager of the new German acquisition, Miguel Martinez. Miguel is the youngest and most educated of the Martinez managerial staff. His background includes a business degree from a university in the United States, as well as years of employment in the family business. Although lacking in practical managerial experience, it was due largely to his influence that Diego saw the wisdom and necessity of expanding operations abroad. Miguel's opportunity has fueled his optimism despite the challenges he faces in the management of a foreign subsidiary.

Treuhandanstalt

Because of the collapse of communism in the German Democratic Republic, the two Germanys were finally going to be reunified. The Treuhandanstalt, or THA, was for a short time the world's largest holding company. It was created in what was the German Democratic Republic. The sole purpose of the THA was to find private buyers for some 13,500 businesses and 15,000 parcels of real estate that had previously been owned by the German Democratic Republic. The government knew that the economy in this sector had to be stimulated quickly. There were hopes that many investors would take advantage of the new markets opening up. However, little thought was given to the immensity of the job. No guidelines were issued, which later led to charges of dubious deals, and limited funds were made available to run the agency.

Therefore, any firm wishing to purchase an existing facility in East Germany had no choice in the matter—they had to deal with the THA. The primary job of the THA was to sell the companies, to try to match existing companies with buyers. However, this proved to be an almost impossible task because the THA has insufficient or no information about the financial positions of the companies it was supposed to sell. In some cases, it could not ascertain what companies were to be sold.

The firms wishing to purchase properties through the THA were initially evaluated on the basis of financial soundness. Second, they were evaluated on potential employment opportunity. Next, they were measured according to the cost of restructuring to the buyer. The speed of the sale was, however, the most important issue to the THA. The sooner the THA finished its work, the sooner the economy would improve.

Price was the main aspect of the sales negotiations. Other facets of the negotiations involved guaranteeing jobs for present employees and arranging for the upgrade and improvement of the companies. This meant the investment of a great deal of time and money on the part of the buyer because many of the firms had fallen into disrepair. In fact, some were no longer operable in their present state.

Negotiations

The THA finally fond what they considered to be a match for Martinez Construction. It was an existing construction firm, Konstruktion Dreizehn, located in Leipzig, Germany. (Leipzig is a city of about 564,000 people located in the eastern part of Germany.)

From the time of his arrival in Germany, Juan felt that he was having a difficult time just getting acquainted with the Germans. He felt pressured by the THA representatives. The Germans were all business. They didn't seem to have time to get to know Juan personally: rush and urgency to complete the sale was the focus of their approach.

The first meeting was scheduled for 9:00 A.M. Juan and Miguel arrived at 9:15. Juan noticed that the THA representative, Helga Schmidt, seemed quite agitated when they arrived. She didn't even offer them coffee. He wondered what had upset her so much.

When he suggested that they be taken on a tour of the city this morning instead of immediately starting the negotiations, he was reminded of the necessity of proceeding with the negotiations. Even though this displeased Juan, he agreed to start negotiations for the sale.

The Germans presented their proposal to Juan. He was amazed. Every detail was in this contract; and yet the THA had not yet ascertained the financial status and position of the construction firm in Leipzig. For this reason, Juan had expected some sort of flexible agreement. This was especially important since there was no way to determine the extent of future problems given the dearth of available financial analysis. Didn't the Germans know this? If the THA was to be trusted, why bother with this type of contract? He told the Germans exactly what his thoughts were on this subject.

Helga was clearly uncomfortable with Juan's emotional outburst. However, she did see his point and decided to compromise by offering a phased contract, which made Juan more comfortable with the situation. However, the Germans felt lost without the technicalities represented in the original contract.

The negotiations proceeded smoothly from this point. The final contract stated that in two years they would review the original price and recalculate it based on new and presumably more reliable data concerning the true value of the firm. Although there were problems with the negotiations, one thing did impress Juan about the Germans. He really appreciated the way the negotiations were organized. When there was a question, Helga always knew whom to contact. She also knew what forms, reports, and so on, needed to be sent to which department of the THA. Helga, on the other hand, was very uncomfortable with Juan's relaxed manner. however, she did value his genuineness and practicality.

Operations

Miguel Martinez arrived tired but excited in Leipzig. The flight provided ample time to consider his actions in the new German subsidiary. After spending a few days setting up household, Miguel met with the three-member management team sent the month before to being studying the situation. It was the consensus of the team, and they quickly convinced Miguel, that human resources would be crucial to the recovery of the company. Under the GDR, the company employed approximately 350 workers. The THA had reduced the workforce to 100. Miguel and his team estimated that 50 employees would be sufficient. However, it was not long before they realized that East Germans did not work nearly as well as West Germans. Further confirmation of the effect of the workers' state on the employees was the lack of initiative and the concept of responsibility among the workers. Miguel was frustrated by the unwillingness of the employees to actively participate in the formulation of ideas and implementation of new procedures and policies. More than 40 years of communism had taught employees to expect all guidance and solutions to come from the top.

Added to the lack of initiative was a fear and distrust of management. This fear was quickly justified when Miguel's new management team investigated a labor union's report criticizing the previous management's hiring practices and competence.

Six months after Miguel's triumphant arrival, his optimism was fading fast. he had just received the latest report concerning the company's financial position, and it was clear that the figures were far from what Martinez Construction had been led to believe. Strict environmental and employee protection regulations forced large investments in plant modifications. Further, there were other costly projects that had not been foreseen during the negotiation process. Cash flow problems were beginning to arise, and this threatened the very existence of the company.

Although reevaluation of the contract was specified after two years, Miguel wondered whether immediate action might be necessary. Sitting in his office overlooking the southern complex of the plant, the heavy rain clouds matched the darkness of his mood.

Appendix 1—A Comparison of Spanish and German Democratic Republic Work Styles

Appendix 2—Neogiating Styles of the Spanish and Germans

Case Questions

1. What was the basis for Martinez Construction's decision to enter the international market? proactive or reactive? Why?

2. Were the Spanish prepared for the problems faced in the negotiations? If not, what might the Spanish have done to better prepare themselves for the negotiations?

3. How did the Spanish interpret the actions of the Germans?

4. Do you think the Germans were aware of the cultural differences that came to the surface during the negotiations?

5. What might the Spanish have done differently to address the concerns of the employees?

6. What are the diverse problems created by the differences between the Spanish and German cultures? communist and capitalist cultures?

Appendix 1: A Comparison of Spanish and German Democratic Republic Work Styles

Spanish

➤ Clear goals not common; work under assumption that goals of past will be goals of future

➤ Hierarchical society with status based on position; line of authority is top-down

➤ Promotions usually determined by seniority

➤ Decisions influenced by human factors

German Democratic Republic

➤ Goals related to politics; what is good for state (society)

➤ Everyone is equal; however, superiors expected to provide all solutions

➤ Lifelong employment common; advancement decisions political

➤ Decisions influenced by what is good for society as a whole

Appendix 2: Negotiating Styles of the Spanish and Germans

Spanish

➤ Prefer to establish trust by taking time to get to know counterparts

➤ Don't attach importance to punctuality

➤ Discuss things at length

➤ Raise their voices and interrupt speakers during disagreements

➤ Make decisions based on general principles and leave details undecided.

Germans

➤ Keep business and pleasure separate

➤ Stress the importance of punctuality

➤ State facts in a concise manner

➤ Reserved and formal during discussions

➤ Exhibit a strong concern for details and exacting contracts

Case Bibliography

This case is based in part on a company discussed in the referenced article by R. W. Frederick and Adolfo de la Fuente Rodriguez; those authors do not indicate the name of the company discussed, nor whether it is real or fictional.

Ames, Helen Watley. *Spain Is Different*. ME: Intercultural Press, Inc., 1992, 89–96.

Cote, Kevin. "Germany's White Elephant." *Fortune*, June 28, 1991.

"Farewell, Sweet Treuhand: Privatisation." *Economist*, 333, 7895, December 1994, 82–85.

"Fast and Loose: East German Privatisation," *Economist*, 331, 7861, April 30, 1994, 75–76.

Frederick, Richard W., and Adolfo de la Fuente Rodriguez. "A Spanish Acquisition in Eastern Germany: Culture Shock." *Journal of Management Development* 13, no. 2 (March 1994): 42–49.

Hampden-Turner, Charles. "The Boundaries of Business: The Cross-Cultural Quagmir." *Harvard Business Review* (September–October 1991).

Hofstede, G. *Cultures and Organization.* New York: McGraw-Hill, 1991, 200–203.

Kanter, Rosabeth Moss. "Transcending Business Boundaries: 12,000 World Mangers View Change." *Harvard Business Review* (May–June 1991): 151–164.

Kanter, Rosabeth Moss, and Richard Ian Corn. "Do Cultural Differences Make a Business Difference?" *Journal of Management Development* 13, no. 2 (1993): 5–23.

Lacher, Michael A. "Creating and Securing Joint Ventures in Central and Eastern Europe: A Western Perspective." *Site Selection* (June 1994): 554–555.

Meschi, Pierre-Xavier and Alain Roger. "Cultural Context and Social Effectiveness in International Joint Ventures." *Mangement International Review* 34 (1994): 197–215.

Miller, Karen Lowery, Jeff Javetski, and Peggy Simson, "Europe: The Push East." *Business Week*, November 7, 1994.

Mueller, Franc. "Societal Effect, Organizational Effect, and Globalization." *Organizational Studies* 15, no. 3 (1994): 407–428.

Olie, Rene, "Shades of Culture and Institutions in International Mergers." *Organizational Studies* 15, no. 3 (1994): 381–405.

"Recognizing and Heeding Cultural Differences Can Be Key to International Business Success." Compiled by staff, *Business America* (October 1994).

Torpey, John. "Growing Together, Coming Apart: German Society Since Unification." *Social Education* 57, no. 5 ( ): 136–239.

West, Judy F., and Judy C. Nixon. "Cultural Diversity Among American and European Business Persons." Paper presented at the annual meeting of the Association of Business Communication International Conference, November 8, 1990.

Comprehensive
Cases

Case 4   TelSys International:
A Marriage of Two Cultures
(Case or Negotiation Simulation)

FINAL NEGOTIATIONS IN KUALA LUMPUR

James R. Chesney, a veteran engineer and former head of the Microelectronic Systems Branch at NASA's Goddard Space Flight Center, allowed his gaze to drift away from the negotiating table toward the view of skyscrapers and blue sky visible through the tall windows on the opposite wall. He smiled faintly, realizing that this was the most he had seen of Kuala Lumpur since his arrival here just three days ago on August 12, 1995. Since then, Chesney and his colleagues had been chauffeured back and forth from their suite at the Hilton. Each day they had encountered intense negotiations over the terms of the pending agreement with the Malaysian

By Christine S. Nielsen, University of Baltimore; Bruce G. Montgomery, Synotinics LLC; Matthew R. Leavenworth, Saltmine LLC; and Geoffrey N. Walters, Meat and Livestock Australia Ltd.

This case was prepared as the basis of class discussion rather than to illustrate effective or ineffective handling of a management situation. The company name TelSys International was used during early stages of Chesney's search for venture capital. All individuals and events in the case are real. The history has been abbreviated in order to fit a case format. Certain names have been disguised. The authors express their gratitude for the graduate research assistance of Asaf Cohen for his research into the world of venture capitalists, and his design of the figure, "ITC and TelSys International." Our thanks to Rhoda Lee for her research into Malaysian customs. We gratefully acknowledge the valuable support of Kathy Webb in document assembly and integration. The authors' appreciate the thorough review of this case by the *CRJ* reviewers. Their advice led to significant improvements in this revision.

Venture Capital Group (VCG). Negotiations revolved around the creation of a new venture, TelSys International, Inc. (TelSys).

Only if Chesney could secure the financing he needed would TelSys be able to produce and market high-quality satellite ground station communications equipment based on his patented designs. While the company's initial customer base would revolve around the world's space agencies and major satellite providers, Chesney knew that there was a huge potential commercial market for TelSys's products as well. So far the negotiations were promising, and the parties were moving toward an arrangement that would allow Chesney to fulfill his dream.

Major concerns were being addressed during the Kuala Lumpur meetings in August 1995. One thorny issue had been settled. As a financial investment firm, each of VCG's holdings had to be in a company that was publicly traded in order that the investment remained liquid. While both VCG and TelSys would have preferred a U.S. stock exchange listing, this was not possible, given the new venture's fledgling status. TelSys was unable to meet the market listing requirements of either the New York Stock exchange or NASDAQ, so an acceptable solution had been reached to utilize a Canadian stock exchange instead. TelSys would become a wholly owned subsidiary of International Technology Contours Incorporated (ITC), a Canadian firm that was already listed on the Toronto Stock Exchange. A major advantage of listing through ITC was that the firm would save underwriting fees and other expenses associated with an initial public offering.

However, other critical issues were yet to be resolved in these final days of negotiations:

1. Determination of the equity split between Chesney's management group and VCG.
2. Decisions regarding leadership of
   (a) the ITC holding company in Canada;
   (b) TelSys International; and
   (c) the ITC Board of Directors.
3. Composition and size of the ITC Board of Directors.
4. Decisions regarding technology-sharing between Chesney and his Malaysian partners.

On this fateful day in Kuala Lumpur, Gary Baker, president of ITC, sat on Chesney's right. Chesney's other advisers during the negotiation were Bruce Montgomery (TelSys vice president of Operations, formerly part of the senior management group with Fairchild), and Peter Campisi, TelSys vice president of Finance, formerly Chief Financial Officer of DavCo Restaurants, Inc.).

THE TENSION BUILDS

Chesney's gaze focused on his VCG counterparts. Less than a year ago, he could not have imagined this scene. The potential saviors of his high-tech venture represented an Islamic banking and finance group. He studied the Malaysian team that faced him: Dr. Nik Bashshâr Ahmad abu Munîr, president and CEO of VCG; Drs. Kalîl 'Abd Al Wâhid and Rafiq Ibn Tammân (both vice presidents of VCG); Mr. Is hâq 'Abd Al 'Aliyy bin Ahmad, managing director of VCG Investments, Inc. (the North American subsidiary located in Connecticut); Ms. Azîzah Hasnâ' Sâlih, financial controller in *purdah* (following the Islamic tradition of wearing veils), and Mr. Yûsuf Sulaymân, director of Finance. (See Exhibit 1, Profiles of Negotiating Team Members.)

Time was running out. Dr. Nik had arranged for a press conference in the Hilton Hotel Ballroom in two hours to announce the agreement. Chesney still had to return to his hotel and

Exhibit 1   Profiles of Negotiating Team Members

James R. Chesney
President
TelSys International

Mr. Chesney, 51, is the founder and president of TelSys International. He retired in 1994 from NASA as a branch head-level manager (GM-15) with over 20 years of professional experience at the Goddard Space Flight Center (GSFC).

At NASA, Mr. Chesney began in 1985 to create the technical team that provided many of the founding employees for TelSys International. With a limited budget, he recruited top engineers, developed a nationally respected organization, and produced the world's leading-edge space telemetry data processing systems and components. He directed the team's efforts to design, develop, and deploy advanced data system architectures and components needed to support NASA's future missions, including such missions as the Earth Observing System (EOS), Gamma Ray Observatory (GRO), and the Space Station Program. His personal success is reflected in the recognized excellence of these systems and components, and their informal identification generally within the industry as "Chesney's systems or components." His other

Please note: Profiles for a majority of negotiating team members are included. Several are not available.

innovations include NASA's first flight application of a commercial VLSI gate array, in 1980.

Mr. Chesney holds a BSEE from Johns Hopkins University and is a member of the ETA KAPPA NU National Electrical Engineering Honor Society. He has written, published, and presented many articles on space telemetry architectures and components and has received numerous awards including NASA's GSFC Exceptional Achievement Award and NASA's Exceptional Engineering Achievement Medal.

Bruce G. Montgomery
Vice President of Operations
TelSys International

Mr. Montgomery has 23 years of engineering, manufacturing, and general management experience in high-technology and aerospace industries. He previously was with Fairchild Space and Defense for 14 years, the last eight as a founder and general manager of a division that grew to 200 employees. Earlier, Mr. Montgomery worked for the management consulting firm Booz Allen & Hamilton; he began his career at the Jet Propulsion Laboratory.

Mr. Montgomery has a B.S. in Science and Engineering from the California Institute of Technology; an M.S. in Civil Engineering from California State University at Los Angeles; and an MBA from the Graduate School of

Exhibit I   (cont.)

Industrial Administration at Carnegie Mellon University. He is a director of the nonprofit Maryland Space Business Roundtable and a registered Professional Engineer in the State of Maryland.

Nik Bashshâr Ahmad abu Munîr
President and CEO
Venture Capital Group

Dr. Nik Bashshâr Ahmad abu Munîr, founder of VCG, obtained his Master's degree in Actuarial Science and his Ph.D. in Finance from a U.S. university. He has vast experience in international fund management, having been deeply involved in the major capital markets of the world, especially the New York Stock Exchange and the Kuala Lumpur Stock Exchange. His specialty is investment analysis and strategy, and he is responsible for developing the investment analysis and strategy of VCG, which has been successful in both the U.S. and Malaysian markets over the years. As the chief executive officer, he oversees the overall investment strategy for VCG and is involved in development of financial and investment instruments, as well as systems development for the financial institutions under the VCG. Given his exposure and experience in international business Dr. Nik also leads VCG in its international business ventures and exercises.

Kalîl 'Abd Al Wâhid
Vice President
Venture Capital Group

Dr. Kalîl 'Abd Al Wâhid graduated with a B.Eng. (Honors) in Electrical Engineering and a M.Eng. in Microwave Communications Engineering from a university in the United Kingdom in 1979 and 1981, respectively. He joined Universiti Kebangsaan Malaysia as a tutor in 1979 and was appointed a lecturer in 1981. In 1984, Dr. Kalîl took a leave of absence to pursue his doctoral degree (funded by the U.S. Office of Naval Research) and graduated with a Ph.D. in Electrical Engineering from a U.S. university.

He was promoted to associate professor in the mid-1990s and shortly thereafter became head of the Electrical, Electronics and Systems Engineering Department, Universiti Kebangsaan Malaysia. Dr. Kalîl is a registered professional engineer with the Board of Engineers Malaysia. He is also a senior member of the Institute of Electrical and Electronics Engineers and a member of the Institute of Engineers Malaysia.

Rafîq Ibn Tammân
Vice President
Venture Capital Group

Dr. Rafîq Ibn Tammân obtained his Ph.D. in Taxation from a university in the United Kingdom. He is a member of the Malaysian Institute of Accountants, and his in-depth experience of the financial sector encompasses over 20 years of professional service. Dr. Rafîq has served on the Boards of Directors of several prominent companies in Malaysia and currently sits on the Board of BIMB Unit Trust Sdn Bhd and other institutions. He has been consultant and adviser to the Ministry of Finance, Malaysia, as well as to the Economic Planning Unit (EPU) of the Prime Minister's Department. His major roles are giving advice on tax matters, leading the advisory and research activities of the group, and aiding in the development of new ventures and financial institutions.

Is hâq 'Abd Al 'Aliyy bin Ahmad
Managing Director
VCG Investments, Inc.

Mr. Is hâq is among the founding members of a pioneering Islamic investment management company in North America. He possesses qualifications in the area of security analysis and fund management from the New York Society of Security Analysis and is a chartered financial analyst candidate. He is a member of a number of professional bodies, including the Association of Investment Management & Research (AIMS).

Azîzah Hasnâ' Sâlih
Financial Controller
Venture Capital Group

Ms. Azîzah Hasnâ' Sâlih is a member of the Australian Society of Certified Public Accountants as well as the Malaysian Institute of Accountants. Graduating in 1981 with a Bachelor of Economics majoring in Accountancy, she began her career as credit officer with Sabah Bank, a Malaysian commercial bank. Her banking experience of nine years spanned all areas from Credit to Finance and Money Market Operations. Ms. Azîzah joined American Express (M) Sdn Bhd in 1990 as manager of Accounting & Financial Control, where she gained valuable experience in the requirements of international financial reporting.

change. Significant conditions of the deal were not yet settled. He turned his attention to the discussion. Fortunately, all members of VCG's negotiating team were fluent in English, so an interpreter was not necessary. Yûsuf Sulaymân, director of Finance, was speaking with an insistent tone. (Sulaymân was responsible for due diligence investigations, and Chesney's group had begun to refer to him among themselves as VCG's "devil's advocate," since he frequently raised questions regarding the feasibility of this undertaking.) Sulaymân was insisting that the venture would not qualify for listing on the Toronto Stock Exchange. "The Exchange regulations will not allow us to increase the total number of shares materially above the number authorized when ITC first listed," Sulaymân declared.

Sulaymân had been a difficult negotiator throughout the process. It appeared that he was out to create obstacles to the deal. Baker responded that there would be "no problem" with the listing. Chesney eased back into his chair and reflected on all the stories he had been told before leaving the states—stories about Americans going to Asia to sign deals, only to find themselves *squeezed* under tight time constraints. Chesney especially remembered all those back home who had warned him: "Be careful. You are dealing with some of the shrewdest deal-makers in the world." (See Exhibit 2, Malaysian Culture: Negotiating Strategies.)

Exhibit 2   Malaysian Culture: Negotiating Strategies*

With Malaysian Partners

- Indicate your willingness to "give and take." Remember, the person who compromises is the most respected and usually receives more than anticipated in negotiations.
- An American meeting a Bumiputra should try at all times to treat that person with great respect. Err on the side of formality until your relationship develops. (A literal translation of Bumiputra is "son of the soil" and refers to the indigenous Malay, the largest ethnic group in Malaysia.)
- Get them "on board" the project so that they are truly part of the team, not perceived as the "opposition."
- Ensure that they fully understand the proposed operations.

With the Government

- Make certain that you are represented by a senior Malaysian executive.
- Use Malaysian partners to promote the project outside formal meetings.

On Technical/Product Issues

- Include senior technical executives on your team.

Negotiation Tactics

- Build solid relationships, but keep them at a formal level.

- Be patient; look at issues from both Malaysian and your own corporate points of view, and work to build solutions of mutual benefit.
- Avoid confrontation and remember the importance of saving face. Never embarrass them, or back them into a corner during negotiations. If you do, you will never have a chance to get the answer or approval that you seek. Do not be averse to asking them their opinion as to how to best address a particular issue. Their answer will provide the opportunity for you to determine how they would address the matter, enable you to develop a "middle ground" position if necessary, and most importantly, learn their thought processes.
- After proposal submission, meet as regularly as possible with your counterparts to ensure they understand the project as well as the benefits to Malaysia and the end users.
- Avoid industry jargon.

Resolving Issues

- The Malaysian way is to resolve by discussion and consensus.
- The court system is rarely used.
- Avoid trying to promote the "American Way" of doing things.

*By Alan J. Wood, of Malwood Global, Inc. This exhibit is provided by Malwood Global, Inc. and Intercultural Communications, Inc. Both companies agree to share with NACRA the right to reproduce the material in this exhibit for a commercially available textbook, and for the Case Research Journal.

Intercultural Communications, Inc.   Malwood Global, Inc.

Alden T. Leavenworth, Executive Director

Chesney was having serious doubts about the wisdom of proceeding. Dr. Nik could tell from the look on Chesney's face that he was running out of patience. At that moment, Dr. Nik interceded to assure Sulaymân that any problems associated with the Canadian listing could be overcome. Chesney breathed a sigh of relief and glanced down at the 20-word speech in Malay that he was expected to deliver at the upcoming press conference. The minister of Entrepreneurial Development would be there, as well as representatives of the Canadian and U.S. embassies. This deal had appeared so much easier to consummate when he first met Dr. Nik in the comforts of his Columbia, Maryland, office.

TWO VISIONARIES MEET

Dr. Nik Bashshâr Ahmad abu Munîr, president and CEO of VCG, met James R. Chesney in July 1995, during Dr. Nik's first visit to Columbia, Maryland. The visit came as no surprise. Teams of VCG executives had been paying visits to TelSys over a period of months since February. "They came in waves," remarked Montgomery, a member of the entrepreneurial team pulled together by Chesney. "There were operations guys, technology and engineering specialists, financial experts. They didn't tell us who was whom; it always took us a while to figure it out."

Both Dr. Nik and Chesney viewed the July 1995 encounter as the most significant in determining whether VCG's investment could represent a "win-win" situation for both parties. During this visit to Columbia, Dr. Nik, and the VCG executives who accompanied him, carefully reviewed the TelSys business plan. VCG's reaction to the plan was enthusiastic, and Dr. Nik made it clear to Chesney that VCG was very interested in exploring investment opportunities in the TelSys start-up.

VCG did have the venture capital Chesney desperately needed to commercialize what he called a Functional Components Architecture that could process data received from space. With VCG's venture capital, TelSys could become a world leader in telemetry for remote sensing satellite communications (a $50 million to $100 million/year business). TelSys technology systems could perform both traditional telemetry processing and the bridging and switching functions that interconnect local area and wide area terrestrial networks to space-ground

and air-ground communications networks. Although TelSys products and technology were developed for satellite telemetry applications, the inherent ability of the equipment to process high rate streams of multimedia data (voice, image, video, and text) makes these products ideal for interconnecting broadband networks using commercial communications satellites. Chesney was enthusiastic about TelSys's abilities to cash in on a *multibillion-dollar* business if the company's technologies were adapted to the needs of other industries, such as telecommunication applications. (See Exhibit 3 for the TelSys International technology proposal.)

Dr. Nik and Chesney discussed their visions of the future for TelSys. With a shared goal of TelSys as a billion dollar company, the men turned their attention to a discussion of *how* this would be accomplished. Dr. Nik assured Chesney that VCG, in the role of venture capitalist, was not out to run TelSys. This was very good news to Chesney. VCG's investors were interested in the liquidity of their investments, so a deal would need to be struck that allowed TelSys stock to be publicly traded.

Of course, both agreed that as the company grew to serve emerging market demands, starting with those in Asia, there would be a need for a local presence. Dr. Nik was interested in establishing a subsidiary of TelSys in Kuala Lumpur for sales and engineering support and for maintenance contracts. A requirement of any agreement would be a training component for young Malaysian engineers to serve on internships in the United States, and then to be transferred to Malaysia. In this way, Dr. Nik would be building indigenous capabilities in the telecommunications field. He knew of a U.S. visa program that would allow foreign engineers to enter the United States for this type of training. Both Dr. Nik and Chesney left their first meeting convinced that they clearly understood each other's motives and requirements. Any difficulty that would arise could be worked out.

HISTORY OF TELSYS

In 1985, NASA's Goddard Space Flight Center had asked Chesney to create a new research unit. Chesney's unit grew into the Microelectronic Systems Branch, complete with prototyping, manufacturing, testing, training, and even marketing

Exhibit 3   Proposal for Telsys International Technology

Overview

TelSys International will offer the technology systems and professional experience required to become a world leader in telemetry and satellite communications. TelSys will design, manufacture, market, and support satellite telecommunications products. TelSys's systems will perform traditional telemetry processing, bridging and switching functions required to seamlessly interconnect local area and wide area terrestrial networks to space-ground or air-ground communications networks.

TelSys's commercial off-the-shelf (COTS) technology will reduce the cost and complexity of accessing and processing satellite data for remote sensing and telecommunications applications. TelSys's reconfigurable systems technology, a new paradigm in communications, will extend object-oriented programming to hardware as well as software. This technology will break price/performance expectations for communications equipment and will set new benchmarks for flexibility, upgradability, and time to market.

TelSys Products

TelSys's family of products will span a broad range of functional and performance capabilities. Products could easily be tailored to meet customer requirements by configuring different sets of standard family components. This will be accomplished using product architecture featuring technologies such as parallel pipelined processing, dynamically reconfigurable computing, object-oriented hardware as well as software and expert systems. TelSys will leverage these technologies by supporting a library of canned configurations for many satellites. Further, standard product capabili-

ties could be easily augmented to address unique telemetry processing requirements or to perform functions such as decompression, decryption, or image processing.

All TelSys products will conform to open systems network standards for seamless integration into distributed computing environments. From a user's perspective, accessing data from satellites will appear to be similar to accessing data from the Internet. TelSys's state-of-the-art network management application software will allow users to remotely control, operate, and monitor the multimission TelSys system, as well as other ground station equipment via a graphical user interface. From a network management perspective, conformance to network management protocols will allow TelSys systems to become an extension of local and wide area networks.

Professional Experience

TelSys's expertise will be based on over 150 man-years of engineering experience with data systems technology supporting both traditional and sophisticated telemetry formats. A leading example is the Consultative Committee for Space Data Systems (CCSDS) protocol, a packet-based communications protocol for satellite data links, used by most of the world's space agencies including NASA, the United States Department of Defense, the European Space Agency (ESA), and the Japanese National Space Development Agency (NASDA). TelSys systems will support space program requirements such as the International Space Station, NASA's Mission to Planet Earth, and the Jet Propulsion Laboratory's Deep Space Network.

functions. Under Chesney's guidance, advanced telemetry data systems were developed that would allow the next generation of satellites to transmit space data back to Earth at the rate of "one Library of Congress" per week. The Microelectronic Systems Branch grew to an 80-person, multimillion-dollar "company within NASA" that built more than 150 high-performance, low-cost systems for NASA and its contractors.

By 1992, Chesney had field-tested a ground system design using what he termed a Functional Components Architecture that could process data

received from space at 20 megabits per second. At NASA's 1992 "spinoff" conference, designed to transfer public sector technologies to the private sector, Chesney's design was featured. More than 40 companies expressed an interest in commercializing the technology. Chesney became convinced that the market for space data was about to explode. So, with the encouragement of NASA's senior management, he announced his intentions in 1993 to "spin off" the technology to the private sector. Chesney had the expertise required to develop the technical aspects of his business plan, but he knew he would need assistance in developing the financial plan. It was at this juncture that he contacted Montgomery, whom he had known through his work with Fairchild Space and Defense. Montgomery had years of experience in the aerospace industry, as well as the business background that Chesney lacked. With Montgomery's help, Chesney developed a business plan for TelSys and began looking for venture capital to underwrite this process.

Chesney knew exactly what would be required: 20 engineers and 10 to 15 businesspeople would need to be on board in order for his dream to become a reality. These human resource requirements could easily be met, provided that Chesney could secure the venture capital to pay their salaries. Chesney was a charismatic leader, sometimes called a "driven, strategic visionary." Engineers from Goddard who had worked under his leadership were ready to abandon their secure jobs for the opportunity to work for him in the private sector. This was "his baby," and they were part of "his family."

Chesney's financial requirements were far more difficult to satisfy. In addition to the $2 million in funds required to hire qualified professionals, Chesney estimated that at least $4 million would be needed to set up a specialized, high-tech manufacturing facility, with an additional $1 million for hardware. All totaled, he would require at least $7 million in investment capital. This was a large request of the venture capital community, given that Chesney wanted to be retained as the firm's president (he had no industry experience), and there was as yet no proven commercial product.

Chesney realized that venture capital firms were becoming more sophisticated and their motivations more varied. Some venture capital firms were most interested in developing businesses and viewed their involvement as a "window on technology," allowing them to access technologies that could be applied profitably to the firm's own operations. Other venture capital firms focused on providing financing and generating high rates of return for their clients. Rates of return in the range of 15 to 30 percent were not uncommon.

Over the many months that Chesney and Montgomery courted U.S. venture capitalists, it became clear that they faced two major stumbling blocks. The first had to do with the issue of control over operations. Chesney was adamant that he should maintain management control. However, he soon learned that venture capitalists would frequently take over 40 to 60 percent of the equity shares of a firm in which they had invested, and in a majority of these cases the venture capitalists would insist on replacing top leadership with their own managers. In public offerings, the original owners were frequently left with as little as 5 to 20 percent of the stock. This arrangement was unacceptable to Chesney.

The second major stumbling block in attracting U.S. venture capitalists was their lack of understanding of satellite telecommunication technology and the potential size of future markets for these systems. Many of the venture capitalists viewed this as a risky scheme. From Chesney's point of view, since the technology and a substantial customer base were already developed through Goddard's Microelectronics Systems Branch, this venture was a "safe bet." He believed that venture capitalists had "hearts of ice." They were most interested in financial forecasts, market projections, and quantitative "number crunching." Chesney learned this the hard way. After retiring from NASA in 1994, he spent the majority of his time seeking venture capital for TelSys. The only success that Chesney had was during a trip to the United Kingdom, where Chesney and Montgomery made a presentation to a group of British investors. A number of these individuals expressed interest in becoming shareholders, provided they could be assured that the total amount of venture capital secured was adequate to meet TelSys needs. In other words, if Chesney and Montgomery could find at least $7 million from other sources, the British investors would come on board as well. "Venture capitalists are like frogs, and when you are looking for money, you've got to kiss a lot of them . . . and some pretty ugly ones," according to Montgomery.

During the summer of 1994, Chesney was introduced to Gary Baker, the president of a Canadian firm, International Technology Contours (ITC), located in Vancouver. ITC was comprised of two subsidiaries engaged in appliance distribution and kitchen retailing. Baker admitted to Chesney that the company's traditional revenue base was shrinking rapidly. Baker had decided that ITC would have to move into new business areas if the company were to survive. Baker offered to serve as Chesney's "broker" with VCG, a venture company based in Kuala Lumpur. Baker had a plan that he thought would satisfy both Chesney's need for capital and

Dr. Nik's requirement of liquidity for VCG's foreign investments. Baker explained that he would suggest to Dr. Nik that ITC serve as a Canadian holding company for TelSys, which could be set up as its U.S. subsidiary. This was a "win-win-win" situation according to Baker.

HISTORY OF THE VENTURE CAPITAL GROUP

During the period 1982–1992, Dr. Nik Bashshâr Ahmad abu Munîr earned his graduate degrees (Master's in Actuarial Science and Ph.D. in Finance) in the United States and returned to Malaysia with his family. He had a mission: to become a leader of the Islamic financial services industry. Given his early achievements, this goal was within reach. Dr. Nik had become a multimillionaire during his sojourn in the United States, balancing his studies with "savvy financial forays" into the stock market, setting up an asset management company that began with an investment of $5,000 (U.S.). The company's investments were *Syariah*-based, that is, in keeping with the Islamic principle that business activities must be founded on allowable profit-making, not interest-earning operations.[1]

Dr. Nik returned to Kuala Lumpur with $12 million (U.S.) on which to build VCG's foundation. He became VCG's president and CEO, strongly believing that his company could *do good while doing well.* "These two goals are mutually inclusive," he said. "It is the creation of wealth that makes it possible to do good works." By the time Chesney first heard of VCG, it was an investment holding company with over $360 million (U.S.) in managed funds, focused on four sectors: (1) banking and financial investment; (2) property development and investment; (3) international business and trading; and (4) information technology.

Dr. Nik was determined to make a substantial contribution to the development of his country and other developing regions. This goal was in keeping with the Malaysian prime minister's "Vision 2020," which was to see Malaysia as a fully developed coun-

try by that time. Dr. Nik was convinced that the telecommunications industry would be the "rising star" of the fast-emerging economies of Asia, so that being a leader in this sector would allow him to take the type of leadership position he wanted. But he was waiting for the right opportunity to stake his claim. He brought Dr. Kalîl 'Abd Al Wâhid on board to assist him in evaluating potential investments in this area. Dr. Kalîl, formerly head of the Electrical, Electronics and Systems Engineering Department at the University of Malaysia, had received his Ph.D. in Electrical Engineering from Penn State.

THE COURTSHIP

In February and March 1995, VCG executives made their first exploratory trips to visit Chesney in Maryland, on the advice of Baker from ITC. Dr. Kalîl, vice president of VCG, was accompanied by Is hâq 'Abd Al 'Aliyy bin Ahmad, managing director of VCG, Inc. (the North American subsidiary located in Stamford, Connecticut). Is hâq and Kalîl liked what they saw: (1) a technology leader in the critical area of space data communications; (2) a small but cohesive group of engineering talent who believed in the technology; and (3) a sense that they could build a business relationship with Chesney that would be based on trust. (In fact, they remarked that TelSys was "almost too open, to the point of naivete.") Clearly, this was a small, emerging company that had not yet become hardened by the business world.

Chesney appreciated Dr. Kalîl's in-depth knowledge of satellite communications technology. Kalîl's understanding of the field and its market potential represented a marked contrast to the situation Chesney had faced when trying to sell the TelSys business plan to U.S. venture capital firms. Also, Kalîl assured Chesney that VCG was not interested in running TelSys operations. VCG would agree to Chesney's continued leadership of the firm's day-to-day operations. Finally, Chesney and Montgomery believed they had found a venture capital partner with whom they could work. Kalîl's message appeared to overcome the two major stumbling blocks TelSys had faced in attempting to secure funds from the U.S. venture community.

In April 1995, Dr. Rafîq Ibn Tammân, vice president of VCG and the person in charge of new ventures, arrived in Columbia, Maryland. Rafîq, with his

---

[1]*According to the* Syariah *principles of Islamic investment and financing, interest-earning instruments are not permitted. rather, business activities emphasize profit and risk-sharing on selected projects. Islamic financial instruments do include such products as Al Bai Bithaman Ajil, "cost plus financing," and* Al-Ijarah, *"lease financing."*

stern countenance and severe manners, emanated an ominous aura. Within just a few days, however, Chesney learned that Rafiq loved to laugh and share good times. They were completely at ease with each other by the end of the first week. Rafiq became actively involved with Baker and Chesney, working to structure a deal that everyone would like. With this groundwork completed, the July 1995 meeting between Dr. Nik and Chesney laid the cornerstone for a contractual agreement. At that meeting, Dr. Nik had invited Chesney to Kuala Lumpur for the final negotiating session, scheduled for August 1995.

NEGOTIATIONS IN THE FINAL HOUR: AUGUST 15, 1995

As negotiations intensified in Kuala Lumpur, Chesney was surprised to learn that the VCG team was offering to invest up to $10.4 million. Before this final phase of negotiations had begun, Chesney understood that VCG's upper limit was closer to $7 million. By August 15, TelSys and VCG negotiators had agreed to the issuance of 43,711,944 total shares in the Canadian company, ITC, which would serve as a holding company for TelSys International in the United States. This approach seemed reasonable, since ITC was already listed on the Toronto stock exchange, and VCG insisted that shares in the new company must be publicly traded. Shares would be issued at $0.52 per share. Of the total shares, several British institutions that had been approached prior to the VCG negotiations would receive 1,800,000 shares for an investment of $936,000. Current ITC shareholders (primarily Baker) would receive 8,761,994 shares. Figure 1 summarizes areas of agreement as well as the issues yet to be determined.

Resolved Equity and Capital Investment Issues:

➤ ITC will become the holding company for TelSys International.

➤ ITC will serve only as a holding company. All technological and manufacturing operations will be conducted by TelSys, its U.S. subsidiary.

➤ ITC's appliance distribution and kitchen retailing businesses will cease.

➤ Prior to the proposed deal with VCG, ITC had 8,761,994 shares outstanding, and these will continue to be held by ITC's shareholders.

➤ British investors, who had shown an interest in TelSys prior to the time VCG appeared on the scene, will be issued 1,800,000 shares of stock for their investment of $936,000.

➤ New shares of ITC will be issued at $0.52 per share. VCG is prepared to invest up to $10,400,000 in ITC.

Figure 1 ITC and TelSys International

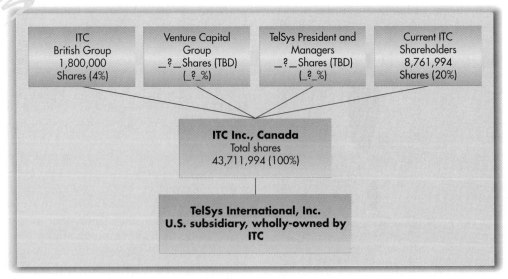

Outstanding Equity and Managerial Issues

➤ What percentage of ITC stock will Chesney's group hold?

➤ What percentage of ITC stock will VCG hold?

➤ What will be the composition and size of ITC's Board of Directors?

➤ Who will be named chairman of the Board of ITC?

➤ Who will be named president of ITC?

➤ Who will be named president of TelSys International?

Chesney knew the final hour of negotiations was at hand. Dr. Nik and he had come too far in this relationship to retreat—or had they? Finally, after many long months seeking financial backing, Chesney knew he was in a position to obtain the investment capital he needed, although from an entirely unexpected source. His spirits were high, but he could not dismiss some nagging doubts in the back of his mind:

1. Would he be able to maintain control over his "baby"?
2. Was VCG truly interested in a long-term relationship or short-term gains? (After all, as a financial investment firm, VCG was very concerned about the liquidity of their investments.)
3. Was VCG interested in sustaining his business in the United States, or transplanting it back to Malaysia?
4. Finally, what did he really know about his potential partners who came from an entirely different culture from his own?

Chesney asked for a half hour in which to confer with his advisers, Montgomery and Campisi. Dr. Nik and his associates appeared to welcome this development. Chesney realized there was very little time left before the scheduled press conference. The pressure was on. He believed this might be his last chance to secure the venture capital he needed; his own investment funds were nearly depleted. He had to consider his responsibilities to Montgomery and Campisi as well. To this point, both men had invested their time in TelSys without any compensation. As the three Americans left the meeting, they promised to return shortly for the "final" negotiation session.

Case 5   Guanxi in Jeopardy
Joint Venture Negotiations in China[1]

"Nothing like this has ever happened before. A nation with a fifth of the world's population has a bad 500 years. It is humiliated by barbarians; it lacerates itself; it sinks from torpor to anarchy. And then, in the space of a few decades, it steps forward.

Its economy grows at a rate for which the word miraculous seems too modest. Its culture shows a new vitality. Its armed forces modernize. And the rest of the world watches, impressed and nervous at the same time, wondering if the new giant still seethes with resentment about the half millennium in which it was slighted."[2]

This case was prepared by John Stanbury, Assistant Professor of International Business at Indiana University, Kokomo, with the considerable assistance of Carole Pelteson and Duwayne Cox, MBA students. The views represented here, are those of the case authors and do not necessarily reflect the views of the Society for Case Research. Authors views are based on their own professional judgements.

The names of the organization and individual's names and the events described in this case have been disguised to preserve anonymity.

Presented to and accepted by the Society for Case Research. All rights reserved to the authors and SCR. Copyright 1996.

INTRODUCTION

Tom Sherman was deeply perplexed as he studied the translation of a cover story from yesterday's edition of the *Beijing Daily*, the only local English newspaper. The article, titled "Motosuzhou/Electrowide, Inc.: Guanxi in Jeopardy," had taken him by surprise. Tom has always know that efforts in securing a joint venture with Motosuzhou, a local Chinese manufacturer, would need an enormous amount of diligence and persistence, which he thought that he and his appointed team members were portraying to their Chinese counterparts. The many sleepless nights Tom and his team worked together in planning the next day's negotiation strategies based on events that transpired with Motosuzhou the day before, coupled with the frustrations of living in a strange place and trying to cope with stark living accommodations, had ultimately accentuated the frustrations of the team.

"Why can't Motosuzhou comply with our objectives?" Tom repeatedly asked himself. The success in securing the joint venture would be a symbolic victory for a man who dedicated this entire career to Electrowide, Inc. Tom could retire from the company knowing that his last "hoorah" might have opened the door to new global opportunities for Electrowide, Inc. After all, China was becoming an enormous window of global opportunity especially for Western firms. Several of the company's competitors were already operational in Malaysia and Hong Kong. In order to compete successfully in today's globally expanding economy, Electrowide realized it needed to quickly serve markets and that the best way to do this was to locate production in Asia. As it appeared, however, Tom was in jeopardy of returning to the United States without the joint venture agreement necessary for Electrowide's entry into the People's Republic of China.

ELECTROWIDE, INC.

Electrowide is a $5B manufacturer of a broad range of automotive electronics products. In an effort to become more proactive in today's ever increasing competitive automotive electronics market, the company is undergoing a massive structural overhaul, streamlining many of its operations and flattening levels of organizational hierarchy. The purpose of this restructuring is to grant more autonomy to the company's various product line departments with respect to operation and business planning decisions so that eventually each will be responsible for its own profit and loss statements. One of the company's key strategic objectives is to become a major, aggressive player in Asia. This is considered a major change in the company's strategic direction. As part of this rapid expansion effort, Electrowide officially opened a regional design center in Tokyo. The center has world-class engineering capabilities

that enable Electrowide to develop original designs at this site. The company employs about 15,000 people in the United States and is aggressively pursuing a policy of increasing its overseas workforce.

Electrowide is looking to find an Asian partner to help manufacture and sell engine management systems that run emission-control, fuel nozzle, and ignition systems for Chinese-made vehicles. Output would be initially sold to the Chinese market with plans to export later. It is projected that the company's first manufacturing JV in China will result in at least $3M in sales its first year. The company also estimates that the JV will have a cooperative life of ten years. The company believes that the facility that its partner can provide will play a major role not only in rapidly promoting Electrowide's business growth, but in providing product development expertise in the region. According to Mike Strong, CEO, "A good part of our growth is going to come from finding the right partners in Asia."

MOTOSUZHOU

Motosuzhou is an enterprise of the Beijing municipal government, from where it takes ultimate direction. Structurally, the company is a top-heavy hierarchy with a deputy director overseeing daily operations and various supervisors in charge of functional units. (See Figure 1.) Decision making is top-down in nature. Approvals for RFCs (Request for Change) must follow a precise, government-audited procedure. Consequently, some decisions take several months to be approved. However, as part of modest experiments in Beijing, the company is on a selected, government-approved list along with 1,000 other companies that enable it to run its own operations free from government interference. Motosuzhou is a small company, operational since 1962. Its labor force is comprised mainly of rural employees, mostly Han Chinese. Although the company's strength is in achieving economies of scale in assembly-line manufacturing of engine control subassemblies, competition in the local market is growing.

The company's objective in teaming with a foreign enterprise is to develop a long-lasting relationship that will work in harmony with local government policies, as well as to gradually acquire technology through transfer by importing equipment and designs and adapt them to the automotive industry in China. The company's facilities and operations are

Figure 1   Motosuzhou Organizational Chart

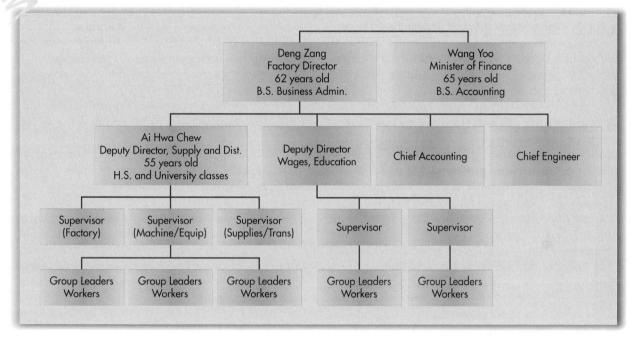

such that to be inundated with new and improved technology techniques too quickly would prove devastating. Certainly, Motosuzhou does not want to fail in the eyes of the government or the community. Electrowide appeared to be keenly interested in Motosuzhou because of the American company's technical proficiency in its design of automotive subsystems. Acquisition of such knowledge would give Motosuzhou a competitive edge in the industry. Also, Motosuzhou would rely on Electrowide for financing most of the cost incurred in establishing the venture. The company is currently on a mission to educate its workforce by providing after-hour English language studies at a local university.

Motosuzhou Team

Deng Zang

Deng Zang is 62 years old, with a B.S. in Business Administration earned from a local evening university. Deng is factory director, a position he has held for ten years. He speaks English poorly.

Ai Hwa Chew

Ai Hwa Chew is 55 years old, a high school graduate with an accumulation of post-high school classes

taken at the factory-run university. Ai Hwa was considered a member of the "delayed generation," that is, one who lost educational opportunities during the Cultural Revolution. His English is very poor, and he relies heavily on an interpreter or one of his managers when English translation is needed. Overall, Ai Hwa is considered a very serious, diligent, and competent deputy director of Supply and Distribution. He is well respected in the company.

Wang Yoo

Wang Yoo is 65 years old, with a B.S. in Accounting from Beijing University, and is relatively fluent in English. He has served as the minister of Finance for 15 years. He is a cousin of Deng Zang.

CHINA: CURRENT BUSINESS ASSESSMENT

China is presently on a course of economic liberalization. It is a country that is increasingly worried about anarchy. Gradually, more and more power is filtering to the provinces and localities. Rich coastal cities such as Shanghai and Guangzhou operate freely. City leaders establish their own economic targets, court foreign investors, and even raise internal trade barriers against the products of other parts of China. The huge rural populations is leaving its ancestral villages for coastal cities, trying to find jobs in the new, growing economy. Chinese cities, in contrast to those in many developing countries, contain high proportions of workers in factories and offices and a low proportion of workers in the service sector. During the "Deng" (i.e., Deng Xiaoping, former premier of the People's Republic) years, from 1978 to 1994, China's real growth rose an average of 9 percent a year. It is predicted that by the year 2025, China's economy will be by far the largest in the world, 1.5 times the size of the U.S. economy.[3]

American firms agree that China has never been an easy place to conduct business. Many foreign investments do not succeed financially. The costs of entering the Chinese market are climbing steeply. Tax preferences for foreign investors have been scaled back. The central government is becoming more restrictive with the JVs that provincial officials used to approve quickly. The Chinese are growing tougher in their bargaining stance. There are tighter limits on certain industries such as utilities and oil refining. One wonders if this will spread to the manufacturing sector as well. The foreign impression is that the Chinese act as if they are in the "driver's seat." As China grows economically, it openly scoffs at the global rules for international trade. The government still controls decisions on imports. Furthermore, contracts in Chinese courts are not enforceable. In the courts' eyes, China is a poor country that should not be held to the same standards as wealthy nations.

With respect to education, it was predicted that by the mid-1990s, 5 percent of its workers and staff in coastal areas, inland cities, and moderately developed areas would have a college education, building a solid intellectual foundation for China. Furthermore, it is anticipated that university entrants will increase by the year 2000.[4] Because only a small percentage of graduates are admitted to universities, China has found alternative ways of meeting demand for education. Schools have been established by government departments and businesses, and in the case of China's factories, workers' colleges exist internally, providing part-time classes. Acquiring literacy is still a problem, particularly among the rural population. The difficulty of mastering written Chinese makes raising the literacy rate particularly difficult. This creates problems in the workplace. An overview of the labor force reveals that males account for slightly more than half of the workforce and occupy the great majority of leadership positions. Though traditional Chinese society is male-centered, on the whole women are better off than their counterparts decades ago.

However, discrimination still exists in hiring for urban jobs, with women offered lower wages and benefits than their male counterparts. In the mid-1980s, less than 40 percent of the labor force had more than a primary education.[5] Skilled workers, engineers, and managerial personnel are still in short supply. Yet, China ranks second to the United States as a host country for foreign investment. However, U.S. firms must forge alliances based on common interests to ensure effective market entry. If the Chinese leaders are threatened and demeaned as is the case when the United States denounces China's MFN (Most Favored Nation) status, China will surely behave in an increasingly disruptive fashion. However, if U.S. firms reach out to the Chinese, the prospects for mutual growth will be somewhat brighter. With China's vast need for the investment and technology that America has to offer, it should not be difficult to gain China's cooperation.

STAGE OF EVENTS

Recently at Electrowide, all employees received an announcement pertaining to structural redesign stemming from a year's worth of BPE (Business Process Engineering) initiatives. The establishment of various councils would eventually assume the majority of decision making within the corporation (see Figure 2). Although specific personnel were not yet appointed to each process council, roles and responsibilities in addition to process definitions were established (see Figure 3). Most of the councils, however, including SMC (Strategy Management Council), were not operational. Electrowide had plans to empower the SMC with responsibilities for establishing processes and guidelines for exploring and establishing acquisitions and joint venture particularly focusing on overseas opportunities. At the same time, the corporation was on another aggressive transformation mission: to seek global pursuits at a rapidly expanding rate in order to become a $10 billion international enterprise by the year 2000. In

Figure 2   Electrowide Restructuring: Establishment of Councils

Process Councils' Definitions

Strategy Management Council: To develop Electrowide's mission, vision, values, and short-term/long-term strategic direction.

Operations Strategy Council: To lead operations transition from a product focus to a process-focused organization with common operating processes and practices.

Product Technology Council: To drive implementation of product line planning, program teams, reuse and technology centers, and to decide Electrowide's strategic enabling technologies.

Information Technology Council: To direct information technology prioritization, policy, alignment, and worldwide infrastructure.

People Process Council: To establish guidelines for selecting, developing, evaluating, and rewarding people to develop a global workforce with the necessary skill sets for Electrowide.

Figure 3   Councils' Roles and Responsibilities

Strategy Management Council

- Set policy, direction, strategy, and pace for the corporate strategy management business processes and assure alignment with corporate objectives.
- Manage the corporate portfolio based on strategic direction; for example, the SMC determines core competencies, makes portfolio decisions, and commissions the Ventures Council to fill gaps in core competencies.
- Balanced scorecard metrics: revenue, earnings before tax margin, net asset turnover x.

Operations Council

- Develop operations strategy, for example, operations planning, quality systems, facilities, integrated supply management.
- Develop the global labor strategy.
- Lead transition from product focus to common process focus.
- Balanced scorecard metrics: best practices of an electronics company, delivery on time.

Information Council

- Set priority for infrastructure development.
- Approve information technology infrastructure projects and overall IT spending.

People Council

- Establish the strategy for rightsizing, re-deployment and re-skilling of the global workforce.
- Establish the framework for global labor strategy implementation.
- Balanced scorecard metrics: employee satisfaction index.

consideration of a study that Electrowide conducted several months ago, China was strongly favored as a revenue gateway for the corporation. Tom was not appointed to sit on any of the newly established councils. However, considering his decades of experience in managing manufacturing operations at Electrowide, and having developed strong bonds to several top corporate executives, he was selected to lead a team to China which was commissioned to pursue a JV with Motosuzhou (see Figure 4).

Tom was assigned a two-person team to carry out this mandate but was not consulted as to its composition. He himself was 55 years old, with a B.S. in Mechanical Engineering from the University of Michigan. He was considered highly technical and knowledgeable about industrial operation and manufacturing techniques. His career has spanned 32 years with Electrowide. He has held various technical management positions within the company and is currently manager of Materials Resource Management, overseeing production inventory for

North American Operations. His only international experience was participating in a technology transfer symposium in Canada two years ago. He plans to retire at the end of the year.

Tom requested the personnel files of his two team members. He noted that Barb Morgan was 42 years old and had a joint B.S. in Psychology and Computer Science from Johns Hopkins University in Baltimore. Barb had begun her career at Electrowide three years ago as a contractor but was hired as a permanent employee upon completion of her first

Figure 4 Request for Approval by the Executive Committee

Electrowide, Inc.	
Recommended Action:	Authorize Electrowide, Inc., to establish a JV with Motosuzhou.
Recommended By:	Mike Strongarm, CEO
Performance Responsibility:	Tom Sherman

Objective: To establish a JV between Electrowide and Motosuzhou of China to conduct manufacturing operations in China.

Electrowide, Inc., seeks to establish a JV entity in the Suzhou Township, Guangzhou Province, China. This request is only for the establishment of the entity. In the event that the Executive Committee does not approve this project, the newly established JV can be dissolved at minimal legal cost. This proposal consists of providing detailed designs, financial, and technical clout necessary to commercialize the JV's technology. Manufacturing cost savings will be realized through low labor costs in China. Long-term objectives will include expanding the manufacturing capabilities to include additional automotive electronic product for both export and for sale to domestic Chinese vehicle manufactures.

The Chinese Government announced plans to withdraw the tax and tariff exemption for imports of capital equipment by foreign-invested companies.

We request that the Executive Committee ratify and confirm the establishment of the JV in order to conduct manufacturing operations in China.

Date: 9/10/95

Approval Recommended:	Mike Strongarm, CEO Electrowide, Inc.

Doyle P. Cunningham, Director of Taxes

Bart C. Chang
Sr. Vice President Marketing and President, Electrowide, Inc.

Suzanne A. Jenkins
Corporate Vice President and Controller

year. Barb's most recent assignment in the company was project manager for an acquisition venture in Sweden. She spoke conversational Chinese as well as fluent French. Apparently, her current assignment was near completion, and she wanted to continue seeking overseas assignments partly as a means of trying to cope with her recent divorce.

Mark Porter's current assignment in Corporate Business Planning was also coming to an end, and he was eager to do some international work. He was 31 years old and had a B.S. in Finance from the University of Pennsylvania and an MBA from Duke University. He was apparently a "fast-tracker" at Electrowide, rotating among various organizational functions every 1.5 years, and had been employed with the company six years. His most recent position was that of business analyst responsible for relaying backlog data to Corporate Finance and Shareholder's Relations. According to his file, he is a type-A personality and a self-starter, focusing on excelling no matter what the cost or sacrifice.

Tom also noted that, as part of the study, Motosuzhou was investigated along with several other possible Eastern Asian partners. Such parameters as the partner's physical location in the country, the size of its labor force, and the strength of the resources that could enhance as well as reduce operational costs for Electrowide were examined. In addition, the company was dependent on finding a local manufacturing company with a strong, established network that could readily market products produced under the JV without additional expense in the effort. Furthermore, finding a local company with ties to government officials was thought to be of benefit. Early warnings about any impending government policy changes that might impact operations within the JV would be advantageous. Above all, management wanted to ensure that its corporate objectives would be achieved upon establishment of the JV. Motosuzhou seemed to fit most closely to the criteria identified in the study.

Tom envisioned that he and the rest of the team would spend the majority of their first several weeks with Motoszhou discussing the specific details of the proposed JV. Instead, their counterparts were keenly interested in learning about their visitors' personal lives, their interests, the size of their families, and the like. Usually, the days were spent touring the city and surrounding countryside, while long hours were spent at night engaging in elaborate dinner get-togethers and nightlife entertainment. Mark never showed much interest or appreciation of the scenery. His thoughts were usually preoccupied with how to steer the course of the next day's discussions on the details of the proposed JV. He was not one for small talk. Barb was quite affable with her Chinese hosts initially. She particularly enjoyed experiencing a night of *quyi*,[6] for which the Motosuzhou team generously paid admission. Yet, her enthusiasm diminished when she took notice that Ai Hwa and this constituents tended not to include her in conversation but rather directed their discussions and eye contact to Barb's male counterparts. One night in particular stood out in Tom's mind. As Ai Hwa Chew was making toasts to his guests thanking them for their interests in his company, he presented Tom with a sterling silver tea set. Tom felt a bit uncomfortable accepting such an expensive gift and even tried to tactfully refuse it. However, Ai Hwa stubbornly refused Tom's insistence. Tom thought that he detected irritation in Hwa's voice but decided not to apologize and prolong the uncomfortable silence that punctuated the room.

By the fourth week, Tom and his team were growing a bit restless. Habitually, they left telephone messages with Ai Hwa's secretary requesting to meet with him and his constituents. Tom even went as far as to establish specific days and times for these proposed discussions. Nothing constructive with respect to these transpired during that week. Tom's patience grew thin as he tried to force smile after smile during long dinner extravaganzas where conversation continued to remain light and disassociated from any issues pertaining to work. Mark was growing extremely impatient, and he frequently excused himself early from get-togethers, or, on occasion, refrained from attending altogether.

A change in routine finally occurred during the fifth week. Deng Zang felt the proper time had materialized when issues concerning the JV should be approached with Electrowide. He commissioned Ai Hwa to put together a formal written invitation that was subsequently hand-delivered to the hotel early in the week. Tom and his team were invited to an arranged meeting to be conducted in Ai Hwa Chew's office the morning following receipt of the letter. Although no agenda was distributed and the time and location for the meeting were changed at 11 P.M. the night before, the team managed to

regain their composure in anticipation of cooperative dialogue with their potential partners. Tom had been instructed by executive staff to remain firm in its pursuit of negotiating specific roles and responsibilities that each party would assume under the JV. Electrowide was to provide and control design, financial, and technical clout necessary to commercialize the JV's technology. Conversely, Electrowide wanted Motosuzhou to provide the manufacturing plant facility, marketing functions utilizing a local sales force, as well as provide the majority of the technical labor force. Furthermore, Electrowide thought it was in its best interest to allow Motosuzhou to continue in its current managerial capacity inasmuch as Electrowide lacked the personnel proficient in Chinese. Moreover, Electrowide planned to hold a 51 percent stake in the venture, with Motosuzhou taking a 39 percent portion, and the remainder to go to the Beijing Municipal government.

Meetings continued throughout the week. Although Mark would have preferred to continue doing research in his hotel room, Tom insisted that his attendance at the meetings was crucial. As the meetings progressed, the American team's overall assessment of whether the objectives of most of their concessions were going to be met was favorable. Barb was instructed not to vocally participate in negotiations, but her keen eye played an important role. She recorded conversations at each meeting and noticed that affirmative nodding by the Chinese counterparts was apparent. Tom's team interpreted this as a sign that concessions outlined by the Electrowide team would be easily confirmed. Barb also noticed, however, that the Chinese team rarely posed specific questions about the details of the JV. The inference was that the Motosuzhou team understood the concessions and, therefore, had no concerns. The interpreter that Motosuzhou provided to the team continually assuaged any doubts about failing progress. This constant reminder renewed the team's faith that Motosuzhou was a compatible fit with Electrowide.

In about the eighth week, however, positive attitudes on the part of Tom and his team began to wane. From the start, HQ promised Tom that his maximum required length of stay would not exceed two months as the company planned at most six weeks to secure agreement for the JV. Tom would certainly miss his daughter's college graduation if negotiations persisted much longer. In addition, Barb, who was a member of the Information Technology Council, was "burning the candle at both ends" as she feverishly worked on several assignments faxed to her from HQ. Mark had contracted the Asian flu and was miserably trying to battle its nasty symptoms while trying to play Tom's right-hand man. Moreover, War Games with Taiwan were growing intense, the threat of which strengthened the team's desire to repatriate as soon as possible. Ai Hwa Chew and his aides were behaving less passively. Questions particular to the concessions proposed by Electrowide were now being raised. Motosuzhou had its own objectives to pursue as commissioned by the minister of Finance, Wang Yoo. Motosuzhou knew it was in its best interest to comply with government mandates; otherwise, the company risked losing its position on the list of free-enterprise entities. Ai Hwa was skeptical about Electrowide's concessions. His assessment was the Electrowide really wanted to gain greater control for itself in the local Asian market. Nowhere in the objective statement as documented on the "Request for Approval" were marketing concessions addressed or implied. One concession Motosuzhou was adamant in winning was control of financial operations of the JV. Moreover, the Chinese company insisted that any profits earned under the JV could be invested only in China, the currency remaining in yuan.

Although this was a crucial point for them, Motosuzhou focused on softer issues initially. For example, Motosuzhou requested that training, consulting, and warranties would be provided to them free of charge. Ai Hwa Chew kept reminding the American team that such provisions were considered free goods in their Chinese system, and hence were perceived as indications of one's sincerity and good will. In addition, Ai Hwa Chew pointed out inconsistencies between the partner's accounting systems which created disagreement regarding allocation of manufacturing costs. Tom was alarmed, for his assessment of Motosuzhou's accounting policies was that they were in complete disarray and that the Chinese firm's management would greatly appreciate it if this function was handled by Electrowide. No formal auditing records had been kept. Ai Hwa Chew kept assuring Tom

that Wang Yoo could provide auditing documentation that the state agency kept on file on all its state-run operations. However, Tom's direct request to the top Finance representative at the Ministry for copies of accounting records fell on deaf ears. Tom knew that he could not allow accounting practices to continue as they were because they would result in the reduction of Electrowide's operating margins, an outcome that violated one of Electrowide's ultimate objective for establishing a JV. HQ also instructed Tom to remain firm on providing training instructors and training materials. However, training costs were to be a necessary expense of Motosuzhou.

To drive a further wedge in objectives, Ai Hwa Chew made it very clear that he was not comfortable continuing management practices as they currently operated. He stressed the need for more harmony in all aspects of the negotiations and JV operations. At the same time, the Executive Committee at Electrowide was enmeshed in activities to finalize formulation, appointments, and operations of each of the council organizations. Consequently, Tom found it increasingly difficult to relay concerns and seek support and approval for changes requested. In addition, the time difference made it difficult for Tom to directly communicate issues to HQ on a timely basis. Delays were not part of Electrowide's plan in securing the JV.

Tom and his team decided to take matters into their own hands. While Ai Hwa called for a few days' reprieve to honor the Chinese Winter holiday, the Electrowide team took advantage of the free days. Unknown to their potential partners, the American team sought the counsel of an American law firm located in Beijing. To circumvent the likelihood of any future misunderstandings between the two parties, Tom instructed the attorney to structure a very formal extensive contract to address every conceivable contingency.

The next morning, over breakfast, as Tom and his team were reviewing their plan of action on how to best present the contract to Ai Hwa Chew, the hotel concierge presented Tom with a Western Union telegram. Tom scanned the contents, shared the information with his team, and then tossed the telegram in the trash, thinking little of its effect on the day's negotiation activities. "Today," Tom assuredly thought, "I feel we're going to come to final agreement." As the telegram started to unfurl in the trash, its contents exposed the following: "Trade Representative, Mickey Kantor, was quoted as bashing Beijing over MFN status on account of China violating intellectual property issues."

Tom wanted to waste little time in presenting the contract to his counterpart. He was anxious to solidify the deal. Almost immediately upon entering Ai Hwa Chew's office, Tom handed over the legal document, which was written entirely in English. As the interpreter read the contract, Ai Hwa's grew dim and his face flushed. While only one-third of the way into listening to the concessions, Ai Hwa motioned Tom and his party to the door of his office. Once outside the office, Tom and his team were quite confused. Shortly, thereafter, Ai Hwa's secretary notified the group that the day's negotiation meetings were canceled. Tom and his team left feeling a bit confused but thought that perhaps Ai Hwa needed some time alone to review the contents of the contract. Unknown to Tom, Ai Hwa was drafting a letter to the Minister of Finance requesting to meet with him. The tone of the letter was rather urgent.

The next morning, Tom spotted the article in the *Beijing Daily*. He was disappointed and at a loss as to how to make reparations.

APPENDIX I[7]
KEY ASPECTS OF CHINESE CULTURE AS THEY RELATE TO NEGOTIATIONS
GUANXI (THE VALUE OF AN ONGOING RELATIONSHIP)

Guanxi is the word that describes the intricate, pervasive network of personal relations that every Chinese cultivates with energy, subtlety and imagination. *Guanxi* is the currency of getting things done and getting ahead in Chinese society. *Guanxi* is a relationship between two people containing implicit mutual obligation, assurances, and intimacy, and is the perceived value of an ongoing relationship and its future possibilities that typically govern Chinese attitudes toward long-term business. If a relationship of trust and mutual benefit is developed, an excellent foundation will be built for future business with the Chinese. Guanxi ties are also helpful in dealing with the Chinese bureaucracy as personal interpretations are used in lieu of legal interpretations.

Because of cultural differences and language barriers, visitors to China are not in a position to cultivate *guanxi* with the depth possible between two Chinese. Regardless, *guanxi* is an important aspect of interrelations in China and deserves attention so that good friendly relations may be developed. These connections are essential to getting things accomplished.[8]

FORMAL AND INFORMAL RELATIONS

At present, it is likely that the majority of social contracts foreigners have with the Chinese are on a more formal than informal level. Informality in China relates not to social pretension or artifice but to the concept of face. Great attention is paid to observance of formal, or social behavior and attendant norms. The social level is the level of form and proper etiquette where face is far more important than fact. It is considered both gauche and rude to allow one's personal feelings and opinions to surface here to the detriment of the social ambience. It is much more important to compliment a person or to avoid an embarrassing or sensitive subject than to express an honest opinion if honesty is at the expense of another's feelings. Directness, honesty, and individualism that run counter to social conventions and basic politeness have no place on the social level; emotions and private relationships tend to be kept private in Chinese society.

CHINESE ETIQUETTE FOR SOCIAL FUNCTIONS

Ceremonies and rules of ceremony have traditionally held a place of great importance in Chinese culture. Confucianism perpetuated and strengthened these traditions by providing the public with an identity, mask, or persona with which a person is best equipped to deal with the world with a minimum of friction. Confucianism consists of broad rules of conduct evolved to aid and guide interpersonal relations. Confucius assembled all the details of etiquette practiced at the courts of the feudal lords during the period c. 551–479 B.C. These rules of etiquette are called the *li* and have long since become a complete way of life for the Chinese.

The *li* may appear overly formalistic to Westerners at first glance. Upon closer inspection, it is apparent that the rules of etiquette play a very important role in regulating interpersonal relations. Some basic rules of behavior are as follows:

➤ A host should always escort a guest out to his car or other mode of transportation and watch until the guest is out of sight.

➤ Physical expression is minimal by Western standards. A handshake is polite, but backslapping and other enthusiastic grasping is a source of embarrassment.

➤ At culture functions and other performances, audience approval of performers is often subdued by American standards. Although the accepted manner of expressing approval varies between functions and age groups, applause is often polite rather than roaring and bravo-like cheers.

➤ A person should keep control over his temper at all times.

➤ One should avoid blunt, direct, or abrupt discussion, particularly when the subject is awkward; delicate hints are often used to broach such a topic.

➤ It is a sign of respect to allow another to take the seat of honor (left of host) or to be asked to proceed through a door first.

➤ The serving of tea often signals the end of an interview or meeting. However, it is also served during extended meetings to quench the thirst of the negotiators.

SMILING AND LAUGHTER

Laughter and smiling in Chinese culture represent the universal reaction to pleasure and humor. They are also a common response to negative occur-rences, such as death and other misfortunes. When embarrassed or in the wrong, the Chinese frequently respond with laughter or smiling, which will persist if another person continues to speak of an embarrassing topic or does not ignore the wrong. Westerners are often confused and shocked by this behavior, which is alien to them. It is important to remember that smiling and laughter in the above situations are not exhibitions of glee, but rather are a part of the concept of face when used in response to a negative or unpleasant situation.

CASE REFERENCES

1. The concept of *guanxi* requires immediate explanation. "Guaanji," as it is pronounced, refers to the special relationship two people develop or already have with each other. Pye (1982: 101) describes it as "friendship with implications of a continual exchange of favors, and the relationship is continuously bound by these exchanges."

2. Kenneth Auchincloss, "Friend or Foe," *Newsweek*, April 1, 1996, p. 32.

3. Robert J. Samuelson, "The Big Game," *Newsweek*, April 1, 1996, p. 37.

4. Worden, Robert L., Savada, Andrea M., and Dolan, Ronald E. *China a Country Study*. Washington, D.C.: Library of Congress, Federal Research Division, 1988, p. 32.

5. Ibid., p. 90.

6. *Quai* is Chinese folk art consisting of various kinds of storytelling and comic monologue and dialogues.

7. This is very largely drawn from James A. Brunner's case, "Buckeye Glass Co. in China," in *International Management: A Cross-Cultural and Functional Perspective* by Kamal Fatehi (Upper Saddle River, N.J.: Prentice Hall).

8. An extremely useful new article that extends this analysis of *guanxi* is "Achieving Business Success in Confucian Societies: The Importance of Guanxi (Connections)" by Irene Y. M. Yeung and Rosalie Tung, *Organizational Dynamics* (Autumn 1996): 54–65. The article is accompanied by an excellent bibliography.

Case 6   Moto
Coming to America

Moto arrived in Chicago in the middle of winter, unprepared for the raw wind that swept off the lake. The first day he bought a new coat and fur-lined boots. He was cheered by a helpful salesgirl who smiled as she packed his lined raincoat into a box. Americans were nice, Moto decided. He was not worried about his assignment in America. The land had been purchased, and Moto's responsibility was to hire a contracting company and check on the pricing details. The job seemed straightforward.

Moto's firm, KKD, an auto parts supplier, had spent 1½ years researching American building contractors. Allmack had the best record in terms of timely delivery and liaisons with good architects and the best suppliers of raw materials. That night Moto called Mr. Crowell of Allmack, who confirmed the appointment for the next morning. His tone was amiable.

Moto arrived at the Allmack office at nine sharp. He had brought a set of *kokeshi* dolls for Crowell. The dolls, which his wife had spent a good part of a day picking out, were made from a special maple in the mountains near his family home in Niigata. He would explain that to Crowell later, when they knew each other. Crowell also came from a hilly, snowy place, which was called Vermont.

When the secretary ushered him in, Crowell stood immediately and rounded the desk with an outstretched hand. Squeezing Moto's hand, he roared, "How are you? Long trip from Tokyo. Please sit down, please."

Moto smiled. He reached in his jacket for his card. By the time he presented it, Crowell was back on the other side of the desk. "My card," Moto said seriously.

"Yes, yes," Crowell answered. He put Moto's card in his pocket without a glance.

Moto stared at the floor. This couldn't be happening, he thought. Everything was on that card: KKD, Moto, Michio, Project Director KKD meant University of Tokyo and years of hard work to earn a

high recommendation from Dr. Iwasa's laboratory. Crowell had simply put it away.

"Here." Crowell handed his card.

"Oh, John Crowell, Allmack, President," Moto read aloud, slowly trying to recover his equilibrium. "Allmack is famous in Japan."

"You know me," Crowell replied and grinned. "All those faxes. Pleased to meet you, Moto. I have a good feeling about this deal."

Moto smiled and lay Crowell's card on the table in front of him.

"KKD is pleased to do business with Allmack," Moto spoke slowly. He was proud of his English. Not only had he been a top English student in high school and university, but he had also studied English in a *juku* (an afterschool class) for five years. As soon as he received this assignment, he took an intensive six-week course taught by Ms. Black, an American, who also instructed him in American history and customs.

Crowell looked impatient. Moto tried to think of Ms. Black's etiquette lessons as he continued talking about KKD and Allmack's history. "We are the best in the business," Crowell interrupted. "Ask anyone. We build the biggest and best shopping malls in the country."

Moto hesitated. He knew Allmack's record—that's why he was in the room. Surely Crowell knew that. The box of *kokeshi* dolls pressed against his knees. Maybe he should give the gift now. No, he thought, Crowell was still talking about Allmack's achievements. Now Crowell had switched to his own achievements. Moto felt desperate.

"You'll have to come to my house," Crowell continued. "I live in a fantastic house. I had an architect from California build it. He builds for all the stars, and for me." Crowell chuckled. "Built it for my wife. She's the best wife, the very best. I call her my little sweetheart. Gave the wife the house on her birthday. Took her right up to the front door and carried her inside."

Moto shifted his weight. Perhaps if he were quiet, Crowell would change the subject. Then they could pretend the conversation never happened. "Moto-san, what's your first name? Here, we like to be on a first-name basis."

SOURCE: Patricia Gercik, *On Track with the Japanese.* 1992 (New York: Kodansha International, 114 Fifth Ave., NY, NY 10011) (OR Kudanske America)

"Michio," Moto whispered.

"Michio-san, you won't get a better price than from me. You can go down the block to Zimmer or Casey, but you got the best deal right here."

"I brought you a present," Moto said, handing him the box of *kokeshi* dolls.

"Thanks," Crowell answered. He looked genuinely pleased as he tore open the paper. Moto looked away while Crowell picked up a *kokeshi* doll in each hand. "They look like Russian dolls. Hey, thanks a lot, my daughter will love them."

Moto pretended that he hadn't heard. I'll help by ignoring him, Moto thought, deeply embarrassed.

Crowell pushed the *kokeshi* dolls aside and pressed a buzzer. "Send George in," he said.

The door opened and a tall, heavyset man with a dark crew cut stepped inside the room.

"George Kubushevsky, this is Moto-san, Michio . . ."

"How do you do?" Kubushevsky's handshake was firm.

Moto took out his card.

"Thanks," Kubushevsky said. "Never carry those." He laughed and hooked his thumbs in his belt buckle. Moto nodded. He was curious. Kubushevsky must be a Jewish name—or was it Polish, or maybe even German? In Japan he'd read books about all three groups. He looked at Kubushevsky's bone structure. It was impossible to tell. He was too fat.

"George, make sure you show Michio everything. We want him to see all the suppliers, meet the right people, you understand?"

"Sure." George grinned and left the room.

Moto turned to Crowell. "Is he a real American?" Moto asked.

"A real American? What's that?"

Moto flushed. "Is he first generation?" Moto finished lamely. He remembered reading that Jews, Lebanese, and Armenians were often first generation.

"How do I know? He's just Kubushevsky."

During the next few weeks Moto saw a great deal of Kubushevsky. Each morning he was picked up at nine and taken to a round of suppliers. Kubushevsky gave him a rundown on each supplier before they met. He was amiable and polite, but never really intimate. Moto's response was also to be polite. Once he suggested that they go drinking

after work, but Kubushevsky flatly refused, saying that he had to work early the next morning. Moto sighed, remembering briefly his favorite bar and his favorite hostess in Tokyo. Yuko-san must be nearly 50 now, he thought affectionately. She could make him laugh. He wished he were barhopping with his colleagues from his *ringi* group at KKD. Moto regretted that he had not brought more *kokeshi* dolls, since Kubushevsky had not seemed delighted with the present of the KKD pen.

One morning they were driving to a cement outlet.

"George."

"Yes, Michio-san."

Moto paused. He still found it difficult to call Kubushevsky by his first name. "Do you think I could have some papers?"

"What kind of papers?" Kubushevsky's voice was friendly. Unlike Crowell, he kept an even tone. Moto liked that.

"I need papers on the past sales of these people."

"We're the best."

"I need records for the past five years on the cement place we are going to visit."

"I told you, Michio-san, I'm taking you to the best! What do you want?"

"I need some records."

"Trust me, I know what I'm doing."

Moto was silent. He didn't know what to say. what did trust have to do with anything? His *ringi* group in Tokyo needed documentation so they could discuss the issues and be involved in the decisions. If the decision to go with one supplier or the other was correct, that should be reflected in the figures.

"Just look at what's going on now," George said. "Charts for the last five years, that's history."

Moto remained silent. George pressed his foot to the gas. The car passed one truck, and then another. Moto looked nervously at the climbing speedometer. Suddenly Kubushevsky whistled and released his foot. "Alright, Michio-san, I'll get you the damned figures."

"Thanks," Moto said softly.

"After we see the cement people, let's go for a drink."

Moto looked uneasily at the soft red light bulb that lit the bar. He sipped his beer and ate a few peanuts. Kubushevsky was staring at a tall blonde at the other end of the bar. She seemed to notice him also. Her fingers moved across the rim of the glass.

"George," Moto said gently. "Where are you from, George."

"Here and there," Kubushevsky said idly, still eyeing the blonde.

Moto laughed. "Here and there."

Kubushevsky nodded. "Here and there," he repeated.

"You Americans," Moto said. "You must have a home."

"No home, Michio-san."

The blonde slid her drink down the bar and slipped into the next seat. Kubushevsky turned more toward her.

Moto felt desperate. Last week Crowell had also acted rudely. When Imai, KKD's vice president, was visiting from Japan, Crowell had dropped them both off at a golf course. What was the point?

He drained his beer. Immediately the familiar warmth of the alcohol made him buoyant. "George," he said intimately. "You need a wife. You need a wife like Crowell has."

Kubushevsky turned slowly on his seat. He stared hard at Moto. "You need a muzzle," he said quietly.

"You need a wife," Moto repeated. He had Kubushevsky's full attention now. He poured Kubushevsky another beer. "Drink," he commanded.

Kubushevsky drank. In fact they both drank. Then suddenly Kubushevsky's voice changed. He put his arm around Moto and purred in his ear. "Let me tell you a secret, Moto-san. Crowell's wife is a dog. Crowell is a dog. I'm going to leave Allmack, just as soon as possible. Want to join me, Michio-san?"

Moto's insides froze. Leave Crowell. What was Kubushevsky talking about? He was just getting to know him. They were a team. All those hours in the car together, all those hours staring at cornfields and concrete. What was Kubushevsky talking about? Did Crowell know? What was Kubushevsky insinuating about joining him? "You're drunk, George."

"I know."

"You're very drunk."

"I know."

Moto smiled. The blonde got restless and left the bar. Kubushevsky didn't seem to notice. For the rest of the night he talked about his first wife and his two children, whom he barely saw. He spoke of his job at Allmack and his hopes for a better job in California. They sat at a low table. Moto spoke of his children and distant wife. It felt good to talk. Almost as good as having Yuko next to him.

As they left the bar, Kubushevsky leaned heavily on him. They peed against a stone wall before getting in the car. All the way home Kubushevsky sang a song about a folk here named Davy Crockett, who "killed himself a bear when he was only three." Moto sang a song from Niigata about the beauty of the snow on the rooftops in winter. Kubushevsky hummed along.

They worked as a team for the next four months. Kubushevsky provided whatever detailed documentation Moto asked for. they went drinking a lot. Sometimes they both felt a little sad, sometimes happy, but Moto mostly felt entirely comfortable. Kubushevsky introduced him to Porter, a large, good-natured man in the steel business who liked to hunt and cook gourmet food; to Andrews, a tiny man who danced the polka as if it were a waltz; and to many others.

Just before the closing, Kubushevsky took him to a bar and told him of a job offer in California. He had tears in his eyes and hugged Moto good-bye. Moto had long since accepted the fact that Kubushevsky would leave.

Two weeks later Moto looked around the conference room at Allmack. Ishii, KKD's president, and Imai had flown in from Tokyo for the signing of the contract for the shopping mall, the culmination of three years of research and months of negotiation. John Crowell stood by his lawyer, Sue Smith. Sue had been on her feet for five hours. Mike Apple, Moto's lawyer, slammed his fist on the table and pointed at the item in question. The lawyers argued a timing detail that Moto was sure had been worked out weeks before. Moto glanced nervously at Ishii and Imai. Ishii's eyes were closed. Imai stared at the table.

Moto shifted uneasily in his seat. Sue was smarter than Mike, he thought. Perhaps a female lawyer wouldn't have been so terrible. While it was not unusual to see females in professional positions in Japan, this was America. Tokyo might have understood. After all, this was America, he repeated to himself. Internationalization required some adjustment. A year ago he would have had total loss of face if confronted with this prolonged, argumentative closing. Today he did not care. He could not explain to Tokyo all he'd learned in that time, all the friends he'd made. When he tried to communicate about business in America, the home office sent him terse notes by fax.

Now the lawyers stood back. President Ishii opened his eyes. Crowell handed a pen to Ishii. They signed the document together. The lawyers smiled. Sue Smith looked satisfied. She should be pleased, Moto thought. Her extensive preparation for the case made him realize again that the Japanese stereotype of the "lazy" American was false. Sue's knowledge of the case was perfect in all details. I'll have to use her next time, Moto thought. She's the smart one. Yes, he thought, his friend Kubushevsky had taught him many things. Suddenly he felt Kubushevsky's large presence. Moto lowered his head in gratitude.

CASE QUESTIONS

1. What was Moto's purpose and agenda for the first meeting with Crowell? How does he try to implement his agenda?
2. What happened to introduce "noise" in the communication from Moto to Crowell, and then from Crowell to Moto?
3. What was the significance of the doll? What went wrong?
4. Why did Crowell's remarks about Allmack threaten a loss of *face* from Moto's perspective?
5. How did Moto feel about Kubushevsky's behavior early on? How did their relationship change?

Part 3
Formulating and
Implementing
Strategy for
International and
Global Operations

C h a p t e r   6

Formulating Strategy

Outline

Opening Profile: FedEx in China—Going Global Through Local Partnering

Federal Express Corporation (FedEx), already the world's largest transportation company, has put its global expansion on fast track with its recent joint venture in Beijing. Tianjin-based Da Tian W. Air Service Corporation has joined with FedEx to form Federal Express-DTW Co. Ltd. to provide international express transportation services for customers with shipping requirements to and from China.

David Cunningham, FedEx Asia Pacific president, recognizes the importance of local connections in doing business in China. This is evident in the plans that he and Wang Shusheng, the Da Tian president, announced when they formed the venture:

> With the continued assistance and support of MOFTEX, SAIC, Customs, CAAC, the new joint venture company plans to establish branch offices in Shanghai, Guangzhou, and Shenzhen by the end of the year 2000 and open offices in an additional 100 cities across the country by 2005.[1]

Eddy Chan, regional vice president for FedEx China and Mid-Pacific, regards this as just another step in FedEx's continued investment in China and states that "companies are operating more and more on an international basis and as such, the importance of international air express is key to remaining competitive."[2]

FedEx started direct flights between China and Japan in 1998, connecting Chinese packages with its direct flights between Osaka, Japan and its U.S. hub in Memphis, Tennessee. "Our focus is on building a network," said Fred Smith, founder and CEO of FedEx. "Once you have a network in place, if that premise is right, then the growth prospects are huge, and we're going to hopefully have a leadership position."[3]

Meanwhile, UPS is trying to play catch-up with FedEx. The company won approval to operate six weekly flights between the United States and China starting in April 2001. UPS, in its continued diplomatic efforts, successfully wooed Chinese officials by flying two pandas free from Beijing Zoo.[4]

As the Opening Profile on FedEx illustrates, companies around the world are spending increasing amounts of money and time on global expansion in search of profitable new markets, acquisitions, and alliances—but are often spending those resources on very different strategies. Experts predict that those companies with operations in major overseas markets (North America, Europe, and Asia) are far more likely to prosper in the twenty-first century than those without such operations.[5] Because these new international opportunities are far more complex than those in domestic markets, managers must plan carefully—that is, strategically—to benefit from them.

The process by which a firm's managers evaluate the future prospects of the firm and decide on appropriate strategies to achieve long-term objectives is called **strategic planning**. The basic means by which the company competes—its choice of business or businesses in which to operate and the ways in which it differentiates itself from its competitors—is its **strategy**. Almost all successful companies engage in long-range strategic planning, and those with a global orientation position themselves to take full advantage of worldwide trends and opportunities. MNCs, in particular, report that strategic planning is essential to contend with increasing global competition and to coordinate their far-flung operations.

In reality, however, that rational strategic planning is often tempered, or changed at some point, by a more incremental, sometimes messy, process of strategic decision making by some managers. When a new CEO is hired, for example, she will often call for a radical change in strategy. That is why new leaders are very carefully chosen, on the basis of what they are expected to do. So, while we discuss the rational strategic planning process here, because it is usually the ideal, inclusive, method of determining long-term plans, we need to remember that, throughout, there are people making decisions, and their own personal judgment, experiences, and motivations will shape the ultimate strategic direction.

REASONS FOR GOING INTERNATIONAL

Companies "go international" for different reasons, some reactive (or defensive) and some proactive (or aggressive). The threat of their own decreased competitiveness is the overriding reason many large companies adopt a strategy of aggressive globalization. To remain competitive, these companies want to move fast to build strong positions in key world markets with products tailored to the common needs of 650 million customers in Europe, Latin America, and Japan.[6] Building on their past success, companies such as IBM and Digital Equipment are plowing profits back into operations overseas. Europe is now attracting much new investment capital because of both the European Union (EU) and the opening of extensive new markets in Eastern Europe.

Reactive Reasons

Globalization of Competitors   One of the most common reactive reasons that prompt a company to go overseas is global competition. If left unchallenged, competitors who already have overseas operations or investments may get so entrenched in foreign markets that it becomes difficult for other companies to enter at a later time. In addition, the lower costs and market power available to these competitors operating globally may also give them an advantage domestically.

Trade Barriers   Restrictive trade barriers are another reactive reason that companies often switch from exporting to overseas manufacturing. Barriers such as tariffs, quotas, buy-local policies, and other restrictive trade practices can make exports to foreign markets too expensive and too impractical to be competitive. Many firms, for example, want to gain a foothold in Europe—to be regarded as an insider—to counteract trade barriers and restrictions on non-EU firms(discussed further in the Comparative Management in Focus section at the end of this chapter). In part, this fear of "Fortress Europe" is caused by actions such as the EU's block exemption for the franchise industry. This exemption prohibits a franchisor, say McDonald's, from contracting with a single company, say Coca-Cola, to supply all its franchisees, as it does in the United States.

Regulations and Restrictions   Similarly, regulations and restrictions by a firm's home government may become so expensive that companies will seek out less restrictive foreign operating environments. Avoiding such regulations prompted U.S. pharmaceutical maker SmithKline and Britain's Beecham to merge. Both thereby guaranteed that they would avoid licensing and regulatory hassles in their largest markets—Western Europe and the United States. The merged company is now an insider in both Europe and America.[7]

Customer Demands   Operations in foreign countries frequently start as a response to customer demands or as a solution to logistical problems. Certain foreign customers, for example, may demand that their supplying company operate in their local region so that they have better control over their supplies, forcing the supplier to comply or lose the business. McDonald's is one company that asks its domestic suppliers to follow it to foreign ventures. Meat supplier OSI Industries does just that, with joint ventures in 17 countries, such as Bavaria, so that it can work with local companies making McDonald's hamburgers.[8]

Proactive Reasons

> From rain forests to remote Chinese villages, the queen of cosmetics (Avon) is cleaning up across the globe.[9]

Economies of Scale   Careful, long-term strategic planning encourages firms to go international for proactive reasons. One pressing reason for many large firms to expand overseas is to seek economies of scale—that is, to achieve world-scale volume to make the fullest use of modern capital-intensive manufacturing equipment and to amortize staggering research and development costs when facing brief product life cycles.[10] Otis Elevator, for example, developed the Elevonic 411 by means of six research centers in five countries. This international cooperation saved over $10 million in design costs and cut the development cycle from four years to two. Economies of scale in production are achieved when higher levels of output spread fixed costs over more units, thus lowering the per-unit cost. Gerrit Jeelof, of Holland's Philips Group, contends that "only with a global market can a company afford the large development costs necessary to keep up with advancing technology."[11]

Growth Opportunities   Companies in mature markets in developed countries experience a growth imperative to look for new opportunities in emerging markets. When expansion opportunities become limited at home, firms such as McDonald's are often driven to seek expansion through new international markets. A mature product or service with restricted growth in its domestic market often has "new life" in another country, where it will be at an earlier stage of its life cycle.[12] Avon Products Inc., for example, has seen a decline in its U.S. market since its traditional sales and marketing strategy of "Avon calling" (house-to-house sales) now meets with empty houses, due to the spiralling number of women who now work outside the home. To make up for this loss, Avon pushed overseas to 26 emerging markets, such as Mexico, Poland, China, India, South Africa, and Vietnam. In Brazil, for instance, Josina Reis Teixeira carries her sample kit to the wooden shacks in the tiny village of Registro, just outside of São Paulo. In some markets Avon adapts to cultural influences, such as in China, where consumers are suspicious of door-to-door salespeople. There, Avon sets up showrooms in its branch offices in major cities so that women can consult cosmeticians and sample products.[13]

In addition, new markets abroad provide a place to invest surplus profits as well as employ underutilized resources in management, technology, and machinery. When entirely new markets open up, such as in Eastern Europe, both experienced firms and those new to international competition usually rush to take advantage of awaiting opportunities. Such was the case with the proactive stance that Unisys took in preparing for and jumping on the newly opened market opportunity in Vietnam.

Resource Access and Cost Savings   Resource access and cost savings entice many companies to operate from overseas bases. The availability of raw materials and other resources offers both greater control over inputs and lower transportation costs.

Lower labor costs (for production, service, and technical personnel), another major consideration, lead to lower unit costs and have proved a vital ingredient to competitiveness for many companies.

Sometimes just the prospect of shifting production overseas improves competitiveness at home. When Xerox Corporation started moving copier rebuilding operations to Mexico, the union agreed to needed changes in work style and productivity to keep the jobs at home.[14] Lower operational costs in other areas—power, transportation, and financing—frequently prove attractive. Trinidad, for example, offers abundant inexpensive energy, a skilled and well-educated workforce with labor rates at about one-fourth of U.S. levels, and government incentives for export-oriented ventures that generate foreign exchange.[15]

Incentives   Governments in countries such as Poland seeking new infusions of capital, technology, and know-how willingly provide incentives—tax exemptions, tax holidays, subsidies, loans, and the use of property.[16] Because they both decrease risk and increase profits, these incentives are attractive to foreign companies. One study surveyed 103 experienced managers concerning the relative attractiveness of various incentives for expansion into the Caribbean region (primarily Mexico, Venezuela, Colombia, Dominican Republic, and Guatemala). The results indicate the opinion of those managers about which incentives are most important; however, the most desirable mix would depend on the nature of the particular company and its operations. The first two issues reflect managers' concerns about limiting foreign exchange risk, where restrictions often change overnight and limit the ability of the firm to repatriate profits. Other concerns are those of political instability in countries such as Haiti and Nicaragua, and the possibility of expropriation, and those of tax concessions.[17]

STRATEGIC FORMULATION PROCESS

Typically, the strategic formulation process is necessary both at the headquarters of the corporation and at each of the subsidiaries. One study reported, for example, that 70 percent of 56 American MNC subsidiaries in Latin America and the Far East operated on planning cycles of five or more years.[18]

The global strategic formulation process, as part of overall corporate strategic management, parallels the process followed in domestic companies. However, the variables, and therefore the process itself, are far more complex because of the greater difficulty in gaining accurate and timely information, the diversity of geographic locations, and the differences in political, legal, cultural, market, and financial processes. These factors introduce a greater level of risk in strategic decisions. However, for firms that have not yet engaged in international operations (as well as for those that do), an ongoing strategic planning process with a global orientation identifies potential opportunities for (1) appropriate market expansion, (2) increased profitability, and (3) new ventures by which the firm can exploit its strategic advantages. Even in the absence of immediate opportunities, monitoring the global environment for trends and competition is important for domestic planning.

The strategic formulation process is part of the strategic management process in which most firms engage, either formally or informally. The planning modes range from a proactive, long-range format to a reactive, more seat-of-the-pants method, whereby the day-by-day decisions of key managers, in particular owner-managers, accumulate to what can be discerned retroactively as the new strategic direction.[19] The stages in the strategic management process described here are shown in Exhibit 6-1. In

Exhibit 6-1   The Strategic Management Process

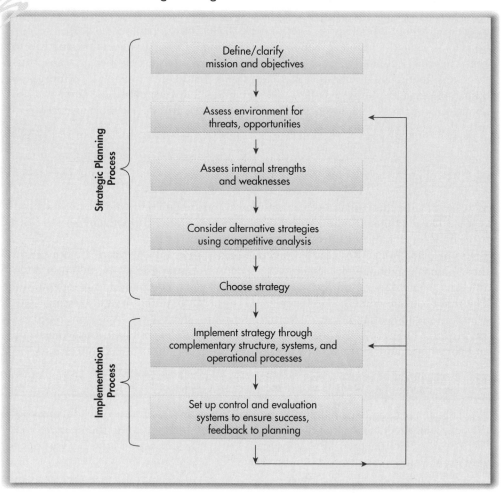

reality, these stages seldom follow such a linear format. Rather, the process is continuous and intertwined, with data and results from earlier stages providing information for the next stage.

The first phase of the strategic management process—the planning phase—starts with the company establishing (or clarifying) its mission and its overall objectives. The next two steps comprise an assessment of the external environment that the firm faces in the future and an analysis of the firm's relative capabilities to deal successfully with that environment. Strategic alternatives are then considered, and plans are made based on the strategic choice. These five steps constitute the planning phase, which will be further detailed in this chapter.

The second part of the strategic management process is the implementation phase. Successful implementation requires the establishment of the structure, systems, and processes suitable to make the strategy work. These variables, as well as functional-level strategies will be explored in detail in the remaining chapters on organizing, leading, and controlling. At this point, however, note that the strategic planning process by itself does not change the posture of the firm until the plans are implemented. In addition, feedback from the interim and long-term results of such implementation, along with continuous environmental monitoring, flows directly back into the planning process.

STEPS IN DEVELOPING INTERNATIONAL AND GLOBAL STRATEGIES

Mission and Objectives

The mission of an organization is its overall raison d'être or the function it performs in society. This mission charts the direction of the company and provides a basis for strategic decision making.

A company's overall objectives flow from its mission, and both guide the formulation of international corporate strategy. Because we are focusing on issues of international strategy, we will assume that one of the overall objectives of the corporation is some form of international operation (or expansion). The objectives of the firm's international affiliates should also be part of the global corporate objectives. A firm's global objectives usually fall into the areas of marketing, profitability, finance, production, and research and development, among others, as shown in Exhibit 6-2. Goals

Exhibit 6-2   Global Corporate Objectives

Marketing
Total company market share—worldwide, regional, national
Annual percentage sales growth
Annual percentage market share growth
Coordination of regional markets for economies of scale

Production
Relative foreign versus domestic production volume
Economies of scale through global production integration
Quality and cost control
Introduction of cost-efficient production methods

Finance
Effective financing of overseas subsidiaries or allies
Taxation—minimizing tax burden globally
Optimum capital structure
Foreign-exchange management

Profitability
Long-term profit growth
Return on investment, equity, and assets
Annual rate of profit growth

Research and Development
Develop new products with global patents
Develop proprietary production technologies
Worldwide research and development labs

for market volume and for profitability are usually set higher for international than for domestic operations because of the greater risk involved. In addition, financial objectives on the global level must take into account differing tax regulations in various countries and how to minimize overall losses from exchange rate fluctuations.

Environmental Assessment

After clarifying the corporate mission and objectives, the first major step in weighing international strategic options is the environmental assessment. This assessment includes environmental scanning and continuous monitoring to keep abreast of variables around the world that are pertinent to the firm and that have the potential to shape its future by posing new opportunities (or threats). Firms must adapt to their environment to survive. How to adapt is the focus of strategic planning.

The process of gathering information and forecasting relevant trends, competitive actions, and circumstances that will affect operations in geographic areas of potential interest is called **environmental scanning**. This activity should be conducted on three levels—multinational, regional, and national—which are discussed in detail later in this chapter. Scanning should focus on the future interests of the firm and should cover the following major variables (as discussed by Phatak and others).[20]

➤   *Political instability.* This variable represents a volatile and uncontrollable risk to the multinational corporation, as illustrated by the upheaval in the Middle East in recent years. MNCs must carefully assess such risk because it may result in a loss of profitability or even ownership.[21]

➤   *Currency instability.* This variable represents another risk; inflation and fluctuations in the exchange rates of currencies can dramatically affect profitability when operating overseas. In early 1995, for example, both foreign and local firms got a painful reminder of this risk when Mexico devalued its peso in 1998 and the currency collapsed in Indonesia, and in 2002 Argentina is suffering the same problems.

➤   *Nationalism.* This variable, representing the home government's goals for independence and economic improvement, often influences foreign companies. The home government may impose restrictive policies—import controls, equity requirements, local content requirements, limitations on the repatriation of profits, and so forth. Japan, for example, protects its home markets with these kinds of restrictive policies. Other forms of nationalism may be exerted through the following: (1) pressure from national governments—exemplified by the United States putting pressure on Japan to curtail unfair competition; (2) lax patent and trademark protection laws, such as those in China in recent years, which erode a firm's proprietary technology through insufficient protection; and (3) the suitability of infrastructure, such as roads and telecommunications.

➤   *International competition.* Conducting a global competitor analysis is perhaps the most important task in environmental assessment and strategy formulation. The first step in analyzing the competition is to assess the relevant industry structures as they influence the competitive arena in the particular country (or region) being considered. For example, will the infrastructure support new companies in that industry? Is there room for additional competition? What is the relative supply and demand for the proposed product or service? The ultimate profit potential in the industry in that location will be determined by these kinds of factors.[22]

Environmental Scanning   Managers must also specifically assess their current competitors—global and local—for the proposed market. They must ask, what are our competitors' positions, their goals and strategies, their strengths and weaknesses, relative to those of our firm? What are the likely competitor reactions to our strategic moves? Managers should compare their company with potential international competitors; in fact, it is useful to draw up a competitive position matrix for each potential international market. For example, Exhibit 6-3 analyzes a U.S. specialty seafood firm's competitive profile in Malaysia.[23]

The U.S. firm in Exhibit 6-3 has advantages in financial capability, future growth of resources, and sustainability, but a disadvantage in quickness. It also is at a disadvantage compared to the Korean MNC in important factors such as manufacturing capability and flexibility and adaptability. Because the other firms seem to have little comparative advantage, the major competitor is likely to be the Korean firm. At this point, then, the U.S. firm can focus in more detail on assessing the Korean firm's relative strengths and weaknesses.

The firm can also choose varying levels of environmental scanning. To reduce risk and investment, many firms take on the role of the "follower," meaning that they limit their own investigations. Instead, they simply watch their competitors' moves and go where they go, assuming that the competitors have done their homework. Other firms go to considerable lengths to gather data carefully and examine options in the global arena.

Ideally, the firm should conduct global environmental analysis on three different levels: multinational, regional, and national. Analysis on the multinational level provides a broad assessment of significant worldwide trends—through identification, forecasting, and monitoring activities. These trends would include the political and economic developments of nations around the world as well as global technological progress. From this information, managers can choose certain appropriate regions of the world to consider further.

Exhibit 6-3   Global Competitor Analysis

Comparison Criteria	A U.S. Firm Compared with Its International Competitors in Malaysia Market				
	A	B	C	D	E
	(U.S. MNC)	(Korean MNC)	(Local Malaysian Firm)	(Japanese MNC)	(Local Malaysian Firm)
Marketing capability	0	0	0	0	—
Manufacturing capability	0	+	0	0	0
R & D capability	0	0	0	—	0
HRM capability	0	0	0	0	0
Financial capability	+	—	0	0	—
Future growth of resources	+	0	—	0	—
Quickness	—	0	+	—	0
Flexibility/adaptability	0	+	+	0	0
Sustainability	+	0	0	0	—

Key:
+ = *firm is better relative to competition.*
0 = *firm is same as competition.*
— = *firm is poorer relative to competition.*
SOURCE: Diane J. Garsombke, "International Competitor Analysis." *Planning Review* 17, no. 3 (May–June 1989): 42–47.

Next, at the regional level, the analysis focuses in more detail on critical environmental factors to identify opportunities (and risks) for marketing the company's products, services, or technology. For example, one such regional location ripe for investigation by a firm seeking new markets is the European Union.

Having zeroed in on one or more regions, the firm must, as its next step, analyze at the national level. Such an analysis explores in depth specific countries within the desired region for economic, legal, political, and cultural factors significant to the company. For example, the analysis could focus on the size and nature of the market, along with any possible operational problems, to consider how best to enter the market. In many volatile countries, continuous monitoring of such environmental factors is a vital part of ongoing strategic planning. In Peru in 1988, inflation had soared to 2000 percent, and leftist terrorists were kidnapping or murdering business leaders. Although key managers fled and many multinational companies pulled out of Peru, Procter & Gamble remained to take advantage of a potentially large market share when competitors left. "Everybody should be dying to come here—you couldn't go to a better business school [than what you learn by managing here]," said Susana Elesperu de Freitas, the 34-year-old Peruvian manager of Procter & Gamble's subsidiary, who was flanked by armed bodyguards wherever she went.[24] Since then, Procter & Gamble, a consumer-products company, has expanded and is now a major force in Peru.

This process of environmental scanning, from the broad global level down to the local specifics of entry planning, is illustrated in Exhibit 6-4. The first broad scan of all potential world markets results in the firm being able to eliminate from its list those markets that are closed or insignificant or do not have reasonable entry conditions. The second scan of remaining regions, and then countries, is done in greater detail—perhaps eliminating some based on political instability, for example. Remaining countries are then assessed for competitor strengths, suitability of products, and so on. This analysis leads to serious entry planning in selected countries; managers start to work on operational plans, such as negotiations and legal arrangements.

Sources of Environmental Information

The success of environmental scanning depends on the ability of managers to take an international perspective and to ensure that their sources of information and business intelligence are global. A variety of public resources are available to provide information. In the United States alone, over 2,000 business information services are available on computer database, tailored to specific industries and regions. Other resources include corporate "clipping" services and information packages. However, internal sources of information are usually preferable—especially alert field personnel who, with firsthand observations, can provide up-to-date and relevant information for the firm. Using its own internal resources extensively, Mitsubishi Trading Company employs over 60,000 market analysts worldwide, whose job it is to gather, analyze, and feed market information to the parent company.[25] Internal sources of information help to eliminate unreliable information from secondary sources, particularly in developing countries. As Garsombke points out, the "official" data from such countries can be misleading: "Census data can be tampered with by government officials for propaganda purposes or it may be restricted. . . . In South Korea, for instance, even official figures can be conflicting depending on the source."[26]

Exhibit 6-4   International Environmental Scanning Process

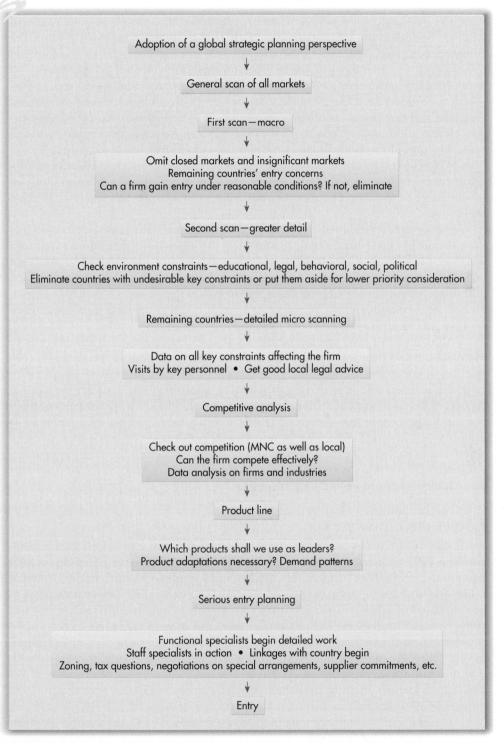

Adoption of a global strategic planning perspective

↓

General scan of all markets

↓

First scan—macro

↓

Omit closed markets and insignificant markets
Remaining countries' entry concerns
Can a firm gain entry under reasonable conditions? If not, eliminate

↓

Second scan—greater detail

↓

Check environment constraints—educational, legal, behavioral, social, political
Eliminate countries with undesirable key constraints or put them aside for lower priority consideration

↓

Remaining countries—detailed micro scanning

↓

Data on all key constraints affecting the firm
Visits by key personnel • Get good local legal advice

↓

Competitive analysis

↓

Check out competition (MNC as well as local)
Can the firm compete effectively?
Data analysis on firms and industries

↓

Product line

↓

Which products shall we use as leaders?
Product adaptations necessary? Demand patterns

↓

Serious entry planning

↓

Functional specialists begin detailed work
Staff specialists in action • Linkages with country begin
Zoning, tax questions, negotiations on special arrangements, supplier commitments, etc.

↓

Entry

SOURCE: John Garland, R. N. Farmer, and M. Taylor, *International Dimensions of Business Policy and Strategy*, 2nd ed. (Boston: PWS-Kent, 1990).

Internal Analysis

After the environmental assessment, the second major step in weighing international strategic options is the internal analysis. This analysis determines which areas of the firm's operations represent strengths or weaknesses (currently or potentially) compared to competitors, so that the firm may use that information to its strategic advantage.

The internal analysis focuses on the company's resources and operations, and on global synergies. The strengths and weaknesses of the firm's financial and managerial expertise and functional capabilities are evaluated to determine what key success factors (KSFs) the company has and how well they can help the firm exploit foreign opportunities. Those factors increasingly involve superior technological capability (as with Microsoft and Intel), as well as other strategic advantages such as effective distribution channels (as with Wal-Mart), superior promotion capabilities (Disney), low-cost production and sourcing position, superior patent and new product pipeline (Merck), and so on.

Using such operational strengths to advantage is exemplified by Japanese car manufacturers: their production quality and efficiency have catapulted them into world markets. As to their global strategy, they have recognized that their sales and marketing functions have proven a competitive weakness in the European car wars, and the Japanese are working on these shortcomings. Japanese automakers—Toyota, Honda, Mazda, and so on—are following Ford and GM in seeking to become more sophisticated marketers throughout Europe.[27]

All companies have strengths and weaknesses. Management's challenge is to identify both and take appropriate action. Many diagnostic tools are available for conducting an internal resource audit. Financial ratios, for example, may reveal an inefficient use of assets that is restricting profitability; a sales-force analysis may reveal that the sales force is an area of distinct competence for the firm. If a company is conducting this audit to determine whether to start international ventures or to improve its ongoing operations abroad, certain operational issues must be taken into account. These issues include (1) the difficulty of obtaining marketing information in many countries, (2) the often poorly developed financial markets, and (3) the complexities of exchange rates and government controls.

Competitive Analysis

At this point, the firm's managers assess its capabilities and key success factors compared to those of its competitors. They must judge the relative current and potential competitive position of firms in that market and location—whether that be a global position or that for a specific country or region. Like a chess game, the firm's managers also need to consider the strategic intent of competing firms and what might be their future moves (strategies). This process enables the strategic planners to determine where the firm has distinctive competencies that will give it strategic advantage as well as what direction might lead the firm into a sustainable competitive advantage—that is, one that will not be immediately eroded by emulation. The result of this process will also help to identify potential problems that can be corrected or that may be significant enough to eliminate further consideration of certain strategies.[28]

This stage of strategic formulation is often called a SWOT analysis (an acronym for Strengths, Weaknesses, Opportunities and Threats), in which the firm's capabilities relative to those of its competitors are assessed as pertinent to the opportunities and threats in the environment for those firms. For example, Philip Morris (PM) considered entry into the Commonwealth of Independent States (CIS) in the early 1990s. The attraction, of course, was the newly opened market of 290 million consumers. Of these, 70 million were smokers and would provide an immediate target market for Philip Morris's cigarette brands. In addition, all 290 million would be a vast potential market for PM's Kraft and General Foods subsidiaries. The next step would be an in-depth assessment of the local and foreign competitors in the region, such as RJR Nabisco.

After its analysis, Philip Morris concluded that the Russian commonwealth presented an attractive opportunity, particularly if the firm could establish a market foothold before RJR Nabisco followed suit. In hindsight, however, Philip Morris might have done some more homework and added other threats to this matrix. After the company set up kiosks to sell packs of Marlboros to people in St. Petersburg in 1992, those booths were blown up overnight—a signal that Russian cigarette distributors didn't want any outside competitors on their turf. Philip Morris subsequently got out of the distribution business. It is also worth noting that, in September 1998, RJR withdrew all operations from Russia as a result of that country's economic problems, after investing about $520 million. The company was among many suffering major losses in Russia's economic collapse in 1998, when the inflation rate reached 84.3 percent by the end of 1999.[29]

Most companies develop their strategy around key strengths, or core competencies. Core competencies represent important corporate resources because, as Prahalad and Hamel explain, they are the "collective learning in the organization, especially how to coordinate diverse production skills and integrate multiple streams of technologies."[30] Core competencies—like Sony's capacity to miniaturize and Philips's optical-media expertise—are usually difficult for competitors to imitate and represent a major focus for strategic development at the corporate level.[31] Canon, for example, has used its core competence in optics to its competitive advantage throughout its diverse businesses—cameras, copiers, and semiconductor lithographic equipment.

Managers must also assess their firm's weaknesses. A company already on shaky ground financially, for example, will not be able to consider an acquisition strategy, or perhaps any growth strategy. Of course, the subjective perceptions, motivations, capabilities, and goals of the managers involved in such diagnoses frequently cloud the decision-making process. The result is that sometimes firms embark on strategies that were contraindicated by objective information because of poor judgment by key players.

Global and International Strategic Alternatives

The fourth major step in the strategic planning process involves considering the advantages (and disadvantages) of various strategic alternatives in light of the competitive analysis. While weighing alternatives, managers need to take into account the goals of their firm and the competitive status of other firms in the industry.

Depending on the size of the firm, a firm must consider two levels of strategic alternatives. The first level, global strategic alternatives (applicable primarily to MNCs), determines what overall approach to the global marketplace a firm wishes to take. The second level, entry strategy alternatives, applies to firms of any size; these alternatives determine what specific entry strategy is appropriate for each country in which the firm plans to operate. Entry strategy alternatives will be discussed in a later section. We now turn to the two main global strategic approaches to world markets—globalization and regionalization.

Approaches to World Markets

Globalization   In the last decade, increasing competitive pressures have forced businesses to consider global strategies—to treat the world as an undifferentiated worldwide marketplace. Such strategies are now loosely referred to as **globalization**—a term that refers to the establishment of worldwide operations and the development of standardized products and marketing. Many, analysts, like Porter, have argued that globalization is a competitive imperative for firms in global industries: "In a global industry a firm must in some way integrate its activities on a worldwide basis to capture the linkages among countries. This includes, but requires more than, transferring intangible assets among countries."[32] The rationale behind globalization is to compete by establishing worldwide economies of scale, offshore manufacturing, and international cash flows. The term *globalization*, therefore, is as applicable to organizational structure as it is to strategy. (Organizational structure is discussed further in Chapter 8.)

The pressures to globalize include (1) increasing competitive clout resulting from regional trading blocs; (2) declining tariffs, which encourage trading across borders and open up new markets; and (3) the information technology explosion, which makes the coordination of far-flung operations easier and also increases the commonality of consumer tastes.[33] Use of Websites has allowed entrepreneurs, as well as established companies, to go global almost instantaneously through e-commerce—either B2B or B2C.[34] Examples are Yahoo!, Landsend, and the ill-fated E-Toys, which met its demise in 2001. In addition, the success of Japanese companies with global strategies has set the competitive standard in many industries—most visibly in the automobile industry. Other companies, such as Caterpillar, ICI, and Sony, have fared well with global strategies.

One of the quickest and cheapest ways to develop a global strategy is through strategic alliances. Many firms are trying to go global faster by forming alliances with rivals, suppliers, and customers. The rapidly developing information technologies are spawning cross-national business alliances from short-term virtual corporations to long-term strategic partnerships.[35] (Strategic alliances are discussed further in Chapter 7.)

Globalization is inherently more vulnerable to environmental risk, however, than a regionalization strategy. Global organizations are difficult to manage because doing so requires the coordination of broadly divergent national cultures. It also means, say Morrison, Ricks, and Roth, that firms must lose some of their original identity—they must "denationalize operations and replace home-country loyalties with a system of common corporate values and loyalties."[36] In other words, the globalization strategy necessarily treats all countries similarly, regardless of their differences in cultures and systems. Problems often result, such as a lack of local flexibility and responsiveness and a neglect of the need for differentiated products. In some recent research into how U.S. companies compete, Morrison et al. discovered that many companies are finding that "globalization is no panacea, and, in fact, global imperatives are being eclipsed by an upsurge in regional pressures."[37] These researchers claim that many companies now feel that regionalization is a more manageable and less risky approach, one that allows them to capitalize on local competencies as long as the parent organization and each subsidiary retain a flexible approach to each other.

Regionalization   For those firms in multidomestic industries—those industries in which competitiveness is determined on a country-by-country basis rather than a global basis—regional strategies are more appropriate than globalization.[38] The regionalization (or multilocal) strategy is one in which local markets are linked together within a region, allowing more local responsiveness and specialization. Top managers within each region decide on their own investment locations, product mixes, and competitive positioning; in other words, they run their subsidiaries as quasi-independent organizations.

Since there are pressures to globalize—such as the need for economies of scale to compete on cost—there are opposing pressures to regionalize, especially for Newly Developed Economies (NDEs) and LDCs. These localization pressures include unique consumer preferences resulting from cultural or national differences (perhaps something as simple as right-hand-drive cars for Japan), domestic subsidies, and new production technologies that facilitate product variation for less cost than before.[39] By "acting local," firms can focus individually in each country or region on the local market needs for product or service characteristics, distribution, customer support, and so on.

As with any management function, the strategic choice as to where a company should position itself along the globalization–regionalization continuum is contingent on the nature of the industry, the type of company, the company's goals and strengths (or weaknesses), and the nature of its subsidiaries, among many factors. In addition, each company's strategic approach should be unique in adapting to its own environment. Many firms may try to "Go Global, Act Local" to trade off the best advantages of each strategy. Matsushita is one firm with considerable expertise at being a "GLOCAL" firm (GLObal, LoCAL). Matsushita has over 150 production and R&D bases in 38 countries. In Malaysia, for example, where Matsushita employs 23,500 people in its 13 subsidiaries, the company diligently follows its policy of trying to keep the expatriate headcount down and train local managers—only 230 employees there are Japanese. Other Matsushita local policies are to develop local R&D to tailor products to markets, to let plants set their own rules, and to be a good coporate citizen in every country.[40] Another global company that works hard to act local in certain markets, such as India, is illustrated in the accompanying Management Focus.

Global Integrative Strategies

Many MNCs have developed their global operations to the point of being fully integrated—often both vertically and horizontally, including suppliers, productive facilities, marketing and distribution outlets, and contractors around the world. Dell, for example, is a globally integrated company, with worldwide sourcing and a fully integrated production and marketing system. It has factories in Ireland, Malaysia, and Texas, and it has an assembly and delivery system from 47 locations around the world. At the same time, it has extreme flexibility. Since Dell builds computers to each order, it carries very little inventory, and therefore can change its operations at a moment's notice.

Although some companies move very quickly to the stage of global integration—often through merger or acquisition—many companies evolve into multinational corporations by going through the entry strategies in stages, taking varying lengths of time between stages. Typically, a company starts with simple exporting, moves to large-scale exporting with sales branches abroad (or perhaps begins licensing), then proceeds to assembly abroad (either by itself or through contract manufacturing), and eventually evolves to full production abroad with its own subsidiaries. Finally, the MNC will undertake the global integration of its foreign subsidiaries, setting up coop-

Management Focus

WHIRLPOOL INDIA'S WHITEMAGIC BLENDS WITH LOCAL CULTURE AND TRADITIONS

Whirlpool India Ltd. launched "Whitemagic Hotwash"—a fully automatic top-loading washing machine—in Kerala. The machine, priced at Rs 19,000, was specially designed for the Indian market.[1] After over a year of research into the values of Indian people, especially homemakers, Whirlpool concluded that hygiene and purity was a matter of intense pride with Indians, and so it was very important to them to have very white clothes for their families.[2] However, after a number of washes in local water in their existing washing machines, the clothes became dull. So Whirlpool designed the "Whitemagic" which has a hot wash option with a super white cycle for special attention to white clothes.[3] A typical advertisement for the machine shows someone in very white clothes, with others in the background in more dull-looking clothes.

These are just some of the ways Whirlpool tries to "act local" while "going global," especially in emerging markets, where it is trying to establish a foothold in anticipation of high growth levels. Other tactics it uses to fall in with the local distribution system are offering incentives to the thousands of Indian retailers to get them to stock Whirlpool products and using local contractors who speak the 18 main languages used in India.[4] The contractors collect payments in cash and deliver the appliances by whatever means works in that area, which may be by bicycle or by oxcart.

Early cooperation with local partners and focusing on local cultures are lessons that Whirlpool learned the hard way after having to shut down two of the four appliance plants it had built in China. Now Whirpool's global strategy is to design basic models of appliances with about 70 percent common parts, leaving the remaining 30 percent to be localized to the needs of the particular market.[5] It looks like they are on to a winning combination: Whirlpool's sales in India have jumped by 80 percent and are expected to reach $200 million for 2001.[6]

[1]"India: Whirlpool's Whitemagic Hits Kerala Market," *Business Line*, November 10, 2000.

[2]P. Engardio and C. Frazier, "Smart Globalization," *Business Week*, August 27, 2001.

[3]www.Whirlpool.com; www.WhirlpoolIndia.com.

[4]Engardio and Frazier.

[5]Ibid.

[6]Ibid.

erative activities among them to achieve economies of scale. By this point, the MNC has usually adopted a geocentric orientation, viewing opportunities and entry strategies in the context of an interrelated global market instead of regional or national markets. In this way, alternative entry strategies are viewed on an overall portfolio basis to take maximum advantage of potential synergies and leverage arising from operations in multicountry markets.[41]

Exhibit 6-5 illustrates the integrated, concurrent strategies used in the global network of the Helicopter Division of France's Société Nationale Industrielle Aerospatiale. The corporation employs a complex pattern of entry strategies and alliances among plants around the world, involving exporting, licensing, joint ventures, importing, and subassembly and maintenance facilities.[42] For example, the company has joint ventures with Brazil and Singapore and also exports parts to those countries for assembly; it licenses certain models to India and Yugoslavia and also exports to them; and it exports rotors and airframes to the United States, which, in turn, direct markets to Canada and Mexico and maintains spares and maintenance facilities for operations in those countries.

Exhibit 6-5   Network of Entry Strategies and Alliances:
Société Nationale Industrielle Aerospatiale: Helicopter Division

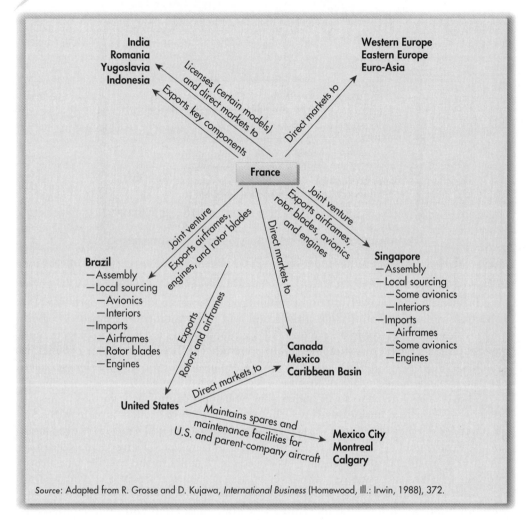

Source: Adapted from R. Grosse and D. Kujawa, *International Business* (Homewood, Ill.: Irwin, 1988), 372.

Using E-Business for Global Expansion

Companies of all sizes are increasingly looking to the Internet as a means of expanding their global operations. However, the Internet is not just about e-business:

> The real story is the profound impact this medium will have on corporate strategy, organization and business models. Our research reveals that the Internet is driving global marketplace transformation and paradigm shift in how companies get things done, how they compete and how they serve their customers.
>
> —www.IBM.com, APRIL 10, 2001

While the benefits of e-business are many, including rapid entrance into new geographic markets, as shown in Exhibit 6-6, less touted are the many challenges

Exhibit 6-6   Benefits of B2B

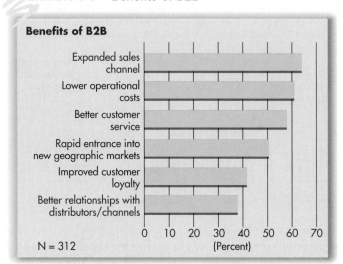

SOURCE: IDC Internet Executive Advisory Council Surveys, 2001.

inherent in a global B2B or B2C strategy. These include cultural differences and varying business models, governmental wrangling and border conflicts, in particular the question over which country has jurisdiction and responsibility over disputes regarding cross-border electronic transaction.[43] Potential problem areas that managers must assess in their global environmental analysis include conflicting consumer protection, intellectual property and tax laws, increasing isolationism even among democracies, language barriers, and a lack of tech-savvy legislators worldwide.[44]

Savvy global managers will realize that e-business cannot be regarded as just an extension of current businesses. It is a whole new industry in itself, complete with a different pool of competitors and whole new sets of environmental issues. A reassessment of the environmental forces in the newly configured industry, using Michael Porter's five forces analytical model, should take account of shifts in the relative bargaining power of buyers and suppliers, the level of threat of new competitors, existing and potential substitutes, as well as a present and anticipated competitor analysis.[45] The level of e-competition will be determined by how transparent and imitable the company's business model is for its product or service as observed on its Website.

It is clear that a competitive global B2B or B2C strategy must offer a technology solution that goes beyond basic transaction or listing service capabilities.[46] To assess the potential competitive position of the company, managers must ask themselves the following:

➤ Does the exchange provide a technology solution that helps industry-trading partners to do business more efficiently?

➤ Is the exchange known to be among the top 3 to 5 within its vertical industry?

➤ Does the exchange offer industry-specific technology and expertise that gives it an advantage over generic exchange-builders?[47]

There is no doubt that the global e-business competitive arena is a challenging one, both strategically and technologically. But many companies around the world are plunging in, fearing that they will be left behind in this fast developing global e-marketplace. Included are Fuji Xerox, which has formed a new e-marketplace with

E-Bix Box

SIEMENS AG LAUNCHES GLOBAL E-COMPANY

Siemens AG, the Munich-based electronics and electrical engineering giant, announced in October 2000 that the company was undergoing radical change and was transforming itself into a company whose entire value chain would be characterized by e-business.

All aspects of Siemens' global value chain—from purchasing, sales, and after-sales service to internal business and production processes, from research and development to training, and the worldwide management of knowledge and expertise—will be networked and handled electronically. In short, Siemens is becoming "one of the world's largest e-business building sites." This was how President and CEO Heinrich V. Pierer described the process at the October 10, 2000 opening of the first Center of E-Excellence. The goal of the centers is to coordinate and control Siemens' transformation into an e-company. The first center was founded at a location near Munich Airport, and others will follow in the United States (Atlanta) and Asia (Singapore). In his opening speech, Heinrich v. Pierer stated that "E-business will transform Siemens into a new company. We will base our entire business on a new foundation, thereby changing all processes, both internal and external ones." He added that an initial investment of 1 billion euros has been earmarked for this purpose. It will be the lever for considerable productivity increases and a corresponding improvement in Siemens' cost position.

Siemens and IBM announced that Siemens will use IBM's WebSphere Commerce Suite, with features including support for dynamic retail models—like on-line catalogs, content management, and modern search engine technologies. Sellers and buyers are able to maintain control in the kind of transaction involving goods or services. Business analysis and personalization tools assist in the creation of individual customer profiles. The Siemens global e-business applications will be jointly developed and implemented by an alliance composed of Siemens' own Siemens Business Services (SBS), i2 Technologies, CommerceOne and IBM. Benefits expected include faster development of new markets, closer customer relationships, and significant reduction of operational costs.

The Siemens program is expected to take around three years to complete. It is based on the concept of a global "e-community" embracing 447,000 Siemens employees as well as all the company's customers.

SOURCES: www.cyberlabsresearch.com/profile/Siemens.html, October 10, 2000; www.ibm.com/press, January 26, 2000.

NEC and other leading e-commerce players, including Simitomo Corporation, Hewlett Packard Japan, Ltd., Sumisho Computer Systems, and U.S. software developer Ariba, Inc. Their site, PLEOMART (plenty of markets) is a B2B marketplace for companies to buy and sell office equipment and supplies, parts, and related solutions services such as consultation, finance, and logistics services on the Web.[48] In Melbourne, Australia, the Broken Hill Proprietary Company, Ltd. (BHP) , which specializes in natural resources and regional steel for the global market, has launched its own one-stop global e-marketplace. The site provides logistics, sample products, and supply procurements to e-business producer marketplaces. Recently, BHP has conducted a series of Internet-based "reverse" auctions, where suppliers agree on starting prices and then bid against each other to lower prices for ferro-alloys. BHP's Francis Egan, vice president for Global Supply, reports that BHP already spends about A$10 billion annually on goods and services on-line. He says that "online auctions allow us to move readily, aggregate our buying power and leverage greater savings . . . they also provide economies of scale and promote greater efficiency in the supply function itself."[49]

Far from Melbourne, but in a world made smaller by the Internet, Germany's Siemens AG has embarked on a Global E-Strategy, as described in the accompanying E-Biz Box.

E-Global or E-Local?

Although the Internet is a global medium, the company is still faced with the same set of decisions regarding how much its products or services can be "globalized" or how much they must be "localized" to national or regional markets. Local cultural expectations, differences in privacy laws, government regulations, taxes, and payment infrastructure are just a few of the complexities encountered in trying to "globalize" e-commerce. Further complications arise because the local physical infrastructure must support e-businesses that require the transportation of actual goods for distribution to other businesses in the supply chain, or to end users. In those instances, adding e-commerce to an existing "old-economy" business in those international markets is likely to be more successful than starting an e-business from scratch without the supply and distribution channels already in place. However, many technology consulting firms, such as Nextlinx, provide software solutions and tools to penetrate global markets, extend their supply chains, and enable new buyer and seller relationships around the globe.

Going global with e-business, as Yahoo! has done, necessitates a coordinated effort in a number of regions around the world at the same time to gain a foothold and to grab new markets before competitors do. Certain conditions dictate the advisability of going **e-global**:

> The global beachhead strategy makes sense when trade is global in scope; when the business does not involve delivering orders; and when the business model can be hijacked relatively easily by local competitors.
> —M. SAWHNEY AND S. MANDAL, "GO GLOBAL," *BUSINESS* 2.0, MAY 2000

This strategy would work well for global B2B markets in steel, plastics, and electronic components.

The **e-local**, or regional strategic approach is suited to consumer retailing and financial services, for example. Amazon and eBay have started their regional approach in Western Europe. Again, certain conditions would make this strategy more advisable:

> [The e-local/regional approach] is preferable under three conditions: when production and consumption are regional rather than global in scope; when customer behavior and market structures differ across regions but are relatively similar within a region; and when supply-chain management is very important to success.
> —SAWHNEY AND MANDAL, 2000, "GO GLOBAL," *BUSINESS* 2.0, MAY 2000

The selection of which region or regions to target depends on the same factors of local market dynamics and industry variables as discussed earlier in this chapter. But for e-businesses, additional variables must also be considered, such as the rate of Internet penetration and the level of development of the local telecommunications infrastructure.

Entry Strategy Alternatives

For a multinational corporation (or a company considering entry into the international arena), a more specific set of strategic alternatives, often varying by targeted country, focuses on different ways to enter a foreign market. Managers need to consider how potential new markets may best be served by their company in light of the risks and the critical environmental factors associated with their entry strategies. The following sections examine the various entry and ownership strategies available to firms, including exporting, licensing, franchising, contract manufacturing, turnkey operations, management contracts, joint ventures, and fully owned subsidiaries set up by the firm. These alternatives are not mutually exclusive; several may be employed at the same time. They are addressed in order of ascending risk.

Exporting   Exporting is a relatively low-risk way to begin international expansion or to test out an overseas market. Little investment is involved, and fast withdrawal is relatively easy. Small firms seldom go beyond this stage, and large firms use this avenue for many of their products. Because of their comparative lack of capital resources and marketing clout, exporting is the primary entry strategy used by small businesses to compete on an international level. Jordan Toothbrush, for example, a small company with one plant in Norway and with limited resources, is dependent on good distributors. Since Jordan exports around the world, the company recognizes the importance of maintaining good distributor relations. A recent survey by Dun and Bradstreet showed that more than half of small to medium-sized businesses anticipate growth in their export sales in the next few years.[50]

An experienced firm may want to handle its exporting functions by appointing a manager or establishing an export department. Alternatively, an export management company (EMC) may be retained to take over some or all exporting functions, including dealing with host-country regulations, tariffs, duties, documentation, letters of credit, currency conversion, and so forth. Frequently, it pays to hire a specialist for a given host country.

Certain decisions need special care when managers are setting up an exporting system, particularly the choice of distributor. Many countries have regulations that make it very hard to remove a distributor who proves inefficient. Other critical environmental factors include export-import tariffs and quotas, freight costs, and distance from supplier countries.

Licensing   An international licensing agreement grants the rights to a firm in the host country to either produce or sell a product, or both. This agreement involves the transfer of rights to patents, trademarks, or technology for a specified period of time in return for a fee paid by the licensee. Anheuser-Busch, for instance, has granted licenses to produce and market Budweiser beer in England, Japan, Australia, and Israel, among other countries. Many food manufacturing MNCs license their products overseas, often under the names of local firms, and products like those of Nike and Disney can be seen around the world under various licensing agreements. Like exporting, licensing is also a relatively low-risk strategy because it requires little investment, and it can be a very useful option in countries where market entry by other means is constrained by regulations or profit-repatriation restrictions.

Licensing is especially suitable for the mature phase of a product's life cycle, when competition is intense, margins decline, and production is relatively standardized.[51] It is also useful for firms with rapidly changing technologies, for those with many diverse product lines, and for small firms with few financial and managerial resources for direct investment abroad. A clear advantage of licensing is that it avoids the tariffs and quotas usually imposed on exports. The most common disadvantage is the licensor's lack of control over the licensee's activities and performance.

Critical environmental factors to consider in licensing are whether sufficient patent and trademark protection is available in the host country, the track record and quality of the licensee, the risk that the licensee may develop its competence to become a direct competitor, the licensee's market territory, and legal limits on the royalty rate structure in the host country.[52]

Franchising   Similar to licensing, franchising involves relatively little risk. The franchisor licenses its trademark, products and services, and operating principles to the franchisee for an initial fee and ongoing royalties. Franchises are well known in the domestic fast-food industry; McDonald's, for example, operates primarily on this basis. For a large up-front fee and considerable royalty payments, the franchisee gets the benefit of McDonald's reputation, existing clientele, marketing clout, and management expertise. The "Big M" is well recognized internationally, as are many other fast-food and hotel franchises, such as Holiday Inn. A critical consideration for the franchisor's management is quality control, which becomes more difficult with greater geographic dispersion.

Franchising can be an ideal strategy for small businesses because outlets require little investment in capital or human resources. Through franchising, an entrepreneur can use the resources of franchisees to expand; most of today's large franchises started out with this strategy. An entrepreneur can also use franchisees to enter a new business. Higher costs in entry fees and royalties are offset by the lower risk of an established product, trademark, and customer base, as well as the benefit of the franchisor's experience and techniques.[53]

Contract Manufacturing   A common means of using cheaper labor overseas is contract manufacturing, which involves contracting for the production of finished goods or component parts. These goods or components are then imported to the home country, or to other countries, for assembly or sale. Alternatively, they may be sold in the host country. If managers can ensure the reliability and quality of the local contractor and work out adequate means of capital repatriation, this strategy can be a desirable means of quick entry into a country with a low capital investment and none of the problems of local ownership. Firms like Nike use contract manufacturing around the world.

Turnkey Operations   In a so-called turnkey operation, a company designs and constructs a facility abroad (such as a dam or chemical plant), trains local personnel, and then turns the key over to local management—for a fee, of course. The Italian company Fiat, for example, constructed an automobile plant in the former Soviet Union under a turnkey agreement. Critical factors for success are the availability of local supplies and labor, reliable infrastructure, and an acceptable means of repatriating profits. There may also be a critical risk exposure if the turnkey contract is with the host government, which is often the case. This situation exposes the company to risks such as contract revocation and the rescission of bank guarantees.

Management Contracts   A management contract gives a foreign company the rights to manage the daily operations of a business but not to make decisions regarding ownership, financing, or strategic and policy changes.[54] Usually, management contracts are enacted in combination with other agreements, such as joint ventures. By itself, a management contract is a relatively low-risk entry strategy, but it is likely to be short-term and to provide limited income unless it leads to another more permanent position in the market.[55]

International Joint Ventures (IJVs)   At a much higher level of investment and risk (though usually less risk than a wholly owned plant), joint ventures present considerable opportunities unattainable through other strategies. A joint venture involves an agreement by two or more companies to produce a product or service together. In an IJV ownership is shared, typically by an MNC and a local partner, through agreed-upon proportions of equity. This strategy facilitates an MNC's rapid entry into new markets by means of an already established partner who has local contacts and familiarity with local operations. IJVs are a common strategy for corporate growth around the world. They also are a means to overcome trade barriers, to achieve significant economies of scale for development of a strong competitive position, to secure access to additional raw materials, to acquire managerial and technological skills, and to spread the risk associated with operating in a foreign environment.[56] Not surprisingly, larger companies are more inclined to take a high equity stake in the IJV, engage in global industries, and are less vulnerable to the risk conditions in the host country.[57] The joint venture reduces the risks of expropriation and harassment by the host country. Indeed, it may be the only means of entry into certain countries, like Mexico and Japan, that stipulate proportions of local ownership and local participation.

In recent years, IJVs have made up about 20 percent of direct investments by MNCs in other countries, including such deals as the robotics venture between Fujitsu and General Electric and the fiber-optic venture between Siemens AG and Corning Glass Works. Many companies have set up joint ventures with European companies to gain the status of an "insider" in the European Common Market. Most of these alliances are not just tools of convenience but are important—perhaps critical—means to compete in the global arena.[58] To compete globally, firms have to incur, and defray, immense fixed costs—and they need partners to help them in this effort.[59]

Sometimes countries themselves need such alliances to improve economic conditions: the Commonwealth of Independent States (CIS) has recently opened its doors to joint ventures, seeking an infusion of capital and management expertise. Philip Morris, discussed earlier, entered a joint venture with Artovaz, a Russian auto manufacturer, to produce Marlboro cigarettes at a converted plant in Samara.

International joint ventures are one of many forms of strategic global alliances that are further discussed in the next chapter.

In a joint venture, the level of relative ownership and specific contributions must be worked out by the partners. The partners must share management and decision making for a successful alliance. The company seeking such a venture must maintain sufficient control, however, because without adequate control, the company's managers may be unable to implement their desired strategies. Initial partner selection and the development of a mutually beneficial working agreement are therefore critical to the success of a joint venture. In addition, managers must ascertain that there will be enough of a "fit" between the partners' objectives, strategies, and resources—financial, human, and technological—to make the venture work. Unfortunately, too often the need for preparation and cooperation is given insufficient attention, resulting in many such marriages ending in divorce. About 60 percent of IJVs fail, usually because of ineffective managerial decisions regarding the type of IJV, its scope, duration and administration, as well as careless partner selection.[60] The list of cross-cultural disappointments is getting longer—as well as the recent DaimlerChrysler problems, Chrysler-Mitsubishi and Fiat-Nissan have, according to *Business Week*, "produced as much rancor as rewards."[61] After years of arguments, GM pulled out of its operations with Korea's Daewoo Motors, citing insufficient care given to their relationship.

Fully Owned Subsidiaries   In countries where a fully owned subsidiary is permitted, an MNC wishing total control of its operations can start its own product or service business from scratch, or it may acquire an existing firm in the host country. Philip Morris acquired the Swiss food firm Jacobs Suchard to gain an early inside track in the European Common Market and to continue its diversification away from its aging tobacco business. With this move, PM became the second U.S. company, after Mars, to assure itself a place in Europe's food industry.[62] Such acquisitions by MNCs allow rapid entry into a market with established products and distribution networks and provide a level of acceptability not likely to be given to a "foreign" firm. These advantages somewhat offset the greater level of risk stemming from the larger capital investments, compared with other entry strategies.

At the highest level of risk is the strategy of starting a business from scratch in the host country—that is, establishing a new wholly owned foreign manufacturing or service company or subsidiary, with products aimed at the local market or targeted for

Exhibit 6-7   International Entry Strategies: Advantages and Critical Success Factors

Strategy	Advantages	Critical Success Factors
Exporting	Low risk No long-term assets East market access and exit	Choice of distributor Transportation costs Tariffs and quotas
Licensing	No asset ownership risk Fast market access Avoids regulations and tariffs	Quality and trustworthiness of licensee Appropriability of intellectual property Host-country royalty limits
Franchising	Little investment or risk Fast market access Small business expansion	Quality control of franchisee and franchise operations
Contract manufacturing	Limited cost and risk Short-term commitment	Reliability and quality of local contractor Operational control and human rights issues
Turnkey operations	Revenue from skills and technology where FDI restricted	Reliable infrastructure Sufficient local supplies and labor Repatriable profits Reliability of any government partner
Management contracts	Low-risk access to further strategies	Opportunity gain longer-term position
Joint ventures	Insider access to markets Share costs and risk Leverage partner's skill base technology, local contacts	Strategic fit and complementarity of partner, markets, products Ability to protect technology Competitive advantage Ability to share control Cultural adaptability of partners
Wholly owned subsidiaries	Realize all revenues and control Global economies of scale Strategic coordination Protect technology and skill base Acquisition provides rapid market entry into established market	Ability to assess and control economic, political and currency risk Ability to get local acceptance Repatriability of profits

export. Japanese automobile manufacturers—Honda, Nissan, and Toyota—have successfully used this strategy in the United States to get around American import quotas.

This strategy exposes the company to the full range of risk, to the extent of its investment in the host country. As evidenced by events in South Africa and China, political instability can be devastating to a wholly owned foreign subsidiary. Add to this risk a number of other critical environmental factors—local attitudes toward foreign ownership, currency stability and repatriation, the threat of expropriation and nationalism—and you have a high-risk entry strategy that must be carefully evaluated and monitored. There are advantages to this strategy, however, such as full control over decision making and efficiency, as well as the ability to integrate operations with overall companywide strategy.

Exhibit 6-7 summarizes the advantages and critical success factors of these entry strategies, which must be taken into account when selecting one or a combination of strategies depending on the location, the environmental factors and competitive analysis discussed here, and the overall strategy with which the company approaches world markets.

Complex situational factors face the international manager as she or he considers strategic approaches to world markets, along with which entry strategies might be appropriate, as illustrated in the accompanying Comparative Management in Focus.

Strategic Planning for the EU Market[63]

Business units [in Europe] still tend to focus on individual countries, and managerial practices still follow long-standing national patterns.

—FRANCESCO CAIO, CEO MERLONI ELETTRODOMESTICI,
FABRIANO, ITALY[64]

Comparative
Management
In Focus

For firms within Europe, the euro eliminates currency risk, and so "Pan European thinking becomes not only practicable but essential."[65] The success of companies within Europe, then, will depend on their efficiency in streamlining and consolidating its processes and in integrating product and marketing plans across Europe. The challenge is to balance the national and the continental view because a common currency does not bring about cultural or linguistic union.[66]

Clearly, both European and non-European companies will need to reconsider their European, and indeed global, strategies now that the EU has become a reality, complete with a common currency, the euro. "Foreign" managers, for example, need to develop an action program to ensure that their products have continued access to the EU and to adapt their marketing efforts to encompass the whole EU. The latter task is difficult, if not impossible, however, because the "citizen of Europe" is a myth; national cultures and tastes cannot be homogenized. With many different languages and distinctive national customs and cultures, companies trying to sell in Europe must thread their way through a maze of varying national preferences. These and other challenges lie ahead, along with numerous opportunities.

UPS is one of many firms experiencing this double-edged sword. Its managers realize that Europe is still virgin territory for service companies, and they expect revenue to grow by 15 percent a year there. However, UPS has run into many conflicts, both practical and cultural. Some of the surprises "Big Brown" had as it put its brown uniforms on 25,000 Europeans and sprayed brown paint on 10,000 delivery trucks around Europe:

> indignation in France, when drivers were told they couldn't have wine with lunch; protests in Britain, when drivers' dogs were banned from delivery trucks; dismay in Spain, when it was found that the brown UPS trucks resembled the local hearses; and shock in Germany, when brown shirts were required for the first time since 1945.[67]

Meanwhile, adventurous European businesses are spreading their wings across neighboring countries as they realize that open markets can offer as much growth and profitability as does protectionism—probably more. British Airways, for example, took the German market under its wing by buying 49 percent of a local airline and using a new Euroname, Deutsche BA. And in one of Europe's biggest mergers, the Zeneca Group P.L.C. of Britain acquired Astra A.B., of Sweden. The resulting pharmaceutical giant was deemed necessary to fund new drug research and to compete in a market dominated by U.S. corporations. Early European mergers were dominated by British companies. But now that Continental European companies will have their shares denominated in euros, there will likely be more cross-border deals among those countries because they will be free of currency-exchange problems.[68]

Companies within the EU are gaining great advantages by competing in a continental-scale market and thereby avoiding duplication of administrative procedures, production, marketing, and distribution. The Italian company Benneton Group SPA is one such company—competing by being technologically efficient. For insiders, a single EU internal market means greater efficiencies and greater economic growth through economies of scale and the removal of barriers, with the consequent lowering of unit costs.

Stiffer competition, however, has resulted both within the market and outside of it, leading to a shakeout of firms; mergers and acquisitions will increase so that larger firms will be strong enough to survive. The 12 "Euroland" countries already have a combined 19 percent of world trade, compared to 17 percent for the United States and 8 percent for Japan, and continued strong growth is projected.

Companies based outside the EU enjoy the same advantages if they have a subsidiary in at least one member state. But they sometimes feel discrimination simply because they will be outside what for the member states is a domestic market. In other words, the EU may build a protectionist wall—of tariffs, quotas, and competitive tactics—to keep out the United States and Japan. However, the EU will also create opportunities for nonmembers—a market with a potential purchasing power of $2.5 trillion, for instance. Many companies, especially MNCs, will start from a better position than some firms based inside the community because of (1) their superior competitiveness and research and development, (2) an existing foothold in the market, and (3) reduced operating expenses (one subsidiary for the whole EU instead of several). But European harmonized standards, while seeking to eliminate trade barriers within Europe, serve to limit access to EU markets by outside companies through the standardized specifications of products allowed to be sold in Europe. The harmonization laws set minimum standards for exports and imports that are EU-wide. However, those standards also frequently hinder European companies from efficient sourcing of raw materials or component parts from "foreign" companies.

Opinions differ about the long-term impact on U.S. firms: the EU could unify its markets, adversely affecting some U.S. industries; market access could be reduced; and demands for reciprocal market access in the United States might ensue.

Others feel that the new single market provides little threat to and considerable opportunity for Americans. Many U.S. firms (in anticipation of protectionism) have invested in Europe since the beginning of the Common Market in 1958, and they now feel satisfied with their current positions. Indeed, U.S. companies (GE, Dow, 3M, Hewlett-Packard) that already have well-established European presences enjoy the same free flow of goods, services, capital, and people as Europeans.

Those U.S. companies not yet established in Europe must examine the EU internal market to decide on their most effective "European strategy." Many firms are opting for joint ventures with European partners, sacrificing their usual preference of 100 percent ownership (or majority control) to extend operations around Europe. This strategy also opens doors to markets dominated by public procurement, as with the AT&T-Philips venture to produce telecommunications equipment. But for a number of firms—both foreign and European—operating in Europe has become cost prohibitive. The average Western European earns more, works fewer hours, takes longer vacations, and receives more social entitlements and job protection than workers in Asia and North America. European MNCs have the highest labor and taxation costs among the TRIAD nations.[69] Siemens AG of Germany, for example, shifted almost all its semiconductor assembly work from its plants in Germany—where it was not permitted to operate around the clock or on weekends—to a plant in Singapore, where it operates 24 hours a day, 365 days a year, and pays $4.40 an hour for workers.[70]

Suzuki, Toyota, Nissan, and other Japanese companies are also experiencing the dilemma of operating in Europe. They are reluctant to freely pour yen into Europe, but they want to keep a foothold in the market. Suzuki, for example, found that in its Spanish plant it took five times the number of workers and cost 46 percent more to produce a Suzuki Samurai than in its Japanese plants.

Strategic Choice

The strategic choice of one or more of the entry strategies will depend on (1) a critical evaluation of the advantages (and disadvantages) of each in relation to the firm's capabilities, (2) the critical environmental factors, and (3) the contribution that each choice would make to the overall mission and objectives of the company. Exhibit 6–7 summarized the advantages and the critical success factors for each entry strategy discussed. However, when it comes down to a choice of entry strategy or strategies for a particular company, there are more specific factors relating to that firm's situation that must be taken into account. These include factors relating to the firm itself, the industry in which it operates, location factors, and venture-specific factors, as summarized in Exhibit 6-8.

After consideration of the factors for the firm as shown in Exhibit 6–8, as well as what is available and legal in the desired location, some entry strategies will no doubt fall out of the feasibility zone. With those options remaining, then, strategic planners need to decide which factors are more important to the firm than others. One method is to develop a weighted assessment to compare the overall impact of factors such as those in Exhibit 6-7, relative to the industry, the location, and the specific venture—on each entry strategy. Specific evaluation ratings, of course, would depend on the country conditions at a given point in time, the nature of the industry, and the focal company.

Based on a study of over 10,000 foreign entry activities into China between 1979 and 1998, Pan and Tse concluded that managers tend to follow a hierarchy of decision-sequence in chosing an entry mode. As depicted in Exhibit 6-9, managers first decide between equity-based and nonequity based. Then, equity modes are split into wholly owned operations and equity joint ventures (EJVs); nonequity modes are divided into contractual agreements and export. Pan and Tse found that the location choice—specifically the level of country risk—was the primary influence factor at the level of

Exhibit 6-8 Factors Affecting Choice of International Entry Mode

Factor Category	Examples
Firm factors	International experience
	Core competencies
	Core capabilities
	National culture of home country
	Corporate culture
	Firm strategy, goals, and motivation
Industry factors	Industry globalization
	Industry growth rate
	Technical intensity of industry
Location factors	Extent of scale and location economies
	Country risk
	Cultural distance
	Knowledge of local market
	Potential of local market
	Competition in local market
Venture-specific factors	Value of firm—assets risked in foreign location
	Extent to which know-how involved in venture is informal (tacit)
	Costs of making or enforcing contracts with local partners
	Size of planned foreign venture
	Intent to conduct research and development with local partners

SOURCE: Excerpted and adapted from *International Management—Concepts and Cases* by A. V. Phatak, pp. 270–275. Copyright © 1997 South-Western College Publishing, Cincinnati, Ohio, a division of International Thomson Publishing Inc.

Exhibit 6-9   A Hierarchical Model of Choice of Entry Modes

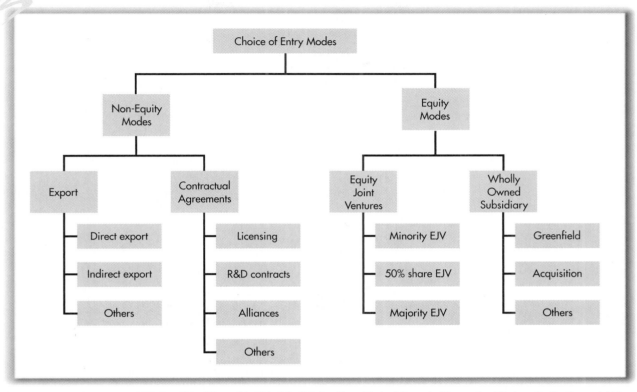

SOURCE: Yigang Pan and David K. Tse, "The Hierarchical Model of Market Entry Modes," *Journal of International Business Studies* 31, no. 4 (4th Quarter 2000): 535–554.

deciding between equity and nonequity modes. Host-country government incentives also encouraged the choice of equity mode.[71]

Gupta and Govindarajan also propose a hierarchy of decision factors but consider two initial choice levels. The first is the extent to which the firm will export or produce locally; the second is the extent of ownership control over activities that will be performed locally in the target market.[72] As shown in Exhibit 6-10, there is an array of choice combinations within those two dimensions. Gupta and Govindarajan point out that, among the many factors to take into account, alliance-based entry modes are more suitable under the following conditions:

➤ Physical, linguistic, and cultural distance between the home and host countries is high.

➤ The subsidiary would have low operational integration with the rest of the multinational operations.

➤ The risk of asymmetric learning by the partner is low.

➤ The company is short of capital.

➤ Government regulations require local equity participation.[73]

Exhibit 6-10 Alternative Modes of Entry

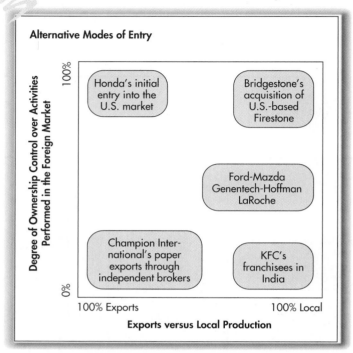

SOURCE: Anil K. Gupta and Vijay Gorindarajan, "Managing Global Expansion: A Conceptual Framework," *Business Horizons*, March/April 2000, pp. 45–54.

The choice of entry strategy for McDonald's, for example, varies around the world according to the prevailing conditions in each country. With its 4,700 foreign stores, McDonald's is, according to *Fortune*, "a virtual blueprint for taking a service organization global."[74] CEO Mike Quinlan notes that, in Europe, the company prefers wholly owned subsidiaries, since European markets are similar to those in the United States and can be run similarly. Those subsidiaries in the United States both operate company-owned stores and license out franchises. Approximately 70 percent of McDonald's stores around the world are franchised. In Asia, joint ventures are preferred so as to take advantage of partners' contacts and local expertise, and their ability to negotiate with bureaucracies such as the Chinese government. Headed by billionaire Den Fujita, McDonald's has over 1,000 stores in Japan; in China it had 23 stores in 1994, with more planned, in spite of conflicts with the Chinese government, such as when it made McDonald's move from its leased Tiananmen Square restaurant. In other markets, such as in Saudi Arabia, McDonald's prefers to limit its equity risk by licensing the name—adding strict quality standards—and keeping an option to buy later. Some of McDonald's implementation policies are given in the next chapter.[75]

Timing Entry and Scheduling Expansions

As with McDonald's, international strategic formulation requires a long-term perspective. Entry strategies, therefore, need to be conceived as part of a well-designed, overall plan. In the past, many companies have decided on a particular means of entry that seemed appropriate at the time, only to find later that it was shortsighted. For instance, if a company initially chooses to license a host-country company to produce a product, then later decides that the market is large enough to warrant its own production facility, this new strategy will no longer be feasible because the local host-country company already owns the rights.[76]

The Influence of Culture on Strategic Choice

In addition, strategic choices at various levels often are influenced by cultural factors, such as a long-term versus a short-term perspective. Hofstede found that most people in countries such as China and Japan generally had a longer-term horizon than those in Canada and the United States.[77] Whereas Americans, then, might make strategic choices with a heavy emphasis on short-term profits, the Japanese are known to be more patient in sacrificing short-term results in order to build for the future with investment, research and development, and market share.

Risk orientation was also found to explain the choice between equity and non-equity modes.[78] Risk orientation relates to Hofstede's uncertainty avoidance dimension.[79] Firms from countries where, generally speaking, people tend to avoid uncertainty (for example, Latin American and African countries) tend to prefer nonequity entry modes in order to minimize exposure to risk. Managers from firms from low-uncertainty avoidance countries are more willing to take risks and therefore are more likely to adopt equity entry modes.[80]

Choice of equity versus nonequity mode has also been found to be related to level of power distance. According to Hofstede, a high power-distance country (such as Arab countries and Japan) is one where people observe interpersonal inequality and hierarchy.[81] Pan and Tse found that firms from countries tending toward high power distance are more likely to use equity modes of entry abroad.[82]

These are but a few of the examples of the relationships between culture and the choices that are made in the strategic planning and implementation phase. They serve to remind us that it is people who make those decisions and that the ways people think, feel, and act are based on their ingrained societal culture. People bring that context to work, and it influences their propensity toward or against certain types of decisions.

Conclusion

The process of strategic formulation for global competitiveness is a daunting task in the volatile international arena and is further complicated by the difficulties involved in acquiring timely and credible information. However, early insight into global developments provides a critical advantage in positioning a firm for future success.

When an entry strategy is selected, the international manager focuses on translating strategic plans into actual operations. Often this involves strategic alliances; always it involves functional level activities for strategic implementation. These subjects are covered in the next chapter.

SUMMARY OF KEY POINTS

1. Companies "go international" for many reasons, including reactive ones, such as international competition, trade barriers, and customer demands. Proactive reasons include seeking economies of scale, new international markets, resource access, cost savings, and local incentives.

2. International expansion and the resulting realization of a firm's strategy are the product of both rational planning and responding to emergent opportunities.

3. The steps in the rational planning process for developing an international corporate strategy comprise defining the mission and objectives of the firm, scanning the environment for threats and opportunities, assessing the internal strengths and weaknesses of the firm, considering alternative international entry strategies, and deciding on strategy. The strategic management process is completed by putting into place the operational plans necessary to implement the strategy and then setting up control and evaluation procedures.

4. Competitive analysis is an assessment of how a firm's strengths and weaknesses vis-à-vis those of its competitors affect the opportunities and threats in the international environment. Such assessment allows the firm to determine where the company has distinctive competences that will give it strategic advantage or where problem areas exist.

5. Corporate-level strategic approaches to international competitiveness include globalization and regionalization. Many MNCs have developed to the point of using an integrative global strategy. Entry and ownership strategies are exporting, licensing, franchising, contract manufacturing, turnkey operations, management contracts, joint ventures, and fully owned subsidiaries. Critical environmental and operational factors for implementation must be taken into account.

6. Companies of all sizes are increasingly looking to the Internet as a means of expanding their global operations. But localizing Internet operations is complex.

DISCUSSION QUESTIONS

1. Discuss why companies "go international," giving specific reactive and proactive reasons.

2. Discuss the ways in which managers arrive at new strategic directions—formal and informal. Which is the best?

3. Explain the process of environmental assessment. What are the major international variables to consider in the scanning process? Discuss the levels of environmental monitoring that should be conducted. How well do you think managers conduct environmental assessment?

4. How can managers assess the potential relative competitive position of their firm in order to decide on new strategic directions?

5. Discuss the relative advantages of globalization versus regionalization.
   What are the relative merits of the entry strategies discussed in this chapter? What is their role in an integrative global strategy?

6. Discuss the considerations in strategic choice, including the typical stages of the MNC and the need for a long-term global perspective.

APPLICATION EXERCISES

1. Choose a company in the microcomputer industry or a chain in the fast-food industry. In small groups, conduct a multilevel environmental analysis, describing the major variables involved, the relative impact of specific threats and opportunities, and the critical environmental factors to be considered. The group findings can then be presented to the class, allowing a specific time period for each group so that comparison and debate of different group perspectives can follow. Be prepared to state what regions or specific countries you are interested in and give your rationale.

2. In small groups, discuss among yourselves and then debate with the other groups the relative merits of the alternative entry strategies for the company and countries you chose in Question 1. You should be able to make a specific choice and defend that decision.

3. For this exercise, research (individually or in small groups) a company with international operations and find out the kinds of entry strategies the firm has used. Present the information you find, in writing or verbally to the class, describing the nature of the company's international operations, its motivations, its entry strategies, the kinds of implementation problems the firm has run into, and how those problems have been dealt with.

EXPERIENTIAL EXERCISE

In groups of four, develop a strategic analysis for a type of company of interest to your group considering entry into Russia. Which entry strategies seem most appropriate? Share your results with the class.

INTERNET RESOURCES

Visit the Deresky companion Web site at http://prenhall.com/Deresky for this chapter's Internet resources.

CASE STUDY: COLA WARS: THE VENEZUELAN COUP

Opening Case Scenario: Disappointed Pepsi Distributor

Stefano:	Hóla Señora Ganser, ¿Como estás?
Sra. Ganser:	Muy bien gracias ¿y usted?
Stefano:	Muy bien, hoy necesito doscientas botellas de Pepsi para mi tienda.
Sra. Ganser:	Lo siento señor, pero tengo solamente Coca-Cola.
Stefano:	¿Qúe? Pero, yo compré trescientas botellas el viemes.
Sra. Ganser:	Sí, pero en el fin de semana la embotelladora de Coca-Cola compró a Pepsi. Ahora todas las tiendas en Venezuela solamente pueden comprar Coca-Cola.
Stefano:	Ay Díos mío, no tengo ninguna selección de refrescos. ¡Qué tipo de país es este!

Translation

Steve:	Hello Mrs. Ganser, How are you?
Mrs. Ganser:	Very well thanks, and you?
Steve:	Very good. Today I need 200 bottles of Pepsi for my store.
Mrs. Ganser:	I'm sorry sir, I only have Coca-Cola.
Steve:	What? But I just bought 300 bottles on Friday.

SOURCE: Adapted from a term project by Steven Davis, Sandra Ganser, and Adam Isen, students at State University of New York, Plattsburgh, Spring, 1998. Copyright © Helen Deresky, 1998.

Mrs. Ganser:	Yes, but over the weekend Coca-Cola bought Pepsi. Now all of the stores in Venezuela can only buy Coca-Cola.
Steve:	Oh My God! I have no selection in drinks. What kind of country is this!

Cola Wars

The Cola wars have been going on for over 65 years, since the establishment of Coca-Cola in 1886. Their first shipment was sent abroad in 1900. From the beginning, Coke had a head start in overseas operations. By 1931 they already had bottling operations in Cuba, Panama, Puerto Rico, The Philippines, and Guam (*The Washington Post,* August 24, 1996).

Pepsi was not far behind; by the 1970's they had captured the Soviet market and scored other international successes, at which time Coke's sales abroad were flat. In 1981, Coca-Cola paid $30 million for a 30 percent equity stake in a Philippine bottler and reversed the 2–1 Pepsi advantage that had previously existed. In 1985, in the United States, Coke suffered legendary humiliation with the launch of New Coke; however, they were quick to replace it with Classic Coke.

By the late 1980's Coca-Cola leapt into Eastern Europe where it bought every available bottling plant in East Germany and moved ahead of Pepsi there. By 1995 Coke had customers in 200 countries, more than 80 percent of its profits came from abroad, compared to 30 percent for Pepsi.

Pepsi was always looking for holes in the cola market where they could get some market share, while trying to fend off counterattacks. Its early links in Moscow gave it a 2–1 advantage in Eastern Europe, but that has changed with Coke jumping into the markets to grab shares in Moscow and India.

The war continued on in Brazil. Pepsi was obliged to take over BAESA (its largest foreign bottler) because the latter company's overly ambitious expansion program had jeopardized its financial viability. The company faced $400 million in debt and possible bankruptcy. Another Latin American disaster occurred in Venezuela. Pepsi lost out again to Coke when their bottler, the Cisneros Group, defected to Coke, without warning. This defection is the focus of this case study, and cause for analysis of Pepsi's competitive strategy.

Pepsi has attempted everything from celebrity advertising and package changes to introducing fast-food chains, in order to keep up with Coke. However, Coke's aggressive strategy seems to always take Pepsi by surprise.

Takeover Events

Roger Enrico, PepsiCo's new CEO, had been on the job for only four months in August of 1996 when the news came. He had received word from Pepsi's regional president in Venezuela, Alberto Uribe that their longtime bottling partner in Venezuela was terminating their partnership; the partner (Hit de Venezuela) had sold a 50 percent stake in its company to arch-rival Coca-Cola and would be bottling under the Coke brand from now on. This was a catastrophe—the third major blow to PepsiCo in as many weeks. First there was the problem with their financially plagued franchise in Argentina (BAESA), which had been struggling for years with financial problems because of mismanagement and overextension. Then, in July of 1996, PepsiCo went in and took over management to try to salvage what remained of this burdensome yet vital behemoth. Then there was the Puerto Rico scandal, where some questionable accounting practices by their bottler in Puerto Rico were undertaken that sent a shock-wave through the company and on to Wall Street. And now this. How could something like this happen? This was PepsiCo's only true conquest in the $350 million-a-year Latin American operation and in a matter of a few days it was gone. This presented the biggest challenge of Mr. Enrico's 24-year career with Pepsi.

Roger considered Oswaldo Cisneros a close and trusted friend. Oswaldo's family owned Hit de Venezuela (the Venezuelan Bottling company) and Oswaldo was in charge of operating it. They had been faithful partners of Pepsi for 47 years. Enrico and Oswaldo had often vacationed together, and their wives were inseparable during their many travels. How could Oswaldo do something so drastic, especially when Pepsi had been in negotiations with him for the past two years, trying to strike an agreement to buy a large part of the Venezuelan operation? He thought Cisneros wanted that, too.

Meanwhile, in Caracas, Venezuela, Oswaldo Cisneros had plenty on his mind. Recently, he had signed an agreement with PepsiCo's arch rival Coca-Cola, selling Coca-Cola a 50 percent share in the Cisneros bottling operation for $300 million up front, and another $300 million over the next 5 years. There was one other clincher. Coca-Cola would put up $100 million in a legal defense fund to cover the expected huge costs of court battles with his ex-partner Pepsi since Cisneros did have a contract with PepsiCo through 2003. All this had happened in such a short time that it was hard for him to believe that his family's whole enterprise was about to take on a new identity.

Oswaldo Cisneros grew up under much different circumstances than his old friend Roger Enrico. Oswaldo was born into wealth. His family emigrated from Cuba in the 1930's, and almost from the beginning they were able to do well in their new homeland. All of the Cisneros kids were immersed in the soda business from the time they were little, and like their father and uncle, became quite good at it. Oswaldo was no exception. He nurtured the business and watched it grow into a multibillion-dollar corporation. Now he was about to embark on a new adventure—one that would surely earn him the scorn of Pepsi and his old friend Roger Enrico. Unfortunately, it was the path he felt Pepsi had forced him to take.

Events Leading Up to Defection

The Cisneros empire was aching to expand to other markets, knowing that their own market in Venezuela was saturated. They controlled 85 percent of the soda industry in their country and had no more growth potential unless they could expand into emerging markets. In order to do this, they would need a lot of capital and a strong partner. Oswaldo Cisneros said he approached Pepsi with his offer to sell. Pepsi gave him the runaround for years, offering to buy at only a small fraction of what Cisneros felt it was worth. Pepsi, on the other hand, says that negotiations had been ongoing for only a couple of years and a favorable deal would have soon been reached. Another disillusioning factor for Cisneros was that he felt Pepsi was not going to allow his company to expand into other Latin American countries, instead reserving them for Pepsi's troubled child in Argentina, BAESA. So, Cisneros felt compelled to approach Coca-Cola through an investment banker to see if Coca-Cola would be interested in a deal. This came as a complete surprise to Roberto Goizueta, chairman and chief executive officer of Coca-Cola, who had no real plans to expand Coca-Cola's market share any further in Venezuela since Pepsi had completely dominated that market for the past five decades. Of course, the possibility of reversing this trend was very appealing since Venezuela was Coca-Cola's only blemish in Latin America, so he decided to take the offer and see what would happen. There were several very secret meetings, which were often argumentative; however, in the end, there was an agreement struck that would be signed in its final form on August 14, 1996.

Meanwhile, at the Pepsi headquarters, there was no apparent reason to be alarmed. Their Venezuelan partner was conducting business as usual, and PepsiCo's corporate team was very busy with a bigger priority—trying to salvage what remained of BAESA, their faltering franchise in Argentina, not to mention the restructuring that had been going on since Roger Enrico took over as CEO of Pepsi. Talks had been underway for some time with the Cisneros family to purchase part of their operation, but there seemed to be no need for immediate action, so this was not given top priority.

The Deal

On Wednesday, August 14, 1996, Oswaldo Cisneros and several of his family members and aides arrived at the Atlanta International Airport, and under a veil of complete secrecy were taken to Coca-Cola's headquarters. There, they signed an agreement turning over 50 percent of their bottling operation to Coca-Cola. After the meeting, there was a grand dinner to celebrate the new $600 million deal. This was a short-lived celebration since there would be an incredible amount of work to do in the next few days.

The Takeover

On Friday, August 16, the last Pepsis were made at the Cisneros' 18 bottling plants, and a rapid transformation took place. Several large cargo planes arrived in Venezuela from the United States. They were stocked full of equipment that would be needed to convert the 18 bottling plants from production of Pepsi to that of Coca-Cola. It was a long, frenzied weekend, with the old going out the door, and the new coming in. Four thousand trucks had to be repainted with Coke emblems, and many thousands of uniforms had to be distributed. There were also customers to notify, many of whom might not like the idea of this sudden change. By the time Monday rolled around, this logistical, tactical, and technical nightmare, which would have been impossible for most corporations, had been completed. The first Cokes were rolling off the assembly line, and on their way to stores and restaurants by that morning. Coke had now completed its conquest of Latin America, taking the last remaining stronghold of Pepsi.

Monday, August 19, 1996

Roger Enrico had watched in disbelief as the transformation took place. In just three days, Pepsi had gone from an 80 percent market share to zero, and from production of 4 million cases a year to zero. Now the stock market was reacting. Pepsi's shares dove $1.50 a share to $30.125, whereas rival Coke's soared to $51.75, a 52-week high (see Exhibit 6-11). Mr. Enrico knew that because of this defection, there could be rough roads ahead in other parts of the globe if he didn't respond to this crisis appropriately. Other partners might consider defecting unless convinced that Pepsi was still a big player in the cola war and could meet Coca-Cola toe-to-toe in any fight. If other emerging markets perceived that Coke would be a better investment than Pepsi, Pepsi's future in those markets could be very grim. There was also the concern of customers. In

Exhibit 6-11

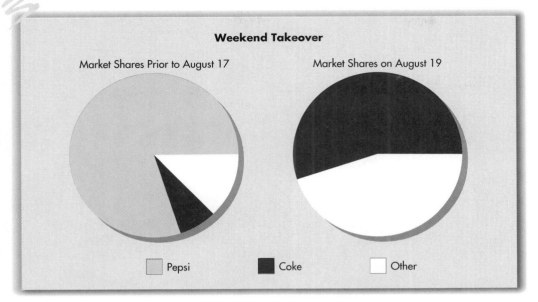

Weekend Takeover

Market Shares Prior to August 17

Market Shares on August 19

Pepsi   Coke   Other

Venezuela, millions of loyal customers were without their favorite soft drink. How to reintroduce Pepsi to that market before they started to forget their loyalties was a paramount concern. One final concern was how to convince the stockholders that Pepsi could recover from this financial embarrassment and still give them a good return.

Competitive Situation

It is evident that Coke has adopted a strategy to consciously aim at markets where Pepsi operates. Coke takes over Pepsi's market shares by buying out the bottlers. The following examples demonstrate the takeover strategy that Coke has recently adopted:

➤ Coca Cola's independent bottler in Morocco bought the only bottler of rival Pepsi in the African country for $55 million. This was more than Pepsi could imagine paying for the bottler, and as a result, Pepsi had to let Coke take over their market share there. Another case of monopolistic pressure was in South Africa. PepsiCo Inc. operated with a franchise bottler New Age Beverages, where they owned 25 percent of the operations. Coke held an 81.3 percent share in South Africa, and in May 1997, Pepsi was forced to cease operations with a challenge from Coke's $1 billion beverage market.

➤ Coca-Cola continued to put Pepsi's shares in peril by purchasing Embotelladora Milca, Nicaragua's largest soft drink bottler. This was one of the few remaining locations where Pepsi accounted for as much as 45 percent of the country's cola market. This share is expected to drop with Coke's recent purchase.

➤ Coca-Cola was charged with engineering the defection of key Pepsi Co. employees, bottlers, and consultants in India through "unfair and illegal means."

Exhibit 6-12   Areas of Coca-Cola's Takeover of Pepsi's Market

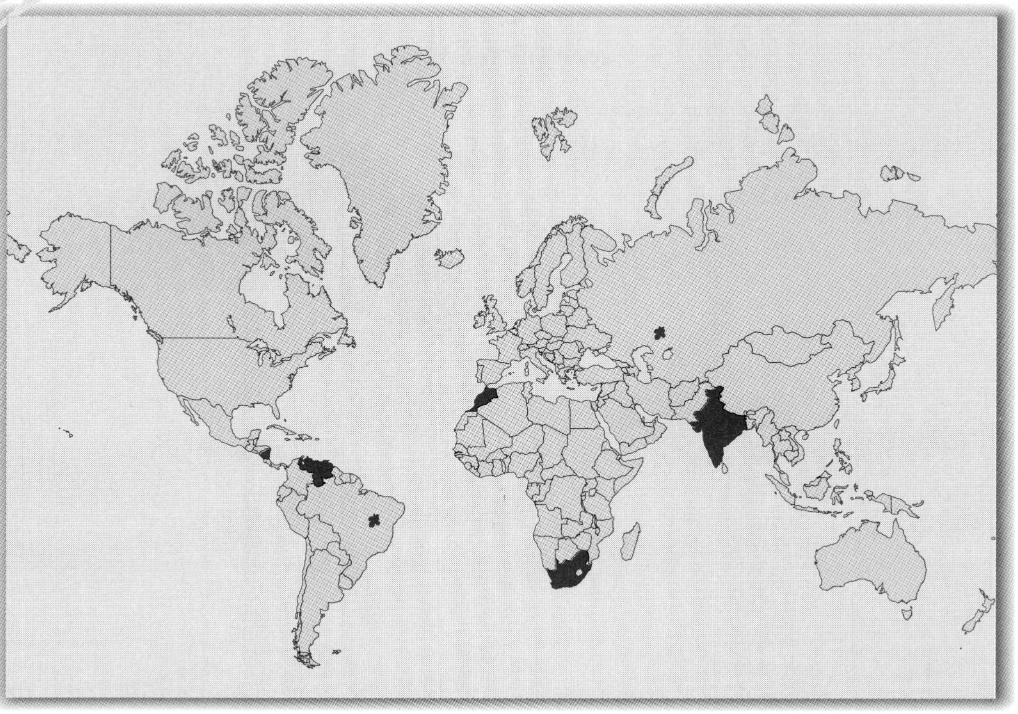

Some of Pepsi Cola's critics feel the company should concentrate on the cola industry, improving bottling and distribution setup rather than focusing on snacks and fast-food restaurants. This is debatable, however; Pepsi may be quite content as number 2 in the cola industry considering that their investments in other industries, such as snack foods and restaurants, brings them a greater profit than their cola sales.

The above map (Exhibit 6-12) indicates the areas where Pepsi had a profitable share of the market until Coke came in and used their aggressive strategies to take over the market share.

Case Questions

1. Could Pepsi have done anything differently to stop the defection in Venezuela?
2. What kind of damage control does PepsiCo need to engage in to minimize financial losses and salvage their reputation?
3. What should Pepsi do in the future to ensure that another "Venezuela" does not happen somewhere else in the world?

Case Bibliography

Alexander, Garth. "Shake-Up to Put Sparkle into Pepsi." *Sunday Times*, January 26, 1997: Lexis Nexis. On-line.

Bums, Jimmy. "Pepsi Co. Secures $8m Argentina Soccer Deal." *Financial Times* (London), March 4, 1997: 23. Lexis Nexis. On-line.

Capos, Claudia. "A Celebration with Fizz: North Carolina Town to Mark Pepsi's 100th Anniversary." *The Boston Globe*, March 22, 1998: MI. Lexis Nexis. On-line.

Collins, Glenn. "A Coke Coup in Venezuela Leaves Pepsi High and Dry." *The New York Times*, August 17, 1996: 35. Lexis Nexis. On-line.

———. "Suddenly, Coke Is Winning Cola War in Venezuela." *The Ottawa Citizen*, August 24, 1996: Lexis Nexis. On-line.

———. "Pepsi Co. Wins $94 Million for Defection by Bottler." *The New York Times*, September 4, 1997: 50. Lexis Nexis. On-line.

———. "Pepsi Co. Bottling Operation in South Africa Is Closed." *The New York Times*, May 24, 1997: 34. Lexis Nexis. On-line.

Colitt, Ray. "Pepsi Offered Venezuela Foothold." *Financial Times* (London), August 10, 1996: 20. Lexis Nexis. On-line.

Dawson, Havis. "Risky Business." *Beverage World*, September 1996: 10. Lexis Nexis. On-line.

Deogun, Nikhil and Karp, Jonathan. "Pepsi Sues Coke Unit to Defend Indian Turf." *Wall Street Journal*, April 20, 1998.

Goering, Laurie. "Coca-Cola Coup Renders Pepsi Flat in Venezuela." *Chicago Tribune*, November 29, 1996: 1. Lexis Nexis. On-line.

Hemlock, Doreen. "Brazilian Pepsi Bottler About to Fizz Out." *Sun Sential* (Ft. Lauderdale, Fla.), November 7, 1996: ID. Lexis Nexis. On-line.

Jabbonsky, Larry. "Room to Run." *Beverage World*, August 1993: 24. Lexis Nexis. On-line.

———. "The Mexican Resurrection." *Beverage World*, August 1993: 38. Lexis Nexis. On-line.

Matthews, Jay. "Coca-Cola and Pepsi Co. Intensify a 65-year Duel for Soda Supremacy." *The Washington Post*, August 24, 1996: AO 1. Lexis Nexis. On-line.

Moody's CD Report. PepsiCo Inc., December 31, 1997.

———. Coca-Cola, December 31, 1997.

Murphy, Helen. "Cola War Erupts in Mexico." *Corporate Finance*, May 1993: 6–7. Lexis Nexis. On-line.

Paulin, David. "Bottled-Up Tension: Pepsi Seeing Red Over Coke's Venezuela Coup." *The Dallas Morning News*, August 22, 1996: 1 0. Lexis Nexis. On-line.

Rotenier, Nancy. "Blue Period." *Forbes*, August 12, 1996: 138. Lexis Nexis. On-line.

———. "PepsiCo. Begins South American Marathon." *The Financial Times* (London), December 13, 1996: 29. Lexis Nexis. On-line.

———. "PepsiCo. Finds New Partner in Venezuela." *The Dallas Morning News*, December 10, 1996: 70. Lexis Nexis. On-line.

———. "PepsiCo. Is Preparing to Return to Venezuela." *The New York Times*, November 14, 1996: 30. Lexis Nexis. On-line.

———. "Tell Me Your Cola and I'll Tell You Your Party? Well Not Quite." *The New York Times*, November 8, 1992: 16. Lexis Nexis. On-line.

Roush, Chris. "Another Loss for Pepsi in Global Competition." *The Atlanta Journal and Constitution*, February 18, 1997: 0 1 E. Lexis Nexis. On-line.

Saporito, Bill. "Parched for Growth; Pepsi Had a Grand Plan for Global Expansion. Alas, Coke Was Thirstier." *Time*, September 2, 1996: 48. Lexis Nexis. On-line.

Sellers, Patricia. PepsiCo's New Generation." *Fortune*, April 1996: 1 10. Lexis Nexis. On-line.

Swafford, David. "The Fizz That Couldn't Last." *Latin Finance*, November 1996: 36. Lexis Nexis. On-line.

Valdmanis, Thor. "Coke Buys Nicaragua's Biggest Bottler." *USA Today*, August 22, 1997: IB. Lexis Nexis. On-line.

Global Alliances and Strategy Implementation

Outline

Opening Profile: The DaimlerChrysler AG Global Alliance Backfires

DaimlerChrysler AG said Monday it plans to cut 26,000 jobs at its ailing Chrysler division, the most dramatic sign yet that the 1998 merger of German and American automakers has not lived up to its promise.
                              —www.charlotte.com/observer, JANUARY 30, 2001

A financial turnaround plan that DaimlerChrysler AG laid out earlier this year appears to be in big trouble as losses accelerate at the company's Freightliner and Chrysler units. Chrysler's losses for 2001 are estimated at three billion euros ($2.74billion).
                              —*WALL STREET JOURNAL*, OCTOBER 11, 2001

Juergen Schrempp, the German chairman and CEO of DaimlerChrysler, had expected to make billions of dollars in cost savings and synergies from the merger of Daimler-Benz and Chrysler. In 1998, Schrempp pledged that the alliance would have the clout and profitability to take on everyone and be the most profitable automotive company in the world. In February 2001, the company announced its plans to take extreme measures to get Chrysler back to profitability, a move expected to take two to four years because of weak sales and spiraling costs. However, in October 2001, the company's turnaround plan was clearly not working as losses were accelerating at the company's Chrysler and Freightliner units. Chrysler's losses for 2001 were estimated at about 3 billion euros ($2.74 billion), considerably more than anticipated in the restructuring plan. Freightliner's losses for 2001 were estimated at about $1 billion. In addition, DaimlerChrysler's market share for U.S. brands had slipped to 11.8 percent from 14.9 percent in September 2000.

What went wrong? Much of the problem seems to stem from culture clashes, in particular Schrempp's attitude toward the merger, Chrysler, and the Americans.

In 1998 Schrempp touted the alliance as a merger of equals, but in 2000 he said that Daimler never intended to be an equal partner with Chrysler and that he had made the statement about equality to gain shareholder approval. Today DaimlerChrysler is essentially a holding company run from Stuttgart that oversees separate business units, which share few products. From the beginning, the marriage was clearly not one made in heaven as Schrempp portrayed because he soon made it evident that he did not view Chrysler as an equal. He also made it obvious that the American executives would have little more privilege in Stuttgart than the use of the men's room. Morale among the Americans was poor from beginning, with the Germans making it clear that it was a takeover, not a merger, and holding meetings only in German, knowing that the Chrysler executives did not understand.

Part of the problem also has been that the synergies expected from the alliance have proven elusive. The macroeconomic forces that led to the alliance in the first place—intense competition, global industry overcapacity, and high need for capital—proved too much for the alliance. Although Daimler needed to spread its R & D spending over a broader sales base, Chrysler's sales were already eroding. Then the Americans complained that the Germans were not allowing Chrysler to follow their own successful strategy to build cars inexpensively and sell at a good profit. So Schrempp, admitting that implementing the alliance was turning out to be much harder than closing the deal in the first place, restructured to allow Chrysler more autonomy. Unfortunately, Chrysler ran into more competition than expected and was forced to give massive incentive plans to move inventory, thus eroding profits.

Dieter Zetsche, a veteran Daimler executive, has been made the new Chrysler's president and chief executive succeeding Robert Eaton. Zetsche plans to idle six plants over the next two years, slashing 26,000 U.S. jobs—about a fifth of the workforce. Wolfgang Bernhard has been assigned as chief operating officer. The other five members on the seven-member rescue team are Americans. So, with 2001 losses for Chrysler estimated at $1.9 billion, perhaps the first cooperative German-American team, born out of necessity, will give Chrysler its best chance at a turnaround. In spite of griping from some Chrysler executives that they didn't want the Germans there, everyone recognized that only a team effort could save the company. Zetsche and Bernhard are making inroads at cultural integration by eating in the employee cafeteria rather than the executive dining room and mingling with Chrysler designers to learn about new products.

In the meantime, Schrempp concedes that the real value of the alliance won't be realized until there is joint production of cars by Daimler and Chrysler, which will take a couple of years. However, DaimlerChrysler's problems have made companies around the world cautious about global megamergers.

SOURCES: *Wall Street Journal*, October 11, 2001; www.charlotte.com/observer, January 30, 2001; www.businessweek.com, January 15, 2001; *Wall Street Journal*, November 8, 2000; *Wall Street Journal*, October 27, 2000; www.FT.com (*Financial Times*, November 2, 2000); *Wall Street Journal*, September 20, 2000.

STRATEGIC ALLIANCES

It is no longer an era in which a single company can dominate any technology or business by itself. The technology has become so advanced, and the markets so complex, that you simply can't expect to be the best at the whole process any longer.

—FUMIO SATO, CEO, TOSHIBA ELECTRONICS CO.[1]

Strategic alliances are partnerships between two or more firms that decide they can better pursue their mutual goals by combining their resources—financial, managerial, technological—as well as their existing distinctive competitive advantages. Alliances—often called cooperative strategies—are transition mechanisms that propel the partners' strategy forward in a turbulent environment faster than would be possible for each company alone.[2] Alliances typically fall under one of three categories:[3]

➤ **Joint Ventures**—in which two or more companies create an independent company. An example is the Nuumi Corporation, created as a joint venture between Toyota and General Motors, which gave GM access to Toyota's manufacturing expertise and provided Toyota with a manufacturing base in the U.S.

➤ **Equity strategic alliances**—in which two or more partners have different relative ownership shares (equity percentages) in the new venture. As with most global manufacturers, Toyota has equity alliances with suppliers, subassemblers, and distributors; most of these are part of their network of internal family and financial links.

➤ **Nonequity strategic alliances**—in which agreements are carried out through contract rather than ownership sharing. Such contracts are often with a firm's suppliers, distributors, or manufacturers, or they may be for purposes of marketing and information-sharing, such as with many airline partnerships.

Global strategic alliances are working partnerships between companies (often more than two) across national boundaries and increasingly across industries. A glance at the global airline industry, for example, tells us that global alliances have become a mainstay of competitive strategy:

Not one airline is competing alone; each major U.S. carrier has established strategic links with non-U.S. companies. Delta is linked with Swissair, Sabena, and Austrian; American with British Airways, U.S. Airways, JAL, and Qantas; Northwest with Continental, KLM, and Alitalia; and United with SAS, Lufthansa, Air Canada, Thai, South African Airways, Varig, Singapore, Air New Zealand, and Ansett Australia.[4]

Alliances are also sometimes formed between a company and a foreign government, or among companies and governments. The European Airbus Industrie consortium comprises France's Aerospatiale and Germany's Daimler-Benz Aerospace, each with 37.9 percent of the business; British Aerospace has 20 percent, and Spain's Construcciones Aeronauticas has 4.2 percent.

Alliances may comprise full global partnerships, which are often joint ventures in which two or more companies, while retaining their national identity, develop a common, long-term strategy aimed at world leadership. The intent of the Daimler-Chrysler global partnership was to achieve these kinds of objectives, though by 2001 it had run into problems (see the Opening Profile). Whereas such alliances have a

E-Biz Box

COVISINT, LLC

Covisint is an e-business exchange developed by DaimlerChrysler AG, Ford, General Motors, Nissan, and Renault to meet the needs of the automotive industry. It is a multimember joint venture with those companies, and Commerce One and Oracle are members. Covisint provides original equipment manufacturers (OEMs) and suppliers the ability to reduce costs and bring efficiencies to their business operations. Covisint has headquarters in Amsterdam, Tokyo, and Southfield, Michigan.

Covisint has more than 250 customers on two continents engaged in activities on the exchange, including catalogs, auctions, quote management, and collaborative design. Its current product and service offering is focused on procurement, supply chain, and product development solutions. The purpose of Covisint is to harness the power of Internet technology to create visibility within a company's supply chain—transforming the linear chain into a far more productive and efficient networked model. Furthermore, the company delivers build-to-order capability with proven, scalable, and secure technologies that reinforce customers' individual competitiveness. Internet technology speeds the flow of material through the supply chain, increases responses to consumer demand, and delivers new products to market faster than ever before. The accompanying diagram presents an overview of Covisint's functions.

Figure 1 Covisint Overview

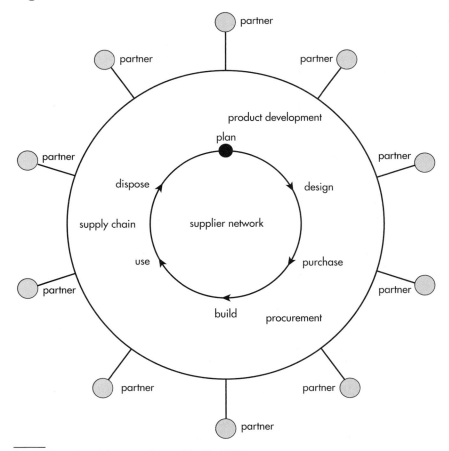

SOURCE: www.covisint.com, September 28, 2001.

Four Japanese car manufacturers—Toyota, Mazda, Honda, and Mitsubishi Motors—are also planning to join the Covisint global automotive online exchange, whereas European-owned firms have been more reluctant to commit to Covisint. PSA Peugeot has already joined Covisint.[5] Covisint expects to generate $300 billion in car sales and save manufacturers up to $263 per car by 2005 as well as reduce delivery periods to a few days and give buyers the opportunity for customized car orders.[6]

broad agenda, others are formed for a narrow and specific function including production, marketing, research and development, and financing. More recently, these have included electronic alliances, such as Covisint, which is redefining the entire system of car production and distribution through a common electronic marketplace (featured in the E-Biz Box on page 262).

Global and Cross-Border Alliances: Motivations and Benefits

1. **To avoid import barriers, licensing requirements, and other protectionist legislation.** Japanese automotive manufacturers, for example, use alliances such as the GM-Toyota venture, or subsidiaries, to produce cars in the United States so as to avoid import quotas.

2. **To share the costs and risks of the research and development of new products and processes.** In the semiconductor industry, for example, where each new generation of memory chips is estimated to cost over $1 billion to develop, those costs and the rapid technological evolution typically require the resources of more than one, or even two, firms. Intel, for example, has alliances with Samsung and NMB Semiconductor for (DRAM) technology development; Sun Microsystems has partners for its (RISC) technology, including N. V. Philips, Fujitsu, and Texas Instruments. Toshiba, Japan's third largest electronics company, has over two dozen major joint ventures and strategic alliances around the world, including partners such as Olivetti, Rhone-Poulenc, and GEC Alstholm in Europe, LSI Logic in Canada, and Samsung in Korea. Fumio Sato, Toshiba's CEO, recognized long ago that a global strategy for a high-tech electronics company such as his necessitated joint ventures and strategic alliances.

3. **To gain access to specific markets, such as the EU, where regulations favor domestic companies.** Market access was one of the enticements for Chrysler to ally with Daimler-Benz. Firms around the world are forming strategic alliances with European companies to bolster their chances of competing in the EU and to gain access to markets in Eastern European countries as they open up to world business. Chun Joo Bum, chief executive of the Daewoo Electronics unit, acknowledges that he is seeking local partners in Europe for two reasons: (1) to provide sorely needed capital (a problem amidst Asia's economic woes); and (2) to help Daewoo navigate Europe's still disparate markets, saying "I need to localize our management. It is not one market."[7]

Market entry into some countries may only be attained through alliances—typically joint ventures. South Korea, for example, has a limit of 18 percent on foreign investment in South Korean firms.

4. **To reduce political risk while making inroads into a new market.** Maytag Corporation, for example, determined to stay on the right side of the restrictive Chinese government while gaining market access, formed a joint venture with RSD, the Chinese

appliance maker, to manufacture and market washing machines and refrigerators. Maytag also invested large amounts in jointly owned refrigeration products facilities to help RSD get into that market. Coca-Cola—a global player with large-scale alliances—is not beyond using some very small-scale alliances to be "political" in China. The company uses senior citizens in the party's neighborhood committees to sell Coke locally.

5. **To gain rapid entry into a new or consolidating industry and to take advantage of synergies.** Technology is rapidly providing the means for the overlapping and merging of traditional industries such as entertainment, computers, and telecommunications in new digital-based systems, creating an information superhighway. As evidenced by such partnerships as the MCI-WorldCom merger in August 1998, such developments are necessitating strategic alliances across industries in order for companies to gain rapid entry into areas in which they have no expertise or manufacturing capabilities. Competition is so fierce that they cannot wait to develop those resources alone. Many of these objectives, such as access to new technology and to new markets, are evident in AT&T's network of alliances around the world, as shown in Exhibit 7-1. Agreements with Japan's NEC, for example, give AT&T access to new semiconductor and chip-making technologies in order to learn how to better integrate computers with communications. Another joint venture with Zenith Electronics will allow AT&T to codevelop the next generation of high-definition television (HDTV).[8]

Challenges in Implementing Global Alliances

Effective global alliances are usually tediously slow in the making but can be among the best mechanisms to implement strategies in global markets. In a highly competitive environment, alliances present a faster and less risky route to globalization. It is extremely complex to fashion such linkages, however, especially where many interconnecting systems are involved, forming intricate networks. Many alliances fail or end up in a takeover in which one partner swallows the other. McKinsey & Company, a consulting firm, surveyed 150 companies that had been in alliances and found that 75 percent of them had been taken over by Japanese partners.[9] Problems with shared ownership, the integration of vastly different structures and systems, the distribution of power between the companies involved, and conflicts in their relative locus of decision making and control are but a few of the organizational issues that must be worked out. But recent economic woes in Asia have turned the tables somewhat, with Western companies having to buy out their financially stressed allies in order to survive.

Often, the form of governance chosen for multinational firm alliances greatly influences their success, particularly in technologically intense fields such as pharmaceuticals, computers, and semiconductors. In a study of 153 new alliances, researchers found that the choice of the means of governance—whether a contractual agreement or a joint venture—depended on a desire to control information about proprietary technology.[10] Thus, joint ventures are often the chosen form for such alliances because they provide greater control and coordination in high-technology industries.

Cross-border partnerships, in particular, often become a "race to learn"—with the faster learner later dominating the alliance and rewriting its terms. In a real sense, an alliance becomes a new form of competition. In fact, according to researcher David Lei,

> Perhaps the single greatest impediment managers face when seeking to learn or renew sources of competitive advantage is to realize that co-operation can represent another form of unintended competition, particularly to shape and apply new skills to future products and businesses.[11]

Exhibit 7-1   AT&T's Alliance Strategy

Partner	Technology	Intent
NEC	Customized chips, computer-design tools	Learn new core technologies from NEC; sales position in Japan
	Mobile phones	Penetrate cellular phone markets; compatible standards
Mitsubishi	SRAM and gallium–arsenide chips	Increase sales in Japan; learn new semiconductor technologies
Italtel	Telecommunications	Expand beachhead in Europe
N.V. Philips	Circuit boards	Market and technology access; purchased 1990
Lucky-Gold Star	Fiber optics, telecommunications, circuits	Entry into Asian markets; technology-sharing agreement
Telefonics	Telecommunications and integrated circuits	Expand European production and marketing
Zenith Technology	High-definition television	Apply and learn digital compression
Intel	Personal computer networks and integrated circuits	Share manufacturing technology and capacity
		Develop UNIX computer operating system for local area networks
Hoya	Photomasks and semiconductor equipment	Develop ion-beam masks and mask design software in Japan and the United States
Mannesmann	Microwave radio gear and cellular phone technology	Serve as OEM supplier to German firm
Go Corp.	Pen-based computers and wireless networks	Set industry standards for telecommunications power and range
Olivetti	Personal computers	Failed in 1988
Eo Corp.	Personal communicator devices	Create new handheld computers
Matsushita	Microprocessors	Encourage new technology standards for Hobbit-based systems
NEC & Toshiba McCaw Cellular	Cellular telephones	Secure downstream market in the United States

SOURCE: D. Lei, "Offensive and Defensive Uses of Alliances," in Heidi Vernon-Wortzel and L. H. Wortzel, *Strategic Management in a Global Economy*, 3rd ed. (New York: John Wiley & Sons, 1997).

All too often, cross-border allies have difficulty in collaborating effectively, especially in competitively sensitive areas; this creates mistrust and secrecy, which then undermine the purpose of the alliance. The difficulty that they are dealing with is the dual nature of strategic alliances—the benefits of cooperation versus the dangers of introducing new competition through sharing their knowledge and technological skills about their mutual product or the manufacturing process. Managers may fear that they will lose the competitive advantage of the firm's proprietary technology or the specific skills that their personnel possess. The cumulative learning that a partner attains through the alliance could potentially be applied to other products or even other industries that are beyond the scope of the alliance, and therefore would hold no benefit to the partner holding the original knowledge.[12] As noted by Lei, the Japanese have far overtaken their U.S. allies in developing and applying new technologies to other uses. Examples are in the power equipment industry (e.g., Westinghouse-Mitsubishi), the office equipment industry (Kodak-Canon), and the consumer electronics industry (General Electric-Samsung). Some of the tradeoffs of the duality of cross-border ventures are shown in Exhibit 7-2.

The enticing benefits of cross-border alliances often mask the many pitfalls involved. In addition to potential loss of technology and knowledge or skill base, other areas of incompatibility often arise, such as conflicting strategic goals and objectives, cultural clashes, and disputes over management and control systems. Sometimes it takes a while for such problems to evidence themselves, particularly if insufficient homework has been done in meetings between the two sides to work out the implementation details. The alliance between KLM Royal Dutch Airlines and Northwest Airlines linking their hubs in Detroit and Amsterdam, for example, resulted in a bitter feud among the top officials of both companies over methods of running an airline business—the European way or the American way—and over cultural differences between the companies, as well as a power struggle at the top over who should call the shots.[13]

Guidelines for Successful Alliances

Many difficulties arise in cross-border alliances in melding the national and corporate cultures of the parties, in overcoming language and communication barriers, and in building trust between the parties over how to share proprietary assets and management processes. Some basic guidelines, as follows, will help to minimize potential

Exhibit 7-2 The Dual Role of Strategic Alliances

Cooperative	Competitive
Economies of scale in tangible assets (e.g., plant and equipment).	Opportunity to learn new intangible skills from partner, often tacit or organization embedded.
Upstream–downstream division of labor among partners.	Accelerate diffusion of industry standards and new technologies to erect barriers to entry.
Fill out product line with components or end products provided by supplier.	Deny technological and learning initiative to partner via out-sourcing and long-term supply arrangements.
Limit investment risk when entering new markets or uncertain technological fields via shared resources.	Encircle existing competitors and preempt the rise of new competitors with alliance partners in "proxy wars" to control market access, distribution, and access to new technologies.
Create a "critical mass' to learn and develop new technologies to protect domestic, strategic industries.	Form clusters of learning among suppliers and related firms to avoid or reduce foreign dependence for critical inputs and skills.
Assist short-term corporate restructurings by lowering exit barriers in mature or declining industries.	Alliances serve as experiential platforms to "demature" and transform existing mature industries via new components, technologies, or skills to enhance the value of future growth options.

SOURCE: David Lei, "Offensive and Defensive Uses of Alliances," in Heidi Vernon-Wortzel and L. H. Wortzel, *Strategic Management in Global Economy*, 3rd ed. (New York: John Wiley & Sons, 1997).

problems. However, nothing is as important as having a long "courtship" with the potential partner to establish compatibility strategically and interpersonally and set up a "prenuptial" plan with the prospective partner. Even setting up some pilot programs on a short-term basis for some of the planned combined activities can highlight areas that may become problematic.

1. Choose a partner with compatible strategic goals and objectives and with whom the alliance will result in synergies through the combined markets, technologies, and management cadre.

2. Seek alliances where complementary skills, products, and markets will result. If each partner brings distinctive skills and assets to the venture, there will be reduced potential for direct competition in end products and markets. In addition, each partner will begin the alliance in a balanced relationship.[14]

3. Work out with the partner how you will each deal with proprietary technology or competitively sensitive information—what will be shared and what will not, and how shared technology will be handled. Trust is an essential ingredient of an alliance, particularly in these areas; but this needs to be backed up by contractual agreements.

4. Recognize that most alliances last only a few years and will probably break up once a partner feels that it has incorporated the skills and information it needs to go it alone. With this in mind, you need to "learn thoroughly and rapidly about a partner's technology and management: transfer valuable ideas and practices promptly into one's own operations."[15]

Some of the opportunities and complexities in cross-border alliances are illustrated in the following section on joint ventures in the Commonweath of Independent States (CIS). Such alliances are further complicated by the different history of the two parties' economic systems and the resulting business practices.

Joint Ventures in the Commonwealth of Independent States

Comparative Management In Focus

Invest early and move as fast as you can. . . . Benefit from the fire-sale prices in the largest market in the world.

I've seen too many westerners fall for the line, "Our license will be arriving any day," which usually means never.
—Vladimir Kvint[16]

These comments reflect both the opportunities and the threats involved in international joint ventures (IJVs) in the CIS. Those opportunities include abundant natural resources and cheap land, a highly educated and low-cost workforce with high-quality basic research skills, and a huge, relatively untapped market of people who have had little previous opportunity for quality consumer products. Those taking advantage of those opportunities include 35,000 Western companies that have set up shop in Moscow alone and over 20,000 joint ventures in Russia. Of those IJVs, 2,800 are U.S.-Russian. They include Caterpillar, IBM, GE, Ford, Hewlett-Packard, Pepsi-Co., Eastman Kodak, and AT&T, as well as thousands of smaller IJVs—primarily in software, hotels, and heavy industrial production. Many, like Bell Labs, are involved in research and development, taking advantage of the Russians' high-level education and technical capabilities.

There are many roadblocks to successful IJVs in the CIS. The overriding concern as of this writing in 2002 continues to be the possibility of a repeat of the 1998 economic collapse with the devalued ruble, the lack of debt and equity capital, and the nonconvertibility of currency. The barter system had taken over, with individuals, companies, and governments trading services and goods and with no money changing hands. Russian teachers were being paid in vodka. Many foreign companies were losing large amounts of money, and some, such as RJR Nabisco, had withdrawn altogether. Most potential new alliances were put on hold by Western companies. As a result of the economic problems, many Russian companies benefited by reinforcing their market positions, with some strong local players gaining a foothold, such as Will-Bill-Dann, which produces dairy products, canned vegetables, and juices.[17]

Western companies had varied reactions to the financial problems. Pizza Hut and KFC (whose food was a luxury at that time) withdrew from Moscow, feeling that the market did not warrant their presence. Pizza Hut was in a joint venture with the city of Moscow, which held 51 percent. But when sales tumbled and at the same time its agreement with the City of Moscow was expiring and the city was demanding excessive increases in rent, the company decided to leave.[18] However, most large global companies—accustomed to economic upheavals in Russia—stuck to their long-term plans.[19] Gillette, for example, which has had a joint venture with Leninets, forming Petersburg Products International (PPI), since 1990, is one that stayed and continues its commitment there. But it was not without its problems during the difficult 1998–1999 period. The effective distribution systems it had painstakingly built up collapsed, as their wholesalers and retailers ran out of money and stopped their orders.

> Overnight, the ability to invoice and receive payment disappeared. So Gillette had to rebuild the distribution system and develop financial support for its suppliers, offering them credit to be paid upon their next orders.[20]

Gillette now employs over 500 people throughout Russia and has built another $40 million razor blade manufacturing plant near St. Petersburg.

Other Western companies are trying to move into locally based production in order to cut down on the expenses of a lot of expatriate staff:

> Danone, the French dairy group, opened its second Russian factory in 2000; Merloni, the Italian fridge manufacturer, bought Stinol, a local competitor with which it already had links; and in 2001, the Greek-based Chipita acquired a bakery in St. Petersburg.[21]

In spite of continued economic progress since then, however, longstanding problems continue, including the lack of clear legal protection for investments, contracts, or rights to natural resources, and the lack of efficient infrastructure for sourcing materials, communication, transportation, and living arrangements. Problems involving organized crime—often referred to in the media as "the Mafia" and called "the racket" by Russians—add considerably to the cost of operating businesses such as hotels. When MNCs refuse to pay for "protection," they often suffer, as with the bazooka attack on the bottling plant that Coca-Cola was building in Moscow.

During 2001, Russia's inflation rate continued to decline, and consumer demand was growing again, especially for Western products. President Vladimir Putin continues to support free-market mechanisms, and Russia's stock market has performed very well.[22] In spite of the continuing political uncertainty and economic risk, joint ventures in the CIS offer great opportunities for both partners. Western companies willing to take the risk can pick up assets very cheaply because of the Russian need for hard currency, capital, new technology, and management skills.[23] Foreigners may now own 100 percent of a venture, although to get office space, supplies, and other essentials, it is often necessary to have the local partner own at least half. All registered citizens may now own and operate a business, and the governments in most parts of the CIS are encouraging the privatization of businesses in order to move rapidly to a market economy—and to stave off economic disaster.

Exhibit 7-3 shows the joint venture relationship between a U.S. firm and a CIS firm, the different goals that they bring to the venture, and the barriers caused by their different operating environments.[24]

Exhibit 7-3   U.S.–CIS Joint Venture

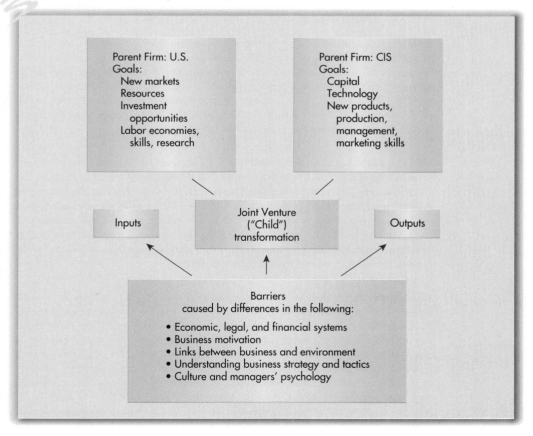

Success requires clearly defined goals, and any proposal must contain solutions to the systemic problems, such as the establishment of efficient supply channels and the repatriation of profits in hard currency. Most managers in the CIS are inexperienced in solving commercial problems based on a capitalist market economy, such as the sourcing of inputs and financing. Western managers still have to teach their joint venture partners about competition, advertising, pricing, distribution networks, and accountability.

The following are some suggestions that may help foreign companies minimize the risk of IJVs in the CIS.

Choose the Right Partner.   The primary reason for IJV failure is a poor match between partners—because of lack of compatible goals or strategy, because the CIS partner company is unreliable, or because it lacks the necessary licenses to either produce a product or to export it, or to be involved in development of natural resources. Check with regional government offices about whether the prospective partner has the requisite licenses, appropriate registrations, and reliable bank backing and history. Also check on the status of future rights to assets that were previously under the control of the state, such as those for property or natural resources, or such as a reserve of shareholdings for future privatization voucher holders.

The choice of a Russian partner can make or break a venture. A local partner may come with risks: you could end up inheriting his "krysha," or laundering money (krysha is the Russian term for paying for "protection").[25]

Businesspeople must realize that there are established procedures for getting out of disputes with partners and that those procedures take place outside of the court system. In Russia a handshake is more binding than a 100-page legal document, so disputes are best solved quietly—"often through the mediation of kryshas." Paul Tatum, U.S. hotel developer, ignored those procedures to his peril. When he took on his fight for control of the Radisson Slavyanskaya Hotel in 1997, he was gunned down in front of his two bodyguards.

Find the Right Local General Manager.   In a survey of 33 successful joint ventures, Lawrence and Vlachoutsicos found that delegating to the right Russian (or Ukrainian, etc.) executive is the secret to success for an IJV because that manager is familiar with the local networks and ministries, the suppliers and markets, and the maze of regulatory issues involved.[26] In addition, local managers are part of the culture of the Russian **mir**, or collective. This involves direct bonds of loyalty between managers and employees, hands-on management practices, and wide consultation but top-down final decision making.

Choose the Right Location.   The political risk of investments in Russia decreases from south to north and west to east, according to the consultant, Vladimir Kvint. Because most people in Siberia have stayed far away from communism and the centers of power and political turmoil in the European parts of Russia, investments there and along the Pacific Coast are more reliable. These areas also have considerable natural resources available. Now that regional leaders have more autonomy, and some have set up economic zones with tax privileges, Kvint recommends that IJVs branch out, away from Moscow to those areas, and to the Russian Far East, where many Japanese IJVs have set up.

Control the IJV   To ensure that hard-currency cash flow will be available, it is best to set up the IJV to provide for more operational self-sufficiency than Western managers are used to. This would avoid world suppliers who require hard currency and local suppliers or distributors who provide poor-quality products or services. The venture's best chance of success is to be vertically integrated to retain control of supplies and access to customers. Not only does this skirt some problems of currency convertibility, but it also controls the high chance of shortages of critical materials and supplies. McDonald's, for example, controlled these elements as well as the quality of its inputs for its Russian restaurants by setting up its own farms for potatoes and beef. Other ways to deal with the hard-currency problem are (1) to sell products to other foreign businesses within the Commonwealth that hold hard currency; (2) to use IJV rubles to buy raw materials or other products that are marketable in the West—and for which hard currency is paid (as when PepsiCo bought vodka and ships); and (3) to export products. Of the 33 joint ventures studied by Lawrence and Vlachoutsicos, most had yet to repatriate profits to the West.

The CIS needs more laws to control business; one less obvious area needing attention is that of cultural differences and how they affect operations.

Although we refer to the new republics by one name—the Commonwealth of Independent States—we must not forget that they are separate republics, each with its own identity, culture, dominant language, ethnic and religious traditions, and economic and labor histories. Different terms are used to differentiate among native Russians (Great Russians), neighboring Ukrainians (Little Russians), and Byelorussians (White Russians). Foreigners need to learn about the particular people in the region where they plan to establish business. Westerners should take time to get to know Russians on a social basis, for example. According to Kvint, "many deals are hatched in saunas between talk of family and philosophy." In particular, it is a mistake to

Exhibit 7-4   Potential Problems and Solutions for U.S.–CIS UVs

Problems	Solutions
Financial infrastructure: hard-currency cash flow and repatriation; capital availability	Reinvest; vertical integration; avoid hard-currency deals; get local bank guarantees
Organized crime	Local relationships
Access to materials and supplies; poor-quality	Vertical integration, make or supply own
Infrastructure: transportation, communication, banking	Set up operational self-sufficiency where possible
Market access and distribution	Set up alliances; own systems where possible
Operational licenses; rights to assets and resources; liablties under old system	Validate with central and local authorities before commitment
Political risk	Minimize by locating in New England or Far East if possible
Strategic and reliability conflicts	Explore compatibility and background of partner
Personnel and operational conflicts	Hire local executives and general manager
Motivation; compensation	Give respect; supply goods and services not accessible to employees

talk down to Russians; they are well educated and advanced in high-technology issues, and they are sensitive to the apparent superiority and wealth of Americans.

Joint ventures in the CIS require a long-term financial and commercial commitment from the foreign partner, including the support of Western on-site personnel. Repatriable profits may not be realized for the first few years of the venture's existence.[26a] (See Exhibit 7-4 for additional information.)

STRATEGIC IMPLEMENTATION

Implementation McDonald's Style

➤ Form paradigm-busting arrangements with suppliers.

➤ Know a country's culture before you hit the beach.

➤ Hire locals whenever possible.

➤ Maximize autonomy.

➤ Tweak the standard menu only slightly from place to place.

➤ Keep pricing low to build market share. Profits will follow when economies of scale kick in.[27]

Decisions regarding global alliances and entry strategies must now be put into motion with the next stage of planning—strategic implementation. Implementation plans are detailed and pervade the entire organization because they entail setting up overall policies, administrative responsibilities, and schedules throughout the organization to enact the selected strategy and to make sure it works. In the case of a merger or IJV, this process requires compromising and blending procedures among two or more companies and is extremely complex. The importance of the implementation phase of the strategic management process cannot be overemphasized. Until they are put into operation, strategic plans remain abstract ideas—verbal or printed proposals that have no effect on the organization.

Successful implementation requires the orchestration of many variables into a cohesive system that complements the desired strategy—that is, a system of fits that will facilitate the actual working of the strategic plan. In this way, the structure, systems, and processes of the firm are coordinated and set into motion by a system of management by objectives (MBO), with the primary objective being the fulfillment of strategy. Managers must review the organizational structure and, if necessary, change it to facilitate the administration of the strategy and to coordinate activities in a particular location with headquarters (as discussed further in Chapter 8). In addition to ensuring the strategy–structure fit, managers must allocate resources to make the strategy work, budgeting money, facilities, equipment, people, and other support. Increasingly, that support necessitates a unified technology infrastructure in order to coordinate diverse businesses around the world and to satisfy the need for current and reliable information. An efficient technology infrastructure can provide a strategic advantage in a globally competitive environment. Jack Welch, while CEO of General Electric (he retired in late 2001), used to refer to his e-commerce initiative, saying:

It will change relationships with suppliers. Within 18 months, all our suppliers will supply us on the Internet, or they won't do business with us.
—JACK WELCH, (THEN) CEO, GENERAL ELECTRIC, FORTUNE, 1999.

An overarching factor affecting all the other variables necessary for successful implementation is that of leadership; it is people, after all, who make things happen. The firm's leaders must skillfully guide employees and processes in the desired direction. Managers with different combinations of experience, education, abilities, and personality tend to be more suited to implementing certain strategies.[28] In an equity-sharing alliance, sorting out which top managers in each company will be in which position is a sensitive matter. Who in which company will be CEO is usually worked out as part of the initial deal in alliance agreements. This problem seems to be frequently settled these days by setting up joint CEOs, one from each company. Setting monitoring systems into place to control activities and ensure success completes, but does not end, the strategic management process. Rather, it is a continuous process, using feedback to reevaluate strategy for needed modifications and for updating and recycling plans. Of particular note here we should consider what is involved in effective management of international joint ventures, since they are such a common form of global alliance, and yet are fraught with implementation challenges.

Managing Performance in International Joint Ventures

Much of the world's international business activity involves international joint ventures (IJVs), in which at least one parent is headquartered outside the venture's country of operation. IJVs require unique controls. Ignoring these specific control requisites can limit the parent company's ability to efficiently use its resources, coordinate its activities, and implement its strategy.[29]

The term *IJV control* can be defined, according to Schaan, as "the process through which a parent company ensures that the way a joint venture is managed conforms to its own interest."[30] Most of a firm's objectives can be achieved by careful attention to control features at the outset of the joint venture, such as the choice of a partner, the establishment of a strategic fit, and the design of the IJV organization.

The most important single factor determining IJV success or failure is the choice of a partner. Most problems with IJVs involve the local partner, especially in less developed countries. In spite of this fact, many firms rush the process of partner selection because they are anxious to "get on the bandwagon" in an attractive market.[31] In this process, it is vital to establish whether the partners' strategic goals are compatible (see Chapter 6). The strategic context and the competitive environment of the proposed IJV and the parent firm will determine the relative importance of the criteria used to select a partner.[32] IJV performance is also a function of the general fit between the international strategies of the parents, the IJV strategy, and the specific performance goals that the parents adopt.[33] Research has shown that, to facilitate this fit, the partner selection process must determine the specific task-related skills and resources needed from a partner as well as the relative priority of those needs.[34] To do this, managers must analyze their own firm and pinpoint any areas of weakness in task-related skills and resources that can be overcome with the help of the IJV partner.

Organizational design is another major mechanism for factoring in a means of control when an IJV is started. Beamish et al. discuss the important issue of the strategic freedom of an IJV. This refers to the relative amount of decision-making power that a joint venture will have, compared with the parents, in choosing suppliers, product lines, customers, and so on.[35] It is also crucial to consider beforehand the relative management roles each parent will play in the IJV because such decisions result in varying levels of control for different parties. An IJV is usually easier to manage if one parent plays a dominant role and has more decision-making responsibility than the other in daily operations. Alternatively, it is easier to manage an IJV if the local general manager has considerable management control, keeping both parents out of most of the daily operations.[36]

International joint ventures are like a marriage—the more issues that can be settled before the merger, the less likely it will be to break up. Control over the stability and success of the IJV can be largely built into the initial agreement between the partners. The contract can specify who has what responsibilities and rights in a variety of circumstances, such as the contractual links of the IJV with the parents, the capitalization, and the rights and obligations regarding intellectual property. Exhibit 7-5 lists some of the major areas of allocation of responsibility that can be delineated in the joint-venture agreement to lessen the potential for strife later.

Of course, we cannot assume equal ownership of the IJV partners; where ownership is unequal, the partners will claim control and staffing choices proportionate to the ownership share. The choice of the IJV general manager, in particular, will influence the relative allocation of control because that person is responsible for running the IJV and for coordinating relationships with each of the parents.[37]

Where ownership is divided among several partners, the parents are more likely to delegate the daily operations of the IJV to the local IJV management—a move that resolves many potential disputes. In addition, the increased autonomy of the IJV tends to reduce many common human resource problems: staffing friction, blocked communication, and blurred organizational culture, to name a few, which all result from the conflicting goals and working practices of the parent companies.[38] Regardless of the number of parents, one way to avoid such potential problem situations is to provide special training to managers about the unique nature and problems of IJVs.[39]

Various studies reveal three complementary and interdependent dimensions of IJV control: (1) the focus of IJV control—the scope of activities over which parents exercise control; (2) the extent, or degree, of IJV control achieved by the parents; and (3) the mechanisms of IJV control used by the parents.[40]

Exhibit 7-5   Control Elements in an IJV Agreement

- Definitions
- Scope of operations
- Management
    Shareholders and supervisory board
    Executive board
    Arrangements in event of deadlock
    Operating management
- Arbitration
- Representations and warranties of each partner

- Organization and capitalization
- Financial arrangements
- Contractual links with parents
- Rights and obligations regarding intellectual property
- Temination agreements
- Force majeur
- Covenants

SOURCE: Timothy H. Collins and Thomas L. Doorley III, *Teaming Up for the Nineties—A Guide to International Joint Ventures and Strategic Alliances*, (Homewood, IL: Basic One Irwin, 1991) p. 230.

We can conclude from two research studies—Geringer's study of 90 developed country IJVs and Schaan and Beamish's study of 10 IJVs in Mexico—that parent companies tend to focus their efforts on a selected set of activities that they consider important to their strategic goals, rather than attempting to monitor all activities.[41] Schaan also found a considerable range of mechanisms for control used by the parent firms in his study (detailed in Exhibit 7-6), including indirect mechanisms such as parent organizational and reporting structure, staffing policies, and close coordination with the IJV general manager (GM). Monitoring the GM typically includes indirect means, perhaps bonuses and career opportunities, and direct mechanisms, such as requiring executive committee approval for specific decisions and budgets. These studies show that a variety of mechanisms are available to parent companies to monitor and guide IJV performance.

The extent of control exercised over an IJV by its parent companies seems to be primarily determined by the decision-making autonomy that the parents delegate to the IJV management—which is largely dependent on staffing choices for the top IJV positions and thus on how much confidence the partners have in these managers. In addition, if top managers of the IJV are from the headquarters of each party, then the more similar are their national cultures, the more compatible their managers will be. This is because there are many areas of control decisions where agreement will be more likely between those of similar cultural backgrounds.[42]

Exhibit 7-6   Control Mechanisms in International Joint Ventures

Ability to make specific decision

Ability to design:
1. Planning process
2. Appropriation requests

Policies and procedures

Ability to set objectives for JVGM

Contracts:
Management
Technology transfer
Marketing
Supplier

Participation in planning or budgeting process

Parent organization structure

Reporting structure

Staffing

Training programs

Staff services

Bonus of JVGM tied to parent results

Ability to decide on future promotion of JVGM (and other JV managers)

Feedback; strategy and plan budgets, appropriation requests

JVGM participation in parent's worldwide meetings

Relations with JVGM; phone calls, meetings, visits

Staffing parent with someone with experience with JV management

MNC level in Mexico

Informal meetings with other parent

Board

Executive committee

Approval required for:
1. Specific decisions
2. Plans, budgets
3. Appropriation requests
4. Nomination of JVGM

Screening/no objection of parent before ideas or projects are discussed with the other parent

SOURCE: J. L. Schaan, "Parent Control and Joint Venture Success: The Case of Mexico, 249" (Unpublished doctoral dissertation, University of Western Ontario, 1983), reprinted in J. Michael Geringer and Louis Herbert, "Control and Performance of International Joint Ventures," *Journal of International Business Studies* 20, no. 2 (Summer 1989).

The many activities and issues involved in strategic implementation—such as negotiating, organizing, staffing, leading, communicating, and controlling—are the subjects of other chapters in this book. Elsewhere we include discussion of the many variables involved in strategic implementation which are specific to a particular country or region, such as goals, infrastructure, laws, technology, ways of doing business, people, and culture. Here, we take a look at three pervasive influences on strategy implementation: government policy, societal culture, and the Internet.

Government Influences on Strategic Implementation

There are many areas of influence by host governments on the strategic choice and implementation of foreign firms. The profitability of those firms is greatly influenced, for example, by the level of taxation in the host country and by any restrictions on profit repatriation. Also important influences are government policies on ownership by foreign firms, on labor union rules, on hiring and remuneration practices, on patent and copyright protection, and so on. For the most part, however, if the corporation's managers have done their homework, all these factors are known beforehand and are part of the location and entry strategy decisions. But what hurts is for managers to set up shop in a host country and then have major economic or governmental policy changes after they have made a considerable investment.

Unpredictable changes in governmental regulations can be a death knell to businesses operating abroad. Although this problem occurs in many countries, one country that is often the subject of concern for foreign firms is China. In a survey of European investment in China, for example, 54 percent of companies questioned said their performance in China was worse than they had anticipated. Caterpillar, Inc. was one of the companies with rapid market growth in producing diesel engines in China in the early 1990s—construction was booming and foreign investment was flooding in. But in 1993, China—afraid that foreign investment was causing inflation—revoked tax breaks and restricted foreign investment. The tables turned on Caterpillar after that because there was not enough domestic demand for their products.[43] In addition, as reported in the *Wall Street Journal*, "the world's auto industry guessed wrong on China."[44] Certainly the market potential is there—only 1 Chinese out of every 110 has a car—but big problems are causing foreign car ventures to withdraw. Peugeot-Citroen SA of France abandoned its factory in China, and Daimler-Benz AG of Germany withdrew before it even started. Beijing is even worrying GM, which has invested millions in China, including 21 joint ventures and other projects. Out of concern that China cannot handle a surge in cars on its inadequate roads, with little parking and few service stations, the government has stopped an auto-loan program, and many cities can no longer issue license plates for private cars. Also Beijing has prohibited government officials below the rank of minister from buying big cars.[45]

Political change, in itself, can of course bring about sudden change in strategic implementation of alliances of foreign firms with host-country projects. This was evident in May 1998 when President Suharto of Indonesia was ousted following economic problems and currency devaluation. The new government began reviewing and canceling some of the business deals linked with the Suharto family, including two water-supply privatization projects with foreign firms—Britain's Thames Water PLC and France's Suez Lyonnaise des Eaux SA. The Suharto family had developed a considerable fortune from licensing deals, monopolies, government "contracts," and protection from taxes.[46] Alliances with the family was often the only way to gain entry for foreign companies.

Cultural Influences on Strategic Implementation

Culture is one variable that is often overlooked when deciding on entry strategies and alliances, particularly when we perceive the target country to be familiar to us and similar to our own. However, cultural differences can have a subtle and often negative effect.

Since many of Europe's largest MNCs—including Nestlé, Electrolux, Grand Metropolitan, and Rhone-Poulenc—experience increasing proportions of their revenues from their positions in the United States, and employ over 2.9 million Americans, they have decided to shift the headquarters of some product lines to the United States. As they have done so, however, there is growing evidence that managing in the United States is not as easy as they anticipated it would be because of their perceived familiarity with the culture. Rosenzweig documents some reflections of European managers on their experiences of managing U.S. affiliates. Generally, he has found that European managers appreciate that Americans are pragmatic, open, forthright, and innovative. But they also say that the tendency of Americans to be informal and individualistic means that their need for independence and autonomy on the job causes problems in their relationship with the head office Europeans. Americans simply do not take well to directives from a foreign-based headquarters. Rosenzweig presents some comments from French managers on their activities in the United States.[47]

> *French Managers Comment on Their Activities in the United States:*
> ➤ "Americans see themselves as the world's leading country, and it's not easy for them to accept having a European in charge."
> ➤ "It is difficult for Americans to develop a world perspective. It's hard for them to see that what may optimize the worldwide position may not optimize the U.S. activities. . . ."
> ➤ "The horizon of Americans often goes only as far as the U.S. border. As a result, Americans often don't give equal importance to a foreign customer. If a foreign customer has a special need, the response is sometimes: 'It works here, why do they need it to be different?'"
> ➤ "It might be said that Americans are the least international of all people, because their home market is so big."

Other European firms have had more successful strategic implementation in their U.S. plants by adapting to American culture and management styles. When Mercedes-Benz of Germany launched its plant in Tuscaloosa, Alabama, U.S. workers and German "trainers" had doubts. Lynn Snow, who works on the door line of the Alabama plant was skeptical whether the Germans and the Americans would mesh well. But now she proudly asserts that they work together, determined to build a quality vehicle. As Jurgen Schrempp, CEO of Mercedes' parent, Daimler-Benz, observed: "'Made in Germany'—we have to change that to 'Made by Mercedes', and never mind where they are assembled."[48]

The German trainers recognized that the whole concept of building a Mercedes quality car had to be taught to the American workers in a way that would appeal to them. They abandoned the typically German strict hierarchy and instead designed a plant in which any worker could stop the assembly line to correct manufacturing problems. In addition, taking their cue from Japanese rivals, they formed the workers into teams that met every day with the trainers to problem-solve. Out the window went formal offices and uniforms, replaced by casual shirts with personal names on the pocket. To add to the collegiality, get-togethers for a beer after work became common. "The most important thing is to bring together the two cultures," says Andreas Renschler, who has guided the M-Class since it began in 1993, "You have to generate a kind of ownership of the plant."[49] The local community has also embraced the mutual goals, often having beer fests and including German-language stations on local cable TV.

The impact of cultural differences in management style and expectations is perhaps most noticeable and important when implementing international joint ventures. The complexity of a joint venture requires that managers from each party learn to compromise in order to create a compatible and productive working environment, particularly when operations are integrated.

Cultural impacts on strategic implementation are often even more pronounced in the service sector, because of many added variables, especially the direct contact with the consumer. Wal-Mart, for example, has not been immune to implementation problems overseas, particularly resulting from culture and lifestyle differences, and from infrastructure problems, as discussed in the accompanying Management Focus.

In China, too, strategic implementation necessitates an understanding of the pervasive cultural practice of *guanxi* in business dealings. Discussed in previous chapters, *guanxi* refers to the relationship networks that "bind millions of Chinese firms into social and business webs, largely dictating their success."[50] Tapping into this system of reciprocal social obligation is essential to get permits, information, assistance to access material and financial resources, and tax considerations. Nothing gets done without these direct or indirect connections. In fact, a new term has arisen—***guanxihu***, which refers to a bond between specially connected firms —that generates preferential treatment to members of the network. Without *guanxi*, implementing a strategy of withdrawal is even difficult. Joint ventures can get hard to dissolve and as bitter as an acrimonious divorce situation. Problems include the forfeiture of assets and the inability to gain market access through future joint ventures partners—all experienced by Audi, Chrysler, and Daimler-Benz. For example:

> Audi's decision to terminate its joint venture prompted its Chinese partner, First Automobile Works, to expropriate its car design and manufacturing processes. The result was an enormously successful, unauthorized Audi clone, with a Chrysler engine and a First Automobile Works nameplate.[51]

E-Commerce Impact on Strategy Implementation

> With subsidiaries, suppliers, distributors, manufacturing facilities, carriers, brokers and customers all over the globe, global trade is complicated and fragmented. Shipments cross borders multiple times a day. Are they compliant with all the latest trade regulations? Are they consistently classified for each country? Can you give your buyers, customers and service providers the latest information, on demand?
>
> —www.Nextlinx.com, SEPTEMBER 10, 2001

As indicated in this quote, global trade is extremely complicated. Deciding on a global strategy is one thing; implementing it through all the necessary parties and intermediaries around the world presents a whole new level of complexity. Because of that complexity, many firms decide to implement their global e-commerce strategy by outsourcing the necessary tasks to companies that specialize in providing the technology to organize transactions and follow through with the regulatory requirements. These specialists are called **e-commerce enablers**; they can help companies sort through the

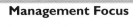

Management Focus

WAL-MART'S IMPLEMENTATION PROBLEMS IN SOUTH AMERICA

Wal-Mart Stores, Inc. is finding out that what plays in Peoria isn't necessarily a hit in suburban São Paulo. Adapting to local tastes has been one thing. But brutal competition, market conditions that don't play to Wal-Mart's ability to achieve efficiency through economies of scale, and some of its own mistakes have produced red ink. Moreover, the company's insistence on doing things "the Wal-Mart way" has apparently alienated local suppliers and employees.

A lot is riding on Wal-Mart's global expansion drive, which is targeting not only South America, but also China and Indonesia, two other markets full of promise and pitfalls. With opportunities for growth dwindling at home, the company is opening fewer than 100 domestic stores a year, down from as many as 150 in the early 1990s. The current rate of openings can't generate the profit gains Wal-Mart wants, and its main hopes lie overseas.

The performance of Wal-Mart's 16 South American stores may well indicate the future outlook. In Canada and Mexico, many customers were familiar with the company from cross-border shopping trips, and by acquiring local retailers it quickly reached the size necessary to hold down costs. In South America and Asia, by contrast, Wal-Mart is building from scratch in markets already dominated by savvy local and foreign competitors such as Grupo Pao de Acucar SA of Brazil and Carrefour SA of France. As of 1998, losses were mounting in Brazil and Argentina.

Squeezing out costs in its supply chain is crucial to Wal-Mart's formula for "everyday low pricing." But timely delivery of merchandise is a relative concept in the bumper-to-bumper traffic of São Paulo, where Wal-Mart depends on suppliers or contract truckers to deliver most of its goods directly to stores. Because it doesn't own its distribution system, it can't control deliveries nearly as well as it does in the United States, vendors say. Stores in Brazil sometimes process 300 deliveries a day, compared with seven a day at U.S. locations, and some shipments have mysteriously disappeared somewhere between the port and the store.

Wal-Mart's troubles in South America stem partly from its own mistakes. Analysts say it failed to do its homework before plunging in. Merchandise flubs—such as unsuitable food products and cordless tools, which few South Americans use—were only the beginning. In Brazil, Wal-Mart brought in stock-handling equipment that didn't work with standardized local pallets. It also installed a computerized bookkeeping system that failed to take into account Brazil's wildly complicated tax system. In addition, Wal-Mart has been slow to adapt to Brazil's fast-changing credit culture, under which they needed to recognize postdated checks, which have become the most common form of credit since Brazil stabilized its currency in 1995. The six South American Sam's Club locations got off to a slow start largely because shoppers weren't used to paying a membership fee and don't have enough room at home to store bulk purchases. In Argentina, the clubs have faced another barrier: small-business customers are reluctant to sign up for fear Wal-Mart could provide information to tax authorities on their purchases.

Although Wal-Mart is learning the hard way about local culture and lifestyles (they want soccer balls in South America, not American footballs), and the managers are finding their way around infrastructure problems, they have learned about the difficulties of strategic implementation in other countries.

SOURCE: Adapted and excerpted from Jonathan Friedland and Louise Lee, "The Wal-Mart Way Sometimes Gets Lost in Translation Overseas," *Wall Street Journal*, October 8, 1997.

Management Focus

NEXTLINX ENABLES GLOBAL STRATEGY IMPLEMENTATION

NextLinx's Trade Collaborator has everything needed to automate, streamline, and manage an entire global trade operation. A Web-based environment, it enables all trading partners to collaborate in a single on-line location, using the same information and processes.

Trade Collaborator, a unique and flexible product suite, simplifies and speeds global trade. It helps companies pay accurate customs charges and reduce their risk of noncompliance. Transaction efficiency will improve and cycle times will be reduced. Plus, NextLinx enables companies to:

- **Calculate accurate landed costs**—Calculate the total cost of delivered products, imports, materials, or components, including customs duties, taxes, other governmental charges, and freight.

- **Automate imports/exports**—Whether buying or selling, Trade Collaborator gives you everything you need to import and export—from classifying products to screening orders to generating the appropriate documentation and creating the right information for a customs entry.

- **Comply with NAFTA 2001**—Take advantage of lower tariffs and reduced compliance costs by getting everything you need to qualify for preferred trading status, generate documentation, and certify compliance.

- **Gain visibility into your shipments**—Rate and book shipments as well as gain crucial visibility into your supply chain so you can track and trace shipments.

POWERED BY GLOBAL KNOWLEDGE™

The most comprehensive and up-to-date database of trade rules and regulations in the market today. So you'll always have the most current and complete information available, without having to maintain it yourself. We give it to you automatically!

SCALABLE, FLEXIBLE, AND PACKAGED TO MEET YOUR BUSINESS NEEDS

At NextLinx, we understand that no two global corporations are the same. That's why we give you multiple options for integrating Trade Collaborator into your organization.

- **Trade Export**—Export intelligently, increase compliance, reduce costs, and maximize efforts. Manage your orders from order to delivery: screen your products and customers, determine licenses, manage letters of credit, generate documents, and archive everything.

- **Trade Agreements**—Utilize trade agreements to their fullest, saving your company millions. Track inventory down to the line item, from country of origin through delivery and qualify your products for preferential tariffs.

- **Trade Import**—Import the products and goods that are critical to your operations with maximum efficiency and compliance. Maintain all information regarding your imports, screen shipments, control all required documentation and manage your trading partners.

- **Trade Fusion**—Trade Fusion offers you access to the most up-to-date trade information available and intelligent tools that will enable your website visitors to legally trade from any location around the world.

SOURCE: www.Nextlinx.com, September 10, 2001.

maze of different taxes, duties, language translations, and so on specific to each country. Such services allow small and medium-sized companies to go global without the internal capabilities to carry out global e-commerce functions. One of these specialist e-commerce enablers is Nextlinx, which we use as an example, in the Management Focus box above, of the application of technology to the wide range of services they provide for strategic implementation.

Conclusion

Cross-border strategic alliances are becoming increasingly common as innovative companies seek rapid entry into foreign markets and as they try to reduce the risks of going it alone in complex environments. Those companies that do well are those that do their homework and pick complementary strategic partners. Too many, however, get "divorced" because "the devil is in the details"—which is what happens when "a marriage made in heaven" runs into unanticipated problems during actual strategic implementation.

SUMMARY OF KEY POINTS

1. Strategic alliances are partnerships with other companies for specific reasons. Cross-border, or global, strategic alliances are working partnerships between companies (often more than two) across national boundaries and increasingly across industries.

2. Cross-border alliances are formed for many reasons, including market expansion, cost- and technology-sharing, avoiding protectionist legislation, and taking advantage of synergies.

3. Technological advances and the resulting blending of industries, such as those in the telecommunications and entertainment industries, are factors prompting cross-industry alliances.

4. Alliances may be short or long term; they may be full global partnerships, or they may be for more narrow and specific functions such as research and development sharing.

5. Alliances often run into trouble in the strategic implementation phase. Problems include loss of technology and knowledge skill-base to the other partner, conflicting strategic goals and objectives, cultural clashes, and disputes over management and control systems.

6. Successful alliances require compatible partners with complementary skills, products, and markets. Extensive preparation is necessary in order to work out how to share management control and technology and to understand each other's culture.

7. Strategic implementation—also called functional level strategies—entail setting up overall policies, administrative responsibilities, and schedules throughout the organization. Successful implementation results from setting up the structure, systems, and processes of the firm, as well as the functional activities that create a "system of fits" with the desired strategy.

8. Differences in national culture and changes in the political arena or in government regulations often have unanticipated effects on strategic implementation.

9. Strategic implementation of global trade is increasingly being facilitated by e-commerce enablers—companies that specialize in providing the software and Internet technology for complying with the specific regulations, taxes, shipping logistics, translations, and so on for each country with which their clients do business.

DISCUSSION QUESTIONS

1. Discuss the reasons that companies embark on cross-border strategic alliances. What other motivations may prompt such alliances?

2. Why are there an increasing number of mergers with companies in different industries? Give some examples. What industry do you think will be the next for global consolidation?

3. Discuss the problems inherent in developing a cooperative alliance in order to enhance competitive advantage, but also incurring the risk of developing a new competitor.

4. What are the common sources of incompatibility in cross-border alliances? What can be done in order to minimize them?

5. Discuss the economic situation in the CIS with your class. What has changed since this writing? What are the implications for foreign companies to start a joint venture there now?

6. What is involved in strategic implementation? What is meant by "creating a 'system of fits'" with the strategic plan?

7. Explain how the host government may affect strategic implementation—in an alliance or another form of entry strategy.

8. How might the variable of national culture affect strategic implementation? Use the Wal-Mart example to highlight some of these factors.

APPLICATION EXERCISES

1. At the time of writing, the Daimler-Chrysler alliance featured in the opening case profile had run into considerable trouble. By the time you are using this textbook, the company's situation may have worsened or improved. How is the alliance doing now? Research the events, successes, and problems that DaimlerChrysler AG has experienced so far and report to the class. Were the problems described in the opening case profile avoidable? Are the strategic goals, which led to the alliance, still attainable?

2. Review the featured Management Focus section on Wal-Mart in South America. Research their recent operations in South America and report to the class. Has Wal-Mart expanded elsewhere in South America? How are their new stores doing? What, if any, problems have they run into?

EXPERIENTIAL EXERCISE: PARTNER SELECTION IN AN INTERNATIONAL CONTEXT

by Professor Anne Smith

Read the following three scenarios and think about the assigned questions before class. Although the names of the specific telecommunications firms have been disguised, each scenario is based on actual events and real companies in the telecommunications service industry.

Scenario 1: TOOLBOX and FROZEN in Mexico

By October 30, 1990, managers from TOOLBOX (A Baby Bell[1] located in the eastern United States) and FROZEN (a Canadian telecommunications service and equipment provider) had been working for months on a final bid for the Telmex privatization. In

---

[1]Seven Baby Bells (also know as Regional Bell Operating Companies, or RBOCs for short) were created in 1984, when they were divested from AT&T. The term *Baby Bell* is really a misnomer given their large size, between $7 billion and $10 billion in revenues, at divestiture. In 1984, the Baby Bells were granted discrete territories where they offered local telephone service; these seven firms also were allowed to offer cellular service in their local service territories. From the AT&T divestiture settlement, the Baby Bells were allowed to keep the lucrative yellow pages and directory assistance services. Yet, these seven firms had no international activities or significant international managerial experience at divestiture.

SOURCE: This exercise was written by Professor Anne Smith, University of New Mexico, based on her research of the firms discussed. Copyright 1998 by Professor Anne Smith. Used with permission.

two weeks, a final bid was due to the Mexican Ministry of Finance for this privatization; TOOLBOX's consortium was competing against four other groups.

Teléfonos de México (Telmex) was a government-run and -owned telecommunications provider, which included local, long-distance, cellular, and paging services in Mexico. Yet, in late 1989, the Mexican government decided to privatize Telmex. Reasons for Telmex's privatization included its need for new technology and installation expertise and the large pent-up demand for phone service in Mexico (where only one in five households had a phone). In early 1990, managers from TOOLBOX's international subsidiary were in contact with many potential partners such as France Telecom, GTE, FROZEN, and Spain's Telefonica. By June 1990, TOOLBOX and FROZEN had chosen each other to partner and bid on the Telmex privatization. During the past six months, discussions had gone smoothly between the international managers at TOOLBOX and FROZEN. With a local Mexican partner (required by the Mexican government), the managers worked out many details related to their Telmex bid, such as who would be in charge of installations and backlog reduction, who would install new cellular equipment, who would upgrade the marketing and customer service function, and who would select and install the central office switches. A TOOLBOX international manager commented, "We got along extremely well with our neighbors to the north. Not surprisingly, given that we speak the same language, have similar business values . . . but, basically we liked their international people, which was essential for our largest international deal ever." A FROZEN international manager stated, "It was ironic that our top executive in charge of business development had been a summer intern at TOOLBOX when he was in college. So, he liked our selection of TOOLBOX for this partnering arrangement, even though he was not familiar with the current TOOLBOX top managers." By September 1990, investment bankers estimated that a winning bid would probably top $1.5 billion. On November 15, 1990, all final bids for the privatization would be due. Having worked out the operational details (contingent on a winning bid), managers from TOOLBOX and FROZEN returned to meet with their top managers one final time to get some consensus on a final bid price for Telmex.

Scenario 2: The Geneva Encounter

At the Telecom 1984 convention in Geneva, Robert and Jim (a GEMS senior vice president and a business development manager, respectively) had just finished hearing the keynote address, and were wandering among the numerous exhibits. This convention, hosted every four years in Geneva, included thousands of exhibits of telecommunications services and hardware providers; tens of thousands of people attended. Though GEMS (a Baby Bell in the southwestern United States) did not have a booth at the 1984 convention, Robert and Jim were trying to learn about international telecommunications providers and activities. On the third day of the conference, Robert and Jim were standing at an exhibit of advanced wireless technologies when they struck up a conversation with another bystander who was from Israel.

"You can get lost in this convention," exclaimed Jim. Daniel from Israel agreed, "Yes, this is my first trip to the Telecom convention, and it is overwhelming. . . . Tell me about GEMS. How is life freed from Ma Bell?" Robert, Jim, and Daniel continued their conversation over drinks and dinner. They learned that Daniel was an entrepreneur who was involved in many different ventures. One new venture that Daniel was pursuing was yellow pages directories and publishing. Daniel was delighted to meet those high-level executives from GEMS because of the Baby Bell's reputation as high-quality telephone service providers. Several months after the conference, Robert and Jim visited Daniel in Israel to discuss opportunities there. Six months later, GEMS and Daniel's firm were jointly developing software for a computerized directory publishing system in Israel. GEMS had committed people and a very small equity stake ($5 to $10 million) to this venture.

Scenario 3: LAYERS and Jack in UK Cable

In early 1990, LAYERS (another Baby Bell from the western United States) was considering investing in an existing cable television franchise in the United Kingdom. In 1984, pioneer/pilot licenses had been awarded in some cities. Many of these initial licenses were awarded to start-up companies run by entrepreneurs with minimal investment capital. Unfortunately, "the 100 percent capital allowances that were seen as vital to make the financial structuring of the cable build a commercial reality" were abolished, creating a "break in the industry's development [from 1985 to 1989] whilst many companies that were interested in UK cable were forced to reexamine their financial requirements."[2]

Jack had obtained one of these early UK cable licenses in 1984, and his investment capital was quickly consumed from installing cable coupled with slow market penetration. By 1986, his efforts toward this venture had waned. In the 1990 Broadcast Act, the government relaxed its rule for cable operators and allowed non-EC control of UK cable companies. This created incentives for current cable operators to sell an equity stake in their ventures. This allowed U.S. and Canadian telephone companies to bring desperately needed cash as well as marketing and installation expertise to these cable ventures. Aware of the impending changes, Jack was once again focusing on his cable operations. He arranged a meeting with several LAYERS international managers in November 1989, in anticipation of the changes. Turning on his charm and sales abilities, Jack explained to the LAYERS' international managers the potential for UK cable television.[3] He also shared with these managers that he was willing to sell a large equity stake in his company to get it growing again. The international managers from LAYERS were impressed by Jack's enthusiasm, but they were even more intrigued by the possibility of learning about the convergence of cable and telephone services from this UK "laboratory." The LAYERS international managers decided that they would discuss this deal with their executive in charge of unregulated activities. By June 1990, LAYERS had an equity stake, estimated to be between $30 and $50 million, in Jack's UK cable venture.

Questions to Consider Before Class

Think about these questions from the perspective of the Baby Bell in each scenario:

1. In your opinion, which one of these scenarios should lead to a long-term successful international partnering relationship? Based on what criteria?

2. In your opinion, which one of these scenarios has the least chance of leading to a long-term, successful international partnering relationship? Why?

---

[2]*The Cable Companion*, The Cable Television Association, pp. 1–11, 1–12.

[3]In the UK, cable operators were allowed to offer both cable and telephone service.

INTERNET RESOURCES

Visit the Deresky companion Web site at http://prenhall.com/Deresky for this chapter's Internet resources.

CASE STUDY: BEN & JERRY'S AND ICEVERKS: ALLIANCE MELTDOWN IN RUSSIA

In 1988, Ben Cohen, president and cofounder of Ben & Jerry's, took a trip to Karelia, Russia (Vermont's Russian sister state) as a representative from Vermont. During his stay in Karelia, he thought of opening up a Ben & Jerry's scoop shop in Russia in hopes of brining the United States and Russia together through ice cream diplomacy. After Mr. Cohen's return from Russia, Ben & Jerry's immediately made a joint venture proposal, and in 1989, they completed the preparations for the first step of expanding their business into Russia. The joint venture was to be called Iceverks and would be located in the city of Petrozavodsk in Russia's Karelia region. Ben's mission was to help promote understanding and communication between Russia and the United States. He also wanted to prove that high-quality ice cream could be produced entirely by using Russian employees and ingredients.

Ben & Jerry's initial investment into the joint venture was approximately $500,000 or 50 percent of the total start-up fees. The other half of the capital was invested by their Russian partners, who raised 20 percent of it by selling interest to a local bank, Petrobank.

With the joint venture came many problems that Ben & Jerry's managers didn't anticipate. First, they had to find a distribution system, which would be a challenge because Russian systems were undeveloped and inefficient. Second, acceptable suppliers had to be located for their ice cream products. They had to determine whether local resources could provide suitable ingredients to produce high-quality ice cream. But a major ingredient for Ben & Jerry's was their philosophy toward social responsibility and philanthropy. The company gives contributions and support to social issues such as acid rain, rain forest destruction, homelessness, and the disabled. It was important to them to encourage Russians to learn more about recycling technology.

In Karelia, Ben & Jerry's donated 10 to 15 percent of its profits to disabled children in the community.

Strategic Implementation

Business Environment   With the collapse of the Soviet Union came political uncertainty for potential foreign investors in the newly democratic Russia. The country had to be rebuilt, and it was questionable what laws would be enacted and what laws would be discarded. Thus, all foreign businesses operating in Russia were doing so under extreme risk. Nevertheless, Ben & Jerry's assumed this risk because their decision to enter Russia was not entirely profit driven. For the most part, they were doing business in Russia for good-will, trying to unite two former cold war countries.

As a result of former communist work ideology, skilled managers were in short supply for the Karelia facilities. Managers, as well as subordinates, needed to be

SOURCE: Adapted by the author from a term paper written by Ryan Gramaglia, Akemia Kikuchi, and Boris Shekhman, students at the State University of New York at Plattsburgh, NY, May 1998. Copyright © Helen Deresky, 1998.

trained both in work habits and in Western capitalistic philosophy. Consequently, managers had to be flown in from the United States until the Russians could learn the intricacies of a free market as well as the production of high-quality ice cream.

With the fall of the USSR, the Russian Mafia has gained enormous power. The underworld is thought to control some 40 percent of the Russian economy. U.S. businesses pay as much as 30 percent of their monthly profit for Mafia "protection." This was a major concern for Ben & Jerry's since their company philosophy for doing business in the East is to not give into extortion or bribery.

Production   Ice cream is a popular dessert in Russia—eaten all year-round. Russians in Moscow consume 170 tons of ice cream per year, 98 percent of which is vanilla. Since Russia is the third largest market in the world, the ice cream business represented enormous potential.

To use the Ben & Jerry's logo, ice cream had to be of superior consistency and quality. Karelia's local milk supply had to be reformed to meet Ben & Jerry's requirements; high-grade eggs and sugar had to be located to make Ben & Jerry's ice cream products in Russia consistent with those in the United States; skilled inspectors, who were in short supply, had to be recruited. In addition, since sanitation standards in Russia's dairy industry are not as strict as those in the United States, Ben & Jerry's had to license a special plate from the 3M Company that disinfects milk from contaminants such as *E. coli* and coliforms. These plates, called, Petffim, react with enzymes produced by bacteria in milk, making it easy to spot contaminants and bacteria growth.

Ben & Jerry's goal was to produce a premium ice cream that Russians could afford. Although their ice cream was slightly more expensive than Russian ice cream, it was still relatively affordable, so they used local suppliers and resources, which reduced cost significantly.

The Ben & Jerry's Company is known for having a wide selection of ice cream flavors. They use a wide variety of ingredients to provide the most satisfying ice cream in the market. But when they introduced some of the American favorite flavors to their new consumers—including Cherry Garcia, Chunky Monkey, and Chocolate Chip Cookie Dough—they ran into problems. The Russians were not accustomed to the chunks of ingredients in the ice cream; they thought it was spoiled or damaged. To adjust to consumer preferences, Ben & Jerry's altered their menu to include more smooth ice creams.

Competition   In 1988, most home refrigerators in Russia had very small freezers—comparable to U.S. models in the 1940s. Thus, ice cream was a dessert commonly sold by street vendors and restaurants for immediate consumption. At this time, street vendors were Ben & Jerry's most substantial competition, selling tons of good-tasting ice cream every day for as little as 35 rubles per unit. However, variety was a weak spot in Russian ice cream—it was vanilla or nothing. Thus, Ben & Jerry's relied on variety and novelty as a competitive advantage.

Local vendors were hostile toward the new Ben & Jerry's facility. Almost all ice cream sold in Petrozavodsk was supplied by a local ice cream monopoly that had ties to the Mafia. Upon hearing of Ben & Jerry's arrival, the local monopoly pressured the dairy not to supply the "outsider" with any cream, forcing them to find a new source of dairy nearly a day's drive away. In addition, they arranged for frequent sanitation inspection visits in an effort to slow Ben & Jerry's operation down and keep them out of the ice cream business in Petrozavodsk.

To add to Ben & Jerry's problems, other imported ice cream products were pushing their way into Karelia, particularly those form nearby Finland and the Czech Republic.

Suppliers   Supply problems plagued Iceverks from 1991 to 1994. Since there were not refrigerated trucks in Russia for their distribution, Ben & Jerry's had to import them. This proved to be time consuming and costly. In addition, there was a lack of refrigeration units in Russian stores, so ice cream would melt and then have to be refrozen, decreasing its quality. In response to this problem, Ben & Jerry's brought in their own refrigerators. They were sold to the stores, or rented, or in some cases, even given to the proprietor of the establishment.

The second problem was the unavailability of many ingredients, such as kahlúa (a cream liqueur) for their White Russian ice cream. The solution was to substitute the kahlúa with vodka, but that altered the flavor of their product.

Conflict in Strategic Goals   In 1993, the Iceverks venture earned about $100,000— a respectable amount for a small distribution operation and franchise in Russia. This unexpected success resulted in conflict and disagreement over expansion between Mr. Morse (head of Ben & Jerry's Russian operation) and Mr. Lukin (one of the Russian partners). Morse felt that they should wait for the right time to expand their Iceverks venture in Russia, and planned this to occur when the demand grew to the point that production was 75 percent of capacity. At that point, they would invest more capital into the venture and expand their market by establishing a distribution network and franchising scoop shops in Moscow and St. Petersburg. They expected this to take about a year. Unfortunately, for ambitious Russian businesspeople who were not getting a taste of real money, this was a year too long. With their newfound capitalistic success, the Russian partners were eager to expand, and Morse's reluctance to do so was a constant frustration for the Russian partners. From the Russians' perspective, they had done all they could in Petrozavodsk. The time to expand was now. This was their country, and they felt that their American partners did not know how to effectively do business on their soil. According to Mr. Lukin, "We didn't know how to make ice cream, and Ben & Jerry's didn't know how to behave in Russia." In addition, the Russian partners received several requests to build other factories throughout Russia, and since loans were available through Russian lending institutions, they saw no reason to delay. "It is difficult to persuade our American partners that our market is—I won't say stable enough—but good enough to move ahead quickly," said Lukin.

Despite their Russian partners' desire to expand, the managers at Ben & Jerry's headquarters preferred to wait for the benefits of nurturing the Iceverks venture before a premature expansion. "We know we have an existing healthy business. If we try to push too hard, we could blow that. I'd rather be a success in Karelia than a failure in Moscow," Mr. Morse said.

In addition to communication problems with Russian partners, the Iceverks venture had to tackle cultural conflicts that affected their performance in the Russian market, primarily in imparting Western business philosophy to the local managers and employees. Simple things like saying "hello" and "thank you" to customers had to be stressed and instilled in every employee's work ethic. In addition, employees had to be trained to keep refrigerators clean and the store sanitary.

Distribution   Three years after the joint venture was established, Ben & Jerry's started to sell if product outside Karelia. This growth was slow and overdue, but they believed that "methodical expansion is the recipe for long-term success here." But they soon found out that distribution channels in Russia, such as railroads were very expensive and prevented them for providing their product at a reasonable price. Distribution in Russia is often controlled by a monopoly, usually with links to organized crime, which means transportation is expensive and arbitrary. Equipment such as refrigerated trucks and warehouses are in short supply, substandard, and expensive.

Partnerships and business contacts in Russia are generally established through friendships and acquaintances. Accordingly, Ben & Jerry's distribution network was established through friends of the Iceverks venture. Iceverks' main distributor, Vessco Co., was headed by a close friend of the Russian partner, which created a favorable business relationship.

Finance   As a joint venture, Ben & Jerry's got a tax break, making its profits tax-free through the end of 1993. After 1993, however, the company would be subjected to tax rates of 30 to 45 percent of earnings.

A major concern for the corporation was the inability to repatriate profits because of the inconvertibility of the ruble. Soviet laws allowed profits to be repatriated in hard currency only if the joint venture produced goods that could be sold abroad for hard currency. Even though rubles were not officially convertible, some Russian banks allowed Ben & Jerry's to buy dollars to wire back to the United States. In 1989, it was almost impossible to estimate the ruble's real value, making it difficult for Ben & Jerry's to value their assets and collateral. When Iceverks was started, the official value of the ruble was $1.65, but its value on the black market at the same time was as little as $0.06. With inflation rates of more than 2,000 percent some years, Ben & Jerry had to periodically adjust their prices. Around that time, prices at other American ventures (such as McDonald's) tripled or quadrupled annually. In one year, for example, the price of Ben & Jerry's cones went up from $0.15 to $0.40 (800 rubles).

Ben & Jerry's produced and sold their ice cream within Russia and used rubles to pay for ingredients, equipment, and salaries. Their revenues were generated partly from their scoop shop operation (in rubles) and partly from selling pints to distributors (in dollars) for sale in Moscow. In the summer of 1993, the Russian government introduced a new law prohibiting the sale of domestically made products wholesale for hard currency. This meant that Ben & Jerry's could no longer sell ice cream to its Moscow distributors for dollars. rather than deal with the uncertainties of the ruble economy, the Moscow distributors quit, leaving Ben and Jerry's unable to sell its products in Moscow.

Case Questions

1. Was Ben & Jerry's premature in entering a business alliance in Russia?
2. What problems did the Iceverks' venture run into? How would you have handled those problems once they arose?
3. In retrospect, what would you have done differently both in setting up the joint venture and in preparing to expand across Russia?
4. What should Ben & Jerry's do now?

Case Bibliography

1. Dexheimer, Ellen and Dtube, Christine. "A Kinder, Gentler Industry: Dairy Companies Answer the Call of Their Social Conscience; News&Trends" Delta Communication Inc., *Daily Food Magazine* 91, no. 5, 13. ISSN: 0888-0050.

2. Liesman, Steve. "Ben & Jerry's at a Fork on a Rocky Road," *Wall Street Journal,* July 30, 1994, 35.

3. Trimble, Jeff. "Ben & Jerry's Big Chill," *U.S. News & World Report,* April 4, 1988. "Mafia Has Death Grip on Russia," *USA TODAY,* November 4, 1996, 4a. www.worldaffairsdc.orp,/news./mafia.html.

4. "Ben & Jerry into Low Fat, Out of Russia, and Gone Phisine," Ben & Jerry Homepage, February 17, 1998. http://www.benjerry.com/international/russia.html.

5. Banerjee, Neela. "Ben & Jerry's Is Trying to Smooth Out Distribution in Russia As It Expands."

6. McKay, Betsy. "Ben & Jerry's Post-Cold War Venture Ends in Russia with Ice Cream Melting," *Wall Street Journal,* February 7, 1997, A14.

7. Freadl-liatt. "Da, We Have No Bananas Karenina; U.S.–Russia Ice Cream Firm Succeeding Despite Crises," *Washington Post,* May 26, 1993.

8. Knobel, Beth. "Doing Business," *Los Angeles Times,* August 31, 1993. P. 2 Column 1: World Report. www.lexisnexis.com/Universe/docum.

9. Andrews, Richard. "Do Business in Russia at Their Leisure," Manning Publications Inc., December 1989. Vol. 17; 12; Sec I: 20. www.lexisnexis.com/Universe./docum.

10. "Frozen Dessert Year in Review," FIND/SVP, Inc., January 20, 1995, 8, 2, I.

11. Burke, Justin. "Russia Gets a Terrible Dip of Caring Capitalism," *The Christian Science Monitor,* May 5, 1993.

12. "Ice Cream Diplomacy; Ben & Jerry's Super Premium Ice Cream Opens Shop in Petrozavodsk," Karelia, Soviet Union: Cahners Publishing Company, August 1991. 92, 8; 66; ISSN: 08880050. www.lexisnexis.com/universe/docum.

13. Shalom, Francois. "Russian Delight: Ben & Jerry's Office Training Exchanges Employees," *Lexis Nexis,* September 1, 1994. DI/BREAK. www.lexisnxi@s.com/universe/doc.um.

14. Doeff, Gail. "Russian Revelation: Ben & Jerry's Homemade Inc. Reports Strong Market Venture in Russia," Delta Communications Inc., January 1994. www.lexisnexis.com.

15. Seplow, Stephen. "Vermont-Style Ice Cream Proves Popular to Russian Taste Buds," *The Houston Chronicle,* May 2, 1993. A 34. www.lexisnexis.com/Universe./docum.

16. "Young Professionals," www.worldaffaris.comLnews./mafia.html.

17. Anderson, Annelise. "The Red Mafia: Legacy of Communism," www.andrsh.stanford.

18. Nadelson, Reggie. "The World in Their Scoop; Artichoke and Lemon Curd Was a Big Mistake, But Chunky Monkey Is a Real Winner," FIND/SVP, Inc., July 14, 1994, 21.

Organization Structure and Control Systems

Opening Profile: Exide's 2000 Global Structure Dilemma— Place versus Product

> Does our future lie in country management or in global business units?
> —ROBERT LUTZ, EXIDE CHAIRMAN AND CEO, *WALL ST. JOURNAL*, JUNE 27, 2001

Robert Lutz, chairman and chief executive of Exide Corporation, was faced with a difficult decision in 2000 as to how to reorganize the company's structure, which was then built around ten separate country organizations. Exide, the world's biggest producer of automotive and industrial batteries, was experiencing mounting losses, a depressed share price, and a heavy debt burden.

Exide's once-booming European business missed profit targets for the fiscal year 1999, and its U.S. losses had widened. Exide's European country managers blamed falling prices. Competitors and clients blamed Exide. "They said, 'Your country managers are exporting into each other's countries,'" recalls Mr. Lutz. "The prices we had to meet were our own." Many of those executives had headed local businesses that Exide had acquired, and they could earn sizable bonuses for hitting local profit goals.

Seeking to build consensus for an organizational overhaul, Mr. Lutz held five management retreats between June 1999 and January 2000. "Where does our future lie?" he asked 30 senior executives assembled for the first retreat at a downtown Madrid hotel. "Does it lie in country management? or in global business units?" At first, Albrecht Leuschner, then head of Exide's six-factory German operation, doubted Exide needed to shift to the business-unit model, organizing by product lines. "My region was in good shape," he says. "I was afraid we would destroy structure and that would damage the [German] business."

Between retreats, managers working in teams were assigned to grapple with various Exide dilemmas, using existing and alternative organizational models. In assessing Asian expansion strategies, one team realized that Exide's geographic focus encouraged construction, even though "it was not profitable for [Exide] to keep putting plants up," says Judith Glaser, a New York consultant who helped run the retreats. The tentative consensus from the teams: Only a product-line structure could cure Exide's ills. The executives debated the proposed management structure for more than two hours. Finally, Mr. Lutz stood and announced, "We don't have 100 percent consensus yet. . . . But I'm going to make a decision, and we are going to go to a global business unit structure."

Santiago Ramirez, then in charge of 1,500 executives and about 8,500 rank-and-file production and sales workers as head of Exide's European operations, "looked disappointed," Ms. Glaser recalls. Several Ramirez lieutenants made sour faces.

"Why don't you give it a try?" Mr. Lutz says he asked the frowning Eduardo Garnica, Exide's managing director of Spain.

"No, I'm out of here," Mr. Garnica replied, according to Mr. Lutz.

The charts also distressed Giovani Mele, a managing director for Italy. At dinner that evening, Ms. Glaser noticed him huddled with two equally morose-looking European associates. "Being a country manager is my life," said Mr. Mele, "It's something I've worked for my whole life. I don't see how I'll have a role going forward." Mr. Mele also dreaded the personal sacrifice that the reorganization would require. Exide moved him to Frankfurt, where he presently makes less money than before. "They said, 'this or nothing,'" he says. His family refuses to leave its home in Naples.

Exide initially formed six global business units, primarily around its product lines. Most remaining country managers were demoted to the post of local coordinator. A few gained power. Dr. Leuschner, for instance, took charge of the global network power business unit, which makes standby industrial batteries for phone systems, computers, and the like. But the new structure didn't last long. "For six weeks," Dr. Leuschner remembers, "I was emperor of the world." In May 2000 Exide agreed to buy international battery maker GNB technologies Inc. for about $368 million in stock and cash. The deal offered a chance to regain a significant and profitable presence in the North American industrial-battery market that it had abandoned more than a decade earlier.

Mr. Lutz feared that Mitchell Bregman, the well-regarded president of GNB's industrial-battery division, might bolt once Exide folded his operation into the newly created global business units. So, just before both sides signed the accord, the Exide leader corralled Mr. Bregman at Exide's Chicago law firm and assured him a significant role in the combined company. "If we had been rigid about our organizational framework, we would have broken up GNB," Mr. Lutz says. Instead Mr. Lutz tilted the structural seesaw back somewhat toward a geographic model by letting Mr. Bregman keep control of the North American industrial-battery business. This triggered a turf battle between Mr. Bregman and Dr. Leuschner over who should run China for Exide. Mr. Bregman finally gave in, in return for his being put in charge of South American operations, while keeping Korea, Japan, and Taiwan.

There are signs of progress from Exide's latest approach: blending the geography and product-line models. As a result of its partially restored geographic focus, Exide still employs separate industrial-battery sales forces on both sides of the Atlantic. But in recent months, the teams have begun making joint pitches to global customers, such as Ford. And Exide has just signed a three-year agreement with Emerson to be their primary world supplier of certain large lead-acid batteries. Mr. Lutz believes the deal never would have happened under the company's old structure. Exide's operating results started to recover in the second half of the fiscal year ended March 31, 2000, reversing first-half operating losses.

The reorganization "is definitely working far better than what we had," Mr. Lutz insists. Yet no one views it as a permanent solution. And Mr. Lutz vows to seesaw again if conditions warrant.

"Come back a year from now and we will look different," says Mr. Mulhauser, his second-in-command. Indeed, Exide is now exploring ways to combine the separate operations now run by Dr. Leuschner, Mr. Bright (Europe) and Mr. Bregman (South America). "We were searching for the Holy Grail. But there isn't one."

SOURCE: Excerpted from Joann S. Lublin, "Place vs. Product: It's Tough to Choose a Management Model," *Wall Street Journal*, June 27, 2001, p. 100.

Strategic plans are abstract sets of decisions that cannot affect a company's competitive position or bottom line until they are implemented. Having decided on the strategic direction for the company, international managers must then consider two of the key variables for implementing strategy—the organizational structure and the control and coordinating mechanisms. The necessity of adapting organizational structures to facilitate changes in strategy is illustrated in the Opening Profile detailing Exide Corporation's struggle to find the most effective global structure.

ORGANIZATIONAL STRUCTURE

> There is no permanent organization chart for the world. . . . It is of supreme importance to be ready at all times to take advantage of new opportunities.
>
> —ROBERTO C. GOIZUETA, (FORMER) CHAIRMAN AND CEO,
> COCA-COLA COMPANY

Organizational structures must change to accommodate a firm's evolving internationalization in response to worldwide competition. Considerable research has shown that a firm's structure must be conducive to the implementation of its strategy.[1] In other words, the structure must "fit" the strategy, or it will not work. Managers are faced with how best to attain that fit in organizing the company's systems and tasks.

The design of an organization, as with any other management function, should be contingency based, taking into account the variables of that particular system at that specific point in time. Major variables include the firm's strategy, size, and appropriate technology as well as the environment in those parts of the world in which the firm operates. Given the increased complexity of the variables involved in the international context, it is no easy task to design the most suitable organizational structure and subsystems. In fact, research shows that most international managers find it easier to determine what to do to compete globally (strategy) than to decide how to develop the organizational capability (structure) to do it.[2] Additional variables affecting structural choices—geographic dispersion as well as differences in time, language, cultural attitudes, and business practices—introduce further layers of complication. We will show how organizational structures need to, and typically do, change to accommodate strategies of increasing internationalization.

EVOLUTION AND CHANGE IN MNC ORGANIZATIONAL STRUCTURES

Historically, a firm reorganizes as it internationalizes to accommodate new strategies. The structure typically continues to change over time with growth and with increasing levels of investment or diversity and as a result of the types of entry strategy chosen. Internationalization is the process by which a firm gradually changes in response to international competition, domestic market saturation, and the desire for expansion, new markets, and diversification. As discussed in Chapter 6, the firm's managers weigh alternatives and decide on appropriate entry strategies. Perhaps the firm starts by exporting or by acting as a licensor or licensee, and then, over time, it continues to internationalize by engaging in joint ventures or by establishing service, production, or assembly facilities, or alliances, abroad, moving into a global strategy. At each stage, the firm's managers redesign the organizational structure to optimize the strategy's chances to work, making changes in the firm's tasks and relationships and designating authority, responsibility, lines of communication, geographic dispersal of units, and so forth. This model of **structural evolution** has become known as the **stages model**, resulting from Stopford's research on 187 U.S. MNCs.[3] Of course, many firms do not follow the stages model because they may start their internationalization at a higher level of involvement—perhaps a full blown global joint venture without ever having exported, for example.

Even a mature MNC needs to make structural changes from time to time to facilitate changes in strategy—perhaps a change in strategy from globalization to regionalization (as discussed in Chapter 6) or an effort to improve efficiency or effectiveness. The reorganization of Aluminum Company of America (Alcoa), for example, split the company into smaller, more autonomous units, thereby giving more focus to growing businesses, such as automotive products, where the market for aluminum is strong. It also enables Alcoa to link businesses with similar functions that are divided geographically—that is, to improve previously insufficient communication between Alcoa's aluminum operations in Brazil and its Australian counterparts.[4]

The typical ways in which firms organize their international activities are shown in the following list. (Larger companies often use several of these structures in different regions or parts of their organization.) After discussing some of these structural forms, we will introduce new, transitional organizational arrangements.

➤ Domestic structure plus export department
➤ Domestic structure plus foreign subsidiary
➤ International division
➤ Global functional structure
➤ Global product structure

As already discussed, many firms—especially the smaller ones—start their international involvement by exporting. For this may simply use the services of an export management company, or they may reorganize into a simple **domestic structure plus export department**.

To facilitate access to and development of specific foreign markets, the firm can take a further step toward worldwide operations by reorganizing into a **domestic structure plus foreign subsidiary** in one or more countries (as illustrated in Exhibit 8-1). To be effective, subsidiary managers should have a great deal of autonomy and should be able to adapt and respond quickly to serve local markets. This structure works well for a company with one or a few subsidiaries located relatively close to headquarters.

With further market expansion, the firm may then decide to specialize by creating an **international division**, organized along functional, product, or geographic lines. With this structure, the various foreign subsidiaries are under the international division, and subsidiary managers report to its head, typically called the vice president, International Division, who in turn reports directly to the CEO of the corporation. The creation of an international division facilitates the beginning of a global strategy. It permits managers to allocate and coordinate resources for foreign activities under one roof, and so it enhances the firm's ability to respond, both reactively and proac-

Exhibit 8-1   Domestic Structure Plus Foreign Subsidiary

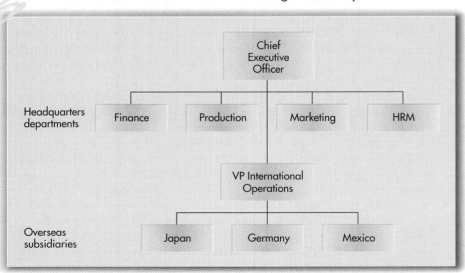

tively, to market opportunities. Some conflicts may arise among the divisions of the firm because more resources and management attention tend to get channeled toward the international division than toward the domestic divisions and because of the different orientations of various division managers.[5] Companies such as IBM, PepsiCo, and Gillette have international divisions, called, respectively, IBM World Trade, PepsiCola International, and Gillette International.

Integrated Global Structures

To respond to increased product diversification and to maximize benefits from both domestic and foreign operations, a firm may choose to replace its international division with an integrated global structure. This structure can be organized along functional, product, geographic, or matrix lines.[6]

The **global functional structure** is designed on the basis of the company's functions—production, marketing, finance, and so forth. Foreign operations are integrated into the activities and responsibilities of each department to gain functional specialization and economies of scale. This form of organization is used primarily by small firms with highly centralized systems. It is particularly appropriate for product lines using similar technology and for businesses with a narrow spectrum of customers. This structure results in plants that are highly integrated across products and that serve single or similar markets.[7]

Much of the advantage resulting from economies of scale and functional specialization may be lost if the managers and the work systems become too narrowly defined to have the necessary flexibility to respond to local environments. An alternative structure can be based on product lines.

For firms with diversified product lines (or services) that have different technological bases and that are aimed at dissimilar or dispersed markets, a **global product (divisional) structure** may be more strategically advantageous than a functional structure. In this structure, a single product (or product line) is represented by a separate division. Each division is headed by its own general manager, and each is responsible for its own production and sales functions. Usually, each division is a **strategic business unit** (SBU)—a self-contained business with its own functional departments and accounting systems. The advantages of this organizational form are market concentration, innovation, and responsiveness to new opportunities in a particular environment. It also facilitates diversification and rapid growth, sometimes at the expense of scale economies and functional specialization. H. J. Heinz Company CEO William R. Johnson came on board in April 1998 and decided that the company should restructure to implement a global strategy. He changed the focus of the company from a multidomestic international strategy using the global geographic area structure to a global strategy, using the global product divisional structure. His goal was further growth overseas by building international operations; this structure also readily incorporated Heinz's Specialty Pet Food division for marketing those products around the world.[8] Particularly appropriate in a dynamic and diverse environment, the global product structure is illustrated in Exhibit 8-2.

With the global product (divisional) grouping, however, ongoing difficulties in the coordination of widely dispersed operations may result. One answer to this problem, particularly for large MNCs, is to reorganize into a global geographic structure.

In the **global geographic (area) structure**—the most common form of organizing foreign operations—divisions are created to cover geographic regions (see

Exhibit 8-2   Global Product (Divisional) Structure

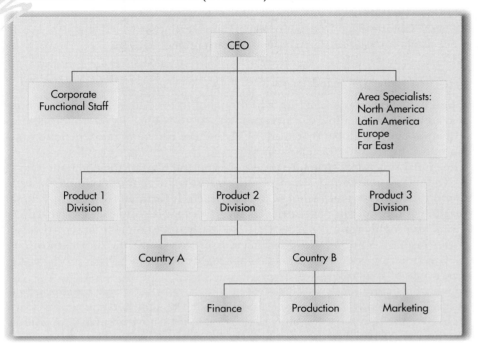

Exhibit 8-3). Each regional manager is then responsible for the operations and performance of the countries within a given region. In this way, country and regional needs and relative market knowledge take precedence over product expertise. Local managers are familiar with the cultural environment, government regulations, and business transactions. In addition, their language skills and local contacts facilitate daily transactions and responsiveness to the market and the customer. While this is a good structure for consolidating regional expertise, problems of coordination across regions may arise. With the geographic structure, the focus is on marketing, since products can be adapted to local requirements. Therefore, marketing-oriented companies, such as Nestlé and Unilever, which produce a range of products that can be marketed through similar (or common) channels of distribution to similar customers, will usually opt for this structure. Nestlé SA, for example, uses this decentralized structure, which is more typical of European companies, because

> it is not Nestlé's policy to generate most of its sales in Switzerland, supplemented by a few satellite subsidiaries abroad. Nestlé strives to be an insider in every country in which it operates, not an outsider.
> —www.Nestle.com (DECEMBER 7, 2000).

Grouping a number of countries under a region doesn't always work out, however, as Ford experienced with its European Group. It soon discovered the tensions among the units in Germany, Britain, and France resulting from differences in their national systems and culture, and in particular management styles. Nevertheless, it has pursued

Exhibit 8-3   Global Geographic Structure

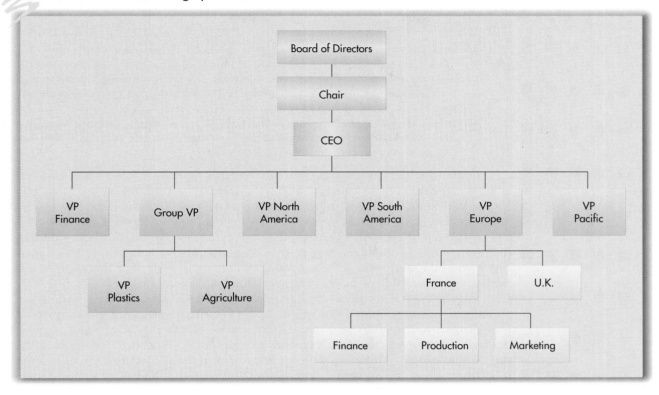

its consolidation into five regionalized global centers for the design, manufacture, and marketing of 70 lines of cars around the world.[9] In 2001, under Ford's CEO Jac Nasser—born in Lebanon and raised in Australia—Ford negotiated a presence in over 200 countries, with 140 manufacturing plants.[10]

A **matrix structure**—a hybrid organization of overlapping responsibilities—is used by some firms but has generally fallen into disfavor recently.

ORGANIZING FOR GLOBALIZATION

> If you misjudge the market [by globalizing], you are wrong in 15 countries rather than only in one.
>
> —FORD EUROPEAN EXECUTIVE.[11]

No matter what the stage of internationalization, a firm's structural choices always involve two opposing forces: the need for **differentiation** (focusing on and specializing in specific markets) and the need for **integration** (coordinating those same markets). The way the firm is organized along the differentiation–integration continuum determines how well strategies—along a localization–globalization continuum—are implemented. This is why the structural imperatives of various strategies such as globalization must be understood to organize appropriate worldwide systems and connections.

As discussed earlier, global trends and competitive forces have put increasing pressure on multinational corporations to adopt a strategy of **globalization**—a specific strategy that treats the world as one market by using a standardized approach to products and markets. Recent examples of companies reorganizing to achieve globalization are the following:[12]

> ➤ **IBM.** Big Blue decided to move away from its traditional geographic structure to a global structure based on its 14 worldwide industry groups, such as banking, retail, and insurance, shifting power from country managers to centralized industry expert teams. IBM hopes the restructuring will help the company take advantage of global markets and break down internal barriers.

> ➤ **Bristol-Meyers Squibb.** The international drug company announced the formation of new worldwide units for consumer medicine businesses such as Bufferin, and for its Clairol and hair-care products.

Organizing to facilitate a globalization strategy typically involves rationalization and the development of strategic alliances. To achieve rationalization, managers choose the manufacturing location for each product based on where the best combination of cost, quality, and technology can be attained. It often involves producing different products or component parts in different countries. Typically, it also means that the product design and marketing programs are essentially the same for all end markets around the world—to achieve optimal economies of scale. The downside of this strategy is a lack of differentiation and specialization for local markets.

Organizing for global product standardization necessitates close coordination among the various countries involved. It also requires centralized global product responsibility (one manager at headquarters responsible for a specific product around the world), an especially difficult task for multiproduct companies. Henzler and Rall suggest that structural solutions to this problem can be found if companies rethink the roles of their headquarters and their national subsidiaries. Managers should center the overall control of the business at headquarters, while treating national subsidiaries as partners in managing the business—perhaps as holding companies responsible for the administration and coordination of cross-divisional activities.[13]

A problem many companies face in the future is that their structurally sophisticated global networks, built to secure cost advantages, leave them exposed to the risk of environmental volatility from all corners of the world. Such companies need to restructure their global operations to reduce the environmental risk that results from multicountry sourcing and supply networks.[14] In other words, the more links in the chain, the more chances for things to go wrong.

Comparative
Management
in Focus

The Overseas Chinese Global Network

The Chinese who left the mother country had to struggle, and that became a culture of its own. Because we have no social security, the Overseas Chinese habit is to save a lot and make a lot of friends.
—LEE SHAU KEE, 65, REAL ESTATE DEVELOPER, HONG KONG (NET WORTH $6 BILLION)[15]

Compared to the Japanese keiretsu, the emerging Chinese commonwealth is an interconnected, open system—a new market mechanism for conducting global business.[16] It is now becoming apparent to many business leaders who have finally figured out Japan's keiretsu that they "now need to understand a distinctively Chinese model, where tycoons cut megadeals in a flash and heads of state wheel and deal like CEOs."[17]

The "Chinese commonwealth" is a form of global network that has become the envy of Western multinationals. It is a network of entrepreneurial relationships spread across continents, though primarily in Asia. What is increasingly being referred to as the "big dragon of Greater China" includes mainland China's 1.3 billion citizens and over 55 million overseas Chinese—most of them from Taiwan, Indonesia, Hong Kong, and Thailand. It is estimated that the Overseas Chinese control $2 trillion in liquid assets and contribute about 80 percent of the capital for the PRC. If the Overseas Chinese lived in one country, their GNP would exceed that of mainland China.[18] In addition, this "bamboo network," which transcends national boundaries, is estimated to contribute about 70 percent of the private sector in Malaysia, Thailand, Indonesia, and the Philippines."[19] Most observers believe that this China-based informal economy is the world leader in economic growth, industrial expansion, and exports. It comprises mostly midsize, family-run firms linked by transnational network channels. "These channels for the movement of information, finance, goods, and capital help to explain the relative flexibility and efficiency of the numerous ongoing informal agreements and transactions that bind together the various parts of the Chinese-based trading area.[20] The network alliances bind together and draw from the substantial pool of financial capital and resources available in the region—including those of entrepreneurial services in Hong Kong, technology and manufacturing capability in Taiwan, outstanding communications in Singapore, and vast endowments of land, resources, and labor in mainland China.[21]

The Overseas Chinese, now models for entrepreneurship, financing, and modernization for the world, and in particular for Beijing, are refugees from China's poverty, disorder, and communism. Business became the key to survival for those Chinese emigrants faced with uncertainties, hardships, and lack of acceptance in their new lands. The uncertainties, a survivor mentality, and the cultural basis in the Confucian tradition of patriarchical authority have led to a way of doing business that is largely confined to family and trusted friends. This business mentality and approach to life has led to many self-made billionaires among the Overseas Chinese. Among them is Y. C. Wang, the Taiwanese plastics king, who had to leave school after the sixth grade but taught himself what was necessary to develop a new industry. At 77, he still never takes a day off and views personal consumption as undue extravagance. His wife sneaks out his worn suits to the tailor to be copied and sneaks the new ones back into his closet.[22] The network of alliances of the ethnic Chinese is based on *guanxi*—personal connections—among families, business friends, and political associations, often rooted in the traditional clans. Massive amounts of cross-investment and trade are restricted primarily to families and long-standing connections, including those from the province of the PRC from which the overseas Chinese or their ancestors migrated. As examples, Chinese ties in Hong Kong have provided about 90 percent of the investment in the adjacent Guangong; and telephone calls from the special economic zone of Xiamen in the PRC to Taiwan now average 60,000 a month, up from 10 a month eight years ago.[23] The web of those connections has created an influential network that is the backbone of the East Asian economy.

The history, culture, and careful, personal approach to business of the Overseas Chinese have led to some underlying values, which Kao calls "life-raft" values, which have shaped a distinctive business culture. These values include thrift and a very high savings level, regardless of need, extremely hard work, trust in family before anyone else, adherence to patriarchal authority, investment based strictly on kinship and affiliations, a preference for investment in tangible goods, and an ever-wary outlook on life.[24] This shared web of culture and contacts has spawned an intensely commercial and entrepreneurial network of capitalists and a dominant power in Asia. Two benefits of such a business culture are speed and patience. Because of their knowledge of and trust in their contacts, the Overseas Chinese can smell profits quickly and make decisions even more quickly; a deal to buy a hotel in Asia can be completed in days, compared to months in the United States.[25] Patience to invest for the long term is an outcome of closely held ownership and management, often in a single family, so that outside shareholders are not demanding short-term profits. There is no doubt that sharing language and cultural bonds is a vital lubricant for business, especially with people in China, where there are few firm laws that businesspeople can rely on.[26]

Organizing to "Be Global, Act Local"

In their rush to get on the globalization bandwagon, too many firms have sacrificed the ability to respond to local market structures and consumer preferences. Managers are now realizing that—depending on the type of products, markets, and so forth—a compromise must be made along the globalization-regionalization continuum, and they are experimenting with various structural configurations to "be global and act local." Colgate-Palmolive's organizational structure illustrates such a compromise. As described by Rosenzweig and illustrated in Exhibit 8-4, the primary operating structure is geographic—that is, localized. The presidents of four major regions—North America, Europe, Latin America, and Asia Pacific—report to the chief operating officer, while other developing regions such as Africa, Eastern Europe, and the Middle East report to the chief of operations of international business development. Then that person reports to the CEO of Colgate-Palmolive, who oversees the centralized coordinating operations (that is, the "globalized" aspects), for technology, finance, marketing, human resources management, and so on.

Colgate-Palmolive's structure has evolved to this point to complement its evolving strategy. As described by Rosenzweig, at first, Colgate-Palmolive structured its international operations on a country-by-country basis, with the foreign subsidiaries each reporting directly to headquarters. With expansion into the 1950s, the structure was changed to a regional one, with regional presidents overseeing subsidiaries. But during the 1970s and 1980s there was increasing global competition in consumer goods, leading Colgate-Palmolive to strive more for global coordination than relying on geographic decentralization. Toward that end, the company reorganized

Exhibit 8-4   Colgate-Palmolive's "Glocal" Organizational Structure

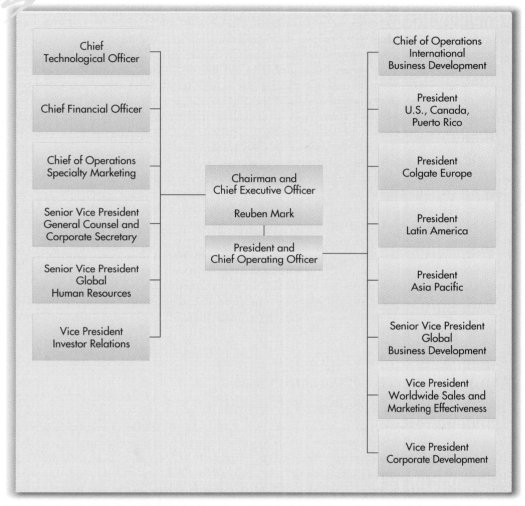

SOURCE: P. M. Rosenzweig, "Colgate-Palmolive: Managing International Careers," Case Study in C. A. Bartlett and S. Ghoshal, *Transnational Management*, 2nd ed. (Boston: Irwin Publishing Co., 1995).

in 1981, setting up a global business development unit to oversee and coordinate some worldwide operations and launch new products. As of 1994, the structure illustrated was a hybrid in order to seek the advantages of global coordination as well as local responsiveness.[27]

Levi Strauss is another example of a company attempting to maximize the advantages of different structural configurations. First, Levi has ensured its ability to respond to local needs in a different way by allowing its managers to act independently: Levi's success turns on its ability to fashion a global strategy that doesn't snuff out local initiative. It's a delicate balancing act, one that often means giving foreign managers the freedom needed to adjust their tactics to meet the changing tastes of their home markets.[28]

Second, Levi's keeps centralized control of some aspects of its business but decentralizes control to its foreign operations, organized as subsidiaries. These subsidiaries are supplied by a global manufacturing network of Levi plants and contract manufacturers. This approach allows local coordination and the flexibility to respond to ever-changing fashion trends and fads in denim shading.[29]

Another company's plan to go global by acting local does not involve changing the company's basic structure. Fujitsu, a Japanese high-technology conglomerate producing computers, telecommunications equipment, and semiconductors, has found a way to internationalize by proxy. Fujitsu has substantial stakes in two foreign companies that account for nearly half of Fujitsu's overseas revenues. They are Amdahl, a Silicon Valley maker of IBM-compatible mainframes, and International Computers Ltd. (ICL), Britain's biggest computer company. These firms are run by westerners, who are given free rein to manage and even compete against each other. The plan is doing so well that Fujitsu is looking for similar deals in Europe. As Fujitsu's president, Takuma Yamamoto, explains, "We are doing business in a borderless economy, but there is a rising tide of nationalism, and you have to find ways to avoid conflict. That is one reason we give our partners autonomy."[30]

Although strategy may be the primary means to a company's competitive advantage, the burden of realizing that advantage rests on the organizational structure and design. Because of the difficulties experienced by companies trying to be "glocal" companies (global and local), researchers are suggesting new, more flexible organizational designs involving interorganizational networks and transnational design.

EMERGENT STRUCTURAL FORMS

Interorganizational Networks

Whether the ever-expanding transnational linkages of an MNC consist of different companies, subsidiaries, suppliers, or individuals, they result in relational networks. These networks may adopt very different structures of their own because they operate in different local contexts within their own national environments.[31] By regarding the MNC's overall structure as a network of interconnected relations, we can more realistically consider its organizational design imperatives at both global and local levels. Exhibit 8-5 illustrates the network structure of N. V. Philips, a multinational with headquarters in the Netherlands and operating units in 60 countries. These units range from large subsidiaries, which might be among the largest companies in a country, to very small single-function operations, such as research and development or marketing divisions for one of Philips's businesses. Some have centralized control at Philips's headquarters; others are quite autonomous.

The network of exchange relationships shown in Exhibit 8-5, say Ghoshal and Bartlett, is as representative of any MNC as it is of Philips. The network framework makes clear that the company's operating units link vastly different environmental and operational contexts based on varied economic, social, and cultural milieus. This complex linkage highlights the intricate task of a giant MNC to rationalize and coordinate its activities globally to achieve an advantageous cost position while simultaneously tailoring itself to local market conditions (to achieve benefits from differentiation).[32] In

Exhibit 8-5   The Network Structure of N.V. Philips

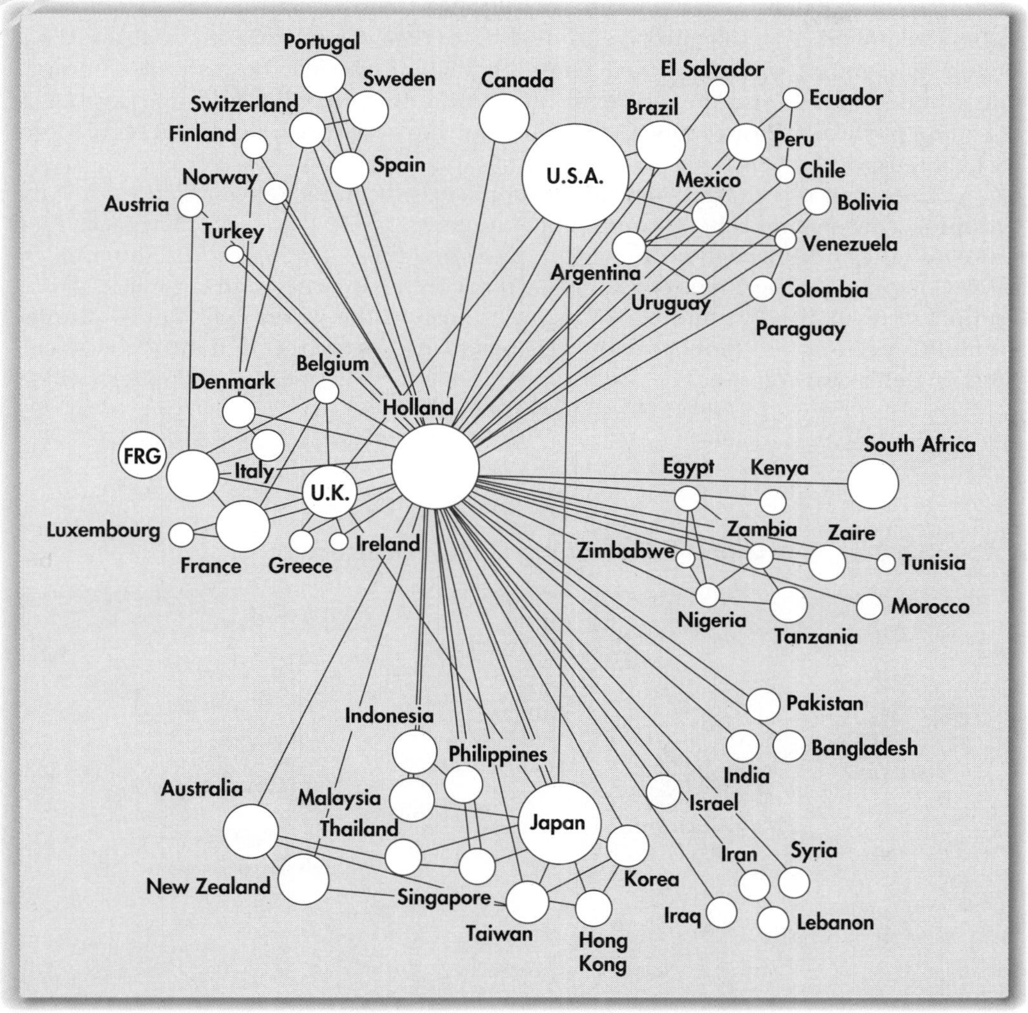

SOURCE: S. Ghoshal and C. A. Bartlett, "The Multinational Corporation as an Interorganizational Network," *Academy of Management Review* 15, no. 4 (1990): 603–625.

fact, N. V. Philips has recently fallen far behind its Japanese competitors in productivity because of its lumbering bureaucratic organization, which it needs to simplify and decentralize.[33]

The Global E-Corporation Network Structure

The organizational structure for global e-businesses, in particular for physical products, typically involves a network of virtual e-exchanges and "bricks and mortar" services, whether those services are in-house or outsourced. This structure of functions and alliances makes up a combination of electronic and physical stages of the supply chain network, as depicted in Exhibit 8-6.

As such, the network comprises some global and some local functions. Centralized e-exchanges for logistics, supplies, and customers could be housed anywhere; suppliers, manufacturers, and distributors may be in various countries, separately or together, wherever efficiencies of scale and cost may be realized. The final distribution system and the customer interaction must be tailored to the customer-location physical infrastructure and payment infrastructure, as well as local regulations and languages.[34]

The result is a global e-network of suppliers, subcontractors, manufacturers, distributors, buyers and sellers, communicating in real time through cyberspace. This spreads efficiency throughout the chain, providing cost effectiveness for all parties.[35] Dell Computer is an example of a company that uses the Internet to streamline its global supply systems. It has a number of factories around the world that supply custom-built PCs to customers in that region. Customers' orders are received through call centers or Dell's own Website. The order for components then goes to its suppliers, which

Exhibit 8-6 The Global E-Corporation Network Structure

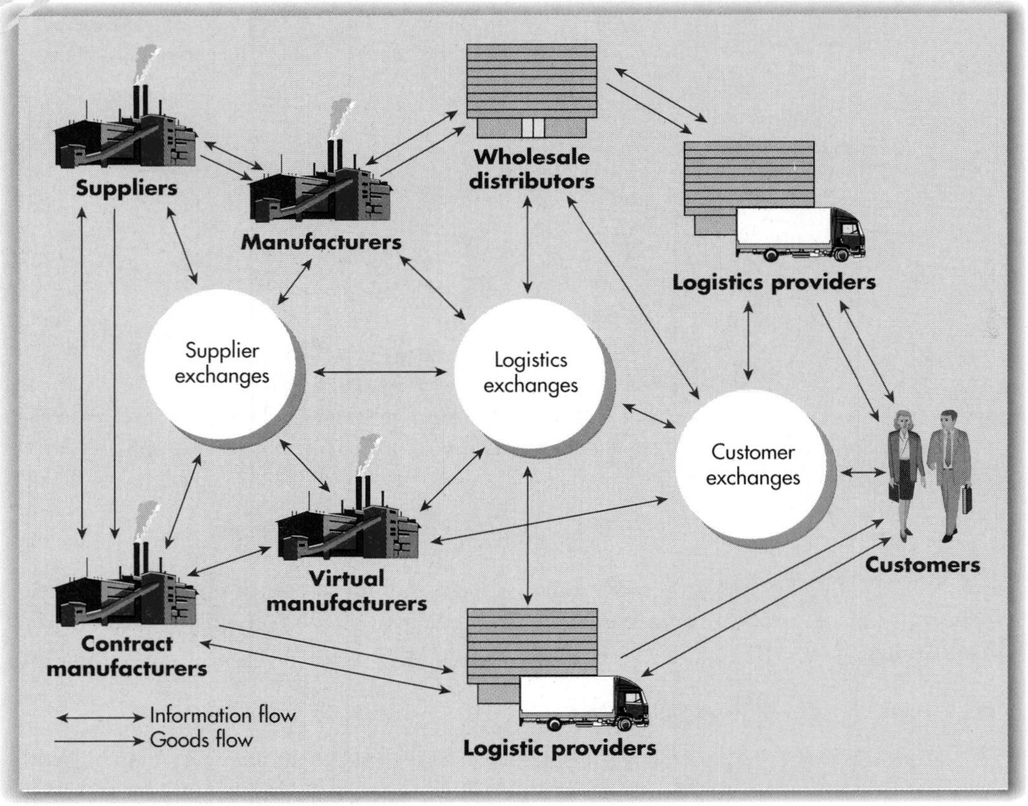

SOURCE: AMR Research.

have to be within a 15-minute drive of its factory. The component parts are delivered to the factory, and the completed customers' orders are collected within a few hours. Dell maintains Internet connections with its suppliers and connects them with its customer database so that they have direct and real-time information about orders. Customers also can use Dell's Internet system to track their orders as they go through the chain.[36]

The Transnational Corporation (TNC) Network Structure

To address the globalization-localization dilemma, firms that have evolved through the multinational form and the global company are now seeking the advantages of horizontal organization in the pursuit of transnational capability—that is, the ability to manage across national boundaries, retaining local flexibility while achieving global integration.[37] This capability involves linking their foreign operations in a flexible way to each other and to headquarters, thereby leveraging local and central capabilities.[38] ABB (Asea Brown Boveri) is an example of such a decentralized horizontal organization. ABB operates in 140 countries with 1,000 companies, with only one management level separating the business units from top management. ABB prides itself on being a truly global company, with 11 board members representing 7 nationalities. Thus, this structure is less a matter of boxes on an organizational chart and more a matter of a network of the company's units and their system of horizontal communication. This involves lateral communication across networks of units and alliances rather than in a hierarchy. The system requires the dispersal of responsibility and decision making to local subsidiaries and alliances. The effectiveness of that localized decision making depends a great deal on the ability and willingness to share current and new learning and technology across the network of units.

Whatever the names given to the organizational forms emerging to deal with global competition and logistics, the MNC organizational structure as we know it, with its hierarchical pyramid, subsidiaries, and world headquarters, is gradually evolving into a more fluid form to adapt to strategic and competitive imperatives. Facilitating this change, Kilmann points out, is the information technology explosion fueled by computers, fax machines, teleconferencing, the Internet, and so forth:

> Competitive companies in the future will be elaborate networks of people and information, each exerting an influence on the other. [These networks will comprise] a small hub of staff connected to each other by their physical proximity, which is electronically connected to global associates who help control assets and negotiate agreements to extend the company's business influence.[39]

In this new global web, the location of a firm's headquarters is unimportant. It may even be, says Reich, "a suite of rooms in an office park near an international airport—a communications center where many of the web's threads intersect."[40] The web is woven by decisions made by managers around the world, both decisions within the company and those between other companies. Various alliances tie together units and subunits in the web. Corning Glass, for instance, changed from its national pyramid-like organization to a global web, giving it the capability of making optical cable through its European partner, Siemens AG, and medical equipment with Ciba-Geigy.[41]

CHOICE OF ORGANIZATIONAL FORM

Two major variables in choosing the structure and design of an organization are the opportunities and need for (1) globalization and (2) localization. Exhibit 8-7 depicts alternative structural forms appropriate to each of these variables and to the strategic choices regarding the level and type of international involvement desired by the firm. This figure thereby updates the evolutionary stages model to reflect alternative organizational responses to more recent environments and to the anticipated competitive environments ahead. The updated model shows that, as the firm progresses from a domestic to an international company—and perhaps later to a multinational and then a global company—its managers adapt the organizational structure to accommodate their relative strategic focus on globalization versus localization, choosing a global product structure, a geographic area structure, or perhaps a matrix form. The model proposes that, as the company becomes larger, more complex, and more sophisticated in its approach to world markets (no matter which structural route it has taken), it may evolve into a **transnational corporation (TNC)**. The TNC strategy is to maximize opportunities for both efficiency and local responsiveness by adopting a transnational structure that uses alliances, networks, and horizontal design formats.

Exhibit 8-7 Organizational Alternatives and Development for Global Competition

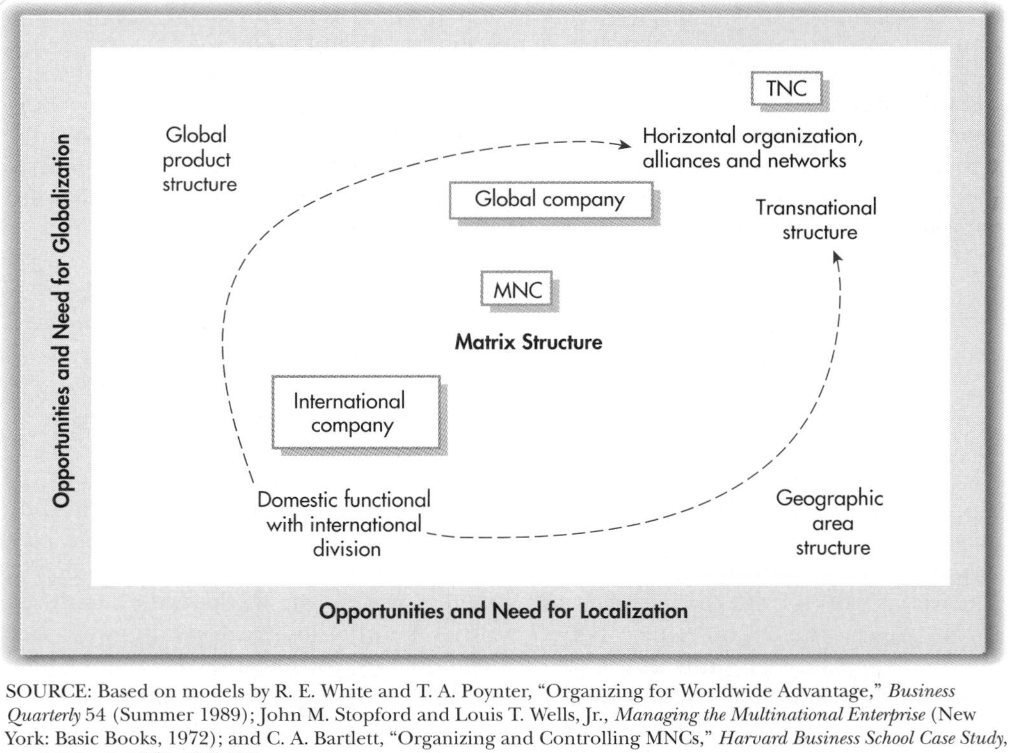

SOURCE: Based on models by R. E. White and T. A. Poynter, "Organizing for Worldwide Advantage," *Business Quarterly* 54 (Summer 1989); John M. Stopford and Louis T. Wells, Jr., *Managing the Multinational Enterprise* (New York: Basic Books, 1972); and C. A. Bartlett, "Organizing and Controlling MNCs," *Harvard Business School Case Study*, no. 9 (March 1987): 365, 375.

Exhibit 8-8   Global Strategy–Structure Relationships

	Multidomestic Strategy	International Strategy	Globalization Strategy	Transnational Strategy
	Low ⟷ Need for Coordination ⟷ High			
	Low ⟷ Bureaucratic Costs ⟷ High			
Centralization of authority	Decentralized to national unit	Core competencies centralized; others decentralization to national units	Centralized at optimal global location	Simultaneously Centralized and Decentralized
Horizontal differentiation	Global area structure	International division structure	Global product group structure	Global Matrix Structure "Matrix in the Mind"
Need for complex integrating mechanisms	Low	Medium	High	Very High
Organizational culture	Not important	Quite important	Important	Very important

SOURCE: C. W. L. Hill and E. R. Jones, *Strategic Management*, 3rd ed. (Boston: Houghton Mifflin, 1995), 390.

The relationships between choice of global strategy and the appropriate structural variations necessary to implement each strategic choice are further illustrated in Exhibit 8-8.

Organizational Change and Design Variables

When a company makes drastic changes in its goals, strategy, or scope of operations, it will usually also need a change in organizational structure. However, other, less obvious, indications of organizational inefficiency also signal a need for structural changes: conflicts among divisions and subsidiaries over territories or customers, conflicts between overseas units and headquarters staff, complaints regarding overseas customer service, and overlapping responsibilities are some of these warning signals. Exhibit 8-9 lists some indications of the need for change in organizational design.

At persistent signs of ineffective work, a company should analyze its organizational design, systems, and work flow for the possible causes of those problems. The nature and extent of any design changes must reflect the magnitude of the problem. In choosing a new organizational design or modifying an existing structure, managers must establish a system of communication and control that will provide for effective decision making. At such times, managers need to localize decision making and integrate widely dispersed and disparate global operations.

Besides determining the behavior of the organization on a macro level (in terms of for what the different divisions, subsidiaries, departments, and units are responsible), the organizational design must determine behavior on a micro level. For example, the organizational design affects the level at which certain types of

Exhibit 8-9   When Is Change Needed?

- A change in the size of the corporation—due to growth, consolidation, or reduction
- A change in key individuals—which may alter management objectives, interests, and abilities
- A failure to meet goals, capitalize on opportunities, or be innovative
- An inability to get things done on time
- A consistently overworked top management that spends excessive hours on the job
- A belief that costs are extravagant or that budgets are not being met
- Morale problems
- Lengthy hierarchies that inhibit the exercise of strategic control
- Planning that has become increasingly staff-driven and is thus divorced from line management
- Innovation that is stifled by too much administration and monitoring of details
- Uniform solutions that are applied to nonuniform situations. The extreme opposite of this condition—when things that should or could function in a routine manner do not—should also be heeded as a warning. In other words, management by exception has replaced standard operating procedures

The following are a few specific indicators of *international* organizational malaise:

- A shift in the operational scope—perhaps from directing export activities to controlling overseas manufacturing and marketing units, a change in the size of operations on a country, regional, or worldwide basis, or failure of foreign operations to grow in accordance with plans and expectations.
- Clashes among divisions, subsidiaries, or individuals over territories or customers in the field
- Divisive conflicts between overseas units and domestic division staff or corporate staff
- Instances wherein centralization leads to a flood of detailed data that is neither fully understood nor properly used by headquarters
- Duplication of administrative personnel and services
- Underutilization of overseas manufacturing or distribution facilities
- Duplication of sales offices and specialized sales account executives
- Proliferation of relatively small legal entities or operating units within a country or geographic area
- An increase in overseas customer service complaints
- Breakdowns in communications within and between organizations
- Unclear lines of reporting and dotted-line relationships, and ill-defined executive responsibilities

SOURCE: Business International Corporation, *New Directions in Multinational Corporate Organization* (New York: Business International Corporation, 1981).

decisions will be made. Determining how many and what types of decisions can be made and by whom can have drastic consequences; both the locus and the scope of authority must be carefully considered. This centralization–decentralization variable actually represents a continuum. In the real world, companies are neither totally centralized nor totally decentralized: The level of centralization imposed is a matter of degree. Exhibit 8-10 illustrates this **centralization–decentralization continuum** and the different ways that decision making can be shared between headquarters and local units or subsidiaries. In general, centralized decision making is common for some functions (finance and research & development) that are organized for the entire corporation, whereas other functions (production, marketing, and sales) are

Exhibit 8-10   Locus of Decision Making in an International Organization

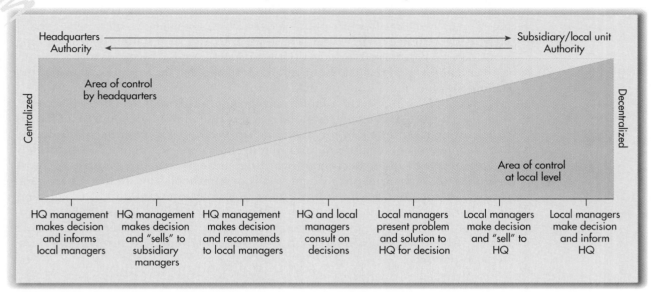

SOURCE: Based on and adapted from R. Tannenbaum and W. Schmidt; and A. G. Kefelas, *Global Business Strategy* (Cincinnati: South-Western, 1990).

more appropriately decentralized. Two key issues are the speed with which the decisions have to be made and whether they primarily affect only a certain subsidiary or other parts of the company as well.

As noted, culture is another factor that complicates decisions on how much to decentralize and how to organize the work flow and the various relationships of authority and responsibility. In Part Four, we discuss more fully how cultural variables affect people's attitudes about working relationships and about who should have authority over whom. At this point, simply note that cultural variables must be taken into account when designing an organization. Delegating a high level of authority to employees in a country where the workers usually regard "the boss" as the rightful person to make all the decisions is not likely to work well. Clearly, managers must think through the interactions of organizational, staffing, and cultural issues before making final decisions.

In sum, there is no one best way to organize. Contingency theory applies to organizational design as much as to any other aspect of management. The best organizational structure is the one that facilitates the firm's goals and is appropriate to its industry, size, technology, and competitive environment. Structure should be fluid and dynamic—and highly adaptable to the changing needs of the company. The structure should not be allowed to get bogged down in the **administrative heritage** of the organization (that is, "the way we do things around here," or "what we've always done") to the point that it undermines the very processes that will enable the firm to take advantage of new opportunities.

Most likely, however, the future for MNC structure lies in a global web of networked companies. Ideally, a company tries to organize in a way that will allow it to carry out its strategic goals; the staffing is then done to mesh with those strategic goals and the way the organizational structure has been set up. In reality, however, the existing structural factors often affect strategic decisions, so the end result may be a trade-off of desired strategy with existing constraints. So, too, with staffing: "ideal" staffing plans have to be adjusted to reflect the realities of assigning managers from various sources and the local regulations or cultural variables that make some organizing and staffing decisions more workable than others.

What may at first seem a linear management process of deciding on strategy, then on structure, and finally on staffing is actually an interdependent set of factors that must be taken into consideration and worked out as a set of decisions. In the next chapter, we will explore how staffing decisions are—or should be—intricately intertwined with other decisions regarding strategy, structure, and so forth. A unique set of management cadre and skills in a particular location can be a competitive advantage in itself, and so it may be a smart move to build strategic and organizational decisions around that resource rather than risk losing that advantage. But first let's look at some other processes that are involved in implementing strategy which are interconnected with coordinating functions through organizational structure.

CONTROL SYSTEMS FOR GLOBAL OPERATIONS

> The establishment of a single currency makes it possible, for the first time,
> to establish shared, centralized accounting and administrative systems.
> —FRANCESCO CAIO, CEO MERLONI ELETTRODOMESTICI, FABRIANO, ITALY,
> *HARVARD BUSINESS REVIEW*, JANUARY/FEBRUARY 1999

To complement the organizational structure, the international manager must design efficient coordinating and reporting systems to ensure that actual performance conforms to expected organizational standards and goals. The challenge is to coordinate far-flung operations in vastly different environments with various work processes, rules, and economic, political, legal, and cultural norms. The feedback from the control process and the information systems should signal any necessary change in strategy, structure, or operations in a timely manner. Often, the strategy, the coordinating processes, or both, need to be changed to reflect conditions in other countries.

Monitoring Systems

The design and application of coordinating and reporting systems for foreign subsidiaries and activities can take any form that management wishes. MNCs usually employ a variety of direct and indirect coordinating and control mechanisms suitable for their organization structure. Some of the typical control methods used for the major organizational structures discussed here are shown in Exhibit 8-11. These are self-explanatory. For example, in the transnational-network structure, decision-making control is centralized to key network nodes, greatly reducing emphasis on bureaucratic control. Output control in this exhibit refers to the assessment of a subsidiary or unit based only on the results attained. Other specific mechanisms are summarized in the next sections.

Exhibit 8-11   Control Mechanisms in Multinational Organizational Structures

Multinational Structures	Output Control	Bureaucratic Control	Decision-Making Control	Organization Control
International division structure	Most likely profit control	Must follow company policies	Some centralization possible	Treated like other divisions
Global geographic structure	Profit center most common	Some policies and procedures necessary	Local units have autonomy	Local subsidiary culture often more important
Global product structure	Unit output for supply; sales volume for sales	Tight process controls for product quality and consistency	Centralized at product division headquarters	Possible for some companies but not always necessary
Transnational network structure	Used for supplier units and some independent profit centers	Less important	Few decisions centralized at head-quarters; more decisions centralized in key network nodes	Organizational culture transcends natioinal cultures; supports sharing and learning; the most important control mechanism

SOURCE: Adapted from John B. Cullen, *Multinational Management: A Strategic Approach, 2ed.* (Cincinnati: South-Western, 1999), 329.

Direct Coordinating Mechanisms

Direct mechanisms that provide the basis for the overall guidance and management of foreign operations include the design of appropriate structures (discussed earlier in this chapter) and the use of effective staffing practices (discussed in Chapter 9). Such decisions proactively set the stage for operations to meet goals, rather than troubleshooting deviations or problems after they have occurred. The accompanying Management Focus describes how McDonald's Corporation. successfully set up direct control systems in advance of its entry into Moscow.

Other direct mechanisms are visits by head-office personnel and regular meetings. Top executives from headquarters may use periodic visits to subsidiaries to check performance, troubleshoot, and help to anticipate future problems. International Telephone and Telegraph Corporation (ITT) holds monthly management meetings at its New York headquarters. Performance data are submitted by each ITT subsidiary general manager from around the world, and problems and solutions are shared.[42] The meetings allow each general manager to keep in touch with her or his associates, with the overall mission and strategy of the organization, and with comparative performance data and new problem-solving techniques. Increasingly, the tools of technology are being applied as direct mechanisms to ensure up front that operations will be carried out as planned, in particular in countries where processes such as efficient infrastructure and goods forwarding cannot be taken for granted. An example of this is the logistics monitoring system set up by Air Express International in Latin America to minimize its many problems there.[43] As another example, Bikeworld.com controls

Management Focus

McDONALD'S IN MOSCOW—A DECADE OF CONTROL CHALLENGES

We have proudly served millions of customers and are looking forward to working with our team of managers and crew to expand our operation to serve many more in communities across Russia.
—KHAMZAT KHASBULATOV, PRESIDENT, MCDONALD'S IN RUSSIA, www.Mcdonalds.com, FEBRUARY 20, 2001

As of 2001, McDonald's had 58 restaurants in the Moscow region, St. Petersburg, Nizhny Novgorod, Yaroslavl, Samara, and Kazan. The restaurants serve over 150,000 customers every day, and, since opening on January 31, 1990, they have served more than 250 million customers and more than 52 million Big Mac sandwiches.

It all started with a chance meeting between George Cohon, senior chairman, McDonald's Canada, and a Soviet Olympic Delegation at the Olympic games in Montreal in 1976. It sparked 14 years of negotiations and culminated in the opening of the first McDonald's in Russia.

When the restaurant finally opened its doors in Moscow's busy Pushkin Square in January 1990, the largest agreement between the former Soviet Union and a food service company became a reality. The 900-seat restaurant broke several of McDonald's previous records—30,000 Russians were served on opening day, and 1 million had been served by March. It took 12 years of negotiations by George A. Cohon, president and founder of McDonald's Restaurants of Canada, to open the doors in Pushkin Square. McDonald's has a 49 percent interest in the joint venture with the Moscow City Council Department of Food Service. In all, McDonald's Canada invested $50 million for construction and personnel training for the processing plant and the restaurant. They agreed to reinvest all their profits in Moscow for a chain of 20 restaurants.

The biggest control problem for McDonald's was that of quality control for its food products. Unlike its Western counterparts, this IJV has had to adopt a strategy of vertical integration for its sourcing of raw materials. To control the quality, distribution, and reliability of its ingredients, McDonald's built a $40 million, 110,000-square-foot plant in a Moscow suburb to process the required beef, milk, buns, vegetables, sauces, and potatoes. The facility includes laboratories for testing to ensure compliance with quality and consistency standards. Peter Frings, an agronomist with McCain Foods Limited, was brought in to introduce the Russian farmers to the nonnative Russet Burbank potato used to make the famous McDonald's fries. Frings and other experts spent several months working on local farms to advise farmers on such aspects as increasing acreage yields and boosting overall quality.

Operational control was a considerable problem for McDonald's in this historic joint venture, specifically in regard to controlling the quality of food and service. The first challenge was the hiring and training of local employees; Craig Sopkowicz, McDonald's quality-control expert, was in charge of the new employees. "We looked for applicants who lived close to the restaurant, among other things, in order to control the timeliness of employees," explains Sopkowicz. Most of the new hires were between 18 and 27 years old, and this was usually their first job: Teenagers seldom work in Russia because labor laws protect them from conflicts with school work. After selecting the 630-member crew, the all-important training and customer control began. To be flexible when positions changed, the new crew was trained in all aspects of the restaurant's functions; the new staff logged in over 15,000 training hours to ensure control similar to that in Western operations. In addition, Roy Ellis, the personnel specialist, had some concern about the employees' appearance and decided to construct an on-site laundry room. "It's more practical . . . and it means we can ensure our standards," explains Ellis. The four Russian managers (Khamzat Khazbulatov, Vladimir Zhurakovskij, Mikhail Sheleznov, and Georgij Smoleevskij) went through the same rigorous training that any other McDonald's manager would, enabling them to manage any of the 11,000 units worldwide. They went to McDonald's Institute of Hamburgerology in Toronto, Canada, for five months—a 1,000-hour program, and from there they went to Hamburger University in Oakbrook, Illinois, for two weeks training along with 235 managers from around the world. The

Russians line up to sample McDonald's fare in Moscow; 30,000 were served on opening day.

operating philosophy underlying the training can be summed up as QSC&V—quality, service, cleanliness, and value.

Innovative control procedures take place in front of the counter in the Moscow unit as well as behind the cash registers. To control for the timeliness of service, McDonald's tried to reduce the long waiting lines by hiring private security people to keep order and by using public-address systems to tell patrons how to place orders. In addition to verbal instructions, customers are given picture-menus to simplify the ordering process. The Russian menu has also been streamlined to help speed up the service and the decision-making process. McDonald's has combated the growing black market problem by installing a one-door policy; this has eliminated large-scale pilferage, which usually occurs out the back door. A limit of ten

Big Macs to each customer helps stop the black market sale to hungry customers anxiously waiting in line.

Top management at McDonald's anticipated difficulties with the setup and daily operations of this IJV and, indeed, had been working toward the opening day for 13 years. Through careful planning for the control of crucial operational factors, they solved the sourcing, distribution, and employment problems inherent in the former Soviet Union.

Over a decade later, in 2001, McDonald's Russia was still importing chickens from France, cheese, fish, and apple segments from Poland, and potatoes—cut and frozen—from the Netherlands. Now a "chain" in Russia with 58 restaurants, McDonald's says that it sources 75 percent of its supplies within the country but that, for continued quality control, it opened its own "McComplex" farm to supply its outlets.

SOURCES: Updates by the author from: www.McDonalds.com February 20, 2001; A. Jack, "Russians Wake Up to Consumer Capitalism," www.FT.com (*Financial Times*), January 30, 2001; earlier material adapted by the author from a term paper written by Gil George and Karsten Fetten, students at the State University of New York–Plattsburgh (December 1990). Copyright © 1993 by Helen Deresky.

their order fulfillment and customer service as they expand globally by incorporating FedEx e-business technologies to develop a fully automated and scalable fulfillment system (described in the accompanying E-Biz Box).

Indirect Coordinating Mechanisms

Indirect coordinating mechanisms typically include sales quotas, budgets, and other financial tools, as well as feedback reports, which give information about the sales and financial performance of the subsidiary for the last quarter or year.

Domestic companies invariably rely on budgets and financial statement analyses, but for foreign subsidiaries, financial statements and performance evaluations are complicated by **financial variables in MNC reports**, such as exchange rates, inflation levels, transfer prices, and accounting standards.

To reconcile accounting statements, MNCs usually require three different sets of financial statements from subsidiaries. One set must meet the national accounting standards and procedures prescribed by law in the host country. This set also aids management in comparing subsidiaries in the same country. A second set must be prepared according to the accounting principles and standards required by the home country. This set allows some comparison with other MNC subsidiaries. The third set of statements translates the second set of statements (with certain adjustments) into the currency of the home country for consolidation purposes, in accordance with FASB Ruling Number 52 of 1982. A foreign subsidiary's financial statements must be consolidated line-by-line with those of the parent company according to the International Accounting Standard Number 3, adopted in the United States.[44]

Researchers have noted comparative differences between the use of direct versus indirect controls among companies headquartered in different countries. One study by Egelhoff examined the practices of 50 U.S., U.K., and European MNCs over their foreign subsidiaries. It compared the use of two mechanisms—the assignment of parent-company managers to foreign subsidiaries and the use of performance reporting systems (that is, comparing behavior mechanisms with output reporting systems).[45] The results of this study show that considerable differences exist in practices across MNC nationalities. For example, says Egelhoff, U.S. MNCs monitor subsidiary outputs and rely more on frequently reported performance data than do European MNCs. The latter tend to assign more parent-company nationals to key positions in foreign subsidiaries and can count on a higher level of behavior control than their U.S. counterparts.[46]

These findings imply that the American system, which measures more quantifiable aspects of a foreign subsidiary, provides the means to compare performance among subsidiaries. The European system, on the other hand, measures more qualitative aspects of a subsidiary and its environment, which vary among subsidiaries—allowing a focus on the unique situation of the subsidiary but making it difficult to compare its performance to other subsidiaries.[47]

MANAGING EFFECTIVE MONITORING SYSTEMS

Management practices, local constraints, and expectations regarding authority, time, and communication are but a few of the variables likely to affect the **appropriateness of monitoring systems**. The degree to which headquarters' practices and goals are transferable probably depends on whether top managers are from the head office, the host country, or a third country. In addition, information systems and evaluation variables must all be considered when deciding on appropriate systems.

E-Biz Box

BIKEWORLD GOES GLOBAL USING FEDEX TECHNOLOGIES AND SHIPPING

- Fully automated and scalable fulfillment system enabled sales value to increase from $1 million to $6 million.

- Access to real-time order status enhances customer service and leads to greater customer retention.

- Bikeworld now has global capacity to service customers.

Since opening its doors in 1971, Bikeworld established itself as the place to go in San Antonio, Texas, for high-quality bicycles and components, expert advice and personalized service. The company came to e-commerce early, opening its Web site in February 1996. Bikeworld's founder, Whit Snell, originally saw the Web as a way to keep customers from using out-of-state mail-order houses. For Bikeworld, the Web represented a 24-hour global retail space where small companies had the same reach and potential for success as much larger ones.

A COMPLETE SHIPPING AND TRACKING SOLUTION

Bikeworld was soon to encounter one of Internet retailing's highest hurdles: fulfillment and after-sale customer service. Sales of its high-value bike accessories over the Internet were steadily increasing, but the time spent processing orders, shipping packages manually and responding to customers' order status inquiries threatened to overwhelm the 16-person operation.

In need of help, Bikeworld looked to FedEx and realized FedEx could offer affordable express delivery on every order; exceeding customer expectations while automating the fulfillment process.

"To go from a complete unknown to a reputable worldwide retailer was going to require more than a fair price. We set out to absolutely amaze our customers with unprecedented customer service. FedEx gave us the blinding speed we needed." says Snell.

The FedEx solution was twofold: To better manage the dramatic increase in sales volume, the FedEx PowerShip® system was integrated with the Bikeworld.com Web server for a seamless exchange of information—from online selling through fulfillment and reporting. When an order is placed at Bikeworld.com, it is assigned a unique FedEx tracking number. As the order proceeds through the assembly process, a FedEx shipping label is generated automatically.

In search of a solution for its customer inquiry issues, Bikeworld utilized FedEx® Ship Manager API software to develop a custom tracking application. The software code embedded FedEx shipping and package tracking functions into Bikeworld's Web site. It allows customers to follow their orders from the moment they're placed until the FedEx courier arrives. Snell says that it's not unusual for customers to check on their orders several times a day, following their packages through the FedEx delivery network.

GROWTH AT THE SPEED OF THE NET

As a traditional shop, Bikeworld's annual sales hovered around $1 million, more than respectable for the category. Four years after venturing online, sales volume has more than quadrupled, and the company is on track to surpass $6 million in 2000. More significantly, Bikeworld.com is consistently profitable, a distinction that places it among the e-commerce elite.

"We had growth but not explosive growth until we went online and chose FedEx as our carrier and offered reliable overnight and two-day service. Just the fact that our product arrives in the FedEx box adds credibility to its value." explains Snell. "The ability to fulfill orders is almost a product by itself. Once you get that done, you can do anything. FedEx helped us get there."

And if you're in San Antonio, you can still visit Bikeworld's Alamo Heights location to buy a bike, find an elusive part or get a flat fixed.

continued

ORDER MANAGEMENT PROCESS

❶ Bikeworld.com customer places an order via the Internet at www.bikeworld.com.

❷ FedEx PowerShip, integrated with Bikeworld.com's server, assigns the customer's order a FedEx tracking number. As the order proceeds through assembly, a FedEx shipping label is generated automatically.

❸ Bikeworld.com assembles the customer order and places the shipping air waybill on the package.

❹ By integrating FedEx Ship Manager API into the Bikeworld.com Web site, customers are able to track their orders from the time they are placed until they are delivered.

❺ FedEx picks up the order and delivers overnight or within two to three days, depending on the customer's specifications.

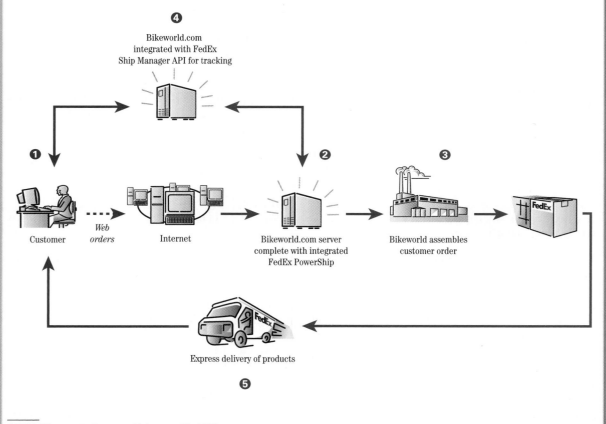

SOURCE: www.Fedex.com, February 22, 2002.

The Appropriateness of Monitoring and Reporting Systems

One example of differences in the expectations regarding monitoring practices, and therefore in the need for coordination systems, is indicated by a study of Japanese and American firms. Exhibit 8-12 shows the mean responses of the American and Japanese managers concerning budget control practices in their firms. Ueno and Sekaran state that their research shows that "the U.S. companies, compared to the Japanese companies, tend to use communication and coordination more extensively, build budget slack to a greater extent, and use long-term performance evaluations to a lesser extent."[48] Furthermore, Ueno and Sekaran conclude that those differences in reporting systems are attributable to the cultural variable of individualism in American society, compared to collectivism in Japanese society. For example, American managers are more likely to use formal communication and coordination processes, whereas Japanese managers use informal and implicit processes. In addition, American managers, who are evaluated on individual performance, are more likely to build slack into budget calculations for a safety net than their Japanese counterparts, who are evaluated on group performance. The implications of this study are that managers around the world who understand the cultural bases for differences in control practices will be more flexible in working with those systems in other countries.

The Role of Information Systems

Reporting systems such as those described in this chapter require sophisticated information systems to enable them to work properly—not only for competitive purposes, but also for purposes of performance evaluation. Top management must receive accurate and timely information regarding sales, production, and financial results to be able to compare actual performance with goals and to take corrective action where necessary. Most international reporting systems require information feedback at one level or another for financial, personnel, production, and marketing variables.

The specific types of functional reports, their frequency, and the amount of detail required from subsidiaries by headquarters will vary. Neghandi and Welge

Exhibit 8-12   Mean Responses of American and Japanese Managers Regarding Their Budget Control Practices

Variables	U.S. Mean	Japan Mean
Communication and coordination	4.03	3.70
Planning time horizons	3.51	3.52
Structuring of budgetary processes	2.95	2.90
Budget slack	3.08	2.89
Controllability of budgets	3.42	3.17
Budget performance evaluation time horizons	2.80	3.11

S.D. = standard deviation.
Response scale: 1–strongly disagree; 2–disagree; 3–neutral; 4–agree; 5–strongly agree
SOURCE: Susumo Ueno and Uma Sekaran, "The Influence of Culture on Budget Control Practices in the U.S.A. and Japan: An Empirical Study," *Journal of International Business Studies* 23 (Winter 1992): 659–674.

surveyed the types of functional reports submitted by 117 MNCs in Germany, Japan, and the United States.[49] They found that U.S. MNCs typically submit about double the number of reports than do German and Japanese MNCs, with the exception of performance reviews. German MNCs submit a few more reports than do Japanese MNCs. U.S. MNCs thus seem to monitor far more through specific functional reports than do German and Japanese MNCs. The Japanese MNCs put far less emphasis on personnel performance reviews than do the U.S. and German MNCs—a finding consistent with their culture of group decision making, consensus, and responsibility.

Unfortunately, the accuracy and timeliness of information systems are often less than perfect, especially in less developed countries, where managers typically operate under conditions of extreme uncertainty. Government information, for example, is often filtered or fabricated; other sources of data for decision making are usually limited. Employees are not used to the kinds of sophisticated information generation, analysis, and reporting systems common in developed countries. Their work norms and sense of necessity and urgency may also confound the problem. In addition, the hardware technology and the ability to manipulate and transmit data are usually limited. The **adequacy of management information systems (MIS)** in foreign affiliates is a sticky problem for headquarters managers in their attempt to maintain efficient coordination of activities and consolidation of results. Another problem is the **noncomparability of performance data across countries**, which hinders the evaluation process.

The **Internet** has, of course, made the availability and use of information attainable instantaneously. Many companies are starting to supply Internet MIS systems for supply-chain management. European partners Nestlé S.A. and Danone Group, world leaders in the food industry, set up Europe's first Internet marketplace for e-procurement in the consumer goods sector, called CPGmarket.com, saying:

> CPGmarket.com will enhance the efficiency of logistics while at the same time reducing procurement costs for businesses producing, distributing and selling consumer goods. CPG (based on mySAP.com e-business platform) allows companies not only to buy and sell, but also to access industry information. . . . Participants will benefit from a more efficient market, reducing costs through higher transaction efficiency and simplified processes.
> —www.Nestle.com, PRESS RELEASE, MARCH 21, 2000.

Evaluation Variables across Countries

A major problem that arises when evaluating the performance of foreign affiliates is the tendency by headquarters managers to judge subsidiary managers as if all of the evaluation data were comparable across countries. Unfortunately, many variables can make the evaluation information from one country look very different from that of another country owing to circumstances beyond the control of a subsidiary manager. For example, one country may experience considerable inflation, significant fluctuations in the price of raw materials, political uprisings, or governmental actions. These factors are beyond the manager's control and are likely to have a downward effect on profitability—and yet, that manager may in fact have maximized the opportunity for long-term stability and profitability compared with a manager of another subsidiary who was not faced with such adverse conditions. Other variables influencing profitability patterns include transfer pricing, currency devaluation, exchange-rate fluctuations, taxes, and expectations of contributions to local economies.

One way to ensure more meaningful performance measures is to adjust the financial statements to reflect the uncontrollable variables peculiar to each country where a subsidiary is located. This provides a basis for the true evaluation of the comparative return on investment (ROI), which is an overall control measure. Another way to provide meaningful, long-term performance standards is to take into account other nonfinancial measures. These measures include market share, productivity, sales, relations with the host-country government, public image, employee morale, union relations, and community involvement.[50]

Conclusion

The structure, control, and coordination *processes* are the same whether they take place in a domestic company, a multinational company with a network of foreign affiliates, or a specific IJV. It is the extent, the focus, and the mechanisms used to organize those activities that differ. More coordination is needed in global companies because of uncertain working environments and information systems and because of the variable loci of decision making. Headquarters managers must design appropriate systems to take into account those variables and to evaluate performance.

SUMMARY OF KEY POINTS

1. An organization must be designed to facilitate the implementation of strategic goals. Other variables to consider when designing an organization's structure include environmental conditions, the size of the organization, and the appropriate technology. The geographic dispersion of operations as well as differences in time, language, and culture affect structure in the international context.

2. The design of a firm's structure reflects its international entry strategy and tends to change over time with growth and increasing levels of investment, diversity, or both.

3. Global trends are exerting increasing pressure on MNCs to achieve economies of scale through globalization. This involves rationalization and the coordination of strategic alliances.

4. MNCs can be regarded as interorganizational networks of their own dispersed operations and other strategic alliances. Such relational networks may adopt unique structures for their particular environment, while also requiring centralized coordination.

5. The transnational structure allows a company to "be global and act local" by using networks of decentralized units with horizontal communication. This permits local flexibility while achieving global integration.

6. Indications of the need for structural changes include inefficiency, conflicts among units, poor communication, and overlapping responsibilities.

7. Coordinating and monitoring systems are necessary to regulate organizational activities so that actual performance conforms to expected organizational standards and goals. MNCs use a variety of direct and indirect controls.

8. Financial monitoring and evaluation of foreign affiliates are complicated by variables such as exchange rates, levels of inflation, transfer prices, and accounting standards.

9. The design of appropriate monitoring systems must take into account local constraints, management practices and expectations, uncertain information systems, and variables in the evaluation process.

10. Two major problems in reporting for subsidiaries must be considered: (1) inadequate management information systems and (2) the noncomparability across countries of the performance data needed for evaluation purposes.

DISCUSSION QUESTIONS

1. What variables have to be considered in designing the organizational structure for international operations? How do these variables interact, and which do you think are most important?
2. Explain the need for an MNC to "be global and act local." How can a firm design its organization to enable this?
3. What is a transnational organization? Since many large MNCs are moving toward this format, it is likely that you could at some point be working within this structure—how do you feel about that?
4. Discuss the implications of the relative centralization of authority and decision making at headquarters versus local units or subsidiaries. How would you feel about this variable if you were a subsidiary manager?
5. As an international manager, what would make you suggest restructuring your firm? What other means of direct and indirect monitoring systems do you suggest.
6. What is the role of information systems in the reporting process? Discuss the statement, "Inadequate MIS systems in some foreign affiliates are a control problem for MNCs."

APPLICATION EXERCISES

1. If you have personal access to a company with international operations, try to conduct some interviews and find out about the personal interactions involved in working with their counterparts abroad. In particular, ask questions about the nature and level of authority and decision making in overseas units compared with headquarters. What kinds of conflicts are experienced? What changes would your interviewees recommend?
2. Do some research on monitoring and reporting issues facing an MNC with subsidiaries in (1) India and (2) the former East Germany. Discuss problem areas and your recommendations to the MNC management as to how to control potential problems.
3. Find out about an IJV in the United States. Get some articles from the library, write to the company for information, or if possible visit the company and ask questions. Present the class your findings on the company's major control issues—both at the beginning of the venture and now. What is the company doing differently in its control process compared to a typical domestic operation? Are the control procedures having the desired results? What recommendations do you have?

EXPERIENTIAL EXERCISES

In groups of four, consider a fast-food chain going into Eastern Europe. Decide on your initial level of desired international involvement and your entry strategy. Draw up an appropriate organizational design, taking into account strategic goals, relevant variables in the particular countries in which you will have operations, technology used, size of the firm, and so on. At the next class, present your organization chart and describe the operations and rationale. (You could finalize the chart on an overhead or flip chart before class begins.) What are some of the major control issues to be considered?

INTERNET RESOURCES

Visit the Deresky companion Website at http://prenhall.com/Deresky for this chapter's Internet resources.

CASE STUDY: FLEXIT INTERNATIONAL

The Flexit Company manufactures and sells athletic conditioning and sports equipment. The primary market is for home use, but approximately 15 percent of the company's profit comes from sales of equipment and spare parts to Aquarius Health Spas Inc. Home use products are sold through sporting goods stores and large retail chain stores such as K mart.

Company History

Flexit began business in 1965 as a small manufacturer of exercise equipment and sold its product—weight sets—to schools and gymnasiums. The product line expanded slowly until the mid-1970s, when the physical fitness craze began. Since 1975, the company has expanded both product line and sales territory. It now sells to the continental 48 states but not to Hawaii or Alaska. However, Flexit's current five-year plan includes exporting to Europe and possible offshore production, as shown in Exhibit 8-13.

    The company president, Jim Goodbody, has always taken pride in the company's self-sufficiency. Flexit manufactures all its products, although it uses outside transportation (commercial trucking) for distribution to retail and wholesale markets.

    At present, Flexit has three manufacturing locations in the United States. The home office and original plant are in Ames, Iowa, where four of the eight Flexit products are made. A plant in Oxnard, California, manufactures two products. The newest plant, in Atlanta, makes two fitness products sold to Aquarius Health Spas. All planning for manufacturing, sales, and distribution is done by the president and his staff at the Iowa facility. Company operations are summarized in Exhibit 8-14 and the organization chart is reproduced in Exhibit 8-15.

Exhibit 8-13   Flexit Corporate Goals

1. Remain a leader in the home physical fitness product market in the United States.
2. Expand domestic market share from 38 to 50 percent within five years.
3. Capture a large market share (at least 10 percent) of the European market in five years.
4. Retain control of operations, but consider international alternatives such as offshore production, import of related products for sale in the United States, subsidiary operations, and countertrade.

SOURCE: M. R. Czinkota, P. Rivoli, I. A. Ronkainen, *International Business* (New York: Dryden, 1989); this case was provided by Lieutenant Colonel Frederick W. Westfall of the United States Air Force Institute of Technology. All rights reserved to the contributor. This case originally appeared in *International Case Histories in Logistics*, published by the Council of Logistics Management, Copyright 1987. It has been adapted with permission of Lieutenant Colonel Frederick W. Westfall and the Council of Logistics Management.

Exhibit 8-14 Flexit Company Operations

1. Each division is responsible for planning each of its product lines. This includes preparing domestic sales forecasts, manufacturing schedules, and inbound and outbound distribution for each product.
2. Raw materials are ordered by each division and trucked to each facility as necessary.
3. All products are manufactured on site. Production schedules are based on sales forecasts from product marketing planners.
4. Outbound distribution of finished products is planned and executed at each division. Shipments are contracted to rail and truck as necessary.
5. The Ames, Iowa, facility includes a manufacturing plant and a corporate staff.

An International Twist

Market research done by Flexit has indicated a large demand for home athletic products in several European countries. Jim Goodbody would very much like to enter that market and eventually become a dominant company in Europe as well as the United States. However, because Flexit has had no experience in international shipments or doing business in a foreign country, he wants initially to limit involvement in overseas operations to exporting.

Exhibit 8-15 Flexit Organization Chart

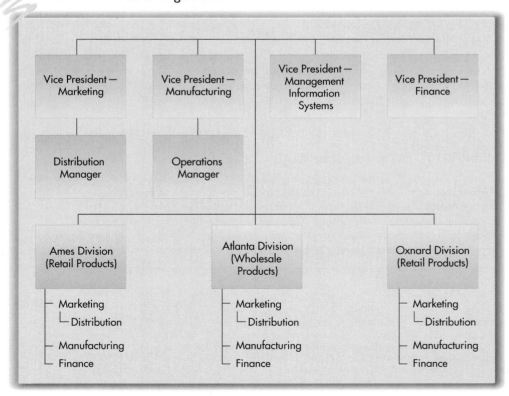

The head of Flexit's marketing department traveled to Europe to meet with officials of several firms interested in representing Flexit. He selected Physique Ltd. as best able to contribute to Flexit's overall marketing goals. Physique Ltd. specializes in home physical fitness products, selling and distributing a full line to all European Economic Community countries and to several non-EEC countries. It also sells to several [former] communist bloc countries on a limited basis. An organization chart for Physique Ltd. is shown in Exhibit 8-16.

Physique Ltd. officials indicated that they see no immediate barriers to handling the Flexit product line. Their distribution channels could easily accommodate the additional products. Physique Ltd. uses rail and truck transportation predominantly and uses air or water services only as necessary.

Physique Ltd. officials believe that Flexit prices would be competitive even after the Physique Ltd. markup is added. They indicated that they would be very interested in establishing either a countertrade or an export business to the United States using Flexit as their distributor if that would be possible in the future. However, such an agreement was not a condition for Flexit's venture into Europe with Physique Ltd.

The Task at Hand

Jim Goodbody has decided to go ahead with the export operation, using Physique Ltd. as distributor, although he has several concerns about the logistics of such an undertaking. Specifically, he is worried that problems may arise because the two companies have different corporate structures. Second, he knows that Flexit managers will be required to take on a number of new tasks. To the head of corporate distribution planning, he gave the broad assignment of determining the best way to get Flexit products to Europe. The only constraint was that he must consult with the head of market planning. The first step taken by the head of corporate distribution planning was to investigate the services offered by freight forwarders. His findings are summarized in Exhibit 8-17.

Exhibit 8-16   Physique Ltd. Organization Chart

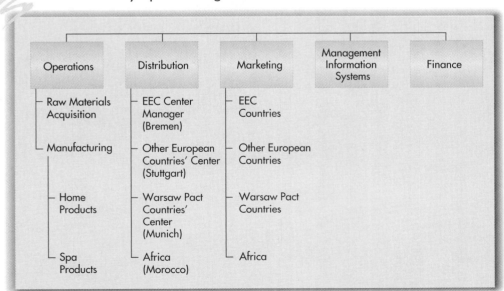

Exhibit 8-17 Typical Freight Forwarder Services

1. Prepare export documentation.
2. Prepare import documentation for destination.
3. Provide for transportation from the exporter to final destination.
4. Prepare and process bills of lading.
5. Arrange for insurance.
6. Prepare documents in the language of the country and provide for certification.
7. Provide for warehouse storage and services as necessary.
8. Prepare and send shipping statement to Banks, other shippers or consignees if necessary.
9. Provide professional assistance on export-related matters.
10. In general, coordinate and facilitate the movement of goods from point of origin to point of destination.

Case Questions

1. Are Flexit's corporate goals realistic for the next five years?
2. Will the existing physical distribution system support the proposed expansion to Europe?
3. Which new tasks can be performed by existing resources, and which must be added or contracted out?
4. What are the benefits and the drawbacks of using an existing distribution channel in Europe?
5. Does the proposed plan have the required flexibility to accommodate expansion for countertrade, import from Europe, offshore production, and subsidiaries in Europe?
6. Is a new organization structure required to support company objectives? What changes do you think should be made? Why? Draw up your recommended new organization chart for Flexit.

Comprehensive Cases

Case 7   Softbank Corporation

Internet and Web-Related Acquisitions, Market Expansion, and Global Strategies in 2001–2002

Syed Tariq Anwar

INTRODUCTION

Softbank Corporation is a Japanese business group that controls over 600 Internet and technology-related companies and other businesses worldwide (see Tables 1–4). The company is headquartered in Tokyo and was started by Masayoshi Son in 1981. Even after the dot.com downturn during 1999–2000, the company ranks as one of the largest distributors of software and technology-related products as well as a provider of Internet-based information in the world. In 2001, Softbank Group was divided into the following segments: IT-related distribution and e-commerce, financial services, publishing and marketing, Internet infrastructure, technology service, and broadcast media (see Table 4). Because of its massive acquisitions, Softbank is often called the Internet *keiretsu* (Lynskey and Yonekura 2001; Webber 1992). The company is the largest investor in the world in the Internet, e-commerce, and technology-related areas. Since 1992, Softbank has grown into one of the most influential and dynamic players in the Internet and e-commerce industry.

Because of Son's unique entrepreneurial style and flamboyant personality, the Western media often called him the Bill Gates of Japan, Cyber-Mogul, Master of the Internet, Japan's Mr. Internet, and the like. Son's entrepreneurial style has become a powerful force in the Internet world. Son started Softbank after receiving his degree in economics from the University of California at Berkeley in 1980. Since 1994, Softbank's shares have been traded on the Tokyo over-the-counter market. In 1998, Softbank's consolidated revenues reached $4.38 billion with a pretax profit of $339 million. In 1999, Softbank's market capitalization surpassed $11.5 billion, and the company employed 7,000 workers worldwide (see Table 1; *Business Week* 1999a&b; *Financial Times* 1997a–c; *Wall Street Journal* 1996,1999a–c).

In the last ten years, Softbank has sought aggressive global diversification by acquiring high-profile Internet companies and invested millions of dollars in long-term Internet technologies. In September 1999, Softbank's selected acquisitions and majority shareholdings included: Yahoo, Yahoo Japan, E-Trade Japan, E-Trade Group, Buy.com, Concentric, E-Loan, USWeb, ZDNet, Ziff Davis, ZD Comdex, Kingston Technology, SB Networks, and Japan Digital Broadcasting Services (see Table 5). Softbank's venture capital subsidiary (Softbank Technology Ventures) has actively pursued and sought

Table I   Softbank Corporation: Selected Financial and Corporate Data (1999 vs. 2001)

A. Financial Data	1999	2001
Consolidated Revenues	$4.3 billion	$4.6 billion
Pretax profit	$339 million	$286 million
Net Profit	$311 million	$75 million
Market Capitalization	$11.3 billion	$12.81 billion
Global Rank	—	447

B. Corporate Data

Head Office	24-1, Nihonbashi-Hakozakicho, Chuco-ku, Tokyo, Japan	
Employees Worldwide (2001)	7,000	7,219
Incorporated	September 3, 1981	
Stock Information	Stock traded on *Tokyo Stock Exchange* (first section) Symbol: *9984*	

Company Structure: Softbank Corporation
Softbank Global Ventures
Softbank International Ventures
Softbank Venture Capital
Softbank Capital Partners
Softbank Europe Ventures
Softbank Latin American Ventures
Softbank China Venture Capital
Softbank Ventures Korea

Board of Directors (as of June 21, 2001)
President & CEO: Masayoshi Son
Directors: Yoshitaka Kitao, Ken Miyauchi; Kazuhiko Kasai, Masahiro Inoue, Ronald Fisher, Jun Murai, Toshifumi Suzuki, Tadashi Yanai, Mark Schwartz.

SOURCE: Softbank Corporation, Tokyo, Japan, September 1999, www.softbank.com/corporate_data.htm: *Forbes.* Master of the Internet, July 5, 1999, pp. 146–151; *Financial Times*, May 11, 2001, pp. 1–55.

equity-related investments in companies from the areas of digital information technology, Internet communications, network services, and e-commerce.

Softbank's shift in its core-competence and long-term strategies results from massive growth in the Internet and technology-related markets in the United States, Japan, and Western Europe. According to industry analysts, Softbank plans to become one of the largest Internet and technology communication companies in the world. Softbank is truly the first-mover company in its product mar-

kets. Analysts believe that in the next five years, Softbank will become a major force in the Internet and technology-related and software distribution areas because of increasing demand and growth. On the other hand, Softbank will be impacted by heightened global competition and will be challenged by newcomers in the industry. The case is intended to have students look at Softbank's future market growth and its global strategies within the concept of internationalization and competitive advantage issues.

Table 2   Softbank Corporation: Major Entities and Product Lines (1999)

A. Media and Marketing

Ziff-Davis, Inc. (NYSE: **ZD**):
  Integrated media & marketing company
  PC Magazine
  PC Week
  Computer Shopper
  50 licensed publication (combined circulation: 8 million readers)
  COMDEX (the largest U.S. show)
ZDNet (NYSE: **ZDZ**)
  Website (news, information, entertainment)
ZDTV
  Cable TV Channel—Digital Information Topics
Ziff-Davis – Market Research Division
  Computer intelligence unit; market research firm

B. Internet and Technology-Related Companies

Softbank Technology Ventures
Asymetrix Learning Systems (NASDAQ: **ASYM**): Online trading programs
BackWeb: Markets software; deliver personalized information
Buy.com: Operates retail Web site
Concentric (NASDAQ: **CNCX**): Provides virtual private networks and extranets; operates the
  Quicken Financial Network for Intuit
E-Loan: On-line mortgage
*E*Trade* (NASDAQ: **EGRP**): On-line Investment brokerage and stock trading services
InterTrust: Develops and sells a software system in the areas of medical records, movies, audio,
  stock transactions, and so on
MessageMedia (NASDAQ: **MESG**): Develops, markets, and installs messaging systems on the
  Internet; two-way communications
Reciprocal: Provides service in the areas of selling software, music, magazines, and other types of
  digital property
USWeb/CKS (NASDAQ: **USWB**): Helps design Web sites for Fortune 1000 companies; deals with
  strategic consulting
Yahoo (NASDAQ: **YHOO**): Premier global Internet media company; Softbank is the largest
  shareholder of Yahoo, which recently acquired *GeoCities*

SOURCE: Softbank Corporation, Tokyo, Japan: September 1999, www.softbank.com/corporate_data.htm.

WHO IS MASAYOSHI SON?

Son was born in 1957 on Kyushu Island and grew up in a small town, Tosu City, Saga Prefecture. He belongs to an ethnic Korean family: his grandparents migrated to Japan from Korea. In 1973, at the age of 16, Son attended high school in California and later moved to Holy Names College in Oakland, California. In 1980, he graduated from the University of California at Berkeley with a B.A. degree in Economics. While an undergraduate student, Son invented a multilingual pocket translator and sold his patent to Sharp Corporation, which later brought him a $1 million windfall (Lynskey and Yonekura 2001). Son also founded Unison Computer Company, which is now owned by Kyocera Corporation. (Webber 1992; www.softbank.com/bios.htm).

Table 3   Softbank Corporation: Company Structure and Portfolio Companies
(December 2001)

A. Company Structure

Softbank in Japan	Softbank Venture Capital (Mountain View, Calif.)
Softbank Corp.	Softbank Capital Partners
Softbank e-Commerce Corp	Softbank Europe Ventures
Softbank Finance Corp.	Softbank Latin America Ventures
Softbank Media & Marketing Corp.	Softbank China Holdings
Softbank Technology Corp.	Softbank Ventures Korea
Softbank Networks Inc.	Softbank Emerging Markets
Softbank Broadmedia Corp.	

B. Portfolio Companies

United States

BUY.COM, Inc.,	SayIt,
CompuBank-National Associates	Sonnet Financial, Inc.
E*Trade	UTStarcom
E-LOAN, Inc.	Viacore, Inc.
Key3media	Yahoo! Inc.
Kinesoft Development Corp.	ZDNet.

SOFTBANK Venture Capital

United States

Neomeo	dbDoctor
ProSavvy	deuxo
ADIR Technologies	Differential Inc.
AppGenesys	Digimarc Corporation
Aqueduct	E-Loan, Inc.
Art Technology Group, Inc.	Electron Economy
Asia Online	etrieve, Inc.
Asymetrix	Evant
Atreus Systems	Everest Broadband Networks, Inc.
B2SB Technologies	Exactis.com
beMANY!	EYT
Blue-Silicon	FastParts, Inc.
BlueLight.com Corporation	FileFish
BlueTiger Networks	Finali Corporation
Broad Daylight, Inc.	FinaPlex
BUY.COM, Inc.	Game Change
CBCA, Inc.	GenericMedia
ChannelWave Software, Inc.	Gold Systems, Inc
Comergent Technologies, Inc.	Group Sense PDA Holdings Limited
Concentric Network Corporation	Guggenheim
Connected Corporation	HeyAnita
Critical Path, Inc.	Hubstorm
Cybercash	HVC Technologies
Danger Research	iBoost Technology, Inc.

Table 3 (cont.)

SOFTBANK Venture Capital (cont.)

United States (cont.)

iGeneration	Raindance Communications
Ignition Corporation	ReachCast Corporation
Intend Change Group, Inc.	REBAR
Interliant, Inc.	Reciprocal, Inc.
InterTrust Technologies	Reelplay.com
Corporation invesmart	Rentals.com
Invisible Worlds, Inc.	Rivio
iPrint.com	SecurityFocus
Kefta	ServiceMagic.com
Latis	ServiceMagic.com
Law.com	ShareWave, Inc.
Legal Knowledge Company	SportBrain
LIMITrader.com	StartSampling
Maaya	Support.com
MessageMedia, Inc.	TelEvoke, Inc
Mondo Media	Terabeam Networks
Net2Phone, Inc.	The Feld Group
Netgov.com	TheStreet.Com, Inc.
NETSEC	Tonos
New Moon	Toysrus.com
Novare	Transilica
Oediv	Trapezo
PayTrust.com	United Devices, Inc
PeoplePC, Inc.	UTStarcom
Perfect Commerce	Veripost
Photopoint	Verisign, Inc.
PocketThis	Viathan
Preview Systems, Inc.	Voice Works
Proxinet, Inc.	Vytek Wireless
Pulse Entertainment	Wideforce Systems
Purple Yogi,Inc	WiredCapital
Quova	Xythos

SOFTBANK Capital Partners

United States

1-800-FLOWERS.Com, Inc.	Mysmart.com, Inc.
AllAdvantage.com	Naviant, Inc.
BlueLight.com Corporation	Odimo.com
BUY.COM, Inc.	Optimark Technologies, Inc.
ClearCross	PeoplePC, Inc.
DoveBid, Inc.	Rivals.com
Electron Economy	SmartAge.com Corporation
Global Sports, Inc.	Toysrus.com
Ignition Corporation	Web MD
Law.com	Webhire
Legal Research Network, Inc.	

Table 3 (cont.)

SOFTBANK Europe Ventures

Finland
  LPG Innovations
France
  CONSUL   Enition
  Cril Telecom Software (CTS)   NeTarget
Israel
  iSeg
Netherlands
  StiVentures
Sweden
  Picofun
  Startupfactory
Switzerland
  uB-mobile
United Kingdom
  Picsel   Venation
  RIOT-E   Volantis
  theworkx.net

SOFTBANK Latin American Ventures

Argentina
  Dineronet
Brazil
  ConnectMed.com
  Springwireless
United States
  BitTime   LearningSoft Corporation
  From2.com (Merged with Arzoon)   Tiaxa

SOFTBANK China Venture Capital

China
  51Marry.com   Good Doctor
  Airoam Technology   Goodbaby
  Alibaba   Guardian Auction
  Asiawise.com   Jia2000
  ChinaQuest   NewLido
  eBao   Precom
  ExhibitionOne   Prosys
  EZnova   Universiti

SOFTBANK Ventures Korea

Korea
  Alibaba Korea   JoyinBox
  Anysteel.com   MediOn (n-Health)
  B2B Cons   MediService (n-Health)
  CrossCert   SecureSoft
  Cyberdigm   SOFTBANK Media
  HeyAnita Korea   SOFTBANK Web Institute
  I-Cube   SOFTBANKnPlatform
  I-Textile Korea   Yahoo! Korea
  I-World

SOURCE: Softbank www.softbank.com.

Table 4   Softbank Group as of December 2001

A. IT-Related Distribution Service and E-Commerce

Softbank EC Holdings Corp., Softbank Commerce Corp., Softbank Frameworks Corp., Onsale Japan K.K., e-Shopping! Information Corp., e-Shopping! Books Corp., e-Shopping! Toys Corp., e-Shopping! Cargoods Corp., e-Shopping! Wine Corp., e-Career Corp., CarPoint K.K., e-Best Corp., Vector Inc., VerticalNet Japan Corp., eEntry Corp., SmartFirm Corp., Tavigator Inc., e-Express Co., Ltd., Style Index Corp., Diamon.com Corp., Softbank Mobile Corp., GWP Japan Corp., eselect Corp., BridalConcierge Corp., Eupholink, Inc., AIP Bridge Corp., CreativeBank Corp., Nihon Ariba K.K., Cmnet Corp., BluePlanet Corp., Ability Design, Ltd.

B. Financial Service

Softbank Finance Corp., E*Advisor Co., Ltd., E*Trade Japan K.K., E8Trade Securities Co., Ltd., Ascot Co., Ltd., E-Loan Japan K.K., Insweb Japan K.K., Softbank Investment Corp., Cognotec Japan K.K., Cybercash K.K., Morningstar Japan K.K., Web Lease Co., Ltd., Softbank Frontier Securities Co., Ltd., SophiaBank Ltd., Office Work Corp., HousePortal Co., Ltd., Goodloan Co., Ltd., e-Commodity Co., Ltd., Online IR Co., Ltd., E-Real Estate Co., Ltd., SF Realty Co., Ltd., Web Portal Co., Ltd., Softbank Asset Management Co., Ltd., SBI Capital Co., Ltd., SBI Promo Corp., Benefit Systems, Inc., Utopian Life Co., Ltd., Finance All Corp., Arsnova Capital Research, Inc., SBF Auction, Inc., Dream Support, Inc., TechTank Corp., SF Aggregation Service Co., Ltd.

C. Publishing and Marketing

Softbank Media & Marketing Corp., Softbank Publishing Inc., Key3Media Events Japan, Inc., Com-Path, Inc., Cyber Communications, Inc., Softbank ZDNet, Inc., WebMD Japan K.K., Barks K.K., Click2learn Japan K.K., Rivals Japan Corp., JaJa Entertainment Inc., Aplix Net Inc., Englishtown Ltd., DirektPlanet Co., Ltd, iWeb Technologies Japan K.K., EC Research Corp.

D. Internet Infrastructure

Softbank Networks Inc., IP Revolution Inc., Internet Facilities Inc., GlobalCenter Japan Corp.

E. Technology Service

Softbank Technology Holdings Corp., Softbank Technology Corp., E-cosmos, Inc., Broadbank Technology Corp., EC Architects Corp., Softbank Mobile Technology Corp., e-Commerce

F. Broadcast and Media

Softbank Broadmedia Corp., Digital Club Corp., Computer Channel Corp., Xdrive Japan K.K., YesNoJapan Corp., Akamai Technologies Japan K.K., Digital Media Factory Inc., Sky Perfect Communications, Inc., J Sky Sports Corp., Nihon Eiga Satellite Broadcasting Corp., Aliss-Net Co., Ltd.

G. Other

Yahoo Japan Corp., AtWork Corp., Softbank Digital Rights Corp., Nasdaq Japan, Inc., Aozora Bank, Ltd., SpeedNet Inc., BB Technologies Corp.

SOURCE: Softbank www.softbank.com.

Table 5 Softbank's Internet and Technology-Related Revenues (as of June 1999)

A. Software and Network Products
Sales (1998): $1.58 billion (9.7% up)
Operating Profit: $30.1 million (38.4% down)
Major Companies: SB Networks, UTStarcom, Trend Micro

B. Media and Broadcasting
Sales (1998): $0.96 billion (17.3% up)
Operating Profit: $114.2 million (10.8% up)
Major Companies: Ziff-Davis, Japan Digital Broadcasting Corp. (TV, radio and data transmission)

C. Technology Events and Trade Shows
Sales (1998): $0.3 billion (30.4% up)
Operating Profit: $78.8 million (8.0% up)
Selected Companies: ZD Comdex & Forums, Inc.

D. Technology Services
Sales (1998): $1.35 billion (185.4% up)
Operating Profit: $48.5 million (22.7% up)
Selected Companies: Kingston Technology (memory modules), Pasona Softbank (computer temp. agency)

E. Internet Sector
Sales (1998): NA
Operating Profit: NA
Selected Companies: Yahoo Japan (ownership: 51%), E-Trade Japan (58%), GeoCities Japan (60%), ZDNet (online news & magazines)

SOURCE: *Wall Street Journal*. "Japan's Softbank Unveils New Internet Deals," June 25, 1999, p. A17.

In 1981, Son returned to Japan and founded Softbank Corporation. The company initially started with two part-time workers and grew to 570 employees by 1991. Softbank supplied computer software, books and magazines, and other technology-related products to 200 dealer outlets. In 1991, the company expanded at a very fast pace and grew to 15,000 dealer outlets because of the changing market conditions and strong consumer demand for software and computer products. That year, Son netted $350 million in sales, and its retailers' network reached 25,000. During this period, Softbank was distributing products from companies such as Microsoft, Novell, Sun Microsystems, and Oracle (Lynskey and Yonekura 2001). After 1991, Son started to expand into the Internet area and made numerous acquisitions. In 1994, Softbank's stock started trading on the Tokyo over-the-counter market. After four years, Softbank's shares were listed on the Tokyo Stock Exchange. Since 1994, the stock has split four times.

Son's recent initiatives, acquisitions, and major alliances include Nihon Cisco Systems, Ziff-Davis trade show, Comdex, Windows World, Yahoo, Yahoo Japan, and Softbank Technology Ventures (see Tables 1–3). In 1994, when the Internet market in North America started to take off, Softbank was the only Japanese company making high-profile acquisitions. This reflects Son's visionary personality and aggressive entrepreneurial style (*Business Week* 1996; *Business Week e-Biz* 1999; *U.S. News & World Report* 1999; Weinberg, 1999). Abrahams and Nakamoto (1999, p. 16) described Softbank as

> a unique Japanese company. Led by Masayoshi Son, its flamboyant president, it has been touted as Japan's answer to Microsoft. Son's multimedia empire has expanded at breathtaking speed to become a global enterprise, but in the past year the group's shares have tumbled, raising concerns about Softbank's future

Forbes (1999, p. 148) commented on Softbank's massive acquisitions:

> Masayoshi Son's golden touch in Web investing has made him fabulously rich. His 42% stake in Softbank gives him a personal worth of $6.4 billion. The $6.4 billion question: Is he really that much smarter than everyone else—or is he just lucky?

Far Eastern Economic Review (1999, p. 11) pointed out Son's bold moves and his entrepreneurial style:

> Son's vision is to build Softbank into a global Internet consortium or zaibatsu,[1] with the same

---

[1] The structure of the *Zaibatsu* group of companies was based on the concept of holding companies. These companies were very strong before World War II. After the war, the United States dissolved these groups, which later took the form of *keiretsu* companies based on the Main-Bank structure and network connections.

landscape-shifting impact as the zaibatsu of the Meiji era who created Japan's first modern industries. He is doing this by identifying businesses where substantial efficiencies can be gained by going on-line. In particular, Son has zoomed in on Japan's stuffy world of brokerage, insurance, and banking.—Should Son succeed, he will be known not just as the man who dominates the Internet, but as a major financial-services player.

ACQUISITIONS, DIVERSIFICATION AND GLOBAL STRATEGIES IN 1999

According to *Forbes* (1999), Softbank has invested $2.4 billion in 100 Internet, technology, communications, and computer publishing companies. As of July 1999, the total market value of these companies had surpassed $14 billion. In many companies, Softbank became one of the major investors (see Table 6). Softbank's venture capital subsidiary (Softbank Technology Ventures) has provided $906 million to many Internet firms in the United States and Japan. Analysts believe that Softbank has plans to invest $1.2 billion in the coming months to seek additional acquisitions and new Internet start-ups. As of September 1999, Softbank held 7 percent to 8 percent ownership in the Internet and e-commerce industry worldwide. Softbank's Internet and technology acquisitions fall into two categories. First, in the area of media and marketing, Softbank owns 70 percent of Ziff-Davis, Inc., which is the largest computer trade show company in the world. Ziff-Davis publishes computer magazines such as *PC Magazine*, *PC Week*, and *Computer Shopper*. Second, in the Internet, communications, and technology sectors, Softbank has invested in some of the top Internet brands—Yahoo, Yahoo Japan, E-Trade Group, E-Loan, Concentric, USWeb, Message Media, and Asymetrix Learning Systems. These acquisitions have placed Softbank among the top Internet and technology players in the world.

Table 6   Softbank's Selected Internet and Technology-Related Acquisitions and Market Value in 1999 and 2001

A. As of July 1999

Acquisition	Date Acquired	Price Paid ($ million)	Current Holding (%)	Market Value ($ million)
E-Trade Group (*On-line Investing*)	July 98	$409	27%	$2,364
Message Media (*Message Technology*)	May–Sept. 98	8	24	124
Pasona Softbank (*Temp. Agency*)	Feb. 95	NA	20	62
Trend Micro (*Anti-Virus Software*)	Dec. 96	64	27	768
USWeb (*Web Consulting*)	Feb. 96	14	7	131
Yahoo (*Internet Portal*)	Nov. 95–Aug. 98	410	27	8,424
Yahoo Japan (*Internet Portal*)	April 96	10	51	2,287
Ziff-Davis (*Media and Marketing*)	Oct. 94–Feb. 96	1,500	70	833
Total:		$2,415		$14,993

B. As of January 2001

Internet/Web Sector		Investment Made Return	Total Companies
Web Infrastructure	$771 million	$2.8 billion	142
Wireless	143 million	238 million	41
Portals and Content	484 million	15 billion	155
Consumer E-Commerce	924 million	1.4 billion	108
Business-to-Business E-Commerce	484 million	612 million	140

SOURCE: *Financial Times.* "Softbank Widens Its Net," July 9, 1999, p. 12; *Forbes.* "Master of the Internet," July 5, 1999, pp. 146–151; *Business Week.* "The Last True Believer," January 22, 2001, pp. EB23–28.

A quick look at Softbank's global strategy reveals two areas. First, Softbank is the main Internet and communications company in the world. This was achieved by acquiring some of the strategic Internet brands in the world markets. Second, Softbank plans to get out of the computer publishing business and will start refocusing on the Internet and e-commerce areas. This could be attributed to high growth in the Internet and e-commerce industry. Although risky in nature, this long-term strategic move by Softbank carries an excellent market share and will place it among the top Internet companies in Japan and other markets. Very few Japanese companies have pursued this kind of risky growth strategy in the Internet and e-commerce areas.

GLOBAL OPPORTUNITIES AND PROBLEM AREAS IN 1999

Company Plans and Global Opportunities

Unlike Microsoft, Dell, AOL, Amazon.com, Intel, and other high-tech and e-commerce companies, Softbank has not been able to become a household name in the Western world. Most of its markets and customers are located in Japan and Asian countries. On the other hand, Softbank ranks as a global player in the Internet and e-commerce. In 1999, Softbank's initial investment of $358 million in the Internet and technology-related industry has grown to a value of $10 billion (*Far Eastern Economic Review* 1999). Most of Softbank's visibility lies in Japan where it has changed the traditional Japanese corporate culture. Unlike the American business environment, the Japanese market has only a limited number of venture capital firms. Analysts believe that Japan lags about four to six years behind in the Internet and e-commerce areas. For this reason, Softbank represents one of the few Japanese companies with significant entrepreneurial potential and future growth prospects. Very few Japanese companies are well positioned to capitalize on the changing Internet and e-commerce industry.

Unlike other Japanese Internet and service companies, Softbank has acquired companies that are complementary in nature and may carry good growth potential in the future. Since its inception in 1981, Softbank has become a small conglomerate influential in many high-tech and Internet sectors.

Although Internet and its related industries are still in their infancy in Japan and other developed markets of Asia, Softbank has fully exploited these markets. This is the main reason Softbank captured a significant market share and changed the mainstream Japanese corporate culture. Son's entrepreneurial style made many inroads in the Japanese corporate environment. Son, the main pace setter in the Internet industry, has forced other competitors to follow him. The change process pursued and managed by Softbank represents a classic textbook case study. As Brown and Eisenhardt (1998, pp. 4–5) state with regard to managing the change process:

> At one level, managing change means reacting to it. . . . But managing change also means anticipating it. . . . Finally, at the highest level, managing change is about leading change. By this we mean creating the change to which others must react. It means launching a new market, raising the industry standard of service, redefining customer expectations, or increasing the pace of industry product cycles. It means being ahead of change or even changing the rules of the game. At the extreme, the best performing firms consistently lead change in their industries.

Softbank fits perfectly within the change process stated by Brown and Eisenhardt (1998) by not only becoming the industry leader but also forcing others to make changes.[2]

Many analysts believe that in the coming years, Softbank's markets will grow significantly. In the areas of product development and worldwide brand visibility, Softbank holds a good position to capitalize on its learning curve and knowledge-related areas. Some of Softbank's investments in the Internet companies doubled in the last three years and have brought a massive fortune to Son (see Table 6). Selected companies include Yahoo, Yahoo Japan, E-Trade, Ziff-Davis, ZDNet, and Geo Cities. In June 1999, Softbank announced a joint venture with NASDAQ to initiate the process of setting up the NASDAQ-type stock market in Japan (*Wall Street Journal* 1999b). In September 1999, Softbank announced another strategic alliance with Microsoft

---

[2]For further discussion, see Kim and Mauborgne (1999a–c).

and Global Crossing to provide telecommunications services in the Asian markets. Global crossing will take 93 percent equity in the venture, whereas Softbank and Microsoft each will invest 3.5 percent in the venture. Softbank and Microsoft may increase their stakes to 19 percent (http://www.quicken.com). These recent alliances and ventures show that Softbank plans to go beyond its traditional Japanese market.

Problem Areas and Weaknesses

In the coming years, Softbank may face problems because of the changing Internet and e-commerce industry (see Table 7). Some of the problems include:

1. Unlike Microsoft, Dell, AOL, Amazon.com, and other high-tech companies, Softbank is not a household name in the United States and the Western world. The company is very well known in Japan but has limited influence in other markets.

2. Softbank stayed mostly in Japan and sought its growth through acquisitions. These acquisitions have accumulated debt that may limit future growth if some of its entities go sour.

3. Ziff-Davis, Inc., which publishes *PC Magazine* and *Computer Shopper*, faces problems because of its declining ad revenues, heightened competition, and debt problems. Analysts believe that Ziff-Davis may take some time to recover since the world PC industry now faces lower profits and an invasion of cheaper machines (*Advertising Age* 1998; *Business Week* 1999a; cbs.marketwatch.com/news/current).

4. Softbank is not listed on either the New York Stock Exchange or NASDAQ. This weakens Softbank's ability to attract mutual fund managers and institutional investors from the United States. In addition, this may hamper Softbank's future growth in Japan and Western Europe.

Table 7   Softbank Corporation: Strengths and Weaknesses

Strengths	Weaknesses
One of the largest and most innovative Internet and communications companies in the world	Not a household name in the United States and Western Europe
Has built/acquired 100 plus Internet companies; aims to be the leader in the Internet and e-commerce industry	Some acquisitions have gone sour; some of the future start-ups may also go sour if Softbank expands into unrelated areas
Excellent potential in the areas of software distribution, Web publishing, and computer trade shows	May encounter more competition in the Internet market
Excellent growth through acquisitions	Softbank's shifting focus on its core strategy may create problems in the coming years
Recent joint venture with NASDAQ looks very promising	
First Mover in the Internet and technology-related industry	May not be able to manage its hundreds of alliances and joint ventures because of changing technologies and competition in the e-commerce areas.
Excellent learning curve; knows the Japanese market	
Knows how to expedite the product development process and target new markets	Stock not listed in the United States (NYSE or NASDAQ)
Plans to bring significant changes in Japan's Internet market	East Asian markets somewhat stagnant; may take some years to recover
Masayoshi Son (president/CEO) is U.S. educated; knows the Western system and culture; also has a good vision	A small player in the e-commerce and retailing industry
Good market share in the niche-oriented Internet and communications industry	Ineffective handling of debt and cash flows have created problems

5. The East Asian crisis has affected Softbank's expansion in the Asian markets. Although economic conditions are improving, Softbank may be affected because of currency depreciations in the weaker economies, that is, Indonesia, Thailand, Malaysia, and others.

6. Historically, Softbank has targeted the distribution of software, computer publications, and selected consumer e-commerce areas. It is still a small player in the e-commerce industry because of entry barriers and heightened competition.

7. Softbank plans to enter into Japan's online financial and insurance industry, which is somewhat untapped. Some analysts believe that Softbank may face tough competition because of its unfamiliarity with these sectors. Softbank's strong know-how in the Internet areas may not be replicated in the finance and insurance sectors.

8. The Internet and e-commerce industry at the global level is a complex industry because of regulations and country-specific standards. Softbank may face these hurdles beyond the Japanese market.

9. Since 1996, Softbank's stock has plunged many times because of its massive acquisitions and debt problems. Some analysts are concerned about Softbank's handling of its debt and negative cash flows since Son owns 43 percent of the company (*Fortune* 1997).

10. In the U.S. market, Softbank has devised a new strategy to cope with its new competitors. Some of the smaller companies in the e-commerce industry are perceived to be more successful and profitable.

GLOBAL STRATEGIES AND PROBLEM AREAS IN 2001–2002

Between 1996 and 1999, Softbank was in a strong position to capitalize on its Internet and technology-related acquisitions worldwide. Since the dot.com downturn, the company has encountered difficulties regarding its consumer markets and new tech-nologies. Like other dot.com and Internet companies, Softbank has lost its market value significantly, and the company was ranked 447 by *Financial Times* (2001) among 1,000 companies worldwide. In the coming years, Softbank may face the following problems (see Table 7):

1. As stated earlier, Softbank is not a household name in the United States and Western Europe. The company is well positioned in Japan but carries limited clout in other markets.

2. As of 2001, Softbank had lost its market value by $188 billion and its share price had declined by 94 percent. On the other hand, the company continues to be the first mover in the Internet areas. In 2000–2001, Softbank incurred some of its heaviest losses in ventures such as Webvan, Buy.com, and other consumer-related Net companies. In 2001, Softbank was concentrating on niche/unique segments in the area of wireless and other Internet technologies (*Business Week e-Biz* 2001; *Wall Street Journal* 2001a–c).

3. Compared with other Internet companies, Softbank's financial position remains to be strong for future growth. As of 2001, the company had a $2 billion venture fund and had accumulated $10 billion in unrealized gains because of its early investments in the Internet area. In addition, Softbank maintains $1.6 billion in corporate cash and marketable securities (*Business Week e-Biz* 2001).

4. Softbank's strategy of seeking expansion in the Web infrastructure, portals/content, consumer e-commerce, and B2B commerce may backfire if markets do not recover. As of 2001, the company had a portfolio of over 600 Internet companies worldwide (see Table 3). Softbank's corporate structure resembles a keiretsu network which may not bring lucrative opportunities if markets go down. On the other hand, as a first-mover company, Softbank's diversifica-

tion strategy has been successful. As of 2001, Softbank continued to amass massive fortune by having partial and full ownerships in technology companies worldwide.

5. Like its earlier initiatives, Softbank's future growth strategies are expected to revolve around three information asymmetries: (a) value-chain asymmetry, which may help coordinate the information industry (between suppliers and buyers); (b) financial asymmetry, which may leverage procurement cost differences; and (c) technology asymmetry, which may leverage technological gaps (Lynskey and Yonekura 2001, pp. 10–12).

6. According to Son, in the coming years, Softbank's core competence will rely solely on the Internet sector and will continue to acquire companies from the areas of infrastructure, hardware, content, commerce, and distribution (Lynskey and Yonekura 2001, p. 12).

WHAT LIES AHEAD?

Many analysts see Softbank as a unique Japanese company. Under Son's leadership, the company stands to reap huge rewards if markets do not tumble in 2001–2002. In the short term, Softbank can acquire all the benefits by being the market leader. More acquisitions are expected in the Internet and mobile commerce. Some analysts believe that Softbank plans to consolidate its position in the Internet market. Softbank is also expected to gradually reduce its holdings in the area of media, publications, and software distribution and to concentrate on the consumer and B2B commerce. A huge growth potential is expected in B2B commerce in the Western world. Of course, it may also carry risks because of competition and changing business markets. At the global level, the Internet and its technology-related markets are highly fragmented (*The Economist* 1999; U.S. Department of Commerce 1999). Companies have to be vigilant to capitalize on the changing technologies, growth, and customers. Softbank is well positioned to be part of the growing market. As

Forbes (1999, p. 151) commented regarding Son's future plans:

> Son wants to be number one in eyeball traffic, finance, e-commerce and content—not by controlling a single behemoth like Amazon.com, but by taking sizable stakes in top players in myriad niches.

Softbank's venture capital subsidiary, Softbank Technology Ventures, has established a 40,000-square-foot site in Mountain View, California (*Fortune* 1999), but the dot.com downturn has impacted its growth. This facility is used as a start-up incubator for promising Internet and technology firms (see Table 3). After having a portfolio of 600 Internet companies, Softbank plans to become a major player in every aspect of technology and e-commerce areas. This includes telecommunications, finance and banking, insurance, publishing, distribution, retailing, and other Web-based service products (see Table 3).

In Japan, Softbank has formed a joint venture with NASDAQ. There is a huge potential in the NASDAQ-style market in Japan (see Table 8). According to one estimate, consumer savings and assets are used inefficiently because of the unavailability of U.S.-style individual investors. Softbank's initiative in this segment with NASDAQ is expected to bring big structural changes in the stock markets in Japan if the economy improves in 2001–2002 (*Financial Times* 1999a–c; *Wall Street Journal* 1999b). In addition, Softbank plans to consolidate its position in Japan's on-line industry in virtually every sector—education, e-commerce (business and retailing), retailing, banking, finance, insurance and bond markets, distribution, and broadcasting. In the present circumstances, Softbank is one of the main Internet companies in the world. It will be interesting to see if it can hold its position as the world Internet company or whether it will just be run over by another Softbank-type company. *Business Week* (2001, p. EB23&24) calls Son "the last true believer in the Internet revolution" and states:

> Undaunted by the tech slump, Softbank's Masayoshi Son is thinking bigger than ever; his master plan: to create a cyberconglomerate that will transform the Net into a truly global phenomenon.

Table 8 Softbank Corporation: Potential Growth Areas and Global Internet Markets

A. Future NASDAQ Market in Japan and Breakdown of Consumer Assets (as of Dec. 1997)

Time Deposits	40.5%
Insurance	24.4%
Demand Deposits	8.6%
Securities	7.3%
Trusts	5.9%
Stocks	4.8%
Cash Currency	3.7%
Bonds	2.5%
Investment Trusts	2.3%
Total Assets	*$10.3 trillion (1,230 yen)*

B. Global Internet Access by Regions (as of May 1999)

Canada & United States	97.0 million consumers (56.6%)
Europe	40.1 (23.4)
Asia/Pacific	27.0 (15.8)
Latin America	5.3 (3.1)
Africa	1.1 (0.6)
Middle East	0.9 (0.5)
Total	*171 million*

C. Selected Countries with Internet Access: Home and Work (as of 1998)

United States	37%
Canada	36
Nordics	33
Australia	31
United Kingdom	15
Germany	10
Japan	10
France	8

SOURCES: *Financial Times,* "Electronic Trading to Open up the World to Japan's Investors" (June 16, 1999), p. 20. U.S. Department of Commerce, *The Emerging Digital Economy–II,* Washington, DC: U.S. Deptartment of Commerce, (June, 1999), p. 3.

CASE BIBLIOGRAPHY

Abrahams, Paul and Michiyo Nakamoto. 1999. Heat Turns up on the Rising Star, *Financial Times* (November 13): 16.

Advertising Age. 1998. Softbank Woes Rattle Clients of Web Ad Firms. (March 23): 1&48.

Brown, Shona L. and Kathleen Eisenhardt. 1998. *Competing on the Edge: Strategy as a Structured Chaos.* Boston: Harvard Business School Press.

Business Week. 1996. Cyber-Mogul: To Conquer the Net, Masayoshi Son Takes to the High Wire. (August 12): 56–62.

Business Week. 1999a. Ziff-Davis Is Printing in Red Ink. (January 25): 107.

Business Week. 1999b. Time for This Behemoth to Evolve? (September 20): 48.

Business Week e-Biz. 1999. The E-Biz 25: Masters of the Web Universe. (September 27): 20–56.

Business Week e.Biz. 2001. The Last True Believer. (January 22): EB23–28.

Butler, Steve. 1999. Empire of the Son. *U.S. News & World Report* (July 5): 48–50.

The Economist. 1999. The Real Internet Revolution. (August 21): 53–54.

Far Eastern Economic Review. 1998. Prodigal Son. (January 22): 42–44.

Far Eastern Economic Review. 1999. Japan's Mr. Internet. (July 29): 11–12.

Far Eastern Economic Review. 2000. Internet Warrior on the Defensive. (November 16): 54–60.

Financial Times. 1997a. Softbank Spree Has Investors in a Jitter. (April 23): 21.

Financial Times. 1997b. Softbank Shares Take Further Dive. (October 4/5): 23.

Financial Times. 1997c. Softbank Falls into the Perception Gap. (December 3): 19.

Financial Times. 1999a. Softbank Set for Online Investors. (April 21): 24.

Financial Times. 1999b. Electronic Trading to Open up the World to Japan's Investors, (June 16): 20.

Financial Times. 1999c. Softbank Widens its Net. (July 9): 12.

Financial Times. 2001. Lehman, Softbank Close Web Venture. (April 10): 17.

Financial Times. 2001. Softbank and Yahoo Japan in Broadband Plan. (July 20): 20.

Forbes. 1999. The World's Working Rich. (July 5): 222.

Fortune. 1997. Japan's Top Technology Investor Takes a Hit. (September 8): 150–151.

Fortune. 1999. How Son Captured Japan's Internet Economy. (August 16): 156–160.

Global Crossing. Microsoft. Softbank Announces Asian Network Venture. (September 8, 1999), http://www.quicken.com

Kim, W. Chan and Renee Mauborgne. 1999a. How to Discover the Unknown Market. *Financial Times* (May 6): 12.

Kim, W. Chan and Renee Mauborgne. 1999b. How Southwest Airlines Found a Route to Success, *Financial Times* (May 13): 20.

Kim, W. Chan and Renee Mauborgne. 1999c. From Trend to Quantum Leap. *Financial Times* (June 10): 24.

Lynskey, Michael, and Seiichiro Yonekura. 2001. Softbank: An Internet Keiretsu and Its Leveraging of Information Asymmetries, *European Management Journal* 19(1): 1–15.

Softbank, Tokyo, Japan. September 1999, www.softbank.com

Softbank, Tokyo, Japan. September 2001, www.softbank.com

U.S. Department of Commerce. June 1999. *The Emerging Digital Economy-II.* Washington, DC.: U.S. Department of Commerce.

Wall Street Journal. 1996. Softbank's Buying Spree May Be Hard Act to Follow. (August 19): B4.

Wall Street Journal. 1999a. Softbank Cleans up on the Internet. (February 3): B4.

Wall Street Journal. 1999b. NASDAQ Plans to Set up a New Stock Market in Japan. (June 16): A19&21.

Wall Street Journal. 1999c. Japan's Softbank Unveils New Internet Deals. (June 25): A15&17.

Wall Street Journal. 2001a. Softbank-Cisco Deal Nourishes Alliance. (January 25): A3.

Wall Street Journal. 2001b. Masayoshi Son's Role as Internet Kingpin in Japan is Shrinking. (March 29): A1&A8.

Wall Street Journal. 2001c. Softbank's Corp.'s Net Profit Quadruples, But Web-Stock Plunge Still Poses Problem. (May 29): A19.

Webber, Alan M. 1992. Japanese Style Entrepreneurship: An Interview with Softbank's CEO, Masayoshi Son. *Harvard Business Review* 70(1): 93–103.

Weinberg, Neil. 1999. Master of the Internet, *Forbes* (July 5): 146–151.

Yip, George S. 1992. *Total Global Strategy: Managing for Worldwide Competitive Advantage.* Englewood Cliffs, NJ: Prentice Hall.

Ziff-Davis Rebuts News Corp. Story. (September 13, 1999). cbs.marketwatch.com/news/current.

CASE QUESTIONS

1. What are your views of Softbank's recent Internet-related diversification and its technology-based acquisitions?

2. Analyze and evaluate Softbank's market niche in the Internet and e-commerce industry.

3. What kind of specific global strategies does Softbank need to undertake to be the key player in the Internet and technology-related markets in Japan, North America, and other global markets?

4. What did you learn from Softbank's global diversification initiatives and expansion strategy?

5. Compare and contrast Softbank with other multinationals from Japan and the Western world regarding internationalization, diversification, and global competition issues.

6. Evaluate Softbank's market expansion and global strategies in 2001–2002.

Case 8   DaimlerChrysler AG

The Making of a New Transnational Corporation

Syed Tariq Anwar

INTRODUCTION

On May 7, 1998, the world auto industry received the stunning news from Daimler-Benz and Chrysler Corporation about their plans to merge as one company. The news was particularly interesting since the proposed merger would create the second largest company in the world considering its combined revenues would exceed $150 billion (see Table 1).[1] The transatlantic combination created a unique merger of German and U.S. corporate systems. The merger was also unusual because it was proposed by a German corporation. In the postwar period in Europe, both companies and their governments often discouraged outside mergers so as to fend off uninvited foreign corporations and foreign direct investment (FDI). Regulatory agencies from the European Union (EU) also kept a close watch on European mergers and acquisitions and seldom approved these initiatives. As the *Wall Street Journal* noted with regard to European corporate structures:

> Many of the biggest deals were negotiated in government offices or between scions of the establishment. Interlocking shareholdings shielded management from the sanctions of the market. Size counted more than profits. Hostile takeovers simply weren't done.[2]

The news of the merger sent shock waves to the world automotive sector since DaimlerChrysler would become the second largest company in the global business after General Motors (GM).[3] Since 1997, both Daimler-Benz and Chrysler had actively

looked for merger partners but had had difficulty finding the right auto manufacturer. Though perceived as "an unconventional marriage, the market as well as auto dealers welcomed it."[4] Harbour associates, automotive consultants' commented:

> Clearly the story of the year was the fusion of Daimler-Benz and Chrysler corporation—resulting in the world's fifth-largest producer of vehicles. The announcement sent shock waves through the industry.—Aside from the culture shock, there was also the sentimental fallout. Without question, the Big Three entity is gone forever.[5]

The DaimlerChrysler merger has two unique features. First, in addition to its nonautomotive operations, Daimler-Benz's Mercedes brand ranks as one of the premier luxury brands in the world as well as an early pioneer in the auto industry. Second, in the case of Chrysler, the company's strength lies in its subcompact cars and utility vehicles and is one of the Big Three auto producers in North America. Chrysler's brand portfolio, comprised of mini vans, Jeep Cherokee, and utility vehicles, provides a big source of income for the company.

In the early 1990s, both companies realized that their future global expansion depended on seeking a merger with another auto manufacturer. Both companies sought partners after 1995 and negotiated with companies such as Fiat, Honda, BMW, and Renault. Because of national barriers, branding incompatibilities, and cultural hurdles, no progress was achieved in the negotiations. To analyze strategic issues, circumstances, and synergies that led to the DaimlerChrysler merger, this case reviews both companies' histories and other circumstances that resulted in the making of a transnational corporation. Even though the merger was welcomed by auto analysts and consumers, there were concerns regarding both companies' future growth potential, corporate compatibility and branding issues.

SOURCE: An earlier version of this work was presented at the 2000 Academy of International Business (AIB) National Conference, Phoenix, Arizona (November 17–20, 2000). The discussion in this case is intended to be used as a basis for class discussion rather than to illustrate either effective or ineffective handling of a managerial situation or corporate strategies. Copyright © Syed Tariq Anwar 2001.

Table 1   Chronology of DaimlerChrysler Merger

January 12, 1998:	Jurgen E. Schrempp (Chairman, Daimler-Benz) proposed a possible merger to Robert J. Eaton (Chairman, Chrysler Corp.), while visiting an auto show in Detroit.
February 12–18, 1998:	Both companies' representatives and advisers met to discuss the merger issues and its feasibility.
March 2, 1998:	Both chairmen (Schrempp & Eaton) met in Lausanne, Switzerland, to chalk out future plans.
March–April, 1998:	Working teams from both companies discussed and outlined details of the merger.
April 23–May 6, 1998:	Working teams from both companies finalized the merger agreement and other documentation.
May 6, 1998:	Both companies signed the merger agreement in London, UK.
May 7, 1998:	Merger agreement is announced in the press.
July 23, 1998:	EU's European Commission approved the DaimlerChrysler merger.
July 31, 1998:	U.S.'s Free Trade Commission approved the merger plan.
August 6, 1998:	DaimlerChrysler announced its plans to list its share as "global stock" instead of ADRs.*
September 18, 1998:	Chrysler shareholders approved the merger with 97.5 percent "yes" votes.
September 18, 1998:	Daimler-Benz shareholders approved the merger with 99.9 percent "yes" votes.
November 6, 1998:	To qualify for pooling-of-interests accounting treatment, Chrysler issued 23.5 million shares.
November 9, 1998:	Daimler-Benz receives 98 percent of stock for its exchange offer.
November 17, 1998:	DaimlerChrysler stock started trading on 21 stock exchanges worldwide under symbol *DCX*.

ADR = American Depository Receipts

SOURCE: Adapted in part from DaimlerChrysler, AG. (History/Group Archives & Investor Relations), www.daimlerchrysler.com

BRIEF HISTORY OF DAIMLER-BENZ AND CHRYSLER CORPORATION

Gottlieb Daimler and Karl Benz were the early pioneers of the motor carriage and two-cylinder V engine between 1886 and 1889. Daimler and Benz's early successes in the automotive sector put them in a competitive position. In 1924, Benz and Cie and Daimler-Motoren-Gesellschaft merged and formed one company, thereby starting the Daimler-Benz era. The company established the foundation of an auto manufacturing that would later produce one of the best luxury brands in the world. Daimler-Benz introduced the concept of commercially feasible vehicles and was the first company to commercialize such vehicles. In the early years, the company remained closely linked to the German state.[6] Daimler-Benz saw its operations expanding to hundreds of countries and became the largest conglomerate out of Germany. The company received credit for bringing varied numbers of innovations, technologies, and new models to the world auto market. In the last 50 years, the Mercedes brand has been one of the legions in the automotive history and has captured the attention of millions of people worldwide because of its high quality and performance, as well as its rigid safety standards. In addition to automotive products, Daimler-Benz aggressively diversified its operations in the areas of aerospace, consumer appliances, electronics, locomotives, and IT services. Unlike its U.S., Japanese, and European counterparts, the company sought limited globalization beyond its automotive exports and remained mostly in Europe because of its rigid corporate environment and Germany's business environment. Ewing further explains this phenomenon, which affected many German corporations in the postwar environment:

> Devastated spiritually and physically, many of Germany's big companies became defensive and risk-averse. In postwar Germany, they created webs of cross-holdings and reciprocal board memberships. The incestuous system functioned well during the cold war. But it couldn't cope with the global competition that accelerated after the 1989 fall of the Berlin Wall and, more recently, the introduction of the euro.[7]

In the post–cold war period, the company became more proactive and took many measures to expand overseas. The major reasons for Daimler-Benz's FDI activities worldwide include the emergence of the single European market and the introduction of euro currency, growth in emerging markets, worldwide consumer convergence, and Germany's higher cost structure.[8]

Chrysler Corporation was formed in 1925. Its original parent company was Maxwell Motors Company. Walter P. Chrysler received his early training at Buick Motor Company. Unlike Daimler-Benz, Chrysler targeted mainstream consumers in America. Between 1941 and 1960, Chrysler introduced many new auto models and technologies in the North American market. As the third largest auto producer in North America, Chrysler never gained "pace-setter" status and always followed GM and Ford in product development, designs, and manufacturing technologies. Chrysler often had difficulty positioning itself in the market regarding consumer ratings and quality standards. In the 1970s, the company struggled to maintain its image and was perceived as the number three auto manufacturer in the United States. Later, Chrysler's problems worsened because of the oil crisis, poor quality, and imports from Japan. Consequently, in 1980, after long negotiations with the management, the

U.S. government decided to rescue Chrysler and provided federal loan guarantees. In the next five years, under the leadership of Lee Iacocca, the company made numerous structural changes in its management and product development areas. During the same period, Chrysler introduced many new lines of vehicles and made huge strides in the market. Chrysler's new line of models included K-cars, mini vans, Jeep Cherokee, and other utility and commercial vehicles, which resulted in huge profits for the company. These models represented the main savior for Chrysler and are still in demand.[9]

After 1990, Chrysler vehicles started to get the same respect as GM and Ford's products but overall, the company remained behind GM, Ford, and other manufacturers (Toyota, Honda, Nissan, Volkswagen, etc.) in the areas of new technologies, quality standards, and consumer ratings. Since the industry was becoming global in the form of transplants and major restructuring and consolidations took place in early 1990s, Chrysler started to face the same kind of problems that had engulfed it in the early 1980s. When Daimler-Benz proposed the merger in January 1998, Chrysler's management and its Board could not reject this offer with its multitude of benefits in R&D, manufacturing, technology sharing, and access to the global markets. In the next four months, both parties conducted extensive meetings and negotiations and eventually announced their plan to the media on May 7, 1998.

WHY DID DAIMLER-BENZ AND CHRYSLER CORPORATION MERGE?

The merger of DaimlerChrysler sheds light on an industry which is highly competitive and global in nature and affects almost every part of the national economies. Since 1990, the competition in the industry has increased because of cost cuttings, changing demographics, and joint ventures and alliances between major players. The top eight manufacturers strain under severe pressure to cut costs and increase market share. In the case of DaimlerChrysler, the major motive was joint product development, access to additional markets, and rationalization.[10] The merger brought Daimler-Chrysler's total revenues to $154 billion with a world market share of 7.4 percent. The major factors that contributed to the merger include:

1. Chrysler, a low-cost producer, has built one of the best design and styling departments in the auto industry. Daimler-Benz, on the other hand, is an excellent quality and technology leader in the industry. Historically, Daimler-Benz's development and manufacturing cost have remained high and often lagged behind in bringing new products to the market. Hence, both companies will exchange know-how by pooling their resources. Both companies planned to save $1.2 billion in the coming years.

2. Over these years, Chrysler has established excellent relations with its suppliers and has practiced efficient outsourcing activities. This may help Daimler-Benz in its small-car project and future subcompact models where the company lacks expertise.

3. Daimler-Benz and Chrysler are considered good manufacturers in the diesel technology and will share each others' know-how in the coming years.

4. Daimler-Benz has a very strong dealer network in Europe, Latin America, and North America. Historically, Chrysler's dealer network has remained weak and inadequate in Europe. This is an additional benefit to Chrysler, which never built strong dealerships in Europe. Both companies can use each other's distribution networks in Europe and Latin America.

5. The euro currency and changing corporate environment in the European markets are other contributing factors behind the merger. Cross-border mergers have been on the rise because of Europe's one market, competition, consolidation among the big companies, and availability of corporate bonds and high-yield debt markets.

6. The North American Free Trade Agreement's (NAFTA) rule-of-origin (64 percent) encouraged and forced foreign auto manufacturers to invest in transplants as well as increase their local content in the United States.[11] To Daimler-Benz, merging with another auto producer was a good strategy to comply with the forthcoming NAFTA rules. Besides this, in the 1990s, Daimler-Benz had started manufacturing its M-series in Tuscaloosa (Alabama) for the North Americam market. Merging with Chrysler made sense and complemented its growing operations and future growth in North America.

7. In the early 1980s, Daimler-Benz progressed nicely and had increased its revenues from core businesses (automotive and vehicles). In 1985, the company's profits had increased by 52 percent to $577 million. In 1986, events started to take a different turn, and the company encountered major problems in its divisions, which included aerospace, computers, and household appliances.[12] In the coming years, the company laid off thousands of workers, and its profit fell by 30 percent.[13] In the 1990s, Daimler-Benz recovered by unloading its unprofitable noncore operations and eventually put its house in order. Further growth and diversification demanded a merger especially from North America because of the NAFTA and healthy business conditions in the European markets.

8. In the cold war era, Daimler-Benz realized that it was critical to globalize not only by shipping products overseas but also by seeking foreign direct investment (FDI) beyond the German market. To establish manufacturing operations, companies spend millions of dollars and must allocate other resources. For this reason, mergers and alliances have become popular in the auto industry. For these reasons, both companies favored a merger since it carried better future prospects.

9. The core products of both companies are in the automotive sectors. Daimler-Benz earns 80 percent of the revenues from cars and commercial vehicles. Chrysler even earns more than this from its automotive sector. The new company's brand portfolio synergy looks bright in the long term after the reorganization. This will help in the development of low-cost and subcompact vehicles where the partners could use common manufacturing platforms.

10. Finally, except in a few segments, the companies have minimum overlap in their brand portfolios. Both companies have complementary technologies in the high-end and low-end segments. Daimler-Benz leads in luxury cars and commercial vehicles, whereas Chrysler's new line of brands continues making good inroads into the low-end market.

DAIMLERCHRYSLER'S NEW ORGANIZATIONAL STRUCTURE

After the merger, DaimlerChrysler management designed an organizational structure that aimed at combining two different business systems and sought a truly transnational corporation. The new management faced the challenge as to how best to combine Daimler-Benz's highly organized and rigid management structure with Chrysler's American management practices. In the making of a new organizational structure, both managements particularly took into consideration the brand portfolios, global markets, and future reorganization. The major goal was to blend an organizational structure that was based on smooth transition and harmony among management. DaimlerChrysler's new mission statement was as follows:

Our mission is to integrate two great companies to become a world enterprise that by 2001 is the most successful and respected automotive and transportation products and service provider. We will accomplish this by constantly delighting our customers with the quality and innovation of our products and services, resulting from the excellence of our processes, our people, and our unique portfolio of strong brands.[14]

Table 2 Daimler-Benz and Chrysler Corporation: Pre-Merger Financial and Corporate Data (1997)

A. Financial Data	Daimler-Benz	Chrysler
Revenues	$71.5 billion	$61.1 billion
Profit	4.6 billion	2.8 billion
Assets	76.1 billion	60.4 billion
Stockholders' Equity:	19.5 billion	11.3 billion
Market Capitalization	86.8 billion	35.9 billion
Fortune Global 500 Rank in 1998	17	25

B. Corporate Data	Daimler-Benz	Chrysler
Head Office	Stuttgart, Germany	Auburn Hills, Michigan
Employees Worldwide:	300,000	121,000
Unit Sales:	1.1 million	2.9 million
Business Units	Cars, Heavy Trucks, Finance, Information Services, Rail, Aerospace, Marine, Equipment	Cars, Light Trucks, Auto Finance
Top Selling Brands/Products in 1998	■ E-Class Sedans and Wagons (38,727 units) ■ M-Class Sport Utilities (35,970 units) ■ C-Class Sedans (29,550 units)	■ Dodge, Plymouth Minivans (443,378 units) ■ Dodge Ram Pickup Trucks (341,765 units) ■ Jeep Grand Cherokee Utilities (185,299 units)

SOURCES: "In High-Tech War Rooms, Giant is Born," *Wall Street Journal,* (November 13, 1998): B1.; "The Fortune Global 500," *Fortune.* (August 3, 1998): F1. The Business Week Global 1000, *Business Week.* (July 13, 1998): 54–87.

The company's six goals reflected its future plans, which were strongly embedded in its ambitions to be one of the key global players in the industry. The goals stated: "Delighted customers, unique portfolio, integrated enterprise, superior profitability, sustained growth, and globalization."[15]

In the first 12 to 18 months, DaimlerChrysler was managed like an alliance in which both companies shared responsibilities and control out of Stuttgart and Auburn Hills. The plans were to make many changes to implement its reorganiza-

tion plan and brand portfolios (see Tables 2, 3, 4, and 5).[16] Both companies wanted to tap into each other's corporate knowledge, market know-how, and R&D activities in Germany and North America. DaimlerChrysler's new supervisory board includes 20 members from DaimlerChrysler's labor union and outside experts. The Board of Management included both chairmen and 12 other senior managers from the company. The shareholders' committee and chairman's integration council were formed to deal with post-merger

Table 3   DaimlerChrysler: Post-Merger Data and Action Plans (1999–2001)

A. Post-Merger Financial Data (1999)

Revenues	$154.6 billion
Profit	5.6 billion
Assets	159.7 billion
Stockholders' Equity:	35.6 billion
Employees	441,502
Shares Outstanding	1 billion

B. Corporate Data

Group Headquarters: Stuttgart, Germany, and Auburn Hills, Michigan, USA.*

Fortune Global 500 rank in 1999	2
Percentage of world's car and truck sales:	7.4 %
Total number of countries selling	200

Manufacturing plants in 34 countries.

Global Brands: Mercedes-Benz, Chrysler, Plymouth, Jeep, Dodge, Smart, Freightliner, Sterling, Setra, Airbus, Eurocopter, Ariane, debis, Adtranz, MTU, TEMIC, and others.

Stock/Stockholder Information: Stock Information: DCX; trading on 21 stock exchanges worldwide (Germany: 8, USA: 4, Austria: 1, Canada: 2, France: 1, Great Britain: 1, Japan: 1, Switzerland: 3); *Location of Stockholders*: Europe—65%, USA—26%, Other—9%; Ownership Structure: 3 main Stockholders—22%, Institutional Investors—17,000 (54%), Retail Investors—24%.

C. Targets and Action Plans for 1999–2001

1999–2000

- Total savings from reorganization and restructuring: $1.4 billion
- Joint procurement, outsourcing, sharing of technologies, and R&D activities
- New brand positioning, implementation of quality standards, worldwide sharing of resources
- Two chairmen in 1999–2000 (*Jurgen Schrempp & Bob Eaton*) 2001 & Beyond
- Reorganization at the top level after 2001
- One Chairman after 2001 (*Jurgen Schrempp*)
- Joint Global R&D and manufacturing activities
- Better cost and quality standards

Note: After 2001, DaimlerChrysler headquarter will move to Stuttgart.
SOURCES: "The Auto Barron," *Business Week* (November 16, 1998); 82–90; Marjorie Sorge and Mark Phelan, "The Deal of the Century," *Automotive Industries* (June 1998): 46–69; "The *Fortune* Global 500," *Fortune* (August 2, 1999): 144–146, F1–F24; DaimlerChrysler, AG (company at a glance) www.daimlerchrysler.com

Table 4   DaimlerChrysler: Products, Businesses and
Manufacturing Facilities (as of December 1999)

Daimler-Benz
Mercedes-Benz Models: A-Class, C-Class, E-Class,
S-Class, SL, M-Class, G-Class, CLK, SLK.

Production Facilities (Germany): Germany (Sindelfingen,
Unterturkheim, Bremen, Berlin, Hamburg, Rastatt)

Production Facilities (other countries): Mercedes-Benz
do Brasil SA, Juiz de Fora; Mercedes-Benz U.S.
International inc., Tuscaloosa, Alabama; Micro Compact
Car smart Gmbh, Renningen smart-Plant, Hambach,
France.

Chrysler
Chrysler Models: Neon, Breeze, Cirrus, Stratus, Intrepid,
Concorde, LHS/300M, Ram Pickup, Durango, Dakota,
Ram Van/Wagon; Jeep: Grand Cherokee, Cherokee,
Wrangler, USA, Canada, Mexico, Europe; Dodge: Viper,
Avenger, Caravan, smart.

Production Facilities (USA): Belvidere, IL, Dayton, OH,
Detroit, MI, Fenton, MI, Huntsville, AL, Indianapolis, IN,
Kenosha, WI, Kokomo, IN, New Castle, IN, Newark, DL,
Sterling Heights, MI, Toledo, OH, Trenton, MI, Twinsburg,
OH, Warren, MI.

Production Facilities (other countries): Graz, Austria,
Bramaelea, Canada, Windsor, Canada, Saltillo, Mexico,
Toluca, Mexico.

Commercial Vehicles
Major Brands: Mercedes-Benz, Freightliner, Sterling, Setra.

Products: Compact Vans, Delivery Vehicles, Semitrailer
Rigs, Coaches, Buses.

Commercial Vehicles (cont.)
Production Facilities: Germany (Mannheim, Worth,
Gaggenau, Dusseldorf, Kassel, Ludwigsfelde, Ulm).

Other Countries: Freightliner Corp, Portland, Cleveland,
St. Thomas, Canada, Mercedes-Benz, Mexico, Mercedes-
Benz do Brasil, Mercedes-Benz Argentina, Mercedes-Benz
of South Africa, Mercedes-Benz Espana, Mercedes-Benz
Istanbul, Turkey, Davutpasa DMM/SMI/SEI, Indonesia.

Aerospace
DaimlerChrysler Aerospace (DASA) is divided into 8
divisions: Commercial Aircraft, Helicopters, Military
Aircraft, Space Infrastructure, Satellites, Defense & Civil
Systems, & Aeroengines.

Debis AG—DaimlerChrysler Services
Financial Services, IT Services & Telecom Services

Chrysler Financial
Subsidiaries: Chrysler Insurance Co., Chrysler Realty
Corp., Chrysler Credit Canada Ltd., Chrysler Capital
Corp.

Rail System
Adtranz: Adtranz is one of the leading suppliers of rail
systems worldwide.

Automotive Electronics
Huntsville Electronics Plant in Alabama; TEMIC.

Diesel Engines
MTU Diesel Engines

SOURCE: DaimlerChrysler, AG (The Businesses of DaimlerChrysler), www.daimlerchrysler.com.

policy matters and other changes. The new organizational structure particularly took into consideration the transition phase and appointed two cochairmen, Jurgen Schrempp from Daimler-Benz and Robert E. Eaton from Chrysler. The president of Chrysler cars and trucks and integration reported to Schrempp and Eaton. Under the president, there were 14 executive vice presidents (EVPs) representing various divisions. (For a complete list of EVPs, see Table 6.)

As one of the largest corporations in the world, DaimlerChrysler maintains a multitude of divisions and a wide array of product lines. The organizational structure paid special attention to both companies' brand portfolio values as well as overseas operations. As stated earlier, since DaimlerChrysler continues its evolution into a major transnational corporation, international and global markets will determine its future organizational structure growth opportunities.

Table 5 Daimler-Benz and Chrysler Corporation: Strengths and Weaknesses before 1998's Merger

Daimler-Benz AG

- Daimler-Benz is Germany's largest conglomerate.
- Well diversified and owns one of the best luxury auto brands.
- Excellent quality reputation and brand visibility; brand loyalty is very high in selected segments.
- Excellent distribution network in Europe.
- One of the largest truck manufacturers in the world.
- Excellent research and development and application of new technologies.
- First mover in many new innovations and safety standards.

Chrysler Corporation

- Third largest auto manufacturer in North America.
- Low development cost in selected segments.
- Excellent distribution network in North America.
- Excellent market share in selected segments, i.e., mini vans, utility vehicles, and utility trucks.
- Maintains one of the best designs facilities.
- Strong contender in low-priced subcompact vehicles.
- Chrysler was the first mover in many technology areas; introduced many innovations in the market.
- Most of the manufacturing is done in the United States, Canada, and Mexico.

Daimler-Benz, AG

- Some acquisitions made in the 1980s did not create synergy and later distracted the company from its core business.
- The company could not manage its noncore (nonauto activities) operations effectively.
- Deutsche Bank is the largest shareholder.
- Daimler-Benz's corporate structure was perceived to be rigid and bureaucratic.
- The board's structure and corporate activities were affected by the rigid German corporate/governance model, which in some areas hindered new innovations and growth opportunities.
- In the 1980s and 1990s, the company's overseas sales suffered form overvalued German Mark.
- Slow in responding to globalization opportunities; 1990s restructuring cost the company 30,000 jobs and loss of revenues.
- Some auto models are overpriced and are unappealing to consumers.
- Manufactures very few models in the subcompact segments.
- Diversification in the areas on noncore segments resulted in problems in early 1990s.
- Difficulty dealing with cost-cutting and reorganization because of rigid German corporate system and labor laws.

Chrysler Corporation

- Chrysler was always perceived to be "the number three" auto manufacturer in the United States.
- Between 1975 and 1980, Chrysler vehicles faced quality problems and tough competition from Japan.
- Consumer satisfaction with Chrysler vehicles always remained low; always trailing behind GM and Ford.
- Oil crisis of 1970s hurt the company badly.
- In the 1970s and early 1980s, Chrysler had limited brand portfolio; slow product development and unappealing designs.
- Chrysler brands were perceived to be out-of-fashion and unappealing to consumers in the early 1990s.
- In the 1970s, the company's strategy was weak and unfocused.
- The company reputation suffered from high cost, production problems and low consumer satisfaction ratings.

Table 6 DaimlerChrysler: Post-Merger Organization Structure

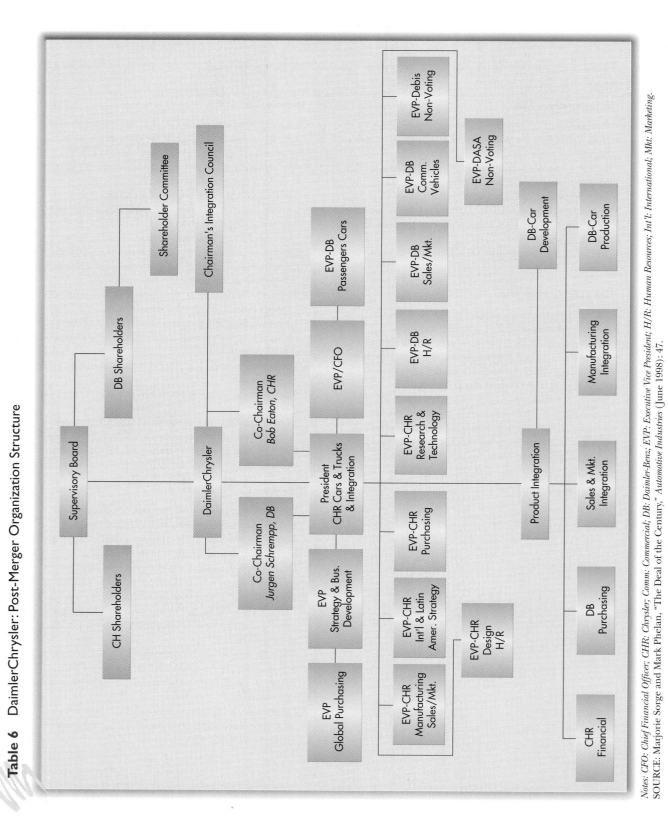

Notes: CFO: Chief Financial Officer; CHR: Chrysler; Comm: Commercial; DB: Daimler-Benz; EVP: Executive Vice President; H/R: Human Resources; Int'l: International; Mkt: Marketing.
SOURCE: Marjorie Sorge and Mark Phelan, "The Deal of the Century," Automotive Industries (June 1998): 47.

PRE-MERGER ISSUES AND OPERATIONS

Pre-Merger Strengths, Weaknesses, and Problem Areas

In the 15 years before the merger, Daimler-Benz had grown into the largest industrial corporation in Germany. The company has frequently diversified beyond its nonauto sectors. In 1998, revenues reached $71.5 billion and made a net profit of $4.6 billion. In the same year, the Daimler-Benz ranked seventeenth on the Global *Fortune* 500 company list and employed 300,000 workers worldwide (see Table 5). The company manufactured products in the areas of automotive sectors, aerospace, consumer electronics, and IT services. The company owned one of the premier luxury auto brands (Mercedes-Benz) in the world and maintained one of the best distribution systems in Europe. Its automotive products were rated among the best quality brands for their safety and customer satisfaction. In commercial vehicles, it was the largest truck manufacturer in the world. In the area of aerospace, Daimler-Benz's DASA is a major player in Europe. With regard to Daimler-Benz's weaknesses, the company lagged behind in global expansion because of Germany's inward corporate structure and cross-shareholdings. After 1990, the company undertook various FDI initiatives to internationalize operations as well as change its corporate culture.

DaimlerChrysler made changes in its accounting practices, which helped the company in listing its stock on the New York Stock Exchange (NYSE).[17] In the product development area, the company is considered conservative in its styling and product features. Daimler lagged regarding responding to Japanese competition in luxury brands. Mercedes-Benz models were considered overpriced and conservative in designs and new technologies.[18] In the late 1980s, Daimler-Benz could not handle its non-core diversifications, especially in the aerospace areas. In the early 1990s, the company was slow to respond to the globalization opportunities and had suffered from its transparency and cross-shareholdings. Unlike its American and Japanese counterparts, Daimler-Benz had to deal with Germany's tougher labor laws, corporate governance, and co-determination issues. Historically, in the last 40 years, Germany's labor unions had become powerful in the areas of wages and worker benefits.

Consequently, German companies responded by investing abroad to deal with rising cost and other labor problems.[19]

Chrysler, on the other hand, was one of the Big Three auto manufacturers in North America. In 1998, Chrysler's revenues reached $61.1 billion and made a net profit of $2.8 billion with a market capitalization of $35.9 billion (see Table 2). In the same year, Chrysler placed twenty-fifth on the Global *Fortune* 500 company list. The company employed 121,000 workers worldwide. Right from its inception, Chrysler produced cars for the masses, and its strength lay in the subcompact cars, mini vans, and utility trucks in North America. Historically, Chrysler had held a strong contender position in the low-end auto market. After recovering from the 1980s crisis, the company introduced a new line of vehicles which included mini vans, the Jeep Cherokee, and the Viper sports car. This shift in branding strategy brought the company good credibility from the consumers. After 1950, Chrysler often established itself as the first mover in many technological advances and innovations but remained behind the market leaders. Chrysler's problems stemmed from poor image and low quality. After the oil crisis, the company continued to manufacture cars with shoddy quality and poor industry ratings. For these reasons, the company frequently ran into financial trouble and had difficulty finding its niche in the market. Even today, Chrysler's cars suffer from quality ratings, and the company is ranked third among the North American auto manufacturers.

Pre-Merger Strategic Alliances and Joint Ventures

As stated earlier, strategic alliances and joint ventures have gained popularity among the auto manufacturers because of cost and global competitive pressures. In the auto industry, hundreds of linkups and alliances have formed all over the world. These cooperative arrangements are in every sector of the industry.[20] Some of the cooperative arrangements are used for market entry and distribution networks. Others aim at creating joint R&D and manufacturing for benchmark competitors and future survival. For example, since the early 1980s, GM and Toyota's joint venture, the New United Motors Manufacturing Industries (NUMMI), has produced thousands of cars and is rated as one of the most successful auto cooperation ventures in North America. The venture has brought a multitude of benefits to GM and Toyota in the areas of technology sharing, distribution, and market access.[21]

Before the merger, Daimler-Benz and Chrysler had created several alliances and joint ventures with other manufacturers (see Table 7). Since the merger, the majority of the alliances and joint ventures formed by both companies have remained active. Daimler-Benz linked up with companies such as Ford, Ballard Power System, Ssangyong, Steyr-Daimler-Puch, Telco, and Volkswagen. In addition, Daimler owns Freightliner, which manufactures commercial vehicles. Chrysler's pre-merger alliances and cooperative agreements included Beijing Automobile Works, BMW, Honda, Peugeot, Renault,

Table 7 Daimler-Benz and Chrysler Corporation's Strategic Alliances and Joint Ventures before 1998 Merger

Daimler-Benz, AG	Chrysler Corp.
• Ford/Ballard Power Systems: Daimler, Ford, and Ballard have a venture to develop fuel cells, which will be used in fuel cell vehicles by 2004. Status in 1999; Active	• Beijing Automobile Works: Chrysler owns 42 percent ownership in Beijing Automobile Works and manufactures Beijing Jeep. Status in 1999: Active.
• Freightliner: Daimler owns Freightliner. Status in 1999: Active	• BMW: Chrysler maintains a joint venture with BMW in Brazil to build 1.4L and 1.6L 4-cylinder gasoline engines. Status in 1999: Active.
• Mitsubishi: Status in 1999: Mitsubishi's joint venture with Daimler has been terminated.	• Honda: Honda distributed Jeep Cherokee in Japan. Status in 1999: Affiliation discontinued in September 1999; Chrysler will start marketing the Jeep in Japan.
• Ssangyong: Daimler-Benz owns 5 percent of Ssangyong; Ssangyong will start manufacturing diesel engines, commercial vehicles, and Mercedes under license by using the Mercedes' W124 platform. Status in 1999: Active.	• Maserati: Status in 1999: Chrysler sold it ownership in Maserati.
• Russia—Ulyanovsk Automotive Plant (UAZ): As of 1999, Mercedes-Benz and UAZ were negotiating to form a joint venture to produce engines and sport/utility vehicles in Russia.	• Mitsubishi: Status in 1999: Chrysler does not own any stock in Mitsubishi, but maintains sourcing relationship in the area of components.
• Steyr-Daimler-Puch: Mercedes and Steyr-Daimler-Puch jointly manufacture G-Wagen. Status in 1999: Active.	• Peugeot: Chrysler owns 49 percent ownership in Arab America Vehicles Limited, Cairo, Egypt. Peugeot plans on manufacturing its 405 model at this plant. Status in 1999: Active.
• Tata Engineering & Locomotive Ltd. (Telco): Mercedes-Benz owns 76 percent of Telco, India. Status in 1999: Active.	• Renault/Volvo/Swedish Motors: Chrysler owns 30 percent of Thai Chrysler which builds Jeep Cherokee. Rest of the ownership (70 percent) is owned by Swedish Motors which in turn is owned by Renault (20 percent) and Volvo (56 percent). Status in 1999: Active.
• Volkswagen: Damiler-Benz and VW each maintain 50 percent ownership in VW-Daug. Status in 1999: Active.	• Steyr-Daimler-Puch: Chrysler and Steyr-Daimler-Puch's joint venture build minivans in Graz, Austria; also produces Jeep Cherokee. Status in 1999: Active.

SOURCES: "Global Joint Ventures and Affiliations for 1998," *Automotive Industries* (February 1998): 16–22. "Global Joint Ventures and Affiliations for 1999," *Automotive Industries*. (February 1999): 18–22.

Volvo, Swedish Motors, and Steyr-Daimler-Puch. Both companies had a cooperative relationship with Steyr-Daimler-Puch before the merger. In the area of developing electric cars and a new generation of fuel cells, DaimlerChrysler has teamed with Ford and Ballard Power System. In the area of e-commerce and business-to-business relationships, both companies are expected to join other auto manufacturers and portal companies in implementing this strategy.[22,23]

GLOBAL OPPORTUNITIES AND PROBLEM AREAS

Competition in the World Auto Industry

In today's world, the strategic importance of the world auto industry is widely recognized. The industry impacts almost every sector of national economies.[24] Competition in the industry is intense and often turns into trade rivalries (see Table 8).[25] In some regions, the competitive environment is further complicated by national subsidies that lead to trade friction among the developed economies. In the last 15 years, U.S. and Japanese governments have argued over trade barriers, market share issues, and tariff and nontariff barriers. In extreme cases, the industry has caused trade wars between the United States and Japan.[26] The industry is so closely linked to their national economies that countries suffer in cases of plant closings and bankruptcies. Chrysler's rescue by the U.S. government was largely motivated by national politics and pressure from the labor unions. The stakes were so high that the Carter administration ended up providing the federal loan guarantees to the company.[27]

From the consumer side, the industry has changed significantly as well. For example, consumers in North America and other developed countries are well informed regarding prices, technical information, and quality ratings. To launch a successful global model requires $500 million to $1 billion. The Internet and other media have played an important role in educating consumers. This has forced the auto producers to change some of their traditional selling and distribution methods. Besides this, on-line selling brings additional opportunities to auto companies as well as consumers. In manufacturing, the auto industry is highly interdependent and global in nature. To

launch a successful global model, it takes about $500 million to $1 billion from the lab to the dealership. In the United States, the industry product life cycle is about eight to ten years. Based on intracompany trade and sourcing strategies, vehicles are assembled with parts from all over the world. The fierce competitive pressures for cost reduction, application of new technologies, and cooperative ventures are mandated to compete and survive in the industry. Competition is no longer restricted to Europe or North America. Other markets such as Asia, Eastern Europe, Latin America, and Africa have altered the profile of the industry. In order to compete effectively, more and more auto manufacturers seek mergers and collaborative arrangements. In the coming years, this activity is expected to intensify among the first eight manufacturers. GM, Ford, Toyota, DaimlerChrysler, Honda, and Volkswagen have been actively expanding and consolidating their worldwide operations in the forms of transplants and joint ventures.

Future Reorganization and Problem Areas

Since its merger, DaimlerChrysler has actively reorganized its worldwide operations, product lines, and management structure. As stated earlier, major motives behind these changes are attributed to cost containment, sharing of resources, and future expansion. Management's recent announcements reveal its intentions to seek diversification in Asia by buying local companies. In the long term, DaimlerChrysler can expect to gain significant benefits from the merger, although problems to date have hindered its implementation process. The merged company faces the following problems:

1. Unlike Chrysler, Daimler-Benz is not a household name in the subcompact market. It may take many years to launch new models unless the company makes a few acquisitions in Asia and Europe.
2. Daimler-Benz has limited globalization in its manufacturing (passenger cars) and assembly operations.
3. Daimler-Benz is viewed as a rigid company in terms of its bureaucracy, rules, and product development process. Chrysler is regarded as a pragmatic

Table 8 DaimlerChrysler and Selected Competitors: Strengths and Weaknesses
(as of December 1999)

Daimler-Chrysler	GM	Ford	Volkswagen	Toyota	Honda
World Market Share: 7.4% Sales: $154.6 bill.	World Market Share: 16.2% Sales: $161.3 bill.	World Market Share: 12.9% Sales: $144.4 bill.	World Market Share: 7.9% Sales: $76.3 bill.	World Market Share: 9% Sales: $99.7 bill.	World Market Share: 4% Sales: $48.7 bill.
Strengths: • Second largest corporation in the world; able to reach many markets worldwide in luxury and subcompact segments. • Combined resources could produce excellent synergy. • Good distribution; conglomerate status. *Weaknesses:* • Will have to deal with two corporate cultures (American and German) in its structures. • Compatibility in branding may create problems; Chrysler brands may hurt the Mercedes name. • May suffer from the German governance structure and cross-shareholdings.	*Strengths:* • Largest corporation in the world. • Major player in global markets; largest exports of vehicles from the United States. • Good expansion in emerging markets. • Good distribution system worldwide; sells many brands. *Weaknesses:* • Slow to change, very big organization with massive bureaucratic structure. • May not be cost effective in product development. • Brand Portfolio is too diverse.	*Strengths:* • Third largest corporation in the world. • Efficient manufacturer; good global sourcing and economies of scale. • Good brand portfolio and visibility • Good manufacturing and quality rating. • Consumer ratings are better. *Weaknesses:* • The "world car" strategy has not been materialized. • Distribution system is weak in some markets. • Losing market share in the North American subcompact segments.	*Strengths:* • Good brand recognition worldwide. • Strong presence in the European markets. • Good distribution network in Europe *Weaknesses:* • Not a strong contender in North America especially in the subcompact market. • Limited product offerings and brand portfolio. *Weaknesses:* • Sales and marketing areas are weak. • Limited diversification from its core business. • Weak in sales and marketing; limited exposure in some markets.	*Strengths:* • Third largest auto manufacturer in the world. • Excellent manufacturing plants worldwide. • Maintains excellent benchmarking standards in its production. • Toyota products get excellent quality ratings worldwide. • Low-cost manufacturer; good overseas expansion plans in the pipeline. *Weaknesses:* • Rigid corporate culture. • Product designs are somewhat unappealing. • Limited market share in the European markets.	*Strengths:* • Strong contender in the subcompact markets. • Excellent quality standards in manufacturing. • Very strong North America; Asia. • Low-cost producer; good economies of scale. • Rapidly expanding worldwide. *Weaknesses:* • Limited presence in Europe and Latin America. • Limited product portfolio in global branding. • Limited diversification from its core business.

SOURCE: Harbour & Associates, Inc., *The Harbour Report 1999: North America* (Troy, Mich.: Harbour & Associates, 1999). "Here Comes the Road Test," *Time.* (May 18, 1998): 66–69; "The Fortune Global 500," *Fortune* (August 2, 1999).

company and considered a leader in minority issues. Daimler-Benz lacks exposure to the American way of management. This mismatch of corporate culture has created problems in the areas of expatriate management, salaries, and other labor relations.[28]

4. Both companies will have difficulty creating a "joint vision" and collective strategies regarding global expansion and acquisitions. Since DaimlerChrysler is now a transnational company dealing with two countries and two national cultures, problems may emerge among the top management in the areas of long-term planning, control, and branding issues.[29] Since Chrysler itself was an independent organization before the merger, American managers dislike Daimler-Benz's control and majority ownership.[30] On Germany's unique corporate governance structure, the *Economist* commented: "The fall from grace of Europe's largest manufacturing firm is an object lesson in the problems created when managers rather than shareholders are in charge."[31]

5. DaimlerChrysler management has limited exposure regarding Daimler-Benz's nonauto operations, creating problems in joint planning and future plans.[32]

6. More and more auto manufacturers seek the Internet to target the markets as well as business-to-business (BtoB) commerce. DaimlerChrysler lags behind in the B2B area. Unlike GM, Ford, Toyota, and Honda, DaimlerChrysler has not announced its plans to go on-line. Toyota has even considered taking customer orders on-line to manufacture custom-built vehicles in five days versus the industry's present standard of 60 days.[33]

7. Chrysler's low-end brands may hurt and cannibalize Mercedes-Benz's high-end products. In some segments, both companies may have difficulty developing a well-defined synergy in their brand portfolio unless a unified small-car strategy is formulated.[34]

8. Neither company has announced any plans regarding sharing their common manufacturing platforms and supplier networks.

9. Analysts believe that the new company suffers from its identity problems, and consumers still identify both companies as separate entities.[35] This will continue to be a major challenge to DaimlerChrysler.

10. Predictably, competition in the global auto industry will intensify because of overcapacity, consolidations, and changing demographics. At present, average auto plant utilization in the world stands at 69 percent versus 1990's 80 percent. This has impacted profits and expansion.[36] DaimlerChrysler will have to devise a new strategy to cope with this situation in the subcompact markets of Asia, Europe, and Latin America. Major competitors such as GM, Ford, Toyota, and Honda are better positioned in the world subcompact market because of their brand portfolio and linkages.

WHAT LIES AHEAD?

In the presence of the growing global economy and changing competition, DaimlerChrysler may seek additional diversifications in the auto and nonauto areas in Asia and Latin America for future consolidation.[37] In the last few years, both companies have faced significant pressure from the stockholders to come up with a new game plan for the twenty-first century. DaimlerChrysler's merger reflects its intentions to become one of the largest global companies in the world. DaimlerChrysler's business plan states:

> DaimlerChrysler is ideally positioned to emerge as the world's leading automotive, transportation, and services company—shaping the future of its industries.[38]

DaimlerChrysler as a company intends to be a global player in world business. The company plans to compete in every part of the world and eventually may capture the status of a superfirm. On the subjects of changing markets, the rise of superfirms, and DaimlerChrysler's merger, the *New York Times* suggested the following: "Superfirms take over in global age.—Latest mergers show how industries are consolidating down to a few mammoth firms to compete in world economy."[39]

As stated earlier, DaimlerChrysler will continue to face problems in its corporate structure because of cultural barriers and management shakeups. German companies in the postwar period developed a very peculiar style of corporate system that relied on cross-shareholdings and a network type of relationships. Unlike American multinationals, German companies turned inward and had limited global expansion. Only in the late 1980s did Germany's large companies and groups start to expand overseas and realize the benefits of direct FDI and transplants.

DaimlerChrysler is a unique transnational company because of the merger of two distinct business systems and the combination of luxury and subcompact brands. While the merger has hit major problems in the early years, a growth potential remains available in selected markets of the emerging markets of Asia, Latin America, and Europe.

POSTSCRIPT

Since the merger, DaimlerChrysler has not performed well and its profitability and market share continues to decline worldwide. In 2000, Chrysler's operating profit declined by 90 percent ($500 million) whereas during the same period, Daimler's profit declined by 49 percent ($4.9 billion).[40] According to industry analysts, the merger has not brought any windfall gains for either company. The logic behind the cross-border merger was to bring significant savings in the areas of production, manufacturing and supplier network, which has not happened yet. Cross-border mergers are very difficult with which to be successful because of differences in corporate cultures, regulatory barriers, and labor issues. It is very difficult to merge two cultures into one company.[41] The *Wall Street Journal* commented:

> DaimlerChrysler turnaround seems to be going in reverse; Stephen Reitman, an analyst at Merrill Lynch, believes the discount war, on top of Chrysler's already-reduced prices, are likely to push Chrysler to an operating loss of about three billion euros ($2.74 billion) for 2001.[42]

In the area of customer incentives, DaimlerChrysler spends $2,394 per vehicle to attract new car buyers which is the highest in the industry. To turn around U.S. operations, Daimler appointed a new CEO (Dieter Zetsche) of Chrysler Group in 2001, who plans on fixing the company in the areas of manufacturing, labor, and dealer network.[43] In the post-merger period, DaimlerChrysler management was reluctant to bring changes in the areas of production/manufacturing, components sharing, and its supplier network.[44] The company plans for 2001/2002 were to cut its workforce by 20 percent (35,000), close six plants in North and South America, and reduce its production by 20 percent.[45] In the coming years, the company will have difficulty integrating its worldwide operations. According to analysts, the turnaround may not be possible in 2002 because of the recessionary environment in North America, Europe and Asia. In addition, outlook in the global auto industry is somewhat stagnant and may not see significant recovery for 2002.[46]

ENDNOTES

1. For details, see *Wall Street Journal*, 1998. Eaton: DaimlerChrysler Will Be Transnational (August 31): B8. Also see: Sorge Marjorie, Sorge and Mark Phelan. 1998, "The Deal of the Century," *Automotive Industries* (June): 46–69; *Wall Street Journal*, 1998, "There Are No German or U.S. Companies, Only Successful Ones" (May 7): A1&11; *The New York Times*. 1998c. "Capitalism Victorious (Thanks, Everyone)" (May 10): B1&8; *The New York Times*. 1998c. "Capitalism Victorious (Thanks, Everyone)" (May 10): B1&8; Kogut, Bruce. 1999. What Makes a Global Company? *Harvard Business Review* (January/February): 165–170.

2. *Wall Street Journal*. 1999. "Europe Marks a Year of Serious Flirtation with the Free Markets" (December 30): A1.

3. *The New York Times*. 1998a. Daimler-Benz Will Acquire Chrysler in $36 Billion Deal that will Reshape Industry, (May 7), pp. 1&C4; *The Economist* 1998. A New Kind of Car Company, (May 9): 61–62; *Wall Street Journal*. 1998b. Chrysler Might Merge with

Daimler-Benz—or be Taken Over, (May 6): A1&8.

4. Harbour & Associates, Inc. 1999. *The Harbour Report 1999: North America.* Troy, Michigan: Harbour & Associates, Inc., p. 3. *Wall Street Journal.* 1998. Chrysler Approves Deal with Daimler-Benz; Big Questions Remains, (May 7): A1&1.

5. Harbour & Associates, Inc. 1999. *The Harbour Report 1999; North America.* Troy, Michigan: Harbour & Associates, Inc., p. 3.

6. *The New York Times.* 1998. Rise of Borderless Corporation (May 8): 1&8.

7. Ewing, Jack. 2000. The Show of Muscle isn't so Scary, *Business Week* (January 10): p. 24.

8. In 1999, Germany was the expensive nation in the world in manufacturing and cost of labor.

9. Levin, Doron, P. 1995. *Behind the Wheel at Chrysler: The Iacocca Legacy.* New York: Harcourt Brace & Co.

10. For recent literature on mergers and acquisitions, see: *Wall Street Journal.* 1999. Daimler Faces Big Test in Small-Car Market (November 29): C14; Cliffe, Sarah. 1999. Can This Merger Be Saved? *Harvard Business Review,* 77(1): 29–44; *The Economist.* 1999. How to Make Mergers Work (January 9) 15–16.

11. Anwar, Syed Tariq. 1996. The Impact of NAFTA on Canada's Automobile Industry: Issues and Analysis, *World Competition,* 19(3): 115–136. For M-series and its development, see: Haasen, Adolf. 1999. M-Class: the Making of a New Daimler-Benz, *Organizational Dynamics,* 27(4): 74–78.

12. The acquired companies included: Dornier, MTU, and AEG.

13. *Financial Times.* 1993. Daimler-Benz Profits to Fall by up to 30 Percent (April 17): 1.

14. www.daimlerchrysler.com/index-e.htm

15. www.daimlerchrysler.com

16. Sorge, Marjorie & Mark Phelan. 1998. The Deal of the Century, *Automotive Industries* (June): 47.

17. For more discussion, see: Radebaugh, Lee H., Gunther Gebhardt and Sidney J. Gray. 1995. Foreign Stock Exchange Listings: A Case Study of Daimler-Benz, *Journal of International Financial Management and Accounting,* 6(2).

18. *Business Week.* 1995. The Shocks for Daimler's New Driver (August 21): 38–39. *The Economist.* 1995. Dismantling Daimler-Benz, (November 18): 67–68; *The Economist.* 1996. Neutron Jurgen? (March 16): 72.

19. As of this writing, Germany is the most expensive nation ($30 per hour) in the area of labor wages.

20. For detail, see: *Automotive Industries.* 1999. Global Joint Ventures and Affiliations for 1999 (February): 16–22.

21. For more discussion on NUMMI's 1998 performance and productivity see: Harbour & Associates, Inc. 1999. *The Harbour Report 1999: North America,* Troy, Michigan: Harbour & Associates, Inc.

22. *Business Week.* 1999. The Global Six (January 25), pp. 68–72.

23. Dyer, Davis, Malcolm Salter and Alan Webber. 1987. *Changing Alliances.* Boston, Massachusetts: Harvard Business School Press; Marston, Richard, C. 1991. Petri, Peter A., 1991. Market Structure, Comparative Advantage, and Japanese Trade Under the Strong Yen, in Krugman, Paul. *Trade with Japan: Has the Door Opened Wider?* Chicago, Il.: The University of Chicago Press, pp. 51–82.

24. Ibid.

25. For further discussion, see: Iacocca, Lee. 1984. *Iacocca: An Autobiography,* New York: Bantam Books; Levin, Doron P. 1995. *Behind the Wheel at Chrysler: The Lee Iacocca Legacy,* New York. Harcourt Brace & Co.

26. *Financial Times.* 1999. Two Tribes on the Same Trail (August 31): 10.

27. Sorge, Marjorie & Mark Phelan. 1998. The Deal of the Century, *Automotive Industries* (June): 47; *Financial Times.* 1998a. Culture Crucial to Synergy Equation (May 8): 22; *Wall Street Journal.* 1998. For Daimler-Benz, a Cultural Road Test (May 8): B1; *Business Week.* 1998. A Secret Weapon for German Reform (October 12): 138; *Wall Street Journal.* 1999. DaimlerChrysler's Transfer Woes (August 24): B1; *Wall Street Journal.* 1999 DaimlerChrysler Readies Management Recall (September 15): A25.

28. *Wall Street Journal.* 1999. Stuttgart's Control Grows with Shakeup at DaimlerChrysler, (September 24): A1&8; *Wall Street Journal.* 1999. DaimlerChrysler Frets Over Loss of U.S. Shareholders (March 24): B4.

29. *The Economist.* 1995. Dismantling Daimler-Benz (November 18): 67.

30. *Wall Street Journal.* 1999. Daimler Faces Big Test in Small-Car Market (November 29): C14.

31. *The Economist.* 1995. Dismantling Daimler-Benz (November 18): 67.

32. *Wall Street Journal.* 1999. Daimler Faces Big Test in Small-Car Market (November 29): C14.

33. *The Economist.* 2000. Wheels and Wires, (January 8): 58–59; *Wall Street Journal.* 1999. Making Digital Decisions, (September 24): B1&4; *Wall Street Journal.* 2000. Ford and GM Sign Pacts with Web Sites (January 10): A3&8.

34. *Wall Street Journal.* 1988a. Daimler-Benz is Struggling to Get off its Bumpy Road (January 8): 10.

35. Biz.yahoo.com/rf/991108/fz.html. 1999. Year Later, DaimlerChrysler Struggles with Identity (November 8): pp. 1–3; also see: *Business Week.* 1999b. Is the King of the Road Moving out of the Fast Lane? (July 19): 48.

36. *The Economist.* 2000. Wheels and Wires, (January 8): 58–59; Sheth, Jagdish N. and Rajendra Sisodia. 1998. Only the Big Three Will Thrive, *Wall Street Journal* (May 11): A22.

37. *Business Week.* 1999c. Desperately Seeking the Right Asian Ally (December 13): 60.

38. www.daimlerchrysler.com

39. *The New York Times.* 1998. Superfirms Take Over in Global Age (May 12): 1&10.

40. *Business Week.* 2001. Can this Man save Chrysler? (September 17): 86–94.

41. *The Economist.* 2000. The DaimlerChrysler Emulsion, (July 29): 67–68; *Financial Times.* 2001. Seeking an Edge in Mergers, (October 22): 8–9

42. *Wall Street Journal.* 2001. DaimlerChrysler Turnaround Seems to be Going in Reverse, (October 2001): B4.

43. For more discussion, see: the *Wall Street Journal.* 2001. Daimler's New Boss for Chrysler Orders Tough, Major Repairs, (January 22); A1&A8; Harbour & Associates. 2001; *The Harbour Report North America 2001*, Harbour & Associates, Inc.

44. *The Economist.* 2001. Schrempp's Last Stand, (March 3): 20–21.

45. *Financial Times.* 2001. Steering Straight with his Foot to the Floor, (February 26): 7; *Financial Times.* 2001. DaimlerChrysler to Cut 35,000 Jobs, (February 26): 15.

46. *Value Line.* 2001. DaimlerChrysler (March): 102.

CASE QUESTIONS

1. What are your views of the DaimlerChrysler merger and its future prospects in the world auto industry?

2. Analyze and evaluate the strengths and weaknesses of Daimler-Benz AG and Chrysler Corporation before the merger.

3. What kind of short-term and long-term plan/global strategies does DaimlerChrysler need to formulate to be one of the key players in the world automotive industry in the 21st century?

4. Compare DaimlerChrysler with other global automotive manufacturers (GM, Ford, Toyota, Honda, Volkswagen, and so on) regarding internationalization, global market share, and competitive issues.

5. Evaluate DaimlerChrysler's non-core activities and product lines. Do you see any complementary synergy visible from the non-automotive diversification in the coming years?

6. Evaluate the merged company's organization structure.

7. Review recent events and results for DaimlerChrysler since this case writing. What do the prospects look like for the industry as a whole and for DaimlerChrysler's position in the world market?

8. What have you learned from the DaimlerChrysler merger and the company's plans for its prominent role in the global auto industry?

Case 9   Reorganization at AB Telecom (1998)[1]

In early 1998, the top managers at AB Telecom were debating how to change its worldwide organization. AB Telecom is a Canadian telecommunications hardware firm that manufactures fixed wireless systems. This $200 million company earned more than 95 percent of its revenues from outside Canada, with 40 percent coming from Asia in 1997. In 1998, AB Telecom conducted all of its manufacturing and R&D within Canada; much of its market development and project engineering is maintained in its Canadian headquarters.

AB Telecom was founded in 1981 and is publicly traded on several Canadian stock exchanges. It had been profitable since 1990, with an average 7 percent net profitability between 1990 and 1997. Given its strong presence outside Canada, ABT has been awarded the prestigious Canadian Export Award several times by the Canadian government.

AB Telecom's traditional customer is a national telephone company that wants to improve telecommunications to its rural locations Sixty percent of ABT's sales in 1997 were turnkey projects for national telephone companies. Its structure had been a regional sales and marketing structure, with three regions: Asia/Pacific, Latin America, and Europe/Middle East/Africa. Each region had a headquarters and several sales subsidiaries in different countries. These regional offices had autonomy in booking small deals, but headquarters became involved with deals worth over 42 million. The regional offices are also reliant on some project engineering support provided by the headquarters.

Several significant changes had created a need for top management to review its current structure:

➤ Early signs of economic difficulty in Malaysia and other Southeast Asian countries could potentially stall or stop agreed-to projects in this region.

➤ Opportunities to use their existing fixed wireless systems for industrial application were growing.

➤ Europe, the Middle East, and Africa provided many opportunities for sales to traditional national telephone companies for rural applications.

➤ Potential is unknown for its new wireless product for urban data transmissions to telephone companies and new competitors.

In March 1998, the CEO, his top management team, and some board members met to discuss how to restructure the company.

Product Applications

Rural Telephony   AB Telecom researches, designs, and manufactures fixed wireless systems mostly for installation in rural and remote areas, to aid in rural telecommunications. ABT manufactures all components required for rural installation. It subcontracts with local contractors to install the systems.

The main application of the AB Telecom product is to connect remote villages and towns to the national telephone system grid. Fixed wireless is a cost-effective solution for many national telephone companies to connect to rural locations; the cost of installing a fixed wireless system is far less than that of laying miles of fiber or copper cable to the same locale. ABT's traditional customers have been national telephone companies.

For this business, ABT considers Alcatel, NEC Japan, and Lucent to be its direct competitors, but the fixed wireless systems are a very small portion of these large multinational firms' sales, whereas ABT specializes in the fixed wireless systems and technology.

Industrial Applications   New applications of ABT's wireless systems have been recently recognized. Companies in industries such a soil, gas, and electricity generation require remote sensing of dispersed operations. In early 1998, this type of business had grown to comprise 25 percent of ABT's revenues. Much of this business was developed "by chance," as explained by one top manager.

We realized that the industrial portion of sales could be more significant. The industrial market

---

[1]This is a real company, but the company name, location, and a few aspects of the firm are disguised because of a pledge of confidentiality by the researcher.

SOURCE: Case written by Professor Anne Smith, University of New Mexico, based on her research of the firm discussed. ©1998 by Professor Anne Smith. Used with permission.

Exhibit I   AB Telecom at Time of Case

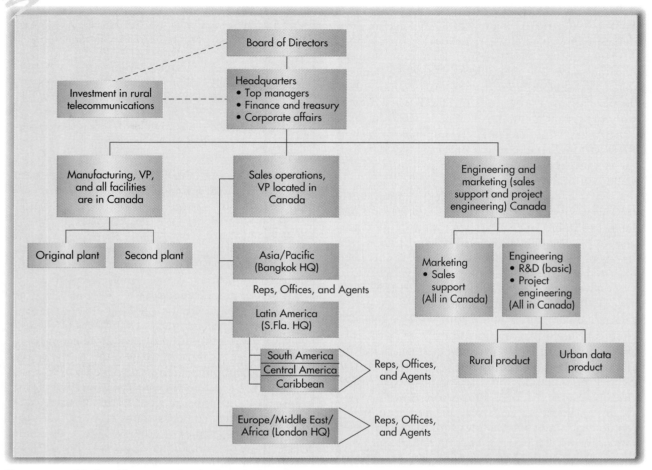

The structure as of the time of the case was a functional organization. Industrial products were being sold by the sales organization "by chance" and without marketing support.

was not properly marketed to, nor were their needs involved in, our R&D efforts. We realized that this area could become significant if we added more products that customers wanted because we are one of the largest companies selling to this fragmented and diverse market.

This manager went on to explain how industrial customers were developed in one Asian country:

Our industrial customers developed just by change [in this country]. Now, we have 100

industrial customers. We had no idea what the customer wanted. Because selling to this national telephone company was slow and government controlled, we stumbled upon the electric companies who were interested. It started off with a change of attention of one salesperson already located in this market, but it developed in a mostly word of mouth way . . . this counts for a lot in [this country]. We gained a reputation for being a reliable supplier, but growing this business was not part of a plan . . . it just happened.

The estimated potential revenue from this market is around $100 million per year, but it is spread among hundreds of industrial customers. One ABT manager explained, "Tremendous sales and marketing efforts are required to obtain a $5 million order but once a customer orders and is satisfied, they are more likely to repeat the purchase. . . . We need more information to develop the business. . . . It is difficult to find out where the big industrial users are worldwide. . . . mostly trial and error," stated one top ABT manager.

Urban Wireless   ABT also had developed and was testing fixed wireless systems in urban settings. The potential customers for this product were telephone companies, both the incumbent telephone company as well as start-up carriers, especially in Europe. A start-up company would offer data services in competition with the original telephone company. The ABT system would be used to transmit data reliably within dense urban settings. This application has required some modification to the original ABT product lines. "With data applications, we are really starting from zero, but we should be able to double or triple them in the future." In 1998, this system was being tested in the U.K. Only a few technical and marketing people were involved and only in a haphazard way.

Investment in Rural License

In 1996, ABT deviated from its sales and delivery of operation systems to invest in the telecommunications infrastructure of a Latin American country. This investment in rural infrastructure in Latin America was a major departure from ABT's short-term, project-oriented, turnkey operations. For several years, top executives had discussed the possibility of pursuing investment as opposed to sales-only deals. This investment was initiated, managed, and controlled by top managers in Montreal, but local managers were hired to help with the installation and operations of this investment.

Top executives outlined several reasons for ABT to pursue an investment in rural telecommunications operations. According to one manager close to this deal, "Many people confuse rural with poverty, but they miss out on a very good investment and tremendous pent-up demand." Most of the large hardware equipment manufacturers have moved form selling equipment and services to investing and buying up licenses in international markets. As one top manager stated, "It was a difficult decision to invest in rural telecom, but our board of directors was convinced it was a good idea . . . we realized that we could supply or equipment at no markup and then sell a 51 percent stake in our investment, perhaps using this to fund future investments in rural telecommunications."

Concerning the challenges inherent in starting this new venture, one manager explained, "We are not experts at running a telephone company; we don't know how to bill or do maintenance." In 1998, ABT hired a local manager away from the national telephone company to run the firm. Consultants with experience with Bell Canada were also helping with the venture. By 1998, ABT had set up 1,000 telephone lines and had 100 employees; the push was to install pay phones, a legal requirement of the license. ABT managers estimated that it would take about 8,000 to 10,000 installed lines to break even, probably in 1999. Once this rural venture establishes a proven track record, ABT managers plan to sell off a portion to a local partner. If this venture is successful, ABT managers are considering future investments in rural telecommunications. One top manager stated, "We are being approached by people in many markets around the world about potential investments."

Current Regional Sales and Marketing Structure

From 1981 until 1988, ABT's Canadian headquarters controlled all of the details of the business. Then, as one top manager explained, "We felt that we had to get closer to the customer, and we went first to Asia because that was where the action was." So, in the late 1980s, ABT placed several sales people in the field in three regions: Asia/Pacific, Latin America, and Europe/Africa/Middle East. In 1997, Asia/Pacific markets were 50 percent of all revenues, Latin America 36 percent, and Europe/Africa/Middle East 19 percent of sales. The United States was not a market for ABT's equipment given the significant rural infrastructure already in place in the United States.

Asia/Pacific   The first subsidiary was in Hong Kong as "an easy way into China," according to a top ABT manager. There were not customers, and it was expensive to maintain an office there. "Because we weren't even paying the light bills, we decided to move the Asia/Pacific headquarters to Manila to save on taxes and expenses, and in order to have access to a skilled labor force." Soon after this move, a sales subsidiary was set up in China, followed by another office in Bangkok after a large project was won there.

By the early 1990s, ABT had more than 60 people on the ground in these three operations. These offices were staffed with technical sales people with an engineering background. They were rewarded on meeting a quota, and they operated autonomously from the headquarters. Their sales efforts centered on selling ABT's equipment and solutions to national telephone companies. These technical sales people placed orders with headquarters and provided service to the firm once the system was installed and in place. Many times, they relied on project engineering for technical details related to a bid or final customer proposal.

In the early 1990s, the Asian headquarters was moved again to Bangkok. As one manager stated, "With these regional offices, we cultivated relationships." If a project or bid was around $1 million, headquarters would rarely get involved. If the order was more strategic (from $5 million to $10 million in size), headquarters would interact closely with sales, working together on pricing, delivery, and technical specifications.

Latin America The Latin America office was located in south Florida. At first, this region was staffed with sales engineers. Then, managers for different areas within Latin America were brought in to strengthen the region's marketing abilities. In 1998, there were three area managers: one each of South America (included Brazil, Argentina, Colombia, and Peru), Caribbean U.S., and Central America. The total number of engineers and managers in this office was 12 in 1998. Sales support and project engineers were still located in Montreal to support Latin America project bids, technical assistance, or operations. Most of the activity within this area involved repeat customers, the national telephone companies. This Latin American sales and marketing area had nothing to do with the 1997 investment in rural telecommunications by ABT. In fact, most of the managers knew very few details about this investment transaction.

With the privatization of many Latin American telephone companies, managers from AB Telecom's Latin American office had developed a close working relationship with Telefónica (Spain's national telephone company) and STET (Italy's national telephone company) because these two companies have purchased significant stakes in many national telephone companies in Latin America. This area had been growing consistently for AB Telecom in the 1990s.

One manager explained how deals are developed in this region: "We follow regulatory changes in countries that are considering privatization. We know that a piece will be rural, and money will be made available for rural according to the bids for this privatization. Our local representatives keep us advised." Another manager explained, "We have not pushed much into the industrial business in Latin American except for one excellent industrial client—an oil company in Venezuela—and this relationship was gained through a technical representative on the ground with this oil company." When asked about how they interact with R&D in Canada, one manager stated, "We don't worry about technology. . . . we worry about satisfying a need . . . we have the best product technically, reflected in our high quality and high price. . . . this combined with being close to the customer lands us deals . . . many of our deals in Latin America are renewals."

One area manager in the Latin American division stated, "The greatest impediment to our international growth is resources—human resources. We are looking for people with language, engineering, project skills, and good interpersonal skills.

Europe/Middle East/Africa In 1998, the Europe/Middle East/Africa region was the most difficult, according to several managers. This was attributed to too many different regulations and frequencies across this region. Sales subsidiaries have been developed where a strong relationship with a national telephone company existed. Sales subsidiaries had been set up in Nairobi, Saudi Arabia, South Africa, Sweden, and the U.K. The head of this regional structure had recently resigned.

Dilemma

In reviewing the evolution of their structure, top managers recognized that they had moved from a domestic functional structure to a geographic regional sales and marketing structure. They realized that each existing sales subsidiary was organized to develop and maintain a close relationship with the national telephone company of countries within its region, focusing mostly on its rural telephony needs.

Salespersons were not rewarded to develop new markets (such as industrial business or urban data transmission) because they were paid on the basis of meeting quarterly sales quotas. According to one top manager, "They could not focus on such a diverse market as industrial because it is going to take two or three years of working closely with an industrial customer or a new telephone competitor to land a deal, and this just doesn't fit within our reward system of sales persons."

In 1998, traditional Asian markets and telephone companies were beginning to suffer, and top managers anticipated that revenues from these markets would be flat or, worse, fall by the end of the year. There were opportunities to expand their presence in non-Asian markets with their traditional customers or to push for entry into other applications such as industrial and urban data.

Therefore, the top managers were focused on developing a structure to manage the tension within its wireless technology division (traditionally housed in the R&D area in Canada), its current regional structure (responsive to customers needs, cultural differences mostly in its current rural applications), and emerging new customer groups (such as the industrial and urban wireless data products).

CASE QUESTION

How should ABT top managers reorganize to resolve the tensions among the regional organization selling to national telephone customers, new applications for industrial and urban data, and investments in rural telephony?

Case 10   Nouvelles Frontières in 2000

The Internet Challenge

In the fall of 2000, Jacques Maillot, CEO of Nouvelles Frontières, called a meeting of the four major shareholders (see Exhibit 1) in order for them to review their company's strategy, as they were preparing to take it public. Of particular concern to him was how investors would view Nouvelles Frontières' aggressive vertical integration into both airlines and hotels; he also wondered how the rapidly growing use of internet in Europe would affect the travel industry as a whole, and the company's position in that industry.

Nouvelles Frontières, created in the mid-sixties as a student association that organized low price holidays, had since grown very rapidly and had become, by the mid-nineties, the largest tour operator in France, ahead of Club Méditerranée. With sales totaling 1.6 billion Euros[1] and over 3 million customers in 1999, Nouvelles Frontières was the sixth largest tour operator in Europe and one of the top twenty in the world. The management of the company considered that, to continue growing at a rapid pace, they had to continue increasing their air transport capacity, and had just recently acquired two brand new Airbus A330 wide-body jets. Nouvelles Frontières was also one of the leading travel services companies in Europe in terms of internet sales but was nevertheless worried that, as more and more of the travel business was shifting to this new channel, they might be losing their competitive advantage.

THE TOUR OPERATING INDUSTRY IN EUROPE IN THE LATE NINETIES

Tour operating consisted in supplying packaged holidays, tours and travel, that were made up on the basis of various components : air transport and a wide variety of other services such as accommodation, excursions, entertainment, sporting activities, car rental,

---

[1]In August 2000, one Euro was worth approximately 0.9 US dollars

SOURCE: This case was developed by Professor Pierre Dussauge as a basis for class discussion and is not intended to illustrate either effective or ineffective handling of a business situation. Copyright © Pierre Dussauge, 2002.

Exhibit I   Nouvelles Frontières' Shareholders

Jacques MAILLOT (CEO)	52%
Patrick BILLEBAULT	14%
Christian PINOT	14%
Noël PICATO	9%
Others (none owning more than 6%)	11%

local transport, etc. Tour operators designed packages that they believed would appeal to customers and assembled them by purchasing all the necessary components from specialized providers such as airlines, hotels, resorts, local tourist organizations, etc. Tour operators published catalogs in which their holiday products were described in detail and from which customers could select the exact package they wished to purchase on the basis of destination, dates, duration, price, specific activities, level of comfort and luxury, etc. By turning to a tour operator, the customer bought a complete and standardized package and no longer had to select the various services one by one. The price of the package was all inclusive (except for particular extras) and it was no longer possible to identify the individual cost of each service provided in the package. Overall, tour operators relieved holidaymakers from the hassle of having to deal with numerous service providers and, in addition, the price of packages tended to be significantly lower than the sum of the prices of services purchased separately.

In carrying out their business, tour operators dealt with three main categories of related service providers:

Air Carriers

Air carriers fell into two main categories: "regular" airlines, that flew scheduled flights, and "charter" airlines flying on demand. Thus, in order to get customers to their holiday destination, tour operators could either reserve seats on a scheduled flight, provided capacity was still available, or charter an entire airplane. The dividing line between scheduled flights and charter flights wasn't very clear, however. First, many airlines had set up specialized charter subsidiaries and therefore offered both services. In addition, airlines often sold block bookings on scheduled flights to tour operators. The latter, instead of chartering a complete plane, could buy a given number of seats on a scheduled flight and were then responsible for marketing them, thus assuming the commercial risk on the seats that they had booked.

The airline industry had traditionally been highly regulated; it was deregulated in the US in the early eighties and began being deregulated in Europe in the nineties. Deregulation, however, mainly applied to domestic flights—or, in the case of Europe, to flights within the European Union. In the late 1990s, international flights continued being organized on the basis of bilateral government to government agreements. These agreements usually specified what routes could be flown, the capacity that could be offered by carriers from each country, and in some cases even regulated fares. Foreign airlines could generally not carry passengers on domestic routes: for instance, although Air France flew from Paris to Los Angeles with a stop in New York, it could not pick up passengers in New York to fly them to LA. Despite the move toward deregulation within Europe, local aviation authorities still exerted considerable influence on air travel in general and on competition between carriers in particular: gates, landing slots and traffic rights were awarded by these local authorities and could not easily be bought and sold. Thus, as major airports were saturated and skies congested, practically the only way for an airline to enter a market or to increase capacity significantly was to acquire an existing carrier that already possessed these scarce slots and rights. British Airways, for example, had chosen to buy out Air Liberté, the fourth largest airline in France (behind Air France, AOM and Corsair), in order to enter the French domestic market—which was the largest by far in Europe—in 1996. By 1998, however, British Airways, whose operations in France were generating considerable losses, chose to withdraw and sold Air Liberté to Swissair. In an attempt to establish a strong presence in France, Swissair also acquired AOM that same year.

Despite the general trend toward privatization, many airlines continued being state-owned or partially state-owned. In 2000, Air France, Alitalia, Iberia, to name just a few of the major airlines in

Europe, were state-controlled, while the German government continued having a significant stake in Lufthansa. In most Third World countries, where national airlines were created shortly after independence, governments continued owning and supporting their flagship carrier.

Overall, since 1970, the airline industry had experienced an average 6% per annum growth in passenger-miles (i.e., the total number of miles flown by all passengers), except for a short but significant downturn in 1991 and 1992, as a consequence of the Gulf War. Prices, however, had declined steadily, which had limited growth in dollar terms to around 3% per annum. The industry had been plagued by structural overcapacity and, for most airlines, the average load factor (i.e., the proportion of available seats actually sold) was well below 75%. In the late nineties, some industry analysts were predicting that a combination of increased deregulation, better use of "yield management" techniques and of computerized reservation systems (such as Sabre, Apollo, Amadeus, Galileo, etc.) would lead to less overcapacity in the future. It must be noted that overcapacity tended to fluctuate according to routes and periods in the year: transatlantic flights, for example, were traditionally very full from May to September and rather empty the rest of the year; flights from Europe to the Caribbean, on the contrary, were full in winter and empty in summer.

A slow but steady shift in demand for air travel had also been occurring in the mid- to late-nineties: the proportion of business travelers had been declining while that of holidaymakers and people traveling for leisure had been going up. Finally, the limited availability of gates and landing slots at major airports was becoming an increasingly crucial factor in the development of air travel. As a whole, the industry had lost over $15 billion from 1975 to 1995.

All these changes were potentially critical for tour operators because air travel accounted for a significant portion of the total cost of packaged tours and holidays.

Providers of Holiday Services

Providers of holiday services supplied all those services that were included in a packaged tour and offered at the place of destination. Such services generally included some form of accommodation, meals and a very wide range of other activities: sports, entertainment, excursions, visits, guided tours, car rental, local transportation, etc. With the exception of hotel chains and car rental companies, most providers of holiday services tended to be local firms. Depending on both the country of destination and the particular kind of service, competition among these local service providers could be very intense or virtually non-existent. Large hotel chains such as Marriott, Sheraton, Hilton, Hyatt, Novotel, etc. or major car rental companies (e.g., Hertz, Avis, Europcar) operated in most countries, where they also had to compete with local rivals; they catered primarily to business travelers but offered discounted fares aimed at holidaymakers in order to fill excess capacity.

On average, services provided to customers at the place of destination accounted for slightly more than half the total cost of packaged tours and holidays sold in the mid-nineties by tour operators in Europe.

Travel Agencies

Travel agencies, which were in contact with the final customer, were responsible for marketing the finished products offered by tour operators. Travel agents in Europe provided a wide variety of services such as airplane ticketing, train ticketing, hotel reservations, car rental, local sightseeing tours, etc. In the mid-nineties, there were some 4000 travel agencies in France, either independent or part of chains; the largest of these chains (Havas Voyages) controlled over 500 outlets and the four largest together about 1500. Almost all travel agents in France were members of the *Syndicat National des Agents de Voyage* (National Association of Travel Agents). They were paid on the basis of a commission granted by airlines, providers of services or tour operators. This commission varied according to the nature of the service distributed: in 1998, it ranged from about 7% for railway ticketing, to around 10% for airline ticketing, and to 15%, sometimes even 18%, for marketing more elaborate tours and holidays. Similar commission rates also applied, with only minor variations, in most other European countries. The commission paid to travel agents by tour operators was the subject of long and often bitter negotiations. In the event of a conflict, the concerted action of the travel agents could easily block the access of a tour operator or of a specific product to the market. In the mid-eighties, Club Méditerranée had had a serious conflict with the travel agents' association on commission issues, was boycotted for several months and, as a result, saw its sales drop notably during that period. For most travel agents in France, packaged tours and holidays accounted for only about 20% of their total business, with over 70% coming from ticketing.

It can be noted that, in France, most travel agents were not affiliated with tour operators or other providers of travel and holiday services. In the UK and Germany, in contrast, several of the large travel agency networks were in fact divisions or subsidiaries of large integrated companies that also provided tour operating services and often controlled their own airline.

THE EVOLUTION OF TOURISM IN EUROPE

It wasn't until the fifties that Europeans began traveling extensively during their holidays. This growth in tourism created a flow of travel toward southern destinations, to countries on the coast of the Mediterranean sea (Spain, Italy, Greece, Turkey, Tunisia, Morocco, etc.), or even farther (the Canary islands, the Caribbean, Indian Ocean islands, etc.). The development of tourism and associated air travel greatly benefited in Europe from the general increase in standards of living as well as from the increased length of legal holidays (a minimum of four to five weeks in most countries).

Demand for packaged tours and holidays developed much earlier and faster in Northern European countries than it did in the south of Europe. First,

standards of living in the UK, Germany and Scandinavia tended to be higher; it was not until the seventies and early eighties that countries like Italy or Spain really started catching up. Second, traveling by air to sunny and warm seaside locations for travelers originating in the UK or Germany made a lot of sense. In those countries with a coast on the Mediterranean such as Spain or Italy, driving to a holiday destination was easy and tended to be a preferred option. As a consequence, the total number of customers for tour operators was significantly larger in northern European countries than it was in the south of Europe (see Exhibit 2).

Very large tour operators such as Airtours and Thomson Travel (UK) or TUI and C&N (Germany) emerged in northern European countries as early as the fifties and sixties. In France, it wasn't until the late sixties and seventies that companies like Club Méditerranée or Nouvelles Frontières achieved a significant size. In Italy and Spain, by the mid-nineties, the industry had not yet grown and concentrated to anywhere near the same extent as it had in the above mentioned countries (see Exhibit 3 for a listing of the largest European tour operators).

Consumer preferences tended to vary somewhat from country to country. Germans appeared to favor destinations such as the Canary islands (which were a Spanish possession off the coast of Africa), Greece, or Turkey. Britons preferred the Baleares islands, southern Spain, or Malta. Favorite destinations for the French were Corsica, the French West Indies and Canada, as well as Tunisia and Morocco. These preferences were actually more obvious at the local level with some resort towns or tourist destinations having become favorite hang-outs for one or another nationality and culture. In such tourist destinations, local staff had often learned how to speak

Exhibit 2

Country	Germany	United Kingdom	France	Italy	Spain
Total population	80 million	60 million	60 million	60 million	40 million
Market for tour operators	16 million to 20 million	14 million to 16 million	6 million to 8 million	4 million to 6 million	2 million to 3 million

Exhibit 3   Leading Tour Operators in Europe

		1998 Sales (million Euros)	Number of Customers
#1	T.U.I. (Germany)	5,000	6,460,000
#2	Airtours (UK)	3,000	5,225,000
#3	C & N (Germany)	2,800	NA
#4	Thomson Travel (UK)	2,400	4,600,000
#5	L.T.U. (Germany)	1,700	2,820,000
#6	Nouvelles Frontières (France)	1,500	2,800,000
#7	Club Mediterranée (France)	1,450	1,500,000
#8	First Choice (UK)	1,300	3,134,000
#9	Kuoni (Switzerland)	1,100	NA
#10	D.E.R. (Germany)	900	2,148,000

SOURCE: Nexotur

the language of the dominant tourist nationality, restaurants offered food that suited their tastes and most other tourist-related activities were influenced accordingly. This was important for tour operators who had to tailor their products and services to particular customer nationalities. It was generally thought it was difficult to offer the same package to customers from different countries and mix nationalities in the same hotel, resort or organized tour.

Since the early sixties, demand for packaged tours and holidays had grown tremendously throughout Europe, on average by over 10% per annum in most countries. By the mid-eighties, this growth had slowed down significantly in Northern European countries and also began declining in France in the nineties. Growth rates for the next five years were not expected to exceed 2% to 3% on average per year in those countries. Industry analysts predicted that most future growth in tour operating in Europe would come from Southern European countries.

NOUVELLES FRONTIÈRES' OPERATIONS

Since it was started in the mid-sixties, Nouvelles Frontières had grown at an extremely rapid pace (1,000 customers in 1967, 4,000 in 1970, 50,000 in 1975, 150,000 in 1980, 500,000 in 1985, 1,200,000 in 1990, 1,900,000 in 1994, and 3,000,000 in 1999). This phenomenal growth was initially marked by considerable risk taking. In order to develop their business as fast as possible, the managers of Nouvelles Frontières chartered large air travel capacities, increasing spectacularly from one year to the next, and offering an ever-expanding range of destinations. An insufficient number of bookings one year could have led to serious problems for the company.

From the very beginning, Nouvelles Frontières was both a tour operator and a travel agent. Nouvelles Frontières had its own network of agencies that exclusively sold Nouvelles Frontières products; Nouvelles Frontières products, in turn, could not be purchased in any other distribution channel. In contrast, holiday packages offered by most other tour operators could be bought from any travel agency. This exclusive distribution organization was supported by a computerized reservation system to which each Nouvelles Frontières agency was connected.

Unlike most other large European tour operators (in the UK and in Germany in particular), Nouvelles Frontières had been able to grow very significantly in the tour operating business without owning an airline. Until 1989, it carried out its business by negotiating with airlines to get discounted fares on scheduled flights or by chartering entire planes. It wasn't until 1990 that Nouvelles Frontières integrated into air travel by acquiring a controlling stake in the equity of Corsair, a small charter airline. By 1998, Corsair had grown significantly and operated fifteen aircraft. Eight of these aircraft were Boeing 747 Jumbo jets (long-haul jets with a 500 passenger capacity which, on average, could fly one to two trips (one way) per day, 300 days a year). Five Corsair aircraft were Boeing 737s (medium-haul jets with a 150 passenger capacity that could make two to three flights a day, 300 days a year on average). In 1998/99 Corsair had started operating two Airbus A330 aircraft (long-haul jets with a 350 passenger capacity which, on average, could fly one to two trips per day). Over the years, Nouvelles Frontières had invested about 150 million Euros of its own funds in Corsair. In 1999, Corsair had transported a little under 2.5 million passengers with a load factor of 94% and its operation had resulted in sales of 450 million Euros and a profit of 2 million (Corsair's sales and profit were consolidated into those of Nouvelles Frontières). Corsair was the only French airline to post a profit every year from 1990 to 1999. 85% of Corsair's sales were to Nouvelles Frontières and were carried out at market prices. For all its air travel purchases, Nouvelles Frontières requested competitive bids from all potential suppliers and only chose Corsair if their prices were the lowest from the start, or if they were willing to at least match the lowest bid. Despite this privileged relationship with Corsair, Nouvelles Frontières remained a significant customer for many other airlines: it was the largest single customer worldwide of such airlines as Royal Air Maroc or Bangladesh Biman and was the largest customer in France of British Airways, KLM or Lufthansa, among others. (See Exhibit 4.)

In a similar fashion, Nouvelles Frontières only began owning and operating its own hotels and resorts in 1986. These resorts offered fairly standardized services and had been grouped into a chain called "Paladien". In 1999 there were 22 Paladien resorts located in such tourist destinations as Greece, Senegal, Tunisia, Morocco, the island of Corsica, the West Indies, etc. On average, Paladien resorts, which had about 100 rooms each (i.e., a 200 guest capacity), had to achieve an occupancy rate of 80% at least 200 days a year to be operated profitably; the average length of stay in Nouvelles Frontières resorts was 10 days in 1999. Accommodation in these Paladien resorts represented only a relatively small portion of all tourist services sold by Nouvelles Frontières, but operating its own facilities made it possible for the company to better control the quality of services provided to customers. Nouvelles Frontières had invested 100 million Euros to develop its Paladien chain. In 1999 all Paladien resorts combined generated total sales of 50 million Euros and profits of 2 million.

Nouvelles Frontières set its prices by adding 11.5% on average to the combined purchase price of flights, accommodation, tours and other services included in the packages to be sold. When air transport or accommodation were procured internally (from Corsair or Paladien resorts), the pricing process remained unchanged with internal transfer

Exhibit 4   The Evolution of Nouvelles Frontières' Activity

		1980	1985	1990	1995	1997	1999
Number of Customers	From France	135,000	410,000	950,000	1,950,000	2,100,000	2,350,000
	From abroad	15,000	90,000	250,000	450,000	550,000	650,000
Breakdown of Purchases (including from Corsair and Paladien)	Air Transport	90%	80%	75%	70%	70%	70%
	Other Services	10%	20%	25%	30%	30%	30%
Breakdown by Destinations	Long Haul	70%	50%	45%	40%	40%	40%
	Short & Med. Haul	30%	50%	55%	60%	60%	60%

prices being used as the basis upon which the 11.5% markup was applied. These internally computed prices were then compared to what was then available on the market and lowered if other competitors offered more attractive prices, or inversely increased if the competitive context made it possible to do so. The aim of this price setting system was to make Nouvelles Frontières the lowest price competitor in the marketplace.

Nouvelles Frontières' total gross margin[2] (which varied slightly from year to year according to a number of parameters such as exchange rates, capacity utilization, etc.) ranged from 9% to 11% of sales and averaged about 10%. This gross margin covered the costs of both the tour operating activity, and the distribution network. The tour operating activity accounted for about 60% of Nouvelles Frontières' internal operating costs, and the distribution activity for 40%. Ultimately, prices were deliberately set for the company's net operating margin to be very low (less than 1% of sales most years). (See Exhibit 5.)

Nouvelles Frontières' management was convinced that the exclusive and specialized distribution system they had created was a significant source of competitive advantage for the company.

---
[2]Gross margin = (sales – purchases)/sales

They pointed to the fact that average sales per salesperson—or per square foot of outlet—were about three times that of non-specialized agencies. Also, Nouvelles Frontières agencies carried out 20% more transactions on average than similar sized generalist travel agencies.

Nouvelles Frontières' management was also convinced that the firm had a cost advantage over its competitors on the tour operating business i.e., tour and trip producing—part of its business. Internally conducted studies seemed to indicate that the cost of the tour operating activity was 10% to 15% lower than that of relatively small competitors (100,000 to 200,000 customers per year) and 2% to 5% lower than that of major competitors (500,000 customers per year and above).

The company's exclusive distribution network was also an asset when dealing with airlines. Any excess capacity airlines were left with at any given time could be put on the market within a matter of hours at highly discounted prices through Nouvelles Frontières' agencies. Because of this, a significant portion of Nouvelles Frontières' business actually came from selling discounted air travel. The sheer size of Nouvelles Frontières' purchases of air travel and the high percentage of total sales that certain airlines made through its distribution network created very favorable bargaining conditions. Nouvelles Frontières could often

Exhibit 5   Income Statements (1980, 1985, 1990, 1995, 1997, 1999) Million Euros

	1980		1985		1990		1995		1997		1999	
Sales	55	*100%*	245	*100%*	610	*100%*	1100	*100%*	1350	*100%*	1600	*100%*
Purchased Services (including from Corsair and Paladien)	49.5	90%	220	89.80%	545	89.34%	985	89.55%	1210	89.63%	1450	90.62%
Gross Margin	5.5	10%	25	10.20%	65	10.65%	115	10.45%	140	10.37%	150	9.38%
Other Expenses	5.2	9.45%	26	10.61%	66	10.82%	110	10.00%	130	9.63%	142	8.88%
Net Operating Margin	0.3	0.55%	−1	−0.41%	−1	−0.17%	5	0.45%	10	0.74%	8	0.50%
Financial Profits	0.9	1.64%	4.9	2%	9.75	1.6%	12	1.09%	13	0.96%	15	0.94%
Net Profit	1.2	2.19%	3.9	1.59%	8.75	1.43%	17	1.54%	23	1.70%	23	1.44%

negotiate fares 50% to 80% lower than the full coach fare and, on average, purchased air transport capacity from regular airlines or charter companies about 10% to 15% cheaper than its main competitors in France.

Finally, having its own exclusive distribution network provided the company with valuable first hand information on the market and allowed it to better take into account changing customer preferences and new trends in tourism when developing its products and services.

In 1999, the Nouvelles Frontières network comprised some 150 travel agencies in France and about 70 offices abroad. About one third of the outlets located in France were franchised. The franchise-holding agencies, which exclusively sold Nouvelles Frontières products and services, got a 5% commission on their total sales and turned in the cash generated from their operation to Nouvelles Frontières on a daily basis. Nouvelles Frontières' suppliers, in turn, were usually paid (as was the habit in France for business-to-business transactions) 45 to 60 days after they delivered their services. Customers paid 30% of the price of the trip as a down payment at the time of reservation, the balance being paid off a month before the departure date at the latest. This system provided Nouvelles Frontières with cash advances in the range of 70 days of sales (i.e., 20% of annual sales), a classic situation in distribution activities in Europe. This excess cash was invested in treasury bonds (for which the interest rate was about 5% in 1999, after having been as high as 8% to 10% in the early nineties).

Several million copies of the various specialized catalogues (by destination, type of holiday, etc.) that Nouvelles Frontières issued each year were mailed out for free to prospective customers. Thus, most customers had already selected the tour, trip or holiday they wanted by the time they stepped into a Nouvelles Frontières agency to make a reservation and secure it by making a down payment. In addition, Nouvelles Frontières offered its customers travel information on most countries in the world, organized preparatory meetings and forums, and published its own series of travel guidebooks.

In the early years of Nouvelles Frontières, the trips and holidays had a clearly marked Third World orientation. For example, the company routinely offered study tours which included working in villages in India, visiting self-managed farms in Algeria, etc. Nouvelles Frontières specialized in very low price travel with little concern for comfort. Over the years, Nouvelles Frontières vastly diversified its product range; nevertheless, in 2000, the founders still defined the goal of their company as "being the cheapest tour operator in all travel categories: from budget holidays to luxury tours and trips".

In 1998, about half of Nouvelles Frontières' customers purchased plain discounted air travel while the other half bought packaged tours and holidays (which included both air travel and accommodation, as well as, in many cases, other services). In comparison, in the early seventies, discounted air travel contributed as much as 80% to 90% of sales, packaged holiday formulas accounting for only 10% to 20%. Since air travel represented on average about 40% of the total cost of a packaged tour or holiday, a significant portion of total sales, even in 2000, was still derived, directly or indirectly, from air travel alone. Availability and cost of air travel strongly affected Nouvelles Frontières' entire business. (See Exhibit 6.)

Exhibit 6 Major Nouvelles Frontières Destinations

Destinations	Number of Customers (1998)
Caribbean/West Indies	560,000
Greece	180,000
Corsica	130,000
United States	120,000
Indian Ocean Islands	120,000
Italy	90,000
Asia	85,000
Canada	80,000
Spain	80,000
Morocco	65,000
Eastern Europe	60,000
Portugal	60,000
Great Britain	55,000
Polynesia	50,000
Senegal	45,000
Tunisia	40,000

NOUVELLES FRONTIÈRES' MANAGEMENT

Nouvelles Frontières was created in 1967 by Jacques Maillot, then a college student, and four of his close friends. Thirty years later, the company was still privately held and continued being run by its founder-owners (see Exhibit 1). Jacques Maillot, a provocative and charismatic individual, had become, over the years, a well know character in France. His frequent diatribes against air transport monopolies and regulations, his constant commitment to make travel accessible to all by striving for low prices had received extensive media coverage for more than twenty years. Within the company, he was highly respected and, though his style was sometimes described as autocratic, he was recognized as a manager with high ethical standards and a genuine concern for his employees.

Nouvelles Frontières' headquarters were functional and modern but far from luxurious. This reflected the emphasis the company put on lowering costs whenever possible in order to pursue its publicly stated corporate goal of offering its customers the lowest possible prices. Though his stake in Nouvelles Frontières' equity made him one of the 50 richest people in France, Jacques Maillot was paid a relatively modest salary (about 10,000 Euros per month). The CEO's salary as well as all others in the company were public information. In addition, the company had rarely distributed any dividends and most of the profits were reinvested in growing Nouvelles Frontières' operations.

Nouvelles Frontières' owner-managers had repeatedly stated that they valued growth more than profits. When asked to justify this position, they argued that the bigger the company could become, the better, and that by expanding they were in fact strengthening its position. They expected a shake-out in the tour operating industry in Europe at some point in the future and were convinced that only the bigger and more cost-effective competitors would survive. And they certainly wanted Nouvelles Frontières to be among the survivors.

COMPETITORS

Aside from Nouvelles Frontières, the only other large tour operator in France was Club Méditerranée. Club Med, as it was usually known, was founded in the mid-fifties and had grown rapidly and successfully by specializing in a very specific type of holiday: customers would be flown to a so-called "village," in fact a closed-in resort in a sunny holiday destination, where they would be offered a wide range of sports and entertainment activities right on the premises, and in almost complete isolation from the surrounding country and population. Club Med was famous for identifying beautiful, yet undeveloped, locations and getting concessions from local governments to build its "villages." In the sixties and seventies, Club Med had cultivated a somewhat "steamy" reputation through advertising campaigns emphasizing "Sea, Sun and S . . ." (i.e., either "Sand" or "Sex", whichever way customers chose to interpret it). Since the mid-eighties, however, Club Med had become much more family oriented, offering such services as child care and supervised children activities in most villages. In the mid-nineties, Club Med operated over 100 villages throughout the world in such exotic locations as Cancun (Mexico), Corfu (Greece), Mauritius, Agadir (Morocco) or Pukhet (Thailand). By the mid-nineties, Club Med had also run into serious problems, losing both customers and money; the company's poor performance was attributed by most analysts to their inability to control costs and to the very high price they charged for their services. This had led to a complete management change with Serge Trigano, the founder's son, being replaced as CEO by Philippe Bourguignon, the former CEO of Disneyland-Paris. In 1999, Club Med had attracted 1.5 million customers and achieved sales of 1.5 billion Euros.

In 1988, Nouvelles Frontières had signed a memorandum of understanding with Club Méditerranée for the two companies to merge. The merger, which would have created one of the largest tour operating companies in Europe at the time, was never carried out because of subsequent disagreements between the top managements of the two firms on a number of strategic issues.

The third largest tour operator in France was FRAM (500,000 customers and 350 million Euros in sales in 1999), a company specializing in tours and trips for retirees, a rapidly growing segment of the population. The purchasing power of retirees made them avid customers of holidays and travel, provided they were offered the kind of attention and assistance they required. The fourth and fifth largest tour operators in France were Jet Tours (350,000 customers and 250 million Euros in sales in 1999) and Frantour (250,000 customers and 150 million Euros in sales in 1999) respectively. Jet Tours had been a subsidiary of Air France, the nation's state-owned flagship carrier, but had not been able to use its close ties with the airline to compete successfully. Jet Tours had been performing very poorly for many years and it was spun off by Air France through a "leveraged management buy-out" in 1997. Frantour was a subsidiary of SNCF, France's nationalized railway system, and was not seen as a serious competitor in the industry. All other tour operators in France were small or medium-sized companies, the most successful of which were very specialized, either by type of tours and holidays (i.e., trekking, cruises, sailing, skiing, scuba diving, etc.) or by destination.

None of the tour operators in France, except Nouvelles Frontières, had an exclusive distribution network. FRAM had a handful of agencies which showcased the firm's services but most of its sales were through traditional travel agents. FRAM paid travel agents a 12% commission but also provided them with specific training and other incentives; total cost of distribution was thus thought to be about 15% for FRAM. In the mid-eighties FRAM had tried to expand its company-owned travel agencies but was pressured into pulling back by its traditional distributors. Club Med operated about 60 travel agencies which it had acquired in 1990 when it took over Club Aquarius, a lower priced copy-cat competitor offering very similar holiday packages, which had gone bankrupt; Aquarius owned these agencies at the time and they were subsequently rebadged as Club Med. Most of Club Med sales in France, however, were still made through the Havas Voyage travel agency network. The commission paid to Havas by Club Med was thought to be about 10% to 12%; the price for Club Med products was the same in both channels though it was rumored that customers willing to bargain could get significant discounts in Club Med's own agencies.

In some other European countries there were very large competitors. In Germany and the United Kingdom the largest tour operators were several times the size of Nouvelles Frontières. None of these large competitors, however, had ventured out of their domestic market in any significant way. Only

T.U.I. (see Exhibit 2) had tried to enter the French market by acquiring a stake in a medium sized local tour operator but had pulled out after a few years, apparently disappointed with its performance. Some observers predicted that the deregulation of air travel in Europe would eventually lead to greater intra-European competition in tour operating. Nouvelles Frontières had established a presence in both Germany and the UK but had not been very successful and remained a marginal player in those markets.

In Spain and Italy, in contrast, the tour operating industry was still not highly developed and nowhere near as concentrated as it was in Northern Europe. Alpitur, the largest Italian tour operator was only one-third the size of Nouvelles Frontières and Tiempo Libre, the largest Spanish tour operator was one tenth its size. In both these countries, Nouvelles Frontières had established a strong presence, becoming the fifth largest tour operator in Italy and the eighth in Spain.

THE INTERNET CHALLENGE

Nouvelles Frontières had started selling on line as early as the mid-eighties by using the French government-sponsored "Minitel" system. Minitel was developed as part as the state-monopoly telephone system: subscribers to a phone line would receive, at no extra charge, a very simple terminal (basically a monitor and keyboard with no computing capability) through which they could access services set up by a variety of providers. Such services included the phone directory, railway or airline information and reservations, banking services, etc. Minitel was in fact an early version of internet, but lack of compatibility and government control prevented it from developing in any significant way and confined it to the French market (though investors did at one point consider importing it to the United States). Nouvelles Frontières' Minitel sales developed rapidly but never accounted for more than 2% to 3% of total sales.

Even before Internet use started spreading significantly in France in the late nineties, Nouvelles Frontières' managers realized this new development would dramatically affect their business. By 1997, travel related services were thought to account for about 45% of all Internet sales worldwide. New competitors in the form of dot.com companies were going after the same customers as Nouvelles Frontières. Location and distance were no longer a factor; providers anywhere in the world could sell travel services to customers located tens of thousands of miles away. Logistic problems, which in many other industries protected traditional competitors from their online rivals to some extent at least, were virtually non existent in travel services. In addition to creating new competition, Internet would undoubtedly affect the relations tour operators had with their suppliers. Most airlines could now reach out directly to their customers without having to invest in costly distribution, as could hotels, resorts or car rental companies.

In this somewhat threatening context, Nouvelles Frontières opened its "nouvelles-frontieres.fr" website in 1997. 1998 Internet sales were 10 million Euros. In 1999, Internet sales increased to 20 million Euros, while total direct sales (Internet, Minitel, and telephone sales combined) exceeded 100 million Euros. Internet sales were expected to be more than 50 million Euros in 2000, 20% of which would come from the weekly auction sale of unsold capacity that the company

organized every Tuesday. In 1999, Nouvelles Frontières opened its English-language website "nouvelles-frontieres.com."

The management of Nouvelles Frontières had been pleasantly surprised by the fact that close to 90% of their online customers were first time clients of the company. Also, they were quite satisfied that, after three years in operation, their website was the third most visited travel-related website in France (see Exhibits 7 and 8).

One issue that Jacques Maillot intended to raise at the upcoming shareholders meeting was how the company should go public. For several years, the main shareholders had been debating whether to take the company public and had finally decided to do so in early 2001. They felt that raising funds on the stock market would allow the company to expand internationally more aggressively and would provide the resources to further strengthen online distribution. They were reluctant, however, to give

Exhibit 7   The Main Online Travel Services Providers in the US

	1999 Sales (million US$)	Market Share
Travelocity.com	808	22%
Expedia	725	20%
Preview Travel	382	10%
Priceline.com	350	10%
ITN.net	260	7%
Cheap Tickets	144	4%
Hotel Reservations Network	131	4%
Travelscape.com	104	3%
Lowestfare.com	70	2%
Trip.com	70	2%
Itravel.com	64	2%
Biztravel.com	40	1%
Others	474	13%

SOURCE: PhoCusWright

Exhibit 8   The Main Online Travel Services Providers in Europe

	% of Internet Users Having Accessed Website
France	
SNCF.fr	8%
Degriftour.fr	3.3%
nouvelles-frontieres.fr	3.3%
Travelprice.com	2.2%
Lastminute.com	2.1%
United Kingdom	
Lastminute.com	5.5%
Railtrack.co.uk	3.1%
Thomascook.co.uk	3%
British-Airways.com	2.6%
TheTrainLine.com	2.5%
Germany	
Deutschbahn.de	11.6%
Lufthansa.de	2.3%
TUI.de	1.5%
Flug.de	1.3%
Reisenplanung.de	1.3%

SOURCE: MMXI Europe

up the controlling stake they had in the company. Jacques Maillot in particular was puzzled by the advice investment bankers had given him: they had suggested that if he lowered his stake in the company to significantly below 50%—as opposed to the current 52% he owned—total market capitalization might be as high as one billion Euros. If, on the other hand, he retained a majority holding, they doubted the market would value Nouvelles Frontières at more than 800 million Euros.

Another issue to be considered was whether Nouvelles Frontières' online activities should remain an integral part of the company, or whether they should be separated from the rest and taken public on their own. The saliency of this question had increased dramatically since Degriftour, one of Nouvelles Frontières' smaller competitors, but the French leader in online travel services sales, had been acquired for 100 million Euros (30 million in cash and 70 million in stock) by Britain's Lastminute.com. Degriftour, which had sales of 100 million Euros in 1999, had specialized in direct sales

(initially by telephone and Minitel, later extended to internet) of travel services. The company had been faltering on the verge of bankruptcy until it was acquired in mid-August 2000.

As he reflected on all these issues, Jacques Maillot realized Nouvelles Frontières was probably facing some of the most difficult challenges in its thirty or so year history.

CASE QUESTIONS

1. Why has Nouvelles Frontières been so successful over the last 30 years? What are the nature and sources of their competitive advantage?
2. In the early 90s, Nouvelles Frontières chose to integrate backward into air travel and resorts; what do you think about such moves?
3. Should Nouvelles Frontières be concerned about foreign competitors ? Should their own international expansion strategy be pursued? Why?
4. How is Internet affecting the company's position? What should they do about it?

Case 11   Whirlpool Corporation's Global Strategy (2000)

We want to be able to take the best capabilities we have and leverage them in all our companies worldwide.

—DAVID WHITMAN, WHIRLPOOL CEO, 1994
QUOTED IN THE *HARVARD BUSINESS REVIEW*

In 1989, Whirlpool Corporation (Whirlpool) embarked on an ambitious global expansion with the objective of becoming the world market leader in home appliances. Beginning with the purchase of a majority stake in an appliance company owned by Philips, the Dutch electronics firm, Whirlpool pur-

chased a majority stake in an Indian firm, established four joint ventures in China, and made significant new investments in its Latin America operations.

By the mid-1990s, however, serious problems had emerged in the company's international operations. In 1995, Whirlpool's European profit fell by 50 percent and in 1996, the company reported a $13 million loss in Europe. In Asia, the situation was even worse. Although the region accounted for only 6 percent of corporate sales, Whirlpool lost $70 million in Asia in 1996 and $62 million in 1997. In Brazil, Whirlpool found itself a victim in 1997, and again in 1998, of spiraling interest rates. Despite the company's investments of hundreds of millions of dollars throughout the 1990s to modernize operations there, appliance sales in Brazil plummeted by 25 percent in 1998. Whirlpool expected that 1999 would be the third straight year of declining sales for the Brazilian subsidiary.

In response to these problems, Whirlpool began a global restructuring effort. In September 1997, the company announced that it would cut 10 percent of its global workforce over the next two years and pull out of two joint ventures in China. In announcing the cuts, Whirlpool's CEO David Whitwam said, "We are taking steps to align the organization with the marketplace realities of our industry."[1] In Latin America, 3,500 jobs were abolished, and significant investments were made to upgrade plants and product lines.

After the optimism of the early 1990s, what went wrong with Whirlpool's global strategy? Was the company overly ambitious? Was there a lack of understanding about how to create an integrated global strategy? Or, were the problems the result of changes in the competitive and economic environments in Europe, Asia, and Latin America? Should Whirlpool have foreseen the problems and reacted earlier?

THE APPLIANCE INDUSTRY IN THE LATE TWENTIETH CENTURY

Approximately 120 million home appliances are sold in developed countries each year.[2] The appliance industry is generally classified into four categories: laundry, refrigeration, cooking, and other appliances. Appliances are constructed in capital-intensive plants, and design usually varies among countries and regions.

The North American Industry

Although it was estimated that 46 million appliances were sold in North America annually, the market was expected to grow little in the late 1990s. Saturation levels were high, with virtually 100 percent of households owning refrigerators and cookers and over 70 percent owning washers. Because of the limited growth opportunities, competition was fierce. In the United States, the industry had consolidated in the 1980s, leaving four major competitors: Whirlpool, General Electric, Electrolux, and Maytag (see Exhibit 1 for more detail). These four firms controlled about 80 percent of the markt.[3] Each firm offered a variety of products and brands segmented along price lines. Distribution of these appliances was generally through sales to builders for new houses or to retailers, such as department stores and specialty resellers.

In a *Harvard Business Review* article in 1994 called "The Right Way to Go Global," David Whitwam, Whirlpool's CEO, described the competitive situation that existed in the early 1990s:

> Even though we had dramatically lowered costs and improved product quality, our profit margins in North America had been declining because everyone in the industry was pursuing the same course and the local market was mature. The four main players—Whirlpool, General Electric, Maytag, and White Consolidated, which had been acquired by Electrolux—were beating one another up everyday.[4]

With limited growth opportunities and a handful of major players in the United States, it was critical that firms focus on cost reduction, productive efficiency, and product quality. Product innovation was also critical, although few major innovations had occurred in recent years. the appliance firms segmented their products according to different consumers' needs, and each strove to achieve greater economies of scale. Still, by the end of the 1990s, the competitive landscape remained unattractive. Profit margins continued to decline for most firms. Many analysts believed that the market for appliances was saturated and that there would be little increase in growth rates. This saturation had left the distributors focusing primarily on replacement purchases and purchases for new housing developments.

[1]C. Quintanilla and J. Carlton, "Whirlpool Announces Global Restructuring Effort," *Wall Street Journal,* September 19, 1997, A3, A6.

[2]David D. Weiss and Andrew C. Gross, "Industry Corner: Major Household Appliances in Western Europe," *Business Economics,* 30, no. 3 (July 1995): 67.

[3]William Echikson, "The Trick to Selling in Europe," *Fortune,* September 20, 1993, 82.

[4]Regina Fazio Maruca, "The Right Way to Go Global: An Interview with Whirlpool CEO David Whitwam," *Harvard Business Review* (March–April 1994): 137.

Exhibit 1   Major Competitors in the United States

GE Appliance

General Electric Appliance was the second-largest manufacturer of household appliances in the United States (behind Whirlpool). Other brand names produced by the company included Monogram, Profile, Profile Performance, Hotpoint, and some private brands for retailers. GE Appliance comprised approximately 6 percent of the parent company's sales and had the top market share position in India and Mexico. In addition, the company had a 50–50 joint venture with General Electric Company, the leading appliance firm in the United Kingdom.

Maytag

Maytag's products were generally aimed at the mid-to-high end of the market and commanded a premium price based on product quality and reliability. Other brand names produced by Maytag included Jenn-Air, Magic Chef, Performa, and Hoover. Maytag entered the European market in 1989, but after a decline in profits, pulled out of Europe in 1995. Maytag had a limited international presence in China.

AB Electrolux

AB Electrolux was the world's largest producer of household appliances. Other Electrolux brand names included Frigidaire, Tappan, and Kelvinator. The Swedish company had the number one market share in Europe and number four market share in North America. Electrolux entered the United States when it bought White Consolidated Industries in 1986. The firm was actively expanding overseas into Eastern Europe, China, India, Southeast Asia, and Latin America.

SOURCES: Hoovers Online. Accessed 2/9/00. Norman C. Remich. "A Kentucky Thoroughbred That Is Running Strong," *Appliance Manufacturer* (July 1995): GEA-3. Greg Steinmetz and Carl Quintanillla. "Tough Target: Whirlpool Expected Easy Going in Europe, and It Got a Big Shock," *Wall Street Journal*, April 10, 1998, Sec. A:1.

The European Industry

In the early 1980s, there were approximately 350 producers of household appliances in Europe. With consolidation in the industry, by the late 1980s the number had shrunk to about one hundred.[5] By early 1995, it was estimated that five of the companies, including Electrolux (with a 25 percent market share), Philips Bauknecht, and Bosche-Siemens, controlled over 70 percent of the market.[6] The industry was highly regionalized, with many of the companies producing a limited number of products for a specific geographic area.

The European market consisted of more than 320 million consumers whose preferences varied by country and by region. For example, Swedes pre-

ferred galvanized washing machines to withstand the damp salty air.[7] The British washed their clothes more often than the Italians did and wanted quieter machines. The French liked to cook on gas at high temperatures, splattering grease on cooking surfaces, and so preferred self-cleaning ovens, while the Germans liked to cook on electric stoves at lower temperatures and did not need such features.[8]

Distribution of the appliances in Europe was different than in the United States. Most appliances were sold through independent retailers, who had become organized in buying groups or as multiple

---

[5]Weiss and Gross

[6]Joe Jancsurak, "Holistic Strategy Pays Off," *Appliance Manufacturer* (February 1995): W-3, W-4.

[7]Greg Steinmetz and Carl Quintanilla, "Tough Target: Whirlpool Expected Easy Going in Europe, and It Got a Big Shock," *Wall Street Journal*, April 10, 1998, Sec. A:1.

[8]Zachary Schiller, et al., "Whirlpool Plots the Invasion of Europe," *Business Week*, September 5, 1988: 70.

store chains.[9] A smaller channel was through independent kitchen specialists who sold complete kitchen packages, including appliances.[10]

The Asian Industry

Asia, the world's second-largest home appliance market, was also the fastest growing market of the 1980s. By the mid-1990s, it was growing at a rate of between 8 percent and 12 percent annually, a rate that was expected to continue well past the year 2000.[11] The industry was highly fragmented, consisting of manufacturers primarily from Japan, Korea, and Taiwan. Matsushita, the market leader, held less than 10 percent market share outside Japan.

Asian consumer preferences were different from those in Europe or North America. Kitchen appliances needed to be smaller to fit in Asian kitchens. Lack of space sometimes required the consumer to store the appliance in an outside hallway and transport it into the kitchen for use.[12] Therefore, high value was placed on appliances that were portable, usually lightweight and on wheels, and easily hooked up to electrical and water supplies. Refrigerators also tended to be smaller and more colorful. Indeed, when Asian countries first began to experience significant economic growth, some East Asians viewed their refrigerators as status symbols and like to display them prominently, perhaps even in the sitting room. Clothes dryers and dishwashers were uncommon in most Asian countries, but most homes had microwaves.

Appliances in Asia were traditionally sold through small retail shops. However, the industry was beginning to witness a shift away from these small shops and toward distribution through national power retailer organizations, especially in China and parts of Southeast Asia.

The Latin American Industry

The economic stability in Latin America in the 1990s made the region an attractive growth proposition. The appliance makers hoped that the days of hyperinflation and economic mismanagement were over, and they were pleased to see that governments were reducing tariffs. Distributors in Latin America were generally responsible for marketing a company's appliances to small independent retailers in the region.[13] In 1994, there were over 65 competitors in the Latin American market, many of them subsidiaries of U.S. parents.

WHIRLPOOL CORPORATION

Whirlpool was founded in 1911 as The Upton Machine Company in St. Joseph, Michigan, to produce an electric motor-driven wringer washer. The company merged with The Nineteen Hundred Washer Company in 1929 and began to sell its first automatic washing machine through Sears, Roebuck & Co. in 1947. The Whirlpool brand was introduced in 1948 and steadily built a strong retail relationship with Sears. Through a series of acquisitions and mergers, the company emerged as a leading force in the U.S. appliance industry with annual revenue reaching $2 billion in 1978 (see Exhibit 2 for more detail on Whirlpool's history). Whirlpool's headquarters was in Benton Harbor, Michigan.

As of 1998, Whirlpool Corporation claimed to be the world's leading manufacturer of major home appliances. The company manufactured in 13 countries and marketed its products under 11 major brand names (including Kenmore, Sears, KitchenAid, Roper, Inglis, and Speed Queen) to over 140 countries. Whirlpool's sales were $8.2 billion in fiscal year 1997.

THE GLOBALIZATION OF WHIRLPOOL

Whirlpool's first international investment was in 1957 when the firm acquired an equity interest in Multibras S.A., a Brazilian manufacturer of white goods. In 1969, the company entered the Canadian market by purchasing an equity interest in Inglis Ltd. and acquired sole ownership in 1990.

By the mid-1980s, Whirlpool saw that, despite increasing efficiencies and product quality, its profit

---

[9]Joe Jancsurak, "Group Sales: Channel Focused," *Appliance Manufacturer*, (February 1995): W-14.

[10]"Group Sales," W-14.

[11]Richard J. Babyak, "Strategic Imperative," *Appliance Manufacturer* (February 1995): W-21.

[12]Richard J. Babyak, "Demystifying the Asian Consumer," *Appliance Manufacturer* (February 1995): W26.

[13]Joe Janesurak, "South American Sales Co.: Linking the Americas, Europe," *Appliance Manufacturer* (February 1995): W-39.

Exhibit 2   Whirlpool History

1911	Upton Machine Company is founded in St. Joseph, Michigan, to produce electric motor-driven wringer washers.
1916	First order for washers is sold to Sears, Roebuck and Co.
1929	Upton Machine merges with Nineteen Hundred Washer Company of Binghamton, New York. The new firm, Nineteen Hundred Corp., operates plants in Michigan and New York until Binghamton is closed in 1939.
1942	All facilities are converted to wartime production until end of World War II in 1945.
1947	The company's first automatic washer is introduced to the market by Sears.
1948	A Whirlpool brand automatic washer is introduced, thus establishing dual distribution—one line of products for Sears, another for Nineteen Hundred.
1950	Nineteen Hundred Corporation is renamed Whirlpool Corporation. Automatic dryers are added to the product line.
1951	LaPorte, Indiana, plant is acquired. It will become the company's parts distribution center. Whirlpool merges with Clyde (Ohio) Porcelain Steel and converts the plant to washer production. All washers eventually will be produced here.
1955	Manufacturing facilities are purchased in Marion, Ohio, from Motor Products Corp., and dryer production is transferred there. Whirlpool merges with Seeger Refrigerator Co. of St. Paul, Minnesota, and the Estate range and air conditioning divisions of R.C.A. RCA Whirlpool is established as the brand name; Whirlpool-Seeger Corporation, as the company name. A refrigeration plant is acquired in Evansville, Indiana, from International Harvester.
1956	First full line of RCA Whirlpool home appliances is introduced. RCA will be used with the Whirlpool brand name until 1967. New administrative center is completed on 100-acre site in Benton Harbor.
1957	Company name is changed back to Whirlpool Corporation. Appliance Buyers Credit Corporation is established as a wholly owned finance subsidiary. It will be renamed Whirlpool Financial Corporation in 1989.

1957	Whirlpool invests in Brazilian appliance market through purchase of equity interest in Multibrás S.A. It is renamed Brastemp S.A. in 1972.
1966	The Norge plant in Fort Smith, Arkansas, is acquired, adding more than one million sq. ft. of refrigeration manufacturing space.
1967	Toll-free Cool-Line® Telephone Service begins. Renamed the Consumer Assistance Center in 1990, it gives customers direct, 24-hour access to Whirlpool. The company's first totally new manufacturing facility is completed in Findlay, Ohio. Dishwashers and, later, ranges will be manufactured there.
1968	The Elisha Gray II Research & Engineering Center is completed in Benton Harbor. For the first time, annual revenues reach $1 billion.
1969	The company enters the Canadian appliance market through purchase of an equity interest in Inglis Ltd. Sole ownership is established in 1990.
1970	Construction is completed on a new plant in Danville, Kentucky. Production of trash compactors and, later, vacuum cleaners is transferred there.
1976	Whirlpool increases its investment in the Brazilian market through purchase of equity interests in Consul S.A., an appliance manufacturer, and Embraco S.A., a maker of compressors.
1978	Annual revenues reach $2 billion.
1983	The company announce a phaseout of washer assembly at St. Joseph. All washers will be made at Clyde.
1984	The St. Paul Division is closed. Production of freezers and ice makers moves to Evansville.
1986	Whirlpool purchases the KitchenAid division of Hobart Corporation. A majority interest is purchased in Apsera s.r.l., an Italian compressor manufacturer. Whirlpool will become sole owner before the business is sold to Embraco of Brazil in 1994. Whirlpool closes most of its St. Joseph Division. The remaining machining operation is renamed the Benton Harbor Division.
1987	Whirlpool and Sundaram-Clayton Limited of India from TVS Whirlpool Limited to make compact washers for the Indian market. Whirlpool will acquire majority ownership in 1994.

Exhibit 2   (cont.)

1988   A joint venture company, Vitromatic S.A. de C.V., is formed with Vitro, S.A. of Monterrey, to manufacture and market major home appliances for Mexican and export markets. Whirlpool acquires the Rope brand name, which it will use to market a full line of value-oriented home appliances.

1989   Whirlpool and N.V. Philips of the Netherlands form a joint venture company, Whirlpool Europe B.V., from Philips major domestic appliance division, to manufacture and market appliances in Europe. Whirlpool will become sole owner in 1991. Appliance operations in the United States, Canada, and Mexico are brought together to form the North American Appliance Group (NAAG). Annual revenues catapult over the $6 billion mark.

1990   A program is launched to market appliances in Europe under the dual brands Philips and Whirlpool. Whirlpool Overseas Corporation is formed as a subsidiary to conduct marketing and industrial activities outside North American and Western Europe. An Estate brand of appliances targeted to national accounts is introduced.

1991   The company commits globally to its Worldwide Excellence System, a total quality management program dedicated to exceeding customer expectations. NAAG repositions its refrigeration business. The Port Credit, Ontario, plant is closed. Top- and bottom-mount refrigerators are consolidated at Evansville, side-by-side refrigerators at Fort Smith.

1992   Whirlpool assumes control of SAGAD S.A., of Argentina. Whirlpool Hungarian Trading Ltd. is formed to sell and service appliances in Hungary. Whirlpool Tatramat is formed to make and sell washing machines and market other major home appliances in Slovakia. Whirlpool will take controlling interest in 1994. A Small Appliance Business Unit is formed to operate on a global basis. revenues top $7 billion. The South American Sales Co. (SASCo), a joint venture with Whirlpool's Brazilian affiliates, begins directing export sales to 35 Latin American countries.

1993   Whirlpool Overseas Corporation is replaced by two separate regional organizations: Whirlpool Asia and Whirlpool Latin America. Whirlpool Asia sets up headquarters in Tokyo with regional offices in Singapore, Hong Kong, and Tokyo. Sales subsidiaries are opened in Poland and the Czech Republic, adding to Whirlpool Europe's growing presence in Eastern Europe. Whirlpool wins the $30 million Super Efficient Refrigerator Program sponsored by 24 U.S. utilities. Inglis Ltd. becomes Canada's leading home appliance manufacturer.

1994   Whirlpool Asia and Teco Electric & Machinery Co. Ltd. form Great Teco Whirlpool Co. Ltd. to market and distribute home appliances in Taiwan. Whirlpool becomes a stand-alone brand in Europe. Brazilian affiliates Consul and Brastemp merge to form Multibrás S.A. Electrodomésticos. Whirlpool breaks ground in Tulsa, Oklahoma, for a new plant to make freestanding gas and electric ranges. Whirlpool's Asian headquarters is moved to Singapore, and the number of operating regions is increased form three to four. Whirlpool exits vacuum cleaner business. To strengthen competitiveness, a major restructuring is announced in North America and Europe. One U.S. and one Canadian plant close. Total revenues top $8 billion.

1995   An executive office is formed in Whirlpool Asia to led the company's rapid growth and manage strategic deployment in the region. Whirlpool acquires controlling interest in Kelvinator of India ltd., one of India's largest manufacturers and marketers of refrigerators. TVS Whirlpool Ltd. changes name to Whirlpool Washing Machines ltd. (WWML). Construction is completed on a new plant in Greenville, Ohio. KitchenAid small appliances will be manufactured there, Whirlpool begins to sell appliances to Montgomery Ward. Whirlpool Europe opens representative office in Russia. Whirlpool Financial Corporation (WFC) is established in India. Whirlpool assumes control of Beijing Whirlpool Snowflake Electric Appliance Group Co. Ltd., a refrigerator and freezer manufacturing joint venture. Beijing Embraco Snowflake Compressor Co. Ltd., a compressor manufacturing joint venture, is formed between Embraco and Beijing Snowflake. Whirlpool has a minority

Exhibit 2   (cont.)

1995 (cont.)	position in the joint venture. Whirlpool acquires controlling interest in the Whirlpool Narcissus (Shanghai) Co. Ltd., a washing machine manufacturing joint venture. Whirlpool acquires majority ownership of SMC Microwave Products Co. Ltd., a microwave oven manufacturing joint venture. Shenzhen Whirlpool Raybo Air-Conditioner Industrial Co. Ltd., an air conditioner manufacturing joint venture, is formed with Whirlpool having a majority stake. Whirlpool investments in Asia increase to over US$350 million, and employees total more than 9,300.	1996	Whirlpool Europe opens sales subsidiaries in Romania and Bulgaria. Production of electric and gas ranges officially begins in Whirlpool's new plant in Tulsa, Oklahoma. the company's new Greenville, Ohio, plant, which manufactures KitchenAid small appliances, begins production. The Ft. Smith Division in Arkansas begins production of trash compactors. Whirlpool Asia employees total more than 12,000. Whirlpool Europe acquires the white goods business of Gentrade of South Africa. The acquisition provides Whirlpool a sales and manufacturing base in this country.

SOURCE: http://www.whirlpool.com

margins were rapidly decreasing in North America. Top management believed that if the company continued to follow its current path, the future would be "neither pleasant nor profitable."[14] They considered restructuring the company financially or diversifying into related businesses but eventually settled on further global expansion for two main reasons: the company wished to take advantage of less mature markets around the world, and it did not want to be left behind by its competitors, which had already begun to globalize.

Whitwam's Vision and Platform Technology

David Whitwam joined Whirlpool in 1968 as a marketing management trainee and rose through the sales and marketing ranks to succeed Jack Sparks as CEO in 1987. Although Whitwam admitted that he had never actually run a multinational company until Whirlpool bought Philips in 1989, he believed that:

> The only way to gain lasting competitive advantage is to leverage your capabilities around the world, so that the company as a whole is greater than the sum of its parts. Being an international company—selling globally, having global brands or operations in different countries—isn't enough.[15]

Whitwam was convinced that most companies with international divisions were not truly global at all, as their various regional and national divisions still operated as autonomous entities rather than working together as a single company. He believed that the only way to achieve his vision of an integrated international company, or one company worldwide, was through intensive efforts to understand and respond to genuine customer needs and through products and services that earn long-term customer loyalty.

Whitwam talked about his vision of integrating Whirlpool's geographical businesses so that the company's expertise would not be confined to one location or product. He forecast appliances such as a World Washer, a single machine that could be sold anywhere, and he wanted to standardize the company's manufacturing processes. According to Whitwam,

> Today products are being designed to ensure that a wide variety of models can be built on the same basic platform. . . . Varying consumer preferences require us to have regional manufacturing centers. But even though the features . . . vary from market to market, much of the technology and manufacturing processes involved are similar.[16]

---

[14]Maruca, p. 136.
[15]Ibid., p. 137.

[16]Ibid., p. 136.

Given this view that standardization should be the focus, Whirlpool planned to base all its products, wherever they were built or assembled, on common platforms. These platforms would produce the technological heart of the product, the portion of the product that varied little across markets. The products could then be diversified to suit individual and regional preferences. In this way, the parts that the customer sees—the dimensions of the appliance, the metal case, and the controls—could be varied by segment or market to fulfill consumers' needs. The products would also have to meet rigorous quality and environmental standards to ensure that they could be used in different countries around the world.

Whitwam believed that the platform technology would bring a $200 million annual savings in design and component costs by the time it was fully implemented in the year 2000.[17] In addition, management was convinced that the platform strategy would put the company two to three years ahead of its competitors.

Platform technology, however, represented only the beginning of Whirlpool's globalization strategy. According to Whitwam in the 1994 interview, Whirlpool could not truly achieve its goal of globalization until:

> we have cross-border business teams . . . running all of our operations throughout the world. . . . There will also come a day when we'll identify a location where the best skills in a certain product area should be concentrated, and that place will become the development center for the type of product. . . . [but] while we may have only one major design center for a given product, not everyone associated with that product will have to be located there.[18]

DEVELOPING AND IMPLEMENTING THE GLOBAL STRATEGY

By 1987 Whirlpool had adopted a five-year plan to develop a new international strategy. The company's 1987 Annual Report included the following statement:

The U.S. appliance industry has limited growth opportunities, a high concentration of domestic competitors, and increasing foreign competition. Further, the United States represents only about 25% of the worldwide potential for major appliance sales. Most importantly, our vision can no longer be limited to our national borders because national borders no longer define market boundaries. The marketplace for products and services is more global than ever before and growing more so every day.

Recent industry forecasts indicated that approximately three-quarters of the growth in domestic appliance sales between 1995 and 2000 would be in East Asia (including Australia), Eastern Europe, and South and Central America. According to the forecasts, by 2000 these three regions (excluding Japan) would account for about 34 percent of sales.

European Expansion

In 1989, Whirlpool bought a major stake in N.V. Philips, a struggling Dutch appliance operation, and then purchased the remaining equity in 1991 for a total of $1.1 billion.[19] Whitwam believed that the U.S. and European markets were very similar and hoped that Whirlpool would be able to replicate their successes in the United States in the new market through implementation of a pan-European strategy. Whirlpool management also believed that the European market was becoming more "American." Research performed by the company indicated that European integration was making it more difficult for smaller companies to survive and that the industry was ripe for consolidation. Whirlpool's plan was to be one of the big players following this consolidation, and Whitwam was expecting a 20 percent share of the $20 billion market by the year 2000.[20] Whirlpool's strategy was to focus on brand segmentation and operational efficiency. It was believed that the company that produced the most innovative products while reducing costs would capture the market.

---

[17]Whirlpool Corporation, Annual Report, 1997.
[18]Maruca, p. 145.

[19]Steinmetz and Quintanilla, A:6.
[20]Ibid., A:1, A:6.

The European subsidiary, Whirlpool Europe BV (WEBV), crated a brand portfolio segmented by price. Bauknecht (Philip's German brand) served as the company's high-end product, while Inglis served as the lower-end, value brand. The Philips/Whirlpool brand filed the middle range.[21] However, the company decided to heavily market the Whirlpool brand name at the expense of managing its other European brands. Managers at Bauknecht in Germany saw their marketing budgets slashed, and Bauknecht's market share fell from 7 percent to 5 percent.[22] By 1995, however, consumer research showed Whirlpool to be the most recognized appliance brand name in Europe, despite the fact that many Germans, Italians, and French had a problem pronouncing the name.

To better manage sales and service throughout the region, Whirlpool set up two centralized distribution centers: one in Cassinetta, Italy, and one in Schorndorf, Germany. Operations were streamlined in order to achieve reduced costs through economies of scale, and considerable efforts were put toward product innovation and increasing operational efficiency. This strategic focus was overlaid with a global outlook, and managers were regularly rotated between Europe and the United States. The rotation generated a crossover of ideas but annoyed retail clients who felt that they had no continuity when dealing with senior managers.

The early years of European expansion were successful. Sales and profits increased steadily, and Whirlpool made a profit of $129 million in Europe in 1993. The company was able to cut costs by reducing the number of suppliers it dealt with and by using common parts in its appliances.

However, Whirlpool was not the only company aggressively attacking the market, and competition subsequent to Whirlpool's entry grew fierce. Electrolux and Bosch-Siemens both greatly improved their efficiency, along with many of the smaller European companies. The European companies laid off large numbers of workers, built up their core businesses, and concentrated on generating profits. Bosch-Siemens expanded its overseas operations while keeping production local, and the company managed to raise its non-German revenue by more than 30 percent in five years. Electrolux shed all of its nonappliance businesses and cut its workforce by 15,000, closing 25 factories. Electrolux invested in new factories and achieved higher efficiency. Both Electrolux and Bosch-Siemens increased their profitability.

Across the industry, European plants doubled their output from 1990 to 1998 and cut the time needed to build a washing machine from five days to eight hours. Companies embraced computer-aided design techniques to speed the development of products. In 1997, it was reported that a new washing machine could move from the ideas stage to the shops in just 2-1/2 years, twice as fast as only a few years before. The "value gap" which existed between appliances in the United States and Europe also closed by an estimated 15 percent to 20 percent for all appliances.[23]

The state of the retail sector also changed. Traditionally, the producers had determined price in the European appliance industry. These producers had been able to reduce their costs through greater operational efficiencies and had allowed the retailers to keep their margins constant. However, by the 1990s, the number of retail outlets across Europe had fallen significantly, giving the larger surviving retailers more power when dealing with manufacturers. Recession in Europe also caused consumers to become more cost-conscious, and brands such as the low-price firm Indesit won considerable market share.

With all companies becoming more efficient as producers, there was a shift toward product innovation as the basis for competition. For example, Whirlpool increased the size of the entrance of its front-loading washing machines, thus allowing clothes to be pushed into the machine more easily and contributing to increased sales. Companies also attempted to improve customer service and to create appliances that were more friendly to the environment. Such changes were not going unnoticed, but the industry appeared to

[21]"Holistic Strategy," W-3.
[22]Steinmetz and Quintanilla, A:6.

[23]Joe Jancsurak, "Marketing: Phase 2," *Appliance Manufacturer* (February 1995): W-10.

be extremely mature. Not only were new entrants, such as Whirlpool, GE, Daewoo of South Korea, and Malaysia's Sime Darby, trying to build up sales from a small base, but the traditional European producers had become more aggressive. More than that, few were making tactical or strategic errors. Seeing the increased costs of competition and the growing intensity of rivalry, Maytag left the European market in 1995, selling its Hoover unit at a $130 million loss. Leonard Hadley, Maytag's chairman, commented, "Europe isn't an attractive place to try to go in and dislodge the established players."[24]

Eastern Europe was seen as the next great battleground and Whirlpool expanded its operations in 1996 to newly developing countries in Eastern and Central Europe. In 1997, Whirlpool opened new offices in Romania, Bulgaria, Turkey, Morocco, and

---
[24] Steinmetz and Quintanilla, A:6.

South Africa from its European headquarters. Sales in the initial years were disappointing.

PROBLEMS FOR WHIRLPOOL

Whirlpool's sales leveled off in the mid-1990s, and profits began to fall. Sales only increased 13 percent from 1990 to 1996, which was far from the levels management had expected. The company initiated a major restructuring in 1995 and laid off 2,000 employees. The restructuring did not solve the problems, and in 1996, the company's European operations recorded a loss of $13 million. Between 1995 and 1997, the company also witnessed a rise in materials and labor costs. Exhibit 3 shows Whirlpool's stock prices versus the S&P 500. Exhibits 3 and 4 show Whirlpool corporate and business unit financial information.

Whirlpool announced a second restructuring in 1997. The company planned to cut a further 4,700

Exhibit 3   Whirlpool Share Price*

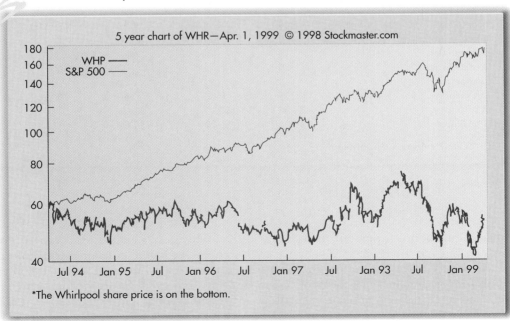

*The Whirlpool share price is on the bottom.

Exhibit 4   Whirlpool Financial Statements

Balance Sheet	Dec-98 US$MM	Dec-97 US$MM	Dec-96 US$MM	Dec-95 US$MM
Cash	636	578	129	149
Securities	0	0	0	0
Receivables	1,711	1,565	2,366	2,117
Allowances	116	156	58	81
Inventory	1,100	1,170	1,034	1,029
Current Assets	3,882	4,281	3,812	3,541
Property and Equipment, Net	5,511	5,262	3,839	3,662
Depreciation	3,093	2,887	2,041	1,883
Total Assets	7,935	8,270	8,015	7,800
Current Liabilities	3,267	3,676	4,022	3,829
Bonds	1,087	1,074	955	983
Preferred Mandatory	0	0	0	0
Preferred Stock	0	0	0	0
Common Stock	83	82	81	81
Other Stockholders' Equity	1,918	1,689	1,845	1,796
Total Liabilities and Equity	7,935	8,270	8,015	7,800

Income Statement	Dec-98 US$MM	Dec-97 US$MM	Dec-96 US$MM	Dec-95 US$MM
Total Revenues	10,323	8,617	8,696	8,347
Cost of Sales	9,596	8,229	8,331	6,311
Other Expenses	39	377	65	31
Loss Provision	45	160	63	50
Interest Expense	260	168	165	141
Income Pretax	564	−171	130	242
Income Tax	209	−9	81	100
Income Continuing	310	−46	156	209
Discontinued	15	31	0	0
Extraordinary	0	0	0	0
Changes	0	0	0	0
Net Income	325	−15	156	209
EPS Primary	$4.09	($0.20)	$2.08	$2.80
EPS Diluted	$4.06	($0.20)	$2.07	$2.76

SOURCES: Whirlpool Annual Reports.

jobs worldwide, or about 15 percent of its workforce, mostly in Europe. In 1998, WEBV had a 12 percent market share and held the number three market position. However, in 1998, the profit margin had reduced further to 2.3 percent, compared to 10 percent in the United States.

Whirlpool's managers blamed a number of causes—reduced consumer demand, poor economic growth, the rising Italian lira, intense competition, and even the European Monetary Union—for its poor performance in Europe, but shareholders were unimpressed. Indeed, Scott

Graham, analyst at CIBC Oppenheimer, commented in 1998, "The strategy has been a failure. Whirlpool went in big [into overseas markets] and investors have paid for it."

In 1998, Whirlpool's goals remained the same, but the timeframes for delivery grew. Whitwam attributed the performance to temporary problems in the newer regions of activity and believed that Whirlpool was now "coming through the challenges." He and the rest of his management team remained resolute: "We were convinced when we first bought [the Philips operation] and we're convinced now. The benefits from Europe have begun to flow. But they have yet to be recognized."[25]

ASIAN EXPANSION

Whirlpool's strategy in Asia consisted of five main points: partnering to build win-win relationships; attracting, retaining, and developing the best people; ensuring quality in all aspects of the business; exceeding customer needs and expectations; and offering four key products (refrigerators, washers, microwaves, and air conditioners). Although Whirlpool announced in 1987 a full-scale cooperation with Daiichi, a department store retailer in Japan, the company decided to focus its efforts in Asia primarily on India and China. There were two main reasons for this decision. First, recent changes in government regulations in both countries made it possible for foreign corporations to own a controlling interest in a manufacturing company. Second, the large populations of India and China reduced the risk of establishing large-scale operations there.

Whirlpool decided that the best way to enter the Asian market was through joint ventures, for they would allow the company to quickly establish a manufacturing presence in Asia. Once it had accomplished this goal, Whirlpool planned to build its own manufacturing facilities in the region. In 1987, Whirlpool announced an agreement with Sundram Clyton of India to manufacture compact washers for the Indian market, a joint venture which later became known as Whirlpool Washing Machines Limited. In 1993, the Asian group established regional headquarters in Tokyo and a pan-Asian marketing, product development, and technology center in Singapore.

Whirlpool intensified its Asian acquisition strategy in 1995 with various acquisitions and joint ventures in both India and China. The company bought controlling interest in Kelvinator in India, combined it with Whirlpool Washing Machines Limited, and renamed the new entity Whirlpool of India (WOI). In addition to giving Whirlpool a 56 percent interest in WOI, the Kelvinator purchase gave the company direct access to more than 3,000 trade dealers in India. Between 1994 and 1995, the company also set up four joint ventures in China, as it believed that China's market for appliances was likely to equal or surpass that of North America within ten years. By 1996, Whirlpool's investment in Asia had reached $350 million, and they employed over 12,000 people. In 1997, the Asian businesses generated over $400 million in sales.

Despite its investments, however, the company suffered operating losses in Asia of $70 million in 1996 and $62 million in 1997. In 1997, Whirlpool decided to restructure its Chinese operations when overcapacity in the refrigerator and air-conditioning markets drove prices down significantly. In 1997, Whirlpool decided to find strategic alternatives for the two money-losing joint ventures which catered to these two markets.

Smaller Chinese companies were also seizing considerable market share away from the multinational foreign competition. Haier, a Chinese producer of air conditioners, microwave ovens, refrigerators, and dishwashers, publicly announced plans to become a global brand by 2002 and had already expanded into Indonesia and the Philippines. In addition, the Chinese government was strongly encouraging consumers to "buy Chinese."[26] Too many producers were making similar goods, and production soon outpaced demand. For example, although Whirlpool believed it would take approximately five to six years for the market to become

---

[25]Ibid., A:6.

[26]Lisa Shuchman, "Reality Check," *Wall Street Journal*, April 30, 1998, Global Investing Section: 1.

saturated, the refrigerator and air conditioning markets were deemed saturated just two years after Whirlpool established its joint ventures in China. In addition, the company's Asian operations produced products of poorer quality than its Japanese rivals.[27]

Competition and overcapacity were not the only problems for Whirlpool. The company had overestimated the size of the market. The Chinese middle class that could afford new home appliances numbered only about 120 million, and there was no tradition in China of changing appliances that worked properly.

Once in China, Whirlpool also realized that it had not properly understood the distribution system. The company discovered that there were huge geographical distances between Chinese cities and that the country lacked strong distribution channels. The company had not expected to face major problems with telecommunications, and, despite the country' huge labor supply, Whirlpool had difficulties finding qualified people for its factories.

The situation in India was similar. Despite having invested heavily in advertising and promotions, Whirlpool blamed overcapacity and difficult trading conditions in the refrigerator sector for its losses. Nevertheless, Whitwam remained confident:

> Our lower cost structure and focus on the remaining majority-owned joint ventures in China, combined with our strong market position in India and Asia-Pacific sales subsidiaries, leave Whirlpool well positioned for future growth and profitability in this region. . . . Our growing knowledge of Asia and ability to draw on the other global resources of Whirlpool will lead to continued improvement in our operating performance in 1998 and beyond, especially as we manage through a difficult market and economic environment.[28]

Whirlpool continued to invest money in India and committed over $100 million to build a new plant near Pune to produce chlorofluorocarbon-free and frost-free refrigerators for the Indian market. The company began construction of the new facility in 1997, and the factory began commercial production in the first quarter of 1998.

LATIN AMERICAN EXPANSION

Throughout most of the 1990s, Brazil was Whirlpool's most profitable foreign operation.[29] The company first bought into the Brazilian market in 1957 and held equity positions in three companies: Brasmotor S.A., Multibras, and Embraco. These companies held a 60 percent market share and after 40 years of operating in Brazil, had extremely high brand recognition and brand loyalty. Whirlpool took over Philip's Argentine subsidiary, SAGAD, in 1992. In the mid-90s, sales and profit figures were good, with sales up 28 percent in 1994–1995, and 15 percent in 1996. In 1997, Brazilian operations recorded approximately $78 million in earnings.

Because Latin America had lower appliance penetration rates than Europe and the United States (e.g., only 15 percent of Brazilian homes owned microwaves, compared with 91 percent in the United States), the region appeared to be a good target for expansion. By the mid-1990s, Latin America was beginning to achieve economic stability, and growth was sure to follow. Consumers felt the same way. Many consumers were not able to replace old and worn-out appliances using budget plans and credit arrangements.

In 1997 in Brazil, Whirlpool spent $217 million to increase its equity share in Brasmotor from 33 percent to 66 percent. Whirlpool then invested another $280 million in 1997 and 1998 to renew plants and product lines. The company introduced data transfer systems, and flexible production lines, and launched new products. Shortly after Whirlpool made these large investments in Brazil, however, interest rates in the country began to climb. The Brazilian government doubled interest rates in October 1997 and again in 1998. As a result, the currency depreciated and the economy suffered. In real terms, the *real* fell more than 50 percent in the six months prior to January 1999. Total foreign investment in Brazil

---

[27]Bill Vlasic and Zachary Schiller, "Did Whirlpool Spin Too Far Too Fast?" *Business Week*, June 24, 1996, 136.
[28]Whirlpool Corporation, Annual Report, 1997.

[29]Ian Katz, "Whirlpool: In the Wringer," *Business Week*, December 14, 1998, 83.

Exhibit 5   Whirlpool Business Unit Sales and Operating Profit

Sales (in millions of US dollars)			
	Dec-97	**Dec-96**	**Dec-95**	**Dec-94**
North America	5263	5310	5093	5048
Europe	2343	2494	2428	2373
Asia	400	461	376	205
Latin America	624	268	271	329
Other	−13	−10	−5	−6
Total	8617	8523	8163	7949

Operating Profit (in millions of US dollars)			
	Dec-97	**Dec-96**	**Dec-95**	**Dec-94**
North America	546	537	445	522
Europe	54	−13	92	163
Asia	−62	−70	−50	−22
Latin America	28	12	26	49
Restructuring charge	−343	−30		−248
Business dispositions	−53			60
Other	−159	−158	−147	−154
Total	11	278	366	370

SOURCE: Whirlpool Annual Reports.

slumped, and the country was eventually forced to request a $41.5 billion credit line from the International Monetary Fund in order to help rescue the economy.

Worse yet, Whirlpool's market research told them that consumers had reacted quickly to the economic problems. Many were afraid of job cuts in the worsening economy and were wondering whether Brazil would resort to the traditional solution of printing money to solve the economic problems. Consumers foresaw inflation and realized that they would not be able to afford to purchase Whirlpool's appliances, especially on credit. As Antonio da Silva, a 37-year-old maintenance worker said, "I'm afraid to pay over many months because you don't know if interest rates or inflation will rise again."[30]

In 1998, Whirlpool's Brazilian sales fell by 25 percent, or $1 billion.[31] Equally important, Whirlpool's *real* reserves had shrunk in value against the dollar, and the company was expecting inflationary pressures. As a result, in late 1998 the company announced more restructuring to its Latin American operations. Whirlpool immediately cut 3,200 jobs (about 25 percent of the workforce) to improve efficiency, and the company planned to cut out levels in the production chain in its seven factories in Brazil, Argentina, and Chile. At the same time, the company increased its marketing efforts in the region.

As of 1998, Whirlpool was still confident of a return to profitability in Latin America. The company believed that industry shipments to Brazil in

[30]Ibid., 83.

[31]Ibid.

1999 would equal those in 1997. *Business Week* characterized the company as bullish:

> The experience of surviving Brazil's many debt crises, bouts of hyperinflation, and military governments has given Whirlpool a been-there, done-that aura of confidence.[32]

But, given Whirlpool's poor showing in the earlier phases of its globalization plan, it still had far to go in convincing the many skeptics and disappointed shareholders that globalization was the best strategy. Many analysts were unsure whether Whirlpool's self-confidence was actually deserved or if it was little more than self-delusion.

---

[32]Ibid., 87.

Staffing and Training for Global Operations

Outline

Opening Profile: Oleg and Mark—Equal Work But Unequal Pay

Oleg and Mark are project managers at the Moscow subsidiary of a multibillion dollar international company. Oleg is a Russian local and Mark an American expatriate. Although raised in vastly different countries, they have a lot in common. Both 30 years old, they graduated from top universities in their home countries with degrees in economics, worked for prestigious organizations, went back to graduate school, and now work side by side in the challenging environment of Russia's emerging market economy. They work long hours, have unpredictable schedules, manage difficult relations with vendors and government agencies, and endure the ups and downs of corporate attitudes toward the Russian market. They often work together, attend the same meetings, face similar problems, and send countless faxes and e-mail messages to corporate headquarters in North America. They have an excellent relationship and often help each other. They like what they do, and their boss sees a bright future for both of them.

But when the working day is over, the similarity abruptly ends. Mark drives his Volvo 760 to a lavish four-room apartment in the prestigious southeast district of Moscow, while Oleg has to take the subway to the dark apartment in a rundown building downtown that he shares with four roommates. On the weekends Mark likes to dine out at the fashionable Savoy restaurant, where dinner costs as much as $200, while Oleg has a few beers at a friend's apartment. Three times a year Mark goes on vacation to Western Europe, the Caribbean, or the United States; once a year Oleg goes to see his parents in Siberia. Neither his car, apartment, nor vacation costs Mark anything—they are part of the "hardship package" he receives as compensation for living in Moscow on top of his regular salary of U.S.$6,000 per month. Oleg does not get any "hardship benefits" since he is a local resident and his salary is $200 per month.

Says Oleg: "I like my job and I like the people I work with. I think we have a great organization here in Moscow. Most of our expatriates are very open and knowledgeable. I think we learn a lot from each other, and the company benefits from having this multinational team.

"My compensation? Well, it's a bit frustrating to know that your buddies, who do the same work you do and who you often help, since many of them don't speak Russian, make 30 times more than you do. This summer we had an intern from an American business school, who worked under me. He used to take me out for lunch to hard-currency restaurants and pay as much as my monthly salary for it! He was a nice guy, but I don't think our relations were quite normal because I could not even buy a bottle of wine for that lunch, and he knew it.

"But at work I don't think about it. I'm too busy to think like that. Sometimes, late at night, some crazy thoughts come to my mind: 'Gee, something must be wrong—they treat you like a second-class citizen, cheap labor, they exploit you'. . . But the next morning, I am up for work and those thoughts are gone. How long will my patience last? I don't know."

According to the company's managing director for Russia: "Some of our Russian managers, such as Oleg, are equally, if not better qualified than expatriates. They perfectly understand our business and they are truly bilingual, while most of our expatriates can barely speak Russian. We are very fortunate to have these Russian employees—their contribution is hard to overestimate. Compensation? We pay them what the market tells us here in Moscow. Yes, it is extremely low pay according to Western standards, but why should I pay a manager $5,000 if I can hire him for $200? Are they bothered by the inequity? I don't think so. I haven't heard any complaints so far, and I think we have very good relations among Russians and expatriates."

Mark comments, "Oleg is a great guy. We get along well, he helps me a lot, especially with my Russian. Do I feel sorry for him? No, I think he has a bright future. One day he will manage this subsidiary. As far as money goes, we live in a market economy. I was hired in the United States and what I get is what the job market pays there. It's different in Russia, so Oleg is being compensated differently. And I think he makes more than Russians working for Russian organizations. Plus, one of the reasons why our company is here is the cheap, skilled labor, and we've got to take advantage of this."

SOURCE: Sheila M. Puffer and Stanislav V. Shekshnia, "Compensating Nationals in Post Communist Russia; The Fit Between Culture and Compensation Systems," Paper presented at the Annual Academy of International Business Conference, Boston, November 1994. Used with permission.

[In the new millennium], the caliber of the people will be the only source
of competitive advantage. . . .
—ALLAN HALCROW, EDITOR, *PERSONNEL JOURNAL*, FEBRUARY 1996

Of the 100 top UK firms surveyed by Cendant International Assignment
Services, 63 reported failed foreign assignments.
—www.expat.FT.com, March 5, 2001

This chapter's Opening Profile describes a contemporary problem of salary differentials between expatriates and their counterpart host-country managers. There
are many challenges to the human resource management function of any organization, domestic or international. However, given the greater complexity of managing
international operations, the need to ensure high-quality management is even more
critical than in domestic operations.

A vital component of implementing global strategy is **international human
resource management (IHRM)**. IHRM is increasingly being recognized as a major
determinant of success or failure in international business. In a highly competitive
global economy, where the other factors of production—capital, technology, raw materials and information—are increasingly able to be duplicated, "the caliber of the people in an organization will be the only source of sustainable competitive advantage
available to U.S. companies.[1] Corporations operating overseas need to pay careful
attention to this most critical resource—one that also provides control over other
resources. Most U.S. multinationals underestimate the importance of the human
resource planning function in the selection, training, acculturation, and evaluation of
managers assigned abroad. And yet the increasing significance of this resource is evidenced by the numbers. Over 37,000 MNCs are currently in business worldwide. They
have control over 200,000 foreign affiliates and have over 73 million employees. In the
United States, foreign MNCs employ three million Americans—over 10 percent of the
U.S. manufacturing workforce.[2] In addition, about 80 percent of mid- and large-size
U.S. companies send managers abroad, and most plan to increase that number.[3] The
National Foreign Trade Council (NFTC) estimates that 300,000 U.S. expatriates are on
assignment at any given time. Of those companies responding to Arthur Andersen's
Global Best in Class Study,

> Those companies generate 43 per cent of their revenues outside their head-
> quarters country; consequently, they need expatriates who can support their
> expansion through both technical expertise and cultural understanding.[4]

However, recent advances in technology are enabling firms to effectively and
efficiently manage the IHRM function and maximize the firm's international management cadre, as illustrated in the accompanying E-Biz Box.

At the first level of planning, decisions are required on the staffing policy suitable for a particular kind of business, its global strategy, and its geographic locations.
Key issues involve the difficulty of control in geographically dispersed operations, the
need for local decision making independent of the home office, and the suitability of
managers from alternate sources.

E-Biz Box

HRMS GOES GLOBAL AT BRITISH AIRWAYS

Companies operating in several countries need to globalize the human resource management systems (HRMS). Compelling reasons for doing so include the need to get an accurate count of the international workforce, to monitor expatriates, to track and analyze employee benefits, to evaluate compensation models, and to streamline payroll. MNCs also need to access data on knowledge and abilities, make up-to-date information easily accessible to line managers, and study career planning and succession planning models. Creating a global HRMS, however, is not an easy task. The different laws, cultures, business practices, and technological limitations of various countries have to be taken into consideration.

Michael P. Corey, head of HR Systems for British Airways, knows how challenging it is to coordinate HR management systems when your company has a presence in 83 countries. Without efficient hardware, software, and HR strategies to back it all up, the corporate data highway can easily resemble a one-lane, unpaved roadway in a developing nation: chaotic, crowded and swarming with obstacles. But Corey is adamant about implementing a system that provides HR with the tools to truly excel. "In an era of intense competition and pressure, at a time when HR must provide value, it's essential to automate and streamline as much as possible," he explains. With more than 50,000 employees working worldwide, and many of them in a different location every day of the week, it's no simple task.

When HR needs to notify employees of a change in benefits or policy, for example, many of the workers are 40,000 feet above the earth. When it needs to track headcount or update employee records, it has to deal with 24 time zones and dozens of languages and cultures. In addition, systems and technologies that work in one place can come to a grinding halt elsewhere. Yet British Airways' automated system handles recruiting, benefits, headcount, basic recordkeeping, and an array of other functions—cutting across technology platforms and breaking language barriers. Moreover, the system, dubbed ACHORD (Airline Corporate Human and Organisation Resources Database), links to 35 other systems that require staff data within British Airways. Plans are now under way to link to 40 additional business systems.

When a manager in Kuala Lumpur needs information on terminations or company share schemes, it's accessible within seconds. When an HR specialist in New York requires data on pensions or concessional travel arrangements, it's visible in a flash. With a network of IBM mainframe computers linked to PCs and dumb terminals, data flows seamlessly between offices and across national boundaries. What's more, the worldwide network has almost eliminated duplicate data input, paperwork, disks and delays in processing work. "It fits into the concept of reengineering and making HR accountable and involved in corporate matters," says Corey. "It provides us with a powerful tool."

SOURCE: Adapted from: S. Greengard, "When HRMS Goes Global: Managing the Data Highway," *Personnel Journal* 7, no. 6 (June 1995): 90–91.

The interdependence of strategy, structure, and staffing is particularly worth noting. Ideally, the desired strategy of the firm should dictate the organizational structure and staffing modes considered most effective for implementing that strategy. In reality, however, there is usually considerable interdependence among those functions. Existing structural constraints often affect strategic decisions; similarly, staffing constraints or unique sets of competences in management come into play in organizational and sometimes strategic decisions. It is thus important to achieve a system of fits among those variables that facilitates strategic implementation.

STAFFING PHILOSOPHIES FOR GLOBAL OPERATIONS

> We found the most successful formula is to hire people in-country and then bring them to our U.S. headquarters to get acquainted and have them interact with our organization.
> —STUART MATHISON, VICE PRESIDENT FOR STRATEGIC PLANNING,
> SPRINT INTERNATIONAL, 1995

Alternate philosophies of managerial staffing abroad are known as the ethnocentric, polycentric, regiocentric, and global approaches. Firms using an **ethnocentric staffing approach** fill key managerial positions with people from headquarters—that is, **parent-country nationals (PCNs)**. Among the advantages of this approach, PCNs are familiar with company goals, products, technology, policies, and procedures—and they know how to get things accomplished through headquarters. This policy is likely to be used where a company notes the inadequacy of local managerial skills and determines a high need to maintain close communication and coordination with headquarters. It is also the preferred choice when the organization has been structured around a centralized approach to globalization and is primarily at the internationalization stage of strategic expansion.

Frequently, companies use PCNs for the top management positions in the foreign subsidiary—in particular, the chief executive officer (CEO) and the chief financial officer (CFO)—to maintain close control. PCNs are usually preferable when a high level of technical capability is required. They are also chosen for new international ventures requiring managerial experience in the parent company and where there is a concern for loyalty to the company rather than to the host country—in cases, for example, where proprietary technology is used extensively.

Disadvantages of the ethnocentric approach include (1) the lack of opportunities or development for local managers, thereby decreasing their morale and their loyalty to the subsidiary, and (2) the poor adaptation and lack of effectiveness of expatriates in foreign countries. Procter & Gamble, for example, routinely appointed managers from its headquarters for foreign assignments for many years. After several unfortunate experiences in Japan, the firm realized that such a practice was insensitive to local cultures and also underutilized its pool of high-potential non-American managers.[5] Furthermore, an ethnocentric recruiting approach does not enable the company to take advantage of its worldwide pool of management skill. This approach also serves to perpetuate particular personnel selections and other decision-making processes because the same types of people are making the same types of decisions.

With a **polycentric staffing approach**, local managers—**host-country managers (HCNs)**—are hired to fill key positions in their own country. This approach is more likely to be effective when implementing a multinational strategy. If a company wants to "act local," there are obvious advantages to staffing with HCNs. These managers are naturally familiar with the local culture, language, and ways of doing business, and they already have many contacts in place. In addition, HCNs are more likely to be accepted by people both inside and outside the subsidiary, and they provide role models for other upwardly mobile personnel.

With regard to cost, it is usually less expensive for a company to hire a local manager than to transfer one from headquarters, frequently with a family and often at a higher rate of pay. Transferring from headquarters is a particularly expensive policy when it turns out that the manager and her or his family do not adjust and have to be transferred home prematurely. Rather than building their own facilities, some companies acquire foreign firms as a means of obtaining qualified local personnel. Local managers also tend to be instrumental in staving off or more effectively dealing with problems in sensitive political situations. Some countries, in fact, have legal requirements that a specific proportion of the firm's top managers must be citizens of that country.

One disadvantage of a polycentric staffing policy is the difficulty of coordinating activities and goals between the subsidiary and the parent company, including the potentially conflicting loyalties of the local manager. Poor coordination among subsidiaries of a multinational firm could constrain strategic options. An additional drawback of this policy is that the headquarters managers of multinational firms will not gain the overseas experience necessary for any higher positions in the firm that require the understanding and coordination of subsidiary operations.

In the **global staffing approach**, the best managers are recruited from within or outside of the company, regardless of nationality—a practice used for some time by many European multinationals. Recently, as more major U.S. companies adopt a global strategic approach, they are also considering foreign executives for their top positions. General Motors hired J. Ignacio Lopez de Arriortua as vice-president for worldwide purchasing, Xerox hired Vittorio Cassoni as executive vice president, and Esprit de Corp hired Fritz Ammann as president.[6]

A global staffing approach has several important advantages. First, this policy provides a greater pool of qualified and willing applicants from which to choose, which, in time, results in further development of an global executive cadre. As discussed further in Chapter 10, the skills and experiences that those managers use and transfer throughout the company result in a pool of shared learning that is necessary for the company to compete globally. Second, where third-country nationals are used to manage subsidiaries, they usually bring more cultural flexibility and adaptability—as well as bilingual or multilingual skills—to a situation than parent-country nationals, especially if they are from a similar cultural background as the host-country coworkers and are accustomed to moving around. In addition, when TCNs are placed in key positions, they are perceived by employees as an acceptable compromise between headquarters and local managers and thus their appointment works to reduce resentment. Third, it can be more cost-effective to transfer and pay managers from some countries than from others because their pay scale and benefits packages are lower. Indeed, those firms with a truly global staffing orientation are phasing out the entire ethnocentric concept of a home or host country. As part of that focus, the term **transpatriates** is increasingly replacing that of expatriates.[7] Firms such as Philips, Heinz, Unilever, IBM, and ABB have a global staffing approach, which makes them highly visible and seems to indicate a trend.[8]

Generally, it seems that "the more distant geographically and culturally the subsidiary, the more expatriates are used in key positions, especially in less developed countries."[9] Clearly, this situation arises out of concern about uncertainty and the ability to control implementation of the corporation's goals. However, given the generally accepted consensus that staffing, along with structure and systems must "fit" the desired strategy,[10] firms desiring a truly global posture should adopt a global staffing approach. That is easier said than done. As shown in Exhibit 9-1, such an approach requires the firm to overcome barriers such as the availability and willingness of high-quality managers to transfer frequently around the world, dual career constraints, time and cost constraints, conflicting requirements of host governments, and ineffective human resource management policies.

In a **regiocentric staffing approach**, recruiting is done on a regional basis—say within Latin America for a position in Chile. This staffing approach can produce a spe-

Exhibit 9-1   Maintaining a Globalization Momentum
through a Global Staffing Policy

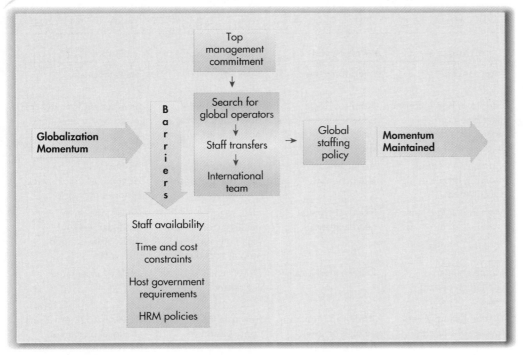

SOURCE: Adapted from D. Welch, "HRM Implications of Globalization," *Journal of General Management* 19, no. 4 (Summer 1994): 52–69.

cific mix of PCNs, HCNs, and TCNs, according to the needs of the company or the product strategy.[11]

What factors influence the choice of staffing policy? Among them are the strategy and organizational structure of the firm as well as the factors related to the particular subsidiary (such as the duration of the particular foreign operation, the types of technology used, and the production and marketing techniques necessary). Factors related to the host country also play a part (such as the level of economic and technological development, political stability, regulations regarding ownership and staffing, and the sociocultural setting).[12] As a practical matter, however, the choice often depends on the availability of qualified managers in the host country. Most MNCs use a greater proportion of PCNs (also called **expatriates**) in top management positions, staffing middle and lower management positions with increasing proportions of HCNs ("inpatriates") as one moves down the organizational hierarchy. The choice of staffing policy has a considerable influence on organizational variables in the subsidiary, such as the locus of decision-making authority, the methods of communication, and the perpetuation of human resource management practices. These variables are illustrated in Exhibit 9-2. The conclusions drawn by the researchers some time ago are still valid today. The ethnocentric staffing approach, for example, usually results in a higher level of authority and decision making in headquarters compared to the polycentric approach.[13]

Exhibit 9-2   Relationships among Strategic Mode, Organizational Variables, and Staffing Orientation

Aspects of the Enterprise	Orientation			
	Ethnocentric	**Polycentric**	**Regiocentric**	**Global**
Primary Strategic Orientation/Stage	International	Multidomestic	Regional	Transnational
Perpetuation (recruiting, staffing, development)	People of home country developed for key positions everywhere in the world	People of local nationality developed for key positions in their own country	Regional people developed for key positions anywhere in the region	Best people everywhere in the world developed for key positions everywhere in the world
Complexity of organization	Complex in home country, simple in subsidiaries	Varied and independent	Highly interdependent on a regional basis	"Global Web": complex, independent, worldwide alliances/network
Authority; decision making	High in headquarters	Relatively low in headquarters	High regional headquarters and/or high collaboration among subsidiaries	Collaboration of headquarters and subsidiaries around the world
Evaluation and control	Home standards applied to people and performance	Determined locally	Determined regionally	Globally integrated
Rewards	High in headquarters; low in subsidiaries	Wide variation; can be high or low rewards for subsidiary performance	Rewards for contribution to regional objectives	Rewards to international and local executives for reaching local and worldwide objectives based on global company goals
Communication; information flow	High volume of orders, commands, advice to subsidiaries	Little to and from headquarters; little among subsidiaries	Little to and from corporate headquarters, but may be high to and from regional headquarters and among countries	Horizontal; network relations
Geographic identification	Nationality of owner	Nationality of host country	Regional company	Truly global company, but identifying with national interests ("glocal")

SOURCE: Updated and adapted by H. Deresky in 2002, from original work by D. A. Heenan and H. V. Perlmutter. *Multinational Organization Development* (Reading, MA: Addison-Wesley, 1979), 18–19.

A study by Rochelle Kopp found that ethnocentric staffing and policies are associated with a higher incidence of international human resource management problems.[14] Exhibit 9-3A shows the breakdown of staffing among PCNs, HCNs, and TCNs of the 81 Japanese, European, and American companies studied. In addition, Kopp found that Japanese firms scored considerably lower than European and American firms in their practice of implementing policies such as preparing local nationals for

Exhibit 9-3A   Nationality of Top Managers in Overseas Operations

Headquarters Country		% Home-Country Nationals	% Local Nationals	% Third-Country Nationals
Japan	(n = 26)	74%	26%	0.2%
Europe	(n = 21)	48%	44%	8%
U.S.	(n = 20)	31%	49%	18%

SOURCE: R. Kopp, "International Human Resource Policies and Practices in Japanese, European, and United States Multinationals," *Human Resource Management* 33, no. 4 (Winter 1994): 581–599.

Exhibit 9-3B   Incidence of International Personnel Problems

Type of Problem	% of Japanese Firms Reporting Problem (n = 34)	% of European Firms Reporting Problem (n = 23)	% of U.S. Firms Reporting Problem (n = 24)
Expatriate-related			
Lack of home-country personnel who have sufficient international management skills	68%	39%	29%
Lack of home-country personnel who want to work abroad	26%	26%	13%
Expatriates experience reentry difficulties (e.g., career disruption) when returning to the home country	24%	39%	42%
Average of expatriate-related problems	39%	35%	28%
Local national staff related			
Difficulty in attracting high-caliber local nationals to work for the firm	44%	26%	21%
High turnover of local employees	32%	9%	4%
Friction and poor communication between home-country expatriates and local employees	32%	9%	13%
Complaints by local employees that they are not able to advance in the company	21%	4%	8%
Local legal challenges to the company's personnel policies	0 (0)	0	8%
Average of local national staff related problems	26%	10%	11%

SOURCE: R. Kopp, "International Human Resource Policies and Practices in Japanese, European, and United States Multinationals," *Human Resource Management* 33, no. 4 (Winter 1994): 581–599.

advancement and keeping inventory of their managers around the world for development purposes. As a result of these ethnocentric practices, Japanese firms seem to experience various IHRM problems, such as high turnover of local employees, more than European and American firms, as shown in Exhibit 9-3B.

Without exception, all phases of human resources management should support the desired strategy of the firm.[15] In the staffing phase, having the right people in the right places at the right times is a key ingredient to success in international operations. An effective managerial cadre can be a distinct competitive advantage for a firm. How the "right" selections are made is the focus of the next section.

GLOBAL SELECTION

The initial phase of setting up criteria for global selection, then, is to consider which overall staffing approach or approaches would most likely support the company's strategy, as discussed above—such as HCNs for localization, the (multilocal) strategic approach, and transpatriates for globalization. These are typically just starting points using idealized criteria, however. In reality, other factors creep into the process, such as host-country regulations, stage of internationalization, and—most often—who is both suitable and available for the position. It is also vital to integrate long-term strategic goals into the selection and development process, especially when rapid global expansion is intended. Insufficient projection of staffing needs for global assignments will likely result in constrained strategic opportunities because of a shortage of experienced managers suitable to place in those positions.

The selection of personnel for overseas assignments is a complex process. The criteria for selection are based on the same success factors as in the domestic setting, but additional criteria must be considered, related to the specific circumstances of each international position. Unfortunately, many personnel directors have a long-standing, ingrained practice of selecting potential expatriates simply on the basis of their domestic track record and their technical expertise.[16] Too often overlooked is the need to ascertain whether potential expatriates have the necessary cross-cultural awareness and interpersonal skills for the position. It is also important to assess whether the candidate's personal and family situation is such that everyone is likely to adapt to the local culture. There are five categories of success for expatriate managers: job factors, relational dimensions such as cultural empathy and flexibility, motivational state, family situation, and language skills. The relative importance of each factor is highly situational and difficult to establish.[17]

These **expatriate success factors** are based on studies of American expatriates. One could argue that the requisite skills are the same for managers from any country—and particularly so for third-country nationals.

A more flexible approach to maximizing managerial talent, regardless of the source, would certainly consider more closely whether the position could be suitably filled by a host-country national, as put forth by Tung, based on her research.[18] This contingency model of selection and training depends on the variables of the particular assignment, such as length of stay, similarity to the candidate's own culture, and level of interaction with local managers in that job. Tung concludes that the more rigorous the selection and training process, the lower the failure rate.

The selection process is set up as a decision tree in which the progression to the next stage of selection or the type of orientation training depends on the assessment of critical factors regarding the job or the candidate at each decision point. The simplest selection process involves choosing a local national because minimal training is necessary regarding the culture or ways of doing business locally. However, to be successful, local managers often require additional training in the MNC companywide processes, technology, and corporate culture. If the position cannot be filled by a local national, but yet the job requires a high level of interaction with the local community, there needs to be a very careful screening of candidates from other countries and a vigorous training program.

Most MNCs tend to start out their operations in a particular region by selecting primarily from their own pool of managers. Over time, and with increasing internationalization, they tend to move to a predominantly polycentric or regiocentric policy because of (1) increasing pressure (explicit or implicit) from local governments to hire locals (or sometimes legal restraints on the use of expatriates) and (2) the greater costs of expatriate staffing, particularly when the company has to pay taxes for the parent-company employee in both countries.[19] In addition, in recent years, MNCs have noted an improvement in the level of managerial and technical competence in many countries, negating the chief reason for using a primarily ethnocentric policy in the past. One researcher's comment represents a growing attitude: "All things being equal, a local national who speaks the language, understands the culture and the political system, and is often a member of the local elite should be more effective than an expatriate alien."[20] However, concerns about the need to maintain strategic control over subsidiaries and to develop managers with a global perspective remain a source of debate about staffing policies among human resource management professionals.[21] A globally oriented company such as ABB (Asea Brown Boveri), for example, has 500 roving transpatriates who are moved every two to three years, thus developing a considerable management cadre with global experience.

For MNCs based in Europe and Asia, human resource policies at all levels of the organization are greatly influenced by the home-country culture and policies. For Japanese subsidiaries in Singapore, Malaysia, and India, for example, promotion from within and expectations of long-term loyalty to and by the firm are culture-based practices transferable to subsidiaries.[22] At Matsushita, however, selection criteria for staffing seem to be similar to those of Western companies. Its candidates are selected on the basis of a set of characteristics the firm calls SMILE: Specialty (required skill, knowledge); Management ability (particularly motivational ability); International flexibility (adaptability); Language facility; and Endeavor (perseverance in the face of difficulty).[23]

Problems with Expatriation

> While 89 per cent of companies formally assess a candidate's job skills prior to a foreign posting, less than half go through the same process for cultural suitability. Even fewer gauge whether the family will cope.
>
> —www.expat.FT.com, MARCH 5, 2001

Deciding on a staffing policy and selecting suitable managers are logical first steps but do not alone ensure success. When staffing overseas assignments with expatriates, for example, many other reasons, besides poor selection, contribute to **expatriate failure** among U.S. multinationals. A large percentage of these failures can be attributed to poor preparation and planning for the entry and reentry transitions of the manager and his or her family. One important variable, for example, often given insufficient attention in the selection, preparation, and support phases, is the suitability and adjustment of the spouse. The inability of the spouse to adjust to the new environment has been found to be a major—in fact, the most frequently cited—reason for expatriate failure in United States and European companies.[24] Yet only about half of those companies studied had included the spouse in the interviewing process. In addition, although research shows that human relational skills are critical for overseas work (a fact acknowledged by the companies in a study by Tung), most of the U.S. firms surveyed failed to include this factor in their assessment of candidates.[25] The following is a synthesis of the factors frequently mentioned by researchers and firms as the major causes of expatriate failure:

➤ Selection based on headquarters criteria rather than assignment needs
➤ Inadequate preparation, training, and orientation prior to assignment
➤ Alienation or lack of support from headquarters
➤ Inability to adapt to local culture and working environment
➤ Problems with spouse and children—poor adaptation, family unhappiness
➤ Insufficient compensation and financial support
➤ Poor programs for career support and repatriation

After careful selection based on the specific assignment and the long-term plans of both the organization and the candidates, plans must be made for the preparation, training, and development of expatriate managers.

TRAINING AND DEVELOPMENT

> Some 81% of companies [around the world] said in 1998 that they expect to send an increasing number of people overseas through 2000. That means more folks confounded by foreign cultures and customs. What's key? Preparation.
>
> —www.businessweek.com, MARCH 5, 2001

It is clear that preparation and training for cross-cultural interactions is critical. In earlier discussions of the need for cultural sensitivity by expatriate managers, we noted that reports indicate that up to 40 percent of expatriate managers end their foreign assignments early because of poor performance or an inability to adjust to the local environment.[26] Moreover, about half of those who do remain function at a low level of effectiveness. The direct cost alone of a failed expatriate assignment is estimated to be from $50,000 to $150,000. The indirect costs may be far greater, depending on the expatriate's position. Relations with the host-country government and customers may be damaged, resulting in a loss of market share and a poor reception for future PCNs.

Both cross-cultural adjustment problems, and practical differences in everyday living present challenges for expatriates and their families. Examples are evident from a 1998 survey of expatriates when they ranked the countries that presented the most challenging assignments to them, along with some pet peeves from their experiences:

China: a continuing problem for expatriates; one complained that at his welcome banquet he was served duck tongue and pigeon head.

Brazil: expatriates stress that cell phones are essential because home phones don't work.

India: returning executives complain that the pervasiveness of poverty and street children is overwhelming.

Indonesia: here you need to plan ahead financially because landlords typically demand rent two to three years in advance.

Japan: expatriates and their families remain concerned that, although there is excellent medical care, the Japanese doctors reveal little to their patients.

After these five countries, expatriates also rank Russia, Mexico, Saudi Arabia, South Korea, and France as challenging.[27]

Even though cross-cultural training has proved to be effective, less than a third of expatriates are given such training. In a 1997 study by Harvey of 332 U.S. expatriates (dual-career couples), the respondents stated that their MNCs had not provided them with sufficient training or social support during the international assignment.[28] Much of the rationale for this lack of training is an assumption that managerial skills and processes are universal. In a simplistic way, a manager's domestic track record is used as the major selection criterion for an overseas assignment.

In most countries, however, the success of the expatriate is not left so much to chance. Foreign companies provide considerably more training and preparation for expatriates than American companies. Therefore, it is not hard to understand why Japanese expatriates experience significantly fewer incidences of failure than their American counterparts, although this may be partially because fewer families accompany Japanese assignees. Japanese multinationals typically have recall rates of below 5 percent, signifying that they send abroad managers who are far better prepared and more adept at working and flourishing in a foreign environment.[29] While this success is largely attributable to training programs, it is also a result of intelligent planning by the human resource management staff in most Japanese organizations, as reported in a study by Tung.[30] This planning begins with a careful selection process for overseas assignments, based on the long-term knowledge of executives and their families. An effective selection process, of course, will eliminate many potential "failures" from the start. Another factor is the longer duration of overseas assignments, averaging almost five years, which allows the Japanese expatriate more time to adjust initially and then to function at full capacity. In addition, Japanese expatriates receive considerable support from headquarters and sometimes even from local divisions set up for that purpose. At NEC Corporation, for example, part of the Japanese giant's globalization strategy is its permanent boot camp, with its elaborate training exercises to prepare NEC managers and their families for overseas battle.[31]

The demands on expatriate managers have always been as much a result of the multiple relationships that they have to maintain as they are of the differences in the host-country environment. Those relations include family relations, internal relations with people in the corporation, both locally and globally, especially with headquarters, external relations (suppliers, distributors, allies, customers, local community, etc.), and relations with the host government. It is important to pinpoint any potential problems that an expatriate may experience with those relationships so that these problems may be addressed during predeparture training. Problem recognition is the first stage in a comprehensive plan for developing expatriates shown in Exhibit 9-4. The three areas critical to preparation are cultural training, language instruction, and familiarity with everyday matters.[32] In the model shown in Exhibit 9-4, various development methods are used to address these areas during predeparture training, postarrival training, and reentry training. These methods continue to be valid and used by many organizations. Two-way feedback between the executive and the trainers at each stage helps to tailor the level and kinds of training to the individual manager. The desired goal is the increased effectiveness of the expatriate as a result of familiarity with local conditions, cultural awareness, and an appreciation of his or her family's needs in the host country.

Exhibit 9-4 A Model for Developing Key Expatriate Executives

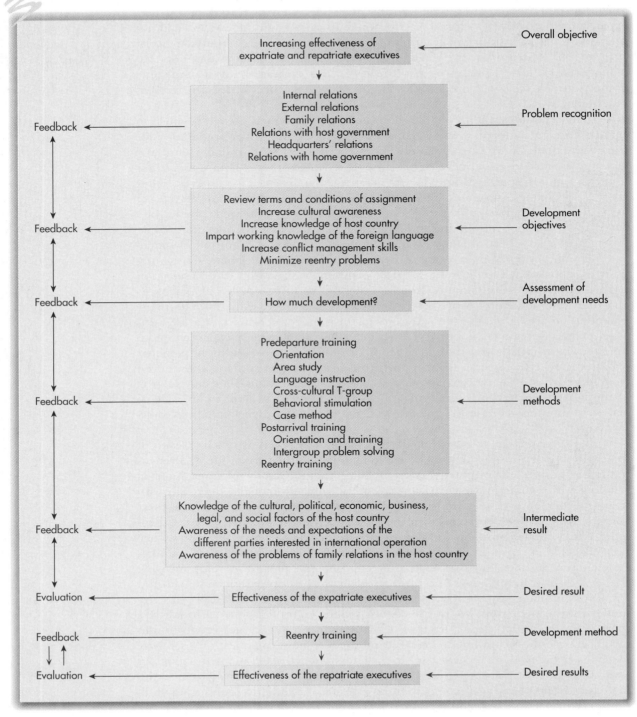

SOURCE: A. Rahim, "A Model for Developing Key Expatriate Executives," *Personnel Journal* (April 1983): 312–337.

Cross-Cultural Training

Training in language and practical affairs is quite straightforward, but cross-cultural training is not; it is complex and deals with deep-rooted behaviors. The actual process of cross-cultural training should result in the expatriate learning both content and skills that will improve interactions with host-country individuals by reducing misunderstandings and inappropriate behaviors. Black and Mendenhall suggest that trainers should apply social learning theory to this process by using the behavioral science techniques of incentives and rehearsal until the trainee internalizes the desired behaviors and reproduces them.[33] The result is a state of adjustment, representing the ability to effectively interact with host nationals.

Culture Shock

The goal of this training is to ease the adjustment to the new environment by reducing **culture shock**—a state of disorientation and anxiety about not knowing how to behave in an unfamiliar culture. The cause of culture shock is the trauma people experience in new and different cultures, where they lose the familiar signs and cues that they had used to interact in daily life and where they must learn to cope with a vast array of new cultural cues and expectations.[34] The symptoms of culture shock range from mild irritation to a deep-seated psychological panic or crisis. The inability to work effectively, stress within the family, and hostility toward host nationals are the common dysfunctional results of culture shock—often leading to the manager giving up and going home.

It is helpful to recognize the stages of culture shock to understand what is happening. Culture shock usually progresses through four stages, as described by Oberg: (1) *honeymoon*, when positive attitudes and expectations, excitement, and a tourist feeling prevail (which may last up to several weeks); (2) *irritation and hostility*, the crisis stage when cultural differences result in problems at work, at home, and in daily living—expatriates and family members feel homesick and disoriented, lashing out at everyone (many never get past this stage); (3) *gradual adjustment*, a period of recovery in which the "patient" gradually becomes able to understand and predict patterns of behavior, use the language, and deal with daily activities, and the family starts to accept their new life; and (4) *biculturalism*, the stage in which the manager and family members grow to accept and appreciate local people and practices and are able to function effectively in two cultures.[35] Many never get to the fourth stage—operating acceptably at the third stage—but those who do report that their assignment is positive and growth oriented.

Subculture Shock

Similar to culture shock, though usually less extreme, is the experience of subculture shock. This occurs when a manager is transferred to another part of the country where there are cultural differences—essentially from what she or he perceives to be a "majority" culture to a "minority" one. The shock comes from feeling like an "immigrant" in one's own country and being unprepared for such differences. For instance, someone going from New York to Texas will experience considerable differences in attitudes and lifestyle between those two states. These differences exist even within Texas, with cultures that range from roaming ranches and high technology to Bible-belt attitudes and laws and to areas with a mostly Mexican heritage.[36]

Training Techniques

Many training techniques are available to assist overseas assignees in the adjustment process. These techniques are classified by Tung as (1) area studies, that is, documentary programs about the country's geography, economics, sociopolitical history, and so forth; (2) culture assimilators, which expose trainees to the kinds of situations they are likely to encounter that are critical to successful interactions; (3) language training; (4) sensitivity training; and (5) field experiences—exposure to people from other cultures within the trainee's own country.[37] Tung recommends using these training methods in a complementary fashion, giving the trainee increasing levels of personal involvement as she or he progresses through each method. Documentary and interpersonal approaches have been found to be comparable, with the most effective intercultural training occurring when trainees become aware of the differences between their own culture and the one they are planning to enter.[38]

Similarly categorizing training methods, Ronen suggests specific techniques, such as workshops and sensitivity training, including a field experience called the host-family surrogate, where the MNC pays for and places an expatriate family with a host family as part of an immersion and familiarization program.[39]

Most training programs take place in the expatriate's own country prior to leaving. Although this is certainly a convenience, the impact of host-country (or in-country) programs can be far greater than those conducted at home because crucial skills, such as overcoming cultural differences in intercultural relationships, can actually be experienced during in-country training rather than simply discussed.[40] Some MNCs are beginning to recognize that there is no substitute for on-the-job training (OJT) in the early stages of the careers of those managers they hope to develop into senior-level global managers. Colgate-Palmolive—whose overseas sales represent two-thirds of its $6 billion in yearly revenue—is one company whose management development programs adhere to this philosophy. After training at headquarters, Colgate employees become associate product managers in the United States or abroad—and, according to John R. Garrison, manager of recruitment and development at Colgate, they must earn their stripes by being prepared to country-hop every few years. In fact, says Garrison, "That's the definition of a global manager: one who has seen several environments first-hand."[41] Exhibit 9-5 shows some other global management development programs for junior employees.

Exhibit 9-5 Corporate Programs to Develop Global Managers

- ABB (Asea Brown Boveri) rotates about 500 managers around the world to different countries every two to three years in order to develop a management cadre of transpatriates to support their global strategy.
- PepsiCo Inc. has an orientation program for its foreign managers which brings them to the United States for one-year assignments in bottling division plants.
- British Telecom uses informal mentoring techniques to induct employees into the ways of their assigned country; existing expatriate workers talk to prospective assignees about the cultural factors to expect (www.expat.FT.com).
- Honda of America Manufacturing Inc. gives its U.S. supervisors and managers extensive preparation in Japanese language, culture, and lifestyle and then sends them to Tokyo for up to three years to the parent company.[42]
- General Electric likes its engineers and managers to have a global perspective whether or not they are slated to go abroad. The company gives regular language and cross-cultural training for them so that they are equipped to conduct business with people around the world (www.GE.com).

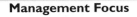

Management Focus

CITIBANK GIVES ADVICE ON CAREER PLANNING

BE MOBILE: TO GET SOMEWHERE, YOU HAVE TO GO PLACES!

As Citibank continues to expand globally, there is a growing need for a cadre of professionals with the global perspective to lead the organization. Two-thirds of Citibank's current management team have already had international experience. While living and working in other countries is probably the most direct way to gain a global perspective, there are alternate routes to accomplish this objective. These are well worth exploring if your road to career growth lies over Citibank's global horizons.

A GLOBAL MOVE IS A GOOD CAREER MOVE

Expatriate assignments offer an extraordinary opportunity for experience, learning, and personal and career enrichment. Our goal is to have each expatriate assignment fulfill a business need and to provide each person who accepts an expatriate assignment with professional as well as personal growth opportunities.

SOME CAREER ADVANTAGES OFFERED BY AN EXPATRIATE ASSIGNMENT

- Develop a global business outlook and an understanding of how to leverage the bank's global position

- Gain the broader perspective through working in different cultures, geographies, businesses and functions

- Interact with a wide range of customers and work with globally focused managers and colleagues, so you can stretch beyond your current environment and add breadth and depth to your work experience

- Apply your solutions to truly unique problems within different cultures and environments

- Take on new challenges that stretch and develop your skills by requiring you to take educated risks

OTHER WAYS TO GAIN A GLOBAL PERSPECTIVE

While advantageous for some, international assignments aren't right for everyone. Only you and those close to you can decide if you want to live and work in a different country, and if so, at which point in time. If success on your career path requires international experience and you are unable to take on an international assignment at this time for any reason, there are other ways to gain global exposure. These might include short-term assignments in other locations, jobs that involve cross-border interaction, or a task force made up of a global team.

SOURCE: www.Citibank.com.

The importance of developing a global orientation in one's career development is illustrated by the advice offered to potential applicants to Citibank given on their Website, as described in Management Focus: Citibank Gives Advice on Career Planning. Citibank is now part of Citigroup—a global financial and insurance institution—since the merger of Citicorp and Travelers Insurance in 1998.

Integrating Training with Global Orientation

In continuing our discussion of "strategic fit," it is important to remember that training programs, like staffing approaches, be designed with the company's strategy in mind. Although it is probably impractical to break those programs down into a lot of variations, it is feasible to at least consider the relative level or stage of globalization that the firm has reached because obvious major differences would be appropriate, for example, from the initial export stage to the full global stage. Exhibit 9-6 suggests levels of

Exhibit 9-6   Stage of Globalization and Training Design Issues

Export Stage	MNC Stage
Degree of Rigor: Low to moderate	*Degree of Rigor:* High moderate to high
Content: Emphasis should be on interpersonal skills, local culture, customer values, and business behavior.	*Content:* Emphasis should be on interpersonal skills, two-way technology transfer, corporate value transfer, international strategy, stress management, local culture, and business practices.
Host-Country Nationals: Low to moderate training of host nationals to understand parent country products and policies.	*Host-Country Nationals:* Moderate to high training of host nationals in technical areas, product and service systems, and corporate culture.
MDC Stage	**Global Stage**
Degree of Rigor: Moderate to high	*Degree of Rigor:* High
Content: Emphasis should be on interpersonal skills, local culture, technology transfer, stress management, and business practices and laws.	*Content:* Emphasis should be on global corporate operations and systems, corporate culture transfer, customers, global competitors, and international strategy.
Host-Country Nationals: Low to moderate training of host nationals; primarily focusing on production and service procedures.	*Host-Country Nationals:* High training of host nationals in global organization production and efficiency systems, corporate culture, business systems, and global conduct policies.

SOURCE: J. S. Black, Mark. E. Mendenhall, Hal B. Gregersen, and Linda K. Stroh, *Globalizing People Through International Assignments* (Reading, MA: Addison Wesley Longman, 1999).

rigor and types of training content appropriate for the firm's managers, as well as those for host-country nationals, for four globalization stages—export, multidomestic, multinational, and global. It is noteworthy, for example, that the training of host-country nationals for a global firm has a considerably higher level of scope and rigor than that for the other stages and borders on the standards for the firm's expatriates.

Training Host-Country Nationals

The continuous training and development of HCNs and TCNs for management positions is also important to the long-term success of multinational corporations. As part of a long-term staffing policy for a subsidiary, the ongoing development of HCNs will facilitate the transition to an indigenization policy. Furthermore, multinational companies like to have well-trained managers with broad international experience available to take charge in many intercultural settings, whether at home or abroad. Such managerial skills are increasingly needed in U.S.-Japanese joint ventures—a good example being G.M.-Toyota in Freemont, California. There, managers as well as employees from both America and Japan learn to work side by side and adjust to a unique blend of country and corporate culture. For the Americans in this organization, helping to acculturate the Japanese employees not only demonstrates friendly goodwill but is a necessary part of securing their own future in the company.

Many HCNs are, of course, receiving excellent training in global business and Internet technology within their home corporations. Kim In Kyung, 24, for example, has a job involving world travel and high technology with Samsung Electronics Company of Seoul, South Korea. Part of Samsung's strategy is to promote its new Internet focus, and this strategy has landed the farmer's daughter a $100,000 job. Her situation reflects Seoul's sizzling tech boom, where IT comprises 11 percent of its $400 billion economy in 2001 and is expected to reach 20 percent by 2010.[43]

In another common scenario also requiring management of a mixture of executives and employees, American and European MNCs presently employ Asians as well as Arab locals in their plants and offices in Saudi Arabia, bringing together three cultures: well-educated Asian managers living in a Middle Eastern, highly traditional society who are employed by a firm reflecting Western technology and culture. This kind of situation involves the integration of multiple sets of culturally based values, expectations, and work habits.

COMPENSATING EXPATRIATES

The significance of an appropriate compensation and benefit package to attract, retain, and motivate international employees cannot be overemphasized. Compensation is a crucial link between strategy and its successful implementation—there must be a fit between compensation and the goals for which the firm wants managers to aim.[44] So that they will not feel exploited, MNC employees need to perceive equity and goodwill in their compensation and benefits, whether they are PCNs, HCNs, or TCNs. The premature return of expatriates or the unwillingness of managers to take overseas assignments can often be traced to their knowledge that the assignment is detrimental to them financially and usually to their career progression.

From the firm's perspective, the high cost of maintaining appropriate compensation packages for expatriates has led many companies—Colgate-Palmolive, Chase Manhattan Bank, Digital Equipment, General Motors, and General Electric among them—to cut back on PCN assignments as much as possible. "Transfer a $100,000-a-year American executive to London—and suddenly he [or she] costs the employer $300,000," explains the *Wall Street Journal*. "Move him to Stockholm or Tokyo, and he [or she] easily becomes a million-dollar [manager]."[45]

Designing and maintaining an appropriate compensation package is more complex than it would seem because of the need to consider and reconcile parent and host-country financial, legal, and customary practices. The problem is that although around the world there may be little variation in typical executive salaries at the level of base compensation, there is often a wide variation in net spendable income. American executives may receive more in cash and stock, but they have to spend more for things that foreign companies provide, such as cars, vacations, and entertainment allowances. In addition, the manager's purchasing power with that net income is affected by the relative cost of living. The cost of living is considerably higher in most of Europe than in the United States. In designing compensation and benefit packages for PCNs, then, the challenge to IHRM professionals is to maintain a standard of living for expatriates equivalent to their colleagues at home, plus compensating them for any additional costs incurred. This policy is referred to as "keeping the expatriate whole."[46]

To ensure that expatriates do not lose out through their overseas assignment, the **balance sheet approach** is often used to equalize the standard of living between the host country and the home country and to add some compensation for inconvenience or qualitative loss. This approach is illustrated in Exhibit 9-7. However, recently some companies have begun to base their compensation package on a goal of achieving a standard of living comparable to that of host-country managers, which does help resolve some of the problems of pay differential illustrated in the opening profile.

In fairness, the MNC is obliged to make up additional costs that the expatriate would incur for taxes, housing, and goods and services. The tax differential is complex and expensive for the company, and generally MNCs use a policy of tax equalization: the company pays any taxes due on any type of additional compensation that the expatriate receives for the assignment; the expatriate pays in taxes only what she or he would be paying at home. The burden of foreign taxes can be lessened, however, by efficient tax planning—a fact often overlooked by small firms. The timing and methods of paying people determine what foreign taxes are incurred. For example, a company can save on taxes by renting an apartment for the employee instead of providing a cash housing allowance. All in all, MNCs have to weigh the many aspects of a complete compensation package, especially at high management levels, to effect a tax equalization policy.

Exhibit 9-7   The Balance Sheet Approach to International Compensation

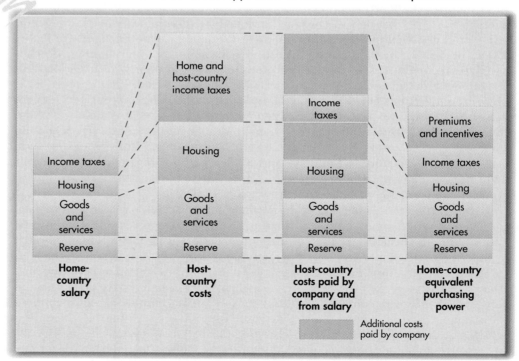

SOURCE: C. Reynolds, "Compensation of Overseas Personnel," in J. Famularo, *Handbook of Human Resource Administration*, 2nd ed., © 1989 McGraw-Hill. Reproduced by permission of McGraw-Hill.

Managing PCN compensation is a complex challenge for companies with overseas operations. Exhibit 9-8 shows the categories that must be considered. All components of the compensation package must be considered in light of both home- and host-country legalities and practices. Most important, to be strategically competitive, the compensation package must be comparatively attractive to the kinds of managers the company wishes to hire or relocate. Some of those managers will, of course, be local managers in the host country. This, too, is a complex situation requiring competitive compensation policies in order to attract, motivate, and retain the best local managerial talent. In many countries, however, it is a considerable challenge to develop compensation packages appropriate to the local situation and culture, while also recognizing the differences between local salaries and those expected by expatriates or transpatriates (that difference itself often being a source of competitive advantage).

Exhibit 9-8   Components of an Expatriate Compensation Package

Salary
- Home rate/home currency
- Local rate/local currency
- Salary adjustments or promotions—home or local standard
- Bonus—home or local currency, home or local standard
- Stock options
- Inducement payment/hardship premium—percentage of salary or lump sum payment, home/local currency
- Currency protection—discretion or split basis
- Global salary and performance structures

Taxation
- Tax protection
- Tax equalization
- Other services

Benefits
- Home-country program
- Local program
- Social Security program

Allowances
- Cost-of-living allowances
- Housing standard
- Education
- Relocation
- Perquisites
- Home leave
- Shipping and storage

SOURCE: P. J. Dowling and R. S. Schuler, *International Dimensions of Human Resource Management* (Boston: PWS-Kent, 1990).

COMPENSATING HOST-COUNTRY NATIONALS

How do firms deal with the kinds of situations posed by Mark and Oleg in the Opening Profile? This issue is explored further in the Comparative Management in Focus later in this chapter. Of course, no one set of solutions can be applicable in any country. There are many variables—including local market factors and pay scales, government involvement in benefits, the role of unions, the cost of living, and so on.

In Eastern Europe, for example, people in Hungary, Poland, and the Czech Republic spend 35 to 40 percent of their disposable income on food and utilities, and that may run as high as 75 percent in the CIS.[47] Therefore, East European managers need to have cash for about 65 to 80 percent of their base pay, compared to about 40 percent for U.S. managers (the rest being long-term incentives, benefits, and perks). In addition, they still expect the many social benefits provided by the "old government." To be competitive, MNCs can focus on providing goods and services that are either not available at all or are extremely expensive in Eastern Europe. Such upscale perks can be used to atttract high-skilled workers.

> Nestlé Bulgaria offers a company car and a cellular phone to new Recruits.
> . . . Fuel prices are about $2 per gallon and cell phones cost $1,200 a year—
> equivalent to half a year's salary.[48]

In Japan, companies are revamping their HRM policies to compete in a global world, in response to a decade-long economic slump. The traditional lifetime employment and a guaranteed tidy pension are giving way to the more Western practices of competing for jobs, of basing pay on performance rather than seniority, and of making people responsible for their own retirement fund decisions.[49]

In China, too, change is under way. University graduates may now seek their own jobs rather than being assigned to state-owned companies, though nepotism is still common. In a study of HRM practices in China, Bjorkman and Lu found that a key concern of Western managers in China was the compensation of the HCNs. In Beijing and Shanghai, top Chinese managers have seen their salaries increase by 30 to 50 percent in the last few years. They have also received considerable fringe benefits such as housing, company cars, pensions, and overseas training. The difficulty, too, was that in Western–Chinese joint ventures, the Chinese partner opposed pay increases.[50] Yet when trying to introduce performance-based pay, the Western companies ran into considerable opposition and usually gave up, using salary increases instead. Setting up some kind of housing scheme, such as investing in apartments, seemed to be one way that foreign-owned firms were able to compete for good managers. Those managers were, understandably, maximizing their job opportunities now that they did not have to get permission to leave the Chinese state-owned companies.[51]

Comparative Management in Focus

Compensation in Russia

How do firms deal with the kinds of situations posed by Mark and Oleg in the Opening Profile? There are many complicating factors involved in compensating Russian nationals: the ongoing transition to a market economy; the Russians' past practices and resultant expectations from their background of employment and compensation in state-owned enterprises; and the cultural norms and work behaviors resulting from their social system.

Puffer and Shekshnia recommend tailoring compensation packages to the Russian culture and the prevailing economic and market situation. They examined compensation surveys conducted by Otis Elevator Company and the U.S. Embassy and found that compensation trends of Western firms to Russian nationals typically included three components: a base salary, incentive pay, and a variety of nonmonetary fringe benefits. Puffer and Shekshnia felt that these three components satisfied the prevailing Russian situation and the Russian culture—which they conclude, using Hofstede's categories, to be that of high power distance, high uncertainty avoidance, high collectivism, high femininity, and high short-term orientation. For example, some hard-currency and some nonmonetary fringe benefits allow Russian employees to have things that are otherwise simply not available to them because of inflation or nonavailability—in other words, to combat the uncertainty avoidance of the value of basic compensation.[52] However, based on their research and experiences in Russia, Puffer and Shekshnia recommend that Western firms need to design compensation packages that will meet their business objectives as well as reward Russians equitably and appropriately. To achieve this end, they give the following recommendations, designed to "reinforce those aspects of Russian culture that help achieve corporate objectives, while reducing the influence of other cultural dimensions that could undermine objectives:"[53]

1. Select Russian employees who are achievement-oriented and willing to take risks (that is, those who do not fit the cultural profile of the majority of Russian workers).
2. Tie individual bonuses to initiative and personal accountability (to encourage individual goal setting).
3. Organize social events and other group activities.
4. Provide small-group incentives (to encourage team achievement with Western managers).
5. Provide a mix of short- and long-term incentives (that is, to transition to a focus on long-term corporate objectives).
6. Tailor the compensation package to individual preferences (to enjoy choices they have not had before).

Conclusion

The effectiveness of managers at foreign locations is crucial to the success of the firm's operations, particularly because of the lack of proximity to, and control by, headquarters executives. The ability of expatriates to initiate and maintain cooperative relationships with local people and agencies will determine the long-term success, even viability, of the operation. In a real sense, a company's global cadre represents its most valuable resource. Proactive management of that resource by headquarters will result in having the right people in the right place at the right time, appropriately trained, prepared, and supported. MNCs using these IHRM practices can anticipate the effective management of the foreign operation, the fostering of expatriates' careers, and ultimately, the enhanced success of the corporation.

SUMMARY OF KEY POINTS

1. Global human resource management is a vital component of implementing global strategy and is increasingly being recognized as a major determinant of success or failure in international business.

2. The main staffing alternatives for global operations are the ethnocentric, polycentric, regiocentric, and global approaches. Each approach has its appropriate uses, according to its advantages and disadvantages.

3. The causes of expatriate failure include the following: poor selection based on inappropriate criteria, inadequate preparation before assignment, alienation from headquarters, inability of manager or family to adapt to local environment, inadequate compensation package, and poor programs for career support and repatriation.

4. The three major areas critical to expatriate preparation are cultural training, language instruction, and familiarity with everyday matters.

5. Common training techniques for potential expatriates include area studies, culture assimilators, language training, sensitivity training, and field experiences.

6. Appropriate and attractive compensation packages must be designed by IHRM staffs to sustain a competitive global management cadre. Compensation packages for host-country managers must be designed to fit the local culture and situation as well as the firm's objectives.

DISCUSSION QUESTIONS

1. What are the major alternative staffing approaches for international operations? Explain the relative advantages of each and the conditions under which you would choose one approach over another.

2. Why is the HRM role so much more complex, and important, in the international context?

3. Explain the common causes of expatriate failure. What are the major success factors for expatriates? Explain the role and importance of each.

4. What are the common training techniques for managers going overseas. How should these vary as appropriate to the level of globalization of the firm?

5. Explain the balance sheet approach to international compensation packages. Why is this approach so important? Discuss the pros and cons of aligning the expatriate compensation package with the host-country colleagues compared to the home-country colleagues.

APPLICATION EXERCISES

1. Make a list of the reasons why you would want to accept a foreign assignment and a list of reasons why you would want to reject it. Does it depend on the location? Compare your list with a classmate and discuss your reasons.

2. Research a company with operations in several countries and ascertain the staffing policy used for those countries. Try to find out what kinds of training and preparation are provided for expatriates and what kinds of results the company is experiencing with expatriate training.

EXPERIENTIAL EXERCISE

This can be done in groups or individually. After the exercise, discuss your proposals with the rest of the class.

You are the expatriate general manager of a British company's subsidiary in Brazil, an automobile component parts manufacturer. You and your family have been in Brazil for seven years, and now you are being reassigned and replaced with another expatriate—Ian Fleming. Ian is bringing his family—Helen, an instructor in computer science, who hopes to find a position, a son, aged 12, and a daughter, aged 14. None of them has lived abroad before. Ian has asked you what he and his family should expect in the new assignment. Remembering all the problems you and your family experienced in the first couple of years of your assignment in Brazil, you want to facilitate their adjustment and have decided to do two things:

1. Write a letter to Ian, telling him what to expect—both on the job and in the community. Tell him about some of the cross-cultural conflicts he may run into with his coworkers and employees, and how he should handle them.

2. Set up some arrangements and support systems for the family and design a support package for them, with a letter to each family member telling them what to expect.

INTERNET RESOURCES

Visit the Deresky companion Website at http://prenhall.com/Deresky for this chapter's Internet resources.

CASE STUDY: FRED BAILEY IN JAPAN: AN INNOCENT ABROAD

Fred gazed out the window of his 24th-floor office at the tranquil beauty of the Imperial Palace amid the hustle and bustle of downtown Tokyo. It had been only six months since Fred Bailey had arrived with his wife and two children for this three-year assignment as the director of Kline & Associates' Tokyo office. Kline & Associates was a large multinational consulting firm with offices in 19 countries worldwide. Fred was now trying to decide whether he should simply pack up an tell the home office that he was coming home or whether he should try to somehow convince his wife and himself that they should stay and finish the assignment. Given how excited they all were about the assignment to begin with, it was a mystery to Fred how things had gotten to this point. As he watched the swans glide across the water in the moat that surrounds the Imperial Palace, Fred reflected on the past seven months.

Seven months ago, Dave Steiner, the managing partner of the main office in Boston, asked Fred to lunch to discuss business. To Fred's surprise, the business they discussed was not about the major project that he and his team had just finished; instead, it was about a very big promotion and career move. Fred was offered the position of managing director of the firm's relatively new Tokyo office, which had a staff of

SOURCE: J. Stewart Black, in *International Human Resource Management*, eds. M. Mendenhall and Gary Oddou (Boston: PWS-Kent, 1991).

40, including 7 Americans. Most of the Americans in the Tokyo office were either associate consultants or research analysts. Fred would be in charge of the whole office and would report to a senior partner. Steiner implied to Fred that if this assignment went as well as his past projects, it would be the last step before becoming a partner in the firm.

When Fred told his wife about the unbelievable opportunity, he was shocked at her less than enthusiastic response. His wife Jennifer (or Jenny as Fred called her) thought that it would be rather difficult to have the children live and go to school in a foreign country for three years, especially when Christine, the oldest, would be starting middle school next year. Besides, now that the kids were in school, Jenny was thinking about going back to work, at least part time. Jenny had a degree in fashion merchandising from a well-known private university and had worked as an assistant buyer for a large women's clothing store before having the two girls.

Fred explained that the career opportunity was just too good to pass up and that the company's overseas package would make living overseas terrific. The company would pay all the expenses to move whatever the Baileys wanted to take with them. The company had a very nice house in an expensive district of Tokyo that would be provided rent free, and the company would rent their house in Boston during their absence. Moreover, the firm would provide a car and driver, education expenses for the children to attend private schools, and a cost-of-living adjustment and overseas compensation that would nearly triple Fred's gross annual salary. After two days of consideration and discussion, Fred told Steiner he would accept the assignment.

The current Tokyo office managing director was a partner in the firm but had been in the new Tokyo office for less than a year when he was transferred to head up a long-established office in England. Because the transfer to England was taking place right away, Fred and his family had about three weeks to prepare for the move. Between transferring things at the office to Bob Newcome, who was being promoted to Fred's position, and getting furniture and the like ready to be moved, neither Fred nor his family had much time to really find out much about Japan, other than what was in the encyclopedia.

When the Baileys arrived in Japan, they were greeted at the airport by one of the young Japanese associate consultants and the senior American expatriate. Fred and his family were quite tired from the long trip, and the two-hour ride to Tokyo was a rather quiet one. After a few days of just settling in, Fred spent his first full day at the office.

Fred's first order of business was to have a general meeting with all the employees of associate consultant rank and higher. Although Fred didn't notice it at the time, all the Japanese staff sat together and all the Americans sat together. After Fred introduced himself and his general idea about the potential and future directions of the Tokyo office, he called on a few individuals to get their ideas about how the things for which they were responsible would likely fit into his overall plan. From the Americans, Fred got a mixture of opinions with specific reasons about why certain things might or might not fit well. From the Japanese, he got very vague answers. When Fred pushed to get more specific information, he was surprised to find that a couple of the Japanese simply made a sucking sound as they breathed and said that it was "difficult to say." Fred sensed the meeting was not achieving his objectives, so he thanked everyone for coming and said he looked forward to their all working together to make the Tokyo office the fastest-growing office in the company.

After they had been in Japan about a month, Fred's wife complained to him about the difficulty she had getting certain everyday products like maple syrup, peanut butter, and good-quality beef. She said that when she could get it at one of the specialty stores it cost three and four times what it would cost in the States. She also complained that since the washer and dryer were much too small, she had to spend extra money by sending things out to be dry cleaned. On top of all that, unless she went to the American Club in downtown Tokyo, she never had anyone to talk to. After all, Fred was gone 10 to 16 hours a day. Unfortunately, while Jenny talked, Fred was preoccupied, thinking about a big upcoming meeting between his firm and a significant prospective client, a top-100 Japanese multinational company.

The next day, Fred, along with the lead American consultant for the potential contract, Ralph Webster, and one of the Japanese associate consultants, Kenichi Kurokawa, who spoke perfect English, met with a team from the Japanese firm. The Japanese team consisted of four members: the vice president of administration, the director of international personnel, and two staff specialists. After shaking hands and a few awkward bows, Fred said that he knew the Japanese gentlemen were busy and he didn't want to waste their time so he would get right to the point. Fred then had the other American lay out their firm's proposal for the project and what the project would cost. After the presentation, Fred asked the Japanese what their reaction to the proposal was. The Japanese did not respond immediately, so Fred launched into his summary version of the proposal thinking that the translation might have been insufficient. But again the Japanese had only the vaguest of responses to his direct questions.

The recollection of the frustration of that meeting was enough to shake Fred back to reality. The reality was that in the five months since that first meeting little progress had been made and the contract between the firms was yet to be signed. "I can never seem to get a direct response from Japanese," he thought to himself. This feeling of frustration led him to remember a related incident that happened about a month after this first meeting with this client.

Fred had decided that the reason not much progress was being made with the client was that he and his group just didn't know enough about the client to package the proposal in a way that was appealing to the client. Consequently, he called in the senior American associated with the proposal, Ralph Webster, and asked him to develop a report on the client so that the proposal could be reevaluated and changed where necessary. Jointly, they decided that one of the more promising Japanese research associates, Tashiro Watanabe, would be the best person to take the lead on this report. To impress upon Tashiro the importance of this task and the great potential they saw in him, they decided to have the young Japanese associate meet with both Fred and Ralph. In the meeting, Fred and Ralph laid out the nature and importance of the task, at which point Fred leaned forward in his chair and said to Tashiro, "You can see that this is an important assignment and that we are placing a lot of confidence in you by giving it to you. We need the report by this time next week so that we can revise and represent our proposal. Can you do it?" After a somewhat pregnant pause, Tashiro responded hesitantly, "I'm not sure what to say." At that point, Fred smiled, got up from his chair and walked over to the young Japanese associate, extended his hand, and said, "Hey, there's nothing to say. We're just giving you the opportunity you deserve."

The day before the report was due, Fred asked Ralph how the report was coming. Ralph said that since he had heard nothing from Tashiro he assumed that everything was under control, but that he would double-check. Ralph later ran into one of the American research associates, John Maynard. Ralph knew that John was hired for Japan because of his language ability in Japanese and that, unlike any of the other

Americans, John often went out after work with some of the Japanese research associates, including Tashiro. So, Ralph asked John if he knew how Tashiro was coming on the report. John then recounted that last night at the office Tashiro had asked if Americans sometimes fired employees for being late with reports. John had sensed that this was more than a hypothetical question and asked Tashiro why he wanted to know. Tashiro did not respond immediately, and since it was 8:30 in the evening, John suggested they go out for a drink. At first Tashiro resisted, but then John assured him that they would grab a drink at a nearby bar and come right back. At the bar, John got Tashiro to open up.

Tashiro explained the nature of the report that he had been requested to produce. He continued to explain that even though he had worked long into the night every night to complete the report it was just impossible and that he had doubted from the beginning whether he could complete the report in a week.

At this point, Ralph asked John, "Why didn't he say something in the first place?" Ralph didn't wait to hear whether or not John had an answer to this question. He headed straight to Tashiro's desk.

Ralph chewed Tashiro out and then went to Fred explaining that the report would not be ready and that Tashiro, from the start, didn't think it could be. "Then why didn't he say something?" Fred asked. No one had any answers, and the whole thing just left everyone more suspect and uncomfortable with one another.

There were other incidents, big and small, that had made the last two months especially frustrating, but Fred was too tired to remember them all. To Fred it seemed that working with Japanese both inside and outside the firm was like working with people from another planet. Fred felt he just couldn't communicate with them, and he could never figure out what they were thinking. It drove him crazy.

Then on top of all this, Jennifer laid a bombshell on him. She wanted to go home, and yesterday was not soon enough. Even though the kids seemed to be doing all right, Jennifer was tired of Japan—tired of begin stared at, of not understanding anybody or being understood, of not being able to find what she wanted at the store, of not being able to drive and read the road signs, of not having anything to watch on television, of not being involved in anything. She wanted to go home and could not think of any reason why they shouldn't. After all, she reasoned, they owed nothing to the company because the company had led them to believe this was just another assignment, like the two years they spent in San Francisco, and it was anything but that!

Fred looked out the window once more, wishing that somehow everything could be fixed, or turned back, or something. Down below the traffic was backed up. Though the traffic lights changed, the cars and trucks didn't seem to be moving. Fortunately, beneath the ground, one of the world's most advanced, efficient, and clean subway systems moved hundreds of thousands of people about the city and to their homes.

Case Questions

1. You are Fred. What should you do now?
2. Turn back the clock to when Fred was offered the position in Tokyo. What, if anything, should have been done differently, and by whom?

Developing a Global Management Cadre

Outline

Opening Profile: The Rise of the NAFTA Manager

The border economy has bred a dynamic new strain of bicultural bosses

If you want to understand the gold rush, you've got to know the prospectors. The reason that Laredo and nearby McAllen, Texas, are two of the top 10 fastest-growing metro areas in the U.S. is mainly owing to NAFTA and is progeny: NAFTA Man.

NAFTA Man is not only bilingual, he's also bicultural. He speaks Spanish on the factory floor in Mexico but yells in English at his kids' T-ball games. He knows when to offer a bribe in Mexico (to a traffic cop) and when not to (during an environmental inspection). He prefers chile rellenos to pot roast, gets his allergy medicine in Mexico but his MRI in the U.S. He has a two-sided wallet for pesos and dollars and would practically kill for a cell phone that works in both countries. "We don't know who we are," laughs John Castany, president of the Reynosa Maquiladora Association, which has 110 mostly gringo members. "We're schizo. Border culture is just, well, different."

These NAFTA Men—and a few women—are genetically engineered by the new border economy. Managers are taught to take a different route to work every day to foil potential kidnappers. They grow accustomed to training—and losing—an entire factory floor of workers every year. And they have discovered that "casual Friday" in McAllen is often a dress-up workday on the other side. Around here, the most valuable asset is their flexibility. "You have to switch gears in Mexico—and not just languages. You have a behavior shift too," says Charles Taliaferro, 49, who runs *maquila* operations for AmMex Products, which makes everything from Siemens electric motors to Smead file folders. Workers cause less trouble, but their bosses have to be more considerate. "In Mexico, you're more polite, more formal," he says.

The man most responsible for NAFTA Man's ascendance in McAllen is a former Catholic priest turned economic hustler named, coincidentally, Mike Allen. As president of the local economic-development office, the 63-year-old executive uses local tax funds to attract business to McAllen—as well as to its Mexican sister city, Reynosa, across the vein-thin river. "I remember back in '88 meeting the mayor of Reynosa. He had an AK-47 in his back seat. We did a handshake deal to bring manufacturers to Mexico," says Allen. Back then, Reynosa had fewer than 20 factories, with 16,000 employees; today there are 209 plants, with 64,000 workers.

Critics point out that the Mexican *maquilas* have drained jobs from the U.S. side. Allen says those jobs were leaving anyway. And even though the Rio Grande Valley remains one of the nation's poorest regions, a lucrative new companion industry—logistics and technical support—has helped boost job growth 7% last year in the McAllen area, the best in Texas. The 2,000 mostly American *maquila* professionals who cross the bridge daily into Reynosa bring in $1 million a year in tolls alone for the city of McAllen. "If Reynosa is not doing well," says city manager Mike Perez, "we're not doing well."

If the real estate market is any barometer, both sides are prospering. The Hunt family of Dallas and its Mexican partners are developing the first planned community on both sides of the border called Sharyland Plantation: 22,000 acres with two landscaped industrial parks and houses ranging up to $500,000. Nearly 70% of the 242 homes were sold to Mexican nationals. "There's an emerging middle class in Reynosa because of NAFTA," says Sharyland's marketing chief, Patrick Brewer. "A lot of *maquila* managers are coming over here, paying cash for $125,000 homes." It's more efficient, since so many of their children actually attend school in the U.S.—the next generation of NAFTA boys and girls.

—By Cathy Booth Thomas/McAllen

SOURCE: *Time*, June 11, 2001.

A crucial factor in global competitiveness is the ability of the firm to maximize its global human resources in the long term. To do this, attention must be paid to several important areas:

1. To maximize long-term retention and use of international cadre through career management so that the company can develop a top management team with global experience.
2. To develop effective global management teams.
3. To understand, value, and promote the role of women and minorities in international management in order to maximize those underutilized resources.
4. To maximize the benefits of an increasingly diverse workforce in various locations around the world.
5. To work with the host-country labor relations system to effect strategic implementation and employee productivity.

PREPARATION, ADAPTATION, AND REPATRIATION

> We began to realize that the entire effectiveness of the assignment could be compromised by ignoring the spouse.
> —STEVE FORD, CORPORATION RELOCATIONS, HEWLETT-PACKARD.[1]

Effective human resource management of a company's global cadre does not end with the overseas assignment. It ends with the successful repatriation of the executive into company headquarters. Long-term, proactive management of critical resources should begin with the end of the current assignment in mind—that is, it should begin with plans for the repatriation of the executive as part of his or her career path. The management of the reentry phase of the career cycle is as vital as the management of the cross-cultural entry and training. Otherwise, the long-term benefits of that executive's international experience may be negated.[2] Shortsightedly, many companies do little to minimize the potential effects of **reverse culture shock** (return shock). In fact, a survey of companies belonging to the American Society of Personnel Administration International (ASPAI) revealed that only 31 percent had formal repatriation programs for executives and only 35 percent of those included spouses. In addition, only 22 percent of those had conducted the programs prior to the executive's departure for the assignment.[3] Those American companies without programs had various explanations: a lack of expertise in repatriation training, the cost of the programs, or a lack of a perceived need for such training.

The long-term implications of ineffective repatriation practices are clear—few good managers will be willing to take international assignments because they will see what happened to their colleagues. If a certain manager lost out on promotion opportunities while overseas and is now in fact worse off than before he or she left, the only people willing to take on foreign assignments in the future will be those who have not been able to succeed on the home front or those who think that a stint abroad will be like a vacation. Research has shown that employees commonly see overseas assignments as negative career moves in many U.S. multinational companies.[4] In contrast, such moves are seen as positive in most European, Japanese, and Australian companies because they consider international experience necessary for advancement to top management.

In a recent study of dual-career couples, "the perceived impact of the international assignment upon returning to the U.S." was one of the most important issues stated by managers regarding their willingness to relocate overseas.[5]

Reverse culture shock occurs primarily because of the difficulty of reintegrating into the organization but also because, generally speaking, the longer a person is away, the more difficult it is to get back into the swing of things. Not only might the manager have been overlooked and lost in the shuffle of a reorganization, but her or his whole family might have lost social contacts or jobs and feel out of step with their contemporaries. These feelings of alienation from what has always been perceived as "home"—because of the loss of contact with family, friends, and daily life—delay the resocialization process. Such a reaction is particularly serious if the family's overall financial situation has been hurt by the assignment and if the spouse's career has also been kept "on hold" while he or she was abroad.

For companies to maximize the long-term use of their global cadre, they need to make sure that the foreign assignment and the reintegration process are positive experiences. This means careful career planning, support while overseas, and use of the increased experience and skills of returned managers to benefit the home office. Research into the practices of successful U.S., European, Japanese, and Australian MNCs indicates the use of one or more of the following support systems, as recommended by Tung, for a successful repatriation program:

> ➤ A mentor program to monitor the expatriate's career path while abroad and upon repatriation.

> ➤ As an alternative to the mentor program, the establishment of a special organizational unit for the purposes of career planning and continuing guidance for the expatriate.

> ➤ A system of supplying information and maintaining contacts with the expatriate so that he or she may continue to feel a part of the home organization.[6]

The Role of the Expatriate Spouse

Many companies are beginning to recognize the importance of providing support for spouses and children—in particular because both spouses are often corporate fast trackers and demand that both sets of needs be included on the bargaining table. Firms often use informal means, such as intercompany networking, to help find the trailing spouse a position in the same location. They know that, with the increasing number of dual-career couples (65 percent in the United States), if the spouse does not find a position the manager will very likely turn down the assignment. They decline because they can't afford to lose the income or because the spouse's career may be delayed entirely if he or she is out of the workforce for a few years. As women continue to move up the corporate ladder, the accompanying ("trailing") spouse is often male—estimated at 25 percent in the year 2000.[7] Companies such as Hewlett-Packard, Shell, Medtronic, and Monsanto offer a variety of options to address the dual-career dilemma.

At Procter & Gamble, employees and spouses destined for China are sent to Beijing for two months of language training and cultural familiarization. Nissho Iwai, a Japanese trading company, gets together managers and spouses who are leaving Japan with foreign managers and spouses who are on their way there. In addition, the firm provides a year of language training and information and services for Japanese children to attend schools abroad. Recent research on 321 American expatriate spouses around the world shows that effective cross-cultural adjustment by spouses is more likely (1) when firms seek the spouse's opinion about the international assignment and the expected standard of living, and (2) when the spouse initiates his or her own predeparture training (thereby supplementing the minimal training given by most firms).[8]

Expatriate Career Management

Support services provide timely help for the manager and therefore are part of the effective management of an overseas assignment. The overall transition process experienced by the company's international management cadre over time is shown in Exhibit 10-1. It comprises three phases of transition and adjustment that must be managed for successful socialization to a new culture and resocialization back to the old culture. These phases are (1) the exit transition from the home country, the success of which will be determined largely by the quality of preparation the expatriate has received; (2) the entry transition to the host country, in which successful acculturation (or early exit) will depend largely on monitoring and support; and (3) the entry transition back to the home country or to a new host country, in which the level of reverse culture shock and the ease of reacculturation will depend on previous stages of preparation and support.[9]

Exhibit 10-1   The Expatriate Transition Process

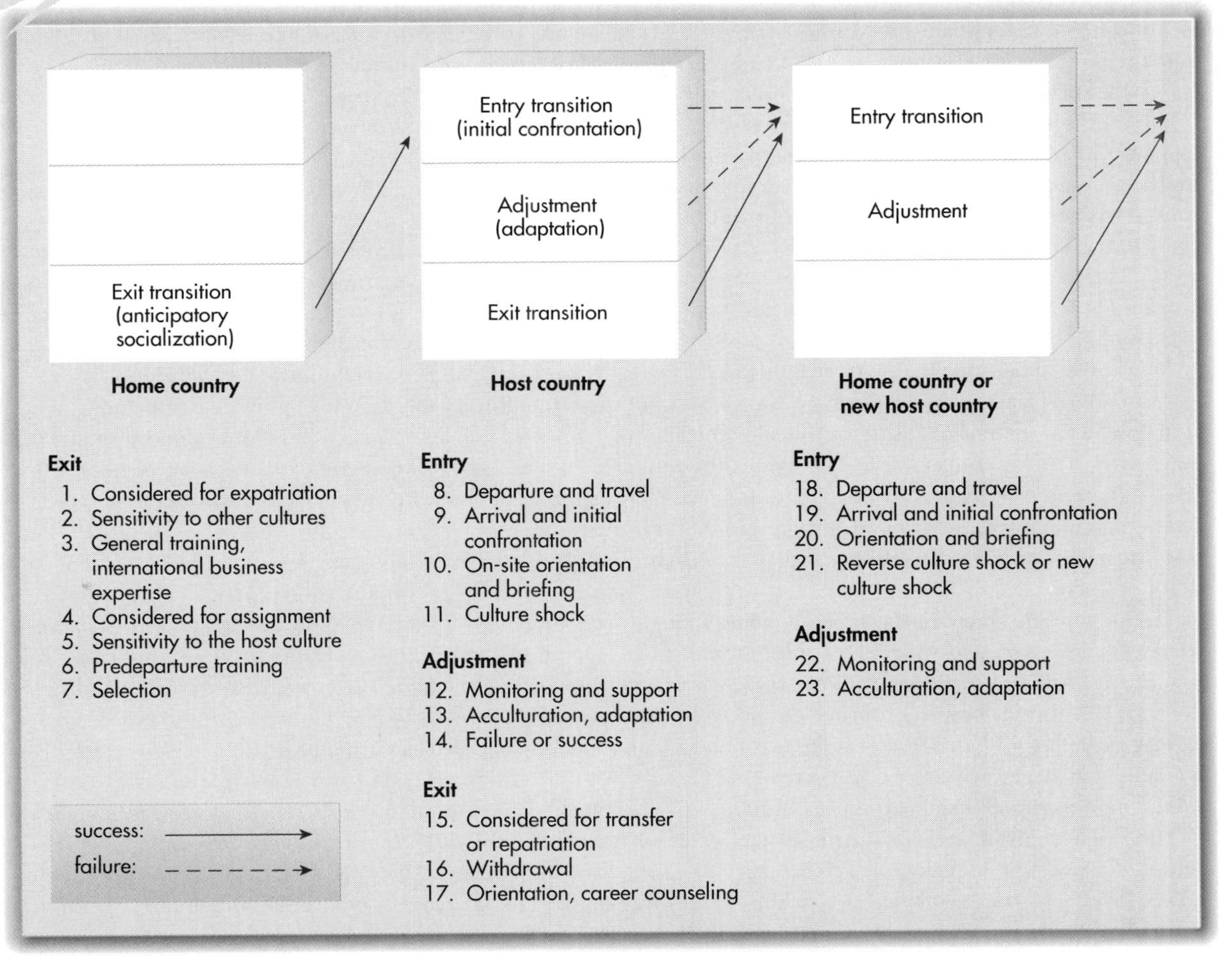

Home country

Exit transition (anticipatory socialization)

Entry transition (initial confrontation)
Adjustment (adaptation)
Exit transition

Host country

Entry transition
Adjustment

Home country or new host country

Exit
1. Considered for expatriation
2. Sensitivity to other cultures
3. General training, international business expertise
4. Considered for assignment
5. Sensitivity to the host culture
6. Predeparture training
7. Selection

Entry
8. Departure and travel
9. Arrival and initial confrontation
10. On-site orientation and briefing
11. Culture shock

Adjustment
12. Monitoring and support
13. Acculturation, adaptation
14. Failure or success

Exit
15. Considered for transfer or repatriation
16. Withdrawal
17. Orientation, career counseling

Entry
18. Departure and travel
19. Arrival and initial confrontation
20. Orientation and briefing
21. Reverse culture shock or new culture shock

Adjustment
22. Monitoring and support
23. Acculturation, adaptation

success: ⟶
failure: - - - ->

SOURCE: P. Asheghian and B. Ebrahimi, *International Business* (New York: HarperCollins, 1990), 470.

Management Focus

MANAGING YOUR CAREER

HOW TO KNOW WHETHER ANOTHER OVERSEAS STINT WILL HELP YOUR CAREER

Gillette human-resources manager Jean Larkin had lived in her Redding, Conn., home just 10 months when she uprooted her family three summers ago to take an overseas assignment. She expected to return to the same U.S. residence after a few years in Johannesburg, South Africa.

Ms. Larkin was wrong. Last September, the 41-year-old expatriate relocated to London so she could play a bigger role as human-resources director for about 950 Gillette workers in seven northern European countries. Five months later, she advanced into regional senior management there. She became HR head for all of Gillette's European commercial operations, covering 2,900 staffers in 20 nations.

In any international move, you risk getting lost in the shuffle toiling far from corporate headquarters. Back-to-back posts in different foreign countries double the chance that key decisionmakers will overlook you. But, as Ms. Larkin's experience shows, careful career management can transform this potentially perilous—and increasingly common—double duty into a positive step.

The trick? Make sure that your second consecutive job abroad will place you in a strong position to fulfill your long-term ambitions inside or outside your company. Two such experiences serve you better than one "as long as you stay visible, and in the loop," says Rita Bennett, managing director of a Chicago intercultural-training concern called Cendant Intercultural, the Bennett Group.

"You have to be kind of critical" about taking a lateral transfer for your second successive international stint, suggests John P. Bohn, a 35-year-old Cargill vice president. He says the agribusiness concern promoted him to a "bigger, better job" in Moscow after two years as an investment manager in Mexico City. He rejoined Cargill's suburban Minneapolis headquarters in fall 1999.

"Before accepting, also look at the track record of returned expats who have completed such assignments," says Gary E. Hayes, a managing partner at Hayes, Brunswick & Partners. The New York management-consulting firm, which specializes in expatriation counseling, advised Ms. Larkin and her husband, a Saab service technician.

Ms. Larkin thought a foreign posting would broaden her breadth at Gillette, a global maker of shaving products that employs about 450 expatriates. But she didn't care to work abroad for the rest of her career. Nor did she have extensive contacts at the company's Boston headquarters before she left the U.S. And while regional human-resources director for Africa, she rarely visited the Boston office because her regional higher-ups operated from London.

Nevertheless, Ms. Larkin's Johannesburg performance attracted internal attention. "She took a number of much needed initiatives . . . in a very difficult environment in South Africa," says Michael Sharp, her Gillette boss until late April. "Jean is never out of sight, out of mind."

Ms. Larkin firmly believes that people considering expatriate double duty must be good advocates for themselves. When Mr. Sharp approached her about the London job last year, she had questions. "She wanted to make sure she wasn't going to miss out on any [U.S.] opportunities," he recalls. "She said, 'Mike, do you really think this is the right move for me?'"

"It definitely was a positive move," she says now.

Because Gillette's assignment letter doesn't spell out duration, Ms. Larkin negotiated an oral agreement with Mr. Sharp: She would stay in London three years, then head home.

In her current high-level position, Ms. Larkin stands out even more than she did in Africa. The youthful-looking executive flies to Boston every quarter to participate in Gillette's human-resources operating committee, for example. She also is aggressively championing a major European role in pilot tests of a plan for cross-functional global career paths.

Ms. Larkin plots her own career path partly by making frequent contacts with headquarters colleagues. Next fall, she intends to make sure everyone still agrees on the length of the U.K. assignment. She will touch base again six months before her anticipated return in fall 2003.

But what if a key home-office sponsor leaves Gillette before then? Ms. Larkin insists she would stay on the headquarters radar screen "by scheduling such appointments with decision makers sooner and by confirming that expectations are aligned."

At the same time, the expatriate recognizes that her growing portfolio of global-management skills could enhance her employment prospects elsewhere. "I could add a lot to any company," Ms. Larkin observes, after five years of progressively bigger foreign assignments. Gillette recently announced plans to eliminate 600 more jobs this year—on top of the 2,700 cuts announced late last year.

Yet Ms. Larkin concedes that she lacks time to pursue professional networking right now because she must make business trips once a week. She may regret her decision, experts warn. "I see savvy expats working their external connections. They have a lot of irons in the fire," reports Cendant Intercultural's Ms. Bennett. When you choose double duty overseas, she adds, networking "is the one thing that should not be dropped."

SOURCE: *Wall Street Journal*, July 3, 2001.

Although we discussed these broad issues earlier, this model offers an interesting overview of the interdependency and the timing of the three transitions.

A company may derive many potential benefits from carefully managing the careers of its expatriates. By helping managers make the right moves for their careers, the company will be able to retain people with increasing global experience and skills. But from the individual manager's perspective, most people understand that no one can better look out for your interests than you can. With that in mind, you need to ask yourself, and your boss, what role each overseas stint will play in your career advancement and what proactive role it will play in your own career. This is illustrated by the experiences of Ms. Larkin, a Gillette manager, in the accompanying Management Focus: Managing Your Career.

The Role of Repatriation in Developing a Global Management Cadre

> Managers returning from expatriate assignments are two to three times more likely to leave the company within a year because attention has not been paid to their careers and the way they fit back into the corporate structure back home.
>
> —www.expat.FT.com, MARCH 5, 2001

In the international assignment, both the manager and the company benefit from the enhanced skills and experience gained by the expatriate. Many returning executives report an improvement in their managerial skills and self-confidence. Some of these acquired skills, as reported by Adler, are shown in Exhibit 10-2.

In addition to the managerial and cross-cultural skills acquired by expatriates, the company benefits from the knowledge and experience those managers gain about how to do business overseas, and about new technology, local marketing, and competitive information. The company should position itself to benefit from that enhanced management knowledge if it wants to develop a globally oriented and experienced management cadre—an essential ingredient for global competitiveness—in particular where there is a high degree of shared learning among the organization's global managers. If the company cannot retain good returning managers, then their

Exhibit 10-2   Skills Learned Abroad

Managerial Skills, Not Technical Skills

Working abroad makes you more knowledgeable about the questions to ask, not the answers.

I learned how to work in two cultures . . . to compromise, not to be a dictator. It's very similar to two domestic cultures . . . like marketing and engineering.

I'm more open-minded . . . more able to deal with a wider range of people . . . because I ran into many other points of view.

Tolerance for Ambiguity

Because I only understood a fraction of what was really going on overseas, maybe 50 percent, I had to make decisions on a fraction of the necessary information. Now I can tolerate nonclosure and ambiguity better.

Things you never thought you'd put up with, you learn to put up with . . . I always thought I was right, until I went overseas.

Multiple Perspective

I learned what it feels like to be a foreigner. . . . I could see things from their perspective.

I learned to anticipate . . . it's the role of a diplomat.

Ability to Work with and Manage Others

I increased my tolerance for other people. For the first time, I was the underdog, the minority.

I became a soft-headed screamer. I'm definitely better with others now.

I used to be more ruthless than I am now. . . . I was the all-American manager. Now, I stop and realize the human impact more. I use others as resources. I do more communicating with others in the organization.

SOURCE: N. J. Adler, *International Dimensions of Organizational Behavior*, 3rd ed. (Boston: PWS-Kent, 1997).

---

potential shared knowledge is not only lost, but is also conveyed to another organization who hires that person. This can be very detrimental to the company's competitive stance. Some companies are becoming quite savvy about how to use technology to utilize shared knowledge to develop their global management cadre, to better service their customers, and—as a side benefit—to store the knowledge and expertise of their managers around the world in case they leave the company. That knowledge, it can be argued, is an asset in which the company has invested large amounts of resources. One such savvy company is Booz-Allen & Hamilton, which instituted a Knowledge On-Line intranet, as featured in the accompanying E-Biz Box.

Black and Gregersen's research of 750 U.S., European, and Japanese companies concluded that those companies that reported a high degree of job satisfaction and strong performance, and that experienced limited turnover, used the following practices when making international assignments:

➤   *They focus on knowledge creation and global leadership development.*

➤   *They assign overseas posts to people whose technical skills are matched or exceeded by their cross-cultural abilities.*

➤   *They end expatriate assignments with a deliberate repatriation process.*[10]

E-Biz Box

BOOZ-ALLEN & HAMILTON USES INTRANET TECHNOLOGY TO SHARE KNOWLEDGE AROUND THE GLOBE

Since 1914, senior executives of world-class organizations in both the public and private sectors have selected Booz-Allen & Hamilton to carry out their management and technology consulting assignments. Booz-Allen recently solved a problem for itself that it is often called upon to solve for its clients: how to bridge islands of information that are isolated due to geographical constraints, computing platforms, and different applications.

After eliminating groupware, document management, and homegrown systems as possible solutions, Booz-Allen decided on intranet technology. For its Knowledge On-Line (KOL) intranet, the firm chose Netscape Enterprise Server and Netscape News Server to support a variety of intranet applications, including:

- A database-driven expert skills directory
- A firmwide knowledge repository able to retrieve information in multiple data types
- Employee directories
- Newsgroups that facilitate global project collaboration

Using a series of benchmarks to evaluate intranet solutions vendors, Booz-Allen determined Netscape software to be the best solution. Netscape met the firm's requirements for:

- Industry-leading Web-based server software
- Outstanding performance, reliability, security, and pricing
- Interoperability, application portability, scalability, and systems network management

Booz-Allen has achieved a tremendous return on investment from its intranet, according to an International Data Corporation study.

SOURCE: Excerpted from Netscape.com case studies.

Booz-Allen & Hamilton relies on its Knowledge On-Line intranet to enhance knowledge sharing among its employees worldwide and to improve client service. By using its intranet to link islands of information separated by geography and platform-specific applications, the renowned consulting firm has enabled its 2,000 private sector consultants to collect and share firmwide their best thinking and expertise.

COLLECTING AND SHARING KNOWLEDGE IN MULTIPLE DATA TYPES

One of the most valued applications supported by KOL is a knowledge repository whereby Booz-Allen can capture, classify, and quantify the firm's knowledge and expertise. The idea behind the knowledge repository is to package knowledge within context. Consultants can do a quick search for best practices, frameworks, business intelligence, competitive data, comparative analysis, business tools, and techniques to help them solve client problems as well as locate the leading experts on a topic.

CYBERSPACE COLLABORATION

Booz-Allen uses the secure Netscape News Server to let global teams of consultants discuss a variety of company- and noncompany-related topics via message threading and real-time discussion groups.

Consultants all over the world take great advantage of the communicative and collaborative capabilities inherent to KOL. Using the news readers built into Netscape Navigator, consultants can engage in either private or public discourse within Booz-Allen. For more general communication across the entire firm, KOL provides public discussion folders accessible to all users.

A successful repatriation program, then, starts before the assignment. The company's top management must set up a culture which conveys the message that the organization regards international assignments as an integral part of continuing career development and advancement, and that it values the skills of the returnees. The company's objectives should be reflected in its long-range plans, commitment, and compensation on behalf of the expatriate. GE sets a model for effective expatriate career management. With its 500 expatriates worldwide, it takes care to select only the best managers for overseas jobs and then commits to placing them in specific positions upon reentry.[11] A study of the IHRM policies of British multinationals indicates that careful planning for foreign assignments pays off. Far-sighted policies, along with selection criteria based more on the adaptability of the manager and her or his family to the culture than on technical skills, apparently account for the low expatriate failure rate—estimated at less than 5 percent.[12]

GLOBAL MANAGEMENT TEAMS

The term **global management teams** describes collections of managers from several countries who must rely on group collaboration if each member is to experience optimum success and goal achievement.[13] Whirlpool International, for example, is a U.S.-Dutch joint venture, with administrative headquarters in Comerio, Italy, where it is managed by a Swede and a six-person management team from Sweden, Italy, Holland, the United States, Belgium, and Germany.[14] To achieve the individual and collective goals of the team members, international teams must "provide the means to communicate corporate culture, develop a global perspective, coordinate and integrate the global enterprise, and be responsive to local market needs."[15] The role and importance of international teams increases as the firm progresses in its scope of international activity. Similarly, the manner in which multicultural interaction affects the firm's operations depends on its level of international involvement, its environment, and its strategy. In domestic firms, the effects of cross-cultural teams are limited to internal operations and some external contacts. In international firms that export

Global management teams play a vital role in global organizations.

products and produce some goods overseas, multicultural teams and cultural diversity play important roles in the relationships between buyers, sellers, and other intermediaries at the boundary of the organization. For multinational firms, the role of multicultural teams again becomes internal to the company; the teams consist of culturally diverse managers and technical people who are located around the world and are also working together within subsidiaries. The team's ability to work together effectively is crucial to the company's success. In addition, technology facilitates effective and efficient teamwork around the world. This was found by the Timberland U.K. sales conference planning team. In the past, their large sales conferences were cumbersome to organize because their offices were in France, Germany, Spain, Italy and the United Kingdom. Then the team started using the British Telecom Conference Call system for the arrangements, which saved them much travel and expense. The company subsequently adopted the BT Conference Calls for the executive teams' country meetings.

> There really was no point in travelling for two hour meetings. So we would lock diaries for a couple of hours over BT Conference Call.
> —www.BritishTelecom.com/cases, FEBRUARY 18, 2001

For global organizations and alliances, the same cross-cultural interactions hold as in MNCs and, in addition, considerably more interaction takes place with the external environment at all levels of the organization. Therefore, global teamwork is vital, as are the pockets of cross-cultural teamwork and interactions that occur at many boundaries.[16] For the global company, worldwide competition and markets necessitate global teams for strategy development, both for the organization as a whole and for the local units to respond to their markets.

As shown in Exhibit 10-3, when a firm responds to its global environment with a global strategy and then organizes with a networked "glocal" structure (discussed in Chapter 8), various types of cross-border teams are necessary for global integration

Exhibit 10-3   Global Teams in the Modern Global Enterprise

Global Environment	Global Strategy	Networked Global Organization	International Teams
Global competition; technological developments; markets; government policies	Optimizing global resources for competitive advantage	Global coordination and integration; local responsiveness; organizational structure; systems; personnel policies and reward systems that support cooperation	Cosmopolitan headquarters' teams; strategic development teams; headquarters' subsidiary teams; technology transfer teams; coalition (joint venture) teams

SOURCE: T. Gross, E. Turner, and L. Cederholm, "Building Teams for Global Operations," *Management Review* (June 1987): 34.

and local differentiation. These include headquarters–subsidiary teams and those coordinating alliances outside the organization. In joint ventures, in particular, multi-cultural teams work at all levels of strategic planning and implementation, as well as on the production and assembly floor.

Increasingly, advances in communication now facilitate **virtual global teams**, with people around the world conducting meetings and exchanging information via the Internet, enabling the organization to capitalize on 24-hour productivity. In this way, too, knowledge is shared across business units and across cultures.[17] Virtual global teams are not without their challenges—including cultural misunderstandings and the logistics of differences in time and space. Group members must build their teams bearing in mind the group diversity and the need for careful communication.[18]

Building Global Teams

The ability to develop effective transnational teams is essential in light of the increasing proliferation of foreign subsidiaries, joint ventures, and other transnational alliances. As noted by David Dotlich of Honeywell Bull Inc. (HBI), an international computer firm, effective international teamwork is essential because cross-cultural "double-talk, double agendas, double priorities, and double interests can present crippling business risks when your storefront stretches for 6000 miles."[19] HBI represents a joint venture of NEC (Japan), Campagnie de Machines Bull (France), and Honeywell (United States). To coordinate this joint venture, HBI considered it important to have transnational teams for front-end involvement in strategic planning, engineering, design, production, and marketing. Dotlich notes that HBI's primary corporate question is how to integrate a diverse pool of cultural values, traditions, and norms in order to be competitive.[20]

The effectiveness of global teams and their ability to integrate with organizational goals depends on the synergy they can attain despite the problems and setbacks that result from the workings of an intercultural group.[21] The advantages of synergy are confirmed by Moran's in a survey of managers from two multinational organizations. He found that the respondents could more quickly generate the advantages of cultural diversity in their organizations than the disadvantages. The advantages they listed included a greater opportunity for global competition (by being able to share experiences, technology, and a pool of international managers) and a greater opportunity for cross-cultural understanding and exposure to different viewpoints. The disadvantages they listed included problems resulting from differences in language, communication, and varying managerial styles; complex decision-making processes; fewer promotional opportunities; personality conflicts, often resulting from stereotyping and prejudice; and greater complexity in the workplace.[22]

How can management find out how well its international teams are performing and what areas need to be improved? The following criteria for evaluating the success of such teams have been proposed by Indrei Ratiu of the Intercultural Management Association in Paris:

➤ Do members work together with a common purpose? Is this purpose spelled out and do all feel it is worth fighting for?

➤ Has the team developed a common language or procedure? Does it have a common way of doing things, a process for holding meetings?

➤ Does the team build on what works, learning to identify the positive actions before being overwhelmed by the negatives?

➤ Does the team attempt to spell out things within the limits of the cultural differences involved, delimiting the mystery level by directness and openness regardless of the cultural origins of participants?

➤ Do the members recognize the impact of their own cultural programming on individual and group behavior? Do they deal with, not avoid, their differences in order to create synergy?

➤ Does the team have fun? (Within successful multicultural groups, the cultural differences become a source of continuing surprise, discovery, and amusement rather than irritation or frustration.)[23]

THE ROLE OF WOMEN IN INTERNATIONAL MANAGEMENT

Around the world, women are remaking companies, society, and themselves. But in each country, women have achieved different things, fought different battles—and made different sacrifices.[24]

Opportunities for female indigenous employees to move up the managerial ladder in a given culture depend on the values and expectations regarding the role of women in that society. In Japan, for example, the workplace has traditionally been a male domain as far as managerial careers are concerned (although rapid changes are now taking place). To the older generation, a working married woman represented a loss of face to the husband because it implied that he was not able to support her. Women were usually only allowed clerical positions, under the assumption that they would leave to raise a family and perhaps later return to part-time work. Employers thus made little effort to train them for upper level positions.[25] As a result, very few women workers have been in supervisory or managerial posts—thus limiting the short-term upward mobility of women through the managerial ranks.[26]

The younger generation and increased global competitiveness have brought some changes to traditional values regarding women's roles in Japan. Over 60 percent of Japanese women are now employed, including half of Japanese mothers.[27] But how and when these cultural changes will affect the number of Japanese women in managerial positions remains to be seen.

Where one finds limitations on managerial opportunities for women in their own country, there are obviously even more limitations on their opportunities as expatriates. Overall, more managerial opportunities are available for American women than for women in most other countries. But even for American women, who now fill over 25 percent of the managerial positions at home, commensurate opportunities are not available to them abroad: about 6 percent of North American expatriate managers are women.[28] The reasons for this anomaly can often be traced to the cultural expectations of the host countries—the same cultural values that keep women in these countries from the managerial ranks.

The lack of expatriates who are female or represent other minority groups does not reflect their lack of desire to take overseas assignments. Indeed, studies indicate their strong willingness to work abroad. Nor can the situation be explained by their lack of success. For example, Adler's major study of North American women working as expatriate managers in countries around the world showed that they are, for the most part, successful.[29]

The most difficult job seems to be getting the assignment in the first place. North American executives are reluctant to send women and minorities abroad because they assume they will be subject to the same culturally based biases as at home, or they assume a lack of understanding and acceptance, particularly in certain countries. Research on 52 female expatriate managers, for example, shows this assumption to be highly questionable. Adler showed, first and foremost, that foreigners are seen as foreigners; furthermore, a woman who is a foreigner (called a *gaijin* in Japan) is not expected to act like a local woman. According to Adler and Izraeli, "Asians see female expatriates as foreigners who happen to be women, not as women who happen to be foreigners." The other women in the study echoed this view. One woman based in Hong Kong noted, "'It doesn't make any difference if you are blue, green, purple, or a frog. If you have the best product at the best price, they'll buy.' "[30]

Women and minorities represent a significant resource for overseas assignments—whether as expatriates or as host-country nationals—that is underutilized by American companies. Adler studied this phenomenon regarding women and recommends that businesses (1) avoid assuming that a female executive will fail because of the way she will be received or because of problems experienced by female spouses; (2) avoid assuming that a woman will not want to go overseas; and (3) give female managers every chance to succeed by giving them the titles, status, and recognition appropriate to the position—as well as sufficient time to be effective.[31]

GLOBAL MULTICULTURALISM: MANAGING DIVERSITY

> Create the dream that all can embrace, and diversity of talent, temperament, ethnicity and gender become valuable.[32]

The potential benefits and difficulties posed by increasing domestic multiculturalism—that is, a culturally diverse workforce and a multicultural marketplace anywhere in the world—are crucial challenges for the future that companies must manage in a positive way. Those benefits go beyond issues of social responsibility to the mandate of competitive necessity. The benefits of managing diversity for competitive advantage can be realized in many ways, including: (1) reducing costs of high levels of turnover and absenteeism; (2) facilitating recruitment of scarce labor; (3) increasing sales to members of minority culture groups; (4) promoting team creativity and innovation; (5) improving problem solving; and (6) enhancing organizational flexibility.[33] In addition, the experience of working with domestic multiculturalism is good training for managers preparing to operate overseas. In a recent survey of 15 Fortune 100 company HRM executives, the top three reasons cited for engaging in diversity management were better utilization of talent, increased marketplace understanding, and enhanced breadth of understanding in leadership positions.[34] Overall, those executives stressed workforce diversity as an advantage in pursuing competitive opportunities rather than as a means to avoid problems.

One way to improve sales to minority groups was suggested by Levi Strauss's Hispanic employees. After watching Levi's "501 Blues" television commercials, they asked "Why is that guy walking down the street alone? Doesn't he have any friends?"[35] The employees explained that Hispanic people would respond more readily to scenes of friends and family. So, Levi developed a new series of 501 ads that emphasized camaraderie, in keeping with the Hispanic culture, rather than individuality. The result has been booming sales in the Hispanic community. This new insight is being echoed by many firms. At IBM, Ted Childs, director of workforce diversity, says, "We think it is important for our customers to look inside and see people like them. If they can't, it seems to me that the prospect of them becoming or staying our customers declines."[36] And at MCI, Timothy Price, president of business markets, says, "We don't encourage homogeneity here; the price you pay for conformity is lack of creativity." In addition, foreign-owned companies are also realizing the value in constructive management of their diverse workforce. Mitsubishi, for example, has incurred a $120 million damages settlement resulting from a sexual harassment lawsuit filed by the EEOC and has since set up a comprehensive diversity training program.

Building Programs to Value Diversity

In recognition of the need to take such a competitive stance toward diversity issues, firms are implicitly moving along the evolutionary curve of a human resources management mandate. This evolution has moved from compliance with Equal Employment Opportunity (EEO) laws in the 1960s to specific affirmative action programs in the 1970s to attempts to develop a balanced workforce in the corporation in the 1980s. Now, led by progressive firms, the move in the 2000s is toward workforce diversity programs that seek out, include, and value employees from various nontraditional backgrounds.

David Kearns, chairman and CEO of Xerox, warns, "We have to manage diversity right now, and much more so in the future. American business will not be able to survive if we do not have a large, diverse work force, because those are the demographics."[37] The demographics that Kearns refers to, indicating the increasing representation of various racial groups, immigrants, and women in the workforce in the United States were discussed in Chapter 1. Projections for civilian labor force representation for the year 2005 are shown in Exhibit 10-4—the largest increase will be from Hispanics and Asians. But firms are now expanding the concept of diversity beyond those of race, ethnicity, and gender to include variables such as age and disabilities and dimensions such as education, and language, as shown in Exhibit 10-5. The goal of such an expanded concept of diversity is as explained at Xerox Company: "to create a workplace in which individuals are unencumbered by traditional barriers, stereotypes, and restrictions."[38]

Exhibit 10-4   Trends in Civilian Labor Force Participation, 1990–2005

Year	All Workers	Males	Females	Whites	Blacks	Hispanics	Asians
1990	100%	54.7%	45.3%	85.9%	10.8%	7.7%	3.3%
Projected 2005	100	52.6	47.4	83.4	11.8	11.1	7.7

SOURCE: Data from U.S. Bureau of Labor Statistics, *Outlook 1990–2005*, Bulletin 2402 (Washington, DC: GPO, 1992): 31–32.

Exhibit 10-5 Dimensions of Workforce Diversity

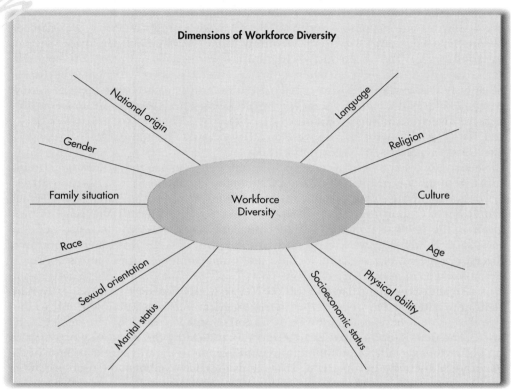

SOURCE: Mark M. Deresky, "Managing in a Diverse Workforce," MBA paper, West Florida University (Spring 1994).

Clearly, managing diversity is a complex and sensitive task; some broad guidelines for managers evolve from the foregoing discussion and corporate examples, as follows:

Diversity Program Guidelines

1. Develop and communicate a broad definition of workplace diversity, including all kinds of differences, such as race, gender, age, work, and family issues.

2. Attain visible commitment from top managers to support programs, and communicate to employees the importance of diversity to the firm's competitive stance—that it is not just a matter of sensitivity training. Hold managers accountable for meeting diversity goals.

3. Avoid stereotyping groups of employees by using titles for them; focus instead on what all employees have in common and on each individual's value to the firm.

4. Set up a broad, diverse pool of talented people to be trained and eligible for job promotion or selection; but let it be known that the best person will get the job—and stick by that.

5. Set up regular training programs with the goal of gradually changing the corporate culture by educating workers about employee similarities as well as differences and the value those differences bring to the firm.

The composition of the labor force worldwide will also experience similar changes.[39] The implications of multiculturalism in the workforce are profound. At Aramco in Dhahran, Saudi Arabia, for example, professionals from 50 countries work together at all levels. The future competitiveness of corporations, both in the United States and abroad, will depend on their ability to attract and manage such diverse talent effectively.

Managing a culturally diverse workforce—that is, managing diversity—requires managers to understand and value diversity in order to maximize the potential of the workforce. A number of companies—Xerox, AT&T, Procter & Gamble, and 3M—are training their executives to be aware of and to manage diversity. Paul Nolan, director of corporate training for the Lincoln Savings Bank in New York, says, "I've never seen an ethnic makeup like the one here; the bank's employee mix includes Hispanics, Chinese, East Indians, blacks [African-Americans] and Italian-Americans." Lincoln has hired a consulting firm to teach its employees how to understand and better manage such diversity.[40]

Generally, the measures many firms are taking indicate the importance they attach to dealing effectively with the issue of workforce diversity, including creating senior staff positions specifically for that purpose. At GE, for example, Eugene Andrews, Manager Workforce Diversity Division, cites the firm's diversity practices (listed as follows), implemented to reach their goal "to be recognized as the world's most competitive company due to our ability to value and fully utilize the contributions of all employees from all cultural and social backgrounds."[41]

GE Diversity Practices

➤ Top management commitment and involvement

➤ Integrated diversity strategy

➤ Campus recruiting

➤ Hires expanded at top level to signal commitment and provide role models

➤ Career management

➤ Management of work/family issues (e.g., child care and flextime)

➤ Diversity education and training

➤ Communications

➤ Community outreach

The ability to manage diversity is a special skill required of today's managers. The word "manage" does not really mean to "control," as it would seem to imply, but, rather, to value diversity; that is, to acknowledge and make use of the different skills and perceptions of people from various backgrounds—and to encourage others to do so. Doing so acknowledges that every culture has something to contribute to the pool of talent necessary to be competitive. Valuing diversity requires that managers create a climate of respect for individual workers and the unique contributions that they can make. When workers come together in committees, task groups, or assembly groups, this climate can create synergistic outcomes.

Maximizing Effectiveness

Much of the potential productivity of diverse work teams depends on the ability of upper management to establish a positive climate for diversity. One way to do this is to set up programs designed to develop an awareness of cultural differences and their potential value. A reevaluation of the organization's recruiting, training, development, and incentive programs can also ensure that these programs support multiculturalism at all levels. Wang Laboratories, for example, has put over a thousand managers—mostly white males—through its training programs on diversity. Wang's program is built on four basic building blocks: (1) an awareness of one's own behavior; (2) a recognition of one's own biases and stereotypes; (3) a focus on job performance; and (4) an avoidance of assumptions.[42]

An important part of creating a positive climate is to show that all people's skills are valued. To do this, managers should develop and promote more minorities and women to upper management levels. At present, very few of these individuals have reached high-level positions. As a result, according to Joan Green, director of employment opportunity programs at Quaker Oats Company, "people in non-traditional roles try to look like the successful people—white males—with the effect that people whose value to the organization lies in their individuality and creativity lose it when they conform."[43]

One of the problems is that the rules for getting ahead in business are made predominantly by white males. This is particularly so in countries like Japan and Mexico. These rules are usually subtle and played out implicitly—on the golf course or over lunch—but they serve to exclude minorities and women from networking and from "the boys' club."[44] Awareness training helps people to confront possible prejudicial assumptions and biases and to deal openly with removing those barriers.

Companies around the world are dealing differently with the issue of managing diversity, depending on their location and situation. Honeywell's home base in Minneapolis, for example, is set among the second largest Laotian, Cambodian, and Vietnamese population in the United States. Honeywell is addressing the resulting problems of language and cultural barriers through the development and administration of special courses and groups for Asian-American employees.

WORKING WITHIN LOCAL LABOR RELATIONS SYSTEMS

> If you have to close a plant in Italy, in France, in Spain or in Germany, you have to discuss the possibility with the state, the local communities, the trade unions; everybody feels entitled to intervene . . . even the Church.
> —JACOB VITTORELLI, FORMER DEPUTY CHAIRMAN OF PIRELLI

An important variable in implementing strategy and maximizing host-country human resources for productivity is that of the labor relations environment and system within which the managers of an MNE will operate in a foreign country. Differences in economic, political, and legal systems result in considerable variation in labor relations systems across countries. Pan-European firms, for example, are still dealing with disparate national labor and social systems as the EC directors wrestle with the goal of the harmonization of labor laws.[45] In addition, European businesses continue to be undermined by their poor labor relations and by inflexible regulations. As a result, businesses are having to move jobs overseas to cut labor costs, resulting from a refusal of unions to grant any reduction in employment protection or benefits in order to keep the jobs at home.[46] In addition, non-European firms wishing to operate in Europe have to carefully weigh the labor relations systems and their potential effect on strategic and operational decisions.

The term **labor relations** refers to the process through which managers and workers determine their workplace relationships.[47] This process may be through verbal agreement and job descriptions, or through a union's written labor contract which has been reached through negotiation in collective bargaining between workers and managers. The labor contract determines rights regarding workers' pay, benefits, job duties, firing procedures, retirement, layoffs, and so on.

The prevailing labor relations system in a country is important to the international manager because it can constrain the strategic choices and operational activities of a firm operating there. The three main dimensions of the labor–management relationship which the manager will consider are: (1) the participation of labor in the affairs of the firm, especially as this affects performance and well-being; (2) the role and impact of unions in the relationship; and (3) specific human resource policies in terms of recruitment, training, and compensation.[48] Constraints take the form of (1) wage levels that are set by union contracts and leave the foreign firm little flexibility to be globally competitive; (2) limits on the ability of the foreign firm to vary employment levels when necessary; and (3) limitations on the global integration of operations of the foreign firm because of incompatibility and the potential for industrial conflict.[49]

Organized Labor Around the World

Exhibit 10-6 shows the percentage of the workforce in trade unions in industrialized countries. Notably, there is a trend of falling union membership. This trend is attributable to various factors, including an increase in the proportion of white-collar and service workers as proportionate to manufacturing workers, a rising proportion of temporary and part-time workers, and a reduced belief in unions in the younger generations.[50] But the numbers do not show the nature of the system in each country. In most countries, a single dominant industrial relations system applies to almost all workers. But in both Canada and the United States there are two systems—one for the organized and one for the unorganized. Each, according to Adams, has "different rights and duties of the parties, terms and conditions of employment, and structures and processes of decision making." Basically, in North America, an agent represents unionized employees, whereas unorganized employees can only bargain individually, usually with little capability to affect major strategic decisions or policies or conditions of employment.[51]

The traditional trade union structures in Western industrialized societies have been in *industrial unions*, representing all grades of employees in a specific industry, and *craft unions*, based on certain occupational skills. More recently, the structure has been conglomerate unions, representing members in several industries, for example, the metal workers unions in Europe which cut across industries, and general unions, which are open to most employees within a country.[52] The system of union representation varies among countries. In the United States, most unions are national and represent specific groups of workers—for example, truck drivers or airline pilots—so a company may have to deal with several different national unions. A single U.S. firm—rather than an association of firms representing a worker classification— engages in its own negotiations.[53] In Japan, on the other hand, it is common for a union to represent all workers in a company. In recent years, company unions in Japan have increasingly coordinated their activities, leading to some lengthy strikes.

Industrial labor relations systems across countries can only be understood in the context of the variables in their environment and the sources of origins of unions. These include government regulation of unions, economic and unemployment factors, technological issues, and the influence of religious organizations.[54] Any of the basic processes or concepts of labor unions, therefore, may vary across countries, depending on where and how the parties have their power and achieve their objectives, such as through parliamentary action in Sweden. For example, collective bargaining in the United States and Canada refers to negotiations between a labor union

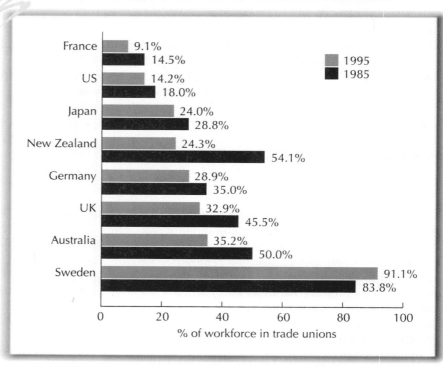

Exhibit 10-6 Trade Union Decline in Industrialized Countries

Legend:
- 1995
- 1985

Country	1995	1985
France	9.1%	14.5%
US	14.2%	18.0%
Japan	24.0%	28.8%
New Zealand	24.3%	54.1%
Germany	28.9%	35.0%
UK	32.9%	45.5%
Australia	35.2%	50.0%
Sweden	91.1%	83.8%

% of workforce in trade unions

SOURCE: Robert Taylor, "Collective Responsibility," *Financial Times*, September 13, 1999.

local and management. But in Europe collective bargaining takes place between the employer's organization and a trade union at the industry level.[55] This difference means that North America's decentralized, plant-level, collective agreements are more detailed than Europe's industrywide agreements because of the complexity of negotiating myriad details in multi-employer bargaining. In Germany and Austria, for example, such details are delegated to works councils by legal mandate.[56]

The resulting agreements from bargaining also vary around the world. A written, legally binding, agreement for a specific period, common in Northern Europe and North America, is less prevalent in Southern Europe and Britain. In Britain, France, and Italy, bargaining is frequently informal and results in a verbal agreement valid only until one party wishes to renegotiate.[57]

Other variables of the collective bargaining process are the objectives of the bargaining and the enforceability of collective agreements. Because of these differences, managers in MNEs overseas realize that they must adapt their labor relations policies to local conditions and regulations. They also need to bear in mind that, while U.S. union membership has declined by about 50 percent in the last 20 years, in Europe overall membership is still quite high—though it, too, has been falling but from much higher levels.

Most Europeans are covered by collective agreements, whereas most Americans are not. Unions in Europe are part of a national cooperative culture between government, unions, and management, and they hold more power than in the United States.

In June 1998, for example, thousands of employees at the state-owned Air France Airline staged protests in Paris airports against proposed job and pay cuts, thereby causing the government to back down.[58]

Increasing privatization will make governments less vulnerable to this kind of pressure. It is also interesting to note that there are labor courts in Europe that deal with employment matters separately from unions and works councils. In Japan, labor militancy has long been dead, since labor and management agreed 40 years ago on a deal for industrial peace in exchange for job security. Unions in Japan have little official clout, especially in the midst of the Japanese recession.

In addition, there is not much to negotiate, since wage rates, working hours, job security, health benefits, overtime work, insurance, and the like, are legislated. Local working conditions and employment issues are all that's left to negotiate. In addition, the managers and labor union representatives are usually the same people, which serves to limit confrontation, as well as does the cultural norm of maintaining harmonious relationships. In the industrialized world, tumbling trade barriers are also reducing the power of trade unions because competitive multinational companies have more freedom to choose alternative productive and sourcing locations. Most new union workers—about 75 percent—will be in emerging nations, like China and Mexico, where wages are low and unions are scarce.[59]

In China the government ordered all 47,000 foreign firms there to be unionized by mid-1996 and new foreign firms to establish unions in their first year of operation. This order was in response to a sharp rise in labor tension and protests about poor working conditions and industrial accidents. The All-China Federation of Trade Unions claimed that "foreign employers often force workers to work overtime, pay no heed to labor-safety regulations and deliberately find fault with the workers as an excuse to cut their wages or fine them."[60] Much of the unrest has been caused by workers who are angry about losing their socialist safety net under the government's new economic reforms. Johnson & Johnson's three consumer-products manufacturing plants in China were already unionized and have a cooperative relationship with the unions.[61]

Convergence versus Divergence in Labor Systems

In South Africa, the elimination of apartheid has given rise to a rapidly growing labor movement. The African National Congress is pro-union, and local unions receive assistance from the AFL-CIO branch in Johannesburg.[62]

Although no clear direction is evident at this point, political changes, external competitive forces, increased open trade, and frequent moves of MNCs around the world are forces working toward convergence in labor systems. **Convergence** occurs as the migration of management and workplace practices around the world reduces workplace disparities from one country to another. This occurs primarily as MNCs seek consistency and coordination among their foreign subsidiaries, and as they act as catalysts for change by "exporting" new forms of work organization and industrial relations practices.[63] It also occurs as harmonization is sought, such as for the EC countries, and as competitive pressures in free-trade zones, such as the NAFTA countries, eventually bring about demands for some equalization of benefits for workers.[64] This trend is highlighted in the accompanying Management Focus: Unions Without Borders? The Case of the Duro Bag Factory in Mexico. It would appear that economic globalization is leading to labor transnationalism and will bring about changes in

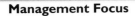

Management Focus

UNIONS WITHOUT BORDERS? THE CASE OF THE DURO BAG FACTORY IN RIO BRAVO

In the dusty border town of Rio Bravo, just across the Rio Grande from Pharr, Texas, the Duro Bag factory churns out the chichi paper bags sold for a dollar at suburban shopping malls throughout the United States.

Eluid Almaguer, an intense, stocky labor activist in his 30s, got a job at the plant in 1998. There he says he saw people lose fingers in machines cutting the cardboard used to stiffen the bottoms of the bags. Safety guards, he explains, were removed from the rollers that imprint designs on the paper lining—the extra time required to clean them was treated as needless lost production. Almaguer recalls that solvent containers didn't carry proper danger warnings, and while workers got dust masks, they were useless for filtering out toxic chemical fumes. "In terms of safety, well, there just wasn't any," he remembers bitterly.

No help was forthcoming from the union at Duro, a *seccion*, or local, of the Paper, Cardboard and Wood Industry Union. The *seccion*—part of the Confederation of Mexican Workers (CTM), a pillar of support for the country's ruling bureaucracy since the 1930s—has a contract with the company, a protection agreement in which government-affiliated union leaders are paid to guarantee labor peace. But Duro workers did find assistance abroad, in a nascent cross-border solidarity movement that is emerging as labor's answer to the globalization of capital.

The battle to change conditions in this plant is one of many labor conflicts that have erupted in the past decade from one end of the border to the other. Duro is just one of 3,611 foreign-owned factories employing more than 1.3 million people in Mexico, according to the National Association of Maquiladoras. In cities like Rio Bravo, Ciudad Juarez, and Tijuana, hundreds of thousands of workers stream through plant gates at each shift change—a human wave pouring into communities of cardboard houses and dirt streets.

As *maquiladora*-style production has transformed the Mexican economy, it has also provided a proving ground for a new model of international relationships between workers and unions. This cross-border solidarity movement has created new leverage against employers and

has energized the rank-and-file union base in Mexico, Canada, and the United States, while providing immediate material support for embattled workers like those at Duro. Five years ago the AFL-CIO administration of John Sweeney broke from the old cold war policy of former AFL-CIO presidents George Meany and Lane Kirkland, which defended free trade, corporate interests, and U.S. foreign policy. Yet, the newest vision of what an international labor movement could become—based on solidarity from below—is being born not in an office in Washington but in shantytowns along the border.

For Duro workers, this support network is based partly in the coalition for Justice in the Maquiladoras (CJM), which brings together unions, churches and community organizations in Mexico, Canada, and the United States. For more than a decade, the coalition has functioned as a resource for Mexican workers trying to fight an economic policy that uses their low wages to encourage further *maquiladora* investment. At Duro, with CJM support, workers began the effort to change conditions by trying to enforce provisions of the union-protection agreement (and Mexican law) that, at least on paper, guarantee overtime pay, profit-sharing, and other rights. As an initial step, they expelled the *seccion's* general secretary, Jose Ángel García Garces, whom they viewed as too close to company managers. In his place the members elected Almaguer.

Duro's vice president of plastics, Bill Forstrom, says wages start at 60 pesos a day (about $6). A gallon of milk in the supermarket costs 20 pesos—a third of a day's work. According to Consuelo Moreno, a Duro worker, "My daughter had to drop out of school this year because we didn't have the money for her to continue."

Nevertheless, says Almaguer, "people were willing to work at bad-paying jobs. But not under those conditions." The new leaders brought repeated grievances before the plant's human relations manager, Alejandro de la Rosa. "We'd take (our complaints) to his office, and he'd throw us out," Almaguer says. "The company was in violation of at least 50 percent of the contract." In October 1999, the company fired Almaguer. The union's leaders in Mexico City cooperated, excluding him from union membership. Police and guards were called into the plant. But after three days of turmoil, workers forced Almaguer's reinstatement as general secretary. Then, on April 14, 2000, 400 workers refused to go to work as a protest against abusive treatment, and they were later joined by 800 more.

In spring 2000, the contract at Duro expired, and workers drew up a list of demands for a new agreement. They asked for two pairs of safety shoes each year, work clothes, contributions to a savings plan, and a doctor at the plant to take care of injuries. "The company said it owned the factory—they would decide what would be done here," Almaguer recalls.

When workers wouldn't budge, their union's national officials signed a new agreement with the company on June 11, ignoring their demands. By then, workers had decided that enforcing the protection agreement was no longer possible. They struck again. And in front of the factory gates, they began organizing a new, independent and democratic union.

With the cooperation of the CJM, there was a public protest in August 2000 of hundreds of advocates of independent unionism from Mexico and the United States. In the face of such pressure, the Tamaulipas labor board finally granted the Duro union legal status.

Workers have yet to negotiate a new contract (as of January 2001), and 150 remain fired. Almaguer's house, made of shipping pallets and cardboard, was burned down in an arson attack on October 31, a crime local police refuse to investigate.

SOURCE: Adapted and excerpted from D. Bacon, "Unions without Borders: A New Kind of Internationalism Is Challenging Neoliberal Globalism," *The Nation*, 272, no. 3 (January 22, 2001): 20.

labor rights and democracy around the world.[65] In East European societies in transition to market economies, for example, newly structured industrial relations systems are being created.[66] Trends in industrial relations, such as the flattening of organizations and the decline in the role of trade unions are viewed by many as global developments pointing to convergence in labor systems.[67]

Other pressures toward convergence of labor relations practices around the world come from the activities and monitoring of labor conditions worldwide by various organizations. One of these organizations is the International Labor Organization (ILO)—comprising union, employer, and government representation—whose mission is to ensure that humane conditions of labor are maintained. Other associations of unions in different countries include various international trade secretariats representing workers in specific industries. These include the International Confederation of Free Trade Unions (ICFTU) and the World Confederation of Labor (WCL). The activities and communication channels of these associations provide unions and firms with information about differences in labor conditions around the world.[68] One result of their efforts to provide awareness and changes in labor conditions was the pressure they brought to bear on MNCs operating in South Africa in the late 1980s. The result was the exodus of foreign companies and the eventual repeal of apartheid laws. Now there is a rapidly growing labor union movement there, thanks to the pro-union African National Congress. The AFL-CIO opened an office in Johannesburg and assists the South African unions.[69]

Political and cultural shifts are also behind the new labor law in South Korea, as the country moves from a system founded on paternalism and authoritarianism to one based on more liberal values.[70]

Although there are forces for convergence in labor relations systems around the world, as discussed earlier, for the most part, MNCs still adapt their practices largely to the traditions of national industrial relations systems, and there is considerable pressure to do so. Those companies, in fact, act more like local employers, subject to local and country regulations and practices. Although the reasons for continued divergence in systems seem fewer, they are very strong: not the least of these reasons are political ideology and the overall social structure and history of industrial practices. It is highly unlikely that China, for example, would accept Western practices that threaten their political ideology. And in the EU, where states are required to maintain parity in wage rates and benefits under the Social Charter of the Maastricht Treaty, there is still a powerful defense of cultural identity and social systems, and considerable resistance by unions to comply with those requirements. Managers in those MNCs also recognize that a considerable gap often exists between the labor laws and the enforcement of those laws—in particular in less developed countries. Exhibit 10-7 shows the major forces for and against convergence in labor relations systems.

The NAFTA and Labor Relations in Mexico

About 40 percent of the total workforce in Mexico is unionized, with about 80 percent of workers in industrial organizations that employ over 25 workers, unionized. However, government control over union activities is very strong, and although there are some strikes, union control over members remains rather weak.[71] Multinational Corporations are required by government regulation to hire Mexican nationals for at least 90 percent of their workforce; preference must be given to Mexicans and to union personnel. In reality, however, the government permits hiring exceptions.

Currently, the only labor issues that are subject to a formal trinational review under the NAFTA labor side pact are minimum wages, child labor, and safety issues. But foreign firms like Honeywell operating in Mexico are faced with pressures from various stakeholders in their dealings with unions. In fact, in early 1998 the AFL-CIO president John Sweeney flew to Mexico to try "to develop coordinated cross-border organizing and bargaining strategies."[72] Although no deals were made at that time, the seeds were sown in the direction of more open union activity and benefits for employees.

Exhibit 10-7   Trends in Global Labor Relations Systems

Forces for Global Convergence ← Current System →	Forces to Maintain or Establish Divergent Systems
Global competitiveness	National labor relations systems and traditions
MNC presence or consolidation initiatives	Social systems
Political change	Local regulations and practices
New market economies	Political ideology
Free-trade zones: harmonization (EU), competitive forces (NAFTA)	Cultural norms
Technological standardization, IT	
Declining role of unions	
Agencies monitoring world labor practices	

Many foreign firms set up production in Mexico at least in part for the lower wages and overall cost of operating there—utilizing the advantages of the NAFTA—and the Mexican government wants to continue to attract that investment, as it has for many years before NAFTA. But Mexican workers claim that some of the large U.S. companies in Mexico violate the basic labor rights and cooperate with progovernment labor leaders in Mexico to break up independent unions. Workers there believe that MNCs routinely use blacklists, physical intimidation, and economic pressure against union organization and independent labor groups that oppose Mexican government policies or the progovernment Confederation of Mexican Workers (CTM). GE, for example, has been accused of firing 11 employees in its Juarez plant who were involved in organizing a campaign for the Authentic Labor Front, Mexico's only independent labor group. The company was also accused of "blacklisting" union activists (a list of "undesirable employees" which is circulated around some employers). In February 1994, formal complaints were filed to the U.S. National Administration office of the Department of Labor by two U.S. unions—the Teamsters and the United Electrical, Radio, and Machine Workers Union. (U.S. unions have an interest in increasing wages and benefits in Mexico so as to offset some of the reasons that American companies take productive facilities there, along with U.S. jobs.) The Labor Department's National Administrative Office (NAO)—set up by the NAFTA to monitor labor policies in the United States, Mexico, and Canada—reviewed complaints that GE may have violated Mexican labor law. That office later ruled that those claims against GE were unsubstantiated; they also ruled that neither that office (the NAO) nor the Mexican counterpart could punish other nations for failing to address union-organization rights, although they could issue formal complaints.[73]

This incident illustrates the complexities of labor relations when a firm operates in other countries—particularly when there are linkages and interdependence among those countries, such as through the NAFTA or the EC. Of interest are the differences in labor law in the private sector among NAFTA nations. For example, while the minimum wage in Mexico is far less than that in Canada or the United States, there are a number of costly required benefits for Mexican workers, such as 15 days pay for a Christmas bonus, and 90 days severance pay.

Labor Relations in Germany

Codetermination has proved to be efficient, and several northern European countries adopted similar systems, while others, such as the UK, did not. The combined influences made dialogue between management and the workers a natural component of decision making.

—ANDRE LEYSEN, CHAIRMAN, SUPERVISORY BOARD, AGLA GEBERT[74]

Comparative Management in Focus

Germany's **codetermination** law (*mitbestimmung*)—which refers to the participation of labor in the management of a firm—mandates representation for unions and salaried employees on the supervisory boards of all large companies and "works councils" of employees at every work site. Unions are well integrated into managerial decision making and can make a positive contribution to corporate competitiveness and restructuring; this seems different from the traditional adversarial relationship of unions and management in the United States.[75] However, the fact is that firms, in the form of affiliated organizations of companies, have to contend with negotiating with powerful industrywide unions. Employment conditions that would be negotiated privately in the United States, for example, are subject to federal mandates in Germany—a model unique in Europe.

Union membership in Germany is voluntary, usually with one union for each major industry, and union power is quite strong. Negotiated contracts with firms by the employers' federation stand to be accepted by firms that are members of the federation, or used as a guide for other firms. These contracts therefore result in setting the pay scale for about 90 percent of the country's workers.[76]

The union works councils play an active role in hiring, firing, training, and reassignment during times of reorganization and change.[77] Because of the depth of works council penetration into personnel and work organization matters, as required by law, their role has been described by some as "co-manager of the internal labor market."[78] This situation has considerable implications for how managers of MNCs plan to operate in Germany. IG Metall, for example, which is Germany's largest metalworking union, with 2.6 million workers, negotiates guidelines regarding pay, hours, and working conditions on a regional basis. Then works councils use those guidelines to make local agreements. IG Metall's proactive role on change illustrates the evolving role of unions by leading management thinking instead of reacting to it. In addition, management and workers tend to work together because of the unions' structure. Indeed, Adams suggests that such institutional accord is a powerful factor in changing deeply ingrained cultural traits.

Codetermination has clearly helped to modify German managerial style from authoritarian to something more akin to humanitarian, without, it should be noted, altering its capacity for efficiency and effectiveness.[79] This system compares to the lack of integration and active roles for unions in the U.S. auto industry, for example, conditions that limit opportunities for change.

DaimlerChrysler, the German-American company headquartered in Germany, includes a works council in its decision making, as mandated by German law. This means that the company's labor representatives pay close attention to U.S. attitudes, which may lead to changes in the tone of the collective bargaining processes. The two-tiered system of a supervisory and a management board will remain. The company will likely exert pressure to bring down the high labor costs and taxes in Germany, under the threat of moving its plants elsewhere in order to remain globally competitive. With the Daimler-Chrysler company accounting for about 13 percent of the DAX index of 30 German blue-chip stocks, U.S. shareholders and managers in the company will no doubt hold some power to bring about change and reduce operating costs in the company—and perhaps eventually in the country. Pay for German production workers is among the highest in the world, about 150 percent of that in the United States and about ten times that in Mexico. German workers also have the highest number of paid vacation days in the world and prefer short work days. The stores are open very little in the evenings or weekends. Termination costs are also very high—including severance pay, retraining costs, time to find another job, and so on—and that is assuming that you are successful in terminating the employee in the first place, which is very difficult to do in Europe. This was brought home to Colgate-Palmolive when it tried to close its factory in Hamburg in 1996. The company offered the 500 employees an average of $40,000 each, but the union would not accept and eventually Colgate had to pay a much higher (undisclosed) amount.

The German model, according to Rudiger Soltwedel of the Institute for the World Economy at Kiel, holds that competition should be based on factors other than cost.[80] Thus, the higher wage level in Germany should be offset by higher-value goods like luxury cars and machine tools, which have been the hallmark of Germany's products. To the extent that the West German unions have established the high-wage, high-skill, and high-value-added production pattern, then, they have also become dependent on the continued presence of that pattern.[81] In recognition of that dependency, German auto firms are in the process of remaking themselves after the Japanese model—reducing supplies and cutting costs in order to compete on a global scale. However, this social contract which has underpinned Germany's manufacturing success is fraying at the edges as Germany's economy weakens under the $100 billion cost of absorbing East Germany and under competitive EC pressures.[82]

Conclusion

The role of the IHRM department has expanded to meet the strategic needs of the company to develop a competitive global management cadre. Maximizing human resources around the world requires attention to the many categories and combinations of those people, including expatriates, host-country managers, third-country nationals, female and minority resources, global teams, local employees, and workforce diversity. Competitive global companies need top managers with global experience and understanding. To that end, attention must be paid to the needs of expatriates before, during, and after their assignments in order to maximize their long-term contributions to the company.

SUMMARY OF KEY POINTS

1. Support programs for expatriates should include information from and contact with the home organization, as well as career guidance and support after the overseas assignment.
2. The expatriate's spouse plays a crucial role in the potential retention and effectiveness of the manager in host locations. Companies should ensure the spouse's interest in the assignment, include him or her in the predeparture training, and provide career and family support during the assignment and upon return.
3. Global management teams offer greater opportunities for competition—by sharing experiences, technology, and international managers—and greater opportunities for cross-cultural understanding and exposure to different viewpoints. Disadvantages can result from communication and cross-cultural conflicts and greater complexity in the workplace.

4. Women and minorities represent an underutilized resource in international manage-ment. A major reason for this situation is the assumption that culturally based biases may limit the opportunities and success of females and minorities.

5. Managing diversity—that is, managing a culturally diverse workforce within a home or a host country—is a crucial competitive issue for the future. The skills required for this task include understanding and valuing diversity to maximize the potential of the workforce.

6. The advantages of multicultural diversity include fuller use of resources through a wider pool of skills, perspectives, and ideas; better understanding of a multicultural market-place; greater innovation and problem solving; and increased motivation and commit-ment in the company resulting from a wider acceptance of decisions.

7. Labor relations refers to the process through which managers and workers determine their workplace relationships. The labor relations environment, system, and processes vary around the world and affect how the international manager must plan strategy and maximize the productivity of local human resources.

DISCUSSION QUESTIONS

1. What steps can the company's IHRM department take to maximize the effective-ness of the expatriate's assignment and the long-term benefit to the company?

2. Discuss the role of reverse culture shock in the repatriation process. What can companies do to avoid this problem? What kinds of skills do managers learn from a foreign assignment, and how can the company benefit from them? What is the role of repatriation in the company's global competitive situation?

3. What are the reasons for the small numbers of American female expatriates? What more can companies do to use women and minorities as a resource for interna-tional management?

4. Discuss the role of international management teams relative to the level of a com-pany's global involvement. Give some examples of the kinds of teams that might be necessary and what issues they would face.

5. Explain what is meant by managing diversity. Describe some important features of a training and development program that could help maximize the effectiveness of multiculturalism in an organization.

APPLICATION EXERCISE

Interview one or more managers who have held positions overseas. Try to find a man and a woman. Ask them about their experiences both in the working environment and in the foreign country generally. How did they and their families adapt? How did they find the stage of reentry to headquarters, and what were the effects of the assignment on their career progression? What differences do you notice, if any, between the expe-riences of the male and the female expatriates?

EXPERIENTIAL EXERCISE

Form groups of six students, divided into two teams, one representing union members from a German company and the other representing union members from a Mexican company. These companies have recently merged in a joint venture, with the sub-sidiary to be located in Mexico. These union workers, all line supervisors, will be working together in Mexico. You are to negotiate six major points of agreement regarding union representation, bargaining rights, and worker participation in management, as discussed in this chapter. Present your findings to the other groups in the class and discuss.

INTERNET RESOURCES

Visit the Deresky companion Website at http://prenhall.com/Deresky for this chapter's Internet resources.

CASE STUDY: MANAGING DIVERSITY AT LUXURY ISLAND RESORT

Patricia Atwell had just accepted a position as a human resource consultant for the Luxury Island Resort in California. The resort's profitability was declining, and Patricia had been hired to evaluate the situation and to make recommendations to the local management and the headquarters management. Feeling a little overwhelmed by this task, Patricia pondered where to start.

There had been an extremely high employee turnover rate in the past few years, the quality of the resort's service had declined, and many regular clients were not returning. Patricia decided to start with the clients by interviewing some of them and asking others to fill out a comment slip about the resort. Many clients criticized the poor service from every type of staff member. One regular client said, "This used to be a happy, efficient place. Now I don't even know if I'll come back next year; the atmosphere among the workers seems dismal; nobody ever looks happy." After reviewing the customer comment cards, Patricia decided to investigate staff relations and job performance at the resort.

At the personnel department, Patricia began to investigate trends and practices regarding hiring and placement. In reviewing the files, she noticed that the labor pool had become increasingly diverse in the last few years, reflecting the general labor market trends in that area. The majority of the employees at the resort represented a number of racial and ethnic backgrounds, and many were recent immigrants. Many were unskilled and had little schooling, yet they were placed straight into their jobs. The management and office staff was also quite diversified; yet, even with their higher education and skill level, there was considerable turnover. While glancing through the files, Patricia noticed a letter of resignation in the file of a reservations office clerk, Maria Martinez. Underneath that letter was a copy of a memo from the resort manager to Ms. Martinez, reprimanding her for consuming alcoholic beverages on the premises. Patricia sought out Ms. Martinez and asked her why she was leaving. Ms. Martinez was clearly angry and hurt as she explained that the previous week she had had a bad cold but did not want to miss any work. So she was in the habit of sipping from a bottle of matta, a nonalcoholic barley beverage popular in the Spanish-speaking Caribbean. She said the manager kept walking past her office and looking in at her. The next day she received the reprimand, but when she tried to talk to him about it, he refused to meet with her.

SOURCE: This case was written by the author and Bethanne Gorenflo, a student at the State University of New York—Plattsburgh (Spring 1993). Copyright © 1993 by Helen Deresky. It is fictional.

The next day, Patricia decided to get out among the employees—to talk to them and observe them on the job. She started her departmental evaluations in the kitchen, where she found a melange of cultures; the French chef was screaming directions, mostly in French, to his assistants and the waiters, who seemed to be Haitian, Spanish, and Asian. Many seemed confused about what they should do but did not say anything.

Case Questions

1. You are Patricia Atwell. Evaluate the situation at the resort. What are your conclusions? Draw up a list of recommendations to the resort management and a list of recommendations to the company president.

2. Assuming your recommendations are accepted; outline your plan for implementing them. What specific steps must be taken, by whom, and when? What results do you anticipate?

Motivating and Leading

**Opening Profile: Success! Starbucks' Java Style Helps to
Recruit, Motivate, and Retain Leaders in Beijing**

When we first started, people didn't know who we were and it was rough finding
sites. Now landlords are coming to us.

—DAVID SUN, PRESIDENT OF BEIJING MEI DA COFFEE COMPANY
(FRANCHISEE FOR NORTHERN CHINA)
(*THE ECONOMIST*, OCTOBER 6, 2001)

Starbucks Coffee International, already operating in London, Japan, Singapore, Taiwan, the
Philippines, and Thailand, is continuing its aggressive global expansion. It plans to have 500 coffee
shops in Europe by the end of 2003. In China, Starbucks had over 35 shops going into 2002, mainly

in Beijing and Shanghai, with plans for five more outlets within a year. This is a remarkable penetration rate, given that China is a country of devoted tea drinkers who do not take readily to the taste of coffee.

No stranger to training leaders from around the world into the Starbucks' style, the company nevertheless has had quite a challenge in recruiting, motivating, and retaining managers for its Beijing outlets. Starbucks' primary challenge has been to recruit good managers in a country where the demand for local managers by foreign companies expanding there is far greater than the supply of managers with any experience in capitalist-style companies. Chinese recruits have stressed that they are looking for opportunity to get training and to advance in global companies rather than for money; they know that managers with experience in Western organizations can always get a job. The brand's pop-culture reputation is also an attraction to young Beijingers.

In order to expose the recruits to java-style culture as well as to train them for management, Starbucks brings them to Tacoma, Washington, for three months to give them a taste of the west coast lifestyle and the company's informal culture, such as Western-style backyard barbecues. Then they are exposed to the art of cappuccino-making at a real store before dawn and concocting dozens of fancy coffees. They get the same intensive training as anyone else anywhere in the world. One recruit, Mr. Wang, who worked in a large Beijing hotel before finding out how to make a triple grand latte, said that he enjoys the casual atmosphere and respect. The training and culture are very different from what one would expect at a traditional state-owned company in China, where the work is strictly defined and has no challenge for employees.

Starbucks has found that motivating their managers in Beijing is multifaceted. They know that people won't switch jobs for money alone. They want to work for a company that gives them an opportunity to learn. They also want to have a good working environment and a company with a strong reputation. The recruits have expressed their need for trust and participation in an environment where local nationals are traditionally not expected to exercise initiative or authority. In all, what seems to motivate them more than anything else is dignity.

SOURCES: www.Starbucks.com; "Coffee with Your Tea? Starbucks in China," *The Economist*, October 6, 2001; "Starbucks' Expansion in China Is Slated," *Wall Street Journal*, October 5, 1998.

MOTIVATING

> In Mexico, everything is a personal matter; but a lot of managers don't get it.
> —ROBERT HOSKINS, MANAGER, LEVITON MANUFACTURING, JUAREZ

After managers set up a firm's operations by planning strategy, organizing the work and responsibilities, and staffing those operations, they turn their attention to everyday activities. This ongoing behavior of individual people carrying out various daily tasks enables the firm to accomplish its objectives. Getting those people to perform their jobs efficiently and effectively is at the heart of the manager's challenge.

As this chapter's Opening Profile illustrates, motivation—and therefore appropriate leadership style—is affected by many powerful variables (societal, cultural, and political). China has a long history behind workers' assumptions about "the way we do things around here," and its strong culture determines attitudes toward work. But in the big cities like Beijing, employees are eager to learn Western ways in order to make themselves more marketable. Foreign companies are challenged to find the right mix of old and new in order to motivate and retain good employees.

Our objective in this chapter is to consider motivation and leadership in the context of diverse cultural milieus. We need to know what, if any, differences there are in the societal factors that elicit and maintain behaviors leading to high employee productivity and job satisfaction. Are effective motivational and leadership techniques universal or culture based?

CROSS-CULTURAL RESEARCH ON MOTIVATION

Motivation is very much a function of the context of a person's work and personal life. That context is greatly influenced by cultural variables, which affect the attitudes and behaviors of individuals (and groups) on the job. The framework of this context was described in Chapter 3 and illustrated in Exhibit 3-1. In applying Hofstede's research on the cultural dimensions of individualism, uncertainty avoidance, masculinity, and power distance, for example, we can make some generalized assumptions about motivation, such as the following.

➤ High uncertainty avoidance suggests the need for job security, whereas people with low uncertainty avoidance would probably be motivated by more risky opportunities for variety and fast-track advancement.

➤ High power distance suggests motivators in the relationship between subordinates and their boss, whereas low power distance implies that people would be more motivated by teamwork and relations with their peers.

➤ High individualism suggests people would be motivated by opportunities for individual advancement and autonomy; collectivism (low individualism) suggests that motivation will more likely work through appeals to group goals and support.

➤ High masculinity suggests that most people would be more comfortable with the traditional division of work and roles; in a more feminine culture, the boundaries could be looser, motivating people through more flexible roles and work networks.

Misjudging the importance of these cultural variables in the workplace may result not only in a failure to motivate, but also in demotivation. Rieger and Wong-Rieger present the following example:

> In Thailand, the introduction of an individual merit bonus plan, which runs counter to the societal norm of group cooperation, may result in a decline rather than an increase in productivity from employees who refuse to openly compete with each other.[1]

In considering what motivates people, we have to understand their needs, goals, value systems, and expectations. No matter what their nationality or cultural background, people are driven to fulfill needs and to achieve goals. But what are those needs, what goals do they want to achieve, and what can motivate that drive to satisfy their goals?

The Meaning of Work

Because our focus here is on the needs that affect the working environment, it is important to understand first what work means to people from different backgrounds. For most people, the basic meaning of work is tied to economic necessity (money for food, housing, and so forth) for the individual and for society. However, the additional connotations of work are more subjective, especially about what work provides other than money—achievement, honor, social contacts, or whatever.

Another way to view work, however, is through its relationship to the rest of a person's life. The Thais call work **ngan**, which is the same as their word for "play," and they tend to introduce periods of play in their workdays. On the other hand, most people in China, Germany, and the United States have a more serious attitude toward work.

Especially in work-oriented China, seven-day work weeks with long hours and few days off are common.[2] A study of average work hours in various countries conducted by Steers found that Koreans worked longer hours and took fewer vacation days than workers in Thailand, Hong Kong, Taiwan, Singapore, India, Japan, and Indonesia.[3] The study concluded that the Koreans' hard work was attributable to loyalty to the company, group-oriented achievement, and emphasis on group harmony and business relationships.

Studies on the meaning of work in eight countries were carried out by George England and a group of researchers who are called the Meaning of Work (MOW) International Research Team.[4] Their research sought to determine a person's idea of the relative importance of work compared to that of leisure, community, religion, and family. They called this concept **work centrality**, defined as "the degree of general importance that working has in the life of an individual at any given point in time." The mean score on the work centrality index for the eight countries studied is shown in Exhibit 11-1.

Exhibit 11-1   The Relative Meaning of Work in Eight Countries

Mean Work Centrality Score

Work is more important and more central in life

Score	Country	N
7.78	Japan (7)	N = 3144
7.30	(former) Yugoslavia (adjusted for sample composition) (5)	N = 521
7.10	Israel (4)	N = 893
6.94	USA (3)	N = 996
6.81	Belgium (1)	N = 446
6.69	Netherlands (1)	N = 976
6.67	Germany (1)	N = 1276
6.36	Britain (0)	N = 409

Numbers in parentheses indicate the number of countries significantly lower (p < 0.05) in work centrality than the country designated.

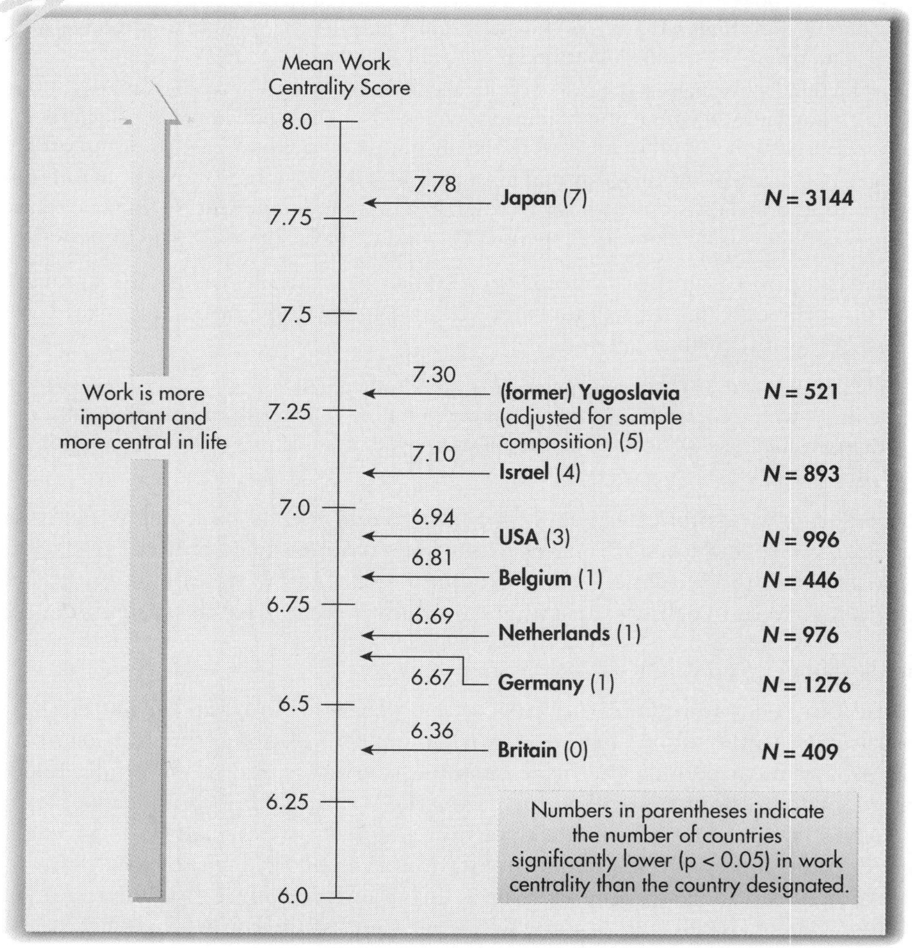

SOURCE: MOW International Research Team, *The Meaning of Working: An International Perspective* (London: Academic Press, 1985).

The obvious general implication from these findings is that the higher the mean work centrality score, the more motivated and committed the workers will be. Of even more importance to managers (as an aid to understanding culture-based differences in motivation) are the specific reasons for valuing work. What kinds of needs does the working environment satisfy, and how does that psychological contract differ among populations?

The MOW research team provided some excellent insights into this question when they asked people in the eight countries to what extent they regarded work as satisfying six different functions: work (1) provides a needed income, (2) is interesting and satisfying, (3) provides contacts with others, (4) facilitates a way to serve society, (5) keeps one occupied, and (6) gives status and prestige. The results are shown in Exhibit 11-2. Note the similarities of some of these functions with Maslow's need categories and Herzberg's categories of motivators and maintenance factors. Clearly, these studies can help international managers to anticipate what attitudes people have toward their work, what aspects of work in their life context are meaningful to them, and therefore what approach the manager should take in setting up motivation and incentive plans.

Exhibit 11-2   The Perceived Utility of the Functions of Work
(Mean Number of Points)

Country	N	Working provides you with an income that is needed	Working is basically interesting and satisfying to you	Working permits you to have interesting contacts with other people	Working is a useful way for you to serve society	Working keeps you occupied	Working gives you status and prestige
Japan	3180	45.4	13.4	14.7	9.3	11.5*	5.6‡
Germany	1264	40.5	16.7	13.1	7.4	11.8	10.1
Belgium	447	35.5	21.3	17.3	10.2	8.7	6.9
Britain	471	34.4	17.9	15.3	10.5	11.0	10.9
Yugoslavia	522	34.1	19.8	9.8	15.1	11.7	9.3
United States	989	33.1	16.8	15.3	11.5	11.3	11.9
Israel	940	31.1	26.2	11.1	13.6	9.4	8.5
Netherlands	979	26.2	23.5	17.9	16.7	10.6	4.9
All countries combined	8792	35.0†	19.5	14.3	11.8	10.8	8.5

*Working keeps you occupied *was translated in Japan in such a manner that there is real question about how similar its meaning was to that intended.*
†*The combined totals weight each country equally regardless of sample size.*
‡*The mean points assigned by a country to the six functions add to approximately 100 points.*
SOURCE: Meaning of Work International Research Team, *The Meaning of Working: An International Perspective* (London: Academic Press, 1985).

In addition to the differences among countries within each category—such as the higher level of interest and satisfaction derived from work by the Israelis as compared with the Germans—it is interesting to note the within-country differences. Although income was the most important factor for all countries, it apparently has a far greater importance than any other factor in Japan. In other countries, such as the Netherlands, the relative importance of different factors was more evenly distributed.

The broader implications of such comparisons about what work means to people are derived from considering the total cultural context. The low rating given by the Japanese to the status and prestige found in work, for instance, suggests that those needs are more fully satisfied elsewhere in their lives, such as within the family and community. In the Middle East, religion plays a major role in all aspects of life, including work. The Islamic work ethic is a commitment toward fulfillment, and so business motives are held in the highest regard.[5] The origin of the Islamic work ethic is in the Muslim holy book, the Qur'an, and the words of the Prophet Mohammed:

> On the day of judgment, the honest Muslim merchant will stand side by side with the martyrs.
>
> —MOHAMMED

Muslims feel that work is a virtue and an obligation to establish equilibrium in one's individual and social life. The Arab worker is defined by his or her level of commitment to family, and work is perceived as the determining factor in the ability to enjoy social and family life.[6] A study of 117 managers in Saudi Arabia by Ali found that Arab managers are highly committed to the Islamic work ethic and that there is a moderate tendency toward individualism.[7]

Exhibit 11-3 shows the results of the study and gives more insight into the Islamic work ethic. Another study by Kuroda and Suzuki found that Arabs are serious about their work and that favoritism, give-and-take, and paternalism have no place in the Arab workplace. They contrasted this attitude to that of the Japanese and Americans who consider friendship to be an integral part of the workplace.[8]

Other variables affect the perceived meaning of work and how it satisfies various needs, such as the relative wealth of a country.[9] When people have a high standard of living, work can take on a different meaning other than simply to provide the basic economic necessities of life. Economic differences among countries were found to explain variation in attitudes toward work in a study by Furnham et al. of over 12,000 young people from 41 countries on all five continents. Specifically, they found that young people in Far and Middle Eastern countries reported the highest competitiveness and acquisitiveness for money, while those from North and South America scored highest on worth ethic and "mastery" (i.e., to continue to struggle to master something).[10] Such studies show the complexity of the underlying reasons for differences in attitudes toward work—cultural, economic, and so on—which must be taken into account when considering what needs and motivations people bring to the workplace. All in all, research shows a considerable cultural variability affecting how work meets employees' needs.

The Needs Hierarchy in the International Context

How can a manager know what motivates people in a specific country? Certainly, by drawing on the experiences of others who have worked there; and also by inferring the likely type of motivational structure present by studying what is known about the

Exhibit 11-3   The Islamic Work Ethic: Responses by Saudi Arabian Managers

Item	Mean
Islamic Work Ethic	
1. Laziness is a vice.	4.66
2. Dedication to work is a virtue.	4.62
3. Good work benefits both one's self and others.	4.57
4. Justice and generosity in the workplace are necessary conditions for society's welfare.	4.59
5. Producing more than enough to meet one's personal needs contributes to the prosperity of society as a whole.	3.71
6. One should carry work out to the best of one's ability.	4.70
7. Work is not an end in itself but a means to foster personal growth and social relations.	3.97
8. Life has no meaning without work.	4.47
9. More leisure time is good for society.	3.08
10. Human relations in organizations should be emphasized and encouraged.	3.89
11. Work enables man to control nature.	4.06
12. Creative work is a source of happiness and accomplishment.	4.60
13. Any man who works is more likely to get ahead in life.	3.92
14. Work gives one the chance to be independent.	4.35
15. A successful man is the one who meets deadlines at work.	4.17
16. One should constantly work hard to meet responsibilities.	4.25
17. The value of work is derived from the accompanying intention rather than its results.	3.16

On scale of 1–5 (5 highest)

SOURCE: Adapted from Abbas J. Ali, "The Islamic Work Ethic in Arabia," *Journal of Psychology* 126 (5) (1992): 507–519 (513).

culture in that region. In addition, some research and comparative studies about needs in specific countries are available and can provide another piece of the puzzle.

Some researchers have used Maslow's hierarchy of needs to study motivation in other countries. A classic study by Haire, Ghiselli, and Porter surveyed 3,641 managers in 14 countries. They concluded that Maslow's needs, in particular the upper-level ones, are important at the managerial level, although the managers reported that the degree to which their needs were fulfilled did not live up to their expectations.[11]

In a similar study, Ronen investigated whether work-related values and needs are similar across nationalities and whether the motivation categories of Maslow and Herzberg apply universally. Studying trained, nonmanagerial male employees (in Germany, Canada, France, Japan, and the United Kingdom), he found that such similarities do exist and that there are common clusters of needs and goals across nationalities. These clusters include (1) job goals, such as working area, work time, physical working conditions, fringe benefits, and job security; (2) relationships with coworkers and supervisors; and (3) work challenges and opportunities for using skills.[12] Ronen concludes that **need clusters** are constant across nationalities and that Maslow's need hierarchy is confirmed by those clusters. In addition, he claims that Herzberg's categories are confirmed by the **cross-national need clusters** in his study.

People's opinion of *how* best to satisfy their needs varies across cultures also. As shown in Exhibit 11-4, there may be varying *priorities* regarding sources of job-related satisfaction. For example, China, Israel, and Korea gave the highest score to "achievement" as satisfying self-actualization needs, whereas the first choice was an "interesting job" for Germany, Holland, and the United States.

One clear conclusion is that managers around the world have similar needs but show differing levels of satisfaction of those needs derived from their jobs. Variables other than culture may be at play, however. One of these variables may be the country's stage of economic development. With regard to the transitioning economy in Russia, for example, a study by Elenkov found that Russian managers stress security

Exhibit 11-4 Comparative Job Motivational Components

Job-Related Sources of Satisfaction for:	China	Germany	Holland	Hungary	Israel	Korea	United States
Self-Actualization Needs							
• Advancement	M	M	H	L	H	H	H
• Use of Ability	H	H	H	H	M	H	H
• Meaningful Work	M	H	M	M	M	M	M
• Achievement	#1	M	H	H	#1	#1	H
• Interesting Job	H	#1	#1	H	H	H	#1
Esteem Needs							
• Recognition	M	L	M	H	M	M	M
• Influence	M	L	M	L	L	L	L
• Esteem	H	M	M	M	H	L	H
Affiliation Needs							
• Co-Worker Support	M	H	H	M	M	H	L
• Supervisor Support	M	H	M	#1	H	H	M
• Interaction	L	L	M	M	L	L	L
Security Needs							
• Work Conditions	L	L	L	M	L	M	L
• Benefits	L	H	L	M	M	M	M
• Security	L	H	M	M	L	H	M
Physiological Needs							
• Base Pay	L	M	L	H	M	M	L

Rankings of the Importance of Job-Related Sources of Need Satisfaction for Seven Countries (H = upper third; M = middle third; L = bottom third; #1 = highest rank)

SOURCE: Data from D. Elizur, L. Borg, R. Hunt, and L. M. Beck, "The Structure of Work Values: A Cross-Cultural Comparison," *Journal of Organizational Behavior* 12 (1991): 21–38; reprinted in J. B. Cullen, *Multinational Management*, 2nd ed. (Cincinnati: South-Western, 2002), 513.

and belongingness needs as opposed to higher-order needs.[13] Whatever the reason, many companies that have started operations in other countries have experienced differences in the apparent needs of the local employees and how they expect work to be recognized. Mazda, of Japan, experienced this problem in its Michigan plant. Japanese firms tend to confer recognition in the form of plaques, attention, and applause, and Japanese workers are likely to be insulted by material incentives because such rewards imply that they would work harder to achieve them than they otherwise would. Instead, Japanese firms focus on groupwide or companywide goals, compared with the American emphasis on individual goals, achievement and reward.

When considering the cross-cultural applicability of Maslow's theory, then, it is not the needs that are in question as much as the ordering of those needs in the hierarchy. The hierarchy reflects the Western culture where Maslow conducted his study, and different hierarchies might better reflect other cultures. For example, Eastern cultures focus on the needs of society rather than on the needs of individuals. Nevis proposes that a hierarchy more accurately reflecting the needs of the Chinese would comprise four levels: (1) belonging, (2) physiological needs, (3) safety, and (4) self-actualization in the service of society.[14] It is difficult to observe or measure the individual needs of a Chinese person because, from childhood, these are intermeshed with the needs of society. Clearly, however, along with culture, the political beliefs at work in China dominate many facets of motivation. As the backbone of the industrial system, cadres (managers and technicians) and workers are given exact and detailed prescriptions of what is expected of them as members of a factory, workshop, or work unit. This results in conformity at the expense of creativity. Workers are accountable to their group, which is a powerful motivator. Because being "unemployed" is not an option in China, it is important for employees to maintain themselves as cooperating members of the work group.[15] Money is also a motivator, stemming from the historical political insecurity and economic disasters that have perpetuated the need for a high level of savings.[16] A Gallup opinion poll cited in the 1998 World Competitiveness yearbook found that a priority among Chinese is to "work hard and get rich," compared to Europeans and Americans who value self-achievement over wealth.[17]

The Intrinsic-Extrinsic Dichotomy in the International Context

The intrinsic-extrinsic dichotomy is another useful model (researched by a number of authors) for considering motivation in the workplace. Herzberg's research, for example, found two sets of needs: (1) motivational factors (intrinsic) and (2) maintenance factors (extrinsic).

Results from others' research using Herzberg's model provide some insight into motivation in different countries and help us to determine whether the intrinsic-extrinsic dichotomy is generalizable across cultures. Research on managers in Greece and on workers in general in an Israeli kibbutz indicate that all these people are motivated more by the nature of the work itself; dissatisfactions resulted from the conditions surrounding the work.[18] Another study in Zambia generally found the same dichotomy. Work motivation was found to result from the intrinsic factors of the opportunity for growth and the nature of the work and, to some extent, physical provisions. Factors that produced dissatisfaction and were not motivators were extrinsic—relations with others, fairness in organizational practices, and personal problems.[19]

In addition to research on single countries, Herzberg's theory has been used to compare different countries on the basis of job factors and job satisfaction. A study of MBA candidates from the United States, Australia, Canada, and Singapore, for example, indicated that Herzberg's motivational factors were more important to these prospective managers than hygiene factors.[20] In a broader study of managers from Canada, the United Kingdom, France, and Japan to determine the relative importance of job factors to them and how satisfied they were with those factors, Kanungo and Wright drew a number of interesting conclusions. Interpreting their results, we can draw some overall conclusions: the managers indicated that internally mediated factors (intrinsic, job content factors) were more important than organizationally controlled factors (extrinsic, job context factors). However, they found differences across countries, in particular between the United Kingdom and France, in how much importance the managers placed on job outcomes and also in their relative levels of satisfaction with those outcomes.[21] As a practical application of their research results, Kanungo and Wright suggest the following implications for motivation in the workplace:

> Efforts to improve managerial performance in the UK should focus on job content rather than on job context. . . . Job enrichment programs are more likely to improve performance in an intrinsically oriented society such as Britain, where satisfaction tends to be derived from the job itself, than in France, where job context factors, such as security and fringe benefits, are more highly valued.[22]

To answer common questions about whether Japanese-style management practices—work groups, quality circles, and long-term employment—make a difference to commitment and job satisfaction, Lincoln studied 8,302 workers in 106 factories in the United States and Japan (though not specifically using Herzberg's factors). He concluded that those practices had similar positive or negative effects on work attitudes in both countries. But while the level of commitment to the company was essentially the same in both samples, the Japanese indicated a lower level of job satisfaction.[23]

The lower level of satisfaction is contrary to popular expectations because of the well-known Japanese environment of teamwork, productivity, long-term employment, and dedication to the company. However, previous research has also found a lower level of job satisfaction in Japan.[24] Lower work satisfaction indicates a higher level of motivation to fulfill personal and company goals (that is, to do better), compared to a lower level of motivation indicated by complacency. As Lincoln points out, however, these research findings could be the result of another cultural variable introducing a measurement bias: the Japanese tendency to "color their evaluations of nearly everything with a large dose of pessimism, humility and understatement" in their persistent quest to do better.[25] This underscores the need to consider carefully all the cultural variables involved in observing or managing motivation.

Although, there is a need for more cross-cultural research on motivation, one can draw the tentative conclusion that managers around the world are motivated more by intrinsic than by extrinsic factors. Considerable doubt remains, however, about the universality of Herzberg's or Maslow's theories because it is not possible to take into account all of the relevant cultural variables when researching motivation. Different factors have different meaning within the entire cultural context and must be considered on a situation-by-situation basis. The need to consider the entire national and cultural context is shown in the accompanying Comparative Management in Focus, which highlights motivational issues for Mexican workers and indicates the importance to them of what Herzberg calls maintenance factors. As you read, consider whether this situation supports or refutes Herzberg's theory.

Motivation in Mexico

> To get anything done here, the manager has to be more of an instructor, teacher, or father figure than a boss.
> —ROBERT HOSKINS, MANAGER, LEVITON MANUFACTURING, JUAREZ

It is particularly important for an aspiring international manager to become familiar with Mexican factory workers because of the increasing volume of manufacturing that is being outsourced there.[26]

To understand the cultural milieu in Mexico, we can draw on research that concludes that Latin American societies, including Mexico, rank high on power distance (the acknowledgment of hierarchical authority) and on uncertainty avoidance (a preference for security and formality over risk). In addition, they rank low on individualism, preferring collectivism, which values the good of the group, family, or country over individual achievement.[27] In Mexico, the family is of central importance; loyalty and commitment to the family frequently determines employment, promotion, or special treatment for contracts. Unfortunately, it is this admirable cultural norm that often results in motivation and productivity problems on the job by contributing to very high absenteeism and turnover, especially in the *maquiladoras*. This high turnover and absenteeism are costly to employers, thereby offsettinig the advantage of relatively low labor cost per hour. "Family reasons" (taking care of sick relatives or elderly parents) are the most common reasons given for absenteeism and for failing to return to work.[28] Workers often simply do not come back to work after vacations or holidays. For many Mexican males, the value of work lies primarily in its ability to fulfill their culturally imposed responsibilities as head of household and breadwinner rather than to seek individual achievement.[29] *Machismo* (sharp role differentiation based on gender) and prestige are important characteristics of the Mexican culture.

As a people, speaking very generally, Mexicans are very proud and patriotic; *respeto* (respect) is important to them, and slights against personal dignity are regarded as a grave provocation.[30] Mexican workers expect to be treated in the same respectful manner that they use toward one another. As noted by one U.S. expatriate, foreign managers must adapt to Mexico's "softer culture"; Mexican workers "need more communication, more relationship-building, and more reassurance than employees in the U.S."[31] The Mexican people are very warm and have a leisurely attitude toward time; face-to-face interaction is best for any kind of business, with time allowed for socializing and appreciating their cultural artifacts, buildings, and so forth. Taking time to celebrate a worker's birthday, for instance, will show that you are a *simpático* boss and will increase workers' loyalty and effort. The workers' expectations of small considerations, that seem inconsequential to U.S. managers should not be discounted. In one *maquiladora*, when the company stopped providing the annual Halloween candy, the employees filed a grievance to the state Arbitration Board—Junta de Conciliación y Arbitraje.

Most managers in Mexico find that the management style that works best there is authoritative and paternal. Paternalism is expected; the manager is regarded as *el patrón* (pronounced pah-trone), or father figure, whose role it is to take care of the workers as an extended family.[32] Employees expect managers to be the authority; they are the "elite"—power rests with the owner or manager and other prominent community leaders. For the most part, if not told to do it, the workers won't do it. Nor will they question the boss or make any decisions for the boss.[33] Nevertheless, employees perceive the manager as a person, not as a concept or a function, and success often depends on the ability of a foreign manager to adopt a personalized management style, such as by greeting all the workers as they come in for their shift.

Generally speaking, many Mexican factory workers doubt their ability to personally influence the outcome of their lives. They are apt to attribute events to the will of God, or to luck, timing, or relationships with higher authority figures. For many, decisions are made on the basis of ideals, emotions, and intuition rather than objective information. However, there is increasing evidence of individualism and materialism, particularly among the upwardly mobile high-tech and professional Mexican employees.

Corrective discipline and motivation must occur through training examples, cooperation, and, if necessary, subtle shaming. As a disciplinary measure, it is a mistake to insult a Mexican directly; an outright insult implies an insult to the whole family. As a motivation, one must appeal to the pride of the Mexican employees and avoid causing them to feel humiliated. Given that "getting ahead" is often associated more with outside forces than with one's own actions, the motivation and reward system becomes difficult to structure in the usual ways. Past experiences have indicated that, for the most part, motivation through participative decision making is not as effective as motivation through the more traditional and expected autocratic methods. With careful implementation, however, the mutual respect and caring the Mexican people have for one another can lead to positive team spirit needed for the team structure to be used successfully by companies such as GM in its highest-quality plant in the world in Ramos Arizpe, near Saltillo, Mexico.[34] Although a study by Nicholls, Lane, and Brechu concluded that there are considerable cultural constraints on using self-managing teams in Mexico, the Mexican executives surveyed suggested that the relative success depends on the implementation.[35] The conflicts are between the norms of behavior in self-managed teams (typical of U.S. and Canadian culture) and typical values in Mexican business culture, as shown in Exhibit 11-5.

Although self-managed teams require individual risk-taking of leaders to spearhead team initiatives, those behaviors, according to the survey of Mexican executives, "are in sharp contrast to the behavioral norms of the paternalistic and hierarchical tradition of managers and workers in the Mexican work place." The workers expect the managers to give instructions and make decisions.[36] The business culture in Mexico is also attributable to prevailing conditions in Mexico's economy of low levels of education, training, and technical skills. The Mexican executives surveyed gave some sugges-

Exhibit 11-5   Contrasting Cultures: Self-Managed Teams and the Mexican Business Culture

Self-managed Teams	Mexican Business Culture
Norms	Value Expectations
Individualism	*Collectivism*
Personal accountability	Shared responsibility
Individual responsibility	Moral obligation
Confidence in ability	Paternalistic management
Confrontation and debate	Harmony
Low uncertainty avoidance	*High uncertainty avoidance*
Take self-initiative	Resist change
Low power distance	*High power distance*
Self-leadership	Respect status roles
Bottom-up decision making	Top-down hierarchical structure
Required Behaviors	Expected Behaviors
Team members solve problems, resolve conflicts, set goals, assess performance, initiate change, and communicate upward. Managers delegate, provide information, and encourage open communication.	Workers follow instructions, respect managers, receive feedback, avoid conflict and criticism, and save face. Managers make decisions, direct, control, and discipline.

SOURCE: C. E. Nicholls, H. W. Lane, and M. B. Brechu, "Taking Self-Managed Teams to Mexico," *Academy of Management Executive* 13, no. 3 (1999).

tions for implementing work teams and cautioned that the process of implementation will take a long time. They suggested the following:

➤ Foster a culture of individual responsibility among team members.
➤ Anticipate the impact of changes in power distribution.
➤ Provide leadership from the top throughout the implementation process.
➤ Provide adequate training to prepare workers for team work.
➤ Develop motivation and harmony through clear expectations.
➤ Encourage an environment of shared responsibility.[37]

For the most part, Mexican workers expect that authority will not be abused but rather that it will follow the family model where everyone works together in a dignified manner according to their designated roles.[38] Any event that may break this harmony, or seems to confront authority, will likely be covered up. This may result in a supervisor hiding defective work, for example, or, as in the case of a steel conveyor plant in Puebla, a total worker walkout rather than using the grievance process.[39] Contributing to these kinds of problems is the need to save face for oneself and to respect others' place and honor. Public criticism is regarded as humiliating. Employees like an atmosphere of formality and respect. They typically use flattery and call people by their titles rather than their names in order to maintain an atmosphere of regard for status and respect.

A context of continuing economic problems and a relatively low standard of living for most workers help explain why Maslow's higher order needs (self-actualization, achievement, status) are generally not very high on most Mexican workers' list of needs. In discussing compensation, Mariah de Forest, who consults for American firms in Mexico, suggests that

> Rather than an impersonal wage scale, Mexican workers tend to think in terms of payment now for services rendered now. A daily incentive system with automatic payouts for production exceeding quotas, as well as daily/monthly attendance bonuses, works well.[40]

As a result of economic reforms and the peso devaluation, money is now a pressing motivational factor for most employees. Since workers highly value the enjoyment of life, many companies in Mexico provide recreation facilities—a picnic area, a soccer field, and so forth. Bonuses are expected regardless of productivity. In fact, it is the law to give Christmas bonuses of 15 days' pay to each worker. Fringe benefits are also important to Mexicans; because most Mexican workers are poor, the company provides the only source of such benefits for them. In particular, benefits that help to manage family-related issues are positive motivators for employees to at least turn up for work. To this end, companies often provide on-site health care facilities for workers and their families, nurseries, free meals, and even small loans in crisis situations.[41] In addition, those companies that understand the local infrastructure problems often provide a company bus to minimize the pervasive problems of absenteeism and tardiness.

The foregoing statements are broad generalizations about Mexican factory workers. There are increasing numbers of American managers in Mexico because the NAFTA has encouraged more U.S. businesses to move operations there. For firms on American soil, managers may employ many Mexican-Americans in an intercultural setting. As the second-largest and fastest-growing ethnic group, Mexican-Americans represent an important subculture requiring management attention as they take an increasing proportion of the jobs in the United States. Yet, they remain the least assimilated ethnic group in the majority mainstream, partially from economic or occupational causes and partially from choice.[42]

Research shows that little conclusive information is available to answer a manager's direct question of exactly how to motivate in any particular culture. The reason is that we cannot assume the universal applicability of the motivational theories, or even concepts, that have been used to research differences among cultures. Furthermore, the entire motivational context must be taken into account. For example, Western firms entering markets in Eastern Europe invariably run into difficulties in motivating their local staff. Those workers have been accustomed to working under entirely different circumstances and usually do not trust foreign managers. Typically, then, the work systems and responsibilities must be highly structured because workers in Eastern Europe are not likely to use their own judgment in making decisions and because managerial skills are not developed.[43]

In sum, motivation is situational, and savvy managers use all they know about the relevant culture or subculture—consulting frequently with local people—to infer the best means of motivating in that context. Furthermore, tactful managers consciously avoid an ethnocentric attitude in which they make assumptions about a person's goals, motivation, or work habits based on their own frame of reference, and they do not make negative value judgments about a person's level of motivation because it differs from their own.

Many cultural variables affect people's sense of what is attainable, and thus affect motivation. One, for example is how much control people believe they have over their environment and their destiny—whether they believe that they can control certain events, and not just be at the mercy of external forces. Although Americans typically feel a strong internal locus of control, others attribute results to, for example, the will of God (in the case of Muslims) or to the good fortune of being born in the right social class or family (in the case of many Latin Americans). Whereas Americans feel that hard work will get the job done, many Hong Kong Chinese believe that outcomes are determined by *joss*, or luck. Clearly, then, managers must use persuasive strategies to motivate employees when they do not readily connect their personal work behaviors with outcomes or productivity.

The role of culture in the motivational process is shown in Exhibit 11-6. An employee's needs are determined largely by the cultural context of values and attitudes—along with the national variables—in which he or she lives and works. Those needs then determine the meaning of work for that employee. The manager's understanding of what work means in that employee's life can then lead to the design of a culturally appropriate job context and reward system to guide individual and group employee job behavior to meet mutual goals.

Reward Systems

Incentives and rewards are an integral part of motivation in a corporation. Recognizing and understanding different motivational patterns across cultures leads to the design of appropriate reward systems. In the United States, there are common

Exhibit 11-6   The Role of Culture in Job Motivation

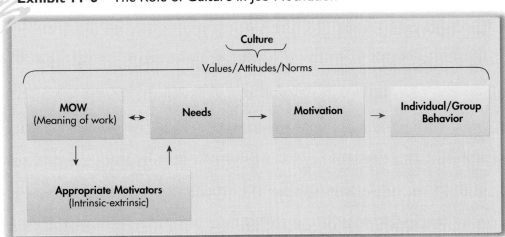

patterns of rewards, varying among levels of the company and types of occupations and based on experience and research with Americans. Rewards usually fall into five categories: financial, social status, job content, career, and professional.[44] The relative emphasis on one or more of these five categories varies from country to country. In Japan, for example, reward systems are based primarily on seniority, and much emphasis is put on the bonus system. In addition, distinction is made there between the regular workforce and the temporary workforce, which usually comprises women expected to leave when they start a family. As is usually the case, the regular workforce receives considerably more rewards than the temporary workforce, both in pay and benefits and in the allocation of interesting jobs.[45] For the regular workforce, the emphasis is on the employee's long-term effectiveness in terms of behavior, personality, and group output. Rewarding the individual is frowned on in Japan because it encourages competition rather than the desired group cooperation. Therefore, specific cash incentives are usually limited. In Taiwan, recognition and affection are important; company departments compete for praise from top management at their annual celebration.

In contrast, the entire reward system in China is very different from that of most countries. The low wage rates are compensated for by free housing, schools, and medical care. While egalitarianism still seems to prevail, the recent free-enterprise reform movements have encouraged **duo lao, duo de** (more work, more pay). One important incentive is training, which gives workers more power. One approach used in the past—and one that seems quite negative to Americans—is best illustrated by the example of a plaque award labeled "Ms. Wong—Employee of the Month." While westerners would assume that Ms. Wong had excelled as an employee, actually this award given in a Chinese retail store was for the worst employee; the plaque was designed to shame and embarrass her.[46] Younger Chinese in areas changing to a more market-based economy have seen a shift towards equity-based rewards, no doubt resulting from a gradual shift in work values.[47]

There is no doubt that culture plays a significant role in determining the appropriate incentive and reward systems around the world. Employees in collectivist cultures such as Japan, Korea, and Taiwan would not respond well to the typical American merit-based reward system to motivate employees because that would go against the traditional value system and would disrupt the harmony and corporate culture.[48]

LEADING

The manager's quintessential responsibility is to help his people realize their own highest potential.
—JACQUES MAISONROUGE, IBM WORLD TRADE CORPORATION

As you read this section on leadership, consider the following questions: To what extent, and how, do leadership styles and practices around the world vary? What are the forces perpetuating that divergence? Where, and why, will that divergence continue to be the strongest? Is there any evidence for convergence of leadership styles and practices around the world? What are the forces leading to that convergence, and how and where will this convergence occur in the future? What implications do these questions have for cross-cultural leaders?

The task of helping employees realize their highest potential in the workplace is the essence of leadership. The goal of every leader is to achieve the organization's objectives while achieving those of each employee. Today's global managers realize that increased competition requires them to be open to change and to rethink their old culturally conditioned modes of leadership.

THE GLOBAL LEADER'S ROLE AND ENVIRONMENT

The greatest competitive advantage global companies in the twenty-first century can have is effective global leaders. Yet this competitive challenge is not easy to meet. People tend to rise to leadership positions by proving themselves able to lead in their home-country corporate culture and meeting the generally accepted behaviors of that national culture. However, global leaders must broaden their horizons—both strategically and cross-culturally—and develop a more flexible model of leadership that can be applied anywhere—one that is adaptable to locational situations around the world.[49] From their recent research involving 125 global leaders in 50 companies, Morrison, Gregersen, and Black concluded that effective leaders must have global business and organizational savvy. They explain global business savvy as the ability to recognize global market opportunities for their company and having a vision of doing business worldwide. Global organizational savvy requires an intimate knowledge of the company's resources and capabilities in order to capture global markets; and to understand each subsidiary's product lines and how the people and business operates on the local level. Morrison, Gregersen, and Black outline four personal development strategies through which companies and managers can meet these requirements of effective global leadership: travel, teamwork, training, and transfers (the four "ts").[50]

Travel, of course, exposes managers to various cultures, economies, political systems, and markets. Working on global teams teaches managers to operate on an interpersonal level while dealing with business decision-making processes that are embraced by differences in cultural norms and business models. Although formal training seminars also play an important role, most of the global leaders interviewed said that the most influential developmental experience in their lives was the international assignment. Increasingly, global companies are requiring that their managers have overseas assignment experience in order to progress to top management positions.[51] The benefits accruing to the organization depend on how effectively the assignment and repatriation are handled, as discussed in Chapter 10.

Effective global leadership involves the ability to inspire and influence the thinking, attitudes, and behavior of people anywhere in the world.[52] The importance of the leadership role cannot be overemphasized because the leader's interactions strongly influence the motivation and behavior of employees, and ultimately, the entire climate of the organization. The cumulative effects of one or more weak managers can have a significant negative impact on the ability of the organization to meet its objectives.

Managers on international assignments try to maximize leadership effectiveness by juggling several important, and sometimes conflicting, roles as (1) a representative of the parent firm, (2) the manager of the local firm, (3) a resident of the local community, (4) a citizen of either the host country or of another country, (5) a member of a profession, and (6) a member of a family.[53]

The leader's role comprises the interaction of two sets of variables—the content and the context of leadership. The **content of leadership** comprises the attributes of the leader and the decisions to be made; the **context of leadership** comprises all those variables related to the particular situation.[54] The increased number of variables (political, economic, and cultural) in the context of the managerial job abroad

Exhibit 11-7   Factors Affecting Leadership Abroad

Content	
Attributes of the Person	**Characteristics of Decisions Situation**
Job position knowledge, experience, expectations	Degree of complexity, uncertainty, and risk
Longevity in company, country, functional area	In-country information needs and availability
Intelligence and cultural learning or change ability	Articulation of assumptions and expectations
Personality as demonstrated in values, beliefs, attitudes toward foreign situations	Scope and potential impact on performance
	Nature of business partners
Multiple memberships in work and professional groups	Authority and autonomy required
Decision and personal work style	Required level of participation and acceptance by employees, partners, and government
	Linkage to other decisions
	Past management legacy
	Openness to public scrutiny and responsibility
Context	
Attributes of the Job or Position	**Characteristics of the Firm and Business Environment**
Longevity and past success of former role occupants in the position	Firm structure: size, location, technology, tasks, reporting, and communication patterns
Technical requirements of the job	Firm process: decision making, staffing control system, reward system, information system, means of coordination, integration, and conflict resolution
Relative authority or power	
Physical location (e.g., home office, field office)	
Need for coordination, cooperation, and integration with other units	Firm outputs: products, services, public image, corporate culture, local history, and community relations
Resource availability	Business environment: social-cultural, political-economic, and technological aspects of a country or market
Foreign peer group relations	

SOURCE: R. H. Mason and R. S. Spich, *Management—An International Perspective* (Homewood, IL: Irwin, 1987), 186.

requires astute leadership. Some of the variables in the content and context of the leader's role in foreign settings are shown in Exhibit 11-7. The multicultural leader's role thus blends leadership, communication, motivational, and other managerial skills within unique and ever-changing environments. We will examine the contingent nature of such leadership throughout this section.

The E-Business Effect on Leadership

An additional factor—technology—is becoming increasingly pervasive in its ability to influence the global leader's role and environment, and perhaps will contribute to a lessening of the differences in motivation and leadership around the world. More and more often, companies like Italtel spa, featured in the accompanying E-Biz Box, are

E-Biz Box

ITALTEL SPA'S LEADERSHIP STYLE EMPOWERS GLOBAL EMPLOYEES WITH TECHNOLOGY

EXECUTIVE SUMMARY

Company: Italtel spa

Industry: Telecommunications

Business Challenge: To "flatten" the organization and expand globally.

Solution: An intranet based on Netscape products that enables Italtel to share knowledge and product information throughout the company.

Plant operations, antenna functioning, and network traffic are monitored on-line.

Solution Features: Employees can access Italtel's technical product documentation on-line.

Employees can book training courses via the intranet.

Reduced costs for information, documentation, and software distribution.

Business Benefits: Network and service monitoring on-line contributes to improved customer service.

Centralized employee database and single network login for every user dramatically reduces system administration time and costs.

Italtel spa is an international supplier of telecommunications networks that specializes in the design, development, and installation of integrated telecommunications systems. The company employs 16,000 people, 21 percent of whom are involved in research and development. Italtel invests 12 percent of its annual revenues in R&D, addressing a wide range of applications.

BUSINESS CHALLENGE

With the globalization of the telecommunications market, Italtel had to expand internationally in order to compete successfully. To do so, Italtel management felt that it should "flatten" the organization, moving from a hierarchical structure to one in which employees are empowered with all the tools and information they need to do their jobs better, thereby improving customer service and time to market.

In addition to the business challenges associated with international expansion, the company faces several technical challenges. Sweeping changes spurred by the convergence of communication and information technologies force Italtel to innovate faster than ever before. As a result, Italtel needs to share knowledge and information and improve communication throughout the company—all within a distributed, extremely heterogeneous computing environment. This environment includes a wide range of client systems, such as Unix workstations and PCs running Windows 3.1, 95, and NT, and servers that include Digital, Hewlett-Packard, IBM, Sun, and Windows NT-based systems. The company needed a new information technology solution that would provide global information access, flexibility, and ease of use. Among the goals for the new system were to create a centralized, easily accessible source for all company information resources, to monitor the company's telecommunications services and network on-line for better performance, to organize training courses, and to set up working groups in different departments.

SOLVING THE CHALLENGE

Italtel selected key components of the Netscape SuitSpot server software family to deploy an enterprisewide intranet and messaging solution. Netscape Enterprise Server distributes Wed-based intranet and Internet services.

SOURCE: www.Netscape.com case studies.

using technology in global leadership techniques to set up systems for their geographically dispersed employees to enable them to expand and coordinate their global operations. In the case of Italtel, this required wide delegation and empowerment of their employees so that they could decentralize.

Individual managers are realizing that the Internet is changing their leadership styles and interactions with employees, as well as their strategic leadership of their organizations. They are having to adapt to the hyperspeed environment of e-business, as well as to the need for visionary leadership in a whole new set of competitive industry dynamics. Some of these new-age leadership issues are discussed in the accompanying Management Focus: Leadership in a Digital World.

CROSS-CULTURAL RESEARCH ON LEADERSHIP

Numerous leadership theories variously focus on individual traits, leader behavior, interaction patterns, role relationships, follower perceptions, influence over followers, influence on task goals, and influence on organizational culture.[55] Our task here is to understand how the variable of societal culture fits into these theories and what implications can be drawn for international managers as they seek to provide leadership around the world. Although the *functions* of leadership are similar across cultures, anthropological studies, such as those by Margaret Mead, indicate that while leadership is a universal phenomenon, what makes effective leadership varies across cultures.[56]

In addition to research studies that indicate variations in leadership profiles, the generally accepted image that people in different countries have about what they expect and admire in their leaders tends to become a norm over time, forming an idealized role for these leaders. Industry leaders in France and Italy, for example, are highly regarded for their social prominence and political power. In Latin American countries, leaders are respected as total persons and leaders in society, with appreciation for the arts being important. In Germany, polish, decisiveness, and a wide general knowledge are respected, with their leaders granted a lot of formality by everyone. Foreigners are often surprised at the informal off-the-job lifestyles of executives in the United States and would be surprised to see them pushing a lawn-mower for example.[57]

Most research on American leadership styles describes managerial behaviors on, essentially, the same dimension, variously termed autocratic versus democratic, participative versus directive, relations-oriented versus task-oriented, or initiating structure versus consideration continuum.[58] These studies were developed in the West, and conclusions regarding employee responses largely reflect the opinions of American workers. The democratic, or participative, leadership style has been recommended as the one more likely to have positive results with most American employees.

CONTINGENCY LEADERSHIP—THE CULTURE VARIABLE

Modern leadership theory recognizes that no single leadership style works well in all situations.[59] A considerable amount of research, directly or indirectly, supports the notion of cultural contingency in leadership. This means that, as a result of culture-based norms and beliefs about how people in various roles should behave, there are

Management Focus

LEADERSHIP IN A DIGITAL WORLD

What does leadership mean in a digital world in which organizations are flexible and fluid and the pace of change is extremely rapid? What's it like to lead in an e-business organization? Jomei Chang of Vitria Technology describes it as follows, "There's no place to hide. [The Internet] forces you to be on your toes every minute, every second." *Is* leadership in e-businesses really all that different from traditional organizations? Managers who've worked in both think it is. How? Three differences seem to be most evident: the speed at which decisions must be made, the importance of being flexible, and the need to create a vision of the future.

Making Decisions Fast. Managers in all organizations never have all the data they want when making decisions, but the problem is multiplied in e-business. The situation is changing rapidly and the competition is intense. For example, Meg Whitman, president and CEO of eBay, says, "We're growing at 40 percent to 50 percent per quarter. That pace absolutely changes the leadership challenge. Every three months we become a different company. In one year, we went from 30 employees to 140, and from 100,000 registered users to 2.2 million. At Hasbro [where she was previously an executive], we would set a yearlong strategy, and then we would simply execute against it. At eBay, we constantly revisit the strategy—and revise the tactics."

Leaders in e-businesses see themselves as sprinters and their contemporaries in traditional businesses as long-distance runners. They frequently use the term *Internet time*, which is a reference to a rapidly speeded-up working environment. "Every [e-business] leader today has to unlearn one lesson that was drilled into each one of them: You gather data so that you can make considered decisions. You can't do that on Internet time."

Maintaining Flexibility. In addition to speed, leaders in e-businesses need to be highly flexible. They have to be able to roll with the ups and downs. They need to be able to redirect their group or organization when they find that something doesn't work. They have to encourage experimentation. This is what Mark Cuban, president and co-founder of Broadcast.com, had to say about the importance of being flexible. "When we started, we thought advertising would be the core of our business. We were wrong. We thought that the way to define our network was to distribute servers all over the country. We were wrong. We've had to recalibrate again and again—and we'll have to keep doing it in the future."

Focusing on the Vision. Although visionary leadership is important in every organization, in a hyperspeed environment, people require more from their leaders. The rules, policies, and regulations that characterize more traditional organizations provide direction and reduce uncertainty for employees. Such formalized guidelines typically don't exist in e-businesses, and it becomes the responsibility of the leaders to provide direction through their vision. For instance, David Pottruck, co-CEO of Charles Schwab, gathered nearly 100 of the company's senior managers at the southern end of the Golden Gate Bridge. He handed each a jacket inscribed with the phrase "Crossing the Chasm" and led them across the bridge in a symbolic march to kick off his plan to turn Schwab into a full-fledged Internet brokerage. Getting people to buy into the vision may require even more radical actions. For instance, when Isao Okawa, chairman of Sega Enterprises, decided to remake his company into an e-business, his management team resisted—that is, until he defied Japan's consensus-charged, lifetime-employment culture by announcing that those who resisted the change would be fired, risking shame. Not so amazingly, resistance to the change vanished overnight.

SOURCE: S. P. Robbins and M. Coulter, *Management*, 7th ed. (Upper Saddle River, N.J.: Prentice Hall), 2001.

variations across nations about what is expected of leaders, what influence they have, and what kind of status they are given. Clearly, this has implications for what kind of leadership style a manager should expect to adopt when going abroad.

The GLOBE Project

Recent research by the Global Leadership and Organizational Effectiveness (GLOBE) Research Program comprised a network of 170 social scientists and management scholars from 62 countries for the purpose of understanding the impact of cultural variables on leadership and organizational processes. Using both quantitative and qualitative methodologies to collect data from 18,000 managers in 62 countries, representing the majority of the world's population, the researchers wanted to find out which leadership behaviors are universally accepted and which are culturally contingent. Not unexpectedly, they found that the positive leadership behaviors generally accepted anywhere are behaviors such as being trustworthy, encouraging, an effective bargainer, a skilled administrator and communicator, and a team builder; the negatively regarded traits included being uncooperative, egocentric, ruthless, and dictatorial.[60] Those leadership styles and behaviors found to be culturally contingent are: charismatic, team-oriented, self-protective, participative, humane and autonomous.

The results for some of those countries researched are shown in Exhibit 11-8. The first column (N) is the sample size within that country. The scores for each country on those leadership dimensions are based on a scale from 1 (the opinion that those leadership behaviors would not be regarded favorably) to 7 (that those behaviors would substantially facilitate effective leadership). The dimensions are explained below. Note that reading from top to bottom on a single dimension allows us to compare those countries on that dimension. For example, being a participative leader is regarded as more important in Canada, Brazil, and Austria than it is in Egypt, Hong Kong, Indonesia, and Mexico. In addition, by reading from left to right for a particular country on all dimensions allows us to develop a profile of an effective leadership style in that country. In Brazil, for example, one can conclude that an effective leader is expected to be very charismatic, team-oriented and participative, and be relatively humane but not autonomous.

The charismatic leader as shown in this research is someone who is, for example, a visionary, an inspiration to subordinates, and performance-oriented. A team-oriented leader is someone who exhibits diplomatic, integrative, and collaborative behaviors toward the team. The self-protective dimension describes a leader who is self-centered, conflictual, and status conscious. The participative leader is one who delegates decision making and encourages subordinates to take responsibility. Humane leaders are those who are compassionate to their employees. An autonomous leader is, as expected, an individualist, so countries that ranked participation as important tended to rank autonomy in leadership as relatively unimportant. In Egypt, participation and autonomy were ranked about equally.[61]

This broad, path-breaking research by the GLOBE researchers can be very helpful to managers going abroad, enabling them to exercise culturally appropriate leadership styles. In another stage of this ongoing research project, interviews with managers from various countries led the researchers, headed by Robert House, to conclude that the status and influence of leaders varies a great deal across countries or regions according to the prevailing cultural forces. Whereas Americans, Arabs, Asians, the English, Eastern Europeans, the French, Germans, Latin Americans, and Russians tend to glorify leaders in both the political and organizational arenas, those in the Netherlands, Scandinavia,

Exhibit 11-8 Culturally-Contingent Beliefs Regarding Effective Leadership Styles

Country	N	Charisma	Team	Self-Protective	Part.	Humane	Auton
Argentina	154	5.98	5.99	3.46	5.89	4.70	4.55
Australia	345	6.09	5.81	3.05	5.71	5.09	3.95
Austria	169	6.03	5.74	3.07	6.00	4.93	4.47
Brazil	264	6.01	6.17	3.50	6.06	4.84	2.27
Canada (English-speaking)	257	6.16	5.84	2.96	6.09	5.20	3.65
China	160	5.57	5.57	3.80	5.05	5.18	4.07
Denmark	327	6.01	5.70	2.82	5.80	4.23	3.79
Egypt	201	5.57	5.55	4.21	4.69	5.14	4.49
England	168	6.01	5.71	3.04	5.57	4.90	3.92
Germany [Former FRG (WEST)]	414	5.84	5.49	2.97	5.88	4.44	4.30
Germany [Former GDR (EAST)]	44	5.87	5.51	3.33	5.70	4.60	4.35
Greece	234	6.02	6.12	3.49	5.81	5.16	3.98
Hong Kong	171	5.67	5.58	3.68	4.87	4.89	4.38
Hungary	186	5.91	5.91	3.24	5.23	4.73	3.23
India	231	5.85	5.72	3.78	4.99	5.26	3.85
Indonesia	365	6.15	5.92	4.13	4.61	5.43	4.19
Ireland	157	6.08	5.82	3.01	5.64	5.06	3.95
Israel	543	6.23	5.91	3.64	4.96	4.68	4.26
Italy	269	5.99	5.87	3.26	5.47	4.37	3.62
Japan	197	5.49	5.56	3.61	5.08	4.68	3.67
Malaysia	125	5.89	5.80	3.50	5.12	5.24	4.03
Mexico	327	5.66	5.75	3.86	4.64	4.71	3.86
Netherlands	289	5.98	5.75	2.87	5.75	4.81	3.53
Nigeria	419	5.77	5.65	3.90	5.19	5.48	3.62
Philippines	287	6.33	6.06	3.33	5.40	5.53	3.75
Poland	283	5.67	5.98	3.53	5.05	4.56	4.34
Portugal	80	5.75	5.92	3.11	5.48	4.62	3.19
Russia	301	5.66	5.63	3.69	4.67	4.08	4.63
Singapore	224	5.95	5.77	3.32	5.30	5.24	3.87
South Africa (Black sample)	241	5.16	5.23	3.63	5.05	4.79	3.94
South Africa (White sample)	183	5.99	5.80	3.20	5.62	5.33	3.74
South Korea	233	5.53	5.53	3.68	4.93	4.87	4.21
Spain	370	5.90	5.93	3.39	5.11	4.66	3.54
Sweden	1790	5.84	5.75	2.82	5.54	4.73	3.97
Switzerland (German)	321	5.93	5.61	2.93	5.94	4.76	4.13
Taiwan	237	5.58	5.69	4.28	4.73	5.35	4.01
Thailand	449	5.78	5.76	3.91	5.30	5.09	4.28
Turkey	301	5.96	6.01	3.58	5.09	4.90	3.83
USA	399	6.12	5.80	3.16	5.93	5.21	3.75
Venezuela	142	5.72	5.62	3.82	4.89	4.85	3.39

Scale 1 to 7 in order of how important those behaviors are considered for effective leadership (7 = highest).

SOURCE: Selected data from Den Hartog, R. House, et al. (GLOBE Project) *Leadership Quarterly*, 10, no. 2 (1999).

and Germanic Switzerland have very different views of leadership.[62] Following are some sample comments made by managers from various countries:

➤ Americans appreciate two kinds of leaders. They seek empowerment from leaders who grant autonomy and delegate authority to subordinates. They also respect the bold, forceful, confident, and risk-taking leader, as personified by John Wayne.

➤ The Dutch place emphasis on egalitarianism and are skeptical about the value of leadership. Terms like leader and manager carry a stigma. If a father is employed as a manager, Dutch children will not admit it to their schoolmates.

➤ Arabs worship their leaders—as long as they are in power!

➤ Iranians seek power and strength in their leaders.

➤ Malaysians expect their leaders to behave in a manner that is humble, modest, and dignified.

➤ The French expect leaders to be "cultivated"—highly educated in the arts and in mathematics. (House et al., *Advances in Global Leadership*, 1999.)

Other research also provides insight on the relative level of preference for autocratic versus participative leadership styles. For example, Hofstede's four cultural dimensions (discussed in Chapter 3) provide a good starting point to study leader–subordinate expectations and relationships. We can assume, for example, that employees in countries that rank high on power distance (India, Mexico, the Philippines) are more likely to prefer an autocratic leadership style and some paternalism because they are more comfortable with a clear distinction between managers and subordinates rather than with a blurring of decision-making responsibility.

Employees in countries that rank low on power distance (Sweden and Israel) are more likely to prefer a consultative, participative leadership style, and they expect superiors to adhere to that style. Hofstede, in fact, concludes that the participative management approaches recommended by many American researchers can be counter-productive in certain cultures.[63] The crucial fact to grasp about leadership in any culture, he points out, is that it is a complement to **subordinateship** (employee attitudes toward leaders). In other words, perhaps we concentrate too much on leaders and their unlikely ability to change styles at will. Much depends on subordinates and their cultural conditioning, and it is that subordinateship to which the leader must respond.[64] Hofstede points out that his research reflects the values of subordinates, not the values of superiors. His descriptions of the types of subordinateship a leader can expect in societies with three different levels of power distance are shown in Exhibit 11-9.

In another part of his research, Hofstede ranked the relative presence of autocratic norms in the following countries, from lowest to highest: Germany, France, Belgium, Japan, Italy, the United States, the Netherlands, Britain, and India. India ranked much higher than the others on autocracy.[65]

Expectations about managerial authority versus participation were also among the managerial behaviors and philosophies studied by Laurent, a French researcher. In a study conducted in nine Western European countries, the United States, Indonesia, and Japan, he concluded that national origin significantly affects the perception of what is effective management.[66] For example, Americans and Germans subscribe more to participation than do Italians and Japanese; Indonesians are more comfortable with a strict autocratic structure. Managers in Sweden, the Netherlands, the United States, Denmark, and Great Britain believe that employees should participate in problem solving rather than simply be "fed" all the answers by managers, compared

Exhibit 11-9   Subordinateship for Three Levels of Power Distance

Small Power Distance	Medium Power Distance (United States)	Large Power Distance
Subordinates have weak dependence needs.	Subordinates have medium dependence needs.	Subordinates have strong dependence needs.
Superiors have weak dependence needs toward their superiors.	Superiors have medium dependence needs toward their superiors.	Superiors have strong dependence needs toward their superiors.
Subordinates expect superiors to consult them and may rebel or strike if superiors are not seen as staying within their legitimate role.	Subordinates expect superiors to consult them but will accept autocratic behavior as well.	Subordinates expect superiors to act autocratically.
Ideal superior to most is a loyal democrat.	Ideal superior to most is a resourceful democrat.	Ideal superior to most is a benevolent autocrat or paternalist.
Laws and rules apply to all, and privileges for superiors are not considered acceptable.	Laws and rules apply to all, but a certain level of privilege for superiors is considered normal.	Everybody expects superiors to enjoy privileges; laws and rules differ for superiors and subordinates.
Status symbols are frowned upon and will easily come under attack from subordinates.	Status symbols for superiors contribute moderately to their authority and will be accepted by subordinates.	State symbols are very important and contribute strongly to the superior's authority with the subordinates.

SOURCE: Geert Hofstede, "Motivation, Leadership, and Organization: Do American Theories Apply Abroad?" *Organizational Dynamics* (Summer 1980): 42–63. Copyright © Geert Hofstede.

with managers in those countries on the higher end of this scale, such as Italy, Indonesia, and Japan. Laurent's findings about Japan, however, seem to contradict common knowledge about Japan's very participative decision-making culture. In fact, research by Hampden-Turner and Trompenaars places Japan as second highest, after Sweden, in the extent to which leaders delegate authority.[67] Findings regarding the other countries are similar—shown in Exhibit 11-10. However, participative leadership should not mean a lack of initiative or responsibility.

Other classic studies indicate cross-cultural differences in the expectations of leadership behavior. Haire, Ghiselli, and Porter surveyed over 3,000 managers in 14 countries. They found that, although managers around the world consistently favored delegation and participation, those managers also had a low appreciation of the capacity and willingness of subordinates to take an active role in the management process.[68]

In addition, several studies of individual countries or areas conclude that a participative leadership style is frequently inappropriate. Managers in Malaysia, Indonesia, Thailand, and the Philippines were found to prefer autocratic leadership,

Exhibit 11-10 Comparative Leadership Dimensions: Participation and Initiative

Managerial Initiative, Managers' Sense of Drive and Responsibility		Extent to Which Leaders Delegate Authority	
0 = low; 100 = high		0 = low; 100 = high	
USA	73.67	Sweden	75.51
Sweden	72.29	Japan	69.27
Japan	72.20	Norway	68.50
Finland	69.58	USA	66.23
Korea	67.86	Singapore	65.37
Netherlands	67.11	Denmark	64.65
Singapore	66.34	Canada	64.38
Switzerland	65.71	Finland	62.92
Belgium/Lux	65.47	Switzerland	62.20
Ireland	64.76	Netherlands	61.33
France	64.64	Australia	61.22
Austria	62.56	Germany	60.85
Denmark	62.79	New Zealand	60.54
Italy	62.40	Ireland	59.53
Australia	62.04	UK	58.95
Canada	61.56	Belgium/Lux	54.55
Spain	61.55	Austria	54.29
New Zealand	59.46	France	53.62
Greece	58.50	Italy	46.80
UK	58.25	Spain	44.31
Norway	54.50	Portugal	42.56
Portugal	49.74	Greece	37.95

SOURCE: C. Hampden-Turner and A. Trompenaars, *The Seven Cultures of Capitalism* (New York: Doubleday, 1993).

whereas those in Singapore and Hong Kong are less autocratic.[69] Similarly, the Turks have been found to prefer authoritarian leadership, as do the Thais.[70]

In the Middle East, in particular, there is little delegation. A successful company there must have strong managers who make all the decisions and who go unquestioned. Much emphasis is placed on the use of power through social contacts and family influence, and the chain of command must be rigidly followed.[71] A comparison of these and other management dimensions between Middle Eastern and Western managers is shown in Exhibit 11-11.

These stereotypical extremes of Middle Eastern and Western leadership styles were exemplified at the highest level by President George Bush and President Saddam Hussein during the 1991 Gulf War. Underlying these styles—and the misunderstandings that persist between Arabs and the West—are many cultural and national factors (including differences in religion, logic, and ideas about truth, freedom, honor, trust, family, and friends). Most of these factors are based on elements of Arab history that Westerners find difficult to comprehend. Arabs tend to use the past as their basis of reference, whereas Americans look to the future.

Exhibit 11-11   Comparison of Middle Eastern and Western Management Practices

Managerial Function	Middle Eastern Stereotype	Western Stereotype
Organizational design	Highly bureaucratic, overcentralized with power and authority at the top. Vague relationships. Ambiguous and unpredictable organization environments.	Less bureaucratic, more delegation of authority. Relatively decentralized structure.
Patterns of decision making	Ad hoc planning, decisions made at the highest level of management. Unwillingness to take high risk inherent in decision making.	Sophisticated planning techniques, modern tools of decision making, elaborate management information systems.
Performance evaluation and control	Informal control mechanisms, routine checks on performance. Lack of vigorous performance evaluation systems.	Fairly advanced control systems focusing on cost reduction and organizational effectiveness.
Manpower policies	Heavy reliance on personal contacts and getting individuals from the "right social origin" to fill major positions.	Sound personnel management policies. Candidates' qualifications are usually the basis for selection decisions.
Leadership	Highly authoritarian tone, rigid instructions. Too many management directives.	Less emphasis on leader's personality, considerable weight on leader's style and performance.
Communication	The tone depends on the communicants. Social position, power, and family influence are ever-present factors. Chain of command must be followed rigidly. People relate to each other tightly and specifically. Friendships are intense and binding.	Stress usually on equality and a minimization of differences. People relate to each other loosely and generally. Friendships not intense and binding.
Management methods	Generally old and outdated.	Generally modern and more scientific.

SOURCE: Copyright © 1980 by The Regents of the University of California. Reprinted from the *California Management Review* 22, no. 3. By permission of The Regents.

From various accounts, Hussein thinks that his strong leadership means the fulfillment of destiny: Iraq was meant to be the dominant power in the region. Others, however, attest to his use of internal power for personal aggrandizement. His leadership style is, obviously, dictatorial, and to most people in the world he seems a ruthless tyrant and a master of manipulation. However, most Iraqis and many other Arabs in the region see him as a hero. Participation and delegation in decision making are clearly not among his leadership behaviors, nor is he likely to seek consensus even on radical plans. In contrast, most Western leaders quietly go about team building—consulting widely and building consensus around whatever action they feel should be taken. After Iraq invaded Kuwait in August 1990, President Bush took time to build strong support behind the scenes, forging a powerful alliance among Arabs, Israelis, Europeans, Japanese, Chinese, and Soviets. Based on continued support, President Clinton ordered further attacks on Iraq in 1998–1999 after Iraq's lack of compliance with agreements made in 1991, and President George W. Bush followed suit in 2001, keeping up the pressure for compliance.[72]

The effects of participative leadership can vary even in one location when the employees are from different cultural backgrounds—from which we can conclude that a subordinate's culture is usually a more powerful variable than other factors in the environment. Research that supports this conclusion includes a study conducted in Saudi Arabia that found participative leadership to be more effective with American workers than with Asian and African employees, and a study in a U.S. plant that found that participative leadership resulted in greater satisfaction and communication among American employees than among Mexican employees.[73]

In Exhibit 11-12 we depict our integrative model of the leadership process—pulling together the variables described in this book and in the research on culture, leadership, and motivation—showing the powerful contingency of culture as it affects

Exhibit 11-12 The Culture Contingency in the Leadership Process: An Integrative Model

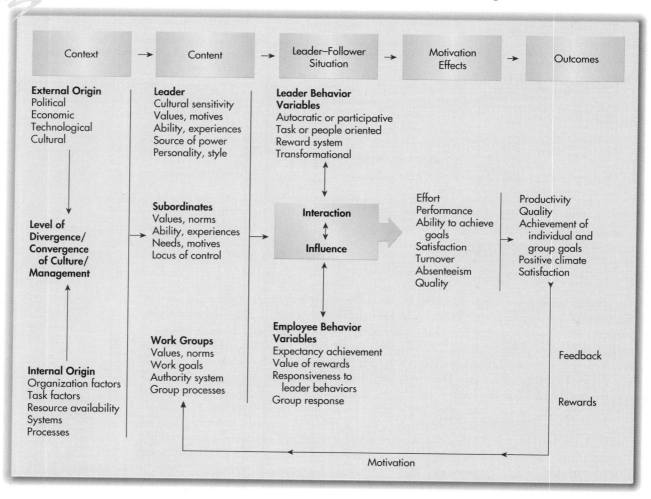

the leadership role. Reading from left to right, it covers the broad environmental factors through to the outcomes affected by the entire leadership situation. As shown in the exhibit, the broad context in which the manager operates necessitates adjustments in leadership style to all those variables relating to the work and task environment and the people involved. Cultural variables (values, work norms, the locus of control, and so forth), as they affect everyone involved—leader, subordinates, and work groups—then shape the content of the immediate leadership situation.

The leader–follower interaction is then further shaped by the leader's choice of behaviors (autocratic, participative, and so on) and by the employees' attitudes toward the leader and the incentives. Motivation effects—various levels of effort, performance, and satisfaction—result from these interactions, on an individual and a group level. These effects determine the outcomes for the company (productivity, quality) and for the employees (satisfaction, positive climate). The results and rewards from those outcomes then act as feedback (positive or negative) into the cycle of the motivation and leadership process.

Clearly, then, international managers should take seriously the **culture contingency** in their application of the contingency theory of leadership: they must adjust their leadership behaviors according to the context, norms, attitudes, and other variables in that society. One example of the complexity of the leadership situation involving obvious contextual as well as cultural factors can be seen from the results of a study of how Russian employees responded to participative management practices of North American managers. It was found that the performance of the Russian workers decreased, which the researchers attributed to a history of employee ideas being ignored by Russian managers, as well as cultural value differences.[74] To gain more insight into comparative leadership situations, the following Comparative Management in Focus highlights the leadership context in India, along with the implications for appropriate leadership by expatriates.

Comparative Management in Focus

Leadership in India

The most effective leadership style in India would thus combine integrity, being organized, an action orientation, being a self starter, charisma, and a collective orientation; with being a problem solver, a visionary, entrepreneurial, and inspirational, in that order.

—JAGDEEP S. CHHOKER, "LEADERSHIP AND CULTURE IN INDIA," THE GLOBE RESEARCH PROJECT, www.ucalgary.ca, NOVEMBER 5, 2001

Results from the recent GLOBE research program confirm the continued diversity and complexity of Indian society and culture, demanding unique skills and behaviors from leaders in India. Although Indian culture is ancient, the society also appears to be transitioning toward power equalization. Although humane orientation and collectivism are still the most important aspects of Indian culture, at the same time there is an increasing preference for individualism.[75]

Many subtle effects of the caste system still remain and affect life in organizations in the form of a strict adherence to hierarchy. Indians are disposed to structure all relationships hierarchically.[76] Management in India is often autocratic, based on formal authority and charisma. Family norms emphasizing loyalty to the family authority figure underlie the limited decision-making experience and unfamiliarity with responsibility found in some employees. Consequently, decision making is centralized, with much emphasis on rules and a low propensity for risk.[77] In addition, intricate family ties and strong authority figures perpetuate a managerial style of paternalism.

Under the pervasive influences of religion, caste, and family on the life of Hindus (about 75 percent of the population), the Indian culture stresses moral orientation and loyalty, as in the pursuit of *dharma*, one's obligation to society, rather than personal goals. Work tends to be viewed primarily in the context of family or intercaste relationships, rather than being valued for itself.[78]

Since the original source of power is family and friends, nepotism is common at both the lowest and highest levels. Unsurprisingly, power based on expertise frequently takes a back seat to power based on position.[79] In India, it is difficult for nonfamily members to advance into upper management. Such strong cultural influences in managers' origins affect managerial style.

Because of the respect for authority and obedience within the Indian family system, attempts by managers—whether Indian or otherwise—to delegate authority often result in confusion and a lack of respect for the manager; Indian employees expect the managers to make the decisions. The norm is to "check with the boss." Any introduction of participative management requires careful training because it is so unlike the cultural norms. Generally, American or other "foreign" managers in India need to make connections with the right families, make contact at the highest levels, and provide incentives for middle managers and assistants to help nudge proposals upward.[80]

> Relationship orientation seems to be a more important characteristic of effective leaders in India than performance or task orientation.
> —J. S. CHHOKER, THE GLOBE RESEARCH PROJECT, 2001

On the micro level of leadership—manager to employees—managers from other cultures are wise to tread slowly while trying to understand the culture and find what works, and to realize that they will encounter a wide range of organizational practices. Research by the GLOBE project researchers found that other important characteristics for effective leadership in India are an action-orientation and charisma. They found that management tends to be formal in what has become known as a "vertical collectivist" culture and that autocratic and bureaucratic leadership styles usually work best.[81]

Various other proposals have been put forward to help managers move toward more effective leadership. Tripathi suggests that "indigenous values, such as familism, need to be synthesized with the values of industrial democracy."[82] Similarly, Sinha proposes that, while a leader in India has to be a "nurturant," taking a personal interest in the well-being of each subordinate, he or she can use that nurturance to encourage increasing levels of participation. The manager may accomplish this by guiding and directing subordinates to work hard and maintain a high level of productivity, reinforcing each stage with increased nurturance.[83] According to Sinha and Sinha, a prerequisite to effective cross-cultural leadership in India is to establish work as the "master value." Once this is done, "other social values will reorganize themselves to help realize the master value."[84]

Multiple problems abound on the macro level of leadership of a global enterprise in India, as discovered by companies such as Gillette, Rank Xerox, Texas Instruments, and Hewlett-Packard. Investment opportunities are very attractive, with a potential for great sales and a pool of cheap, highly educated, and skilled labor. But even after getting through the entrenched bureaucracy to set up business, managers may face many operating problems because of the undeveloped infrastructure and difficult climate. Gaining control and integrating leadership styles with local managers are additional hurdles. Western managers, used to being boss in their own companies, may have difficulty taking orders from Indian partners and prefer to operate at a faster pace.[85] Gill, of Gillette, suggests, "You've got to find the right partner and convince him to give you complete management control."[86] Failure to include an Indian partner or to build local support was behind the cancellation of Enron's $2.8 billion power project in Dhabol, as part of a resurgence of economic nationalism in India in 1995 pending national elections. The project was reinstated in 1999; but as of 2001, problems between Enron and the Indian government continued and Enron decided not to build more plants in India.[87] In other areas, such as telecommunications, liberalization is progressing well, to the benefit of companies such as AT&T, Motorola, and Texas Instruments (TI). It is noteworthy that these companies have Indian joint-venture partners and Indian CEOs. TI India's managing director, Srini Rajam, noted that the Bagalore plant was responsible for one-third of TI's design automation for semiconductor products worldwide.[88]

India is expected to be an economic giant someday. Meanwhile, American managers must realize that setting up and running a successful business in India requires astute leadership skills, including integrating and collaborating at all levels of the community for the long term.

As we have said, leadership refers not just to the manager–subordinate relationship, but to the important task of running the whole company, division, or unit for which the manager is responsible. In Japan, for example, in spite of recent economic distress, many companies there continue to provide a model for quality control techniques. One executive, who has worked ten years for Japanese companies, says that a key to Japanese-style success is "to take many small steps, consistently, every day."[89] One of the areas in which Japanese managers use this process of **continuous improvement**— or *kaizen*—is quality control, which has been the hallmark of success for many Japanese industries.

Although anecdotal evidence in late 2001 indicated that Japan's long economic decline and the increased global competitiveness were eroding the system of lifetime employment and causing Japanese employees to be more independent, it is still common for employees to have a great sense of loyalty and duty to the firm. Hard work and loyalty have resulted in widespread workaholism among Japanese because of "the intense pressures on them to conform and to identify with their corporate 'family.'"[90] Conformity and dedication are instilled in the individual from childhood; for example, it is typical for a group of employees to participate in a company song and creed recitation before work.

For some time, American companies have studied successful Japanese companies for the purpose of emulating management styles in order to improve productivity, in particular the practice of employee involvement. Recently, increased global competitiveness and further exposure to Western culture and managerial practices have led Japanese firms to adopt more American practices. This partial blending of management practices indicates a trend toward convergence of leadership styles. Nevertheless, management processes, though ostensibly similar, will usually manifest themselves differently as a function of the entire cultural context in which they are enacted.

Conclusion

Because leadership and motivation entail constant interactions with others (employees, peers, superiors, outside contacts), cultural influences on these critical management functions are very strong. Certainly, other powerful variables are intricately involved in the international management context, particularly those of economics and politics. Effective leaders carefully examine the entire context and develop a sensitivity to others' values and expectations regarding personal and group interactions, performance, and outcomes—and then act accordingly.

SUMMARY OF KEY POINTS

1. Motivation and leadership are factors in the successful implementation of desired strategy. But while many of the basic principles are universal, much of the actual content and process is culture-contingent—a function of an individual's needs, value systems, and environmental context.

2. One problem in using content theories, such as those created by Maslow and Herzberg, for cross-cultural research is the assumption of their universal application. Because they were developed in the United states, even the concepts, such as achievement or esteem, may have different meanings in other societies, resulting in a noncomparable basis of research.

3. Implicit in motivating an employee is an understanding of which of the employee's needs are satisfied by work. Studies on the "meaning of work" indicate considerable cross-cultural differences.

4. Other studies on cross-cultural motivation support Herzberg's two-factor theory. They also indicate, as do studies using Maslow's theory, support for the greater importance of intrinsic factors to motivation, at lease on the managerial level. One problem with Herzberg's theory is that it does not account for all relevant cultural variables.

5. A reexamination of motivation relative to Hofstede's dimensions of power distance, uncertainty avoidance, individualism, and masculinity provides another perspective on the cultural contexts that can influence motivational structures.

6. Incentives and reward systems must be designed to reflect the motivational structure and relative cultural emphasis on five categories of rewards: fiancial, social status, job content, career, and professional.

7. Effective leadership is crucial to the ability of a company to achieve its goals. The challenge is to decide what is effective leadership in different international or mixed-culture situations.

8. The perception of what makes a good leader—both traits and behaviors—varies a great deal from one society to another. The recent GLOBE leadership study across 62 countries provides considerable insight into culturally appropriate leadership behaviors.

9. Contingency theory is applicable to cross-cultural leadership situations because of the vast number of cultural and national variables that can affect the dynamics of the leadership context. These include leader–subordinate and group relations, which are affected by cultural expectations, values, needs, attitudes, perceptions of risk, and loci of control.

10. Joint ventures with other countries present a common but complex situation in which leaders must work together to anticipate and address cross-cultural problems.

DISCUSSION QUESTIONS

1. Discuss the concept of work centrality and its implications for motivation. Use specific country examples and discuss the relative meaning of work in those countries.

2. What are the implications for motivation of Hofstede's research findings on the dimensions of power distance, uncertainty avoidance, individualism, and masculinity?

3. Explain what is meant by the need to design culturally appropriate reward systems. Give some examples.

4. Develop a cultural profile for workers in Mexico and discuss how you would motivate them.

5. Describe the variables of content and context in the leadership situation. What additional variables are involved in cross-cultural leadership?

6. Explain the theory of contingency leadership and discuss the role of culture in that theory.

7. How can we use Hofstede's four dimensions—power distance, uncertainty avoidance, individualism, and masculinity—to gain insight into leader–subordinate relationships around the world? Give some specific examples.

8. Describe the autocratic versus democratic leadership dimension. Discuss the cultural contingency in this dimension and give some examples of research findings indicating differences among countries.

9. Discuss how you would develop a profile of an effective leader from the research results from the GLOBE project. Give an example.

APPLICATION EXERCISES

1. Using the material in the chapter on motivation in Mexico, design a suitable organizational reward system for the workers in your company's plants in each of those countries.

2. Choose a country and do some research (and conduct interviews, if possible) to create a cultural profile. Focus on factors affecting behavior in the workplace. Integrate any findings regarding motivation or work attitudes and behaviors. Decide on the type of approach to motivation you would take and the kinds of incentive and reward systems you would set up as manager of a subsidiary in that country. Use the theories on motivation discussed in this chapter to infer motivational structures relative to that society. Then decide what type of leadership style and process you would use. What major contingencies did you take into account?

3. Try to interview several people from a specific ethnic subculture in a company or in your college regarding values, needs, expectations in the workplace, and so on. Sketch a motivational profile of this subculture and present it to your class for discussion.

EXPERIENTIAL EXERCISES

1. Bill Higgins had served as the manager of a large U.S. timber company located in a rather remote rain forest in a South American country. Since it began its logging operations in the 1950s, a major problem facing the company has been the recruitment of labor. The only nearby source of labor is the sparsely populated local Indian group in the area. Bill's company has been in direct competition for laborers with a German company operating in the same region. In an attempt to attract the required number of laborers, Bill's company invested heavily in new housing and offered considerably higher wages than the German company, as well as a guaranteed 40-hour work week. Yet the majority of the available workers continued to work for the German company, despite its substandard housing and minimum hourly wage. Bill finally brought in several U.S. anthropologists who had worked among the local Indians. The answer to Bill's labor recruitment problem was quite simple, but it required looking at the values of the Indian labor force rather than simply building facilities that would appeal to the typical U.S. laborer.
   What did the anthropologists tell Bill?
2. Meet with another student, preferably one whom you know well. Talk with that person and draw up a list of leadership skills you perceive him or her to possess. Then consider your research and readings regarding cross-cultural leadership. Name two countries where you think the student would be an effective leader and two where you think there would be conflict. Discuss those areas of conflict. Then reverse the procedure to find out more about yourself. Share with the class, if you wish.

SOURCE: Gary P. Ferraro, *The Cultural Dimensions of International Business*, 2nd ed. (Upper Saddle River, NJ: Prentice Hall, 1994).

INTERNET RESOURCES

Visit the Deresky companion Website at http://prenhall.com/Deresky for this chapter's Internet resources.

CASE STUDY: TOYOTA'S TOUGH BOSS

Hiroski Okuda isn't afraid to speak his mind or impose radical change in an organization. And because of these traits, he is memorable at Toyota Motor Corporation (www.global.toyota.com), where he is the chairman of the board. Prior to becoming chairman, Okuda served as Toyota's president—the first nonfamily member in over 30 years to head the company. He also is unusual among other Japanese executives because, in Japan, executives are supposed to be unseen. Okuda justifies his outspoken and aggressive style as necessary to change a company that had become lethargic and overly bureaucratic.

SOURCE: S. P. Robbins and M. Coulter, *Management*, 7th ed. (Englewood Cliffs, N.J.: Prentice Hall, 2001).

Hiroski Okuda, chairman of the board. Toyota Motor
Corporation

Okuda moved ahead at Toyota by taking jobs that other employees didn't want.
For example, in the early 1980s, the company was trying to build a manufacturing facility in Taiwan, but the Taiwanese government's demands for high local content, technology transfer, and guaranteed exports convinced many at Toyota that the project
should be scrapped. Okuda thought differently. He successfully lobbied for the facility
in the company, and it's now very profitable for Toyota. As Okuda noted, "Everyone
wanted to give up. But I restarted the project and led it to success." His drive and ability to overcome obstacles were central to his rise in the company's hierarchy.

When Okuda ascended to the presidency of Toyota in early 1995, the company
was losing market share in Japan to both Mitsubishi and Honda. Okuda attributed this
problem to several factors. Toyota had been losing touch with Japanese customers for
years. For example, when engineers redesigned the Corolla in 1991, they made it too
big and too expensive for Japanese tastes. Then, four years later, in an attempt to
lower costs significantly, they stripped out so many features in the car that the Corolla
looked too cheap. Competitors, on the other hand, had also done a much better job
at identifying the boom in recreational vehicles—especially the sport-utility market.
Toyota's burdensome bureaucracy also bothered Okuda. A decision that took only
five minutes to filter through at Suzuki Motor Corporation would take upwards of
three weeks at Toyota.

In his first 18 months on the job, Okuda implemented some drastic changes. In
a country where lifetime employment is consistent with the culture, he replaced
nearly one-third of Toyota's highest-ranking executives. He revamped Toyota's long-
standing promotion system based on seniority, adding performance as a factor.
Some outstanding performers moved up several management levels at one time—
something unheard of in the history of the company.

Okuda also worked with the company's vehicle designers to increase the speed
at which a vehicle went from concept to market. What once took 27 months was short-
ened to 18. And now the company is making a custom car within five days of receiving
an order.

Finally, Okuda is using the visibility of his job to address larger societal issues facing all Japanese businesses. For instance, he accused Japan's Finance Ministry of trying to destroy the auto industry by driving up the yen's value. And he has been an audible voice in the country, condemning the tax lending practices that forced Japanese banks to write off billions of dollars in bad loans that led, in part, to that country's economic crisis in the late 1990s and early 2000.

Unfortunately, some of Okuda's actions may have backfired. Speculation that he overstepped his boundary at times by his blunt demands for change and his refusal to bail out other members of the Toyota *keiretsu* may have offended the founding Toyota family, leading to his removal as president of the company in June 1999. However, even though he was no longer president of the company, his strategic leadership helped him to be appointed to the chairman's job.

Discussion Questions

1. How would you describe Hiroski Okuda's leadership style? Cite specific examples supporting your choice.

2. When a company is in crisis, do you believe that a radical change in leadership is required to turn the company around? Support your position.

3. Would you describe Okuda's leadership style as (1) charismatic, (b) visionary, and (c) culturally consistent with Japanese practices? Explain.

Case Bibliography

Information on company from Hoover's Online (www.hoovers.com), November 27, 2000, and from company's Web site (www.global.toyota.com), November 27, 2000; R. L. Simison, "Toyota Finds Way to Make a Custom Car in 5 Days," *Wall Street Journal*, August 6, 1999, p. A4; N. Shirouzu, "Toyota Is Tightening Control of Key Suppliers in Bid to Block Encroachment by Foreign Firms," *Wall Street Journal*, August 3, 1999, p. A18; N. Shirouzu, "Toyota Plans an Expansion of Capacity Due to Demand," *Wall Street Journal*, June 29, 1999, p. A8; B. McClennan, "New Toyota Chief Has U.S. Credentials," *Ward's Auto World*, June 1999, p. 42; E. Thornton, "Mystery at the Top," *Business Week*, April 26, 1999, p. 52; N. Shirouzu, "Top-Level Reshuffle Expected at Toyota," *Wall Street Journal*, April 8, 1999, p. A20; E. Thornton, "This Isn't Your Simple Flat Tire," *Business Week*, February 1, 1999, p. 54; N. Shirouzu, "Toyota President Expected to Quit Post—Hiroski Okuda Is to Become Auto Maker's Chairman; Firm to Revamp," *Wall Street Journal*, January 11, 1999; and A. Taylor, III, "Toyota's Boss Stands Out in a Crowd," *Fortune*, November 25, 1996, pp. 116–22.

Comprehensive Cases

Case 12   West Indies Yacht Club Resort

When Cultures Collide

Jeffrey P. Shay
University of Montana

Patrick Dowd, a 30-year-old management consultant, stared out his office window at the snowy Ithaca, New York, landscape. Dowd reflected on his recent phone conversation with Jim Johnson, general manager of the 95-room West Indies Yacht Club Resort (WIYCR) located in the British Virgin Islands. Johnson sounded desperate on the phone to pull the resort out of its apparent tailspin and noted three primary areas of concern. First, expatriate manager turnover was beginning to become problematic. In the past two years the resort had hired and then failed to retain three expatriate Waterfront Directors and three expatriate Food and Beverage Directors. Second, although the resort had not initiated a formal guest feedback program, Johnson estimated that guest complaints had increased from 10 per week to more than 30 per week over the past two years. The complaints were usually given by guests to staff at the front desk, written down, passed on to Johnson, and usually centered on the deteriorating level of service provided by local British Virgin Islands' employees. Many repeat guests claimed, "The staff just doesn't seem as motivated as it used to be". And third, there appeared to be an increasing level of tension between expatriate and local staff members. In the past, expatriates and locals seemingly found it natural to work side by side, now there was a noticeable gap between these groups that appeared to be growing.

Johnson had come to know Dowd and his reputation for being one of the few expatriate management consultants in the region who seemed to have a real grasp on what it took to manage effectively in the Caribbean. The two had become better acquainted in 1993 when the world-renowned sailing school that Dowd was working for, Tradewind Ventures, was contracted to develop new family-focused programs to be offered by the resort. Through this experience, Dowd gained in-depth knowledge of the resort. Dowd's reputation and knowledge of the resort prompted Johnson's call to see if Dowd would be interested in working as a participant-observer at the resort to determine the underlying reasons behind his three major concerns. Johnson requested that Dowd work at the resort during three Christmas holiday weeks to observe resort staff during the peak season. Dowd would then present an analysis of his observations and make recommendations regarding what actions could be taken to improve the situation. Although Dowd had never provided consulting in this specific area (i.e., an analysis of the cultural influences on the behavior of workers in the Caribbean), he gladly accepted the challenge as it coincided with his personal experience in the region and recent courses on cross-cultural management that he had taken at Cornell University. Dowd moved over to his bookcase and pulled books, brochures, and other information off the shelf and began reading. He was departing for the British Virgin Islands in one week and wanted to get a head start on his background research.

THE BRITISH VIRGIN ISLANDS' TOURISM MARKET

Thirty-six islands, 16 of which are inhabited, comprise the 59 square mile chain of British Virgin Islands (BVIs) (see Exhibit 1). Unlike neighboring islands, St. Thomas and St. Croix, that underwent extensive tourism development during the 1970s and 1980s, the BVI government carefully planned and restricted growth. The result was a carefully carved niche in the Caribbean market—positioning the island chain in the exclusive/ecotourism market segment.

From 1950 to 1970, the BVIs hosted the traveling elite. During the early 1970s, the introduction and rapid growth of bareboat chartering (boats

ranging from 28 to 50 feet, chartered [rented] to tourists qualified to take the boats out without the assistance of a licensed captain) made the small island chain affordable for tourists with moderate budgets as well. Bareboat charters offered a unique vacation opportunity—one that connected tourists with the islands' rich natural beauty and intriguing history by allowing tourists to visit quiet harbors and villages that were void of larger cruise ships and large hotels. The BVI's calm waters and steady trade winds were soon filled with charter boats as the chain of islands quickly became known as the premier chartering location in the world. By the early 1990s, there were more than 500 charter boats available in the Virgin Islands, with the largest company, The Moorings, managing more than 190 charter boats in the BVIs alone. Although charter industry growth in the BVIs drew the attention of major developers, the combination of strict government regulations constraining the size of new hotels and resorts, along with limited access pro-

Exhibit 1   The British Virgin Islands and Its Luxury Hotels

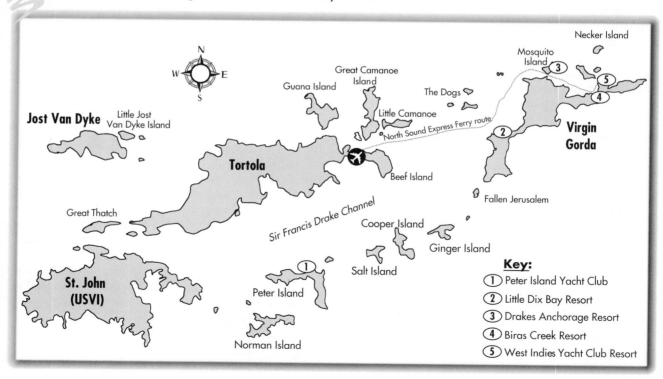

vided by the small Beef Island Airport kept these developers and mass tourism out. As a result, smaller midscale to upscale hotels and resorts were developed in the BVIs.

UPSCALE HOTELS IN THE BRITISH VIRGIN ISLANDS

Although several midscale hotels were developed and operating in the BVIs by the mid-1980s, there were only four truly upscale hotels in the island chain in addition to WIYCR (discussed in detail below) (see Exhibit 1 for hotel locations). Each of these hotels provided three meals per day (not including alcoholic drinks) and access to activities (e.g., water sports equipment) as part of the price for the room. Biras Creek was an independent resort located adjacent to WIYCR's property and overlooked North Sound of Virgin Gorda (see Exhibit 2). This resort featured 34 rooms, one restaurant, three tennis courts, a private beach with a bar, a small marina, and several miles of nature trails. Peak season double occupancy rates in 1994 for Biras Creek ranged from $395 to $695 per night and, similar to WIYCR, this resort was only accessible by sea. After facing high turnover of expatriate resort managers and expatriate assistant managers for the past five years, Biras Creek implemented a policy of hiring individuals for these positions for three-year contracts. After the contract was completed, managers were required to seek employment elsewhere. The owners felt that most managers became less effective after three years because they suffered from burnout.

Drakes Anchorage was an independent resort located on the 125-acre Mosquito Island, an island

Exhibit 2   Virgin Gorda and Its Luxury Hotels

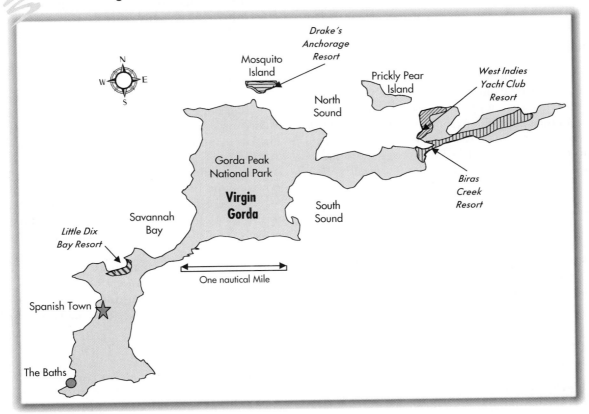

situated at the northern entrance to North Sound (see Exhibit 2). This small resort offered 12 rooms, a beachfront restaurant, a protected anchorage for charter boats, a picturesque hiking trail, and four secluded sandy beaches. Peak season double occupancy rates in 1994 ranged between $400 and $600 per night. Expatriate managers oversaw operations at this resort as well. Guests staying at this resort were primarily interested in a relaxing, secluded vacation with limited activities.

Little Dix Bay Resort opened in 1964 as part of the Rockefeller Resort chain. In 1993, after a multi-million-dollar renovation project, Rosewood Hotels and Resorts, a Dallas-based company, acquired the management contract for the resort. This resort offered 98 rooms ranging in price from $480 to $1000 per night in 1994 during peak season for a double occupancy room. This resort was located on the northwestern shore of Virgin Gorda and overlooked the Sir Francis Drake Channel, a channel cutting through the heart of the BVI chain (see Exhibit 2). In addition to a fine dining restaurant, the resort offered small boats (i.e., sunfish, lasers, whalers, etc.), water-skiing, and day excursions to snorkeling and diving sites for guests. These amenities made Little Dix the WIYCR's strongest local competitor. Under the management of Rosewood Hotels and Resorts, expatriate managers often rotated every two to three years from one Rosewood property to another. Its prices and impeccable service attracted some of the most affluent tourists visiting the region.

Located on Peter Island, the Peter Island Yacht Club was operated by JVA Enterprises, a Michigan-based firm that acquired the resort in the early 1970s (see Exhibit 1). The resort had 50 rooms, a fine dining restaurant, a marina, and a beautiful secluded beach. Peak season double occupancy rates ranged from $395 to $525 per night in 1994. This resort was also managed by expatriates and had been recently remodeled after being struck by two hurricanes in the early 1990s. Similar to Drake's Anchorage, this resort primarily attracted guests looking for a secluded island vacation with limited activity.

BVI LABOR MARKET LAWS AND REGULATIONS

All hotels operating in the BVIs faced a number of challenges beyond the strict regulations on development. Perhaps the most significant challenge was dealing with local labor market laws and regulations. Despite the restricted growth in tourism, the supply of qualified service employees severely lagged demand. Four general government restrictions and policies exacerbated the challenge of hiring and managing staff. First, organizations were granted only a limited number of work permits to attract more experienced service employees from foreign countries. Expatriate work permits were granted based on the total number of employees working at a resort (i.e., the more employees a resort had, the greater number of expatriates it could get permits for) and the availability of locals who possessed the skills requisite for the position. The latter meant that resorts had to post positions in local newspapers for at least one month before requesting a permit for an expatriate.

Second, organizations were not permitted to lay off staff during slow seasons. This created significant challenges for resorts like WIYCR that ran at nearly 100 percent occupancy during the peak season (December through May) and as low as 40 percent during the off season (June through November). Especially hurt by this were luxury resorts that required high staffing levels to provide the services that guests expected during the peak months but were then left overstaffed during the off season periods.

Third, policies restricting the conditions under which an employee could be fired severely limited an organization's ability to retain only the best workers. For example, one hotel manager claimed, "It is hard to fire a local employee even if he steals from us. We are often required to file documents with the government and then attend a formal hearing on why we dismissed an employee. Since it is so difficult to fire someone who steals, imagine how difficult it is to fire someone who doesn't work hard, is always late, or forgets to come to work! Our hands are really tied by these regulations."

Finally, organizations were under extreme pressure to promote BVI locals into management positions whenever possible. As noted above, before hiring an expatriate manager a resort had to advertise the position for at least a month. In addition, if a local approached the resort with minimal requisite skills for the job but was enthusiastic and willing to learn, the resort found it difficult in the current environment to overlook the local and hire the expatriate. As a result of these restrictions and policies, managers often found themselves overstaffed with underqualified workers.

Managers overcame these dilemmas in a number of ways. To combat regulations on foreign employees, organizations often paid foreign staff through their offshore corporate headquarters and limited the amount of time they actually spent at the resort, hotel, or other service site. In response to restrictions on laying off staff, organizations offered attractive vacation components to their employment contracts. This allowed the organization to pay lower wages and to decrease excess labor during off-seasons. Managers, forced to retain staff regardless of their productivity levels, rationalized that excess labor costs were offset by lower wages in the region, avoidance of costs associated with training a new employee, and the need for extra staff during peak season.

Hotels and resorts also realized that although many entry-level employees could continue to be trained on-the-job, locals seeking managerial positions would require more formalized training. Unfortunately, neither the BVI nor the United States Virgin Islands had developed hospitality management training programs because there wasn't the critical mass of local managers required to start such programs. Instead hotels and resorts sent promising young staff to service training programs in the Bahamas and Bermuda in an effort to prepare them for management positions.

THE WEST INDIES YACHT CLUB RESORT

In 1964 the Kimball family sailed into the North Sound of Virgin Gorda (see Exhibit 2). The Sound's natural beauty captivated the family, and they knew it was a place to which the family would soon return. Nestled on the mountainside of the innermost point, the Kimballs found a shorefront pub and five cottages known as The West Indies Resort. The cottages were rustic with only cold water running in the bathrooms. It was at the resort's pub that Joe Kimball met Armin Dubois, the property's eccentric owner. Dubois had been a pioneer Virgin Islands yachtsman who had found paradise on these shores and never left.

Under Dubois' management, an old diesel generator supplied lighting, and water was collected on the roofs and stored in cisterns that doubled as cot-

tage foundations. The pub and restaurant served mariners when Dubois felt like it. Dubois established his own protocol. Mariners blew foghorns just off the main dock and Dubois responded as to whether or not he was open for business. Even after being invited ashore, guests were unsure as to how long the hospitality would last. Dubois was notorious for turning off the generator to let guests know they had outstayed their welcome.

By early 1973, after several visits to North Sound, Kimball asked Dubois if he would sell or lease property so that he could build a family cottage. Dubois replied several months later that he wasn't interested in selling or leasing a small piece of property but would entertain an offer to buy out the whole property. In late 1973, Kimball did just that.

Kimball's painstaking attention to detail fostered development of the property's unique character. His vision was to provide a truly eco-conscious and comfortable place for travelers to enjoy an environment perfect for sailing, fishing, snorkeling, diving, and combing beaches. To accomplish this, Kimball maintained many of Dubois' earlier practices. For example, the resort continued to generate its own electricity, and collect and distill its own water. In addition, the resort used gray water (partially treated water) to irrigate the hillsides and used solar power wherever possible. In sharp contrast to the multistory designs used by other Caribbean developers, Kimball constructed 55 individual bungalows that were scattered along the hillside and preserved the natural beauty for which the resort was known. Kimball differentiated the resort from others in the region by acquiring the world's largest resort fleet of sailboats (e.g., J24's, JY15's, Cal 27's, Freedom 30's, Lasers, Sunfish, Rhodes 19's, Mistral sailboards) and powerboats (e.g., Boston Whalers and sport fishing boats). These carefully selected boats were easy for even inexperienced guests to handle. These acquisitions in conjunction with the resort's sailing instruction program established the resort's reputation as one of the premier water sports resorts in the world. Subsequently, Kimball changed the resort's name to The West Indies Yacht Club Resort to leverage the distinct aquatic recreational activities that the resort offered.

In 1987, with the resort's reputation growing and business booming, Kimball acquired a 15-year renewable management contract for The Sandy Point Resort, located adjacent to his property. The additional facilities, including 40 more rooms, a second restaurant, a swimming pool, a fuel dock, and beach, gave the property the critical mass necessary to compete with local and international competitors. The resort also outsourced the provision of Scuba services from the Virgin Islands Dive Company. By 1990, the property had become a fully operational, water sports-oriented, ecology-conscious resort that encompassed more than 75 acres and a mile of beachfront.

The resort faced two major challenges: an occupancy cycle with high peaks and low valleys and changing market demographics. Resort managers estimated that occupancy rates from 1985 to 1990 had ranged from between 80 and 100 percent during the peak season from mid December until the end of May and between 40 and 60 percent from June until early December. These fluctuations were thought to occur because key customer markets sought Caribbean vacations during the colder winter months but found it hard to justify a trip to the tropics during spring, summer and fall when the weather at home was more acceptable. It wasn't until the resort was forced to carry Sandy Point's additional overhead that management realized the need to address occupancy rate fluctuations. One of the most difficult costs to manage was labor. To provide the high-end service that the resort was known for, the number of staff employed by the resort had increased substantially. According to Jim Johnson, the resort was barely able to meet its guests' needs during peak season, while during slow season the resort was overstaffed.

Changing market demographics also posed a challenge. In the past, the resort predominantly attracted couples of all ages. However, changing market demographics severely hampered its ability to attract both new and repeat guests. Former guests who had begun to raise families of their own recalled the intimate moonlit dinners and walks on the beach but couldn't recall ever seeing any children and therefore did not identify the resort as "family friendly." The resort had never turned away families but had focused marketing efforts primarily on affluent couples without children. Changing demographics forced the resort to reexamine the message conveyed by its advertising.

As a result, the resort launched a new marketing campaign in 1990. Advertising targeted families, and the staff prepared to cater to family-specific needs. The resort created sailing instruction programs for children and a host of activities designed to keep children busy while their parents enjoyed quiet time together. Family excursions onboard some of the resort's larger yachts provided the opportunity for families to sail together and explore some of the less inhabited islands. In addition, the resort added special Christmas, Easter, and Thanksgiving family programs that offered an entertaining atmosphere for the whole family. The resort changed, and the market was responding favorably as occupancy rates began to climb, even during the difficult slow season. Tom Fitch, the director of Marketing and Special Promotions, also implemented several additional marketing initiatives in an attempt to increase occupancy during slower periods (see Exhibit 3 for examples).

By 1994, the resort began to see initial indications that the marketing initiatives were working. Although the resort still had some difficulty in attracting guests during the period between June and August, the resort increased its occupancy rates during the period between September and December to between 70 and 80 percent. The resort was rated as one of the best tropical resorts in the world by *Conde Nast Traveler* and maintained a strong position in the upscale segment of the BVIs. Peak season rates for double occupancy rooms ranged from $390 to $595 per day with meals and access to all water sports equipment included.

Despite the resort's prime location for water sports activities and strong reputation as the premier water sports resort in the Caribbean, management remained concerned about being able to match the service levels provided by their competitors. Increased availability of water sports at competing resorts threatened the resort's differentiated market position. WIYCR managers knew that some of their former guests were vacationing at nearby Little Dix Bay because that resort now offered similar water sports activities, had rates that overlapped those offered at WIYCR, and guests had been dissatisfied with the declining level of service they experienced during their last visit to WIYCR. WIYCR managers feared that this trend might continue if changes were not implemented soon.

Exhibit 3   Recent Marketing Initiatives

Fast Tacks Weeks: Initial efforts to fill slow-season periods centered on leveraging the resort's competitive advantage. Fitch developed The Fast Tack Program which targeted specific sailing groups and utilized the resort's vast sailing resources. These groups ranged from racing to cruising, from families to couples, from senior citizens to young adults. During certain weeks in the historically slow fall season, sailing celebrities were invited and gave specialized seminars to guests. Perhaps the most widely noted week is the ProAm week in which guests are assigned to teams with some of the top match racing skippers in the world. In addition to becoming a major source of income to the resort, the weeks have become a key free advertising vehicle. Articles in sailing magazines have served not only to promote the weeks themselves, but have increased reader awareness of the sailing experience that the resort can offer.

Family Weeks: To change the resort's image, Fitch marketed special programs during traditional school break periods to families. These weeks provided special services, including instructional and recreational programs, for children and young adults. By providing a fun, yet safe, environment for

children, parents were free to spend time alone enjoying activities designed for their tastes (e.g., harbor sunset cruises). In additional, there were several family excursions planned throughout the week which offered an opportunity to enjoy exploring reefs and other islands together.

Capturing the Market Earlier: In addition to the family weeks and Fast Tacks weeks, marketers realized that there was another market that they had been ignoring which could significantly reduce some of its occupancy cycle troubles. Instead of waiting until a couple had established themselves or started a family, why not get them when they were tying the knot? After all, the resort provided one of the most romantic atmospheres in the Caribbean. Moreover, the majority of weddings in North America, the primary market for the resort, occur during the slow periods of summer and fall. In response to this revelation the resort began to actively market wedding and honeymoon packages. The resort hoped that these guests would return for future second, third, and fourth honeymoons as well as bring their children when they started their families.

THE WIYCR ORGANIZATION

Company Headquarters. Kimball insisted on managing strategic planning, finance, and reservations activities from an office in Chicago, Illinois (see organization chart in Exhibit 4). He wanted to live in the United States and attend to other investments (none of which was in hospitality) and argued that these activities were easily separated from the day-to-day operations management activities that took place at the resort. As the resort expanded and Kimball grew older (he was now in his seventies), he visited WIYCR less frequently and never during peak weeks. Moreover, Kimball, who once prided himself for knowing the names of each employee at the resort, knew fewer and fewer of his employees by name. As a result, when he did visit the resort the local employees thought that Kimball seemed increasingly removed and distant.

Marketing and Special Promotions. Kimball firmly believed that marketing activities should take place close to the consumer. As a result, Tom Fitch,

the 32-year-old Marketing and Special Promotions director, managed from a small office in the southwestern corner of Connecticut. Fitch grew up as an active sailing competitor on the Long Island Sound (an area that stretches from New York City to the southeastern tip of Connecticut) sailing circuit and was well connected within the sailing industry. Fitch's strong sailing background coupled with being centrally located within the United States' largest sailing community afforded great opportunities for promoting the resort with its most major target market area. Unlike Kimball, Fitch was always on-property during the high season and special promotions weeks. Fitch believed that it was important during these weeks for him to tend to the special needs of guests he had attracted to the resort. Local employees often underestimated the work required to plan and market these programs. Seeing him socialize with guests while on property, local employees questioned whether or not his job was really full-time once he left the resort and returned to the states. After all, they only saw him periodically

Exhibit 4 West Indies Yacht Club Resort Organizational Chart

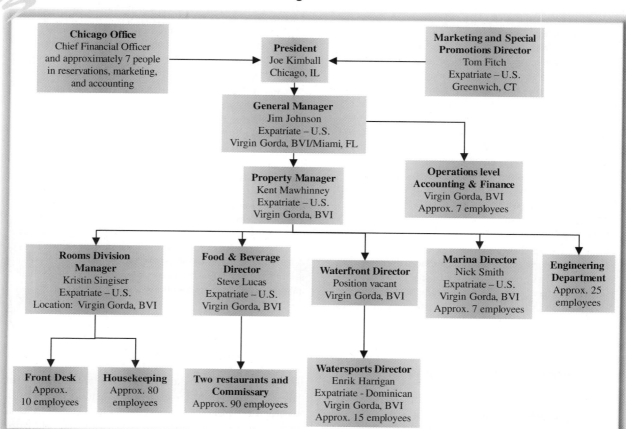

when he came in for a few weeks, threw large parties, and frantically tried to assure that the guests' needs were met.

Jim Johnson, General Manager. In the WIYCR organization, the general manager traditionally oversaw all functional areas of the hotel and also played an important role in strategic planning. Jim Johnson, the 48-year-old expatriate general manager originally from the United States, was hired in 1990 based on his extensive hospitality experience and academic training. His experience included several years as assistant manager of Little Dix Bay Resort and a Master's degree in hospitality management from Cornell University. Johnson worked

from his home in Miami, Florida most of the time in order to spend more time with his family, provide his children with stronger educational opportunities than those offered in the BVIs, and reduce the number of expatriate permits that the resort required. Johnson averaged approximately two weeks at the resort per month, staying for longer periods of time during the high season and shorter periods of time during the low season. Johnson spent most of the time while at the resort in his office and in meetings with the heads of the various departments. Local employees often referred to him as a "behind-the-scenes" type manager; he provided detailed goals, objectives, and actions for his staff but was not present for the execution of plans.

Johnson generally felt confident in his management team, especially his Property Manager whom he personally recruited and hired.

Kent Mawhinney, Property Manager.

The property manager was generally the second in command at the WIYCR and was responsible for implementing the general manager's plans and monitoring the results. Kent Mawhinney, the 40-year-old property manager from the United States, was hired by Johnson in 1992 and had an impressive background that included working on the management staff for six years at Caneel Bay, a Rockefeller Resort located on nearby St. John (in the United States' Virgin Islands). Mawhinney was a "hands-on" manager who believed that "management by walking around" was needed in the Caribbean. Resort employees knew Mawhinney as a manager who was willing to get his hands dirty, and they greatly appreciated this attitude.

Kristin Singiser, Rooms Division Manager.

The Rooms Division manager was responsible for two departments at the WIYCR: Housekeeping and the Front Desk. To many guests it seemed like Singiser had been at the resort forever. In fact, Singiser had been hired in 1985 as part of the front desk staff and was now 35 years old. She was born and raised in the Midwestern United States. She came to the resort with little hotel industry experience, had only been to the Caribbean as a tourist prior to taking the job, and proceeded to work her way up in the WIYCR organization to her current position. She was well respected by the guests and local staff because of her never-ending energy and constant smile. However, after 11 years at the property Singiser was beginning to get more frustrated with problems she faced over and over again. Her staff knew how Singiser felt but also knew that the issues were mainly between her and the Chicago office.

Steve Lucas, Food and Beverage Director.

The Food and Beverage director was responsible for two restaurants, a commissary, an employee dining facility, and three bars that were located on the WIYCR property. The resort had experienced high turnover in this position with three Food and Beverage directors resigning to return to the United States within the past two years alone. Steve Lucas, a 28-year-old with recent experience working as the Food and Beverage director for an exclusive California resort, was currently filling this position. Lucas was from the United States and had an impressive restaurant industry track record. He was hired by the resort in the middle of November 1994 and arrived at the property during the first week of December. Lucas had no previous experience working outside of the United States.

Nick Smith, Marina Director.

The Marina director was responsible for the resort's growing marina operations, run largely out of the Davey Jones marina. This marina included dock space for up to 35 boats, a fuel and water dock, and yacht maintenance services. The marina attracted yachting enthusiasts who were seeking a short stay in a resort environment. Nick Smith was promoted eight years before to his current position as Marina Director. Smith, now 45 years old, was originally from the United States and had been working at the resort for nearly 15 years. He lived on the property along with his wife and their six-year-old daughter.

Waterfront Director.

The Waterfront director's position was created to assign responsibility to oversee the growing waterfront activities at the resort. The director's responsibilities included overseeing the Watersports Department and its director, as well as the resort's fleet of day excursion boats, planning and promoting day excursions, and developing and maintaining relationships with the sites that day excursions visited. The resort hired several expatriates for the Waterfront director position. For a variety of reasons these expatriates didn't work out. Two had become alcoholics, and one had mysteriously packed his belongings and departed in the middle of the night. This position was currently vacant, with most responsibilities assumed by Nick Smith and Enrik Harrigan (the Watersports director—see below).

Enrik Harrigan, Watersports Director.

The Watersports director was primarily responsible for the resort's fleet of small to medium-sized boats and its windsurfing program. From 1986 until 1992, the Watersports Department had been under the leadership of Bill Jones, a Canadian who fell in love with the resort while staying there as a guest. His easygoing management style was well respected by a staff that would seemingly do anything for him.

Unfortunately for the resort, Bill returned to Canada in 1992. The next most senior member of the water sports staff was 27 year old Enrik Harrigan, a windsurfing guru from Dominica (part of the Windward Island chain located in the Southern Caribbean Sea) who had been working at the resort for about five years. Harrigan assumed the responsibilities as Watersports director and was well respected by the staff as well but found he had difficulty assigning tasks and managing the operation.

DOWD ARRIVES IN THE BRITISH VIRGIN ISLANDS

On December 15, 1994, Dowd arrived at WIYCR. He found it hard to imagine the imminent transformation of the serene British Virgin Islands into an environment overwhelmed by a frenzy of holiday tourist activity. Within a few days thousands of tourists would invade the BVIs, stretching its natural, human, and capital resources to their limits. The natural beauty that the islands offered was a familiar sight for Dowd who had spent ten years working as a management consultant for small to medium sized hotels in the Caribbean. Tradewind Ventures, a world renowned sailing school, introduced him to the British Virgin Islands through summer employment as a Skipper and Operations Director in 1986. For the next six years, Dowd worked year-round for Tradewind Ventures as a management consultant during the winter months and Operations Director during the summer. During his tenure with Tradewind Ventures, Dowd added the Cabarete Beach Hotel (Cabarete, Dominican Republic) and the West Indies Yacht Club Resort (Virgin Gorda, British Virgin Islands) to his client base. In addition, Dowd had completed his Bachelor of Science and Master's in Business Administration at Babson College. The primary point of differentiation between Dowd's consulting services and those offered by the larger consulting companies rested in his understanding of the Caribbean market and, most importantly, its people. His understanding had evolved through interactions both professionally and socially with local nationals from the region. Mike McClane, manager of a nearby charter boat company, respected Dowd's ability to understand the local nationals, saying "You really must understand my employees. Heck, Small Craft (employee's nickname) considers you a friend and I'm the only other outsider

I know of to accomplish that. It took me five years, you've done it in two summers!"

Dowd had entered the doctoral program in Hotel Administration at Cornell University in September 1994; driven largely by his desire to study the challenges associated with expatriate management assignments. Dowd hoped that his understanding of the local culture was enhanced by what he had learned over the past semester in the classroom at Cornell. His first semester introduced him to new theoretical explanations for differences in behaviors across cultures. He wondered whether these tools would be helpful for interpreting behaviors and then communicating what they meant to Johnson and his managers.

DOWD'S OBSERVATIONS OF OPERATIONS

Checking In.   Night had fallen on the Caribbean, and as the North Sound Express ferry (a ferry that takes passengers from the Beef Island Airport on Tortola to various resort locations on Virgin Gorda (see Exhibit 1) approached the main dock at WIYCR, Dowd noticed the familiar stride of a former colleague from Tradewind Ventures. Dave Pickering, a 22-year-old Cleveland native, had been working in the water sports department for nearly a month and was looking forward to Dowd's arrival. Pickering had worked with Dowd for the past three summers as a Skipper and Program Director at Tradewind Ventures. Although Pickering worked in the Caribbean for these three summers, his interactions had been primarily with the expatriate staff that Tradewind Ventures brought down each summer. Working side-by-side with the locals was a much different experience. Pickering had been hired by WIYCR in early December of 1994 as part of the water sports staff. He was primarily responsible for teaching sailing lessons, taking guests out on the larger boats, and signing out water sports equipment to guests.

Pickering extended an enthusiastic and firm handshake as Dowd got off the ferry. "Welcome to The Rock," he said. "The Rock" was the phrase coined by expatriates to describe living at the secluded resort. The two walked up the dock, and Pickering paused for a minute. "Looks like someone forgot to come out and greet the guests again. It will take me a few minutes to give the briefing so go along to the front desk if you want. I'm sure you're familiar with the routine. We're going out to Saba Rock (a small island about 300 feet off the resort's North beach) in about a half-hour so why don't you drop your stuff in your room and meet me at the dinghy dock." Dowd nodded and headed for the front desk.

Kristin Singiser met Dowd at the front desk, exchanged greetings, and then Singiser suddenly looked confused. "Who met you down on the docks?", she asked.

"Dave was down there and is giving the guest briefing," he replied.

"That's odd. Dave is supposed to be off tonight. I wonder who was supposed to meet you down there?", Singiser said with a disturbed look on her face. She assigned Dowd to his room, picked up the radio microphone, and called one of the golf cart chauffeurs to come pick him up. As Dowd walked out of the lobby he thought, "What would have happened if nobody showed up to greet us? Sure I'm working here, but those people who were on the boat with me are paying thousands of dollars to be here, what would they think?"

A Night at Saba Rock.   Although Dowd knew that he had an 8:00 A.M. meeting with Johnson, he couldn't help but enjoy the company of his island friends. Saba Rock was the only real hideout for expatriates and local national employees from WIYCR. A few tourists managed to find a dinghy ride out to the small pub on the one-half acre island, but they were usually the more adventurous types and were always welcome.

Pickering always had such a positive disposition; however, tonight a hint of irritability seemed to come across in his voice. "You know why I am here . . . right?" Dowd asked.

"Yes, I think so. Kent Mawhinney told me something about you coming down here to observe operations and make some suggestions for improvements. Boy, do I have some suggestions. How about firing everyone and bringing down our old staff from Tradewind Ventures?" he candidly replied. Dowd couldn't help but inquire further. Pickering said that when he arrived a few weeks prior the employees really welcomed him aboard. This seemed normal; Pickering had always been consid-

ered one of the more affable members of the Tradewind Ventures staff. Pickering said that each day coworkers in the water sports department distanced themselves more and more. Pickering said, "The harder I work, the greater the distance between us becomes."

"I don't understand," Pickering continued, "I've even tried to do some of their work to get back in good favor with them. But nothing seems to work. It's gotten to the point where I think some of these guys don't like me at all."

As Pickering continued, he questioned whether the resort's compensation system could ever work. Employees were paid an hourly rate based on their tenure at the resort. As Pickering understood the resort's compensation system, each year resort employees were given a raise without any performance review. Dowd asked Pickering for some concrete examples of why the system wasn't working. Pickering explained, "Even some of the most senior guys in the water sports department hide from work. These senior employees know that they will get raises even if they don't do a good job . . . excuse me, these guys get raises even if they don't do their job at all."

Pickering was very confused why the locals weren't taking advantage of the opportunity to get tips. Pickering was making $US50 to 100 extra per day on tips alone and when he told his fellow employees this they laughed and said it wasn't worth that much to them to have to work so hard. Dowd asked if Pickering had discussed his concerns with any of the managers. Pickering replied that he had a few conversations with Mawhinney about it but hadn't been able to find an opportunity to speak with Johnson. The discussion continued until Dowd's eyes began to grow heavy and he climbed in a resort dinghy and headed back to the resort.

Meeting with Johnson.   Johnson arrived in the Clubhouse Restaurant just a few minutes past eight. Dowd had already found his way to the breakfast buffet and sat with a plate full of local fruits and pastries. Johnson seemed rushed and told Dowd that he would have to keep the meeting short. Johnson told Dowd that he didn't want to influence Dowd's observations by explaining what he thought were the problem areas at the resort. Instead, Johnson would rather point out departments generating complaints and let Dowd observe without any biases. Dowd realized that this would be difficult because he knew so many of the employees but it was a role in which Dowd had been successful in the past. Dowd found that getting to the bottom of problems in organizations in the Caribbean often required gaining acceptance by the group, a status that was only achieved through gaining local employees' trust and establishing friendships. It was only then that employees would open up. Johnson wanted Dowd to focus on Front Desk, Food and Beverage, and Water Sports services and indicated that the resort's staff was at Dowd's service in terms of discussing operations. Johnson finished his coffee, wished Dowd luck, and left. As he watched Johnson walk out the door, Dowd thought, "Its always so easy to pick out the expatriate down here . . . we always seem to be in such a hurry."

Property Tour with Kent Mawhinney: Dowd finished up his breakfast and made his way down the shoreline to meet with Mawhinney, the property manager. He was greeted by Mawhinney at the top of the spiral staircase leading to the administrative offices. Mawhinney informed Dowd that he was leaving on his daily rounds and asked Dowd to join him. Mawhinney had extensive experience working in the Caribbean, and Dowd knew he would be a rich resource. As they walked off to their first stop Dowd bluntly asked Mawhinney what he thought the main problems were at the resort. Mawhinney replied that the most basic problem was getting plans implemented. When Mawhinney managed in the United States, his employees were concerned with the opportunity for advancement and really worked hard to prove themselves. In the Caribbean, things were different. Local employment laws almost guaranteed jobs and employees knew this. As a result, employees were more concerned with fitting in with their coworkers than with making any type of an impression. The resort had provided opportunities for some of the locals to be promoted, but few seemed interested. In his opinion, locals didn't want the added responsibility even if it meant more money. In some cases, the resort thought that rewarding the best employees with a title and some authority would help management gain more control over their employees. The result was an employee with a title who was unwilling to take on any of the job's responsibilities.

"If the employees only realized what they could have if they worked a little harder, took these positions seriously, and moved up in the organization," Mawhinney commented.

The property tour took about an hour. Mawhinney visited with each department head, a mix of local nationals, and expatriates (see Exhibit 4). His conversations instilled a sense of urgency to get the resort in shape for the coming week. In each case, he offered assistance in any way necessary to ensure reaching the resort's desired goals and objectives. Dowd was particularly impressed by the amount of detail that Mawhinney recalled regarding each manager's immediate challenges. Mawhinney pointed out to Dowd that one of the main differences between managing in the United States and managing in the Caribbean is how managers have to communicate with employees. Because there is a 70 percent functional illiteracy rate on the property, he could not rely on memos as he had in the States. Instead, he managed by physically demonstrating to his staff what had to be done. For example, Mawhinney's maintenance staff had been told several times that garbage was to be placed in a specific storage area. The staff continued storing the trash in the wrong place until Mawhinney physically showed them where and how it was to be stored.

Steve Lucas: By 10:30 A.M., Mawhinney and Dowd had completed the tour of the resort with the exception of the restaurants. As the two approached the Clubhouse dining area, Dowd noticed a man in his early thirties arguing with a local cook who looked to be in his fifties (later Dowd would find out that this was the Head Chef who had worked at the resort for more than 20 years).

"Why didn't you tell me that you couldn't get the ingredients for cheesecake? The menus have already been printed, and now we're going to look like fools! What is wrong with you people?" the man asked the cook.

Mawhinney interrupted, "Steve, what seems to be the problem?"

"Well, once again they failed to tell me that something was wrong," Lucas replied.

Mawhinney looked at the cook and asked if he could have a moment alone with Lucas. The cook welcomed the opportunity to leave the tense situation. Mawhinney calmed Lucas down and said that it was just part of the challenge of working in paradise. Mawhinney guided Lucas back over to Dowd, introduced the two, and informed Dowd that he had to get back to his office for a conference call with the resort's head office in Chicago.

Lucas and Dowd exchanged stories of their background. Lucas had been hired two weeks ago because the former Food and Beverage director quit. When Dowd asked him whether he liked his new job, Lucas replied:

It's a bit early to tell. One thing is for sure . . . it's a lot more challenging than I ever imagined! I know the staff has been here for a while but I don't know how they ever managed. They seem to work as a "seat of your pants" type operation. No planning, no commitment, no enthusiasm. It's surprising because I have heard that this resort is one of the best places for people down here to work. I guess the biggest challenge is the fact that I know the people in Chicago expect big things from me and I plan to deliver . . . no matter what it takes. I just wish I had more time to train these people properly before we are hit with the big rush next week. Did you know that The Clubhouse and The Carvery are expected to serve 1,000 dinners on New Year's Eve? After dinner we expect that another 500 to 800 charterboat tourists will be coming ashore for the entertainment at the bar. Meanwhile, my staff is accustomed to our average nightly seating of about 100 for the rest of the year. This will be a big test for them . . . and, I guess for me as well.

Dowd asked Lucas how he was adjusting to the local culture. "I am having a great time so far. It's so much fun hanging out with a different group of guests every week. I am not looking forward to the slow season around here though. Then, who will I have to hang around with? I haven't made very many local friends and that's mostly because I want to keep business and pleasure separate anyway."

Their conversation went on for another 20 minutes. Finally, Lucas looked anxious to get back to overseeing the preparations for tonight's meal, so Dowd closed the conversation and moved on. As Dowd walked away, he stopped to take a glance back at Lucas. Lucas was hovering over one of his staff,

checking to make sure that each ingredient was properly measured before being added to the pot. "What a way to have to manage!" Dowd thought.

Meeting with Kristin Singiser: Singiser entered the restaurant with an apologetic look on her face. "Sorry I am so late. Glad you found yourself a Piña Colada to keep you occupied", she said.

"So, what took you so long?" Dowd asked jokingly.

Singiser explained that it had been a long day. The Chicago office had overbooked the resort by 20 percent for the coming week without telling the guests that there might be some inconveniences. Therefore, it was her job to greet guests on the dock and inform some of them that they would have to stay onboard one of the resort's larger charter boats for a few nights until rooms became available. Meanwhile, other families were informed that the children and parents would be staying at opposite ends of the resort. As if dealing with understandably irate guests wasn't enough, her staff made several disturbing remarks.

They asked me, "Why is everyone always coming down on us about providing good service when Chicago pulls a stunt like this?" I just don't know how to reply. My staff faces angry guests all day as a result of this fiasco. How can I expect them to be courteous when the guests are so mad and the staff had no influence on the situation? The worst part is that Chicago has done this to us for the past three years, and each time I tell my staff to just manage this time and I'll try to make sure it doesn't happen again. I go to bat for them but seem to strike out every time."

Over a lobster dinner, the two discussed many other challenges that Singiser had faced over the years. Much of the local's behavior she had become accustomed to, but some things were still frustrating. "Sometimes you feel like the only way you can manage these people is to bash them over the head with it," she commented. Apparently, her style was to demonstrate exactly what she expected of her front desk staff a few times, knowing that some of them would get it right and others would continue to do it their own way. When they continued to do it their own way, it was time for "bashing them over the head with it." Despite all of her frustrations, Singiser was probably the most respected expatriate on the WIYCR staff. Over her long tenure she had adapted to the local culture, made close friends with the locals, and recognized what it took to get things done. However, she still felt challenged when trying to motivate her staff. "Money, opportunity for advancement, all of the normal incentives, they all don't seem to make any impact", she said.

In previous conversations with Singiser's staff, Dowd had solicited their opinions. Most staff said that Singiser was "different." She had a sincere interest in them and was involved with the local culture. She frequently took trips with her staff to the neighboring islands and had them over to her bungalow for dinner on occasion. Sure, she was tough, but her staff felt that managers had to be that way sometimes.

A Day at Water Sports: As they finished their meals and enjoyed an after-dinner drink, Singiser suggested that Dowd spend at least one day working alongside the staff at water sports. That would give him an inside look at a department critical to the resort's success. After all, water sports were the main reason why guests chose the resort for their vacation.

Walking down the path to the water sports shack, Dowd knew that he had an interesting day ahead of him. He had extensive water sports experience but had only observed WIYCR's operations from a guest's perspective. Throughout the day, Dowd took mental notes on how the department operated and how the locals worked (or didn't work). Harrigan was behind the desk at the shack most of the day, while his assistant, Mitchell (a 25-year-old local Virgin Gordan) raced about the harbor on a 15-foot whaler (a small power boat) taking guests out to boats. It was surprising that Harrigan allowed some of his senior staff to noticeably avoid work. Fergus and Muhammad (both in their late twenties and from Virgin Gorda), for example, conveniently wandered off during the peak morning rush. Guests were left standing in line for 15 minutes because the desk was short-staffed. With Fergus and Mohammad's help at the desk, Dowd thought that the wait could be reduced to 5 minutes. The daylight sun was waning and guests wanted to get out on the water. When some of the senior staff did interact with guests, they were reserved and not overly courteous. Guests asked questions, and the staff mumbled incoherent responses. However, one group of guests did have an advantage—guests who had bought several rounds of drinks for the staff the night before. When one of these guests arrived at the desk, the senior staff would jump to their feet and greet them like these guests were part of the local family. Dowd jokingly referred to this as "pre-service tipping."

Working at the Water Sports Department, Dowd found himself hustling the whole day, thinking that maybe some of it would rub off on his fellow workers. He had a slight advantage over Pickering's socialization into the group because Dowd had worked alongside the local staff during the three previous Thanksgiving vacations as part of a joint project between WIYCR and Tradewind Ventures. The group accepted him long ago. He thought, "Maybe if they see me working hard they will think it's OK." By the end of his first day, Dowd had earned $100 in tips. He told the local staff, and they didn't believe him until he laid the money out on the counter. He explained how they could easily do the same thing and make a killing this week. They reluctantly replied, "Yeah, right, like we could do that."

At the end of the day Dowd, Fergus, and Muhammad stopped for a beer at the Commissary (a small snack bar). Dowd asked them how they thought things were going in the Water Sports Department. Fergus replied, "Things went more smoothly when Bill (Jones) was around. He gave us clear directions regarding what we had to do for the day and we did it. Things are different with Enrik (Harrigan). He's really laid back, and we often don't know what we're supposed to be doing." Dowd also inquired about how they felt about the expatriates who worked at the resort, and Muhammad's comments summarized the discussion, "We have so many managers from the States and they don't stay here very long. Many of them think they can just come in here and we'll instantly be their friends. I'm tired of making friends just to have them leave a year later. The worst part is that they think we want to become managers like them. Managing people takes too much effort. I'm just not interested in leaving my friends behind just to make a little more money."

Talking with Guests: When Dowd was not speaking with the resort's management or its employees, he spent his time with the guests. The following quotes summarized the comments made by guests regarding guest interactions with the resort's staff:

> "There was nothing for us to do at night from December 23 until December 26. I know that the staff has to celebrate Christmas, but it would have been nice for us to have something to do."

> "I was waiting in line for almost 10 minutes at the bar. They only had two bartenders on and they moved so slowly. Plus, since all the guests are getting their own drinks, why do they have five waitresses. They just stood there. Can't they work behind the bar too?"

> "We were out on the Almond Walk (a terrace area attached to the resort's main restaurant) and thought that a waiter would come by. When we asked one of the waitresses she said that she was assigned to the dining room. The dining room had served its last guest an hour before and was located about 25 feet from the Almond Walk. Someone should tell them that it's OK to go out onto the Walk and serve other guests."

> "I asked the restaurant manager to call a waiter over for me, but I'll never do that again. He went over to his wait staff and told them that they were incompetent. I felt so bad. I think that the staff purposely avoided our table for the rest of the night because they were afraid of getting into trouble again."

> "I was looking forward to being greeted at the docks by someone who would help me with my bags. After all, I'd just finished a 10-hour trip and am paying a lot of money to be here. When I asked the front desk staff they apologized and said that someone must have forgotten. It's surprising that I am paying this much money for people to forget. What's that about first impressions being the most important?"

> "Reading the brochure, I really thought that the programs for the kids sounded great. However, the first few days my kids said that the staff weren't very interested in making them have a good time. They seemed like they were more interested in when they got off work than with making my kids have a good time. Then they had Dave. What a difference! The kids came back excited about everything they did that day. He was so energetic and interested in my kids."

> "I told the front desk that they should really spray for bugs out on the terrace or get one of those bug lamps. There are so many mosquitoes out there in the evening. The staff doesn't seem to be too interested in responding though."

> "We called maintenance the other day to tell them that our rooms are not fully operational in terms of things like showers, screens and faucets working. It's kind of surprising to be at a resort like this without at least the basics. They said they would send someone by today, but that was three days ago. I think I will go to one of the other managers next."

> "Today I went to the beach at around 10 am and they were already out of towels again. The beach attendant said that he would bring some back as soon as he found them. I guess he didn't find any because it's been three hours, although I did see him standing around at the other end of the resort talking with some friends. Do you think he ever even looked for them?"

Listening to these comments, Dowd wondered which problems related to poor management relations with local staff, which related to simply poor work by the local staff, and which related to poor managing by the expatriates. One thing was sure—issues in all of these areas were beginning to affect the guests.

MAKING SENSE OF IT ALL

Dowd had been at the resort for just one week and the information from interviews with managers, local employees, and resort guests along with personal observations filled his head as he sat down to begin preparing for his meeting with Johnson the following morning. It was clear that there needed to be some changes at the resort if Johnson was going to resolve the issues concerning expatriate turnover, increasing guest complaints, and the level of tension between some of the expatriate managers and the local employees. The first wave of peak season guests, those coming for the Christmas holiday, would arrive tomorrow and stretch the resort's resources to their limits. Dowd wondered how he could best utilize the information gathered to analyze the current situation and provide some course of action for Johnson to take that would address his concerns. Dowd sat at his table and began to organize his thoughts.

Case 13 · A First-Time Expatriate's Experience in a Joint Venture in China

THE LONG TRIP HOME

James Randolf was traveling back to his home state of Illinois from his assignment in China for the last time. He and his wife were about three hours into the long flight when she fell asleep, her head propped up by the airline pillow against the cabin wall. James was exhausted, but for the first time in many days he had the luxury of reflecting on what had just happened in their lives.

He was neither angry nor bitter, but the disruption of the last few weeks was certainly unanticipated and in many ways unfortunate. He had fully expected to complete his three-year assignment as the highest ranking U.S. manager of his company's joint venture (JV) near Shanghai. Now, after only 13 months, the assignment was over, and a manager from the regional office in Singapore held the post. Sure, the JV will survive, he thought, but how far had the relationship that he had been nurturing between the two partnered companies been set back? His Chinese partners were perplexed by his company's actions and visibly affected by the departure of their friend and colleague.

Was this an error in judgment resulting from Control's relative inexperience as a multinational company and a partner in international joint ventures, James wondered? Or, had something else caused the shift in policy which resulted in the

This case was prepared by John Stanbury, Assistant Professor of International Business at Indiana University, Kokomo, with enormous assistance from Rina Dangarwala, and John King, MBA Students. It is not intended to illustrate either effective or ineffective handling of a managerial situation. The views represented here are those of the case author and do not necessarily reflect those of the Society for Case Research. The author's view is based on his own professional judgments.

The names of the organization, and the industry in which it operates, and individuals' names and the events described in this case have been disguised to preserve anonymity.

Presented to and accepted by the Society for Case Research. All rights reserved to the author and SCR. Copyright © 1997 by John Stanbury.

earlier-than-planned recall of several of the corporation's expatriates from their assignments? There had always been plans to reduce the number of expatriates at any particular location over time, but recently the carefully planned timetables seem to have been abandoned. Next week, James had to turn in his report covering the entire work assignment. How frank should he be? What detail should he include in his report? To whom should he send copies? There had been rumors that many senior managers were being asked to take early retirement. James did not really want to retire but could hardly contain his dissatisfaction as to how things had turned out. Maybe it would be better to take the offer, if it was forthcoming, and try to find some consulting that would make the best use of his wide spectrum of technical and managerial experience which now included an expatriate assignment in what was considered to be one of the most difficult locations in the world.

James reflected with satisfaction on his accomplishment of the initial primary objectives which were to establish a manufacturing and marketing presence. In fact, he was quite pleased with his success at putting many things in place which would allow the operation to prosper. The various departments within the joint venture were now cooperating and coordinating and the relationships he had established were truly the evidence of this achievement. He would like to have seen the operations become more efficient, however.

The worklife that awaited him upon his return was a matter of considerable concern. Reports from the expatriates who preceded him in the last few months indicated that there were no established plans to utilize their talents, and often early retirement was strongly encouraged by management. Beyond the obligatory physical examinations and debriefings, he had been told there was little for them to do. Many of the recalled expatriates found themselves occupying desks in Personnel waiting for responses about potential job opportunities.

He gazed at his wife, Lily, now settled into comfortable slumber. At least she had had a pretty good experience. She was born in Shanghai but left China in 1949. The country was then in the middle of a revolution, but, aside from her memory of her parents appearing extremely anxious to leave, she remembered little else about the issues surrounding their emigration to the United States. Most of her perceptions about "what it was like" in China came from U.S. television coverage, some fact, some fiction.

As the plane droned on into the night, James thought back to how this experience began.

THE COMPANY

Control's world headquarters were in Chicago, Illinois. It had operations in several countries in Europe, Asia and South America but, with the exception of several *maquiladoras*, all of its expansion had occurred very recently. Its first involvement in joint ventures began only three years ago. As an in-house supplier to "Filtration Inc.," a huge Chicago-based international manufacturing conglomerate, specializing in the design and production of temperature control and filtration systems, it had been shielded from significant competition, and most of its product lines of various electronic control mechanisms had been produced in North America. Ten years ago, however, Controls became a subsidiary of Filtration Inc. and was given a charter to pursue business beyond that transacted with its parent. At the same time, the rules for acquiring in-house business changed as well. Controls now bid for Filtration Inc.'s business against many of the world's best producers of this equipment. The need to utilize cheaper labor and to be located closer to key prospective customers drove the company to expand internationally at a rate that only a few years earlier would have been completely outside its corporate comfort zone.

A JV in China would provide Controls with an opportunity to gain a foothold in this untapped market for temperature control systems. This could pave the way for a greater thrust into the expanding Chinese economy. If the JV was successful, it could also lead to the establishment of plants to manufacture various products for the entire Asia/Pacific market.

The corporation's involvement in the joint venture seemed less planned than its other expansion efforts. The Freezer and Cooler Controls Business Unit (one of Controls' key business units), headquartered in Lakeland, MN, sent a team of four, consisting of two engineers and two representatives from the Finance and Business Planning Departments, to investigate the possibility of partnering with a yet-to-be-identified Chinese electronics assembly operation. The team was not given an adequate budget and was limited to a visit of one month. Not being experienced international negotiators, they were only able to identify one potential partner, a Chinese state-owned firm. They quickly realized that they did not have time to conclude negotiations, and returned to HQ without having met their objective. After debriefing them upon their return to the United States, the corporation's planners decided that the Chinese JV presented a good opportunity and sent another team to continue these negotiations. Eventually, an agreement was reached with the Chinese state-owned firm. Exhibit 1 shows the organizational relationships between Filtration Inc. and its subsidiaries.

HOW IT ALL BEGAN

James had always been intrigued by the idea of securing an international assignment. His interest heightened on the day that Controls, Inc. announced its intentions to expand the business

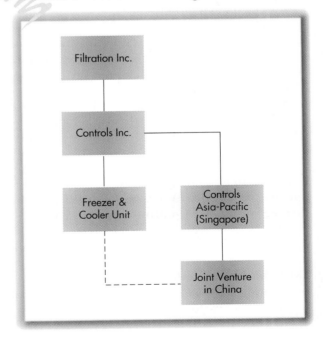

Exhibit I   Filtration Inc. Organization Chart

through establishing a more international presence, worldwide. By age 51, James had worked in managerial positions in Engineering, Quality, Customer Support and Program Management for the last 15 of his 23 years with the company, but always in positions geographically based in Pauley, Illinois. He frequently mentioned the idea of working on an international assignment to his superiors during performance reviews and in a variety of other settings. He did not mentally target any specific country, but preferred an assignment in the Pacific Rim, due to his lifelong desire to gain an even deeper understanding of his wife's cultural heritage.

Finally, two years ago, he was able to discuss his interests with the corporation's International Human Resources manager. During this interview he was told of the hardships of functioning as an expatriate. There could a language problem as well as difficulties caused by the remoteness from home office. He remained interested.

A year later, James was first considered for a position that required venture development in Tokyo. At one point he was even told he had been chosen for that position. With little explanation, the company instead announced the selection of a younger, more "politically" connected "fast-tracker."

When, a few months later, a discussion about the position in China was first broached by Personnel, it was almost in the context of it being a consolation prize. The position, however, appeared to be one for which James was even better suited and one which would be challenging enough to "test the mettle" of any manager in the company. The assignment was to "manage a joint venture manufacturing facility" located on Chongming Dao Island, about 25 miles north of Shanghai. The strategic objective of the JV was market entry into China.

Soon thereafter, in mid-August of 1992, James was asked to go immediately to Lakeland to meet one-on-one with Joe Whistler, the director of the Freezer and Cooler Controls Business Unit to discuss the JV. The negotiating team was still in China in the process of "finalizing" the JV agreement with the Chongming Electro-Assembly Company, a state-owned electronic device assembly operation. The corporation felt that there was a dire need to put someone on site. Joe asked if he could leave next week! James indicated that he was interested in

accepting the position and that he was willing to do whatever the corporation required of him to make it happen as soon as possible. It was understood that a formal offer for the position would be processed through Personnel and communicated through James's management. When this trip didn't materialize, James wondered if this was going to be a repeat of the Tokyo assignment. Finally, in late September, James's supervisor approached him and said, "if you still want it, you've got the prize."

ORIENTATION

Filtration, Inc. has a defined set of procedures to deal with expatriate work assignment orientation. When it was determined that James was a strong candidate to go overseas, it was arranged for James and his wife to go to Chicago for orientation training. The training began with a day-long session conducted by Filtration Inc.'s International personnel function. James thought the training was exceptionally well done. Filtration Inc. brought in experts to discuss pay, benefits, moving arrangements and a multitude of other issues dealing with working for the corporation in an international assignment. Part of the orientation process was a "look-see trip," the normal length of which was seven days. The trip was quickly arranged to begin two weeks later. The Randolfs were extremely excited. This would be Lily's first trip back to China. They even extended the duration of the trip to ten days to do some investigation on their own time.

There was a considerable mix-up in the planning of the "look-see" trip. Although the Personnel Department in Pauley wanted to arrange the entire trip, Controls' Asia-Pacific regional office in Singapore insisted it was better for them to handle it locally. The Randolfs were supposed to have a rental car available upon arrival but discovered that no arrangements had been made, and so they were forced to secure their own car. Their itinerary indicated that they had reservations at the Shanghai Inn, but they soon discovered that no reservations had been made there either.

In Shanghai they went sightseeing on their own for three days. Afterward, they were scheduled for seven days of official activities. They spent the following two days with an on-site consultant, who was on retainer from the JV, and who showed the potential expatriates around the city. Her tour consisted of what she perceived a typical American might most like to see.

The wife of an expatriate herself, the consultant didn't speak Shanghainese or any other Chinese dialects. Travel with her was somewhat of a nightmare. As opposed to discussing the planned locations with the Chinese driver at the beginning of a day, she directed the trip one step at a time. She would show the driver a card on which was written the address of the next location and say "go here now." This approach caused considerable delays due to the inefficiencies of transversing the city numerous times and touring in a disorderly sequence. They were shown American-style shopping, American-style restaurants, and potential living accommodations. The Randolfs were told that leasing a good apartment commonly required a "kickback."

After visiting the JV's factory near Shanghai they traveled to the regional headquarters, Controls Asia-Pacific, in Singapore to participate in an extensive orientation workshop. Again, the topics included compensation policies and other matters of interest to potential expatriates, this time from the perspective of Controls, Inc. James and Lily both noted a significant contrast in dealings with the regional Controls, Inc. personnel staff as opposed to the "first rate" Filtration Inc. International Human Resources people. The former was by far a less polished and informed operation. Even as they departed Singapore for the United States, they were still unsure that the move was right for them. They spent the next several days reflecting on the trip and discussing their decision. They were discouraged by the lack of maintenance apparent in the factory, which was clearly inferior to U.S. standards. Things were dirty, and little effort was expended on environmental controls. The days seemed awfully gray. However, they had quickly become enamored with the Shanghai people and this became a key factor in their ultimate decision to accept the position. As the result of their interactions with the Chinese partners and Shanghai area residents, James and Lily truly felt the promise of exciting, new, deep, long-lasting relationships.

Once they were firmly committed to the assignment, they attended a two-day orientation on living and working in China. This was provided by Prudential Relocation Services Inc. in Boulder, Colorado, and was tailored to the needs and desires of the participants. Optional curriculum tracks included: the history, culture, political climate, business climate and the people of the region. James focused his training on a business-related curriculum which was taught by professors from a local university. Additionally, whenever an expatriate returned from China to the home office on home leave, James was given an opportunity to interface with him. Exhibit 3 summarizes the key characteristics of Chinese culture and management.

Between November (1992) and January (1993), James worked an exhausting schedule, alternating two-week periods in Pauley and at the JV in China, where lodging and meals were provided in a hotel. During this time, his wife, Lily, remained in Lakewood preparing for their permanent relocation to China. Also, Filtration, Inc. held scheduled, intensive Mandarin language courses in Chicago, which James planned to attend, but due to his work schedule he was unable to take advantage of the opportunity. Finally, in January, James attended the language school for a week. Fortunately, he and Lily already spoke some Cantonese, another Chinese dialect. After James was finally on-site full-time in February, he hired a language tutor to supplement this training. The orientation procedure concluded with a checklist of things that James and Controls were to accomplish after the commencement of his on-site assignment. While all of these checklist items were eventually accomplished, priorities on the job didn't allow them to be completed in a very timely manner.

WORKPLACE ORIENTATIONS

Mandarin, China's official language, was spoken at the factory. In regions where Mandarin is not the primary language of the people, it is the language most commonly used in industry and trade, and in dealing with the government. Most residents were not proficient in Mandarin, although the oldest members of the population had learned it only after they had completed their formal education, if at all. Mandarin became China's official language when the alphabet was standardized in 1955. Away from the workplace, people preferred to speak Shanghainese or Chongming Dao's own similar dialect.

Chongming Dao, the actual site of the factory, was situated in the Chuang Yangtze River. At approximately 50 miles long and 18 miles wide, it is

China's third largest island. Its population is approximately one million people. The residents were perceived by the Shanghainese to be poor, backward farmers.

James found that he was able to maintain residencies in Shanghai and in Chongming Dao, although all the Chinese workers, including managers, lived close to their place of work. The trip from downtown Shanghai to the plant took more than two hours. First there was a 1½-hour trip to the site of the ferry departure, then came a 20-minute ferry ride, followed by another 20 minutes of travel by car. Work days at the factory were scheduled from Tuesdays through Saturdays. As is common in China, the schedules were centrally planned to alternate with those of other factories in a manner which conserved power consumption.

The Chinese partner had warehouses and a business center on the island, which, in addition to the factory, became part of the JV. The people worked under conditions that would be totally unacceptable to most American workers. There were no temperature or humidity controls. In the winter the plant was so cold that workers wore up to six layers of clothing. In contrast, summers were very hot and humid. None of the machinery had safety guards. Tools were generally either nonexistent or inadequate. Lighting was also very poor.

The Chinese factory's workforce was primarily young women. This was in contrast to the Chinese partner's factories that James had visited, where most of the workers were men who appeared to be over the age of 40. The plant's organization and operation fostered considerable inefficiencies. There were not process controls to prevent errors and scrap. The only visible methods of quality control were extensive amounts of 100 percent testing and inspection performed after the product was completely assembled. The layout of the plant was awkward. There were numerous little rooms and no large expansive production areas. Operations were not laid out sequentially or even in a line. The typical mode of operations was to have numerous workers working elbow to elbow around the perimeter of a large table.

Material movement was most commonly performed by dragging large tubs of materials across the floor. Storage was disorderly and bins were generally not stacked, due to a lack of shelving. Consequently,

containers of parts, partially assembled products, scrap materials and finished assemblies could be found anywhere and everywhere. Instead of scheduling plant output, the system scheduled only the number of man-hours to be expended. This lack of direction caused a considerable amount of confusion and inefficiency. It was really more of a way of accounting for the use of the excessive labor force that existed in the factory and in the area. James often commented that he could produce as much or more output with only the number of Quality Control (QC) operators that were in the plant. By his estimates, the JV employed three times as many people as were needed. James did not think that he could change this immediately but felt that he could convince the Chinese management that this practice needs to be change eventually.

ADAPTING TO LIFE IN CHINA

Beyond some terrific people in the Personnel Department in Pauley, who could help with specific employment-related issues, James quickly came to realize that there would be little operational support from the home office. His links back to his corporation came more from Filtration Inc. than from Controls. Filtration Inc. at least sent a monthly package of news clippings, executive briefs and memos that had been specifically prepared for expatriates. The package allowed James to keep up somewhat on what was happening in the larger corporate setting.

Filtration Inc. had a couple of dozen employees in Shanghai. It was their role to establish and implement a joint venture that the parent had negotiated with a different Chinese manufacturer than the one with which Controls had partnered. As part of this team, there were also a few representatives from Controls, Inc. They were all co-located in a small office building in downtown Shanghai. It was in this corporate office environment that James found a great deal of support, a lot of helpful advice and his unofficial mentor, a Filtration Inc. manager who had spent four years in China. At the time, James wondered why he hadn't visited this office during his orientation trip.

The help that James received from Controls Inc.'s subsidiary, Controls Asia-Pacific, was often ineffective and inconsistent. Nagging policies and obligatory paperwork were typical characteristics of their assistance. There were ongoing problems finding and retaining a qualified translator for James. In the agreement, the JV was responsible for providing each expatriate with a translator. Controls Asia-Pacific was responsible for the wage structure at the JV. The Personnel Dept. in Singapore established a maximum wage rate for the translator position at 2,000 yuan. This rate was fair for the area, but there were few high quality translators available. When an area translator was identified, he would often be lost to another multinational company in the area who offered a salary of 3,000 yuan. To attract translators from Shanghai would require a wage comparable to the wages one would receive in Shanghai, and 2,000 yuan was significantly lower than that paid in the city.

Another aspect of employment in China which merited consideration was the movement of one's "personnel file" from a former employer to the present one. This is the rough equivalent of changing one's residency to another state in the United States. The reputation and perception of Chongming Dao was that of a rural community. This would have a negative impact on transferring a translator's file back to Shanghai in the future. Singapore didn't understand the economics and implications of this situation and refused to increase the wage rate to a level that would entice qualified translators to accept the position. James, as a result, was without a qualified translator for significant periods during his time in China. The impact on his ability to function in that setting was therefore also significant, resulting in less being accomplished than if Singapore had been more flexible.

The residence in Shanghai was available because the JV had committed to a two-year lease of an executive apartment on the 22nd floor of the Shanghai Inn. These accommodations were quite nice and offered most of the comforts of home. The hotel complex included a supermarket, exercise facilities, a theater, and several restaurants, including Shanghai's Hard Rock Cafe. The three-bedroom apartment, which James measured to be around 1,500 square feet, was converted into a two-bedroom apartment to his specifications. Amenities included cable TV with five English language channels. Accommodations on the island were significantly rougher. The original plan was for James to temporarily stay at the government's guest house on the factory grounds, until a 12-unit housing compound was constructed in the immediate vicinity. The small rooms, intense heat, and fierce mosquitoes at the guest house proved to be unbearable and, by June, James decided to make other arrangements. These entailed staying in a hotel 17 miles away with the two other expatriates from Controls, Inc. to manage the JV. Although the building was new, the quality of the construction was quite poor, which seemed to be common in China. The costs associated with constructing their compound were, by this time, estimated to be much larger than expected. Eventually, a solution was reached to fix up certain aspects of the guest house and retain it as the long-term island living arrangements for them. After this Lily always traveled with him to and from the factory.

ADAPTING TO THE WORK

In addition to James, there were three other Controls, Inc. expatriates assigned to the JV. The director of Engineering and the director of Manufacturing were on assignment from the United States. The director of Finance was from Singapore. Each of these individuals had dual roles, that of heading up their respective departments, and the assignment to bring to the JV new technology associated with their departments. The Finance director had the particularly challenging assignment of introducing a new accounting system to the JV, one that was compatible with the Controls, Inc. system. The existing system, installed by the Chinese partner, was not designed to report profits and losses, irrelevant concepts in the formerly state-owned company.

The other expatriates occasionally complained of not getting good cooperation from the Chinese workers. James never encountered this problem, as he always communicated his requests directly to the workers.

One of the first problematic situations that evolved related to differences between expatriate conditions of employment for Filtration Inc. and Controls Inc. employees. Most Filtration employees enjoyed a per diem of US$95 but Controls employees, were limited to US$50 per day. Additionally, the Filtration Inc.'s visitation policies were more liberal in terms of allowing college-age children to visit their expatriate parents.

ONGOING NEGOTIATIONS

In China, a JV contract is "nice framework" from which to begin the real negotiation process. The Controls JV negotiating team viewed the contract as a conclusion to negotiations and returned to the United States in late December of 1992. James soon discovered that the process of negotiations would be ongoing. On almost a daily basis, some element of the agreement was adjusted or augmented with new understanding.

A misconception held by the Controls negotiating team related to the ease of obtaining appropriate governmental approvals. There were various annexes and subcontracts which were yet to be finalized and approved when they departed. Some of these approvals were required from government officials with whom they had had very little interface. The impact of this miscalculation was that production in the JV didn't commence on January 1, 1993, as anticipated. Instead it took until August 1, 1993 to get the operation going.

One of the most serious issues affecting the operation of the JV which directly impacted James' effectiveness was the JV's organization structure which was negotiated by the Controls team. The organization chart for the JV is shown in Exhibit 2. Controls perceived the position of Chairman (COB) of the Board of Directors to be of greater importance in operating the company than that of managing director, thinking that they could "run the company" from that position. Consequently, when the organization chart was drawn up, Controls conceded the position of managing director to the Chinese partner in exchange for the right to appoint the COB for the first three of the five years. James noted that in Chinese JVs negotiated by Filtration Inc., the U.S. partner always secured the position of managing director.

OBSERVATIONS OF CHINESE MANAGEMENT METHODS

James observed that when Chinese managers were dealing with subordinates, decision making was very top-down. This resulted in virtually all decisions of any consequence being made by the managing director. James was extremely fortunate that the managing director appointed by the Chinese part-

Exhibit 2   Controls' Joint Venture in China: Organization Chart

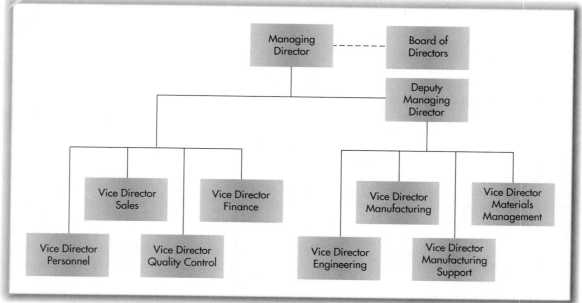

ner was willing to share his power. He and the managing director developed an excellent relationship, which James consciously worked on in the firm belief that this was the key to business success in China. Toward the end of his time at the JV, James was frequently left in charge of running the factory while the managing director was visiting outside friends of influence, customers, and potential customers. The only other manager who shared this distinction was the director of Personnel.

The Personnel Department, in this JV, as in the state-owned Chinese companies, was unusually powerful when compared to most U.S. companies that James was familiar with. They maintained the all-important employment files and were very connected to the Communist Party.

OBSERVATIONS OF CHINESE MANAGEMENT TEAM

Chinese managers at the JV were considerably more educated than the workers. They had matriculated at various universities and graduated with degrees in Engineering, Management, and the like. In one case, the manager's experience and education came from his time as a career-soldier in the Army.

INTERACTIONS WITH THE CHINESE GOVERNMENT

Prior to the formation of the JV, the secretary for the Communist Party and the managing director were coequals when it came to "running the Chongming Electro Assembly Company." About 325 of the 1,819 employees at the JV were communists. After James's arrival, there was always a question as to what would happen to the party office, which was located adjacent to the managing director's office. In many ways the party served a function similar to that of labor unions in the United States. It represented the workers and entered into discussions related to labor relations issues. The Communist Party could be viewed as a different channel to deal with issues and James quickly recognized it as an ally.

James's only personal experience with a government bureau was while getting his residency papers established. The rules he encountered were extremely inflexible, everything had to be just right, and no copies were allowed as the Bureau required originals. The Bureau office, which was the size of a walk-in closet in the United States, was extremely crowded and the process required forcing one's way up through the lines to get to the table where female police officers would process the paperwork. After it was all over, he noticed that they had spelled his name wrong. He did not return to correct the mistake.

INTERACTION WITH THE UNION

The JV also had a labor union, but by comparison to the United States, the organization was extremely weak and superficial. James's only dealing with the union related to a request for donations for a retirees' party the union wanted to hold. Since the JV had no retirees, and this was new ground for him, he referred them to the managing director.

GETTING IT TOGETHER

James loved to walk the floor and see what was happening in the factory. His position gave him the authority to direct actions to be taken, but often he did not have to use this authority in that way. The Chinese workers seemed to be influenced by his every action. If he would make a point to pick up trash in the parking lot, the next day he would observe that the trash had all been cleaned up. Another example was when he straightened some papers in the pigeon holes of a filing system. The next day every stack of papers was perfectly arranged. He felt that there was never a time where he walked the floor and it didn't pay off in some way. He found Chinese workers to be very attentive to detail.

He was often tested by the Chinese managers and workers alike, as is not uncommon in other parts of the world. He perceived that they would test his commitment, leadership and his decision-making ability. They would determine how far this Manager could be pushed. These tests provided him with the opportunity to do the right thing. A case in point was when a drunken salesperson accosted a woman in a nightclub. James took him to a private place and severely chastised him.

During his assignment, he remained cognizant of the fact that one of his jobs was to make the MD look good. This required him to fire a translator on the spot when the translator remarked that anyone who wanted to stay in China was stupid.

He had great admiration for the Chinese workers at the JV. They proved to be very cooperative people. They had a great deal of pride and were very loyal to their company and the industry in which they worked. James often commented that, with informed leadership, Chinese workers would be as good as workers anywhere in the world.

What James liked best however, was his interactions with the Chinese people. Every day brought him a new experience.

OBSERVATIONS ABOUT THE CHINESE PEOPLE

Most of the Chinese people were not communists. They would rather ignore the political situation going on around them and get on with their lives. They were eager to learn anything they could about what Westerners could teach them. Almost without exception, they looked up to Americans and would begin to imitate them after a while. James found it very gratifying. He was also delighted with their treatment of his wife Lily, which bordered on reverence. James wondered as to the reasons for this. Perhaps it had something to do with the fact that she, through her parents, had previously escaped communist oppression and found a better life, which symbolized to the Chinese that there was hope for all.

James never saw a Chinese man leering at a woman, as is common in the United States. In China, sexuality was a private matter. They tended to live a simpler life than do most westerners. Their children were treated with reverence, even doted on. Their chaotic traffic jams seemed always to be dealt with very calmly. James never observed swearing or anger, as is common in the United States. James also found that the Chinese have an attitude that they know more than westerners do, but that this never manifested itself in a boastful way. The attitude was more that at some point in time, westerners would come around to their way of thinking. It was almost as though they played the role of a wiser urban patriarch guiding his young country cousin during the latter's first visit to the city. See Exhibit 3 for more information on Chinese culture and management.

ACTIVITIES AWAY FROM THE JOB

James and Lily had a different social life than that enjoyed in the United States. They spent hours walking and talking. Occasionally, when they were in Shanghai they had the opportunities to see shows. They saw the acrobats, went to symphony concerts and ballet, even joining crowds when Foster Beer brought Australian bands to perform in a Shanghai park.

The concerns Lily had expressed prior to expatriating disappeared as she made friends and became integrated into the social fabric of the area. Because her appearance was indistinguishable from the indigenous Shanghai-area people, she was more readily accepted and learned more about local happenings that most Westerners. At one point, two months after their arrival, Lily was hospitalized with a lung infection. Even this was resolved satisfactorily. She particularly noted that the skill level of the medical practitioners seemed to be very good, from the diagnosis to the way they painlessly took blood samples. Overall she found it easy to occupy her time. She was a traditional wife, who had not worked full time since her children were born and never had difficulty occupying the time in her life as she was a woman who was compelled to learn about everything and everybody. She spent much of her time traveling with James to and from the site, and when he was working she sought out the people and assisted at a mission nearby as she had some experience in nursing, having earned her RN before marrying James.

The Randolfs preferred to eat food with fresh ingredients and were happy away from the "supermarket" society, so Lily also spent a lot of time shopping. They felt that they were able to eat quite well in China.

James and Lily learned as much of the local Shanghai dialect as they could. In spite of never becoming fully proficient, the fact that they attempted to speak it greatly pleased the local residents. They spent much of their spare time interacting with the people of the area.

Sometimes Filtration Inc. would put on a social affair for the expatriates in Shanghai. James and Lily were always invited. While on the island, however, they always ate at the restaurant in the factory. Contrary to what they were told at their

Exhibit 3   Survey of Key Characteristics of Chinese Culture and Management[1]

Culture

One of the strong cultural beliefs among the Chinese is that their culture is the oldest and the best. It is the center of the universe, the *Zhong guo*—center country. They believe themselves to be totally self-sufficient. In Chinese, the character of the word China means "middle kingdom," thus implying that everyone other than themselves is beneath them.

Concept of Face and Time

The concept of face is of paramount importance in China. It is a person's most precious possession. Without it, one cannot function in China. It is earned by fulfilling one's duties and other obligations. Face often requires little effort, but merely an attention to courtesy in relationships with others. Face involves a high degree of self-control, social consciousness and concern for others. In Chinese society, display of temper, sulking, loss of self-control or frustration create further loss of face rather than drawing respect.

Despite having invented the clock, the Chinese never define or segment time in the way that it is approached in the West. Even today, for Chinese, time simply flows from one day to another. If a job is not completed today, they will carry it forward to the next day or the day after next. This is a manifestation of the concept of Polychronic (non-linear) time. In Western cultures, people see time as Monochronic (linear).

An important cultural difference between the West and China is the Chinese custom of giving precedence to form and process in completing a task, over the task itself, an approach which is typically more time-consuming.

Behavior

Chinese behavior is influenced by their brutal history. This has created a careful people. They give consideration to the repercussions of every move or decision that they make.

An important aspect of behavior involves the way the Chinese think. They think about thinking and relationships, whereas the Westerner would think in linear patterns of cause and effect.

Another aspect, which confuses the Westerner, is the willingness to discuss endless possibilities even when things look hopeless.

A Chinese philosophy that relates to interacting with Westerners, can be stated: Whereas a westerner will try to tell you everything he knows in a conversation, a Chinese will listen to learn everything the westerner knows, so that, at the end of the day, he would know both what he knew and what the westerner knew.

Gift Giving

Chinese are conditioned to express appreciation in tangible ways, such as by giving gifts and other favors. They regard the westerner's frequent use of "thank you" as a glib and insincere way of passing off obligations to return favors. When they do someone a favor, they expect appreciation to be expressed in some very concrete way. If all you choose to do is say "thanks," it should be very specific and sincere, and then stop. The Chinese do not like gushy thanks. Gift giving in China is a highly developed art. Although it has greatly diminished today (there is a law forbidding government officials from accepting gifts of any kind or value), the practice remains a vital aspect of creating and nurturing relationships with people.

Living as a Foreign Guest in the People's Republic of China

Foreigners who have gone to the People's Republic of China in the last decade, to help the Chinese, have been given preferential treatment. Their quarters are often far more modern than those of a typical Chinese. The expatriate is given perquisites in excess of those available to all but the top officials, fed with highest quality food, and paid salaries many times higher than paid to their Chinese counterpart of the same status. They are sheltered from the harsh realities of Chinese life and are recipients of enormous courtesy and care.

There are three main reasons for this preferential treatment. First, as a poverty-stricken nation, the Chinese need to attract and retain foreigners to help them achieve a higher standard of living, by increasing their economic and technical level. Second, the Chinese believe that people from the developed nations are so used to modern comforts that they would not be able to function competently without them. Finally, there is simple pride. They want their country to be thought of favorably.

Exhibit 3   (cont.)

Social

Generally, the sociocultural behavior of the Chinese differs greatly from that of Western societies. Family is very important to them, and obligation to them takes precedence when it conflicts with work responsibilities. Those outside the family are treated with indifference and sometimes with contempt. Decision making evolves from the opinion and support of the family. The highest respect is given to elders and ancestors. The reverence for authority and order explains why the Chinese are so careful about getting consensus from everyone. An important ideal that is fostered by the family is harmony.

The Chinese do not believe in the concept of privacy. This absence of individuality and freedom is a way of life in China.

Laws Made to Be Broken

Due to their history of being encumbered by rules and taboos, the Chinese have developed a perverse and seemingly contradictory attitude toward laws and regulations. They tend to ignore them and break them to suit their purpose, as long as they think they can get away with it. A significant proportion of public Chinese behavior is based on political expediency, and not on their true feelings. Since their public, official behavior is more of a survival technique than anything else, they do not feel guilty about ignoring or subverting the system. It is something they do naturally as a way of getting by.

Importance of Human Resources Management in Organizations in China

The labor environment in China is influenced by six major factors. They are National Economic Plans, the Four Modernization Programs, Political Leadership, Chinese Cultural Values, Labor Unions, and the Special Economic Zones that is, SEZs. The SEZs were created specially for the conduct of the joint ventures with overseas countries. The main characteristics of the SEZs that are found in a joint venture are their dominating influence on matters pertaining to the employment wage system, organizational structure, management roles and decision making.

One of the most interesting aspects of Chinese HRM is the unmistakable influence of some of the traditional cultural values such as *guanxi* (relationship), *renqing* (favor), *mianzi* (face), and *bao* (reciprocation) in recruitment and selection, training and development, and placement and promotion.

There is a definite political element involved in the behavior of Chinese Personnel managers; those who are more party-oriented base their decisions on party policies rather than for the good of the company.

Maintaining Personnel Files and Their Implications

Chinese-style personnel management generally does not forgive or forget any real or imagined past transgressions by employees under their jurisdiction. Any past mistakes or offenses committed by the employee are duly recorded in the employee's file and are often used against that person.

To hire someone from another company, the other company must release the prospective employee's file. This contains the employee's work record and entitles him or her to benefits accorded to workers in the state sector. If the employer is not willing to release the file and the employee leaves, he or she loses the benefits, a risk few Chinese are willing to take. Many foreign companies have been able to complete transfers only after compensating the other company. The average payoff has been about 1,000 yuan (in 1992), a very modest amount in $US but one half of one month's salary for a translator.

The Chinese can be said to be ethnocentric, that is, the belief that one's own national or regional management practices are superior. This can carry over into the review and acceptance of an employee's file from other provinces. The employee's previous place of employment can impact his future job prospects. In this case, the Shanghainese would look with disfavor on an employee file (and therefore the individual) from the poorer, less sophisticated Chongming Dao area.

A related culture difference is that a foreign manager would examine an employee's file from the perspective of performance, whereas a Chinese manager would review the file to learn of an individual's seniority and to see if there is a history of causing dissention.

Rank

There are no official class distinctions in China, but rank among businesspeople and government bureaucrats is very important. It is very important that you know the rank of the individual you are likely to deal with and your response should be consistent with the rank. Connections and rank gain one access to the *tequan* or special privileges. If the top official is accompanied by the second in rank, all the discussion should be directed toward the top official and the second in rank might as well not be present.

Exhibit 3   (cont.)

Manufacturing and Quality Control in China

In general, the Chinese have only a rudimentary understanding of quality concepts. They almost always carry out 100 percent inspections to "control" quality. Because the Chinese have become accustomed to inferior quality goods, producing goods of high quality is often not perceived by workers to be important. Those items that do not pass quality control are offered to the employees free of charge.

There is great variety in the quality of technology used in China. For the most part the technological level resembles that of the United States in the 1950s. There is scant computerization. Materials handling is done manually. Machinery is bulky and frequently needs repair.

Scheduling of work is almost nonexistent, though work itself is assigned to groups. A typical manufacturing operation is very labor-intensive, and in most cases there is an excessively large workforce. Production planning is usually based on the number of hours to be worked rather than on the number of units to be manufactured.

Infrastructure

China's economy suffers from weak infrastructure. Electricity is unavailable at times (especially if the firm has exceeded its quota). Roads need repairs, train shipments are more often than not late, factory allocations of raw materials are (occasionally) routed to other units, and the communication systems can be considered a nightmare.

Additional Note

Neither Geert Hofstede's original study (Hofstede, 1980) nor his later work (Hofstede and Bond, 1988) included China as a country of analysis. However, Hong Kong and Taiwan were included in both instances. The results were similar for Power Distance (Large), Individualism (Low), Uncertainty Avoidance (Low), and Confucianism (High), differing only in Masculinity (Hong Kong, high and Taiwan, low). We would therefore expect top-down decision making, centralized authority, little participative management, tolerance of uncertainty, and authority vested only in the most senior employees. This confirms the events described in the case.

orientation training, they found the Chinese to be gregarious and fun-loving during meals. Meals were used as an opportunity to build relationships and share experiences.

JAMES'S RECALL AND DEPARTURE

Then one day, early in February 1994, James received the call from Singapore, which proved to be the most disappointing news he had heard during his entire China experience. Controls had chosen to recall him back to home office. He was directed to train his replacement and return home within the month.

Things had been going very well for several months now, and he was accomplishing a great many things. There was still so much he planned to do, including to convince the Chinese JV partner that they needed to reduce the number of workers significantly.

While he and Lily handled the news and the return arrangements with a great deal of dignity,

there was a great sense of disbelief and sadness associated with the recall. Jimmy Chao, his replacement, arrived two weeks later. Jimmy was a Singaporean engineer whose experience was limited to supervising production at one of Control's factories in that country. James spent as much time getting him up to speed as was possible. Jimmy was 18 years younger than James, quite cocky and very opinionated and aggressive. While James provided all the coaching that he could, Jimmy was bound to do things his way.

The scene at the ferry when they departed the island for the last time was incredible. Many of the workers and all of the managers supplied by the Chinese partner were there to see them off. Many tokens of appreciation and affection were exchanged.

The plane droned inexorably on. James had, by this point in the trip, "rerun the tapes" of his whole experience over and over in his mind, and again thought about how blessed he felt to have had the experience at all. What recommendations should I make in my report and during my debriefings? If I really think they are heading for the "ditch" it is my responsibility to steer them away from it. Oh well, these questions will have to wait until another day. It is time to get some sleep. I wonder what the temperature is in Pauley?

NOTES

Hendryx, Steven R. "The China Trade: Making the Deal Work." *Harvard Business Review* (July–August 1986): 75–84.

Hofstede, Geert. *Cultures' Consequences: International Differences in Work Related Values*, Beverly Hills, CA: Sage Publications, 1980.

———, and Bond, Michael H. "The Confucius Connection: From Cultural Roots to Economic Growth." *Organizational Dynamics* (Spring 1988): 5–21.

Hu, Wenzhong, and Grove, Cornelius. *Encountering the Chinese: A Guide for the Americans.* Yarmouth, ME: Intercultural Press Inc., 1993.

Kumar, Saha Sudhir. "Managing Human Resources in China." *Canadian Journal of Administrative Science* 10, no. 2 (Summer 1991): 167–177.

Macleod, Roderick. *How to Do Business with the Chinese.* New York: Bantam Books, 1988.

Wall, Jr., James J. "Managers in the People's Republic of China." *Academy of Management Executives* 4, no. 2 (1990): 19–32.

Yeung, Irene Y. M., and Tung, Rosalie L. "Achieving Business Success in Confucian Societies: The Importance of Guanxi." *Organizational Dynamics* (Autumn 1996): 54–65.

Case 14 South African Breweries Group

Wealth is not created in a vacuum. Our commitment to generating profits is matched by our regard for good corporate citizenship.
—GROUP CHIEF EXECUTIVE GRAHAM MACKAY

Mission: South African Breweries is an international company committed to achieving sustained commercial success, principally in beer and other beverages, but with strategic investments in hotels and gaming. We achieve this by meeting the aspirations of our customers through quality products and services and by sharing fairly among all stakeholders the wealth and opportunities generate. Thereby, we fulfill our goals of business growth and maximized long-term shareholder value, while behaving in a socially responsible and progressive manner.

As Graham Mackay looked out of his office window, he reflected on the just-announced joint venture project with Narang Industries, Ltd. in India. The venture created South African Breweries India and gave the new company 60 percent control of Narang Breweries located in Nawabganj, Uttar Pradesh, northeast of Delhi.

As he pondered the expansions, Mackay turned and looked at the Corporate Governance Award which South African Breweries (SAB) received in 1998 and thought about how the company had grown since he took over almost a decade ago. In its corporate profile of SAB, the judges for the award noted that SAB excelled in "ethical expression" and outstanding integrity in conducting its business operations.

With that in mind, he turned his attention to the Beer South Africa Division and the follow-up of their implementation of the Equity III plan. While good progress had been made towards making the upper ranks of the division more ethnically diversified, there were shortfalls which needed to be addressed. He thought about how the press, the trade unions and the South African government would perceive

SAB's efforts to strengthen diversity, equity, and dignity throughout their South African operations. It had been a year since the plan was implemented, and the internal audit would take place in a few weeks. The audit's findings would be forwarded to the South African government in accordance with the dictates of the Equity Employment Act of 1998. He had scheduled a meeting with the Managing Director of the Beer South Africa Division, Norman Adami, and his Human Resources Director, R. J. Davis, to discuss the issues surrounding Equity III.

THE GLOBAL BEER INDUSTRY

Four companies dominate the global beer industry: Anheuser-Busch, Heineken, South African Breweries, and Miller Brewing Company. Each of the companies enjoyed a home market profit center for decades; Anheuser-Busch and Miller in the United States, Heineken in Europe, and SAB in South Africa. In order to grow their respective businesses, each company sought to expand their operations internationally in order to capitalize on new opportunities.

SOUTH AFRICAN BREWERIES LTD.

South African Breweries was founded in 1895 in response to the demand by gold miners in the Witwatersrand region and Johannesburg. Prior to the introduction of beer, the miners' drink of choice in the dusty prospecting fields was raw potato spirits mixed with tobacco juice and pepper. Small wonder that the new beer was well received.

In 1897 SAB listed on the Johannesburg Exchange and a year later their premium brand, Castle Lager, was launched. The company grew steadily throughout the Twentieth Century and underwent extensive growth by buying several other breweries in 1956. In the late 1960s, the company diversified into food products and property management. The diversification reached is zenith in 1974 when the company went into mass market retailing by buying the Bazaars Department Store chain. By 1976, though, after stockholders had punished the company by pushing the stock price to an all-time low, SAB reorganized and reevaluated its mission and objectives. SAB decided to focus its strategy on its core competency of manufacturing and distributing beer and reorganized accordingly.

Once those changes were made, the SAB Group structure began to reflect its current form.

South Africa was excluded from the United Nations from 1974 to 1990. Throughout these sixteen years, SAB pursued a domestic policy of purchasing cross-holdings in other South African firms. At the same time, they hedged their international holdings by purchasing properties through the Westgate International Group in Holland and the United Kingdom. During this period, the company bought several breweries in South Africa and eventually controlled 98 percent of the South African beer market.

Cross-holding was a form of capitalization for South African companies because the local capital markets were drying up due to the international boycott of the country. As the boycott dragged on, many multinationals left the country, taking with them badly needed capital and jobs. The cross-holdings led to the creation of six mega-corporations, one of which was SAB, which had an incredible amount of control over the local economy.

Once apartheid ended in 1990 and international sanctions were lifted, SAB began a massive sell-off of its cross-holdings. It divested itself of most of its diversified assets, but still maintained a sizeable number of glass retail outlets for automotive and construction supplies. This injection of fresh capital gave SAB the flexibility to pursue new opportunities.

SAB invested over US $650 million between 1995 and 1998 to upgrade its South African facilities. The company committed US $825 million for international expansion, and throughout the 1990s the company expanded extensively in sub-Saharan Africa, Central and Eastern Europe, and in China. As SAB focused on emerging and developing markets, it had to reorganize itself for the process.

THE MOVE TO LONDON 1999— SOUTH AFRICAN BREWERIES PLC

In order to access cheaper capital for expansion and investments, South African Breweries PLC was formed in December 1998 and listed on the London Stock Exchange on March 8, 1999. With the listing, the firm raised over US $500 million and promptly used the funds to buy the China operations of Fosters, buy the Czech brewers Pilsner Urquell and Radegast, and to retrench itself by repurchasing stock from its largest shareholders. This strategy made SAB the third largest beer distributor in the world.

In 1998, SAB had US $5.653 billion in sales, which was a 2.9 percent increase over that of the previous year. Its net income was US $240 million, which was a 50 percent increase over the net income earned in 1997. This was due in large part to a decrease of 24,000 personnel over twelve months in an effort to streamline operations. In December 1999, the South African Breweries Group had 49,000 employees worldwide.

ORGANIZATION

South African Breweries Group is a multi-division company which operates in nineteen countries worldwide, with Graham Mackay as the Group Chief Executive directing operations from London. The Beer South Africa Division (known as Beer South Africa) is Johannesburg-based, and is the country's largest brewer with 98 percent market share. Its Castle Lager brand accounts for half of its domestic sales. Other local brands include Hansa Pilsner, Ohlsson's Lager, along with a dozen other micro brands throughout the country.

The South African Breweries International Division (SABI) concentrates on international operations and has extensive interests in Africa (outside South Africa), China and Eastern Europe. SABI has thirty brewing operations in eighteen countries producing 30.5 million hectoliters annually. SABI has been the main growth engine for the SAB Group during the past decade. The division is organized by region: SABI-Africa, SABI-Europe, and SABI-Asia.

In Africa, SABI employs 7,000 people and has a brewing capacity of 10 million hectoliters. SABI-Africa operates in Angola, Ghana, Kenya, Mozambique, Tanzania, Uganda, Zambia, and Zimbabwe.

SABI-Europe has operations in Poland, Romania, Hungary, Slovakia, Russia, and the Czech Republic. In 1999, with the acquisition of the Czech producers Pilsner Urquell and Redegast, SAB became the largest beer producer in Eastern Europe.

SABI-Asia acquired the minority interest in five Fosters' breweries in China in 1999. SABI owns 49 percent of CRE, a joint venture with China Resources Enterprises Limited (CRE) which holds the remaining 51 percent. CRE is listed on the Hong Kong Stock Exchange. China is the second largest beer market in the world in terms of consumption, with 187 million hectoliters sold in 1997, and is currently growing at over 10 percent annually. The Chinese beer market was projected to become the largest beer market in the world within five years of 1998, and SABI is the top foreign brewer in the country.

The Other Beverage Division had a mixture of a large number of niche market companies that mainly operated in Africa. From joint ventures with Coke, to providing fruit and soft drinks to the various African markets, this division was very adept at finding niches and capitalizing on the opportunities.

The Hotel and Gaming Division under the South Sun name operated numerous hotels and casinos primarily in South Africa. They controlled 75 hotels with 12,600 rooms and held the exclusive right to the Inter-Continental and Holiday Inn brands in South Africa. Southern Sun also has a 50% stake in Tsogo Sun, which currently operates three casinos in South Africa.

The Plate Glass & Shatterprufe Industries Division is an automobile glassmaker that SAB purchased in the 1980s. SAB's move into producing windshields was more an extension of its bottling expertise than a direct desire to get into the automotive supplies business. It had been, and continued to be, a quite profitable business.

Eighty percent of the Group's corporate profits were from the Beer South Africa and South African Breweries International Divisions.

SOUTH AFRICA

The Republic of South Africa is composed of nine provinces covering approximately 473,000 square miles, which is roughly twice the size of Texas. The topography is that of a plateau with rolling hills and coastal plains. The Limpopo and Orange are the major river systems, although fast-flowing seasonal rivers traverse Natal and parts of the Cape. Surface water is always in short supply and is becoming more of a sustainability issue with each passing year.

There were approximately 40 million people in South Africa in 1998, and there is a wide range of cultural diversity. The ethnically mixed population is 76 percent black, 12 percent white, and 12 percent mixed and Asian. The African language groups represented include Zulu (39 percent), Xhosa (11 percent), Sotho (27 percent), and Tswana (6 percent), with several other smaller dialects making up the rest. This diversity makes South Africa one of the most pluralist societies in the world. Often known as the "Rainbow Society," this diversity poses both opportunities and challenges for business leaders and their employees.

THE PAST

In 1948, institutionalized apartheid became law. The legislation prohibited Blacks from owning property or businesses. With all businesses in the hands of the Whites, powerful Black unions emerged as a voice for the disenfranchised. Throughout the 1970s and 1980s, the clash between Whites and Blacks intensified, and the distinction between the haves and hav-nots became more pronounced, particularly in the Black townships.

In 1990, South Africa began dismantling the apartheid system and in April 1994, South Africa held its first democratic and universal election ushering in a new era in the turbulent history of the country. The multiparty election was won by Nelson Mandela's African National Congress (ANC). The ANC was an outlawed political movement from its inception in the early days of apartheid until 1990, when the White-led South African government yielded to international pressures, recognized the party, and released its leader from political imprisonment.

The ANC political power base had two factions. The left-wing faction is concerned with social justice and addressing the issues of prior inequalities. Often this faction points to the fact that unemployment and under-employment in South Africa stands at 40+ percent. They note that 90 percent of South Africa's economy is controlled by 15 percent of the population and six large conglomerates, including South African Breweries. The left's aim was to socially engineer South Africa so that the wealth would be more evenly distributed among the population.

The center-faction of the ANC was known as the Realists. While they sought to redress many of the injustices done under apartheid, they realized that in order to provide employment for the people, South Africa must be a place where businesses, both local and foreign, wanted to invest.

The new South African constitution was described as one of the most liberal in the world.

Observers pointed to the series of laws that were passed, which sought to redress the injustices of the past. One law, strongly supported by the unions, required the unbundling of the mutually owned businesses in order to give non-Whites a chance at ownership. New laws also required that companies show in the three- to five-year business plans a dedicated effort to make the demography of South Africa represented in all levels of the company, particularly in management.

THE EMPLOYMENT EQUITY ACT OF 1998

In October 1998, the South African government passed the Employment Equity Act. It was the government's affirmative action policy. The Act sought to remedy the imbalances in employment opportunities that resulted from the apartheid policies. The law mandated that all companies operating in South Africa implement an affirmative action program using measures designed to further the diversity of the workforce based on equal dignity and respect of all people. These measures included the elimination of unfair practices that affected people from designated groups; the making of reasonable accommodation for these groups such that they could enjoy equal opportunities; and representation of such groups in all levels of the workforce. Additionally, the retraining and developing of these groups could include preferential treatment but not quotas.

The new legislation required companies to focus on three areas; the first banning unfair discrimination in hiring, promoting, training, pay and benefits, and layoffs. The second was an organizational transformation to remove unreasonable barriers to employment for any South African regardless of ethnicity. The third was the acceleration of appointing, training, and promoting persons from disadvantaged communities.

THE CHANGING BUSINESS ENVIRONMENT

When apartheid ended in 1990, sanctions were lifted and South African firms were forced to compete globally. In the past, the sanctions insulated South African businesses, and government subsidies provided a form of price protection from foreign competition. Also, government regulations, particularly labor laws, made it difficult for companies to cut back on wages and jobs. These practices slowed South African businesses' responses to global pressures and competition.

There were attempts by South African and foreign companies to employ workers from outside of South Africa who were very willing and ready to work for lower wages. These actions caused great resentment, and South Africans accused the foreigners of "taking our jobs."

DEVELOPING PEOPLE

Management research and practice suggested that poor personnel management in organizations led to hidden costs such as decreased productivity and an increase in missed deadlines, poor customer service, accidents, absenteeism, and high employee turnover. The cost effectiveness of good personnel management was a widely held belief in business, but evidence of its practical implementation in South Africa was not common. Historically, in South Africa, there was a tendency for employees to be promoted because of their technical efficiency rather than their people-management skills. During the 1970s and 1980s, managerial domination of the corporate hierarchy meant that the individualistic and patronizing style of people-management survived and thrived. However, global trends made these attitudes obsolete, and the current competitive environment forced personnel management issues to the forefront as one of the most important strategic issues in companies.

BEER SOUTH AFRICA

A staff of seven department heads supported N. J. Adami, Managing Director of Beer South Africa. The departments were broken out by function: Northern and Southern South African Operations, Marketing, Finance, Technical Assistance, Corporate Affairs (Public Relations), and Human Resource (HR) Management. R. J. Davies was the HR department head and was supported by a staff divided into planning, staffing, and personnel policy functions. It was this department that was responsible for ensuring that Beer South Africa complied with the Employment Equity Act of 1998.

EQUITY I

Twenty-seven years before the 1998 Act, in 1971, SAB had an Equity Employment Plan. It was at the forefront of addressing social inequities in its hiring, promoting, and training practices. The intention was to significantly increase the number of African, Asian, and Black people throughout the salaried staff ranks so that the salaried ranks were more demographically representative of the markets they served. In 1971, only 1 percent of Blacks occupied salaried positions, but by 1978 they constituted 13 percent of the total Beer South Africa's salaried staff. The significant increase was achieved by appointing and promoting them into salaried jobs that were required as a consequence of the ongoing growth in demand for beer during this period.

The shortcomings of this period were that the staff profile still failed to reflect the market profile in terms of race, and most Blacks were appointed in functions outside of the technical fields. The technical fields, such as brewmaster, productions controller, etc., were still predominantly filled by Whites, and it was from these career areas that senior managers were selected.

After thirty-six months, the equity program was reviewed and several lessons were learned. The first was that the line managers had to be held accountable for implementing the equity plan. The second was that the plans had to be realistic in their scope and in their timeframe in terms of execution. The third was that line positions had to be targeted and Blacks identified and developed to fill those positions. This meant strategic manpower plans and career plans for Black and White employees needed to be developed. Once there were plans, then there had to be extensive education and training throughout the company to change the organizational culture and climate so that these diversity plans were seen, not as a hindrance, but rather as an enabler to success.

EQUITY I REVISIONS

After the shortfalls were identified, the company then took action and made adjustments to the program. The most significant development of this phase was that the Revised Equity I initiatives were placed on par with Beer South Africa's other main business strategies such as marketing, personnel staffing and training, production quality, and cost reductions.

A target was set to achieve a 50/50 mix between Black and White salaried employees on an integrated basis by 1990, with all employees being competent in their positions. Individual managers' promotions and bonuses would depend as much on performance in equity as on performance in the traditional areas of sales growth and cost control. And there would be no token jobs, because everyone in the company had to have a real job and would be evaluated by common performance standards.

From 1975 to 1990, the number of salaried Blacks increased to 46 percent, and although the target of 50 percent was not reached, the company came very close to achieving it. While the results were substantial during this time period, the drive to continue equity initiatives further had significantly slowed within the division. In 1990, another equity assessment was conducted in Beer South Africa's plants and operational centers to evaluate the overall effectiveness of the program. This survey revealed that the equity program had lost its momentum among managers who felt that it had a negative effect on their bottom line. These managers preferred to put equity on the back burner and to concentrate instead on dealing with the difficulty of operating a profitable business unit during the economic downturn.

EQUITY II

Graham Mackay, who believed that this program had to be championed by the most senior people in the organization, launched Equity II in 1992. In particular, he recognized the need to tighten up on discipline and monitoring in order to eliminate the inertia that sought to put the equity initiatives on the back burner.

The primary thrust of this initiative was to affirmatively integrate Beer Division's employees so that they were representative of South Africa's race groups at all levels and in all disciplines. The next part of the program was to ensure that all work practices and facilities were standardized and that job descriptions were uniform across the division. The division was committed to education and training the quest to eradicate social prejudices and attitudes in the workplace. Finally, the company pro-actively directed corporate social investment toward redressing past social inequities. This involved directing contracts of non-core services and products to Black-owned businesses.

Between 1992 and 1998, tremendous progress was made. Blacks constituted 53 percent of salaried staff, and by 1994 there were detailed three-year Equity II plans in all plants countrywide. The development and implementation of shared values and vision created teamwork and an esprit de corps throughout the company. All product teams, stakeholders, and individuals were required to commit themselves to the necessary behavioral changes demanded by this program, and it provided a rallying point for the whole organization.

EQUITY III

When the Employment Equity Act became law in 1998, SAB conducted another review in order to learn from Equity II and develop a new plan. The requirements in the Employment Equity Act were very similar to the existing equity initiatives at SAB.

The challenge in conceptualizing and developing a new Equity III program was to go beyond the paradigms of the past and devise a strategy that would take both global and local trends into account and provide the possibility for further change and improvement. Championed by Graham Mackay and Norman Adami, Beer South Africa's Equity III program was launched in late 1998, and its primary thrust was to leverage the human resource diversity throughout the division to create a global competitive advantage for the firm. Diversity was central to supporting all other core strategies in achieving the corporate goals and ultimately the firm's vision and mission.

Increased productivity, channel marketing, and personnel development focused on international growth and expansion were the core strategies that the Equity III initiatives supported. Equity III's strategy was complex, multifaceted and multi-layered. The strategy had four primary objectives: headcount targets, personnel management, human dignity initiatives, and commercial equity investments in the communities.

Setting personnel numbers that were representative of the demographic market that the employees came from was seen as a top priority. This was also to be extended to disabled persons. Ensuring that facilities and operations were modified, where possible, to accommodate and take advantage of this talent pool was seen as a way to gain and retain top personnel talent.

Personnel development was to receive even more resources, particularly in the area of hiring, training, and retaining top Black managerial talent. Competency standards were to be further developed and then, through a system of education and training, these standards would be met and internal certificates issued to those who showed that they had learned the material. Target numbers were set for promoting Black managers into the upper levels of SAB management.

The third prong of Equity III was the focus on human dignity. The objective was to move from the elimination of discrimination to the valuing of diversity in the organization. This education and training process was designed to positively impact the subtle and unwritten norms that affected interactions at every level of the organization. By conducting training, self-assessment, and practical skills development, the firm sought to eliminate all forms of structural discrimination within the division. The elimination of the more subtle, residual, and discriminatory behaviors was going to be difficult because it dealt with personal core values and beliefs that had been ingrained for years in each person. Overcoming mistrust and suspicion was seen as necessary to creating a cohesive working environment among the division's employees.

Commercial equity was Beer South Africa's commitment to good social responsibility. The objective was to contribute to the development of a stable socioeconomic environment by supporting the growth and development of small, micro, and medium Black-owned entrepreneurial ventures. To further this, efforts were undertaken to facilitate the transfer and sharing of technical and business skills through the promotion of partnerships and joint ventures.

INITIAL RESULTS

At the end of 1999, there were 49,000 people in nineteen countries working for the South African Breweries Group; 59 percent of them had been with the company for at least five years.

In South Africa, the remuneration for employees amounted to 40 percent of the after-tax profits (only taxation took a bigger share of the sales revenue). Benefits included accident, medical, and health insurance, and included welfare in the form of housing subsidies, education, and training benefits. Within the country, Beer South Africa was consistently at the high end of the spectrum in terms of pay and benefits.

With the goal of developing its people, 34,000 employees were trained and over US $17 million was spent to ensure that the training was aligned with the goals outlined in Equity III. The Beer South Africa Training Institute was named a benchmark candidate by the International Benchmark Forum, the judges of the best world-class training practices. Additionally, the Competency Acquisition Process (CAP) was one of the best in South Africa and the world for assuring world-class brewing standards in its production facilities.

In the area of knowledge management, the Beer Division established BEERnet, the firms Intranet. Managed by Human Resources, the system provided access to internal and external courses, journals, magazines, key training documents, web sites, videos, seminars, and conferences. There was an exponential increase in the use of these tools to develop the skills of the employees during the first eighteen months of use.

THE FUTURE

In order to be competitive in the global market, Graham Mackay felt that valuing and utilizing the diversity throughout the organization would provide a tremendous strategic advantage. Even though there had been shortfalls, he remained passionately committed to the Equity III program. As the Group Chief Executive, he knew that he had to reaffirm his vision through communication and action. Upon reflecting on the rapid changes his firm had undergone, he knew that he needed to ensure that more leaders were trained and given the resources to help them achieve their objectives. Now he had to prepare for his meeting with Norman Adami to discuss what the upcoming Equity III audit would reveal.

Case 15   Maywood Inc.

Establishing a Regional Branch Office in Singapore[1]

INTRODUCTION

Gary Lowery had just completed the first year of a three-year assignment with Maywood Inc. in Singapore. Gary was reflecting on his assignment and how much progress both he and the company had made in the past year. Certainly he had enjoyed the assignment and all the excitement. He did not mind the long working hours required to complete all the days' tasks, but he was somewhat concerned that he was not able to spend as much time with his family as he would like.

Even though Gary had made significant progress in setting up the Asia-Pacific Sales and Marketing Headquarters, he still wondered if he had accomplished all that he should have. Was he handling personnel issues in a manner that was legal and ethical? Had he effectively communicated his concerns and experiences back to corporate staff in the United States? Gary pondered the question of whether he had adjusted his management style enough or gone too far in accepting the management style and business methods that were expected by the Singaporeans. He thought back to his MBA training, remembering the subject of Hofstede's dimensions, specifically the power distance concept (see Appendix I), and wondered if his management style was appropriate for Singapore.

In addition, Gary was pondering a recent meeting where he seemed to have upset the power bal-

ance. Had he lost face so badly that he could not recover, or should he press on with his ideals? Moreover, had he also caused an Indian engineer and his Chinese managers to lose face? Was his participative management style really appropriate for the business culture in Singapore? Reflecting on these thoughts, Gary wondered what, if anything, he could or should do differently in the coming year to improve his performance and assist in achieving corporate goals associated with penetrating the Asia-Pacific market.

Finally, Gary thought about the company as a whole—was it prepared for international expansion? Did the company have the knowledge and resources to effectively implement its defined strategy to develop and penetrate international markets, in particular the Asia-Pacific region?

COMPANY BACKGROUND

Maywood Inc. is a multinational manufacturing firm that produces electronic products. Its world headquarters are located in an upper Midwestern state in the United States. Maywood Inc. began in the mid-1950s as a high-quality producer of both finished television sets and component parts. At that time, Maywood's products were designed and manufactured in North America. Over the years, Maywood Inc. grew domestically and its product lineup grew to include many other electronic products. In the mid-1980s, Maywood Inc., determined to increase both revenues and profits, decided to expand into global markets. At first, Maywood Inc. focused on exporting—selling its domestically designed and manufactured products in international markets. However, it soon became apparent that this strategy would not result in the company meeting its objectives and Maywood Inc. would have to manufacture products in the region in which they were to be sold. First, competitors had the advantage of lower wage rates compared to those Maywood Inc. was paying in North America. Maywood's prices for comparable products were 20 to 40 percent higher than those that competitors were offering. Second, customers were

This case was prepared by John Stanbury, Assistant Professor of International Business at Indiana University, Kokomo, and Gary Mitchell, MBA Student, with additional assistance from Mary Green, MBA Student. It is not intended to illustrate either effective or ineffective handling of a managerial situation. The views represented here are those of the case authors and do not necessarily reflect those of the Society for Case Research. The authors' views are based on their own professional judgments.

The names of the organization, and the industry in which it operates, and individuals' names and the events described in this case have been disguised to preserve anonymity.

Presented to the Society for Case Research. All rights reserved to the authors and SCR. Copyright 1998.

demanding that products be manufactured locally. This pressure came in the form of nationalistic pride, prohibitively high import tariffs, and direct government legislation. Thus, in the late 1980s, Maywood Inc. decided to expand manufacturing facilities to include sites in strategic regions of the world.

Maywood's management determined that one of its first overseas manufacturing facilities should be located in or near the large Asian market. There were several reasons for this strategy. First, the Asian market was already fairly well developed. There was a large demand for the type of products that Maywood Inc. made since the consumers in this part of the world had the disposable income to purchase the products. Second, there was a large supply of relatively skilled, low-cost labor in this region that would help Maywood Inc. with competitive pricing pressures. Third, manufacturing in the targeted sales region would substantially reduce transportation costs to ship finished goods to customers.

The company eventually decided to build a manufacturing plant in Singapore. Singapore was attractive for several reasons. First, Singapore was centrally located to the markets that Maywood Inc. desired to serve in Asia. Second, Singapore had a large workforce of highly skilled and educated employees. Third, the labor cost in Singapore, though not as low as in China or other developing nations, was attractive and would allow Maywood Inc. to meet its cost targets for its products. Fourth, English was the primary language in the Singaporean business community, and that would facilitate communications with corporate offices in the United States. Conversely, this would also allow the American expatriates to communicate easily with the Singaporean workers. Fifth, the cost of living in Singapore was reasonable, which means that employees at the plant could enjoy a decent standard of living. Sixth, the government in Singapore was stable, resulting in a low risk of capital investment loss due to erosion of inflationary pressure or nationalization of the plant by the Singapore government. Finally, Singapore accepted and gave much better treatment to female employees than either Japan or Korea; this was deemed important since the manufacturing facility would employ a large proportion of women.

For the past several years, the Maywood Inc. plant in Singapore has been run almost entirely by nationals. The plant director's position, formerly held by an American expatriate, has recently been turned over to a Singaporean employee. Only two expatriates remain at the facility—a production manager and an engineering manager.

The Singapore Manufacturing Facility is run very efficiently, and the outgoing product quality is world class. The plant is currently building several of Maywood's product lines. However, Maywood Inc. had yet to win many significant contracts in the Asian markets in the first few years of operations of the manufacturing plant, and most of the products manufactured there were shipped back to North America. Asian customers seemed to be hesitant to source products from such a new production facility. It was thought that unproven quality was a main reason for this reluctance. However, with the manufacturing plant in operation and producing high-quality goods for several years, Maywood Inc. has begun to win several significant contracts to supply its products in various Asian markets.

By the early 1990s, Maywood Inc. realized that it needed to increase its presence in this growing Asian market. A manufacturing facility alone was not enough to support this enormous market potential in the region. Maywood Inc. desperately needed a coordinated team of sales and marketing personnel located in the region to support its many current and potential customers. Along with this, it needed applications engineers who could understand the requirements of the markets and create product designs or develop appropriate product modifications. Therefore, Maywood Inc. created an Asia-Pacific division and named a vice president to establish a regional marketing operation. Maywood Inc. decided that Singapore would be an ideal location in which to establish this organization. (See Appendix II for a partial organizational chart of Maywood Inc.)

SINGAPORE

History

Singapore is an island equivalent in size to Chicago (640 km^2) and is located at the lower tip of Malaysia. The population in Singapore is a little more than 2.8 million people, yielding more than 4,200 people per km^2. Virtually everyone lives in urban areas.

Prior to World War II, Singapore had been a territory of Britain; however, during the war, the island was captured and occupied by the Japanese. Near the conclusion of World War II, the British recaptured control of Singapore. In 1963, Malaya, Singapore, North Borneo, and Sarawak joined to become the country of Malaysia. Then, in 1965, Singapore detached from Malaysia to become an independent republic and a member of the United Nations. Lee Kuan Yew, who had been prime minister since 1959, continued to lead Singapore until 1990 when he resigned. He has been credited with shaping Singapore into a solid economic power with racial harmony and national unity. He is still the leader of the People's Action Party and is a government adviser. Goh Chok Tong took over the leadership of Singapore and has continued Lee's policies. However, Goh's leadership is more liberal, allowing freer speech and fewer rules.

The Chinese comprise about 76 percent of the population, the Malays about 15 percent, and the Indians about 6 percent. The Indian population includes a number of different groups speaking various languages and following several religions including Hinduism, Islam, Buddhism, Jainism, and Sikism. Malay, Chinese, Tamil, and English are all official languages of Singapore! Malay is the indigenous language. English is the "language of administration," which all Singaporeans are expected to learn. Although there are a number of Chinese dialects, Standard Chinese (Putonghua or Mandarin) is predominant.

Singaporeans are free to worship, unless the religion is labeled as antigovernment. The following is a breakdown of the religious community:

Religion	Practiced By
Buddhism or Taoism	About 50% of the population, mostly the Chinese
Islam	About 15% of the population, mostly the Malays with some Indians
Christianity	About 10% of the population, including Chinese, Indians, Caucasians, and Eurasians
Hinduism	About 5% of the population
Atheist or agnostic	A significant minority of the Chinese

Politics

Politically, Singapore is very stable. Wee Kim Wee is president and head of state, but Prime Minister Goh exercises executive authority and heads the government with his cabinet. The government owns the radio and television facilities, and licenses the privately owned newspapers. Education is highly valued in Singapore. All children aged 6 to 16 are required to go to school, which is free. Medical care, which is subsidized by the government, is considered excellent. Some strictly enforced laws include littering, jaywalking, spitting, and possession of drugs (potentially a capital offense). The government had previously launched a campaign (including monetary incentives) not to have more than two children per family. But the Singaporean growth rate slowed so much that now three children are recommended. The family system in Singapore is very strong, and there is a great respect for elders. It is not generally socially acceptable to live together or have children without being married.

Economy[2]

In comparison to most other nations in Asia, Singapore is very prosperous and stable economically due to fairly rapid industrial growth during the 1970s and 1980s. Major industries include electronics, clothing, plastic materials, and pharmaceuticals. In addition to industrial manufacturing, Singapore is also known for its shipping ports. It handles a variety of goods produced in Asia and shipped to the United States, Germany, and other Southeast Asian nations. Tourism and banking also play a large role in the Singaporean economy. Singapore has membership in the economic partnership called ASEAN—Association of Southeast Asian Nations. Similar to the NAFTA (North American Free Trade Association) or the EC (the European Community), member nations enjoy duty-free or reduced-rate trading with other ASEAN countries. The people of Singapore currently enjoy a rather high standard of living.

Maywood Inc. in Singapore

Although Maywood Inc. already employed several sales and engineering personnel throughout various Asian regions including Singapore, Japan, China, Korea, Malaysia, Thailand, Vietnam, the Philippines, Australia, India, and others, there was no coordination of Asian operations in the region. Maywood's upper management, the vice president of the Asia/Pacific Division in particular, saw this as a weakness in the organization. All the Asian staff were reporting to the Asia/Pacific director who was based in Kokomo, Indiana, in the United States. This arrangement was becoming very cumbersome due to the increasing number of overseas personnel as well as the 12- to 14-hour time difference. In order to become a viable entity in the Asian market, Maywood Inc. needed a focus in the Asian region. The vision was to create a Sales and Marketing Headquarters that could coordinate the activities of the existing Asian personnel as well as expand operations to meet the growing needs in this region. The plan was to have five Asian directors—Operations, Finance, Engineering, Sales, and Manufacturing—located in the headquarters and reporting back to the vice president of the Asia/Pacific Division in the United States. The Manufacturing director, already in place at the Singapore plant, would remain at the plant, however, rather than move to this new regional headquarters. The Operations director, in addition to his other responsibilities, would coordinate the activities of the other four directors. The Operations director, therefore, would be the focal point for all communications with corporate offices in the United States. However, as stated earlier, each of the five directors reports directly to the vice president of the Asia/Pacific Division who is located in the United States.

Maywood Inc. embarked on its expansion journey by selecting from its domestic facilities a small management team that could set up the new Sales and Marketing Headquarters facility. The expatriate management team to be selected consisted of a finance director, an engineering director, and an operations director, Gary Lowery. (The sales director's position would not be filled by an expatriate.) Gary has spent 20+ years with Maywood Inc. in a variety of assignments. He was hired out of college with a Bachelor of Science in Industrial Engineering to be a line supervisor in one of Maywood's U.S. manufacturing plants. When he had been at Maywood Inc. eight years, Gary completed his Master's degree in Business Administration from a nearby university. He had attended evening classes for four years to complete the degree. Eventually, Gary worked his way up to manager of Manufacturing Planning for one of

Maywoods' primary product lines. In this position, Gary was responsible for setting the manufacturing strategy, including where and how to build the products for his particular product line. He reported to Maywood's vice president of Operations. Also in that role, Gary had the opportunity to work with personnel in Europe and Asia. In particular, he has spent the last three years dealing (from a distance) with the Maywood Inc. manufacturing plant currently established in Singapore. Gary's performance was always top notch and he had gained the respect of several of the company's top management. When the Asian marketing Headquarters opportunity evolved, the vice president of the Asia/Pacific region, to whom the operations director would report, approached Gary and asked if he would be interested in the assignment. After a quick check with his wife and family, Gary enthusiastically agreed to be interviewed and considered for the position.

Each candidate was carefully selected based on qualifications, desire for international exposure, career potential, and experience, including prior international assignments. Strangely, there were no formally written job descriptions for any of the positions. This was new territory for Maywood Inc., and it was felt that roles and responsibilities would be documented as the team progressed in the assignment. The Finance, Engineering, and Operations directors passed through an initial interview with the vice president of the Asia/Pacific Region. About two weeks later, the potential new directors and their families were briefed and interviewed by a team of corporate human resource personnel. About a week later, Gary was informed that he had been chosen for the position of Operations director for the Asian Marketing Headquarters. Although Maywood's formal policy stated that all candidates were to be given a preliminary trip to Singapore with their spouses to check out the country and living conditions, Gary was never given this opportunity. He found that the procedure in place was for the candidate to accept the position first and then work out the details afterward. Fortunately, Gary has a very easygoing personality and was not bothered by this.

In the days following his acceptance, Gary found that his role for the Singapore assignment was viewed by the company as a "jack-of-all-trades." His responsibilities in Singapore, in addition to being the office manager, would cover many duties including public relations, human resources, maintenance, facilities, and security. Through his various assignments in manufacturing engineering and supervision, Gary had some experience in the areas of human resource management as well as facilities and maintenance; however, Gary had no experience dealing with security or public relations issues. Furthermore, his depth of knowledge in human resource management, maintenance, and facilities was certainly not as extensive as the new role would require. Even though many of these duties would be new to Gary, he looked forward to the increased responsibility and the ability to learn and deal with new challenges. He had the self-confidence to assure himself that he could resolve new issues as they occurred.

Approximately two weeks before the move to Singapore, Gary, along with the newly selected Finance and Engineering directors and their families, was sent to a three-day workshop in a neighboring state conducted by a company that specialized in training employees and their families in what to expect of an international work assignment. The company tailors the training to the specific country of the assignment—in this case, Singapore. The participants were given information on various aspects of living outside the United States. Separate training sessions were held for Gary, Linda (Gary's wife), Gary's children, and the whole family. The family training stressed that the family should expect differences, that differences were acceptable rather than necessarily right or wrong, and not to question any moral dilemmas that might develop. The family was also taught about the diversity of religions that they would encounter in Singapore. In addition, they learned some basic Malay and Chinese vocabulary and language skills, but nothing very extensive. Gary's training was intense, focusing on business practices, and started with the proper method of presenting a business card. Linda remembers being told what products she would and would not be able to purchase in Singapore. The children sampled various foods and were given assistance on projects that would be typical of those faced in Singapore schools.

Upon reflection, Gary thought the training was not particularly helpful or enlightening and could have been much better. Specifically, the training had focused on the culture of Singapore but had ignored the need to relate to the business environment in general and management practices, specifically. He had heard similar comments from other Maywood Inc. employees who had been through this training and wondered why Maywood Inc. continued to send its people to this expensive training if it was not seen as being effective. Prior to and during the assignment, Gary bought several books on Asian cultures which he thought gave much more useful insight than the training in Colorado. Gary often found such history and cultural books in airports as he traveled to the various locations in the region. Gary finished another of these books on the flight from the United States to Singapore. When he was done reading the books, he placed them in a small reference library at the Singapore plant so that other would-be travelers might gain use from them.

After the exhausting flight from the United States, Gary arrived at the Singapore airport at 1:00 A.M. Monday morning. The Singapore plant director met him at the airport and escorted Gary to the hotel where he would stay for the next several days. he settled into his hotel room and climbed into bed by 2:00 A.M. for a brief nap. He was expected to meet with a team of personnel at the existing Maywood Inc. manufacturing facility in Singapore only five hours from now, at 7:00 A.M. Personal matters kept Gary from leaving a day earlier, which would have given him a day to relax before going to work. Feeling the effects of the long flight, the 13-hour time change, and the short-night's sleep, he met with the local personnel and engineers in the manufacturing plant with whom he would be working closely. They were responsible for assisting him in setting up policies for the new Asian Marketing Headquarters. Gary would have preferred to take a day off to rest on Monday, but he thought it was important to begin to build relationships as soon as possible. Moreover, through the cultural training he received, Gary felt it would have given the wrong appearance if he had not gone right to work on his first day there. Gary spent most of the day touring the plant and meeting key individuals; he took time to jot down notes about the people and conversations so he would have a record of people's positions and other key information. Gary perceived that getting to know the people and developing relationships would be a key to cultivating *guanxi*. (*Guanxi* is a Chinese concept similar to networking in the United States.) *Guanxi* networks, however, are based on close personal relationships. [Putti] Building these relationshipss is extremely important, as they will help accomplish tasks more quickly. The development of *guanxi* is "a kind of social investment and incurs responsibility and obligation." [Chen] That is, *guanxi* relationships are reciprocal.

Toward what Gary thought was the end of his first day—around 4:30 in the afternoon—he retired to his temporary office and started to browse through the day's e-mails and voice mails he had received. At around 5:30, he was surprised to see that almost nobody in the office had left yet! Not wanting to be the first to leave, he decided to stay and compose a few responses to the many e-mails that required his attention. Six o'clock came and went, but the employees remained. At 6:30, however, Gary was exhausted and ready to go home, but many in the office still remained. At 7:00, he finally decided that he had to get back to the hotel for some much needed rest. This happened again the next several days—nobody was leaving before 7:00 or 7:30 in the evening. Finally, Gary approached one of the managers with whom he was beginning to confide and asked why people were staying so late. Gary, expecting to hear a response that the employees did not want to make a bad impression by leaving before he did, was surprised to hear that this was normal practice. The work ethic in Singapore was that one stayed at work until all the work for that day was done. Astonished, Gary pondered what would happen if the workers back in the States adhered to this practice.

In the days to follow, Gary's first task was to find a building or office space to house the new Marketing and support staff. Two managers from the plant accompanied him to various potential sites. They were selected by the Singapore Manufacturing Plant director, who chose them based on the relevance of their experience, personalities, and willingness to accept such a special assignment. It was expected that they would work closely with Gary for the first several months and then return to their previous jobs at the manufacturing plant. During the search for the new office site, the two Singaporean managers pointed out historical sites and other points of local interest. This helped Gary immensely in understanding the Singapore culture as well as just familiarizing him

with things the island nation had to offer. It took only about a week to locate what Gary thought would be an excellent location for the new office. It was a high-rise building less than 10 kilometers from the current manufacturing plant. The entire eighteenth floor of the building amazingly happened to be vacant. The floor number has particular significance in Singapore as Chinese tradition holds that the number eight signifies success! For this reason, the eighteenth floor rented for a premium in excess of the other floors in the building. However, the lease payment was just within the limit set by corporate offices, so Gary, conferring with his Singaporean associates, decided that it would be the best location for the new office.

During this same time, Gary's Singaporean work colleagues helped him locate suitable living quarters for him and his family. They found a very nice apartment located in a high-rise complex. Although this was quite a change from Gary's suburban home in the United States, which was a large ranch on more than one half of an acre of land, he was pleased with the accommodations.

In the next several days, Gary's task was to determine a layout for the new office. He worked very diligently planning the offices for the executives and the cubicles for the engineers, clerical employees, and other support staff. When he showed his plans to his Singaporean associates, they politely told him that his layout would not work in the Singapore culture. Gary had placed the executive offices along the perimeter of the building so as to give them the "window seats" that he was accustomed to seeing in Maywood's American facilities. The Singaporeans explained that placing the executives in a more central location would better promote *guanxi* and a good working environment. They further explained that physical layout and surroundings are a very important part of the Chinese culture and that the office should incorporate principles of Feng Shui. Gary reluctantly discarded his plans and asked the others to help him draft a layout proposal that would be more acceptable. (*Feng Shui* is the concept of trying to align man-made creations such as homes and office buildings with the natural environment. Man-made surroundings and environments should be designed to exist in harmony with the natural environment as well as to reflect elements of nature in their design.)

Soon after, Gary's wife and children traveled to Singapore. They were met at the airport by a manager from the Singapore manufacturing plant and taken to their apartment, since Gary was tied up at the office. He had signed the lease and moved into the high-rise apartment about a week earlier. They settled in quickly, being particularly pleased to see Gary for they had been separated for several weeks. On the day of their arrival Gary returned home at around 7:30 that evening, and found his family somewhat worried by his late arrival. They were glad to see each other, however, and the mood soon improved. Gary's family congratulated him on choosing such a nice apartment. Gary reflected on the generous help provided by his associates to locate this place. He was becoming more and more comfortable with these people and fully respected their recommendations for personal, business, cultural, and other matters.

The family cheer did not last very long, however, as Gary informed them that he had faxes to send, e-mail to both read and send, as well as a conference call with the United States at 9:00 that evening. His family was somewhat disappointed to learn that Gary's work had not ended when he left the office. The family knew from phone conversations over the past few weeks that Gary had been putting in long hours, but they assumed this would change when they arrived. They were in denial about the reality that their father and husband would have less time to spend with them than when they were back in the United States. Gary still had several hours of work ahead—phone calls to corporate management, faxes to send, and conferences with teams in the United States. Gary knew that he had adjusted fairly quickly to the amount of work required in this assignment and hoped his family would acclimate as quickly.

With the signing of the office lease, Gary set about trying to get it arranged for occupancy. Since Gary had developed a good relationship with the two managers who helped him select the office space and his apartment, he decided to ask the Singapore Manufacturing director if one of the two, J. L. Ong, could transfer to the new office to be his personal assistant. Gary was surprised, but delighted to hear that this was possible and that JL was honored to be chosen for this role. JL proved to be an invaluable asset—giving Gary cultural advice, knowledge of professional practices, and helpful hints.

Gary's next responsibility as Operations director was to hire the new employees who would staff the Asian Marketing Headquarters. Specifically, support staff was needed such as secretaries, accountants, and entry-level engineers. Gary developed profiles of the types of people he needed and gave these descriptions and qualifications to JL who worked with human resources personnel at the Singapore Manufacturing Plant to select candidates for interviews. Gary would have preferred to hire a head of human resources, but that was not in the budget. The human resources team ran an advertisement in the local newspaper, in part stating the following:

> Maywood Inc. has come to Singapore. Staffing is now in progress for its new regional Sales and Marketing headquarters. Get in on the ground floor of the Singapore extension of this US$7 Billion multinational company!"

In addition, candidate were sought for the position of director of Sales for this region. Because of the importance of this position, however, a search was conducted using an executive recruiting firm rather than the company's HR staff.

The newspaper advertisement generated great interest in Singapore, and soon the HR staff was swamped with resumes of highly qualified potential employees. Since Gary had many other responsibilities, JL and the human resources group from Maywood's Singapore manufacturing facility pre-screened resumes and candidates before Gary ultimately conducted the formal interview and employment screening meetings. Gary was pleased with the work JL and the HRM staff were doing, for the candidates he ultimately interviewed were well qualified for their respective positions. The candidates whom Gary met seemed to be from diverse races and religions. However, Gary had noticed that at the Maywood Inc. manufacturing plant in Singapore, every secretary and receptionist whom Gary met was Chinese. In addition, during the selection processes underway, Gary noticed that he was gently guided by JL and the other personnel to select Chinese candidates over Indians or Malays, for example, even for secretarial positions. Gary wondered whether the Chinese candidates were better qualified than the non-Chinese candidates, or if personal or systemic bias was involved in the employment selection process.

Gary was somewhat concerned because, if there were true biases being expressed by his selection committee, he felt the company might be liable for discrimination. In addition, treating others unfairly on racial grounds was a practice that Gary knew was illegal in the United States, and he considered it unethical as well. Gary was not particularly familiar with the governing laws in Singapore relating to such issues, so he confided in JL. He could tell that JL was uncomfortable with the question being posed, and JL did not seem to give a clear or direct answer. Gary desperately wanted and needed some legal advice. To Gary's surprise, the company did not have any lawyers either on staff or on retainer in Singapore who could be accessed directly for such issues. Thus far, Maywood's legal staff in the United States appeared to have handled all domestic as well as international legal issues. Hence, Gary asked his boss back in the United States, the vice president of the Asia/Pacific region, if he would check with the legal department about these issues. Gary's boss agreed, but Gary did not receive a quick response. Later, Gary learned that this boss had found from the legal department that U.S. law would not apply in Maywood's Asian operations except in the case of U.S. expatriates. The legal department was apparently not in a position to give Gary any counsel or direction on Singaporean law.

The issues of legality and application of America's Equal Employment Opportunity (EEO) laws were still gnawing at Gary. Thus, having had little success with Maywood's legal staff, Gary decided to do a bit of research himself. Through this research, Gary found that Title VII of the Civil Right Act contains the Equal Employment Opportunity information. Upon investigation, Gary determined that EEO laws could be applied to expatriates working for American multinational firms but not to indigenous employees. In other words, the American multinational firm needed to adhere to U.S. EEO laws in hiring and dealing with U.S. expatriates, but local laws govern how the other foreign workers can be treated. However, if the host country's laws contradict EEO, the American company may be exempt from prosecution emanating from those laws. Gary thus concluded that Singapore law, rather than U.S. law, would govern the treatment of the Singaporean employees. The fact that JL indicated the practices did not violate Singapore law

brought some closure to Gary's uncertainty. Gary also learned later that Maywood's U.S. legal department did have legal contacts in Singapore and other countries in the Asia-Pacific region, but they preferred that all questions and inquiries pass through the U.S. legal department for resolution.

During the actual interviewing process, Gary was initially shocked by the questioning and testing that was permissible and customary in Singapore. In stark contrast to U.S. employment laws, it seemed that very personal and private questions could be asked or any test could be given during the interview. Furthermore, the applicants answered the questions openly and honestly and seemed to accept this practice as much as JL and the HR representatives did. The questions were really aimed at getting to know the applicant at a personal level and to establish a relationship. Typical questions in an interview included the following that would be similar to those asked in the United States:

- ➤ Why did you leave your previous job?
- ➤ What type of position would you desire with our company?
- ➤ Where do you currently live?

Other typical questions asked in an interview included the following that would not generally be acceptable in the United States:

- ➤ What nationality are you?
- ➤ Where were you born?
- ➤ What type of immigration papers do you own?
- ➤ How much money did you make in your previous job?
- ➤ What organizations do you belong to?
- ➤ What does your spouse do?
- ➤ What do the other members of your family do, and what are their affiliations?

After a few weeks of these interviews and reassurance from JL that this was acceptable, Gary no longer felt uncomfortable about asking these types of questions in the interviewing process. In fact, he appreciated the wealth of knowledge such questioning gave him about each applicant and how the applicant would fit within the organization. The interviewing process allowed applicants to raise any questions they had about employment with Maywood Inc. Many applicants expressed a desire to work for an international company. Later, Gary discovered this was because expatriate managers were generally thought to be not as harsh or demanding as their Chinese counterparts. Nearly all applicants were concerned about the stability of the company and, oddly enough, about what job title they would receive. It seemed that without a suitable title, Singaporeans would not hire into a company or, if hired, might even quit. JL proposed appropriate job titles to Gary, and he accepted these almost without question.

Hiring began almost immediately, and soon there was an office full of employees. Only two months after having selected the Asian Marketing headquarters office location, a grand opening ceremony was conducted. Much thought, planning, and effort went into making this a successful and memorable event. Along with employees and their families, suppliers and customers were also invited. This ceremony was a large event that included food, speeches by Gary and other directors, and even a Chinese Lion dance accompanied by beating drums. The grand opening turned out to be a great success and served to promote the superstition that the business would now be granted good luck.

Gary's role broadened after the initial hiring and grand opening were complete. Even though the Asian Marketing Headquarters was not a subsidiary but really just a branch sales office, Gary had a great deal of responsibility to bring revenue and profits to the company. He was responsible for making the Asian Marketing Headquarters a success. He had to coordinate meetings to facilitate the flow of information between the regional Sales and Marketing forces, the engineering design team, the manufacturing plant, and corporate headquarters in the United States. The goal of the entire Asia/Pacific operating unit was to locate new customers, determine their needs, and then design and manufacture products that would satisfy those markets. Along the way, Gary tried to bring the Maywood Inc. culture to the Singaporean employees. In addition, Gary desperately desired to transfer some of the Singapore culture back to corporate headquarters in an attempt to educate those at corporate headquarters.

As Gary continued interfacing with different groups of people working at the Asian Marketing Headquarters as well as the Singapore manufacturing plant, he was surprised to hear certain conversations—generalizations he interpreted as ethnic stereotypes—about certain races, nationalities, and religions of people. Various people would openly state their beliefs such as "Filipinos are always . . ." or "Muslims are always. . . ." Gary was rather shocked that statements like these were discussed, even in the workplace! Gary wanted to reprimand individuals on occasion for making such comments, but he remembered from his cultural training that he should not judge people and their actions by his standards but rather by the standards of the indigenous people. However, he was still bothered by the comments because stating such stereotypes back home in the United States could cause a lot of problems.

Maywood Inc., like other companies in Singapore, was very accommodating to the needs of its diverse workforce. For example, in the manufacturing facility there were many Muslim workers who had special needs for eating and worshipping. Maywood Inc. met these needs by equipping the cafeteria with two separate lines. One line served traditional Singaporean Chinese cuisine, while the other line served Muslim food. This was important because the Muslims didn't eat meat from split-hoofed animals, and their plates were not even allowed to touch those used by non-Muslims. Therefore, there were completely different serving as well as dish-cleaning operation lines for Muslims. Maywood Inc. also supplied a room where the Muslims could worship, as required by their religious beliefs, throughout the day.

Even though the company was accommodating to its workforce's diverse needs, Gary noticed that all the workers were not necessarily given the same opportunities in the company. There appeared to be a glass ceiling above which only those of Chinese origin could rise. It appeared that all management positions were filled by either Malaysians or Singaporeans of Chinese decent, and of the Buddhist religion. The Malays, Indians, and Filipinos appeared destined for lower level jobs. For example, when Gary indicated interest in promoting a non-Straits Chinese for managerial jobs, his local human resources staff commented that "You don't want her." or "He is not experienced enough to interface with the people which the job requires." or "He is much more suited to do the job which he is currently doing." Gary felt he was being screened and fed the Straits Chinese—the equivalent of the United States' "white males."

One encounter in particular stuck in Gary's mind. A technical problem relating to a customer's request arose and required a meeting for its resolution. Gary joined several engineers and managers in a conference room to discuss the current issue at hand. Vineet Bhali was one of the engineers present. Vineet was an Indian who had spent 12 years as an electrical engineer with an electronics firm in India. He has been employed at Maywood Inc. in Singapore for five years. Vineet's manager, Kuan Lee Tan, was also present. Gary started the meeting by summarizing the problem. When Gary asked for input, Vineet eagerly expressed his idea for a solution to the problem. But before Vineet was finished explaining his idea, Kuan Lee interrupted him. Kuan Lee commented to Vineet that Gary did not want to hear about his idea. Kuan Lee firmly stated that Vineet's proposal was **not** the way the company should handle the problem. Vineet, though obviously not pleased, appeared as if he was used to interruptions like this from his boss, and he sat back in his chair, silenced into submission.

Several managers had been conversing about the problem for several minutes when Vineet again persisted in trying to enter the conversation. This time, Kuan Lee's manager interrupted Vineet and tried to silence him one more time. Gary was very impressed by Vineet's understanding of the problem and his clear, structured solution, and he was struck by Vineet's managers' actions. After Vineet was interrupted for the second time, Gary, as the senior manager of the meeting, said, "Wait, Vineet may have a valid point. Let's hear him out."

Gary was met by a dead silence, and he felt a chill come over the room. Then Vineet spoke, uninterrupted, for 15 minutes. Gary now felt that Vineet was given the respect and attention that he, as an experienced engineer, deserved. A few days later when Gary was alone, Vineet discretely approached him and thanked him for listening to his point of view. After further reflection on the events that took place in the meeting, Gary concluded that Vineet was treated the way he was because of his race. Gary spoke to his confidant, JL, who explained about the pecking order of who can say what in a meeting: the engineer should not speak out directly to the people in the meeting. If he had something to say, he should have said it only to his boss, in private. By speaking up in the meeting, Vineet and his boss had both lost face.

In a conversation a few days later with JL, Gary learned many interesting points about the treatment of Indians and other non-Chinese in the Singapore culture. Credit or recognition was almost never given to a person of non-Chinese origin, especially in a public setting. There is no career development for the non-Chinese. In a nutshell, the Chinese ran the show, and all others had to show their respect to this system. Gary was very uneasy with this situation and wondered what he should do. In addition, he was now wondering if he too had lost face. Would the others in that meeting room still respect him? Could he continue to be an effective leader? What could he do to ensure that future expatriate managers assigned from corporate headquarters to the regional office did not have to deal with these problems on an ad hoc basis? Could a policy be developed to deal with these concerns? Gary was in a position that pitted his personal ethics against hundreds of years of Singaporean culture.

NOTES

1. The authors acknowledge with thanks the assistance of Catherine Schaidle, a Singaporean national; Judith Ogden, Assistant Professor of Law and Taxation who read drafts of the case; and Fang Yan, MBA student at American University, Washington, DC, a national of the People's Republic of China, who worked for several months in Singapore. All provided valuable comments.
2. Summarized from "Republic of Singapore: Economy," *Encarta 97 Encyclopedia*, Microsoft Corporation, 1996.

APPENDIX I

FURTHER BACKGROUND ON SINGAPORE

Culture

Singapore is a society in which ambiguity and uncertainty are highly accepted and not considered threatening. Tolerance of others and harmony and solidarity among people are highly valued. It is known for it diversity of cultures and people. There are three major Asian cultural groups in Singapore: Chinese, Malay, and Indian. The various cultures blend together harmoniously, each one maintaining its original homeland practices, adding to the uniqueness of this multicultural society. Because of the cultural and religious diversity of its people, festivals and events occur year-round and Singapore celebrates them all.

All Singaporeans view the family as central and honored. Because it helps support the family, work is given a very high value. Asians have a reputation of being very industrious with a strong work ethic. Punctuality is expected; however, it is seldom maintained, especially for social occasions. Singaporeans tend to also look beyond their family circle and are concerned about the contribution of their work to both their company and society in general. Collectivism, rather than individualism, is emphasized. This collectivism has led to a society in which cooperation and compromising are highly valued.

Business

Foreign companies like those of the United States and Japan dominate the manufacturing sector in Singapore, employing roughly 55 percent of the workforce. However, American managers tend to be consultative in their leadership style, while Singaporean managers are more paternalistic and autocratic.

Work is very important to Singaporeans. Cooperation and diversity in the workplace are especially valued and encouraged, as are training (especially in the foreign companies) and recognition for one's accomplishments. Because there is a chronic shortage of labor in Singapore, an employee's job satisfaction is crucial to a stable workforce within a company.

Because of the high context nature of the Asian culture, formality is not generally stressed in the Singaporean business environment; hence, policies, rules, and procedures often are limited in use. Managers are more willing to take risks in making decisions. They tend to give great attention to detail. Company leaders appear more paternalistic than their American counterparts: there is often clear and strong authority that is accepted by their subordinates. They also tend to have less trust and confidence in their subordinates, as compared to their American counterparts. Because of their authority, they often remain somewhat aloof, tending to keep their distance from their subordinates

in social situations. In addition, leaders seldom show anger or emotion. However, leaders must show signs of moral character, caring, and protection of their subordinates. They tend to build harmony among employees, diffuse conflict, and show dignity and "face" to subordinates. In some cases, these paternalistic managers will treat all employees as members of a large extended family. For example, it would not be uncommon for certain Singaporean managers to visit employees or their family members when they are sick. The Singaporean manager may even subsidize their medical expenses!

Decision Making in Business

Whereas American managers tend to ask and consider the opinions of their subordinates before making decisions, Singaporean mangers tend to make decisions quickly and expect their subordinates to comply with their decisions, regardless of whether they understand the reasoning behind them.

Singapore has more of a directive style of decision making than the West. Usually only a small, centralized group of managers make business decisions. They are not open to suggestions or input from subordinates when deliberating or making decisions. Hence, they are less likely to inform or include subordinates until the decisions are already made and are ready for implementation.

When groups are trying to form a decision, direct objections, heated debates, and confrontation, all traits of Western society, are not welcomed. Rather, negotiations are more subtle, more restrained, and much less confrontational. Group discussions tend to be very polite and emotionless, with indirect objections.

Face and Loss of Face

"Face" stands for an individual's social position or prestige, both of which are achieved by successfully fulfilling one's social roles. "Saving face," a concept that is central to all Asian cultures, is an important aspect of interpersonal interactions. Children are taught at a very early age how to be courteous and self-controlled when interacting with others, so that everyone "saves face." It is very poor manners to shout, swear, or even speak in a raised voice. To publicly criticize, shame, or insult someone, to display a violent temper, or to make someone feel inferior are all ways of "losing face." Importantly, **face is lost by both parties involved** . . . both the offender and the offended.

A loss of face is most noticeable in the interactions between superiors and their subordinates. The following are some examples in which face is lost:

➤ A student questions a teacher.

➤ One publicly disagrees with one's parents.

➤ In a business setting, a subordinate questions or disagrees with his superior.

In the business world, the concern for "face" often leads to compromising and conflict avoidance. For instance, an Asian may say "yes" when he means "no" or "maybe" to preserve face, since stating an untruth is considered better than making someone "lose face" or hurting someone's feelings. It is not uncommon to see two parties come to the negotiation table with their bargaining positions buffered with wide margins. During the negotiation process, both sides will then gradually give in until a solution is reached. This tactic helps both parties save face since neither one emerges as an outright winner or loser.

If a Singaporean seems to laugh out of context, it could be because he feels shy, nervous, embarrassed, or humiliated—because he has lost face.

Hofstede's Dimensions

Hofstede wrote extensively about varying degrees of power distance. Of importance is the fact that the United States is low on the power distance scale. This means that managers tend to be democratic and involve peers as well as subordinates in the decision-making process. Singapore, on the other hand, tends to be much higher in power distance. This implies that, in general, Singaporean managers tend to be more autocratic and infrequently involve others in decision making.

APPENDIX II

PARTIAL MAYWOOD INC. ORGANIZATIONAL CHART

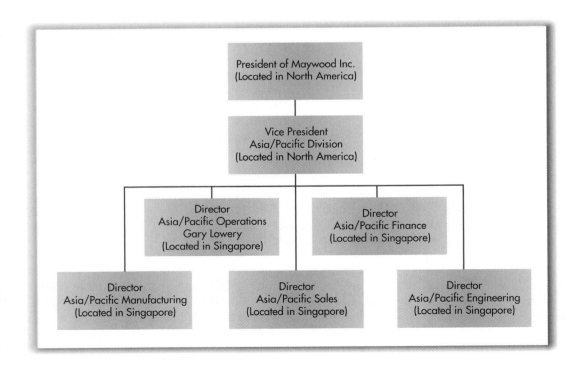

CASE BIBLIOGRAPHY

Chen, Min. *Asian Management Systems: Chinese, Japanese, and Korean Styles of Business,* Routledge, NY: 1995, 61.

Craig, JoAnn. *Culture Shock,* Singapore: Times Books International, 1986, 1–14.

"Culturgram '95: Republic of Singapore." Brigham Young University, Provo, Utah, 1994.

Hofstede, Geert. *Cultures' Consequences: International Differences in Work Related Values.* Beverly Hills, CA: Sage Publications, 1980.

Putti, Joseph M. *Management: Asian Context.* Singapore: McGraw-Hill Book Co., 1991, 83–87 and 93–94.

Redding, S. G. *The Spirit of Chinese Capitalism.* New York: Walter de Gruyter & Co., 1990, 231–236.

"Republic of Singapore: Economy." *Encarta 97 Encyclopedia.* Microsoft Corporation, 1996.

Westwood, R. I. *Organizational Behavior.* Hong Kong: Longman Group, 1992, 36–38, 87, 134–137, 213–216, 236–237, 358, and 370–372.

"What Feng Shui Can Do for You." *The Sunday Times.* June 29, 1997, Section 4, 7.

Integrative Term Project

This project requires research, imagination, and logic in applying the content of this course and book.

In groups of three to five students, create an imaginary company that you have been operating in the domestic arena for some time. Your group represents top management, and you have decided it is time to go international.

➤ Describe your company and its operations, relative size, and so forth. Give reasons for your decision to go international.

➤ Decide on an appropriate country in which to operate, and give your rationale for this choice.

➤ State your planned entry strategy, and give your reasons for this strategy.

➤ Describe the environment in which you will operate and the critical operational factors that you must consider and how they will affect your company.

➤ Give a cultural profile of the local area in which you will be operating. What are the workers going to be like? What kind of reception do you anticipate from local governments, suppliers, distributors, and so on?

➤ Draw up an organization chart showing the company and its overseas operations, and describe why you have chosen this structure.

➤ Decide on the staffing policy you will use for top-level managers, and give your rationale for this policy.

➤ Describe the kinds of leadership and motivational systems you think would be most effective in this environment. Give your rationale.

➤ Discuss the kinds of communication problems your managers might face in the host-country working environment. How should they prepare for and deal with them?

➤ Explain any special control issues that concern you for this overseas operation. How do you plan to deal with them?

➤ Identify the concerns of the host country and the local community regarding your operations there. What plans do you have to deal with their concerns and to ensure a long-term cooperative relationship?

Integrative Case

AT&T Consumer Products: The Mexico Decision

In the fall of 1988, Nick Stevens, the vice president of manufacturing at AT&T Consumer Products, had to select a site for a new answering systems manufacturing facility. He was inclined to choose Mexico, but he had not ruled out Malaysia or the United States.

As Stevens pondered the many factors that would affect his decision, he could not help reflecting on the profound changes that had occurred at AT&T in recent years. AT&T in 1988 was vastly different from the company he had joined 22 years earlier. Some changes were clearly reflected on the organizational chart, others involved new policies, but the most challenging ones related to AT&T's role in society, and Stevens had to consider all these factors in making his decision.

HISTORY

Like Singer with its sewing machines and Gillette with its razors, American Telegraph and Telephone was an American icon. Long known as Ma Bell, AT&T had been the world's largest corporation. In the early 1980s, it had more than $150 billion in assets, and its annual revenues of $70 billion repre-sented almost 2 percent of the U.S. gross national product. Until January 1984, AT&T employed one million people and had more than three million shareholders (see Exhibit IC-1).

Alexander Graham Bell, who patented the telephone in 1876, founded the Bell Telephone Company in 1877. Though Bell was credited with inventing the telephone, it was Theodore Vail who created the Bell System. Vail, one of the first managers hired by the founders of what would become AT&T, stated as early as 1879 that AT&T's goal was "one system, one policy, universal service."[1] Since Vail's time and until the 1984 divestiture, AT&T's annual reports consistently reiterated a commitment to furnishing "the best possible service at the lowest possible cost."[2]

Vail devised an organizational structure that lasted for a century without fundamental change. Local telephone companies, known as Bell Operating Companies, were organized as nominally independent subsidiaries. They provided local telephone service and access to the long-distance network (see Exhibit IC-2). They also billed customers for long distance and international service provided by the AT&T Long Lines Department.

Western Electric Manufacturing Company was founded in Cleveland in 1869 as an electric-equipment shop. In the 1870s, it became a mecca for inventors. In 1881, Bell Telephone bought an interest in Western Electric, and the following year, it formally became the manufacturer of Bell telephones and equipment.

In addition to producing or procuring practically all Bell System telephone equipment, Western Electric developed the high vacuum electronic amplifying tube that made possible coast-to-coast telephone calls and cleared the way for radio broadcasting, sound motion pictures, and television; it

SOURCE: Research Associate Wilda White prepared this case under the supervision of Professor Joseph Badaracco as the basis for class discussion rather than to illustrate either effective or ineffective handling of an administrative situation. Copyright ©1992 by the President and Fellows of Harvard College. To order copies or request permission to reproduce materials, Call 1-800-545-7685, or write the Publishing Division, Harvard Business School, Boston, MA 02163, or go to http://www.hbsp.harvard.edu/ No part of this publication may be reproduced, stored in a retrieval system, used in a spreadsheet, or transmitted in any form or by any means—electronic, mechanical, photocopying, recording, or otherwise—without the permission of Harvard Business School. Rev. October 19, 1994.

Exhibit IC-1   Seven-Year Summary of Selected AT&T Financial Data
(dollars in millions; except per share amounts)

	1982	1983	1/1/84	1984	1985	1986[a]	1987	1988[a]
Results of Operations								
Total revenues	$70,022	$72,357		$33,187	$34,496	$34,213	$33,773	$35,218
Total costs and expenses	50,678	57,338		30,892	31,476	33,847	30,252	38,276
Net Income (loss)	7,279	249		1,370	1,557	139	2,044	(1,669)
Dividends on preferred shares	142	127		112	110	86	23	1
Income (loss) applicable to common shares	7,137	122		1,258	1,447	53	2,021	(1,670)
Earnings (loss) per common share	$8.06	$6.00		$1.25	$1.37	$0.05	$1.88	($1.55)
Dividends declared per common share	5.81	6.10		1.20	1.20	1.20	1.20	1.20
Assets and Capital								
Property, plant and equipment-net			$20,569	$21,343	$22,262	$21,101	$20,808	$15,280
Total assets	$150,004	$140,229	35,545	39,773	40,688	39,534	39,473	35,152
Long-term debt including capital leases			9,137	8,718	7,794	7,660	7,919	8,128
Common shareowners' equity			12,368	13,763	14,633	13,550	14,455	11,465
Other Information (data at year end except 1/84)								
Market price per share	$62.86	$63.02	$17.88	$19.50	$25.00	$25.00	$27.00	$28.75
Employees	1,000,000		373,000	365,200	337,600	316,900	303,000	304,700

[a]1988 data was significantly affected by a charge for accelerated digitization program costs; 1986 data was significantly affected by major charges for business restructuring, an accounting change and other charges.

Exhibit IC-2   Pre-divestiture AT&T

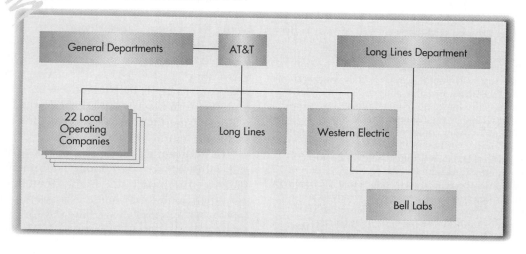

produced the first air-to-ground radio telephones; made and installed one of the pioneer commercial radio broadcasting systems, WEAF in New York; developed the first motion-picture sound system; built all the radar used by the U.S. armed forces in World War II; and in the space age, built the Nike missile systems, the DEW line radar defense system, the Sentinel and Safeguard antiballistic missile systems, and much of the communications and control equipment for the U.S. space program.

Western Electric was the largest component of the Bell System. Had it not been wholly owned by AT&T, Western Electric would have been the 12th largest industrial company in the United States. At its height, Western Electric operated 23 major plants scattered around the United States from Atlanta, Georgia, to Phoenix, Arizona, to North Andover, Massachusetts.

Bell Telephone Laboratories was formed out of the Western Electric engineering research department in 1925. It was equally owned by Western Electric and AT&T. Bell Labs developed and designed the equipment that Western Electric manufactured and the Bell System used. Originally a small organization, Bell Labs grew into a giant as a result of World War II military hardware requirements. Before divestiture, it had 25,000 employees, an annual budget of $2 billion, and employed 20,000 PhDs. It maintained 17 locations in 9 states. Its inventions included the electrical digital computer (1937), transistors (1947), lasers (1958), the communications satellite Telstar (1962), radar, semiconductors, fiber optics, and electronic switching equipment.

REGULATORY HISTORY

In 1934, the United States Congress created the Federal Communications Commission (FCC) to regulate the telephone industry. Its mission was "to make available, so far as possible, to all the people of the United States a rapid, efficient, nationwide and worldwide wire and radio communications service with adequate facilities at reasonable charges." Under FCC regulation, each Bell Operating Company was guaranteed an area of operation without competition and assured a certain maximum profit margin. Local operating companies were required to serve anyone within their operating area who requested telephone service. Charges for local telephone service were subject to state or local government approval.

As of the late 1960s, all telephone sets, private branch exchanges, and other standard equipment used in residences or by businesses were owned by the telephone company and leased to users. Nearly all telephone equipment (referred to as customer premises equipment, CPE, by the telephone industry) was manufactured by Western Electric and sold to the operating companies.

Carterfone   In 1968, the FCC issued its *Carterfone* decision. This case arose when AT&T refused to permit the *Carterfone*, a non-Bell device that linked mobile car radios with the national telephone network, to be connected to the Bell System. AT&T threatened service termination to anyone connecting the device to the network, arguing that non-Bell equipment could harm the system. When Tom Carter appealed to the FCC, the commission ruled in his favor and ordered AT&T to allow customers to connect their own telephone equipment to the Bell System. However, customers were required to lease a protective device from AT&T to link the non-Bell device and the Bell System telephone line.

Many consumers and competitive telephone equipment manufacturers complained that the protective devices constituted a barrier to competition, intended to protect AT&T's monopoly. In 1972, the FCC reexamined its *Carterfone* ruling and held that any equipment could be connected to the network without a protective device, if it had been certified as safe for use on the network. This decision became effective in 1980.

1982 Modified Final Judgment Decree   In January 1982, AT&T and the U.S. Department of Justice announced that they had reached a settlement of the government's long-standing antitrust case against the company. The 1974 lawsuit had charged AT&T with monopolizing the market for telephone equipment and long-distance service. The government maintained that as long as AT&T controlled the local circuits that provided the only access to most consumers, competition could not exist in long-distance service, data services, private branch exchanges, key telephone systems, large telephone switching machines, or other telephone equipment and services.

The settlement, which became known as the Modified Final Judgment called for the divestiture of the Bell Operating Companies by AT&T on January 1, 1984. The 22 BOCs would be regrouped under 7 separate and independent Regional Bell Operating Companies and restricted to providing local telephone service. They could not offer long-distance services and would be barred from manufacturing telephone equipment. They could, however, sell telephone equipment manufactured by others.

Under the terms of the settlement, AT&T would retain part of Bell Labs, all of Western Electric, and its long-distance and customer premises equipment operations. The settlement forbade AT&T's use of the "Bell" name, except for Bell Laboratories. It permitted AT&T to enter other electronics businesses, including computers. Many observers expected the settlement to initiate a great commercial contest between IBM and AT&T in the telecommunications and computing fields.

THE NEW AT&T

Organizational Structure   In anticipation of divestiture, AT&T's vertically integrated, functional organizational structure was replaced by an organizational structure built around the lines of business in which the company would now be engaged. Each line of business would be responsible for its own profitability and its contribution to AT&T's revenues.

Two sectors were created and given responsibility for the overall management of resources to support the lines of business. AT&T Communications would handle the long-distance service, and AT&T Technologies encompassed the unregulated parts of the business and included AT&T Consumer Products (see Exhibit IC-3).

Regulation   After 1984, only telephone equipment was fully deregulated. All telephone services remained under federal and state regulation. For example, AT&T's prices for long-distance services still had to be approved by the FCC.

Exhibit IC-3   Post-divestiture AT&T

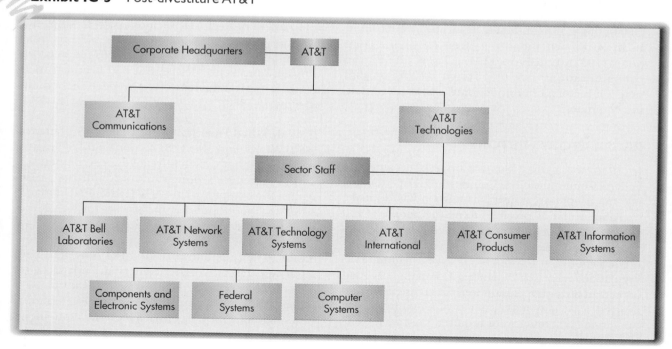

Labor   Before divestiture, three unions represented more than two-thirds of the Bell System's one million workers. The Communications Workers of America (CWA) represented 675,000 AT&T workers, the International Brotherhood of Electrical Workers (IBEW) represented 100,000 AT&T workers, and the Telecommunications International Union (TIU) represented 50,000 AT&T workers.

On August 7, 1983, after the antitrust settlement was announced but before it became effective, a nationwide strike against the Bell System began after the unions representing Bell System employees rejected the Bell Systems' wage package. The strike was the first since a six-day walkout in 1971. Beyond the wage dispute, the pending January 1984 divestiture of AT&T's 22 operating companies had cast a shadow across the bargaining table. The unions pushed for an "employment security" package that would provide training and retraining for members and protect jobs after divestiture. AT&T, faced with nonunion competition in a deregulated environment, was trying to control costs and maintain maximum flexibility in the way it utilized its workforce.

After 22 days, AT&T and the unions reached an accord. In addition to wage increases for each of the three years of the contract, AT&T agreed to increases in retirement pay, better pension protection for workers transferred to lower-paying jobs, and additional training, transfer rights, and retraining for laid-off workers.

After divestiture, the unionized workers were spread throughout AT&T and the divested Bell Operating Companies. Of AT&T's 375,000 workers remaining after divestiture, 63.6 percent were members of a union.

Range of Businesses   After divestiture, AT&T described its primary business as "moving and managing information." It provided consumers with basic long-distance service, special calling plans, and other miscellaneous services. AT&T also sold and leased telephones and answering systems to consumers. To businesses, the company offered communications and networked computer systems and telemarketing services. It also provided communications services and products and computer systems to all levels of government in the United States and abroad.

Dealings with the U.S. Government   AT&T's largest customer was the U.S. government. It sold its full range of customized and standard products to such agencies as the U.S. Army, Navy, and Air Force, and the Federal Aviation Administration. AT&T also managed Sandia National Laboratories as a service to the U.S. government on a nonprofit, no-fee basis. Sandia was one of the United States's largest research and development engineering facilities, with projects in areas such as the safety, security, and control of weapons systems, and the development of new energy sources.

International Activities, Joint Ventures, and Alliances   AT&T did business in more than 40 countries and had approximately 21,000 employees outside the United States. It was involved in numerous joint ventures and alliances, both in the United States and abroad. For example, it had agreements and alliances with British Telecom, France Telecom, and Kokusai Denshin Denwa of Japan. It had an agreement to share technology with Mitsubishi and to make and market worldwide a static random access memory chip. AT&T was also cooperating with NEC in Japan on a wide range of semiconductor products and technologies. AT&T also had an agreement with Zenith to codevelop an all-digital, high-definition television system using AT&T's microchips and video compression research and Zenith's television technology.

AT&T CONSUMER PRODUCTS

Although consumers were permitted as early as 1980 to connect non-Bell telephone equipment to the Bell System, the market for residential telephones did not take off until 1983, when leasing charges were listed separately from service charges on consumers' bills. The unbundling of leasing charges alerted consumers to the economic benefits of owning their own telephones. In 1983, retail telephone sales jumped 230 percent to about $1.1 billion.[3] In the first nine months of 1983, imports of telephones from Taiwan, Hong Kong, Japan, and Korea increased 568 percent over the same period in 1982, to 25.7 million telephones.[4]

The imported telephones were unlike the old U.S.-manufactured electromechanical telephones that were built to operate over a 30-year depreciation period. Some were one-piece models selling for as little as $20. Japanese companies, led by Matsushita under the Panasonic label, introduced feature-laden electronic telephones with integrated chips that made possible the inclusion of a variety of features at a reasonable cost.

The onslaught of new competition spelled trouble for AT&T Consumer Products (CP). This unit, formed after the telephone equipment market was deregulated, had never sold as much as a telephone cord before 1983. Moreover, AT&T's telephones were never designed to be marketable. In many ways, AT&T's attitudes toward its customers had been "we make it, you take it." Its telephones had cost $20 to make, while a repair call cost $60, so AT&T's goal had been to make highly reliable telephones, even if they were somewhat overengineered. As Jim Bercaw, a 35-year AT&T veteran described it: "We would bring pellets and metal in the back door, and send telephones out of the front door. We even made our own screws."

In the face of daunting competition, declining revenues, and unacceptable profit levels, CP consolidated its residential telephone production in AT&T's Shreveport, Louisiana, facility and spent tens of millions of dollars to upgrade and automate the facility. After the expense of integrating new technology and methods, CP discovered that its labor costs were still too high. A McKinsey & Company competitive analog study revealed that CP was out of line with its competitors on all points and scores, including such critical areas as cost of goods sold and SO&A. In fact, the cost of goods sold was 90 percent of revenues, and CP executives reasoned that it had to be at 65 percent in order to be competitive. In late 1984, AT&T corporate leaders told CP management to "fix the business or exit the business."

CP soon began making changes. In recalling their impact on its people, Ken Bertaccini, a 25-year veteran of AT&T and President of CP since 1985, said:

On January 1, 1984, our people went from a world of guaranteed customers, guaranteed profits and guaranteed jobs—to the much less certain world of a fiercely competitive consumer electronics world—with the only guarantee of success coming from excellent and sustained performance.

CP'S COMPETITORS

In the mid-1980s, there were three types of competitors in the telephone equipment market: (1) telephone companies, (2) consumer electronic companies, and (3) housewares companies. The telephone companies included AT&T, other traditional providers of service and equipment, such as GTE and ITT, and some of the divested Bell Operating Companies. As providers of telephone services, these companies had a strategic interest in the telephone equipment market. But like AT&T, these companies were, for the most part, unfamiliar with the world of competitive consumer marketing.

The consumer electronic companies ranged from sophisticated Japanese manufacturers like Matsushita and Sony, which offered full lines of consumer products, to smaller, specialized companies like Code-A-Phone, Unisonic, and PhoneMate. The consumer electronic companies were market-driven competitors with well-developed distribution networks and considerable expertise in designing products for the consumer market.

Consumer electronics companies' interest in the market was based on long-term possibilities and not just short-term profit and loss. As homes became more and more automated, telephones seemed likely to take on more the role of a home computer terminal. Therefore, the consumer electronics companies wanted the telephone terminal business as a platform for new generations of higher value-added products.

The housewares companies were primarily represented in the telephone equipment market by General Electric. It had a good reputation for reliability and quality and significant experience designing, marketing, and distributing consumer products.

Matsushita, a $40 billion Japanese company that manufactured under the Panasonic label, was CP's most formidable competitor. Panasonic was the predominant residential telephone vendor in Japan. Its strategy had been to provide products that competed with the market leader, but offered marginally more functions for the price. Matsushita manufactured its telephone products entirely in Japan. It used a highly automated manufacturing process and did not subcontract any of its production. Because of the volume of business it did and the wide range of associated products it manufactured,

Matsushita was able to operate its manufacturing operations at full capacity year round.

CP'S SURVIVAL PERIOD: 1985–1986

Establishing a Foundation and Culture for CP
CP's management realized that it had to be transformed from a regulated monopoly to a highly flexible organization that not only accepted change, but embraced it. "Business Passion" and "Shared Values" were established as the new foundation of CP. They were created to provide the basis and guidelines for all CP decisions and actions. Said

Nick Stevens, CP's vice president of manufacturing: "The passion is truly part of the decision process, and there is seldom a decision not made in its frame of reference."

"Business Passion," depicted in Exhibit IC-4, signified CP's commitment to "Be the Best" for its owners, customers and people. CP referred to its workers as "people." Executives strongly discouraged the use of the term employees, and they incurred a fine for using what they called the "E-word." Management believed that to achieve long-term success it had to weigh equally the effect of each business decision on all three stakeholder groups. The pyramid in the

Exhibit IC-4   AT&T Consumer Product Business Foundation: Business Passion and Shared Values

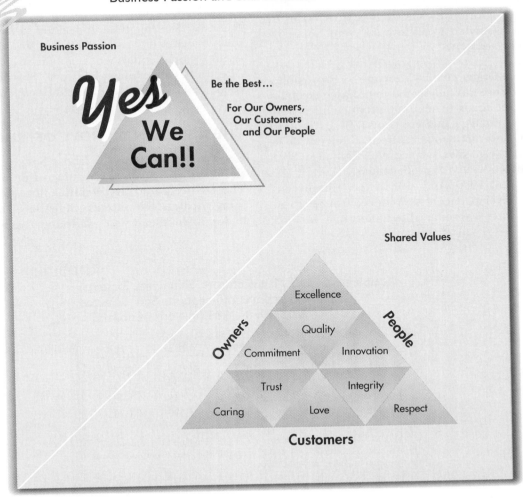

background of the "Business Passion" graphically represents the relationship between the "Business Passion" and "Shared Values."

CP's "Shared Values" described what the business was and aspired to be. On an individual level, the business wanted to create an environment of caring, trust, love,[5] integrity, and respect. On a business level, CP wanted to create an environment that valued commitment, quality, and innovations and achieved excellence in everything it did. CP managers placed a significant part of their compensation "at risk," making it dependent upon the unit's performance.

CP made what its executives called a "huge" investment in its people. It developed education programs as well as honor and recognition programs. Everyone had the opportunity for two weeks of business education each year. There were also several recognition events each year. Spouses or guests were invited to an annual event honoring CP's top performers.

Creating an Organizational Structure   CP's organizational structure was redesigned to promote flexibility and market focus. The nine product lines were turned into Strategic Business Units (SBUs).[6] Product managers and representatives from all relevant functional areas (e.g., sales, finance, etc.) formed an SBU. These SBUs operated as profit centers.

Between 1985 and 1988, the number of executive-level managers was reduced from 40 to 16. The workforce was reduced by almost half. In 1985,

CP had as many as six layers of supervision between its operational levels and its president. In 1988, CP had as few as three. A comprehensive measurement system was also developed and implemented. The system focused on assessing owner, customer, and people satisfaction on a regular basis by looking at profits, needs, and attitudes, respectively.

Developing a Business Strategy   In late 1984, Jim Bercaw, who was vice president of manufacturing at the time, was told to develop a "global manufacturing plan." To that end, he traveled to the Far East. His trip revealed that all of CP's competitors were manufacturing in Asia. He later said: "I have a second-fastest-gun-in-the-West philosophy. If you can't be the fastest gun in the West, it is better to travel in crowds."

With all its competitors in Asia, CP decided that it also had to move its manufacturing operation there. At the same time, it decided to contract out the remainder of its manufacturing requirements to Asian original equipment manufacturers (OEMs). After 1986, CP no longer had any U.S. production of residential telephone equipment (see Exhibit IC-5).

THE DECISION TO MOVE OFFSHORE

Choosing a Location   CP chose Singapore as the site of its first offshore manufacturing operation. The facility would first manufacture corded and then cordless telephones. Singapore, an island nation in Southeast Asia, was founded as an *entrepôt*

Exhibit IC-5   U.S. Manufacturers' Shipments, Exports, and Imports of Telephone Sets, Selected Years, 1978–1988 (millions of dollars)

	1978	1982	1988
Shipments	$824	$1,065	$359
Exports	10	24	56
Imports	42	149	1,408
Apparent consumption	856	1,190	1,703

SOURCE: United States Bureau of Census, "Selected Electronic and Associated Products, 1979, 1983," series MA36N, and "Communications Equipment, 1988," series MA36P.

because of its strategic position and excellent natural harbor. In 1988, however, manufacturing employed almost a third of the labor force, and the Singaporean government played a major role in managing the economy.

CP management chose Singapore in part because it was an English-speaking country and its Economic Development Board provided a kind of one-stop shopping for foreign companies that wanted to do business there. Corruption was not a problem: "The place was squeaky clean," recalled a CP manager. In addition, an existing building was available immediately for lease. According to Jim Bercaw, Singapore was not the lowest cost option, but it was considerably cheaper than the United States. Jim Bercaw described the decision this way:

> It was a jiffy quick decision. In January 1985, we began to negotiate, in March 1985, we received budgetary and financial approval. In May 1985, we buttonholed a lease in an existing factory. By January 1986, we shipped our first product.
>
> Logically, the decision to go to Singapore and sacrifice 500 jobs to save 10,000 jobs was a "no-brainer." However, culturally the decision created a struggle around taking jobs from our own facility out of America.[7]
>
> We also had to decide what kind of facility we wanted Singapore to be. We knew we wanted to attract the right kind of people there. We wanted to treat our people well. The labor rate was not crucial because the gap was so large. We wanted the facility to be world-class. And, we had a notion, that at some point we wanted the factory to be solely operated by Singaporeans. We did not want to create an American factory in Singapore.

The move to Singapore reduced CP's labor costs 90 percent and its overhead costs 40 percent. Overall, CP saved 30 percent of its manufacturing costs by moving to Singapore, even after accounting for tariffs and transportation costs.

Impact on Labor   In 1985, the Shreveport Western Electric plant employed between 6,000 and 7,000 workers and was the largest employer in northwestern Louisiana. Some 750 workers at the plant were involved in the production of telephones. These workers were represented by the International Brotherhood of Electrical Workers (IBEW).

In July 1985, AT&T laid off 875 workers at the plant, 100 of whom made residential telephones. The remaining 650 residential telephone workers were phased out through later layoffs, transfers, or attrition. At the time of the July 1985 layoffs, AT&T announced that it was shifting the manufacture of residential telephones from the Shreveport facility to a new leased building in Singapore to cut costs and remain competitive.

The Singapore announcement came in the second year of the union's three-year contract. Under the union contract, union workers were not permitted to strike while the contract was in force. The local union officials in Shreveport characterized the union as extremely vocal and unified in its opposition to the move to Singapore. According to the union local, AT&T did not attempt to discuss or negotiate alternatives to moving offshore with the union.

In recalling this period, Ken Bertaccini said:

> The decision to downsize was very difficult but clear. It cost American jobs and sacrificed the livelihoods of people who were part of the AT&T family. It meant moving jobs to parts of the world without any associations or relationships with AT&T. Patriotic emotions were involved, as well as the pain of looking great people in the eye and telling them that they would no longer have jobs.

Laid-off workers received Trade Readjustment Payments, as well as the benefits outlined in the union contract. These included severance pay based on years of service as well as extended medical benefits.

During the 1986 contract talks, the union negotiated retraining programs for its membership to help prepare them for life after AT&T. An Enhanced Training Opportunity Program was adopted that provided educational opportunities for workers, including computer training and classes at community colleges.

EXCELLENCE PERIOD: 1987–1988

When Nick Stevens joined CP in November 1987, he noticed that the Singapore facility had strayed from its original manufacturing strategy. Stevens decided CP needed another manufacturing location. The new facility would focus exclusively on manufacturing corded telephones.

According to Nick Stevens, the new location had to be able to sustain a world-class facility. Geographic proximity to Singapore, the cost and availability of labor, government incentive packages, and infrastructure were all among the criteria considered by Stevens. Ultimately, he decided on Bangkok, Thailand.

Thailand, known earlier as Siam, was one of the world's largest producers of rubber. Thai was spoken by approximately 97 percent of the population and was the official language, although English was used in government and commerce. Manufacturing accounted for about one-fifth of the country's gross national product and employed about 11 percent of the workforce. In the late 1980s, the country had one of the highest rates of economic growth in the world.

In February 1988, Stevens presented his Bangkok proposal to the AT&T Board and received approval. By June 1988, the facility was announced in Bangkok.

Answering System Market In 1987, CP adopted a five-year plan to make CP's answering systems the market share leader by 1992. As early as 1985, industry experts predicted a robust market for telephone answering systems. Unit sales in 1986 exceeded four million (see Exhibit IC-6).

The answering systems market had two segments: adjuncts and integrated. Adjunct answering systems did not include a telephone, but integrated systems did. In both segments, the strongest competitors were Panasonic, PhoneMate, and GE/Thompson. The market set the price for answering systems, and there were no real differences in the margins between the segments. In both segments, however, low-end prod-ucts (those with less features) commanded smaller margins. In general, the market for answering systems was in affluent countries. In 1987, the largest market by far was the United States. Europe, especially Germany, was expected to develop in future years.

CP's goal for answering systems required it to look for another site for an answering systems manu-facturing facility. Stevens's goal for 1988 was to explore the opportunities in Mexico and Europe. In June 1988, he saw an item in the *Wall Street Journal* advertising a seminar in Tucson, Arizona, on Mexican *maquiladoras*.[8] The seminar included a side trip into Nogales and Hermisillo, Mexico, to tour var-ious *maquiladora* operations (see Exhibit IC-7).

MEXICO

Mexico was the third largest country in Latin America, after Brazil and Argentina. In 1988, more than 83.5 million people lived in Mexico, making it the 11th most populous country in the world. Officially known as the United States of Mexico, it was organized into 31 states and a *distrito federal*. It shared a 2,000 mile border with the United States of America.

Although Mexico secured its independence from Spain in 1821, it was the Mexican Revolution in 1910 that initiated a period of dramatic social change. A new constitution was adopted in 1917 that restricted foreign economic control and gave workers new protections. In 1929, the *Partido Revolucionario Institucional* (PRI) was formed. Since its founding, it never lost an election. Rapid indus-trial growth after 1940 improved living standards for much of Mexico. Import substitution, which

Exhibit IC-6 Growth of U.S. Telephone Equipment Markets, 1984–1988 (millions of current dollars, 1990)

Type of Market	1984	1985	1986	1987	1988
Telephone sets—corded	$1,200	$1,585	$1,685	$1,750	$1,825
Telephone sets—cordless	410	305	410	438	474
Answering systems	298	371	535	557	634

SOURCE: North American Telecommunications Association, Telecommunications Market Review and Forecast (1990 Edition): 12, 144, 154, 162, 178.

Exhibit IC-7   Map of Mexico

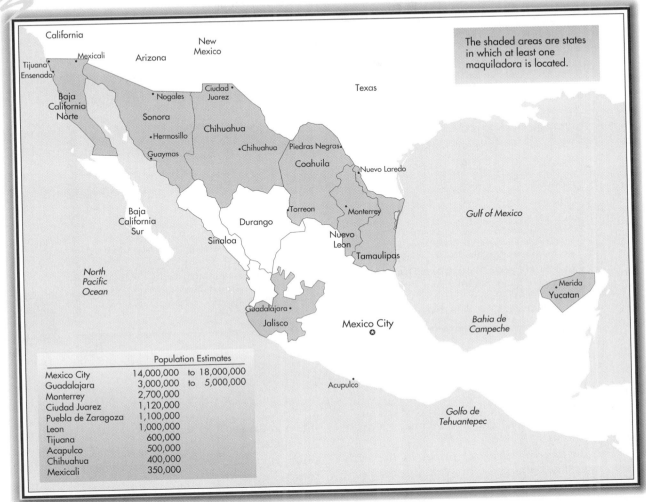

The shaded areas are states in which at least one maquiladora is located.

Population Estimates		
Mexico City	14,000,000	to 18,000,000
Guadalajara	3,000,000	to 5,000,000
Monterrey	2,700,000	
Ciudad Juarez	1,120,000	
Puebla de Zaragoza	1,100,000	
Leon	1,000,000	
Tijuana	600,000	
Acapulco	500,000	
Chihuahua	400,000	
Mexicali	350,000	

entailed manufacturing locally what had been previously imported, and aggressive promotion of Mexican products for Mexican consumption were adopted as the country's strategy for development.

Unrest in the late 1960s spurred increased government investment in the infrastructure as well as increased spending on social programs. Despite these aggressive policies, the six-year term (from 1970 to 1976) of President Luis Echeverrea Alvarez was marked by 30 percent annual inflation, budget deficits, and political unrest.

In the late 1970s, major new oil fields were discovered in Mexico that gave it easy access to foreign credit at low interest rates. Public debt nearly doubled between 1979 and 1981 from US$40 billion to US$78 billion. Despite the growth in government expenditures, by the end of the 1970s, about 50 percent of all Mexican households lacked running water and sewage services, 25 percent lacked electricity, and 22 percent had neither running water, sewer services, nor electricity. Twenty percent of the population suffered from malnutrition, and 45 per-

Exhibit IC-8 Hourly Compensation of Production Workers in Manufacturing

	Wages (US$ per hour worked)								
Country	**1980**	**1981**	**1982**	**1983**	**1984**	**1985**	**1986**	**1987**	**1988**
United States	$9.84	$10.84	$11.64	$12.10	$12.51	$12.96	$13.21	$13.40	$13.85
Japan	5.61	6.18	5.70	6.13	6.34	6.43	9.31	10.83	12.80
Singapore	1.49	1.79	1.96	2.21	2.46	2.47	2.23	2.31	2.67
Hong Kong	1.51	1.55	1.67	1.52	1.58	1.73	1.88	2.09	2.40
Taiwan	1.00	1.18	1.22	1.27	1.42	1.50	1.73	2.26	2.82
Thailand	NA	NA	NA	NA	NA	NA	NA	NA	1.40
Brazil	1.38	1.64	1.86	1.26	1.07	1.12	1.47	1.38	1.46
Mexico	NA	3.71	2.54	1.85	2.04	1.60	1.09	1.06	1.32
Malaysia	NA	NA	NA	NA	NA	NA	NA	NA	1.60

Note: Hourly compensation is defined as (1) all payments made directly to the worker, pay for time worked, pay for time not worked, all bonuses and other special payments, and the costs of payments in kind, and (2) employer contributions to legally required insurance programs and contractual and private benefit plans.

SOURCE: Except Malaysia and Thailand, 1980, 1984–1988, United States Department of Labor, Bureau of Labor Statistics, May 1991, Report 803: 1981–1983, unpublished data from United States Department of Labor Bureau of Labor Statistics, Office of Productivity and Technology. Malaysia and Thailand, 1988, Bank Swiss.

cent of the population did not receive adequate health care.[9]

The decline of world oil prices in the early 1980s, as well as a sharp rise in world interest rates, plunged Mexico into economic crisis. In August 1982, Mexico announced that it could not meet the interest payments on its foreign debt of US$88 billion. In September, banks were nationalized, and new currency controls were put in place.

In December 1982, foreign debt exceeded US$91 billion. Mexico turned to the International Monetary Fund (IMF) for assistance. The government budget was slashed, food subsidies were eliminated, and the peso was sharply devalued. The combination of inflation and the peso devaluation substantially reduced the real wages of workers (see Exhibit IC-8). In 1986, in exchange for new foreign loan agreements with the IMF, the World Bank, and its commercial bank creditors, Mexico agreed to major reforms of its economic policies, including liberalization of foreign investment, reductions in public spending, tax reform, and divestiture of state-owned enterprises.

In July 1988, Carlos Salinas de Gortari, the PRI's candidate, won the presidency with 50.4 percent of the vote,[10] amid widespread charges of irregularities in the polling. Cuauhtemoc Cárdenas, the son of the Mexican president who had nationalized the oil companies in 1938, had mounted a strong campaign against the PRI. Cárdenas was critical of the PRI for abandoning Mexico's history of national self-determination. According to the PRI, Cárdenas won 31.1 percent of the vote in the election, including four states and the distrito federal. However, many Mexicans believe that Cárdenas actually won the election. As president, Salinas renegotiated the foreign debt, continued the austerity plan, and continued privatizing government-owned businesses.

Maquiladoras

In 1965, the government of Mexico initiated the Border Industrialization Program. The program permitted foreign corporations to establish wholly owned subsidiary operations in Mexico. Under the program, the subsidiary could import into Mexico duty free, machinery, raw materials, and component parts to be used in processing or assembling goods in Mexico.[11] So long as the end product was exported, Mexican duties were not levied on the imported components. Under the laws of the United States and most industrialized countries, when the imported components are exported back to their country of origin in the form of finished products, only the value added in Mexico—labor, overhead, raw materials—and not the value of the imported raw materials or components—was subject to duty.[12] Operations established under this program were commonly known as *maquiladoras*, *maquilas*, or in-bond assembly operations.[13]

Maquiladora or *maquila* is derived from the Spanish verb "*maquilar*," which means to measure or take payment for grinding corn. In colonial times, the *maquila* was the portion of flour that the miller kept as payment for grinding the corn. In the 1980s, *maquiladora* or *maquila* referred to the system under which foreign companies provide the corn (for example, electronic components), Mexico keeps its portion for assembling or processing (for example, foreign currency changed into pesos for wages and production costs), and the assembled goods return to their country of origin with a duty paid only on the value added in Mexico.

Twin plant is another term often associated with *maquilas*. Originally, the Border Industrialization Program envisioned the establishment of complementary plants across the border from one another. The Mexican twin was intended to provide labor-intensive assembly of components fabricated in the United States. The assembled components would then be shipped to the twin in the United States where they would be finished, inspected, distributed, and sold. However, in most cases, the complementary U.S. plant was not located along the border but elsewhere within the United States at preexisting facilities. In 1987, fewer than 10 percent of all Mexican *maquilas* had a U.S. twin.[14]

The Border Industrialization Program was adopted to provide permanent employment for Mexico's rapidly growing population along the U.S.–Mexico border. The program sought to create jobs by attracting foreign manufacturing facilities that would not compete directly with domestic Mexican producers. The program also attempted to absorb migrant agricultural workers displaced by the expiration of the U.S. Bracero Program.[15] To address the problems resulting from the end of the Bracero Program, the law initially required that all foreign owned assembly operations be located within a 20-kilometer strip along the U.S.–Mexican border. New regulations were adopted in 1977 that permitted *maquilas* to locate in the economically depressed interior regions of Mexico. In 1983, the Mexican government extended the program to all regions of Mexico. However, by 1986, over 88 percent of all *maquila* operations were still concentrated along the border. *Maquiladoras* located near the border accounted for approximately 87 percent of the total *maquiladora* workforce.[16]

The number of *maquiladoras* grew from 12 in 1965 to over 1,450 in 1988.[17] Over the same period, the number of *maquiladora* workers grew from 3,000 to over 361,800 (see Exhibit IC-9). The type of *maquila* production had also changed. In 1965 and 1966, the vast majority of *maquiladoras* were textile firms. In 1988, *maquiladora* production included automobiles and auto parts, electronics, telecommunications equipment, and scientific instruments.

Beginning in the early 1980s, a substantial number of major U.S. multinationals, including many Fortune 500 companies, established *maquiladoras*. Several European and Japanese firms also established *maquiladoras* or employed subcontractors to perform their assembly in Mexico. In 1987, there were 20 Japanese *maquiladoras* in Mexico. The most prominent Japanese manufacturers operating *maquiladora* facilities were Sanyo, Sony, Toshiba, Hitachi, Matsushita, and TDK.[18]

MAQUILADORAS FOR MEXICO

Impact on the Economy Mexico earned foreign exchange on the value added to products assembled or processed in Mexico and then exported (see Exhibits IC-9 and IC-10). In fewer than 25 years, the *maquiladora* industry had become Mexico's second largest industry after oil and oil-related production. In 1987, the *maquiladora* industry accounted for

Exhibit IC-9 Selected Data on the Maquiladoras

	1980	1981	1982	1983	1984	1985	1986	1987	1988
Number of firms	620	605	585	600	672	760	891	1,125	1,450
Average annual employment (000)	119.5	131	127	151	200	212	250	305	362
Imported materials (million $)	1,750	2,227	1,979	2,823	3,749	3,825	4,351	5,507	7,808
Exported material (million $)	2,523	3,202	2,830	3,641	4,904	5,092	5,646	7,105	10,146
Value added (million $)	773	975	851	818	1,155	1,267	1,295	1,598	2,337
Wages, salaries, loans	458	596	463	385	595	660	586	739	1,141
Domestic raw materials and packaging	30	29	26	37	51	36	54	86	132
Utilities and other expenses	129	153	174	183	206	238	295	314	388
Miscellaneous expenses	155	197	189	213	303	334	360	458	676

Note: Figures may not add up due to rounding

SOURCE: Banco de Mexico, "La Industria Maquiladora de Exportación, 1980–1986," mimeo. Mexico, 1987; 1987 and 1988, INEGI, "Advances de Informacion Economica—Industria Maquiladora de Exportación," November 1988 and November 1989.

Exhibit IC-10 Selected Data on Mexico's Balance of Payments

	1980	1981	1982	1983	1984	1985	1986	1987	1988
Merchandise exports	16,070	19,940	21,230	22,312	24,196	21,663	16,031	20,655	20,566
Merchandise imports	(18,900)	(24,040)	(14,435)	(8,550)	(11,255)	(13,212)	(11,432)	(12,222)	(18,898)
Trade balance	(2,830)	(4,100)	6,795	13,762	12,941	8,451	4,599	8,433	1,668
Foreign direct investment	2,090	2,540	1,655	461	390	491	1,160	1,796	635
Current account balance	(8,160)	(1,390)	(6,307)	5,403	4,194	1,130	(1,673)	3,968	(2,443)

SOURCE: Balance of Payments Statistics Vol. 41, Yearbook, Part 1 (IMF: 1990).

Trade Balance, also known as Balance of Trade, is a country's exports of goods minus its imports of goods.

Foreign Direct Investment is the acquisition of physical assets outside the home country with substantial management control (usually defined as 10 percent or more of the ownership of a company) held by the parent corporation of the home country.

Current Account Balance is the net of the country's imports, exports, services and government unilateral transfers (sums sent outside the home country by the government for foreign aid, emergency relief, etc.).

Balance of Payments is the record of the goods and services an economy has received from and provided to the rest of the world and of the changes in the economy's claims on and liabilities to the rest of the world.

SOURCE: Michael G. Rukstad (ed.), *Macroeconomic Decision Making in the World Economy: Text and Cases* (FL: Holt, Rinehart and Winston, Inc., 1989): 485.

approximately 44 percent of Mexican exports to the United States. That year, *maquiladoras* contributed approximately US$1.6 billion in foreign exchange earnings. Between 1982 and 1987, the industry created 178,000 new jobs out of a total of 408,000 jobs created over this period.[19]

Impact on the Environment   It was estimated that *maquiladoras* generated more than 20 million tons of hazardous waste annually. Such wastes included corrosive acids and bases, sludge from electroplating processes, cyanide solutions, paint sludge and thinners, and heavy metals such as cadmium, chromium, lead, mercury, and silver.[20] Under the Mexican law that had regulated *maquiladoras* since 1983, hazardous wastes had to be returned to their country of origin.[21] American owned *maquiladoras* had to comply with both Mexican and U.S. laws regulating hazardous waste disposal. U.S. law required would-be generators of hazardous waste to obtain an EPA identification number. In addition, *maquiladoras* that planned to transport hazardous waste for off-site treatment, storage, or disposal within the United States had to prepare a manifest. Each time the waste changed hands, the manifest had to be signed. Biennial reports were required to be submitted to the EPA by all companies shipping hazardous waste to the United States.

EPA records showed that in 1987 only 20 out of more than 1,000 U.S. *maquiladoras* returned their hazardous waste to the United States.[22] A study by the Texas Center for Policy Studies found that in a 2½ year period only 33 of the approximately 600 *maquiladoras* in the Texas–Mexico border area had filed the required notices for return of their hazardous wastes to the United States.[23] A November 1990 study by the Secretaria de Desarrollo Urbano y Ecología (the Ministry of Urban Development and Ecology or SEDUE), the Mexican Government's equivalent of the U.S. Environmental Protection Agency, revealed that only 19 percent of the plants using toxic materials could show that they had disposed of wastes properly.[24] Other studies revealed that primary sources of drinking water in the border area had been contaminated with industrial solvents and other chemicals.[25]

Historically, Mexico had less stringent environmental standards than the United States and lax enforcement of its standards.[26] In a 1988 survey of

maquiladoras in Mexicali, a Mexican city near the California border, by El Colegio de la Frontera Norte, 10 percent of the 100 *maquiladoras* surveyed freely admitted that "environmental legislation" in Mexico was one of the main factors in their decision to leave the United States and relocate in Mexico. Seventeen percent of those surveyed considered it a factor of importance.[27]

In 1988, Mexico enacted the General Law on Ecological Balance and Environmental Protection. The administrator of the U.S. Environmental Protection Agency said about the law:

> . . . what we know about Mexico's 1988 comprehensive environmental law indicates that it may be sufficiently stringent to rebut the "pollution haven" argument. Properly enforced, the law should result in greatly improved environmental protection.[28]

SEDUE was the federal Mexican agency charged with enforcing the 1988 environmental law. Its annual budget for pollution control was approximately US $3.1 million. In contrast, in the same year, the annual budget for pollution control in Texas was US$50 million. In Ciudad Juarez, a Mexican state near El Paso, Texas, there was one Mexican federal inspector for more than 300 *maquiladora* plants and all Mexican domestic industry.[29]

Most of the *maquiladoras* were clustered around Tijuana–San Diego in California and Ciudad Juarez–El Paso in Texas. The resulting population growth in these cities severely strained the water supply and infrastructure. A 1981 University of Mexico study on border resources found that the aquifer under El Paso–Ciudad Juarez was being depleted faster than it was being replenished. In the lower Rio Grande Valley, closer to the Gulf of Mexico, municipal and industrial needs were expected to reduce drastically the water available for crop irrigation by the year 2000.[30]

Wages and Working Conditions   The Mexican Constitution and federal Mexican labor law set forth the minimum rights and benefits to which Mexican workers were entitled. The law regulated employment conditions such as work schedules, overtime, vacation periods, legal holidays, payment of salaries, employment of women and minors, occupational risks, and minimum wages. Article Three of Mexico's federal labor law provided:

> Work is a social right and social obligation. It is not an article of commerce; it requires respect for the freedom and dignity of the person performing it and it shall be carried out under conditions protecting the life, the health, and a decent standard of living for the worker and his family.[31]

Mexican workers also had the right to unionize. In major Mexican cities, nearly all workers were members of a union. Under Mexican law, the union had the right to approve or disapprove an employer's hiring decisions.

A survey conducted by the International Trade Commission found that U.S. companies viewed the Mexican minimum wage as the major attraction of foreign investment in Mexico[32] (see Exhibit IC-11). Minimum wages in Mexico were set by commissions comprised of members of the government, organized labor, and private industry. These commissions set the minimum wage for 86 different unskilled and skilled occupational classifications in 11 different economic zones in Mexico. The highest minimum wages had traditionally been along the northern border.[33]

Base *maquiladora* wages averaged about $3.50 to $4.00 per day for production workers[34] (see Exhibit IC-11). According to the American Friends Service Committee, comparable Mexican manufacturers in major cities paid two to three times *maquiladora* wages.[35] Common fringe benefits, such as attendance bonuses and transportation subsidies, could raise the wage from $7 to $9 per day. Attendance bonuses were in response to the 10 to 35 percent turnover rate that came to characterize *maquiladoras*. The average hourly wages paid to *maquiladora* workers placed strict limits on their purchasing power. In the town of Matamoros, for example, the average worker had to work an hour and a half to buy a half gallon of milk, three hours to buy a box of cereal, five and a half hours to buy two pounds of beef, and 17 hours to buy a toddler-size dress.[36]

Limited studies of *maquiladora* working conditions indicated that employees experienced many work-related health and safety problems. Eye disease and the weakening of the optic nerve were prevalent among electronics workers. Among textile workers, inadequate seating was associated with the development of lumbago.[37]

In a Tijuana, Mexico *maquiladora* of one of CP's Asian competitors, the casewriter observed an assembly line of workers, 98 percent of whom were women, hunched over a moving conveyor belt that carried printed circuit boards (PCBs) in various stages of completion. The plant made cable boxes and tuners. The women workers sat on nonergonomic stools while placing capacitors or other minute components on PCBs. Some workers used magnifying glasses to place components on the printed circuit boards. Some women soldered or tested PCBs. Testing was done by manually manipulating a component on a PCB or by staring at a computer screen as the PCB was tested by a machine.

The *maquiladora* employed a handful of male workers. These workers attended the automated processes in the plant, though there seemed to be little for them to do. No women were assigned to the machines. All employees worked a nine and one-half hour day, from 8:00 A.M. to 6:00 P.M., with a half-hour break for lunch. Outside the plant a trailer was used for the storage of hazardous waste.

Exhibit IC-11 Average Hourly Compensation Cost for Maquiladora Workers

Year	Compensation
1980	$1.42
1981	1.67
1982	1.23
1983	0.91
1984	1.06
1985	1.07
1986	0.80
1987	0.75
1988	0.80

SOURCE: 1980–1986, U.S. International Tariff Commission (USTIC), *The Use and Economic Impact of TSUS Items 806.30 and 807*, Publication No. 2053 (Washington, D.C.: USTIC, January 1988): 8–9; 1987 and 1988, Leslie Sklair; *Assembling for Development* (Boston: Urwin Hyman, Inc., 1989): 72.

Half of Mexico's population was below the age of 18. Although it was illegal in Mexico to hire children under 14, the Mexico City Assembly estimated that between 5 million to 10 million children were employed illegally, often in hazardous jobs.[38] The *Wall Street Journal* profiled Vincente Guerrero, a 12-year-old Mexican boy who had been compelled to leave the 6th grade to work in a shoe factory.[39]

… Vincente spends most of his time … smearing glue onto the soles of shoes with his hands. The glue he dips his fingers into is marked "toxic substances … prolonged or repeated inhalation causes grave health damage; do not leave in the reach of minors." All [the boys who work in the factory] ignore the warning.

Impossible to ignore is the sharp, sickening odor of the glue. The only ventilation in the factory is from slits in the wall where bricks were removed from a window near Vincente that opens only halfway. Just a matter of weeks after he started working, Vincente was home in bed with a cough, burning eyes and nausea.

When a teacher came by the factory to chide school dropouts [the plant superintendent's 13-year old son] rebuked her. "I'm earning 180,000 pesos a week," he said. "What do you make?" The teacher, whose weekly salary is 120,000 could say nothing.[40]

Exhibit IC-12   Distribution of Men and Women in the Maquila Workforce in 1986

Various Manufacturing Activities	Men	Women
Electrical and electronic machinery and equipment	9,610	29,001
Furniture and fixtures	5,803	1,910
Nonelectrical equipment and parts	1,857	897
Footwear and leather products	1,776	2,052
Transportation equipment and accessories	17,850	23,144
Total industry	64,812	139,076

SOURCE: USTC, Publication No. 2053, January 1988, 8–11.

Estimates placed the savings, compared to average *maquiladora* wages, from hiring younger (ages 14–18) and less skilled workers at 30%–40%.

Some critics charged that *maquiladoras* had disrupted the social and family structure of Mexican society by discriminating against Mexican males, the traditional breadwinners, and hiring predominantly women. The critics also contended that women were preferred over men because they were more docile, politically unaware, inexperienced, and less demanding. In the 1970s, women comprised 23 percent of the Mexican labor force overall but 72.3 percent of the *maquila* industry[41] (see Exhibit IC-12).

Living Conditions   In the Mexican border towns, many *maquiladora* workers lived in dwellings fashioned from cardboard and scraps of wood taken from *maquiladora* trash bins. Some of the cardboard had once contained polyvinyl chloride; written on the cardboard walls were warnings that the former contents could release hazardous fumes. The workers' water supply was stored in 55-gallon drums also found in *maquiladora* trash bins. The drums contained labels indicating that they formerly contained fluorocarbon solvents whose vapors are harmful if inhaled.

MAQUILADORAS AND THE UNITED STATES

Impact on the Economy   Advocates argued that *maquiladoras* help keep U.S. manufacturing internationally competitive, saving jobs that would otherwise be lost if U.S. manufacturers went to the Far East, since *maquiladoras* primarily use components made in the United States. According to a U.S. Department of Commerce report, nearly 75,000 U.S. workers were employed during 1986 to produce and ship $2.9 billion worth of components and raw materials used annually by *maquiladoras*.[42]

Organized labor in the United States contended that *maquiladoras* take jobs out of the United States—some of which could be held by the estimated 27 million workers and unemployed people in the United States who were functional illiterates. The Communications Workers of America (CWA) estimated that had there been no increase in foreign production by U.S. companies, more than 20,000 of the 120,000 jobs lost in the telecommunications industry since 1981 would have been saved.[43] In 1988, the jobless rate in the U.S. electronics industry was 86 percent higher than it was in 1979. In the five years between January 1979 and January 1984, employment for production workers manufacturing telephone and telegraph equipment declined in the United States by 23.4 percent.[44]

Maquiladora workers tended to shop in US border towns which returned a portion of their *maquila* wages to the United States. Studies have suggested that *maquila* workers spent more than half of their wages in the United States, mainly in the stores and shopping malls of the U.S. border towns.[45]

Impact on the Environment The *maquiladoras* brought rapid development on the U.S. side of the border. The pace of development outstripped the ability of the region to absorb it. Mexican officials have complained that growing development on the U.S. side of the border threatened surface-water supplies promised to Mexico under a 1944 treaty. A legal advisor to the Mexican Foreign Ministry believed that by the mid–1990s the United States would be unable to deliver the volume of water promised Mexico.[46] The primary source of drinking water on the Texas border was the Rio Grande, which was consistently drunk dry.[47]

Not only was there a shortage of water, but the water that was available was frequently contaminated. Most Mexican border towns did not have sewage treatment plants. Ciudad Juarez dumped all its raw sewage into a canal that paralleled the Rio Grande. A study in San Elizario, Texas, showed that everyone there had been exposed to hepatitis at least once by the time he or she was 20 years old.[48] More than 20 million gallons of untreated sewage and chemicals ran into the Tijuana River each day. Some ended up on the Imperial Beach on the California coast, which has been closed for ten years.[49] Recreational use of the Rio Grande below Laredo, Texas, has long been considered unsafe because its sister city in Mexico, Nuevo Laredo, dumps about 25 million gallons of untreated sewage into the river every day.[50]

The air quality along the border had also been affected. On the Mexican side of the border across from El Paso, Texas, firewood was the chief cooking and heating fuel for most of the 1.2 million residents of Ciudad Juarez, Mexico. Rubber tires were burned in kilns that made decorative tiles. Along with pollution from motor vehicles and industry, the smoke from these fires produced an acrid cloud over both cities under certain weather conditions.[51]

CONSIDERATIONS ON PLANT LOCATION

In late 1988, Stevens enrolled in the seminar advertised in the *Wall Street Journal* and toured the *maquiladora* operations situated around the U.S.–Mexico border. Stevens described his reactions to the tour: "I did not like what I saw. I saw exploitation in the form of sweatshops, I saw wage inflation, horrible environmental conditions, and huge workforce turnover." CP management had also heard that bribery and corruption were a way of life in Mexico.

Stevens was considering other sites in Mexico including Monterrey, Hermisillo, Chihuahua, and Guadalajara. He was also considering locations outside Mexico: Malaysia, a U.S. greenfield operation in Texas, and a U.S. AT&T "factory-within-a-factory" operation. A plant outside the United States would employ approximately 1,800 people at full capacity of 3.5 million units per year. The work week would average 45 hours.

Projections indicated that a *maquiladora* plant in the border region was the lowest cost option. (See Exhibit IC-13.) Wages elsewhere in Mexico were likely to be higher—by 15%–20%, for example, in Guadalajara. Expenditures on pollution controls were another cost issue. Complying with U.S. "good citizen" standards with on-site facilities would add $2–$3 million to the estimates in Exhibit IC-13 during the first few years. However, a number of companies avoided those expenditures by paying local firms relatively small amounts to dispose of waste—though some of these disposal firms did not actually comply with Mexican laws and regulations.

Malaysia offered several advantages. AT&T had significant experience in Asia, as well as infrastructure and support systems in the area, and the Malaysian Industrial Development Authority offered, like Singapore, a central, one-stop shopping opportunity for foreign companies. On the negative side, Stevens was concerned about putting too many eggs in one basket in Asia and feared that Malaysian wages and salaries would rise as more companies moved there.

Exhibit IC-13   Initial Estimates of Average Cost per Unit at Alternative Sites (labor costed at average maquilidora rates)

	Existing AT&T Factory				
	Greenfield	*Full*	*Incremental*	*Malaysia*	*Mexico*
Landed Cost[a]	$47.33	$52.33	$51.89	$41.48	$39.44
Additional Cost[b]	.72	−.66	.65	3.40	2.96
Total cost	$48.04	$52.99	$52.54	$44.89	$42.39
Incremental carrying costs			0.49		
					$45.37

[a]*Landed Cost includes material, labor, and overhead.*
[b]*Additional Cost includes transportation fees, duties, asset tax, and a charge for AT&T's internal hurdle rate.*
Data has been disguised. The essential relationships have, however, been preserved.

At the time Stevens was considering where to locate CP's new manufacturing facility, AT&T's senior management was reviewing its capital budgeting process. It seemed it would be more difficult to get approval for the current project than for the Singapore and Thailand operations.

Wherever the plant was located, it would be devoted to manufacturing answering systems. Electronic components, printed circuit boards, power adapters, pellets, and cardboard boxes would be brought into the plant. The plant would make the body of the answering systems in-house using plastic injection molding. Completed answering systems would leave the plant boxed and ready to ship.

Even if the project were approved, Stevens and CP management still had to reach decisions on wages and benefits, the profile of its workforce in terms of gender, age, and educational background, the sourcing of components, as well as a host of other issues.

CASE QUESTIONS

1. Should AT&T build its telephone answering machine plant in Mexico? Justify your answer.
2. What decisions should Nick Stevens make about wage levels, benefits, waste management, teenage workers, gender-based hiring, and bribery in the event he chooses a Mexican site?

3. What obligations, if any, do AT&T managers have to their U.S. employees or the United States?

CASE ENDNOTES

1. Robert W. Garnet, *The Telephone Enterprise: The Evolution of the Bell System's Horizontal Structure, 1878–1909* (Baltimore: Johns Hopkins University Press, 1985): 173.
2. Ibid.
3. "The Big and Bruising Business of Selling Telephones," *Business Week*, March 12, 1984, 103.
4. Ibid.
5. "Love" had not always been a part of CP's "Shared Values." After extensive discussion, it was included in 1989 in order to deepen, in the words of one manager, "CP's commitment to live up to its personal values of caring, trust, and respect." This decision was reinforced by the outpouring of support for a CP executive who successfully battled cancer during the mid-1980s.
6. CP's product lines were (1) leased telephones, (2) corded telephones, (3) cordless telephones, (4) answering systems, (5) special needs systems (communications products for people with hearing, speech, motion, and vision impairments), (6) telephone accessories, (7) home security systems, and (8) public pay telephones.

7. Approximately 10,000 people worked throughout CP. According to CP management, these jobs were at risk if CP did not make competitively priced telephones.

8. A *maquiladora* is a plant that assembles components that are usually imported into the home country of the *maquiladora* duty free. The assembled components are then reexported. On reexport, a duty is paid only on the value of the labor that assembled the components and the value of any other home-country inputs.

9. Helen Shapiro, "Mexico: Escaping from the Debt Crisis?" (Cambridge, MA: President and Fellows of Harvard College, 1991), p. 6.

10. In comparison, de la Madrid received 71.6 percent of the vote in 1982 and López Portillo received 95 percent of the vote in 1976. M. Deiai Baer, "Electoral Trends," in *Prospects for Mexico*, ed. George W. Grayson (Washington, DC: Center for the Study of Foreign Affairs, Foreign Service Institute, Department of State, 1988), p. 43.

11. Without the provisions of the Border Industrialization Program, products could not be imported into Mexico without an import license. After Mexico joined the General Agreement on Tariffs and Trade (GATT) in 1986, tariffs at an initial level of 50 percent were substituted for import licenses. At the end of 1987, the tariff ceiling for most items was lowered to 20 percent. Import licenses are still required for electronic and computer equipment and automotive imports. Sidney Weintraub, *Transforming the Mexico Economy: The Salinas Scenerio* (Washington, DC: National Planning Association, 1990), p. 5.

12. In the United States, tariff items 806.30 and 807.00 permit the portion of the product made of U.S. components to reenter the United States duty free.

13. All *maquiladora* facilities that export the assembled products are part of the "In-Bond Industry." The in-bond feature of the BIP requires that an importing *maquiladora* plant guarantee the payment of duties on imported materials that would otherwise be due. The guarantee usually consists of a surety bond. After processing, if the assembled products are exported, the bond is canceled.

14. U.S. International Tariff Commission (USTIC), *The Use and Economic Impact of TSUS Items 806.30 and 807*, Publication No. 2053 (Washington, DC: U.S. International Trade Commission, January 1988), pp. 8–12.

15. The Bracero, or Mexican Labor Program, allowed migrant Mexican workers to enter the United States on a temporary (seasonal) basis from 1942 through 1964. It was initiated to alleviate labor shortages in the U.S. agricultural and railroad industries during World War II. The Bracero Program attracted to the border unemployed workers from the Mexican interior who were seeking the guaranteed U.S. minimum wage. The railroad portion of the program ended in 1946. The agricultural program expired in 1964. A large segment of the border population became dependent on income earned by Braceros in the United States.

16. U.S. International Tariff Commission (USTIC), *The Use and Economic Impact of TSUS Items 806.30 and 807*, Publication No. 2053 (Washington, DC: U.S. International Trade Commission, January 1988), p. 84.

17. Khosrow Fatemi, ed., *The Maquiladora Industry: Economic Solution or Problem?* (New York: Praeger Publishers, 1990), pp. 4 and 28.

18. U.S. International Tariff Commission (USTIC), *The Use and Economic Impact of TSUS Items 806.30 and 807*, Publication No. 2053 (Washington, DC: U.S. International Trade Commission, January 1988), pp. 8–12.

19. Instituto Nacional de Estadfstica, Geograffa e Informtica (INEGI), National Income and Product Accounts, 1988.

20. Douglas Alexander and Roberto L. Fernandez, "Environmental Regulation of Business in Mexico," *Doing Business in Mexico* (New York: Matthew Bender, 1990), pp. 79–29, 79–30.

21. 1982 Decree for Promotion of the Maquiladora Industry (Diario Oficial, August 15, 1983), Art. 26.

22. "Transfrontier Health and Environmental Risks," *Natural Resources Journal* (Winter 1990), p. 177.

23. Remarks of Mary E. Kelly, Executive Director, Texas Center for Policy Studies, before the Senate Finance Committee, February 20, 1991, p. 3.

24. "Border Industry's Nasty Byproduct Imperils Trade," *New York Times*, March 31, 1991, 16, col. 3.

25. Ibid., p. 4.

26. "The Texas Border: Whose Dirt?" *The Economist*, August 18, 1990, pp. 24–25.

27. "Transfrontier Health and Environmental Risks," Natural Resources Journal (Winter 1990), p. 177.

28. William K. Reilly, "Mexico's Environment Will Improve With Free Trade," *Wall Street Journal*, April 19, 1991, A15, col. 2.

29. Remarks of Mary E. Kelly, Executive Director, Texas Center for Policy Studies before the Senate Finance Committee, February 20, 1991, p. 6–7.

30. "The Texas Border: Whose Dirt?" *The Economist*, August 18, 1990, pp. 24–25.

31. Commercial, Business and Trade Laws, Mexico, F. Labor Law (Title first to ninth) (United States of America: Oceana Publications, Inc., 1983): p. 3.

32. U.S. International Tariff Commission (USTC), *The Use and Economic Impact of TSUS Items 806.30 and 807*, Publication No. 2053 (Washington, DC: U.S. International Trade Commission, January 1988).

33. Barbara Chrispin, "Manpower Development in the Maquiladora Industry: Reaching Maturity" in Khosrow Faterni ed., *The Maquiladora Industry: Economic Solution or Problem?* (New York: Praeger Publishers, 1990), p. 75.

34. Ibid., p. 76.

35. *Background and Perspectives on the U.S.–Mexico–Canada Free Trade Talks* (Pennsylvania: American Friends Service Committee, April 10, 1991), p. 6.

36. Simon Billenness and Kate Simpson, "Franklin's Insight," September 1992, Boston MA., p. 8.

37. Judith Ann Warner, "The Sociological Impact of the Maquiladoras" in Khosrow Fatemi ed., *The Maquiladora Industry: Economic Solution or Problem?* (New York: Praeger, 1990): 193. Lumbago is pain in the lower back (lumbar region) often caused by muscle strain.

38. Matt Moffett, "Working Children: Underage Laborers Fill Mexican Factories, Stir U.S. Trade Debate," *Wall Street Journal*, April 8, 1991, 1, col. 1.

39. Ibid.

40. Ibid., A14, col. 1.

41. Leslie Sklair, *Assembling for Development: The maquila Industry in Mexico and the United States* (Boston: Unwin Hyman, 1989), pp. 165–166.

42. U.S. International Tariff Commission (USTIC), *The Use and Economic Impact of TSUS Items 806.30 and 807*, Publication No. 2053 (Washington, DC: U.S. International Trade Commission, January 1988), pp. 8–15.

43. John Cavanagh, Lance Compa, et al., *Trade's Hidden Costs: Worker Rights in a Changing World Economy* (Washington, DC: International Labor Rights Education & Research Fund, 1988), p. 21.

44. Full Employment Action Council, "Economic Dislocation and Structural Unemployment: The Plight of America's Basic Industries," September 6, 1985.

45. Leslie Sklair, "Mexico's Maquiladora Programme," in George Philip (ed.), *The Mexican Economy* (London: Routledge, 1988), p. 299.

46. "The Natural Limits to Growth," *The Economist*, April 20, 1991, p. 24.

47. Ibid.

48. "Border Industry's Nasty Byproduct Imperils Trade," *New York Times*, March 31, 1991, 16, col 3.

49. "The Texas Border: Whose Dirt?" *The Economist*, August 18, 1990, p. 24.

50. "Border Industry's Nasty Byproduct Imperils Trade," *New York Times*, March 31, 1991, p. 16, col. 3.

51. "Border Industry's Nasty Byproduct Imperils Trade," *New York Times*, March 31, 1991, p. 16, col. 3.

Glossary

acculturation The process of cultural change and adaptation among groups, in particular where one or more minority groups are being merged with a majority group.

affective appeals Negotiation appeals based on emotions and subjective feelings.

appropriability of technology The ability of an innovating firm to protect its technology from competitors and to obtain economic benefits from that technology.

assimilation A one-way process of adaptation in which people are expected to conform to the values and norms of the dominant culture, causing gradual erosion of minority groups' cultures.

attribution The process in which a person looks for the explanation of another person's behavior.

axiomatic appeals Negotiation appeals based on the ideals generally accepted in a society.

B2B Business-to-business electronic transactions.

B2C Business-to-consumer electronic transactions.

balance sheet approach An approach to the compensation of expatriates that equalizes the standard of living between the host and home countries, plus compensation for inconvenience.

chaebol South Korea's large industrial conglomerates of financially linked, and often family-linked, groups of companies that do business among themselves whenever possible—for example, Daewoo.

codetermination The participation of labor in the management of a firm.

collective bargaining In the United States—negotiations between a labor union local and management; in Sweden and Germany, for example, negotiations between the employer's organization and a trade union at the industry level.

collectivism The tendency of a society toward tight social frameworks, emotional dependence on belonging to an organization, and a strong belief in group decisions.

comparative advantage A mutual benefit in the exchange of goods between countries, where each country exports those products in which it is relatively more efficient in production than other countries.

competitive advantage of nations The existence of conditions that give a country an advantage in a specific industry or in producing a particular good or service.

context in cultures (low to high) Low-context cultures, such as Germany, tend to use explicit means of communication in words and readily available information; high-context cultures, such as those in the Middle East, use more implicit means of communication, in which information is embedded in the nonverbal context and understanding of the people.

control system appropriateness The use of control systems that are individually tailored to the practices and expectations of the host-country personnel.

convergence (of management styles, techniques, and so forth) The phenomenon of increasing similarity of leadership styles resulting from a blending of cultures and business practices through international institutions, as opposed to the **divergence** of leadership styles necessary for different cultures and practices.

core competencies Important corporate resources or skills that bring competitive advantages.

creeping expropriation A government's gradual and subtle action against foreign firms.

creeping incrementalism A process of increasing commitment of resources to one or more geographic regions.

cross-cultural management (research), or comparative management (research) That field of management that studies the behavior of people interacting within and among organizations around the world.

cultural noise Cultural variables that undermine the communications of intended meaning.

cultural sensitivity (cultural empathy) A sense of awareness and caring about the culture of other people.

culture The shared values, understandings, assumptions, and goals that over time are passed on and imposed by members of a group or society.

culture shock A state of disorientation and anxiety that results from not knowing how to behave in an unfamiliar culture.

culture-specific reward systems Motivational and compensation approaches that reflect different motivational patterns across cultures.

deculturation The process by which people in transition between culture groups lose their cultural identity through insufficient ties to either group.

degree of enforcement The relative degree of enforcement, in a particular country, of the law regarding business behavior, which therefore determines the lower limit of permissible behavior.

direct control The control of foreign subsidiaries and operations through the use of appropriate international staffing and structure policies and meetings with home-country executives (as compared with **indirect control**).

distinctive competencies Strengths that allow companies to outperform rivals.

divergence See **convergence**.

domestic multiculturalism The diverse makeup of the workforce comprising people from several different cultures in the home (domestic) company.

E-commerce The selling of goods or services over the Internet.

E-commerce enablers Fulfillment specialists that provide other companies with services such as Web-site translation.

economic risk The level of uncertainty about the ability of a country to meet its financial obligations.

environmental assessment The continuous process of gathering and evaluating information about variables and events around the world that may pose threats or opportunities to the firm.

ethical relativism An approach to social responsibility in which a country adopts the moral code of its host country.

ethnocentric staffing approach An approach that fills key managerial positions abroad with persons from headquarters—that is, with parent-country nationals (PCNs).

ethnocentrism The belief that the management techniques used in one's own country are best no matter where or with whom they are applied.

expatriate One who works and lives in a foreign country but remains a citizen of the country where the employing organization is headquartered.

expropriation The seizure by a local government of the foreign-owned assets of an MNC with inadequate or no compensation.

Foreign Corrupt Practices Act A 1977 law that prohibits most questionable payments by U.S. companies to officials of foreign governments to gain business advantages.

Foreign Direct Investment (FDI) Multinational firm's ownership, in part or in whole, of an operation in another country.

franchising An international entry strategy by which a firm (the franchiser) licenses its trademark, products, or services and operating principles to the franchisee in a host country for an initial fee and ongoing royalties.

fully owned subsidiary An overseas operation started or bought by a firm that has total ownership and control; starting or buying such an operation is often used as an entry strategy.

generalizabilty of leadership styles The ability (or lack of ability) to generalize leadership theory, research results, and effective leadership practices from one country to another.

geocentric staffing approach A staffing approach in which the best managers are recruited throughout the company or outside the company, regardless of nationality—often, third-country nationals (TCNs) are recruited.

global corporate culture An integration of the business environments in which firms currently operate, resulting from a dissolution of traditional boundaries and from increasing links among MNCs.

globalism Global competition characterized by networks of international linkages that bind countries, institutions, and people in an interdependent global economy and a one-world market.

globalization The global strategy of the integration of worldwide operations and the development of standardized products and marketing approaches.

global strategic alliances Working partnerships that are formed around MNCs across national boundaries and often across industries.

governmentalism The tendency of a government to use its policy-setting role to favor national interests rather than relying on market forces.

high-context communication One in which people convey messages indirectly and implicitly.

horizontal organization (dynamic network) A structural approach that enables the flexibility to be global and act local through horizontal coordination, shared power, and decision making across international units and teams.

host-country nationals (HCNs) Workers who are indigenous to the local country where the plant is located.

indirect control The control of foreign operations through the use of reports, budgets, financial controls, and so forth. See also **direct control**.

individualism The tendency of people to look after themselves and their immediate family only and to value democracy, individual initiative, and personal achievement.

integration of immigrant workers Providing programs to integrate the foreign-born into the workplace and local community.

intercultural communication This type of communication occurs when a member of one culture sends a message to a receiver who is a member of another culture.

internal versus external locus of control Beliefs regarding whether a person controls his own fate and events or they are controlled by external forces.

international business The profit-related activities conducted across national boundaries.

international business ethics The business conduct or morals of MNCs in their relationships to all individuals and entities with whom they come in contact when conducting business overseas.

international codes of conduct The codes of conduct of four major international institutions that provide some consistent guidelines for multinational enterprises relative to their moral approach to business behavior around the world.

international competitor analysis The process of assessing the competitive positions, goals, strategies, strengths, and weaknesses of competitors relative to one's own firm.

internationalization The process by which a firm gradually changes in response to the imperatives of international competition, domestic market saturation, desire for expansion, new markets, and diversification.

international joint venture (IJV) An overseas business owned and controlled by two or more partners; starting such a venture is often used as an entry strategy.

international management The process of planning, organizing, leading, and controlling in a multicultural or cross-cultural environment.

international management teams Collections of managers from several countries who must rely on group collaboration if each member is to achieve success.

international social responsibility The expectation that MNCs should be concerned about the social and economic effects of their decisions regarding activities in other countries.

keiretsu Large Japanese conglomerates of financially linked, and often family-linked, groups of companies, such as Mitsubishi, that do business among themselves whenever possible.

kibun Feelings and attitudes (Korean word).

kinesics Communication through body movements.

labor relations The process through which managers and workers determine their workplace relationships.

licensing An international entry strategy by which a firm grants the rights to a firm in the host country to produce or sell a product.

locus of decision making The relative level of decentralization in an organization, that is, the level at which decisions of varying importance can be made—ranging from all decisions made at headquarters to all made at the local subsidiary.

love–hate relationship An expression describing a common attitude of host governments toward MNC investment in their country—they love the economic growth that the MNC brings but hate the incursions on their independence and sovereignty.

low-context communication One in which people convey messages directly and explicitly.

managing diversity The effective management of a culturally diverse workforce through understanding and valuing diversity; achieved by acknowledging and using the different skills and perceptions of people from various backgrounds and encouraging others to do so.

managing environmental interdependence The process by which international managers accept and enact their role in the preservation of ecological balance on the earth.

managing interdependence The effective management of a long-term MNC subsidiary–host-country relationship through cooperation and consideration for host concerns.

maquiladoras U.S. manufacturing or assembly facilities operating just south of the U.S.–Mexico border under special tax considerations.

masculinity The degree to which traditionally "masculine" values—assertiveness, materialism, and the like—prevail in a society.

MIS inadequacy The inability to gather timely and accurate information necessary for international management, especially in less developed countries.

monochronic cultures Those cultures in which time is experienced and used in a linear way; there is a past, present, and future, and time is treated as something to be spent, saved, wasted, and so on (as compared with **polychronic cultures**).

moral idealism The relative emphasis on long-term, ethical, and moral criteria for decisions versus short-term, cost-benefit criteria. See also **utilitarianism**.

moral universalism A moral standard toward social responsibility accepted by all cultures.

multicultural leader A person who is effective in inspiring and influencing the thinking, attitudes, and behavior of people from various cultural backgrounds.

multidomestic strategy Emphasizing local-responsiveness issues.

multinational corporation (MNC) A corporation that engages in production or service activities through its own affiliates in several countries, maintains control over the policies of those affiliates, and manages from a global perspective.

nationalism The practice by a country of rallying public opinion in favor of national goals and against foreign influences.

nationalization The forced sale of the MNC's assets to local buyers with some compensation to the firm, perhaps leaving a minority ownership with the MNC; often involves the takeover of an entire industry, such as the oil industry.

negotiation The process by which two or more parties meet to try to reach agreement regarding conflicting interests.

noncomparability of performance data across countries The control problem caused by the difficulty of comparing performance data across various countries because of the variables that make that information appear different.

nontask sounding (*nemawashi*) General polite conversation and informal communication before meetings.

nonverbal communication (body language) The transfer of meaning through the use of body language, time, and space.

objective–subjective decision-making approach The relative level of rationality and objectivity used in making decisions versus the level of subjective factors, such as emotions and ideals.

open systems model The view that all factors inside and outside a firm—environment, organization, and management—work together as a dynamic, interdependent system.

parochialism The expectation that "foreigners" should automatically fall into host-country patterns of behavior.

pluralism A process of acculturation in which there is a two-way integration of cultural groups.

political risk The potential for governmental actions or politically motivated events to occur in a country that will adversely affect the long-run profitability or value of a firm.

polycentric staffing approach An MNC policy of using local host-country nationals (HCNs) to fill key positions in the host country.

polychronic cultures Those cultures that welcome the simultaneous occurrence of many things and emphasize involvement with people over specific time commitments or compartmentalized activities (as compared with **monochronic cultures**).

posturing General discussion that sets the tone for negotiation meetings.

power distance The extent to which subordinates accept unequal power and a hierarchical system in a company.

privatization The sale of government-owned operations to private investors.

projective cognitive similarity The assumption that others perceive, judge, think, and reason in the same way.

proxemics The distance between people (personal space) with which a person feels comfortable.

protectionism A country's use of tariff and nontariff barriers to partially or completely close its borders to various imported products that would compete with domestic products.

quality control circle (QC circle) A group of workers who meet regularly to find ways to improve the quality of work.

questionable payments Business payments that raise significant ethical issues about appropriate moral behavior in either a host nation or other nations.

regiocentric staffing approach An approach in which recruiting for international managers is done on a regional basis and may comprise a specific mix of PCNs, HCNs, and TCNs.

regionalization The global corporate strategy that links markets within regions and allows managers in each region to formulate their own regional strategy and cooperate as quasi-independent subsidiaries.

regulatory environment The many laws and courts of the nation in which an international manager works.

relationship building The process of getting to know one's contacts in a host country and building mutual trust before embarking on business discussions and transactions.

repatriation The process of the reintegration of expatriates into the headquarters organization and career ladder as well as into the social environment.

Ringi system "Bottom up" decision-making process used in Japanese organizations.

self-reference criterion An unconscious reference to one's own cultural values; understanding and relating to others only from one's own cultural frame of reference.

separation The retention of distinct identities by minority groups unwilling or unable to adapt to the dominant culture.

stereotyping The assumption that every member of a society or subculture has the same characteristics or traits, without regard to individual differences.

strategic alliances (global) Working partnerships between MNCs across national boundaries and often across industries.

strategic freedom of an IJV The relative amount of control that an international joint venture will have, compared with the parents, in choosing suppliers, product lines, customers, and so on.

strategic implementation The process by which strategic plans are realized through the establishment of a system of fits throughout an organization with the desired strategy—for example, in organizational structure, staffing, and operations.

strategic planning The process by which a firm's managers consider the future prospects for their company and evaluate and decide on strategy to achieve long-term objectives.

strategy The basic means by which a company competes—the choice of business or businesses in which it operates and how it differentiates itself from its competitors in those businesses.

structural evolution The stages of change in an organizational structure that follow the evolution of the internationalization process.

subsidiary A business incorporated in a foreign country in which the parent corporation holds an ownership position.

synergy The greater level of effectiveness that can result from combined group effort than from the total of each individual's efforts alone.

technoglobalism A phenomenon in which the rapid developments in information and communication technologies (CTSs) are propelling globalization and vice versa.

terrorism The use of, or threat to use, violence for ideological or political purposes.

total quality management (TQM) A philosophy practiced by an entire organization working together with an interdepartmental collective responsibility for the quality of products and services.

transnational corporations (TNCs) Multinational corporations that are truly globalizing by viewing the world as one market and crossing boundaries for whatever functions or resources are most efficiently available; structural coordination reflects the ability to integrate globally while retaining local flexibility.

uncertainty avoidance The extent to which people feel threatened by ambiguous situations; in a company, this results in formal rules and processes to provide more security.

utilitarianism The relative emphasis on short-term cost-benefit (utilitarian) criteria for decisions versus those of long-term, ethical, and moral concerns. (See also **moral idealism**.)

values A person or group's ideas and convictions about what is important, good or bad, right or wrong.

work centrality The degree of general importance that working has in the life of an individual at any given time.

workforce diversity The phenomenon of increasing ethnic diversity in the workforce in the United States and many other countries because of diverse populations and joint ventures; this results in intercultural working environments in domestic companies.

works council In Germany, employee group that shares plant-level responsibility with managers.

World Trade Organization (WTO) A formal structure for continued negotiations to reduce trade barriers and settling trade disputes.

Booknotes

CHAPTER 1: ASSESSING THE ENVIRONMENT—POLITICAL, ECONOMIC, LEGAL, TECHNOLOGICAL

1. "Nokia's China Strategy: Exchanging Technology for Market Access," www.businessweek.com, January 22, 2001.
2. D. Pearl and A. Freedman, "Behind Cipla's Offer of Cheap AIDS Drugs," *Wall Street Journal*, March 12, 2001.
3. K. Ohmae, "Putting Global Logic First," *Harvard Business Review* (January–February 1995): 119–125.
4. *Business Week*, August 31, 1998.
5. *Buisness Week*, November 10, 1998.
6. Jeremy Kahn, "The Fortune Global 500," *Fortune*, August 3, 1998.
7. K. Ohmae, *The Borderless World* (New York: Harper Business, 1990).
8. Ibid.
9. "EU Members Play the Numbers Game," *Financial Times*, November 17, 2000.
10. *Wall Street Journal*, February 28, 1995.
11. "South Korean Chaebol Enter Series of Mergers," *Wall Street Journal*, September 4, 1998.
12. "How Japan's Toshiba Got Its Focus Back," *Wall Street Journal*, December 28, 2000.
13. "A Kinder, Gentler Way to Open Up Japan," *Wall Street Journal*, January 12, 2001.
14. G. Becker, "It's Time for NAFTA to Look Further South," *Business Week*, January 8, 2001.
15. *Fortune Investors' Guide*, December 18, 2000.
16. W. E. Halal and A. I. Nikitin, "One World: The Coming Synthesis of New Capitalism and a New Socialism," *Futurist* (November–December 1990): 8–14.
17. J. A. Quelch, E. Joachimsthaler, and J. L. Nueno, "After the Wall: Marketing Guidelines for Eastern Europe," *Sloan Management Review* (Winter 1991): 82–93.
18. "Piling into Central Europe," *Business Week*, July 1, 1996.
19. M. Forney and P. Yatski, "No More Free Lunch," *Far Eastern Economic Review*, October 16, 1997, 62–63.
20. Naomi Koppel, Associated Press, "Agreement Reached Allows China Entry into WTO," *The Press Republican*, September 16, 2001.
21. UPI Newswire, November 7, 1995.
22. K. Ohmae, 1990.
23. W. B. Johnston, "Global Work Force 2000: The New World Labor Market," *Harvard Business Review* (March–April 1991): 115–127.
24. Ibid.
25. N. J. Adler, "Cross-Cultural Management: Issues to Be Faced," *International Studies of Management and Organization* 13 (Spring–Summer 1983): 7–45.
26. B. Weiner, president of Probe International, "What Executives Should Know about Political Risks," *Management Review* (January 1991): 19–22.
27. Ibid.
28. S. H. Robock and K. Simmonds, *International Business and Multinational Enterprises*, 4th ed. (Homewood, IL: Irwin, 1989), 378.
29. Ibid.
30. D. F. Simon, "After Tiananmen: What Is the Future for Foreign Business in China?" *California Management Review* (Winter 1990): 106–108.
31. A. Jack, "Europe Reinvented: Russians Wake Up to Consumer Capitalism," January 30, 2001.
32. A. Clark, "Japan Goes to Europe," *World Monitor* (April 1990): 36–40.
33. E. F. Micklous, "Tracking the Growth and Prevalence of International Terrorism," in *Managing Terrorism: Strategies for the Corporate Executive*, ed. P. J. Montana and G. S. Roukis (Westport, CT: Quorum Books, 1983), 3.
34. Robock and Simmonds.
35. G. M. Taoka and D. R. Beeman, *International Business* (New York: HarperCollins, 1991).
36. Rahul Jacob, "Asian Infrastructure: The Biggest Bet on Earth," *Fortune*, October 31, 1994, 139–146.
37. D. R. Beeman, "An Empirical Analysis of the Beliefs Held by the International Executives of United States Firms Regarding Political Risks and Risk Reduction Methods in Developing Nations" (unpublished doctoral diss., Indiana University Graduate School of Business, 1978), reprinted in G. M. Taoka and D. R. Beeman, *International Business* (New York: HarperCollins, 1991), 36–41.
38. T. W. Shreeve, "Be Prepared for Political Changes Abroad," *Harvard Business Review* (July–August 1984): 111–118.
39. M. C. Schnitzer, M. L. Liebrenz, and K. W. Kubin, *International Business* (Cincinnati, OH: South-Western, 1985).

40. C. Erol, "An Exploratory Model of Political Risk Assessment and the Decision Process of Foreign Direct Investment," *International Studies of Management and Organization* (Summer 1985): 75–90.

41. T. Morrison, W. Conaway, and J. Bouress, *Dun & Bradstreet's Guide to Doing Business Around the World* (Englewood Cliffs, NJ: Prentice Hall, 1997).

42. Schnitzer, Liebrenz, and Kubin.

43. P. Smith Ring, S. A. Lenway, and M. Govekar, "Management of the Political Imperative in International Business," *Strategic Management Journal* 11 (1990): 141–151.

44. Ibid; L. D. Howell and B. Chaddick, "Models of Political Risk for Foreign Investment and Trade," *Columbia Journal of World Business* (Fall 1994).

45. Taoka and Beeman.

46. Ibid.

47. Overseas Private Investment Corporation, *Investment Insurance Handbook*, 4.

48. Schnitzer, Liebrenz, and Kubin.

49. B. O'Reilly, "Business Copes with Terrorism," *Fortune*, January 6, 1986, 48.

50. *Wall Street Journal*, December 29, 2000.

51. J. Dahl, "Firms Warn Workers Traveling Abroad," *Wall Street Journal*, April 10, 1989, B1.

52. *Wall Street Journal*, February 20, 2002.

53. F. John Mathis, "International Risk Analysis," in *Global Business Management in the 1990s*, ed. R. T. Moran (Washington, DC: Beacham, 1990): 33–44.

54. Mathis, 40.

55. Ibid.

56. Much of this section is drawn from A. Paul, "Indonesia," *Fortune*, April 13, 1998.

57. Ibid.

58. "Why Sweet Deals Are Going Sour in China," *Business Week*, December 19, 1994, 50–51.

59. M. Loeb, "China: A Time for Caution," *Fortune*, February 20, 1995.

60. P. Hui-Ho Cheng, "A Business Risk in China: Jail," *Asian Wall Street Journal*, April 22, 1994.

61. M. Litka, *Inernational Dimensions of the Legal Environment of Business* (Boston: PWS-Kent, 1988), 5.

62. Ibid.

63. Jacob.

64. Litka.

65. Jacob.

66. Ibid.

67. R. J. Radway, "Foreign Contract Agreements," in *Global Business Management in the 1990s*, ed. R. T. Moran (Washington, DC: Beacham, 1990), 93–103.

68. S. P. Robbins and R. Stuart-Kotze, *Management* (Scarborough, Ontario: Prentice Hall, Canada, 1990), 4–11.

69. Ibid.

70. "Lacking Roads, Village Building Information Highway," *Wall Street Journal*, December 29, 2001.

71. Sylvia Ostry, "Technological Productivity and the Multinational Enterprise," *Journal of International Business Studies* 29, no. 1 (1st quarter, 1998): 85–99.

72. Ibid.

73. "Where Technology Is the Appropriate Word," *The Economist*, April 18, 1987, 83.

74. "How to Sell Soap in India," *The Economist*, September 1988, 82.

75. Hans Dieter Zimmerman, "E-Business." www.businessmedia.org.

76. "What Is E-Business," PriceWaterhouseCoopers, www.pwcglobal.com, July 21, 2000.

77. J. Rajesh, "Five E-Business Trends," Net.Columns; www.indialine.com, February 18, 1999.

78. Ibid.

79. "E-Management," *The Economist*, November 11, 2000.

80. "E-Commerce Report, *New York Times*, March 26, 2001.

81. PriceWaterhouseCoopers. This section draws from a term paper by Ms. Laura Harrison, student at the State University of New York, December 2000.

82. "What Is E-Business," PriceWaterhouseCoopers, www.pwcglobal.com, July 21, 2000.

83. B. James, "Reducing the Risks of Globalization," *Long-Range Planning* 23, no. 1 (1990): 80–88.

CHAPTER 2: MANAGING INTERDEPENDENCE: SOCIAL RESPONSIBILITY AND ETHICS

1. "Killer in a Bottle," *The Economist* 279, no. 7184, May 9, 1981, 50.

2. A. M. Freeman and S. Stecklow, "As Unicef Battles Baby-Formula Makers, African Infants Sicken," *Wall Street Journal*, December 5, 2000.

3. Ibid.

4. J. C. Laya, "Economic Development Issues," in *Multinational Managers and Host Government Interactions*, ed. Lee A. Tavis (South Bend, IN: University of Notre Dame Press, 1988).

5. John A. Quelch and James E. Austin, "Should Multinationals Invest in Africa?" *Sloan Management Review* (Spring 1993): 107–119.

6. Milton Friedman, *Capitalism and Freedom* (Chicago: University of Chicago Press, 1962).

7. S. Prakash Sethi, "A Conceptual Framework for Environmental Analysis of Social Issues and Evaluation of Business Response Patterns," *Academy of Management Review* (January 1979): 63–74.

8. A. B. Carroll, "A Three Dimensional Conceptual Model of Corporate Performance," *Academy of Management Review* 4 (1979): 497–505.

9. John Dobson, "The Role of Ethics in Global Corporate Culture," *Journal of Business Ethics* 9 (1990): 481–488.

10. Ibid.

11. N. Bowie, "The Moral Obligations of Multinational Corporations," in *Problems of International Justice*, ed. Luper-Fay (New York: Westview Press: 1987), 97–113.

12. A. C. Wicks, "Norman Bowie and Richard Rorty on Multinationals: Does Business Ethics Need 'Metaphysical Comfort'?" *Journal of Business Ethics* 9 (1990): 191–200.

13. Joanna Ramey, "Clinton Urges Industry to Enlist in the War Against Sweatshops," www.labordepartment.com, April 15, 1997.

14. Shu Shin Luh, "Report Claims Abuses by Nike Contractors," *Wall Street Journal*, February 22, 2001.

15. *Asian Wall Street Journal*, April 8, 1994.

16. "Staunching the Flow of China's Gulag Exports," *Business Week*, April 13, 1992.

17. J. Carlton, "Ties with China Will Be Severed by Levi Strauss," *Wall Street Journal*, May 5, 1993, A3.

18. G. P. Zachary, "Levi Tries to Make Sure Contract Plants in Asia Treat Workers Well," *Wall Street Journal*, July 28, 1994.

19. "Sweatshop Police," *Business Week*, October 20, 1997.

20. Kathleen A. Getz, "International Codes of Conduct: An Analysis of Ethical Reasoning," *Journal of Business Ethics* 9 (1990): 567–577.

21. Swee Hoon Ang, "The Power of Money: A Cross-Cultural Analysis of Business-Related Beliefs," *Journal of World Business* 35, no. 1 (Spring 2000): 43.

22. D. Vogel, "Is U.S. Business Obsessed with Ethics?" *Across the Board* (November/December 1993): 31–33; A. Singer, "Ethics—Are Standards Lower Overseas?" *Across the Board* (September 1991): 31–34.

23. Parviv Asheghian and Bahman Ebrahimi, *International Business* (New York: Harper and Row, 1990), 640–641.

24. Ibid.

25. Vogel.

26. A. Singer, "Ethics—Are Standards Lower Overseas?" *Across the Board*, September 1991, 31–34.

27. Ibid.

28. J. G. Kaikati and W. A. Label, "American Bribery Legislation: An Obstacle to International Marketing," *Journal of Marketing* (Fall 1980): 38–43.

29. G. R. Laczniak and J. Naor, "Global Ethics: Wrestling with the Corporate Conscience," *Business*, July–August–September, 1985, 152.

30. Singer.

31. G. A. Steiner and J. F. Steiner, *Business, Government and Society*, 6th ed. (New York: McGraw-Hill, 1991).

32. Larry Luxner, "IBM Feeling Blue in Argentina," *Multinational Monitor* 17, no. 10 (October 1996): 14(4).

33. T. L. Carson, "Bribery and Implicit Agreements: A Reply to Philips," *Journal of Business Ethics* 6 (1987): 123–125.

34. M. Philips, "Bribery," *Ethics* 94 (July 1984).

35. Ibid.

36. Laczniak and Naor, 1985.

37. L. H. Newton and M. M. Ford, *Taking Sides* (Guilford, CT: Dushkin, 1990).

38. Ibid.; K. Gillespie, "Middle East Response to the U.S. Foreign Corrupt Practices Act," *California Management Review* (Summer 1987): 9.

39. K. M. Bartol and D. C. Martin, *Management* (New York: McGraw-Hill, 1991).

40. Vogel.

41. A. Cadbury, *Harvard Business Review* (September–October 1987): 63–73.

42. M. E. Shannon, "Coping with Extortion and Bribery," in *Multinational Managers and Host Government Interactions*, ed. Lee A Tavis (South Bend, IN: University of Notre Dame Press, 1988).

43. Laczniak and Naor.

44. "A World of Greased Palms," *Business Week*, November 6, 1995.

45. D. E. Sanger, "Nippon Telegraph Executive Demoted for Role in Scandal," *New York Times*, December 10, 1988.

46. Susan Chira, "Another Top Official in Japan Loses Post in Wake of Scandal," *New York Times*, January 25,1989, 1, 5; and "Remember the Recruit Scandal? Well . . ." *Business Week*, January 8, 1990, 52.

47. Sadehei Kusomoto, "We're Not in Honshu Anymore," *Across the Board* (June 1989): 49—50.

48. Ibid.

49. P. W. Beamish et al., *International Management* (Homewood, IL: Irwin, 1991).

50. J. N. Behrman, *National Interests and the Multinational Enterprise* (Englewood Cliffs, NJ: Prentice Hall, 1970), 31.

51. Adapted from Asheghian and Ebrahimi.

52. R. Grosse and D. Kujawa, *Inernational Business* (Homewood, IL: Irwin, 1988), 705.

53. R. H. Mason and R. S. Spich, *Management, An International Perspective* (Homewood, IL: Irwin, 1987).

54. Yves L. Doz and C. K. Prahalad, "How MNCs Cope with Host Government Intervention," *Harvard Business Review* (March–April 1980).

55. Mason and Spich.

56. Simcha Ronen, *Comparative and Multinational Management* (New York: John Wiley and Sons, 1986), 502–503.

57. R. T. De George, *Competing with Integrity in International Business* (New York: Oxford University Press, 1993), 3–4.

58. *The Nation,* January 22, 2001.

59. "A Whole New World," *Time,* June 11, 2001.

60. Ibid.

61. "Interfaith Center on Corporate Responsibility," *Wall Street Journal,* June 28, 2001.

62. *Automotive News,* February 12, 2001.

63. L. F. Tomasi, "Borderless Economy and Barricaded Borders," *Migration World Magazine,* January 2001, 4.

64. *Time.*

65. *Fortune*—Investors' Guide, December 18, 2000.

66. "Two Years Later, the Promises Used to Sell NAFTA Haven't Come True, but Its Foes Were Wrong, Too," *Wall Street Journal,* October 26, 1995.

67. *Wall Street Journal,* October 28, 1994.

68. Ibid.

69. *Fortune,* 2000.

70. *Wall Street Journal,* 1994.

71. "The Border," *Business Week,* May, 1997.

72. Ibid.

73. *Wall Street Journal,* June 29, 1994.

74. Felipe A. M. de la Balze, "Finding Allies in the Back Yard—NAFTA and the Southern Cone," *Foreign Affairs,* July–August, 2001, v80 i4, p. 7.

75. "NAFTA for the Americas," *Earth Island Journal,* Summer, 2001, v16, i2, p. 24.

76. B. Ward and R. Dubois, *Only One Earth* (New York: Ballantine Books, 1972).

77. Ronen.

78. S. Tifft, "Who Gets the Garbage," *Time,* July 4, 1988, 42–43.

79. Jang B. Singh and V. C. Lakhan, "Business Ethics and the International Trade in Hazardous Wastes," *Journal of Business Ethics* 8 (1989): 889–899.

80. R. A. Peterson and M. H. Sauber, "International Marketing Ethics: Is There a Need for a Code?" (paper presented at the International Studies Association Southwest, Houston, TX, March 16–19, 1984).

81. M. Reza Vaghefi, S. K. Paulson, and W. H. Tomlinson, *International Business Theory and Practice* (New York: Taylor and Francis, 1991): 249–250.

82. T. E. Graedel and B. R. Allenby, *Industrial Ecology* (Englewood Cliffs, NJ: Prentice Hall, 1995).

83. M. Sharfman, Book Review of Graedel and Allenby, *Academy of Management Review* 20, no. 4 (1995): 1090–1107.

84. Ronen, 1986.

85. P. Asheghian and B. Ebrahimi, *International Business* (NY: Harper and Row, 1990) 640–641.

86. Becker and Fritzsche.

CHAPTER 3: UNDERSTANDING THE ROLE OF CULTURE

1. David A. Ricks, *Big Business Blunders: Mistakes in Multinational Marketing* (Homewood, IL: Dow-Jones-Irwin, 1983).

2. Carla Joinson, "Why HR Managers Need to Think Globally," *HR Magazine,* April 1998, 2–7.

3. Ibid.

4. J. Stewart Black and Mark Mendenhall, "Cross-Cultural Training Effectiveness: A Review and a Theoretical Framework for Future Research," *Academy of Management Review* 15, no. 1 (1990): 113–136.

5. Adapted from Bernard Wysocki, Jr., "Global Reach: Cross-Border Alliances Become Favorite Way to Crack New Markets," *Wall Street Journal,* March 26, 1990, A1, A4.

6. Geert Hofstede, *Culture's Consequences: International Differences in Work-Related Values* (Beverly Hills, CA: Sage Publications, 1980), 25; E. T. Hall, *The Silent Language* (Greenwich, CT: Fawcett, 1959). For a more detailed definition of the culture of a society, see A. L. Kroeber and C. Kluckholhn, "A Critical Review of Concepts and Definitions," in *Peabody Museum Papers* 47, no. 1 (Cambridge, MA: Harvard University Press, 1952), 181.

7. David Dressler and Donald Carns, *Sociology, The Study of Human Interaction* (New York: Knopf, 1969), 56–57.

8. K. David, "Organizational Processes for Intercultural Management," Paper presented at the Strategic Management Association, San Francisco, CA, 1989.

9. *Wall Street Journal,* February 20, 2001; and *Wall Street Journal,* February 2, 1990, A15.

10. Lane Kelley, Arthur Whatley, and Reginald Worthley, "Assessing the Effects of Culture on Managerial Attitudes: A Three-Culture Test," *Journal of International Business Studies* (Summer 1987): 17–31.

11. J. D. Child, "Culture, Contingency and Capitalism in the Cross-National Study of Organizations," in *Research in Organizational Behavior,* ed. L. L. Cummings and B. M. Shaw (Greenwich, CT: JAI Publishers, 1981), 303–356.

12. Jangho Lee, T. W. Roehl, and Soonkyoo Choe, "What Makes Management Style Similar and Distinct Across Borders? Growth Experience and Culture in Korean and Japanese Firms," *Journal of International Business Studies* 31, no. 4 (4th Quarter 2000): 631–652.

13. James A. Lee, "Cultural Analysis in Overseas Operations," *Harvard Business Review* (March–April 1966).

14. E. T. Hall, "The Silent Language in Overseas Business," *Harvard Business Review* (May–June 1960).

15. "American Culture Is Often a Puzzle for Foreign Managers in the U.S.," *Wall Street Journal*, February 12, 1986, 34.

16. "One Big Market," *Wall Street Journal*, February 6, 1989, 16.

17. D. A. Ralston, Yu Kai-Ceng, Xun Wang, R. H. Terpstra, and He Wel, "An Analysis of Managerial Work Values across the Six Regions of China" Paper presented at the *Academy of International Business*, Boston, November 1994.

18. Philip R. Harris and Robert T. Moran, *Managing Cultural Differences* (Houston, TX: Gulf Publishing, 1987).

19. K. David, "Field Research," in *The Cultural Environment of International Business*, 3rd ed., ed. V. Terpstra and K. David (Cincinnati, OH: SouthWestern, 1991), 176.

20. "Sharia Loosens Its Grip," *Euromoney* (May 1987): 137–138.

21. Ibid.

22. Mansour Javidan and Robert J. House, "Cultural Acumen for the Global Manager: Lessons from Project GLOBE," *Organizational Dynamics* (Spring 2001): 289–305.

23. Geert Hofstede, "National Cultures in Four Dimensions," *International Studies of Management and Organization* (Spring–Summer 1983).

24. Elizabeth Weldon and Elisa L. Mustari, "Felt Dispensability in Groups of Coactors: The Effects of Shared Responsibility on Cognitive Effort" (unpublished manuscript, Kellogg Graduate School of Management, Northwestern University).

25. P. Christopher Earley, "Social Loafing and Collectivism: A Comparison of the United States and the People's Republic of China," *Administrative Science Quarterly* 34 (1989): 565–581.

26. H. K. Steensma, L. Marino, and K. M. Weaver, "Attitudes towards Cooperative Strategies: A Cross-Cultural Analysis of Entrepreneurs," *Journal of International Business Studies* 31, no. 4 (4th Quarter 2000): 591–609.

27. Simcha Ronen and Oded Shenkar, "Clustering Countries on Attitudinal Dimensions: A Review and Synthesis," *Academy of Management Review* 10, no. 3 (1985): 435–454.

28. F. Trompenaars, *Riding the Waves of Culture* (London: Nicholas Brealey, 1993).

29. L. Hoeklin, *Managing Cultural Differences: Strategies for Competitive Advantage* (The Economist Intelligence Unit/N.Y. Addison-Wesley, 1995).

30. Ross A. Webber, *Culture and Management, Text and Reading in Comparative Management* (Homewood, IL: Irwin, 1969), 186.

31. "Korea's Digital Quest," www.businessweek.com, September 25, 2000.

32. H. Jeff Smith, "Information Privacy and Marketing: What the U.S. Should (and Shouldn't) Learn from Europe," *California Management Review* 43, no. 2 (Winter 2001).

33. Ibid.

34. Ibid.

35. "Data Privacy Deal," *Journal of Commerce*, March 28, 2000, 4.

36. R. Howells, "Update on Safe Harbor for International Data Transfer," *Direct Marketing* 63, no. 4 (August 2000): 40.

37. Smith, 2001.

38. D. Darlin and J. B. White, "GM Venture in Korea Nears End, Betraying Firm's Fond Hopes," *Wall Street Journal*, January 16, 1992, 1.

39. Geert Hofstede, *Culture's Consequences: International Differences in Work-Related Values* (Beverly Hills, CA; Sage Publications, 1980).

40. George W. England, "Managers and Their Value Systems: A Five-Country Comparative Study," *Columbia Journal of World Business* (Summer 1978): 35–44.

41. Lennie Copeland and Lewis Griggs, *Going International* (New York: Random House, 1985); Boye De Mente, *Japanese Etiquette and Ethics in Business* (Lincolnwood, IL: NTC Business Books, 1989); Boye De Mente, *Korean Etiquette and Ethics in Business* (Lincolnwood, IL: NTC Business Books, 1989); George W. England and R. Lee, "Organizational Goals and Expected Behavior among American, Japanese and Korean Managers: A Comparative Study," *Academy of Management Journal* 14, no. 4 (1971): 425–438; R. L. Tung, *Business Negotiations with the Japanese* (Lexington, MA: Lexington Books, 1984); W. G. Ouchi and A. M. Jaeger, "Theory Z Organization: Stability in the Midst of Mobility," *Academy of Management Review* 3, no. 2 (1978): 305–314; T. Seth, "Management and Its Environment in India," in *Management in an International Context*, ed. Joseph L. Massie and J. Luytjes (New York: Harper and Row, 1972): 201–225; Nam-Won Suh, "Management and Its Environment in Korea," in *Management in an International Context*, ed. Joseph L. Massie and Jan Luytjes (New York: Harper and Row, 1972),

226–244; Philip R. Harris and Robert T. Moran, *Managing Cultural Differences* (Houston, TX: Gulf Publishing, 1991); Fernando Quezada and James E. Boyce, "Latin America," in *Comparative Management*, ed. Raghu Nath (Cambridge, MA: Ballinger Publishing, 1988), 245–270; Simcha Ronen, *Comparative and Multinational Management* (New York: John Wiley and Sons, 1986); and V. Terpstra and K. David, *The Cultural Environment of International Business*, 3rd ed. (Cincinnati, OH: South-Western, 1991).

42. R. G. Linowes, "The Japanese Manager's Traumatic Entry in the United States: Understanding the American-Japanese Cultural Divide," *Academy of Management Review* (1993): 21–38.

43. Ibid.

44. Yumiko Ono and Wm. Spindle, "Japan's Long Decline Makes One Thing Rise—Individualism," *Wall Street Journal*, December 29, 2000.

45. Ibid.

46. E. T. Hall and M. R. Hall, *Understanding Cultural Differences* (Yarmouth, ME: Intercultural Press, 1990), 4.

47. P. R. Haris and R. T. Moran, *Managing Cultural Differences*, 4th ed. (Houston, TX: Gulf Publishing Co., 1996).

48. Robert Moore, "Saudi Arabia," Chapter 11, in Harris and Moran.

49. John A. Pearce II and Richard B. Robinson, Jr., "Cultivating Guanxi as a Foreign Investor Strategy," *Business Horizons* 43, 1 (January 2000): 31.

50. M. Chen, *Asian Management Systems: Chinese, Japanese and Korean Styles of Business* (New York: Routledge, 1995).

51. Anne Marie Francesco and Barry Allen Gold, *International Organizational Behavior* (Upper Saddle River, NJ: Prentice Hall, 1997).

52. J. Lee, "Culture and Management—A Study of Small Chinese Family Business in Singapore," *Journal of Small Business Management*, July 1996.

53. R. Sheng, "Outsiders' Perception of the Chinese," *Columbia Journal of World Business* 14 (2) (Summer 2000), 16–22.

54. Lee.

55. Ralston, et al.

CHAPTER 4: COMMUNICATING ACROSS CULTURES

1. E. T. Hall and M. R. Hall, *Understanding Cultural Differences* (Yarmouth, ME: Intercultural Press, 1990), 4.

2. E. Wilmott, "New Media Vision," *New Media Age*, September 9, 1999, p. 8.

3. Hall and Hall; K. Wolfson and W. B. Pearce, "A Cross-Cultural Comparison of the Implications of Self-discovery on Conversation Logics," *Communication Quarterly* 31 (1983): 249–256.

4. H. Mintzberg, *The Nature of Managerial Work* (New York: Harper and Row, 1973).

5. L. A. Samovar, R. E. Porter, and N. C. Jain, *Understanding Intercultural Communication* (Belmont, CA: Wadsworth Publishing Co., 1981).

6. P. R. Harris and R. T. Moran, *Managing Cultural Differences*, 3rd ed. (Houston, TX: Gulf Publishing, 1991).

7. Samovar, Porter, and Jain.

8. Hall and Hall, 15.

9. J. Child, "Trust—The Fundamental Bond in Global Collaboration," *Organizaional Dynamics* 29, no. 4 (Spring 2001): 274–288.

10. Ibid.

11. World Values Study Group (1994), *World Values Survey, ICPSR version* (Ann Arbor, MI: Institute for Social Research); R. Inglehart, M. Basanez, and A. Moreno, *Human Values and Beliefs: A Cross-Cultural Sourcebook* (Ann Arbor: University of Michigan Press, 1998).

12. Mansour Javidan and Robert J. House, "Cultural Acumen for the Global Manager," *Organizational Dynamics* 29, no. 4 (Spring 2001), 289—305.

13. Harris and Moran.

14. M. L. Hecht, P. A. Andersen, and S. A. Ribeau, "The Cultural Dimensions of Nonverbal Communication, in *Handbook of International and Intercultural Communication*, ed. M. K. Asante and W. B. Gudykunst (Newbury Park, CA: Sage Publications, 1989), 163–185.

15. H. C. Triandis, *Interpersonal Behavior* (Monterey, CA: Brooks/Cole, 1977).

16. Harris and Moran.

17. Adapted from N. Adler, *International Dimensions of Organizational Behavior*, 2nd ed. (Boston: PWS-Kent, 1991).

18. D. A. Ricks, *Big Business Blunders: Mistakes in Multinational Marketing* (Homewood, IL: Dow-Jones-Irwin, 1983).

19. Vern Terpstra and K. David, *The Cultural Environment of International Business*, 3rd ed. (Cincinnati, OH: South-Western, 1991).

20. L. Copeland and L. Griggs, *Going International* (New York: Random House, 1985).

21. J. R. Schermerhorn, "Language Effects in Cross-Cultural Management Research: An Empirical Study and a Word of Caution," *National Academy of Management Proceedings* (1987): 103.

22. Jiatao Li, Katherine R. Xin, Anne Tsui, and Donald C. Hambrick, "Building Effective International Joint Venture Leadership Teams in China," *Journal of World Business* 34, no. 1 (1999): 52–68.

23. R. L. Daft, *Organizational Theory and Design*, 3rd ed. (St. Paul, MN: West Publishing, 1989).

24. Li et al., 1999.

25. O. Klineberg, "Emotional Expression in Chinese Literature," *Journal of Abnormal and Social Psychology* 33 (1983): 517–530.

26. P. Ekman and W. V. Friesen, "Constants Across Cultures in the Face and Emotion," *Journal of Personality and Social Psychology* 17 (1971): 124–129.

27. J. Pfeiffer, "How Not to Lose the Trade Wars by Cultural Gaffes," *Smithsonian* 18, no. 10 (January 1988).

28. E. T. Hall, *The Silent Language* (New York: Doubleday, 1959).

29. Hall and Hall.

30. Ibid.

31. N. M. Sussman and H. M. Rosenfeld, "Influence of Culture, Language, and Sex on Conversational Distance," *Journal of Personality and Social Psychology* 42 (1982): 66–74.

32. Copeland and Griggs.

33. Hecht, Andersen, and Ribeau.

34. Li et al., 1999.

35. Pfeiffer.

36. Hall and Hall.

37. Ibid.

38. Hecht, Andersen, and Ribeau.

39. P. A. Andersen, "Explaining Differences in Nonverbal Communication," in *Intercultural Communication: A Reader*, ed. L. A. Samovar and R. E. Porter (Belmont, CA: Wadsworth, 1988); S. Scott Elliot, A. D. Jensen, and M. McDonough, "Perceptions of Reticence: A Cross-Cultural Investigation," in *Communication Yearbook* 5, ed. M. Burgoon (New Brunswick, NJ: Transaction, 1982).

40. Hall and Hall.

41. R. Axtell, ed., *Dos and Taboos Around the World*, 2nd ed. (New York: John Wiley and Sons, 1985).

42. Copeland and Griggs.

43. M. K. Nydell, *Understanding Arabs* (Yarmouth, ME: Intercultural Press, 1987).

44. Harris and Moran.

45. E. T. Hall, *The Hidden Dimension* (New York: Doubleday, 1966), 15.

46. A. Almaney and A. Alwan, *Communicating with the Arabs* (Prospect Heights, IL: Waveland, 1982).

47. E. T. Hall, "The Silent Language in Overseas Business," *Harvard Business Review* (May–June 1960).

48. Ibid.

49. Based largely on the work of Nydell; and R. T. Moran and P. R. Harris, *Managing Cultural Synergy* (Houston, TX: Gulf Publishing, 1982), 81–82.

50. Ibid.

51. Copeland and Griggs.

52. Hall and Hall.

53. D. C. Barnlund, "Public and Private Self in Communicating with Japan," *Business Horizons* (March–April 1989): 32–40.

54. Hall and Hall.

55. A. Goldman, "The Centrality of "Ningensei" to Japanese Negotiating and Interpersonal Relationships: Implications for U.S.-Japanese Communication," *International Journal of Intercultural Relations* 18, no. 1 (Winter 1994).

56. Jean-Louis Barsoux and Peter Lawrence, "The Making of a French Manager," *Harvard Business Review* (July–August 1991): 58–67.

57. D. Shand, "All Information Is Local: IT Systems Can Connect Every Corner of the Globe, But IT Managers Are Learning They Have to Pay Attention to Regional Differences," *Computerworld*, April 10, 2000, p. 88 (1).

58. T. Wilson, "B2B Links, European Style—Integrator Helps Apps Cross Language, Currency and Cultural Barriers," *InternetWeek*, October 9, 2000, 27.

59. Shand.

60. Wilmott.

61. *Business Week*, February, 1998, 14–15.

62. Wilson.

63. www.manheimauctions.com, April 2001.

64. Shand.

65. Ibid.

66. D. Ricks, *Big Business Blunders* (Homewood, IL: Dow-Jones-Irwin, 1983).

67. Adler.

68. P. G. W. Keen, "Sorry, Wrong Number," *Business Month* (January 1990): 62–67.

69. R. B. Ruben, "Human Communication and Cross-Cultural Effectiveness," in *Intercultural Communication: A Reader*, ed. L. Samovar and R. Porter (Belmont, CA: Wadsworth, 1985): 339.

70. D. Ruben and B. D. Ruben, "Cross-Cultural Personnel Selection Criteria, Issues and Methods," in *Handbook of Intercultural Training*: vol. 1, *Issues in Theory and Design*, ed. D. Landis and R. W. Brislin (New York: Pergamon, 1983), 155–175.

71. Young Yun Kim, *Communication and Cross-Cultural Adaptation: An Integrative Theory* (Clevedon, England; Multilingual Matters, 1988).

72. Ibid.

73. R. W. Brislin, *Cross-Cultural Encounters: Face-to-Face Interaction* (New York: Pergamon, 1981).

CHAPTER 5: CROSS-CULTURAL NEGOTIATION AND DECISION MAKING

1. John Pfeiffer, "How Not to Lose the Trade Wars by Cultural Gaffes," *Smithsonian* 18, no. 10 (January 1988): 145–156.
2. Nancy J. Adler, *International Dimensions of Organizational Behavior*, 2nd ed. (Boston: PWS-Kent).
3. Philip R. Harris and Robert T. Moran, *Managing Cultural Differences*, 2nd ed. (Houston, TX: Gulf Publishing).
4. John L. Graham and Roy A. Herberger, Jr., "Negotiators Abroad—Don't Shoot from the Hip," *Harvard Business Review* (July–August 1983): 160–168; Adler; John L. Graham, "A Hidden Cause of America's Trade Deficit with Japan," *Columbia Journal of World Business* (Fall 1981): 5–15.
5. Phillip D. Grub, "Cultural Keys to Successful Negotiating," in *Global Business Management in the 1990s*, ed. F. Ghader et al. (Washington, DC: Beacham, 1990): 24–32.
6. R. Fisher and W. Ury, *Getting to Yes* (Boston: Houghton Mifflin, 1981).
7. "Soviet Breakup Stymies Foreign Firms," *Wall Street Journal*, January 23, 1992.
8. S. Weiss, "Negotiating with 'Romans,'" *Sloan Management Review* (Winter 1994): 51–61.
9. John A. Reeder, "When West Meets East: Cultural Aspects of Doing Business in Asia," *Business Horizons* (January–February 1987): 72.
10. Adler, 197.
11. Fisher and Ury.
12. Lennie Copeland and Lewis Griggs, *Going International* (New York: Random House, 1985), 85.
13. Ibid.
14. Adler, 197–198.
15. Fisher and Ury.
16. R. Tung, "Handshakes across the Sea," *Organizational Dynamics*, Winter 1991, 30–40.
17. John L. Graham, "The Influence of Culture on Business Negotiations," *Journal of International Business Studies* 16, no. 1 (Spring 1985): 81–96.
18. G. Fisher, *Inernational Negotiation: A Cross-Cultural Perspective* (Chicago: Intercultural Press, 1980).
19. Pfeiffer.
20. *Wall Street Journal*, February 2, 1994.
21. John L. Graham, "Brazilian, Japanese, and American Business Negotiations," *Journal of International Business Studies* (Spring–Summer 1983): 47–61.
22. T. Flannigan, "Successful Negotiating with the Japanese," *Small Business Reports* 15, no. 6 (June 1990): 47–52.
23. Graham, 1983; Boye De Mente, *Japanese Etiquette and Ethics in Business* (Lincolnwood, IL: NTC Business Books, 1989).
24. Robert H. Doktor, "Asian and American CEOs: A Comparative Study," *Organizational Dynamics* (Winter 1990): 49.
25. Harris and Moran, 461.
26. Adler, 181.
27. These profiles are adapted from Pierre Casse, *Managing Intercultural Negotiations: Guidelines for Trainers and Negotiators* (Washington, DC: Society for Intercultural Education, Training and Research, 1985).
28. D. K. Tse, J. Francis, and J. Walls, "Cultural Differences in Conducting Intra- and Inter-Cultural Negotiations: A Sino-Canadian Comparison," *Journal of International Business Studies* (3rd Quarter 1994): 537–555.
29. B. W. Husted, "Bargaining with the Gringos: An Exploratory Study of Negotiations between Mexican and U.S. Firms," *International Executive* 36, no. 5 (September–October 1994): 625–644.
30. Pierre Casse, *Training for the Cross-Cultural Mind*, 2nd ed. (Washington, DC: Society for Intercultural Education, Training, and Research, 1981).
31. Nigel Campbell, John L. Graham, Alain Jolibert, and Hans Meissner, "Marketing Negotiations in France, Germany, the United Kingdom, and the United States," *Journal of Marketing* 52 (April 1988): 49–63.
32. Neil Rackham, "The Behavior of Successful Negotiators" (Reston, VA: Huthwaite Research Group, 1982).
33. J. Teich, H. Wallenius, and J. Wallenius, "World-Wide-Web Technology in Support of Negotiation and Communication," *International Journal of Technology Management* 17, nos. 1/2 (1999): 223–239.
34. Ibid.
35. Ibid.
36. J. A. Pearce II, and R. B. Robinson, Jr., "Cultivating Guanxi as a Foreign Investor Strategy," *Business Horizons* 43, no. 1 (January 2000): 31.
37. Ibid.; R. L. Tung, *U.S.-China Trade Negotiations* (New York: Pergamon Press, 1982).
38. Joan H. Coll, "Sino-American Cultural Differences: The Key to Closing a Business Venture with the Chinese," *Mid-Atlantic Journal of Business* 25, no. 2, 3 (December 1988/January 1989); 15–19.
39. M. Loeb, "China: A Time for Caution," *Fortune*, February 20, 1995, 129–130.
40. O. Shenkar and S. Ronen, "The Cultural Context of Negotiations: The Implications of Chinese Interpersonal Norms," *Journal of Applied Behavioral Science* 23, no. 2 (1987): 263–275.

41. Tse et al.

42. J. Brunner, teaching notes, the University of Toledo.

43. Ibid.

44. Joanna M. Banthin and Leigh Stelzer, "Ethical Dilemmas in Negotiating Across Cultures: Problems in Commercial Negotiations between American Businessmen and the PRC," Paper presented at 1st International Conference on East-West Joint Ventures, October 19–20, 1989, State University of New York–Plattsburgh; and J. M. Banthin and L. Stelzer, "'Opening' China: Negotiation Strategies When East Meets West," *The Mid-Atlantic Journal of Business* 25, no. 2, 3 (December 1988/January 1989).

45. Brunner.

46. Pearce and Robinson.

47. Ibid.

48. Ibid.

49. C. Blackman, "An Inside Guide to Negotiating," *China Business Review*, 27, no. 3 (May 2000): 44–45.

50. Brunner.

51. Boye De Mente, *Chinese Etiquette and Ethics in Business* (Lincolnwood, IL: NTC Business Books, 1989), 115–123.

52. S. Stewart and C. F. Keown, "Talking with the Dragon: Negotiating in the People's Republic of China," *Columbia Journal of World Business* 24, no. 3 (Fall 1989): 68–72.

53. Banthin and Stelzer, "'Opening' China."

54. Blackman.

55. Ibid.

56. Lucian Pye, *Chinese Commercial Negotiating Style* (Cambridge, MA: Oelgeschlager, Gunn and Hain, 1982).

57. W. B. Gudykunst and S. Ting Tomey, *Culture and Interpersonal Communication* (Newbury Park, CA: Sage Publications, 1988).

58. L. Copeland and L. Griggs, *Going International* (New York: Random House, 1985), 80.

59. M. A. Hitt, B. B. Tyler, and Daewoo Park, "A Cross-Cultural Examination of Strategic Decision Models: Comparison of Korean and U.S. Executives," in *Best Papers Proceedings of the 50th Annual Meeting of the Academy of Management* (San Francisco, CA, August 12–15, 1990): 111–115; G. Fisher, *International Negotiation: A Cross-Cultural Perspective* (Chicago: Intercultural Press, 1980); G. W. England, "Managers and Their Value Systems: A Five-Country Comparative Study," *Columbia Journal of World Business* 13, no. 2 (Summer 1978); W. Whitely and G. W. England, "Variability in Common Dimensions of Managerial Values Due to Value Orientation and Country Differences," *Personnel Psychology* 33 (1980): 77–89.

60. Hitt, Tyler, and Park, 114.

61. B. M. Bass and P. C. Burger, *Assessment of Managers: An International Comparison* (New York: Free Press, 1979), 91.

62. D. K. Tse, R. W. Belk, and Nan Zhan, "Learning to Consume: A Longitudinal and Cross-Cultural Content Analysis of Print Advertisements from Hong Kong, People's Republic of China and Taiwan," *Journal of Consumer Research* (forthcoming).

63. Copeland and Griggs; M. K. Badawy, "Styles of Mideastern Managers," *California Management Review* 22 (1980): 51–58.

64. N. Namiki and S. P. Sethi, "Japan," in *Comparative Management—A Regional View*, ed. R. Nath (Cambridge, MA: Ballinger Publishing, 1988), 74–76.

65. De Mente, *Japanese Etiquette*, 80.

66. S. Naoto, *Management and Industrial Structure in Japan* (New York: Pergamon Press, 1981); Namiki Sethi.

67. Harris and Moran, 397.

68. S. P. Sethi and N. Namiki, "Japanese-Style Consensus Decision-Making in Matrix Management: Problems and Prospects of Adaptation," in *Matrix Management Systems Handbook*, ed. D. I. Cleland (New York: Van Nostrand, 1984), 431–456.

CHAPTER 6: FORMULATING STRATEGY

1. "FedEx Forms Joint Venture in China," November 11, 1999.

2. Ibid.

3. D. Blackmon and D. Brady, "Orient Express: Just How Should a U.S. Company Woo a Big Foreign Market?" *Wall Street Journal*, April 6, 1998.

4. A. Hill, "International Economy: UPS Granted Application to Fly Direct to China," *Financial Times*, November 27, 2000.

5. Bernard Wysocki, Jr., "U.S. Firms Increase Overseas Investments," *Wall Street Journal*, April 9, 1990.

6. Herbert Henzler and Wilhelm Rall, "Facing Up to the Globalization Challenge," *McKinsey Quarterly* (Winter 1986): 52–68.

7. "The Stateless Corporation," *Business Week*, May 14, 1990, 100–101.

8. A. E. Serwer, "McDonald's Conquers the World," *Fortune*, October 17, 1994.

9. "The Avon Lady of the Amazon," *Business Week*, October 24, 1994.

10. Ibid.

11. A. K. Gupta and V. Govindarajan, "Managing Global Expansion: A Conceptual Framework," *Business Horizons* (March/April 2000).

12. G. Melloan, "Global Manufacturing Is an Intricate Game," *Wall Street Journal*, November 29, 1988.

13. "The Avon Lady of the Amazon."

14. "The Stateless Corporation."

15. "Trinidad and Tobago," *Wall Street Journal,* May 23, 1990, special advertising section.

16. Robert Weigand, "International Investments: Weighing the Incentives," *Harvard Business Review* (July–August 1983): C1.

17. M. McCarthy, M. Pointer, D. Ricks, and R. Rolfe, "Managers' Views on Potential Investment Opportunities," *Business Horizons* (July–August 1993): 54–58.

18. Anant R. Negandhi, *International Management* (Boston: Allyn and Bacon, 1987), 230.

19. Henry Mintzberg, "Strategy Making in Three Modes," *California Management Review* (Winter 1973): 44–53.

20. Arvind V. Phatak, *International Dimensions of Management,* 2nd ed. (Boston: PWS-Kent, 1989).

21. Joseph V. Micallef, "Political Risk Assessment," *Columbia Journal of World Business* 16 (Summer 1981): 47–52; Mark Fitzpatrick, "The Definition and Assessment of Political Risk in International Business: A Review of the Literature," *Academy of Management Review* 8 (1983): 249.

22. M. Porter, *Competitive Strategy* (New York: Free Press, 1980).

23. D. J. Garsombke, "International Competitor Analysis," *Planning Review* 17, no. 3 (May–June 1989): 42–47.

24. A. Swasy, "Procter & Gamble Fixes Aim on Tough Market: The Latin Americans," *Wall Street Journal,* June 15, 1990.

25. W. H. Davidson, "The Role of Global Scanning in Business Planning," *Organizational Dynamics* 19 (Winter 1991).

26. Garsombke.

27. Joann S. Lublin, "Japanese Auto Makers Speed into Europe," *Wall Street Journal,* June 6, 1990.

28. K. R. Andrews, *The Concept of Corporate Strategy* (Homewood, IL: Dow-Jones-Irwin, 1979).

29. A. Shama, "After the Meltdown: A Survey of International Firms in Russia," *Busienss Horizons* 43, no. 4 (2001): 73.

30. C. K. Prahalad and Gary Hamel, "The Core Competence of the Corporation," *Harvard Business Review* (May–June 1990): 79–91.

31. Ibid.

32. M. E. Porter, "Changing Patterns of International Competition," in *The Competitive Challenge,* ed. D. J. Teece (Boston: Ballinger, 1987), 29–30.

33. P. W. Beamish et al., *International Management* (Homewood, IL: Irwin, 1991).

34. A. Palazzo, "B2B Markets—Industry Basics," www.FT.com, January 28, 2001.

35. N. S. Levinson and M. Asahi, "Cross-National Alliances and Interorganizational Learning," *Organizational Dynamics* (Autumn 1995): 50–62.

36. A. J. Morrison, D. A. Ricks, and K. Roth, "Globalization versus Regionalization: Which Way for the Multinational?" *Organizational Dynamics* 19 (Winter 1991).

37. Ibid.

38. G. M. Taoka and D. R. Beeman, *International Business* (New York: HarperCollins, 1991).

39. Beamish et al.

40. B. Schlender, "Matsushita Shows How to Go Global," *Fortune* July 11, 1996.

41. Yoram Wind and Susan Douglas, "International Portfolio Analysis and Strategy: The Challenge of the 1980s," *Journal of International Business Studies* (Fall 1991): 69–82.

42. R. Gross and D. Kujawa, *International Business* (Homewood, IL: Irwin, 1989), 372.

43. P. Greenberg, "It's Not a Small eCommerce World, After All," www.ecommercetimes.com, February 23, 2001.

44. Ibid.

45. M. Porter, *The Competitive Advantage of Nations* (New York: Free Press, 1990).

46. S. Butler, "Survivor: B2B Style," www.emarketer.com/ analysis/ecommerce, April 13, 2001.

47. "eBusiness Trends," www.idc.com/ebusinesstrends, April 12, 2001.

48. "Fuji-Xerox Teams Up for New E-Marketplace." www.fujxerox.com, April 14, 2001.

49. "Online Auctions Free Procurement Savings," BHP Corporate Services, www.bhp.com, April 20, 2001.

50. "Small Businesses Take Part in Export Boom," *Investor's Daily,* July 10, 1991.

51. John Garland, Richard N. Farmer, and Marilyn Taylor, *International Dimensions of Business Policy and Strategy,* 2nd ed. (Boston: PWS-Kent, 1990), 106.

52. Phatak, 58.

53. R. J. Radway, "International Franchising," in *Global Business Management in the 1990s,* ed. R. T. Moran (Washington, DC: Beacham, 1990), 137.

54. Franklin R. Root, *Entry Strategies for International Markets* (Lexington, MA: Lexington Books, 1987).

55. Ibid.

56. S. Zahra and G. Elhagrasey, "Strategic Management of IJVs," *European Management Journal* 12, no. 1 (1994): 83–93.

57. Yigang Pan and Xiaolia Li, "Joint Venture Formation of Very Large Multinational Firms," *Journal of International Business Studies* 31, no. 1 (First Quarter 2000): 179–181.

58. Dorothy B. Christelow, "International Joint Ventures: How Important Are They?" *Columbia Journal of World Business* (Summer 1987): 7–13.

59. Kenichi Ohmae, "The Global Logic of Strategic Alliances," *Harvard Business Review* (March–April 1989): 143–154.

60. Zahra and Elhagrasey.

61. "The Partners," *Business Week*, February 10, 1992.

62. John Templeman and Richard A. Melcher, "Supermarket Darwinism: The Survival of the Fattest," *Business Week*, July 9, 1990.

63. Many of the facts and opinions in this section are from the following sources: R. Hudson, "Investing in Euroland," *Wall Street Journal, World Business R.25*, September 28, 1998; Dana Milbank, "Can Europe Deliver?" *Wall Street Journal*, September 30, 1994; Tamar Almor and Seer Hirsch, "Outsider's Response to Europe 1992: Theoretical Considerations and Empirical Evidence," *Journal of International Business Studies* 26, no. 2 (2nd Quarter 1995): 223–237; S. Tully, "Europe 1992—More Unity Than You Think," *Fortune*, August 17, 1992; S. Lee, "An Impossible Dream?" *Forbes*, July 25, 1988; R. E. Gut, "The Impact of the European Community's 1992 Project," *Vital Speeches of the Day* 65, no. 2, November 1, 1988; D. Oliver, "Antitrust as a 1992 Fortress," *Wall Street Journal*, April 24, 1989; C. W. Verity, "U.S. Business Needs to Prepare Now for Europe's Single Internal Market," *Business America*, August 1, 1988; L. H. Clark, Jr., "Europe '92? It's Mostly a Break for the Americans," *Wall Street Journal*, May 21, 1990; and Barbara Toman, "Now Comes the Hard Part: Marketing," in "World Business Special Report," *Wall Street Journal*, September 22, 1989.

64. N. G. Carr, "Managing in the Euro Zone," *Harvard Business Review* (January/February 1999): 47–57.

65. Ibid.

66. Ibid.

67. Milbank.

68. A. Cowell, "Zeneca Buying Astra as Europe Consolidates," *New York Times*, December 10, 1998.

69. L. E. Brouthers, S. Werner, and E. Matulich, "The Influence of Triad Nations' Environments on Price-quality Product Strategies and MNC Performance," *Journal of International Business Studies* 31, no. 1 (First Quarter, 2000): 39–62.

70. Ibid.

71. Yigang Pan and David K. Tse, "The Hierarchical Model of Market Entry Modes," *Journal of International Business Studies* 31, no. 4 (Fourth Quarter 2000): 535–554.

72. Gupta and Govindarajan.

73. Ibid.

74. A. E. Serwer, "McDonald's Conquers the World," *Fortune*, October 17, 1994.

75. K. R. Harrigan, "Joint Ventures and Global Strategies," *Columbia Journal of World Business* 19, no. 2 (Summer 1984): 7–13.

76. Ibid.

77. G. Hofstede, *Cultures and Organizations: Software of the Mind* (London: McGraw-Hill, 1991).

78. Pan and Tse.

79. Hofstede, 1994.

80. Pan and Tse.

81. Hofstede, 1994.

82. Pan and Tse.

CHAPTER 7: GLOBAL ALLIANCES AND STRATEGY IMPLEMENTATION

1. B. R. Schlender, "How Toshiba Makes Alliances Work," *Fortune*, October 4, 1993, pp. 116–120.

2. D. Lei and J. W. Slocum, Jr., "Global Strategic Alliances: Payoffs and Pitfalls," *Organizational Dynamics* (Winter 1991).

3. M. A. Hitt, R. D. Ireland, and R. E. Hoskisson, *Strategic Management* (Cincinnati, OH: South-Western, 1999).

4. Arvind Parkhe, "Global Business Alliances," *Business Horizons* 43, no. 5 (September 2000): 2.

5. www.e4engineering.com, January 4, 2001.

6. www.businessweek.com, October 14, 2000.

7. J. E. Hilsenrath, "Tiger Trouble," *Wall Street Journal*, September 28, 1998, R.17.

8. D. Lei, "Offensive and Defensive Uses of Alliances," in Heidi Vernon-Wortzel and L. H. Wortzel, *Strategic Management in a Global Economy*, 3rd ed. (New York: John Wiley & Sons, 1997).

9. J. Main, "Making Global Alliances Work," *Fortune*, December 17, 1990.

10. R. N. Osborn and C. C. Baughn, "Forms of Interorganizational Governance for Multinational Alliances," *Academy of Management Journal* 33, no. 3 (1990): 503–519.

11. Lei.

12. Ibid.

13. T. L. Wheelen and J. D. Hunger, *Strategic Management and Business Policy*, 6 ed. (Reading, MA: Addison-Wesley, 1998).

14. Lei.

15. Wheelen and Hunger.

16. Vladimir Kvint, consultant at Arthur Anderson & Co., New York, originally from Siberia.

17. A. Jack, "Russians Wake Up to Consumer Capitalism," www.FT.com, January 30, 2001.

18. A. Shama, "After the Meltdown: A Survey of International Firms in Russia," *Business Horizons* 43, no. 4 (July 2000): 73.

19. Ibid.
20. Ibid.
21. Jack.
22. Shama.
23. S. B. Novikov, "Soviet-American Joint Ventures: The Problems of Establishment and Activities," Paper presented to the 1st International Conference on East-West Joint Ventures, State University of New York, Plattsburgh, October 19–20, 1989.
24. K. R. Harrigan, "Joint Ventures and Global Strategies," *Columbia Journal of World Business* 19, no. 2 (Summer 1984): 7–13.
25. M. Brzezinski, "Foreigners Learn to Play by Russia's Rules," *Wall Street Journal*, May 14, 1998.
26. P. Lawrence and C. Vlachontsicos, "Joint Ventures in Russia: Put the Locals in Charge," *Harvard Business Review*, January–February 1993, 44–54.
26a. Vladimir Kvint, "Don't Give Up on Russia," *Harvard Business Review* (March–April 1994): 62–73; "The Russian Investment Dilemma: Perspectives," *Harvard Business Review* (May–June 1994): 35–44; Robert Starr, "Structuring Investments in the CIS," *Columbia Journal of World Business* (Fall 1993): 12–19; Paul Lawrence and Charalambos Vlachoutsicos, "Joint Ventures in Russia: Put the Locals in Charge," *Harvard Business Review* (January–February 1993): 44–54; "Investments in the CIS," *Columbia Journal of World Business* (Fall 1993): 12–19; Paul Lawrence and Charalambos Vlachoutsicos, "Joint Ventures in Russia: Put the Locals in Charge," *Harvard Business Review* (January–February 1993): 44–54.
27. A. E. Serwer, "McDonald's Conquers the World," *Fortune*, October 17, 1994.
28. Theodore Herbert and Helen Deresky, "Should General Managers Match Their Strategies?" *Organizational Dynamics* 15, no. 3 (Winter, 1987): 12; R. H. Mason and R. S. Spich, *Management—An International Perspective* (Homewood, IL: Irwin, 1987), 177.
29. E. Anderson and H. Gatignon, "Modes of Foreign Entry: A Transaction Cost Analysis and Propositions," *Journal of International Business Studies* (Fall 1986): 1–26.
30. J. L. Schaan, "Parent Control and Joint Venture Success: The Case of Mexico" (unpublished doctoral dissertation, University of Western Ontario, 1983).
31. H. W. Lane and P. W. Beamish, "Cross-Cultural Cooperative Behavior in Joint Ventures in Less Developed Countries," *Management International Review* 30 (Special Issue 1990): 87–102.
32. J. M. Geringer, "Strategic Determinants of Partner Selection Criteria in International Joint Ventures," *Journal of International Business Studies* (First Quarter 1991): 41–62.
33. J. M. Geringer and L. Hebert, "Control and Performance of International Joint Ventures," *Journal of International Business Studies* 20, no. 2 (Summer 1989).
34. Geringer.
35. P. W. Beamish et al., *International Management* (Homewood, IL: Irwin, 1991).
36. J. P. Killing, *Strategies for Joint Venture Success* (New York: Praeger, 1983).
37. J. L. Schaan and P. W. Beamish, "Joint Venture General Managers in Less Developed Countries," in *Cooperative Strategies in International Business*, ed. F. Contractor and P. Lorange (Toronto: Lexington Books, 1988), 279–299.
38. Oded Shenkar and Yoram Zeira, "International Joint Ventures: A Tough Test for HR," *Personnel* (January 1990): 26–31.
39. Ibid.
40. J. M. Geringer and L. Hebert, "Control and Performance of International Joint Ventures," *Journal of International Business Studies* 20, no. 2 (Summer 1989): 235–254.
41. M. Geringer, "Criteria for Selecting Partners for Joint Ventures in Industrialized Market Economies" (doctoral dissertation, University of Washington, Seattle, 1986); Schaan and Beamish.
42. R. Mead, *International Management* (Cambridge, MA: Blackwell Publishers, 1994).
43. Lisa Shuchman, "Reality Check," *Wall Street Journal*, April 30, 1998.
44. C. S. Smith, "GM Bets Billions on Shaky Car Market in China," *Wall Street Journal*, May 10, 1998.
45. Ibid.
46. J. Pura, "Backlash Builds Against Suharto-Lined Firms," *Wall Street Journal*, May 27, 1998.
47. P. Rosenzweig, "Why Is Managing in the United States So Difficult for European Firms?" *European Management Journal* 12, no. 1 (1994): 31–38.
48. "In Alabama, the Soul of a New Mercedes?" *Business Week*, March 31, 1997.
49. Ibid.
50. J. A. Pearce II, and R. B. Robinson, Jr., "Cultivating Guanxi as a Foreign Investor Strategy," *Business Horizons* 43, no 1 (January 2000): 31.
51. Ibid.

CHAPTER 8: ORGANIZATION STRUCTURE AND CONTROL SYSTEMS
1. A. D. Chandler, *Strategy and Structure: Chapters in the History of the American Industrial Enterprise*

(Cambridge, MA: MIT Press, 1962); R. E. Miles et al., "Organizational Strategy, Structure, and Process," *Academy of Management Review* 3, no. 3 (July 1978): 546–562; and J. Woodward, *Industrial Organization: Theory and Practice* (Oxford University Press, 1965).

2. C. A. Bartlett and S. Ghoshal, *Managing Across Borders* (Boston: Harvard Business School Press, 1989).

3. J. M. Stopford and L. T. Wells, Jr., *Managing the Multinational Enterprise* (New York: Basic Books, 1972).

4. D. Milbank, "Alcoa Chairman Plans to Begin Reorganization," *Wall Street Journal*, August 9, 1991.

5. P. Asheghian and B. Ebrahimi, *International Business* (New York: Harper and Row, 1990).

6. Ibid.

7. R. H. Mason and R. S. Spich, *Management—An International Perspective* (Homewood, IL: Irwin, 1987).

8. "Heinz's Johnson to Divest Operations, Scrap Management of Firm by Regions," *Wall Street Journal*, December 8, 1997, B22.

9. A. Taylor III, "Ford's Really Big Leap at the Future," *Fortune*, September 18, 1995, 134–144.

10. L. Greenhalgh, "Ford Motor Company's CFO Jac Nasser on Transformational Change, E-Business, and Environmental Responsibility (Interview)," *Academy of Management Executive* 14, no. 13 (August 2000): 46.

11. "Borderless Management," *Business Week*, May 23, 1994.

12. Ibid.; "Power at Multinationals Shifts to Home Office," *Wall Street Journal*, September 9, 1994; "Big Blue Wants the World to Know Who's Boss," *Business Week*, September 26, 1994.

13. H. Henzler and W. Rall, "Facing Up to the Globalization Challenge," *McKinsey Quarterly* (Fall 1986): 52–68.

14. T. Levitt, "The Globalization of Markets," *Harvard Business Review* (May–June 1983): 92–102; and S. P. Douglas and Yoram Wind, "The Myth of Globalization," *Columbia Journal of World Business* (Winter 1987): 19–29.

15. L. Kraar, "The Overseas Chinese," *Fortune*, October 31, 1994.

16. J. Kao, "The Worldwide Web of Chinese Business," *Harvard Business Review* (March–April 1993): 24–35.

17. "Asia's Wealth," *Business Week*, November 29, 1993.

18. Kao.

19. "The New Power in Asia," *Fortune*, October 31, 1994.

20. M. Weidenbaum, "The Rise of Great China: A New Economic Superpower," in *Annual Editions, 1995/96* (Guilford, CT: Dushkin Publishing Group), 180–185.

21. Weidenbaum.

22. Ibid.

23. Kraar.

24. Weidenbaum.

25. Kao.

26. Kraar.

27. P. M. Rosenzweig, "Colgate-Palmolive: Managing International Careers," Harvard Business School Case, 1995.

28. "For Levi's, a Flattering Fit Overseas," *Business Week*, November 5, 1990, 76–77.

29. Ibid.

30. B. R. Schlender, "How Fujitsu Will Tackle the Giants," *Fortune*, July 1, 1991.

31. S. Ghoshal and C. A. Bartlett, "The Mulinational Corporation as an Interorganizational Network," *Academy of Management Review* 15, no. 4 (1990): 603–625.

32. R. E. White and T. A. Poynter, "Organizing for Worldwide Advantage," *Business Quarterly* 54 (Summer 1989): 84–89.

33. B. Hagerty, "Philips to Eliminate 35,000 to 45,000 Jobs by End of 1991," *Wall Street Journal*, October 26, 1990, A12.

34. Mohanbir Sawhneyand Sumant Mandal, "Go Global," *Business 2.0* (May 5): 178–213.

35. J. D. Daniels, L. H. Radebaugh, and D. P. Sullivan, *Globalization and Business* (Englewood Cliffs, NJ: Prentice Hall, 2002).

36. "Energizing the Supply Chain," *The Review*, Deloitte & Touche, January 17, 2000, p. 1.

37. C. A. Bartlett and S. Ghoshal, "Organizing for Worldwide Effectiveness: The Transnational Solution," *California Management Review* (Fall 1988): 54–74.

38. Ibid., 66.

39. R. H. Kilmann, "A Networked Company That Embraces the World," *Information Strategy* 6 (Spring 1990): 23–26.

40. R. B. Reich, "Who Is Them?" *Harvard Business Review* (March–April 1991): 77–88.

41. Ibid.

42. A. V. Phatak, *International Dimensions of Management*, 2nd ed. (Boston: PWS-Kent, 1989).

43. G. Rohrmann, CEO, AEI Corp., press release.

44. Phatak.

45. W. G. Egelhoff, "Patterns of Control in U.S., U.K., and European Multinational Corporations," *Journal of International Business Studies* (Fall 1984): 73–83.

46. Ibid.

47. Ibid.

48. S. Ueno and U. Sekaran, "The Influence of Culture on Budget Control Practices in the U.S.A. and Japan: An Empirical Study," *Journal of International Business Studies* 23 (Winter 1992): 659–674.

49. A. R. Neghandi and M. Welge, *Beyong Theory Z* (Greenwich, Conn.: J.A.I. Publishers, 1984), 18.

50. Phatak.

CHAPTER 9: STAFFING AND TRAINING FOR GLOBAL OPERATIONS

1. J. L. Laabs, "HR Pioneers Explore the Road Less Traveled," *Personnel Journal* (February 1996): 70–72, 74, 77–78.

2. Ibid.

3. J. Stewart Black and Hal B. Gregersen, "The Right Way to Manage Expats," *Harvard Business Review* (March/April 1999): 52–62.

4. C. Joinson, "Why HR Managers Need to Think Globally," *HR Magazine*, April 1998, 2–7.

5. C. A. Bartlett and S. Ghoshal, "Matrix Management: Not a Structure, a Frame of Mind," *Harvare Business Review* (July–August 1990).

6. J. S. Lublin, "Foreign Accents Proliferate in Top Ranks as U.S. Companies Find Talent Abroad," *Wall Street Journal*, May 21, 1992.

7. S. J. Kobrin, "Is There a Relationship Between a Geocentric Mind-Set and Multinational Strategy?" *Journal of International Business Studies* (Third Quarter 1994); N. J. Adler and S. Bartholomew, "Managing Globally Competent People," *Academy of Management Executive*, August 6, 1992, 52–65; P. Dowling and R. S. Schuler, *International Dimensions of Human Resource Management* (Boston: PWS-Kent, 1990).

8. G. Hedlund, "Who Manages the Global Corporation," unpublished working paper, Stockholm School of Economics, 1990.

9. D. Welch, "HRM Implications of Globalization," *Journal of General Management* 19, no. 4 (Summer 1994): 52–69.

10. T. T. Herbert and H. Deresky, "Should General Mangers Match Their Business Strategies?" *Organizational Dynamics* 15, no. 3 (Winter 1987); and "Senior Management Implications of Strategic Human Resource Management Programs," *Proceedings of the Association of Human Resource Management and Organizational Behavior Conference* (New Orleans, November 1986).

11. Heenan and Perlmutter.

12. S. B. Prasad and Y. K. Krishna Shetty, *An Introduction to Multinational Management* (Englewood Cliffs, NJ: Prentice Hall, 1979).

13. Rochelle Kopp, "International Human Resource Policies and Practices in Japanese, European, and United States Multinationals," *Human Resource Management* 33, no. 4 (Winter 1994): 581–599.

14. Ibid.

15. Herbert and Deresky.

16. M. Mendenhall and G. Oddou, "The Dimensions of Expatriate Acculturation: A Review," *Academy of Management Review* 10, no. 1 (1985): 39–47.

17. Ronen; and R. L. Tung, "Selection and Training of Personnel for Overseas Assignments," *Columbia Journal of World Business* (Spring 1981): 68–78.

18. Tung, "Overseas Assignments."

19. Dowling and Schuler.

20. S. J. Kobrin, "Expatriate Reduction and Strategic Control in American Multinational Corporations," *Human Resource Management* 27, no. 1 (1988): 63–75.

21. P. J. Dowling, "Hot Issues Overseas," *Personnel Administrator* 34, no. 1 (1989): 66–72.

22. Hem C. Jain, "Human Resource Management in Selected Japanese Firms, the Foreign Subsidiaries and Locally Owned Counterparts," *International Labour Review* 129, no. 1 (1990): 73–84.

23. Bartlett and Ghoshal.

24. Tung, "U.S., European, and Japanese Multinationals."

25. R. D. Hays, "Expatriate Selection: Insuring Success and Avoiding Failure," *Journal of International Business Studies* 5, no. 1 (1974): 25–37; Tung, "U.S., European, and Japanese Multinationals."

26. J. S. Black, "Work Role Transitions: A Study of American Expatriate Managers in Japan," *Journal of International Business Studies* 19 (1988): 277–294.

27. "They're Sending You Where?" www.businessweek.com, January 3, 2000.

28. M. Harvey, "Dual-Career Expatriates: Expectations, Adjustment and Satisfaction with International Relocation," *Journal of International Business Studies* 28, no. 3 (1997).

29. Tung, "U.S., European, and Japanese Multinationals."

30. Ibid.

31. B. Wysocki, Jr., "Prior Adjustment: Japanese Executives Going Overseas Take Anti-Shock Courses," *Wall Street Journal*, December 4, 1987.

32. Mendenhall and Oddou.

33. J. S. Black and M. Mendenhall, "Cross-Cultural Training Effectiveness: A Review and a Theoretical Framework for Future Research," *Academy of Management Review* 15, no. 1 (1990): 113–136.

34. K. Oberg, "Culture Shock: Adjustments to New Cultural Environments," *Practical Anthropology* (July–August 1960): 177–182.

35. Ibid.

36. Ibid.

37. P. R. Harris and R. T. Moran, *Managing Cultural Differences*, 4th ed. (Houston, TX: Gulf Publishing, 1996), 139.

38. Tung, "Overseas Assignments."

39. P. C. Earley, "Intercultural Training for Managers: A Comparison of Documentary and Interpersonal Methods," *Academy of Management Journal* 30, no. 4 (December 1987): 685–698.

40. Ronen.

41. Kealey, 81.

42. J. S. Lublin, "Younger Managers Learn Global Skills," *Wall Street Journal*, March 31, 1992.

43. "Seoul Is Supporting a Sizzling Tech Boom," www.businessweek.com, September 25, 2000.

44. Herbert and Deresky.

45. "Living Expenses," www.economist.com, July 22, 2000; "Runzheimer International Compensation Worksheet," www.runzheimer.com, 2000.

46. B. W. Teague, *Compensating Key Personnel Overseas* (New York: Conference Board, 1972).

47. D. Kiriazov, S. E. Sullivan, and H. S. Tu, "Business Success in Eastern Europe: Understanding and Customizing HRM," *Business Horizons* (January/February 2000): 39–43.

48. Ibid.

49. Y. Ono and W. Spindle, "Japan's Long Decline Makes One Thing Rise: Individualism," *Wall Street Journal*, January 3, 2001.

50. Ingmar Bjorkman and Yuan Lu, "The Management of Human Resources in Chinese-Western Joint Ventures," *Journal of World Business* 34, no. 3 (Fall 1999): 306.

51. Ibid.

52. M. Selz, "Hiring the Right Manager Overseas," *Wall Street Journal*, February 27, 1992.

53. Sheila M. Puffer and Stanislav V. Shekshnia, "Compensating Nationals in Post-Communist Russia: The Fit Between Culture and Compensation Systems," Paper presented at the Annual Academy of International Business Conference, Boston, November 1994).

CHAPTER 10: DEVELOPING A GLOBAL MANAGEMENT CADRE

1. Charlene M. Solomon, "One Assignment, Two Lives," *Personnel Journal* (May 1996): 36–47.

2. N. J. Adler, *International Dimensions of Organizational Behavior*, 2nd ed. (Boston: PWS-Kent, 1991); M. Mendenhall, E. Dunbar, and G. Oddou, "Expatriate Selection, Training, and Career-Pathing: A Review and Critique," *Human Resource Management* 26 (1987): 331–345.

3. M. G. Harvey, "Repatriation of Corporate Executives: An Empirical Study," *Journal of International Business Studies* 20 (Spring 1989): 131–144.

4. Tung, "Career Issues in International Assignments," *Academy of Management Executive* 2, no. 3 (1988): 241–244.

5. M. Harvey, "Dual-Career Expatriates: Expectations, Adjustments and Satisfaction with International Relocation," *Journal of International Business Studies* 28, no. 3 (1997): 627.

6. Tung.

7. Solomon.

8. R. Pascoe, *Surviving Overseas: The Wife's Guide to Successful Living Abroad* (Singapore: Times Publishing, 1992); and R. Pascoe, "Employers Ignore Expatriate Wives at Their Own Peril," *Wall Street Journal*, March 29, 1992.

9. J. S. Black and H. B. Gregersen, "The Other Half of the Picture: Antecedents of Spouse Cross-Cultural Adjustment," *Journal of International Business Studies* (Third Quarter 1992): 461–477.

10. Ibid.

11. Based on D. C. Feldman, "The Multinational Socialization of Organization Members," *Academy of Management Review* 6, no. 2 (April 1981): 309–318.

12. J. Hamill, "Expatriate Policies in British Multinationals, *Journal of General Management* 14, no. 4 (Summer 1989): 18–33.

13. Based on W. Dyer, *Team Building* (Reading, MA: Addison-Wesley, 1987).

14. R. B. Reich, "Who Is Them?" *Harvard Business Review* (March–April 1991): 77–88.

15. T. Gross, E. Turner, and L. Cederholm, "Building Teams for Global Operations," *Management Review* (June 1987): 32–36.

16. Based largely on Adler, 1991.

17. C. Solomon, "Building Teams Across Borders," *Global Workforce* (November 1998): 12–17.

18. Ibid.

19. T. Brown, "Building a Transnational Team," *Industry Week*, May 16, 1988, 13.

20. Ibid.

21. R. T. Moran, "Cross-Cultural Contact: A Formula for Success in Multicultural Organizations," *International Management* (December 1988): 74.

22. Ibid.

23. I. Ratiu, "International Consulting News," in *Managing Cultural Differences*, 3rd ed., ed. P. R. Harris and R. T. Moran (Houston, TX: Gulf Publishing 1991).

24. *Wall Street Journal*, July 26, 1995.

25. M. Kaminski and J. Paiz, "Japanese Women in Management: Where Are They?" *Human Resource Management* 23, no. 2 (Fall 1984): 277–292.

26. P. Lansing and K. Ready, "Hiring Women Managers in Japan: An Alternative for Foreign Employers," *California Management Review* 26, no. 4 (1988): 112–127.

27. "Japan's Working Mothers," *Japan Report* 37, no. 5 (August 1991).

28. "Women in Business: A Global Report Card," *Wall Street Journal*, July 26, 1995.

29. N. J. Adler and D. N. Izraeli, *Women in Management Worldwide* (Armonk, NY: M. E. Sharpe, 1988), 245.

30. Ibid.

31. Jelinek and Adler. "Women: World Class Managers for Global Competition," *Academy of Management Executive* 11, no. 1 (February 1988): 11–19.

32. L. S. Lewan, "Diversity in the Workplace," *Human Resource Management* (June 1990): 42–45.

33. T. Cox and S. Blake, "Managing Cultural Diversity: Implications for Organizational Competitiveness," *Executive* 5 (1991): 45–56.

34. J. R. W. Joplin and C. S. Daus, "Challenges of Leading a Diverse Workforce," *Academy of Management Executive* 11, no. 3 (August 1997).

35. "Managing by Values," *Business Week*, August 1, 1994.

36. "How to Make Diversity Pay," *Fortune*, August 8, 1994.

37. J. Braham, "No, You Don't Manage Everyone the Same," *Industry Week*, February 6, 1989, 28–35.

38. Speech by Xerox Company Diversity Manager at the 1994 Meeting of the Middle Atlantic Association of Colleges of Business Administration, New York.

39. W. B. Johnston, "Global Work Force 2000: The New World Labor Market," *Harvard Business Review* (March–April 1991): 115–127.

40. A. Edwards, "Cultural Diversity in Today's Corporation," *Working Woman* (January 1991): 45–51.

41. Speech by E. Andrews, Manager Workforce Diversity Division, General Electric Company, at the 1994 Meeting of the Middle Atlantic Association of Colleges of Business Administration, New York, 590–602.

42. Braham.

43. L. Copeland, "Making the Most of Cultural Differences in the Workplace," *Personnel* (June 1988): 52–60.

44. R. T. Jones, "How Do You Manage a Diverse Workforce?" *Training and Development Journal* (February 1989): 13–21.

45. P. J. Dowling, R. S. Schuler, and D. E. Welch, *International Dimensions of Human Resource Management*, 2 ed. (Belmont, CA: Wadsworth, 1994).

46. "Taking the Pledge," *The Economist*, November 23, 1996, S15(2).

47. R. M. Hodgetts and F. Luthans, *International Management*, 2nd ed. (New York: McGraw-Hill, 1994).

48. M. R. Czinkota, I. A. Ronkainen, and M. H. Moffett, *International Business*, 3rd ed. (New York: Dryden Press, 1994).

49. C. K. Prahalad and Y. L. Doz, *The Multinational Mission: Balancing Local Demands and Global Vision* (New York: Free Press, 1987).

50. R. Taylor, "Challenge Facing Endangered Species," *Financial Times*, August 14, 1995, 10.

51. R. J. Adams, *Industrial Relations under Liberal Democracy* (University of South Carolina Press, 1995).

52. Dowling, Schuler, and Welch.

53. J. S. Daniels and L. H. Radebaugh, *International Business*, 6th ed. (Reading, MA: Addison-Wesley, 1992).

54. M. Poole, *Industrial Relations: Origins and Patterns of National Diversity* (London: Routledge, 1986).

55. Dowling, Schuler, and Welch.

56. Adams.

57. Ibid.

58. "Unions Feel the Beat," *U.S. News and World Report*, January 24, 1994.

59. Ibid.

60. "World Wire: China to Unionize Foreign Firms," *Wall Street Journal*, May 1, 1994.

61. Ibid.

62. J. T. Barrett, "Trade Unions in South Africa: Dramatic Change after Apartheid Ends," *Monthly Labor Review* 199, no. 5 (May 1996): 37.

63. M. M. Lucio and S. Weston, "New Management Practices in a Multinational Corporation: The Restructuring of Worker Representation and Rights?" *Industrial Relations Journal* 25, no. 2, 110–121.

64. Ibid.

65. D. B. Cornfield, "Labor Transnationalism?" *Work and Occupations* 24, no. 3 (August 1997): 278(10).

66. R. Martin, A. Vidinova, and S. Hill, "Industrial Relations in Transition Economies: Emergent Industrial Relations Institutions in Bulgaria," *British Journal of Industrial Relations* 34, no. 1 (March 1996): 3.

67. "Labour Relations: Themes for the 21st Century," *British Journal of Industrial Relations* 33, no. 4 (December 1995): 515.

68. Daniels and Radebaugh.

69. Barrett.

70. "Culture Clash: South Korea," *The Economist* 342 (7999), January 11, 1997.

71. A. M. Rugman and R. M. Hodgetts, *International Business* (New York: McGraw-Hill, 1995).

72. This section is drawn from a term project by Joy Kennley and Tim Lemos, students at the State University of New York, Plattsburgh, Spring 1995; and articles by Tim Shorrock, such as "GE, Honeywell Are Focus of NAFTA Labor Complaints," *Journal of Commerce and Commercial* 399, no. 2814, February 15, 1994.

73. Daniels and Radebaugh.

74. R. Calori and B. Dufour, "Management European Style," *Academy Management Executive* 9, no. 3 (August 1995).

75. J. Hoerr, "What Should Unions Do?" *Harvard Business Review* (May–June 1991): 30–45.

76. Hodgetts and Luthans.

77. Hoer.

78. H. C. Katz, "The Decentralization of Collective Bargaining: A Literature Review and Comparative Analysis," *Industrial and Labor Relations Review* 47, no. 1 (October 1993).

79. Adams.

80. "The Perils of Cosy Corporatism," *The Economist*, May 21, 1994.

81. Wofgang Streeck, "More Uncertainties: German Unions Facing 1992," *Industrial Relations* (Fall 1991): 30–33.

82. "Germany's Economic Future Is on the Bargaining Table," *Business Week*, March 30, 1992.

CHAPTER 11: MOTIVATING AND LEADING

1. F. Rieger and D. Wong-Rieger, "A Configuration Model of National Influence Applied to Southeast Asian Organizations," *Proceedings of the Research Conference on Business in Southeast Asia*, Mary 12–13, 1990, University of Michigan.

2. M. J. Gannon & Associates, *Understanding Global Cultures: Metaphorical Journeys Through 17 Countries* (Beverly Hills, CA: Sage Publications, 1994).

3. R. M. Steers, *Made in Korea: Chung Ju Yung and the Rise of Hyundai* (New York: Routledge, 1999).

4. Meaning of Work International Research Team, *The Meaning of Working: An International Perspective* (New York: Academic Press, 1985).

5. D. Siddiqui and A. Alkhafaji, *The Gulf War: Implications for Global Businesses and Media* (Apollo, PA: Closson Press, 1992), 133–135.

6. Ibid.

7. A. Ali, "The Islamic Work Ethic in Arabia," *Journal of Psychology* 126 (1992): 507–519.

8. Yasamusa Kuroda and Tatsuzo Suzuki, "A Comparative Analysis of the Arab Culture: Arabic, English and Japanese Language and Values," Paper presented at the 5th Congress of the International Association of Middle Eastern Studies, Tunis (September 20–24, 1991), quoted in Siddiqui.

9. J. R. Hinrichs, "Cross-National Analysis of Work Attitudes," Paper presented at the American Psychological Association Meeting, Chicago, 1975.

10. A. Furnham, B. D. Kirkcaldy, and R. Lynn, "National Attitudes to Competitiveness, Money, and Work among Young People: First, Second, and Third World Differences," *Human Relations* 47, no. 1 (1994): 119–132.

11. M. Haire, E. E. Ghiselli, and L. W. Porter, "Cultural Patterns in the Role of the Manager," *Industrial Relations* 12, no. 2 (February 1963): 95–117.

12. S. Ronen, *Comparative and Multinational Management* (New York: John Wiley and Sons, 1986).

13. D. S. Elenkov, "Can American Management Concepts Work in Russia? A Cross-Cultural Comparative Study," *California Management Review* 40, no. 4 (Summer 1998): 133–157.

14. E. C. Nevis, "Cultural Assumptions and Productivity: The United States and China," *Sloan Management Review* 24, no. 3 (Spring 1983): 17–29.

15. R. L. Tung, "Patterns of Motivation in Chinese Industrial Enterprises," *Academy of Management Review* 6, no. 3 (1981): 481–489.

16. Swee Hoon Ang, "The Power of Money: A Cross-Cultural Analysis of Business-Related Beliefs," *Journal of World Business* 35, no. 1 (Spring 2000): 43.

17. *World Competitiveness Yearbook (1998)* (Lausanne, Switzerland: Institute for Management Development).

18. D. D. White and J. Leon, "The Two-Factor Theory: New Questions, New Answers," *National Academy of Management Proceedings* (1976): 358; D. Macarov, "Work Patterns and Satisfactions in an Israeli Kibbutz: A Test of the Herzberg Hypothesis," *Personnel Psychology* (Autumn 1973): 483–493.

19. P. D. Machungwa and N. Schmitt, "Work Motivation in a Developing Country," *Journal of Applied Psychology* (February 1983): 31–42.

20. G. E. Popp, H. J. Davis, and T. T. Herbert, "An International Study of Intrinsic Motivation Composition," *Management International Review* 26, no. 3 (1986): 28–35.

21. R. N. Kanungo and R. W. Wright, "A Cross-Cultural Study of Managerial Job Attitudes," *Journal of International Business Studies* (Fall 1983): 115–129.

22. Ibid., 127–128.

23. J. R. Lincoln, "Employee Work Attitudes and Management Practice in the U.S. and Japan: Evidence from a Large Comparative Survey," *California Management Review* 32, no. 1 (Fall 1989): 89–106.

24. J. R. Lincoln and K. McBride, "Japanese Industrial Organization in Comparative Perspective," *Annual Review of Sociology* 13 (1987): 289–312.

25. Lincoln.

26. "Detroit South," *Business Week*, March 16, 1992.

27. Hofstede.

28. M. B. Teagarden, M. C. Butler, and M. Von Glinow, "Mexico's Maquiladora Industry: Where Strategic Human Resource Management Makes a Difference," *Organizational Dynamics* (Winter 1992): 34–47.

29. T. T. Herbert, H. Deresky, and G. E. Popp, "On the Potential for Assimilation and Integration of Sub-Culture Members into the U.S. Business System: The Micro-Cultural Effects of the Mexican-American National Origin, Culture, and Personality," *Proceedings of the International Business Association Conference* (London, November 1986).

30. John Condon, *Good Neighbors: Communication with the Mexicans* (Yarmouth, ME: Intercultural Press, 1985).

31. G. K. Stephens and C. R. Greer, "Doing Business in Mexico: Understanding Cultural Differences," *Organizational Dynamics* (Summer 1995): 39–55.

32. Teagarden, Butler, and Von Glinow.

33. Stephens and Greer.

34. Ibid.

35. C. E. Nicholls, H. W. Lane, and M. B. Brechu, "Taking Self-Managed Teams to Mexico," *Academy of Management Executive* 13, 3 (1999): 15–25.

36. Ibid.

37. Ibid.

38. Mariah E. de Forest, "Thinking of a Plant in Mexico?" *Academy of Management Executive* 8, no. 1 (1994): 33–40.

39. Ibid.

40. Ibid.

41. Teagarden, Butler, and Von Glinow.

42. Herbert, Deresky and Popp; R. S. Bhagat and S. J. McQuaid, "Role of Subjective Culture in Organizations: A Review and Direction for Future Research," *Journal of Applied Psychology Monograph* 67, no. 5 (1982): 669.

43. Malgorzata Tarczynska, "Eastern Europe: How Valid Is Western Reward/Performance Management?" *Benefits and Compensation International* 29, no. 8 (April 2000): 9–16.

44. M. A. Von Glinow and M. B. Teagarden, "The Transfer of Human Resource Management Technology in Sino-U.S. Cooperative Ventures: Problems and Solutions," *Human Resource Management* 27, no. 2 (1988): 201–229.

45. M. A. Von Glinow and Byung Jae Chung, "Comparative HRM Practices in the U.S., Japan, Korea and the PRC," in *Research in Personnel and HRM, A Research Annual: International HRM*, ed. A. Nedd, G. R. Ferris, and K. M. Rowland (London: JAI Press, 1989).

46. A. Ignatius, "Now If Ms. Wong Insults a Customer, She gets an Award," *Wall Street Journal*, January 24, 1989, 1, 15.

47. T. Saywell, "Motive Power: China's State Firms Bank on Incentives to Keep Bosses Operating at Their Peak," *Far Eastern Economic Review* (July 8, 2000): 67–68.

48. Steers.

49. A. Morrison, H. Gregersen, and S. Black, "What Makes Savvy Global Leaders?" *Ivey Business Journal* 64, no. 2 (1999): 44–51; and *Monash Mt. Eliza Business Review* 1, no. 2 (1998).

50. Ibid.

51. Ibid.

52. Morrison et al.; J. W. Gardner, *John W. Gardner on Leadership* (New York: Free Press, 1989); W. Bennis and B. Nanus, *Leaders* (New York: Harper and Row, 1985); and R. D. Robinson, *Internatinalization of Business* (Hinsdale, IL: Drysden Press, 1984), 117.

53. R. H. Mason and R. S. Spich, *Management—An International Perspective* (Homewood: IL: Irwin, 1987).

54. Ibid., 184.

55. B. M. Bass, *Bass & Stogdill's Handbook of Leadership* (New York: Free Press, 1990).

56. See, for example, M. Mead, *Sex and Temperament in Three Primitive Societies* (New York: Morrow, 1935); and M. Mead et al., *Cooperation and Competition among Primitive Peoples* (New York: McGraw-Hill, 1937).

57. L. Copeland and L. Griggs, *Going International* (New York: Random House, 1985), 131.

58. D. McGregor, *The Human Side of Enterprise* (New York: McGraw-Hill, 1960). See, for example, R. M. Stogdill, *Manual for the Leader Behavior Description Questionnaire—Form XII* (Columbus: Ohio State University, Bureau of Business Research, 1963); R. R. Blake and J. S. Mouton, *The New Managerial Grid* (Houston, TX: Gulf Publishing, 1978).

59. F. E. Fiedler, "Engineering the Job to Fit the Manager," *Harvard Business Review* 43, no. 5 (1965): 115–122.

60. Den Hartog, Deanne N., R. J. House, Paul J. Hanges, P. W. Dorfman, S. Antonio Ruiz-Quintanna, and 170 associates, "Culture Specific and Cross-Culturally Generalizable Implicit Leadership Theories: Are Attributes of Charismatic/Transformational Leadership Universally Endorsed?" *Leadership Quarterly* 10, no. 2, (1999): 219–256.

61 Ibid.

62. R. House et al., "Cultural Influences on Leadership and Organizations: Project GLOBE," *Advances in Global Leadership*, Vol. 1, (JAI Press, 1999).

63. Geert Hofstede, "Motivation, Leadership and Organization: Do American Theories Apply Abroad?" *Organizational Dynamics* (Summer 1980): 42–63.

64. Ibid.

65. Geert Hofstede, "Value Systems in Forty Countries," *Proceedings of the 4th International Congress of the International Association for Cross-Cultural Psychology* (1978).

66. Andre Laurent, "The Cultural Diversity of Western Conceptions of Management," *International Studies of Management and Organization* 13, no. 1–2 (Spring–Summer 1983): 75–96.

67. C. Hampden-Turner and A. Trompenaars, *The Seven Cultures of Capitalism* (New York: Doubleday, 1993).

68. M. Harie, E. E. Ghiselli, and L. W. Porter, *Managerial Thinking: An International Study* (New York: John Wiley and Sons, 1966).

69. S. G. Redding and T. W. Case, "Managerial Beliefs among Asian Managers," *Proceedings of the Academy of Management* (1975).

70. I. Kenis, "A Cross-Cultural Study of Personality and Leadership," *Group and Organization Studies* 2 (1977): 49–60; F. C. Deyo, "The Cultural Patterning of Organizational Development: A Comparative Case Study of Thailand and Chinese Industrial Enterprises," *Human Organization* 37 (1978): 68–72.

71. M. K. Badawy, "Styles of Mid-Eastern Managers," *California Management Review* (Spring 1980): 57.

72. Various Newscasts, 2001.

73. A. A. Algattan, *Test of the Path-Goal Theory of Leadership in the Multinational Domain,* Paper presented at the Academy of Management Conference, 1985, San Diego, CA; J. P. Howell and P. W. Dorfman, "A Comparative Study of Leadership and Its Substitutes in a Mixed Cultural Work Setting" (unpublished manuscript, 1988).

74. D. H. Welsh, F. Luthans, and S. M. Sommer, "Managing Russian Factory Workers: The Impact of U.S.-Based Behavioral and Participative Techniques," *Academy of Management Journal* 36 (1993): 58–79.

75. Jagdeep S. Chhoker, "Leadership and Culture in India: The GLOBE Research Project," www.mgmt3.ucalgary.ca/web/globe.nsf/index, November 10, 2001.

76. Jai B. P. Sinha and D. Sinha, "Role of Social Values in Indian Organizations," *International Journal of Psychology* 25 (1990): 705–715.

77. Hofstede, "Motivation, Leadership and Organization."

78. Jai B. P. Sinha, "A Model of Effective Leadership Styles in India," *International Studies of Management and Organization* (Summer–Fall 1984): 86–98.

79. Ibid.

80. B. M. Bass and P. C. Burger, *Assessment of Managers: An International Comparison* (New York: Free Press, 1979).

81. Chhoker.

82. R. C. Tripathi, "Interplay of Values in the Functioning of Indian Organizations," *International Journal of Psychology* 25 (1990): 715–734.

83. Sinha.

84. Sinha and Sinha.

85. A. Spaeth, "India Beckons—and Frustrates: The Country Needs Foreign Investment, But Investors May Find That Hard to Believe," *Wall Street Journal,* September 22, 1989, R23–R25.

86. Ibid.

87. "Enron Switches Signals in India," *Business Week,* January 8, 2001. "Enron Calls on Guarantees by India to Collect Debts," *Wall Street Journal,* February 9, 2001.

88. S. S. Rao, "Yankee, Be Good," *Financial World,* November 7, 1995, 54–68.

89. J. J. Curran, "Why Japan Will Emerge Stronger," *Fortune,* May 18, 1992.

90. Yumiko Ono and Wm. Spindle, "Japan's Long Decline Makes One Thing Rise—Individualism," *Wall Street Journal,* December 29, 2000.

Credits

Chapter 1: "Nokia's China Strategy" reprinted from January 28, 2001 issue of *Business Week* by special permission, copyright © 2001 by The McGraw-Hill Companies, Inc.

Exhibit 1.2: From *Dun & Bradstreets Guide to Doing Business Around the World* by T. Morrison, W. Conaway and J. Douress. Copyright © 1997. Reprinted with permission of Prentice Hall Direct.

Exhibit 1.3: "Revised Forecast" from *The New York Times*, March 26, 2001. Copyright © 2001 by The New York Times Co. Reprinted by permission.

Exhibit 1.5: "Why It Isn't Easy" from *The Economist*, November 11, 2000. Copyright © 2000 The Economist Newspaper Group, Inc. Reprinted with permission. Further reproduction prohibited. www.economist.com.

Exhibit 1.6: "It's Barely Started" from *The Economist*, November 11, 2000. Copyright © 2000 The Economist Newspaper Group, Inc. Reprinted with permission. Further reproduction prohibited. www.economist.com.

Exhibit 2.4: "2001 CPI Score" from *Transparency International*, 2001. Reprinted with permission of Transparency International.

Exhibit 2.5: "Bribe Payers Index" from *Transparency International*, 2000. Reprinted with permission of Transparency International.

Exhibit 2.6: From *Management: An International Perspective* by R.H. Mason and R.S. Spich, p. 202. Homewood, IL: Irwin, 1987. Reprinted by permission of the authors.

Chapter 3: "The Net Is Transforming the West, but Companies in the East Lag Behind" reprinted from www.businessweek.com, October 23, 2000 by special permission, copyright © 2000 by The McGraw-Hill Companies, Inc.

Exhibit 3.2: From *Managing Cultural Differences* by Philip R. Harris and Robert T. Moran, 5th ed. Copyright © 2000 by Butterworth–Heinemann. Reprinted by permission.

Exhibit 3.3: Reprinted from "Cultural acumen for the global manager: lessons from Project GLOBE" by Mansour Javidan and Robert J. House in *Organizational Dynamics*, Spring 2001, pp. 289–305. Copyright © 2001, with permission from Elsevier Science.

Exhibit 3.4: "Comparative Analysis, Conclusions, and Future Directions" by Raghu Nath and Kunal K. Sadhu in *Comparative Management—A Regional View*, © 1988, p. 273. Reprinted by permission of the author.

Exhibit 3.5: From "Clustering Countries on Attitudinal Dimensions: A Review and Synthesis" by S. Ronen and O. Shenkar in *Academy of Management Review*, September 1985, p. 449. Copyright © 1985 by Academy of Management. Reproduced with permission of Academy of Management via Copyright Clearance Center.

Exhibit 3.7: From "The Influence of Mexican Culture on the Use of Japanese Manufacturing Techniques in Mexico" by J.J. Lawrence and Ryh-song Yeh in *Management International Review* 34, No. 1 (1994): 49–66. Reprinted with permission.

Exhibit 3.8: From "Information Privacy and Marketing: What the U.S. Should (and Shouldn't) Learn from Europe" by H. Jeff Smith. Copyright © 2001, by The Regents of the University of California. Reprinted from the *California Management Review*, Vol. 43, No. 2. By permission of The Regents.

Exhibit 3.9: From *Managing Cultural Differences* by Philip R. Harris and Robert T. Moran, 5th ed. Copyright © 2000 by Butterworth–Heinemann. Reprinted by permission.

Exhibit 3.10: From "The Japanese Manager's Traumatic Entry into the United States: Understanding the American-Japanese Cultural Divide" by R. G. Linowes from *Academy of Management Executive VII*, No. 4, November 1993, p. 24. Copyright © 1993 by Academy of Management. Reproduced with permission of Academy of Management via Copyright Clearance Center.

Exhibit 3.11: From *Managing Cultural Differences* by Philip R. Harris and Robert T. Moran, 5th ed. Copyright © 2000 by Butterworth–Heinemann. Reprinted by permission.

Exhibit 3.12: From *Managing Cultural Differences* by Philip R. Harris and Robert T. Moran, 4th ed. Copyright © 1996 by Butterworth–Heinemann. Reprinted by permission.

Exhibit 3.13: From "Comparing Chinese and Western Cultural Roots" by J. Scarborough reprinted with permission from *Business Horizons*, November–December 1998, Figure 1, p. 21. Copyright © 1998 by The Trustees at Indiana University, Kelley School of Business.

Exhibit 3.14: From "Culture and Management—A Study of Small Chinese Family Business in Singapore" by Dr. Jean Lee in *Journal of Small Business Management* (July 1996). Reprinted by permission of Blackwell Publishing Ltd.

Exhibit 4.5: Source: Based on information drawn from Edward T. Hall and M.R. Hall, *Understanding Cultural*

Name and Subject Index